DB971641

Special Envoy to Churchill and Stalin
1941–1946

SPECIAL ENVOY
to Churchill and Stalin
1941–1946

by

W. AVERELL HARRIMAN
and
ELIE ABEL

RANDOM HOUSE NEW YORK

Library of Congress Cataloging in Publication Data

Harriman, William Averell, 1891–
Special envoy to Churchill and Stalin, 1941–1946.

Includes index.
1. World War, 1939–1945—Diplomatic history. 2. World War, 1939–1945—United States. 3. United States—Foreign relations—1933–1945. 4. Harriman, William Averell, 1891–   I. Abel, Elie, joint author. II. Title.
D753.H28   940.53′2   75–10275
ISBN 0–394–48296–4

Manufactured in the United States of America

9 8 7 6 5 4 3 2

FIRST EDITION

FOREWORD

THIS BOOK HAS BEEN THIRTY YEARS IN THE MAKING. I have long felt an obligation to record my experiences, observations and assessments of the World War II period. More than any other American, I had both a close personal association with Winston Churchill and intimate dealings with Josef Stalin. Of course, I had known Franklin Roosevelt since my childhood.

But other activities kept getting in the way. In 1953, I started to work with Herbert Feis on my papers of the 1941–46 period. At that time I wrote extensive memoranda amplifying the hurried notes I had made earlier. When I decided to run for governor of New York in 1954, however, that collaboration had to end. Feis completed his excellent book, *Churchill, Roosevelt, Stalin: The War They Waged and the Peace They Sought*, on his own. I believe it was a major contribution, but the Feis book, under the circumstances, could not include my personal impressions and point of view.

In the intervening years I was so involved with current events, whether in government or in opposition, that I could not contemplate the degree of concentration a comprehensive book of this nature demands.

Not until Elie Abel suggested some three years ago that we might write this book together did I feel ready at last to undertake it. I had long admired his writings—their clarity, the skill with which he assembled facts and illuminated recent history. After considerable discussion we decided to adopt the literary model devised by Henry Stimson and McGeorge Bundy in their book, *On Active Service in Peace and War*. Our book would be written in the third person except, of course, when it quoted from my notes, memoranda, letters, telegrams and recollections.

Although I did not keep a diary, I tried whenever possible to make notes and memoranda of significant conversations, in addition to my telegrams and personal letters to Roosevelt, Hopkins and others. My work at the time was so absorbing, so wholly directed toward action in support of the war, that many of the notes were necessarily brief. In London, there were many late nights with Churchill, and my need to be up and doing early the next morning left hardly a moment for keeping detailed records. In Moscow, however, owing to the need for translation, there was time to make detailed notes of my talks with Stalin and other Soviet officials.

Over the past two years, Elie Abel and I have worked closely together. To paraphrase Stimson on Bundy's role, the style and composition of this book is entirely Elie's. He has skillfully placed my own account of events in the broader context of the war. On substance we have been in constant consultation; the analysis and the judgments expressed conform to my own. He has accurately recorded what I thought and felt at the time, together with my retrospective assessments.

I want to record my gratitude for the scholarly assistance of Charles Maier, a member of the Harvard University Department of History and a research associate of the John F. Kennedy School of Government. He is currently an associate of the Lehrman Institute in New York. Through his tireless research and wise advice, he helped greatly in compiling the raw material that went into this book and in many discussions with us helped sharpen our focus and avoid pitfalls.

IN LOOKING BACK OVER MY EXPERIENCES of some fifty years with the Soviet Union, I find that my basic judgments remain little altered, although conditions have changed radically. I have been attacked for those judgments from both ends of the political spectrum. Some have called me a warmonger; others denounced me as too soft on Communism. I continue to maintain, as in 1945, that on ideology there is no prospect of compromise between the Kremlin and ourselves, but that we must find ways to settle as many areas of conflict as possible in order to live together on this small planet without war.

I have constantly believed that internal pressures by the Russian people and the influence of world opinion would lead in time to some relaxation in the Soviet system, and that greater respect for human rights would gradually develop. This has certainly been happening, though unevenly and far too slowly.

I heartily approve the policy of détente. It seems to me dangerous, however, to use a French word, the meaning of which is not clear to the American people. *Détente* means the relaxation of tensions between nations. I fail to see how anyone can oppose that objective. But it is my impression that people have been oversold on the actual achievements of the détente policy. A visiting Russian editor told me recently that the people he met in the United States believed that *détente* meant the Soviet Union had accepted the status quo everywhere in the world; and if Soviet activities anywhere were found to be in conflict with the status quo, that necessarily meant the Russians had broken the understanding. Our understandings with the Soviet Union are, in fact, specific and so are strictly limited. They were entered into in the hope of preventing nuclear war and of making further agreements possible, but we have a long way to go.

In a talk with Mr. Brezhnev in June 1974, I found that he shared my understanding of the concept of détente. He indicated that we ought to try to make progress step by step, year by year. He hoped that the annual exchange of visits—the President going to Russia one year and his own return visit to the United States the next—would improve the climate and the prospects for such progress. Within the Soviet Union, Brezhnev has committed himself unequivocally to détente. It would be reckless on our part not to try to meet him halfway. It seems to me important, however, that the public at large not confuse the idea of détente with other French words such as *rapprochement* or *entente*, both of which connote the establishment of generally harmonious and more complete understandings between governments. The time has come, perhaps, to say what we mean and to mean what we say in plain English.

We have made progress in the easing of tension, particularly in the nuclear field and in Europe on Berlin. But there is a great deal more to be done. I decry those who contend that any relaxation of tensions must inevitably benefit the Russians, to our disadvantage. It seems to me we have no choice. In this nuclear age, war is unthinkable. Our interest is bound to be served by relieving tensions as much as we can, by working for what I have called "competitive coexistence." I for one do not fear the competition. The strength of the ideals on which our nation is founded gives us an opportunity to expand our constructive influence in the world. Our military strength, essential as it is, should be basically defensive. I have found in my travels that our ideals have a powerful appeal for men everywhere. People want us to live up to them. In my experience, the American Presidents who have had the greatest influence are those who spoke most eloquently to the people of the world. I can remember Russian women weeping in the streets of Moscow when Roosevelt died. They felt they had lost a friend—a friend who, they hoped, would lead the world to peace.

When John F. Kennedy was killed, peasants in South America and in Africa tacked up his photograph in their huts. They saw in him a man who had cared about their future. This may sound like sentimentality. It is, I am convinced, practical world politics.

We ought to recognize that American policy has not always been in tune with the thinking of ordinary people around the world, particularly in the developing countries. Now that the tragedy of Vietnam is behind us, the time has come for a reappraisal of our objectives, in collaboration with like-minded nations, in order that we can once again give inspiration, hope and leadership to the world.

My latest mission to Moscow was to head a delegation of distinguished Americans appointed by President Ford to represent the United States at the Soviet 30th Anniversary Celebration of VE Day—May 8 and 9, 1975.

In Brezhnev's keynote address, he stressed peace as the theme of the celebration. He paid tribute to the heroism of the Red Army and the supreme sacrifices of the Soviet people in the victory that has brought thirty years of peace. He pointed out that the effective collaboration between us had been achieved in spite of "differences of social system" and now called for peaceful coexistence and détente to prevent another world disaster. He also stated "the high-principled . . . support of the liberation movement . . . invests our peace policy with even greater strength . . ."

Many aspects of the two-day celebration gave striking evidence that the Kremlin is determined to avoid the horrors of another war and yet continue to support "liberation movements" wherever the opportunity unfolds.

IN EXPRESSING MY GRATITUDE to those associated with me during the war, I want first to mention my daughter Kathleen. She was with me during the five years I spent overseas in London and in Moscow. For reasons of health, my wife was unable to make these difficult journeys. Kathleen got a job with the International News Service in their London bureau and later with *Newsweek*. I was, of course, personally anxious to have Kathleen with me. I knew it would be a great experience for her. Also, the British at the time were still sending children to Canada and the United States in fear of German bombing and the threat of invasion. I felt that Kathleen's presence would be looked upon as a mark of American confidence. I remember that even Mrs. Churchill showed surprise when I told her that Kathleen was coming over.

Kathleen wrote a great many letters home, and we have quoted generously from them. She combined an astute perception of the people and the scenes around her with a vivid style of expression. In Moscow, at first she helped in the Office of War Information and later handled its activities. In addition, she ran Spaso House, no easy task in those difficult days. Stalin once remarked on her presence in wartime Moscow as a great contribution to public morale.

I was fortunate in having as my assistant Robert P. Meiklejohn, who had been associated with me in my prewar business activities. Meiklejohn did everything for me. He not only took my particularly secret dictation but ran the Mission in London single-handed. He kept copious notes and wrote a report on the two-and-a-half-year history of the Harriman Mission, which has been an invaluable source of information for this book. Before we went to Moscow, Meiklejohn was commissioned in the Navy as a lieutenant.

I shall always be grateful to Edward Stettinius, who, when he took on responsibility for the Lend-Lease program, sent me two able young lawyers, Winthrop Brown and Charles Noyes. They were unusually effective.

Perhaps the most remarkable member of my staff was Sam Berger. I wanted someone close to the American labor movement to deal with manpower problems in Britain. At my request Isadore Lubin, who was then working in the White House, got Sam's name from Sidney Hillman. As I was pressed for time, I had to interview Sam in a taxi-cab driving from the White House to the Pentagon during a visit to Washington in January 1942. I hired him then and there; Sidney Hillman's character reference was enough for me. Sam proved of immense value. For example, to make up for the lag in coal production, we got the British to undertake strip mining, then unknown in Britain. I sent Berger to the United States to negotiate for large shovels, which were then in short supply. He took with him a promising young official of the Ministry of Supply, Harold Wilson. Sam made a career of the foreign service and recently retired after an impressive record, having served effectively as ambassador in several critical posts.

There were a great many others who came and went during the wartime years that I served in Britain. I am particularly grateful to the Army, Navy and Air Force officers assigned to the Mission. For all of them I opened doors to the British ministries, but they did the job that proved so effective in our common cause.

In London, I had built the staff up from scratch. But I brought only Kathleen, Bob Meiklejohn and General John R. Deane with me to Moscow. General Deane was to head our newly established military mission to the Soviet Union. I soon felt the need of a Russian expert as minister counselor and was determined to have George Kennan. It took nine months of pressure on the State Department, with the aid of Harry Hopkins, to get him reassigned to Moscow. My determination

was richly rewarded. Kennan's knowledge of Russia—language, litera-
ture, history, politics—was of inestimable value.

With General Deane, George Kennan served as my principal
adviser over the last year and a half of my term as ambassador. We
were supported by a fine staff of foreign service officers, to whom I
will ever be grateful, particularly to Tommy Thompson and Eddie
Page. I greatly respected the work of John Paton Davies and John
Melby, two capable, loyal foreign service officers who were unjustly
sacrificed during the McCarthy purge.

I must add a word about Chip Bohlen's brother-in-law, my close
friend Charlie Thayer, who helped me enormously during my first
wartime visit to Moscow in September 1941. Unhappily, he was
another victim of the McCarthy terror, and our country lost a most
effective and imaginative officer.

There were others who served us well—Francis Stevens, Bob
Tucker and Tom Whitney, for example, together with occasional
stimulating visits from Elbridge Durbrow, an expert on Poland.

I also want to record my gratitude to the British ambassador, Sir
Archibald Clark Kerr. We kept in almost daily touch with one
another, exchanging information of the most highly classified nature.
I must confess that I got the better of the bargain, as the Foreign Office
kept Archie much better informed of world-wide developments than
the State Department kept me. Our staffs also learned to work together
as a team.

The fact that I saw Stalin frequently induced other members of
the diplomatic corps to share their problems with me. I can recall, for
example, visits from the ambassador of Afghanistan, Sultan Ahmad,
then the dean of the diplomatic corps. A dispute was raging at the time
between his country and the Soviet Union over rival claims to certain
islands in the Oxus River, the border between the two countries. The
Afghan peasants were continuing to cut hay on the islands, as they had
for generations, and the Red Army from its side of the river would
take potshots at them from time to time, occasionally with unfortunate
results. At the ambassador's request, I did my best to interest Molotov
and Vishinsky in halting this practice. The dispute was finally settled.
I doubt whether I contributed much to it, but in postwar years I have
been warmly received as a friend in my visits to Afghanistan. My talks
with these diplomats helped to educate me about Russian policies in
other parts of the world. Only the Japanese embassy doors were closed
both ways.

W. AVERELL HARRIMAN

CONTENTS

Special Envoy to Churchill and Stalin
1941–1946

CHAPTER I

All Aid to Britain, Short of War

I T WAS AN EXTRAORDINARY ASSIGNMENT that President Roosevelt outlined for William Averell Harriman on February 18, 1941. "I want
you to go over to London," the President said, "and recommend everything that we can do, short of war, to keep the British Isles afloat."
Harriman would be the President's personal representative. He would
report to the White House, not the State Department. He would
concern himself with all matters affecting the conduct of the war—
Lend-Lease, shipping, strategy—dealing directly with Prime Minister
Churchill and his service and supply ministers. The newly appointed
American ambassador to the Court of St. James's, John Gilbert
Winant, would take care of the normal business of American represen-
tation, deal with the Foreign Office and report to the Secretary of
State, Cordell Hull.

Harriman had known Eleanor and Franklin Roosevelt since his
school days at Groton, where he had been a classmate of Eleanor's
younger brother, Hall Roosevelt. With his sister, Mary Harriman
Rumsey, Averell Harriman had broken the family's solid Republican
tradition by voting for Alfred E. Smith in 1928 and then for Roosevelt in 1932, 1936 and 1940. Although never completely sold on all
aspects of the New Deal, he had been one of the few men prominent
in Wall Street who, instead of damning Roosevelt for his economic
heresies, had been willing to serve in the National Recovery Administration. He had also been an original member of the Business Advisory Council to the Department of Commerce, established by

Roosevelt in 1933, which included such leading industrialists as Walter
Teagle of Jersey Standard and Gerard Swope of General Electric.
Harriman later served as its chairman for three years. He was forty-
nine years old, a partner in the private banking firm of Brown Brothers
Harriman & Company, chairman of the board of the Union Pacific
Railroad and chairman of the Executive Committee of the Illinois
Central.

Some six weeks earlier his friend Harry Hopkins had alerted Harriman to the possibility of an important war job in England. Hopkins
had then flown off to England in January, at Roosevelt's request, to
meet Churchill for the first time. Now Hopkins had returned and
Harriman called on the President to learn precisely what assignment
he had in mind.

> The President talked to me as if it was mutually under-
> stood that it had been decided I should go for some time past
> [Harriman recorded in his notes a few days later]. He was a
> bit foggy as to whom I was to work with on this side as he
> had not set up the Lend-Lease organization. He explained,
> however, it would not be OPM and, at all events, entirely in-
> dependent of the State Department. He said I was to communi-
> cate with him on any matters that I thought were important
> enough . . . All in all, rambling on as he does on many sub-
> jects, he was far more humble, less cocksure and more human
> than in any conversation I had with him since he was Presi-
> dent.[1]

Their rambling conversation touched on the confused status of
the OPM, the Office of Production Management (headed jointly by
William S. Knudsen of General Motors and Sidney Hillman of the
Amalgamated Clothing Workers of America), an organization with a
split personality which Roosevelt had created to speed the task of
industrial mobilization. Sensing that Harriman, who worked for Knudsen in charge of the raw materials branch, did not greatly admire his
bureaucratic handiwork, Roosevelt disarmed his visitor by admitting,
"You know, Averell, I am by nature a compromiser."

Harriman immediately accepted the London mission. He urged
Roosevelt to announce the appointment without delay so that he could
begin preparing for the difficult task ahead and recruiting a staff. The
President made his announcement the same afternoon to the White
House reporters clustered around his desk:

THE PRESIDENT: I don't think there is much news that you haven't
    already got. You saw Averell Harriman when he went out, and
    that is a thing that has been in the process of discussion for a

month or six weeks; and finally, when Harry Hopkins came back, what we thought probably would be a need has rather definitely become a need; so Averell Harriman is going over in about ten days. As soon as the defense program under the Lend-Spend, Lend-Lease—whatever you call it—bill is perfected, more or less, he will go over and—Oh, I suppose you will ask all about his title, so I thought I would invent one; I talked over with him what his title would be, and we decided it was a pretty good idea to call him an "Expediter." There's a new one for you. I believe it is not in the diplomatic list or any other list. So he will go over as "Defense Expediter."

PRESS: What is the salary?

(The President did not reply.)*

THE PRESIDENT: That doesn't conform with anything you ever heard before—but that doesn't mean it isn't an excellent idea. We won't send his name to the Senate—it won't be that kind of job; and that is neither here nor there.

Roosevelt was enjoying the mystification. He had just appointed Winant, former head of the International Labor Organization, to take Joseph P. Kennedy's place in London on the theory that the new ambassador would get along well with British Labor; the President preferred not to be too closely identified with the Conservative party of Winston Churchill. The reporters, naturally, were curious about the relationship between Winant's embassy and Harriman's as-yet-undefined mission. One of them asked whether Harriman would report through the embassy or directly to the President.

"I don't know," Roosevelt replied, "and I don't give a —— you know."

There could be no question where Averell Harriman stood in the great debate then raging across the land—isolation or intervention to help the beleaguered British. Speaking at the Yale Club in New York on February 4, he tried to rouse his audience by calling the roll of Yale men (Dean Acheson at the State Department, Robert A. Lovett in the War Department, Archibald MacLeish at the Library of Congress) who had put aside their private occupations to enter the government because they cared deeply whether Britain or Hitler's Germany would win the war. Harriman left no room for doubt concerning his own position on the question of Lend-Lease for Britain:

"If we are to aid Britain, let's be practical and grant the President power to make our aid effective. The most fatal error would be half-hearted and insufficient help. Let those who are

* Harriman in fact took no salary.

ready to accept a totalitarian world vote 'no' to aid to Britain.
Don't let the issue be confused by cries of dictatorship at
home."

The cry of presidential dictatorship from the isolationist camp
had started with Roosevelt's proclamation of Lend-Lease on December 17, 1940. "What I am trying to do," the President said that day,
"is eliminate the dollar sign." He used an analogy that seemed to
Harriman brilliant in its simplicity: "Suppose my neighbor's home
catches fire, and I have a length of garden hose . . ." The Lend-Lease
decision plunged the country into a long, bitter debate, which Harriman joined with his Yale Club speech and an address before the Traffic
Club of Washington on February 13, five days before his meeting with
Roosevelt:

> "I see no place in this debate for the cry of dictatorship at
> home. This cry has been sounded in each of the war emergen-
> cies in our history and yet democracy has survived. Those
> who have such fears have little faith in democracy. If we are
> to aid Britain, someone must have power to act in the chang-
> ing scene of war, to lend our power when and where it can
> be effective. The founding fathers gave the Congress the
> authority to grant the President [that] power . . .
>
> "So I come back to the simple question: Will we aid
> England? This is a decision that should not be made in emo-
> tion or in heat, it must be thought through clearly.
>
> "I have made my decision. I am not willing to face a
> world dominated by Hitler."

In quickly accepting Roosevelt's offer, Harriman demonstrated
his impatience for action. He had long regretted the family and business circumstances that had kept him out of action in the world war.
Newly married before America entered the war, he had bought a
shipbuilding company on the Delaware River, near Chester, Pennsylvania, which was assembling prefabricated ships in a few months
instead of building them from the keel up, in the slower, traditional
fashion. As soon as war was declared he went to Washington and
negotiated a government contract to build forty steel cargo ships for
the merchant marine. "I was quite conscious of a young man's responsibility," Harriman recalled some fifty-five years later. "I felt
very strongly that there should be a draft. Intellectually, I could
reason that I had done the right thing, because I thought that shipping
was the real bottleneck of World War I. But emotionally, I never felt
entirely comfortable. Some people said I worked in the second war
because of a sense of guilt. I'm not going to try to psychoanalyze

myself. But I did get a lot of satisfaction, having the opportunity to serve overseas in World War II. That tended to square the balance."

The winter of 1940–41 was the season of despair for all free men. Hitler's armies had subjugated Poland, overrun the Low Countries and brought France to her knees. Britain stood alone, braced for a German invasion. The United States, its power and wealth as yet unmobilized, was still ostensibly neutral when Roosevelt decided to send Harriman to London. The President had met Churchill briefly in 1918. He now felt the need to establish a closer personal link than was possible through correspondence. They had started exchanging letters in September of 1939, when Roosevelt congratulated Churchill upon his return to office as First Lord of the Admiralty in the Cabinet of Neville Chamberlain. Churchill, who regretted that there had been "no opportunity for anything but salutations" when he met Roosevelt twenty-one years earlier, responded gratefully, signing his letter "Naval Person."[2] Their long, memorable correspondence was to continue over the next five and a half years, although it seemed to both men a poor substitute for the face-to-face meeting they craved; all the more so after Churchill in May 1940 succeeded Chamberlain at No. 10 Downing Street and had taken to signing his letters "Former Naval Person."

His first message to Roosevelt as Prime Minister, dated May 15, foretold the horrors to come with astonishing prescience:

> The small countries are simply smashed up, one by one, like matchwood. We must expect, though it is not yet certain, that Mussolini will hurry in to share the loot of civilisation. We expect to be attacked here ourselves, both from the air and by parachute and air-borne troops, in the near future, and are getting ready for them. If necessary we shall continue the war alone, and we are not afraid of that. But I trust you realise, Mr. President, that the voice and force of the United States may count for nothing if they are withheld too long. You may have a completely subjugated, Nazified Europe established with astonishing swiftness, and the weight may be more than we can bear. All I can ask now is that you should proclaim non-belligerency, which would mean that you would help us with everything short of actually engaging armed forces.
>
> We shall go on paying dollars for as long as we can but I should like to feel reasonably sure that when we can pay no more, you will give us the stuff all the same.[3]

Harriman was one of those Americans who refused to haggle with the beleaguered British over the terms of payment for fifty overage destroyers Churchill had requested from the United States, together with late-model American war planes, anti-aircraft guns, ammunition, steel and other essential materials. He had worried himself sick over the menace of Hitlerism since the German occupation of the Rhineland in 1936, to the point of developing a duodenal ulcer in the spring of 1940. It was his first serious illness and he attributed it solely to his concern over the lack of action by the Western powers. He did exactly what the doctor ordered: gave up smoking, lived on milk and cream, spent some time in bed and recovered his health just as the "phony war" was turning real in the summer of 1940.

When Roosevelt took his first cautious step toward industrial mobilization in late May of 1940 by creating his National Defense Advisory Commission, Harriman was ready. He went down to Washington at once to join Edward R. Stettinius of U.S. Steel, who was in charge of industrial materials, as transportation adviser. NDAC, the parent of the Office of Production Management, was a distinctly Rooseveltian improvisation. Instead of having one chairman, it had seven heads.* Harriman's enthusiasm and energy soon overflowed the less than full-time demands of his job. Unlike many of his colleagues in the Stettinius office, all senior executives of large corporations who were thrown together in a single large room on the ground floor of the Federal Reserve Board Building "with one desk, one telephone and a lot of straight-back chairs," Harriman did not wait to be told what to do. Knowing his way around Washington from his NRA days, he quickly organized the work assigned to him and in a matter of weeks became more concerned with the short supply of raw materials than with their transportation. Supplies of crude rubber from the Far East having been cut by the Japanese occupation of French Indochina, synthetic rubber plants had to be built in a hurry. As for aluminum, the industry's capacity had been outstripped by the sudden demand for military aircraft. Harriman's quick and total immersion in these problems prompted a change of assignment when NDAC, the seven-headed monster, gave way after several months to OPM, a two-headed organization headed by Knudsen and Hillman. Knudsen suggested to Harriman that he had been "flitting around" long enough and should now take charge of the industrial materials branch.

In search of more aluminum, which called for vast quantities of hydroelectric power, Harriman ran head-on into the irascible Secretary of the Interior, Harold Ickes. He went to see Ickes with Robert P.

* Apart from Stettinius, the Defense Commission was made up of William S. Knudsen, industrial production; Sidney Hillman, labor; Leon Henderson, price stabilization; Ralph Budd, transportation; Chester C. Davis, farm products; Dr. Harriet Elliott, consumer protection.

Patterson, Under Secretary of War, to ask that a bloc of power from the Bonneville Dam on the Columbia River be allocated to the Aluminum Company of America so that it could rapidly expand production. Ickes refused with characteristic bluntness. He was not about to strengthen Alcoa's monopoly, he said, arguing that the power contract ought to go to the Reynolds Metals Company, which in Harriman's view lacked the experience or the staff for expanded production. "We argued with Ickes," Harriman recalled, "that awarding the contract to Reynolds would mean delays in production that were bound to hurt the defense effort. We also made the point that the government could dispose of the new aluminum plant after the war as it saw fit. But Ickes turned a deaf ear. In his diary, published after the war, he accused Patterson and myself of using our government positions to build up monopolies. Bob Lovett, then Assistant Secretary of War for Air, estimated that Ickes' stubborn position cost the country many hundreds of vitally needed aircraft by delaying our aluminum expansion."

By Christmas of 1940 Roosevelt had taken several additional strides toward committing the industrial strength of the United States to the defense of Britain. He turned over to the Royal Navy the fifty destroyers Churchill had requested, although the hard-boiled temper of the Congress required him to get in exchange ninety-nine year leases on several British air and naval bases in the West Indies and Newfoundland. The President moved no faster than congressional and public opinion would tolerate. It was not until March 11, 1941, that a wary Congress completed passage of the Lend-Lease Act, which he had put forward in December. This legislation, shrewdly designated H.R. 1776, an act "to promote the defense of the United States," was to make possible a steady and steadily expanding flow of arms and essential raw materials to Britain, in spite of the Neutrality Act, without payment and without subterfuge.

As the New Year beckoned ("the New Year of storm that is opening upon us," in Churchill's words), Roosevelt also proclaimed common cause with the people of the British Isles. "If Britain should go down," he said in a "fireside chat" broadcast around the world on December 30, 1940, "all of us in all the Americas would be living at the point of a gun . . . We must produce arms and ships with every energy and resource we can command . . ." On New Year's Eve, Churchill thanked the President with characteristic flourish:

> They burned a large part of the City of London last night, and the scenes of widespread destruction here and in our provincial centres are shocking; but when I visited the still-burning ruins today, the spirit of Londoners was as high as in

the first days of the indiscriminate bombing in September, four
months ago.

I thank you for testifying before all the world that the
future safety and greatness of the American Union are intimately concerned with the upholding and the effective arming
of that indomitable spirit.[4]

Roosevelt was grateful for Churchill's rolling prose. But he felt
the need for a personal meeting. When Hopkins volunteered to fly
over and make the arrangements, the President at first dismissed the
idea. There was so much to be done in the White House—plans for
his third inaugural, a new State of the Union message to be drafted
and a new budget, swollen by the cost of preparing for the war he
still hoped to avoid. Then, without alerting Hopkins to his change of
heart, the President announced on January 3, 1941, that he was sending him over to see Churchill "just to maintain—I suppose that is the
word for it—personal relations between me and the British Government." There was loud laughter among the White House reporters
that morning as the President insisted that Hopkins would have no
special mission, no title, no powers and that he would be traveling
alone.

Hopkins had just heard the news from Stephen Early, the President's press secretary, when Harriman telephoned from Sun Valley,
Idaho, where he was on a skiing holiday with his family. "Let me
carry your bag, Harry," Harriman said, pointing out that he could be
useful. "I've met Churchill several times and I know London intimately." Hopkins insisted that he must travel alone but that he wanted
to see Harriman upon his return. The President, he added vaguely,
might have something for him to do, something that would come out
of the trip to London.

It is a matter of record that Hopkins, a social worker from Iowa
who had never before been involved in world affairs, left Washington
holding no very exalted opinion of Churchill. The Prime Minister, in
turn, was somewhat flabbergasted by the news that Roosevelt was
sending over Hopkins, of all people. The Foreign Office had help-
fully provided a dossier on the unknown presidential emissary, showing that he had been chiefly concerned with relief work during the
Great Depression. To Churchill, 1941 seemed the wrong year for an
earnest discussion of British welfare policies after the war was won.
But Brendan Bracken, Churchill's parliamentary private secretary, had
heard that Hopkins was close to Roosevelt, at least as close as Bracken
was to the Prime Minister. So Bracken met Hopkins at the airport,
took him to see Churchill at Downing Street and then escorted him to
Ditchley, the stately home of Ronald Tree, M.P. Churchill spent week-

ends at Ditchley when the moon was full, his security men having decided that the Prime Minister's official country residence at Chequers could be pinpointed too easily by German bombers.

After dinner that Saturday of the full moon, when the ladies had withdrawn, leaving the Prime Minister and his male guests to their coffee, brandy and cigars, Churchill invited Hopkins to share with them his vision of the postwar world. "After the war we must make a good life for the cottagers," Churchill said, as if to put Hopkins, the social worker, at his ease. Hopkins responded with a degree of violence the Prime Minister had not bargained for. "I don't give a damn about your cottagers," he said. "I came here to see how we can beat that fellow Hitler." That brief outburst laid to rest the Prime Minister's preconceptions about the presidential emissary. "Mr. Hopkins," he said, "we had better go into the library."* They remained in the library until four o'clock in the morning, talking about that fellow Hitler and how he could be beaten.

Before leaving Washington, Hopkins had been advised by the economist Jean Monnet, who after the fall of France had joined the British Purchasing Commission in the United States, that "Churchill is the British War Cabinet and no one else matters." Perhaps out of loyalty to Roosevelt, the only great man he acknowledged, Hopkins had dismissed that notion scornfully. A close friend, hearing Hopkins run Churchill down as a Tory prima donna, was sufficiently concerned to warn him that he had better stay home if he insisted on behaving "like a damned little small-town chauvinist." But a few days in London were enough to transform Hopkins' attitude. He wrote to Roosevelt on the note paper of Claridge's Hotel:

> The people here are amazing from Churchill down and if courage alone can win—the result will be inevitable. But they need our help desperately and I am sure you will permit nothing to stand in the way. . . .
>
> <u>Churchill</u> is the gov't in every sense of the word—he controls the grand strategy and often the details—labor trusts him—the army, navy and air force are behind him to a man. The politicians and upper crust pretend to like him. I cannot emphasize too strongly that he is the one and only person over here with whom you need to have a full meeting of minds.
>
> Churchill wants to see you—the sooner the better—but I have told him of your problem until the [Lend-Lease] bill is

* The account of Hopkins' first evening at Ditchley differs somewhat from other published accounts. Harriman heard it from David Margesson, Churchill's Secretary of State for War, who was present at the dinner. The story, Harriman felt, fairly described Churchill's attitude toward Hopkins on his arrival.

passed. I am convinced this meeting between you and Churchill is essential—and soon—for the battering continues and Hitler
does not wait for Congress.[5]

When Hopkins flew home, Harriman and Winant went out to
meet him at the Marine Terminal of LaGuardia Airport. Mayor
Fiorello H. LaGuardia was there to deliver a short speech of welcome,
together with an impressive turnout of reporters, who got little information out of Hopkins. He was still climbing out of the Boeing
Clipper when Winant, in a state of high excitement, called out, "Are
they going to hold out?" Hopkins shouted back, "Of course they are."
It was plainly impossible for Hopkins to have said anything else with
a crowd of strangers listening. Only after Harriman, Winant and
Hopkins had arrived in his suite at the Roosevelt Hotel could he re-
count his impressions of England at war with any degree of confiden-
tiality.

For all his outward optimism, Hopkins had come back with
certain misgivings. "He was impressed by the determination of the
British to resist," Harriman recalled, "but appalled by their lack of
means to do so and the need for immediate American help—on a scale
we had not till then imagined." Hopkins also was troubled by the
great expectations of the British. Many of the people he had met
appeared to believe that Roosevelt would have the United States in
the war by summer. They looked upon Lend-Lease as the decisive
step in a rapid American escalation, leading to outright belligerency.
Although Hopkins, in all his private discussions with British leaders,
had emphasized the persistent strength of isolationist sentiment in
Congress and the country at large, many of his listeners were not
persuaded. They could not imagine that the American people—having
followed the President through eight years of domestic crisis—would
now repudiate his leadership. While Hopkins came away convinced
that the United States would have to increase its help immediately and
that this would call for strong leadership by Roosevelt, he was not yet
prepared to commit U.S. naval vessels to convoy duty in the North
Atlantic by way of making certain that Lend-Lease supplies would
reach the British Isles safely. He favored turning over ten destroyers
a month to the British, a step that would inevitably call for a rapid
expansion of the American destroyer program, and doubling the 1942
goals for the emergency merchant shipbuilding program.

THE HARRIMAN-HOPKINS FRIENDSHIP, which had taken root in the
New Deal years, was to flower in wartime. They had met almost
casually in 1933 when they happened to be traveling from New York

to Washington on the same train. Their club-car conversation that first day led to further meetings and a lasting friendship. Harriman liked Hopkins' irreverent attitude toward the high and mighty. He could be cynical and iconoclastic; he also could be a warm, loyal friend. On the surface the two had little in common: Hopkins, the son of a harness maker, born in Sioux City, Iowa, graduate of Grinnell College, transplanted to the slums of New York, where he worked for a succession of welfare organizations; a man whose clothes were perpetually rumpled, always short of cash, frail and ailing. His idea of the high life was an afternoon at the race track. Harriman, by contrast, was the son of a railroad millionaire, born in New York, schooled at Groton and Yale, a world traveler from childhood; at home on the polo field and the ski slope; a railroad executive, international banker and collector of Impressionist paintings.

A friendship that seemed to thrive on contrasts, it was in fact firmly based on a shared sense of public obligation and common objectives, which allowed for frequent differences about how to get there. Hopkins, for example, was aghast when Harriman came to see him in behalf of the Business Advisory Council to argue for decentralization of the federal relief programs he administered. "I thought he was going to jump across the table and throttle me," Harriman recalled. "Harry had a very high sense of honor about his federal relief program. He was absolutely certain that if the money were distributed locally, much of it would be stolen. It was an article of faith with him that local control in those days meant more corruption."

When Roosevelt considered appointing Hopkins as Secretary of Commerce toward the end of 1938, he sent his close friend and adviser Thomas J. Corcoran to sound out Harriman. "That's the greatest idea you ever thought of," Harriman responded. He felt that Hopkins' close relationship with Roosevelt was bound to make the Commerce Department far more influential and effective than it had been under Daniel C. Roper, the outgoing Secretary. "I had developed a great respect for Harry," Harriman recalled. "I knew he was open-minded and that his views were quite different from the general public impression of a wild spender. I wanted him to get to know more businessmen. If the Business Advisory Council could sell Hopkins on some new ideas, that would mean Roosevelt, too, was about three-quarters sold."

The Hopkins nomination to Commerce raised a loud outcry across the land. Even newspapers that were moderately friendly to Roosevelt considered Hopkins an incongruous choice. Republican papers and congressmen were openly hostile. "Surely, this is the most incomprehensible, as well as one of the least defensible, appointments the President has made in his six and one-half years in the White

House," the Chicago *Daily News* thundered. The Senate echoed with bitter opposition through three days of hearings before the Commerce Committee and a full week of frequently ill-tempered floor debate.

Harriman's enthusiasm for Hopkins, shared by remarkably few captains of industry, led him to rally the entire membership of the Business Advisory Council behind the appointment. It was not an easy task. When Harriman was called before the Senate Commerce Committee to testify on Hopkins' fitness for Cabinet office, the chairman, Senator Walter F. George of Georgia, could scarcely contain his astonishment. Harriman had no sooner reported that the Business Council was unanimous in supporting Hopkins than George, totally incredulous, exclaimed, "They are?" Harriman replied, "Yes, Mr. Chairman, they are." He later recalled, "I was on and off the stand as fast as any man who ever appeared before Senator George." Hopkins' few close friends in the business world—Harriman and Stettinius chief among them—were still viewed with suspicion by the much larger number of businessmen hostile to the New Deal as "Hopkins' tame millionaires." But the Senate confirmed Hopkins by a vote of 58 to 27, five Democrats voting against him with the Republicans, and at least three others abstaining.

Hopkins undoubtedly had proposed the London assignment for his friend Harriman, who enjoyed the President's full confidence. It was another of Roosevelt's improvisations, designed in part to keep Cordell Hull and the State Department at arm's length while he and Churchill, using the Harriman channel, worked out their strategic decisions. "I think Roosevelt knew that we would get involved in the war, sooner or later," Harriman recalled. "He knew the country was not ready for it. He wanted to learn what he could do for the British, short of war, and he wanted that information to come to him directly. He didn't want it filtered through other channels. Above all, he didn't want a personality as strong and stubborn as Mr. Hull to get involved in those decisions, which step by step were becoming more unneutral. I think, however, that Hopkins was responsible for the creative conception that Roosevelt and Churchill needed to develop an intimate relationship going beyond the limits of traditional diplomacy."

HARRIMAN SET ABOUT PREPARING for his London mission through a process of total immersion. He called on Hull and Henry L. Stimson, the Secretary of War; General H. H. Arnold of the Army Air Forces; Admiral Harold R. Stark, Chief of Naval Operations; General George C. Marshall, Army Chief of Staff; and his old Wall Street friends James V. Forrestal and Robert A. Lovett, then Under Secretary of the Navy and Assistant Secretary of War, respectively. He also talked with Dean Acheson, the brand-new Assistant Secretary of State for economic affairs, while waiting to see Hull, and with as many assorted generals and admirals as he could collar before departing. What Harriman heard from these men in commanding positions was not altogether reassuring. Acheson, for example, confessed that he was still in the dark as to the State Department's policy on just about every important question on the international agenda. He indicated to Harriman that although Secretary Hull had "rather definite views" of his own, he was unwilling to set policy when he encountered a significant divergence of opinion within the Department, for example over economic policy toward Japan.

The military men whom Harriman talked with, in late February and early March, wanted to deal fairly with the British but for the most part betrayed a certain skepticism over the requests for arms and munitions coming out of London. They disliked the President's informal way of doing business with Churchill through a tenderfoot like Hopkins. "We can't take seriously requests that come late in the evening over a bottle of port," Lieutenant Colonel James L. Hatcher complained to Harriman. The root of the matter was the overall shortage of ships, airplanes and matériel of every description. The British, already at war and besieged, wanted all the help they could get; the Americans, still technically at peace but fearful that they too would soon be fighting, determined to keep what they could. Harriman quickly realized that every British request would have to be justified, the comparative urgencies carefully calibrated. "There was the unanimous feeling," he recorded in a memorandum summarizing his talks with the military leaders, "that they must have more information on which to base their judgment as to whether a particular [item of] munition was of greater value in British or American hands. We are so short that everything given up by the Army or Navy comes out of our own blood; there is practically nothing surplus and will not be for months." Admiral John Towers, for example, then chief of the Navy's Bureau of Aeronautics, was being pressed to assign larger numbers of PBY (Catalina) flying boats to the Royal Air Force for antisubmarine duty. Harriman found that Towers would have to be persuaded that Britain's need was greater than his own. "Towers would be willing to give up more PBY's now only if he knows that the British have crews enough, bases enough, etc., to operate them, and that the use to which they are going to put them is more important than his," Harriman wrote in his memorandum dated March 11, 1941. "No one has given me any instructions or directions as to what my activities should be. These conversations, however, have made my job quite clear. I must attempt to convince the Prime Minister that I, or someone, must convey to our people his war strategy or else he cannot expect to get maximum aid. Without understanding and acceptance of his war strategy, our military men will drag their feet."

On March 1 Harriman lunched with Stimson and his wife at Woodley, an old Southern colonial building set in spacious grounds which looked over and across Rock Creek Park to the center of Washington. Stimson had bought the place in 1929, when he moved to Washington from New York upon becoming Secretary of State in the Hoover Administration. Roosevelt had invited Stimson to join his Cabinet in June 1940, along with Colonel Frank Knox, who became Secretary of the Navy. Both were Republicans of the internationalist stripe; both supported Roosevelt in matters of foreign policy, opposing the isolationist tendencies of their own party. At luncheon that day Stimson told Harriman that his personal position on the war had not changed since the resounding address he had delivered at New Haven on June 18, 1940, while still a private citizen. In the New Haven speech, which fell an inch or two short of declaring war upon Germany, Stimson proposed outright repeal of the Neutrality Act, calling it "a shackle to our true interests for over five years." He wanted all American ports opened to British and French warships for repairs and refueling. He favored sending American planes and other munitions to Britain and France "on a scale which would be effective" and, if necessary, in American ships under American convoy. He also pressed for the immediate adoption of a system of universal military training.

Stimson now appeared to recognize that Roosevelt could not act so boldly or so fast. He assured Harriman that he was a member of the President's team; he had no doubt Roosevelt shared his own convictions and would move as swiftly as public opinion allowed.

In response to Harriman's questions, Stimson foreshadowed the Europe-first strategy that in later years so infuriated some senior naval officers, the reconstructed isolationists and General Douglas MacArthur. The Atlantic was the crucial theater of war, Stimson said, and the United States "must not be diverted into engagements in the Far East which would have the effect of diluting its aid to Britain." The paramount problem, as he saw it, was to protect the British supply line. According to Harriman's notes of their talk, Stimson said he was prepared to draw a line southward from Greenland or Iceland and then use the United States Navy to convoy all merchant ships, British or American, that far across the Atlantic; if German submarines or other naval vessels ventured west of the mid-Atlantic line they should be hunted down. He argued that Hitler had breached all international law by his aggressions in Europe, and the United States, accordingly, must now feel free to defend its own interests, "without regard to anyone's legalistic objections."

Harriman called on Cordell Hull on March 7. The Secretary of State arrived some forty-five minutes late from a Cabinet meeting, looking weary and worried. Hull nevertheless received Harriman warmly, showing no resentment of the odd arrangements the President had proposed for the Harriman Mission. "I was relieved to find," Harriman recorded in his notes, "that there was not the slightest indication of any fear of complications [arising from] my mission's independence of the State Department." On the contrary, he wrote, Hull said that "he was ready at all times to be of assistance to me, not only in government affairs but personally."

Hull told Harriman that he was disturbed over the Navy's inactivity in the Pacific lest trouble with Japan should develop. He complained that the Navy resisted his advice to keep "cruising about" the waters off Singapore and the Dutch East Indies, by way of deterring Japanese adventures. He had pointed out, Hull said, that the Japanese might be tempted to seize control of certain strategic points in the Far East. The Navy's insistence upon keeping so many of its major warships tied up in Hawaii, Hull warned, could lead to an "ignominious result."

"What is the name of that harbor?" Hull inquired.

"Pearl Harbor."

"Yes," said Hull, and moved on to other matters. Harriman had a final opportunity to sound the President's own views. They covered a great deal of ground together, discussing affairs of state somewhat inconclusively, and Harriman came away greatly troubled by the President's vagueness. The meeting started with a gastronomic horror:

I lunched with the President, Friday, March 7, at his desk. An extraordinary meal. Spinach soup—didn't taste bad but looked like hot water poured over chopped-up spinach. White toast and hot rolls. Main dish—cheese soufflé with *spinach!!* Dessert—three large fat pancakes, plenty of butter and maple syrup. Tea for the President, coffee for myself.

I note the above because he was just recovering from a cold and it struck me as the most unhealthy diet under the circumstances . . . we discussed the British food situation and their increasing need for vitamins, proteins and calcium. As the President was obviously tired and mentally stale . . . it struck me that, in the British interest, fortification of the President's diet should be first priority.

The President asked Harriman to look into the British food situation. He spent considerable time—too much for Harriman, who had heard all this before from Claude Wickard, the Secretary of Agriculture—explaining the need for vitamins, cheese and pork. After considerable effort, Harriman managed to change the subject. He recorded:

> I finally got him over to shipping and he "yes, yessed"
> me when I urged the necessity for the establishment of a
> strong shipping control with greater power than he had given
> so far to Jerry Land.*
> I told him Jerry was overworked. If he decided to use
> Jerry Land . . . which I hoped he would, I urged him to
> instruct Jerry to relieve himself of the details of the Maritime
> Commission operations and concentrate his attention on the
> emergency, including British maritime problems.
> He agreed but in the manner which I have long since
> learned, cannot be accepted as a commitment. Incidentally,
> lack of understanding of what the President means when he
> nods or says "yes" has led to much bitterness on the part of
> certain types of businessmen who assume they have the agreement of the President when all they have, really, is an indication that the President is not prepared to argue the point with
> them . . . I blame the caller, not the President, because it is
> so obvious that [this] is simply the President's pleasant way of
> dodging a discussion which he does not care to enter into. It
> means that he hears and understands what you are saying, but
> not necessarily that he agrees to it. Anyone who assumes
> otherwise is engaging in wishful thinking, or is not very astute.

Harriman then brought up the fearful losses the British convoys were suffering and the plan he had discussed with Stimson to provide American naval escorts for British convoys as far as Iceland.

The President stressed the difficulties of convoying. He was ready, he said, to go as far as American public opinion would permit. But it would do the British no good if, as the result of a clash between an American ship and a German submarine, Hitler were to decide that he was in a state of war with the United States and thus free to attack American vessels anywhere on the seven seas. The thing to do now, Roosevelt contended, was to load supplies for Britain in American merchant ships, have the U.S. Navy escort them as far as Iceland, and there transship the supplies into British bottoms. Harriman, who between the wars had run a transatlantic shipping line, did not think of this as a practical suggestion.

Before Harriman left, Roosevelt outlined another pet scheme for installing flights of helicopters on the decks of merchant ships in con-

* Admiral Emory S. Land, head of the Maritime Commission, had been a close friend of Harriman's since his entry into the shipbuilding business during World War I.

voy. The helicopters, so the President explained, could hover over the convoys, spot German submarines, drop a depth charge or two and then, if they had difficulty landing on a wobbly deck, could be plucked from the sea in great nets trailing behind the base ship. Harriman had been exposed to these flights of presidential fancy more than once in the past—he called it "romancing." He also recognized that he would be leaving in a few days on a mission the President had not cared to define precisely, without specific instructions and without real assurance of getting quick decisions at the White House. His mandate was broad enough: "Recommend everything that we can do, short of war, to keep the British Isles afloat." It was "an excellent mandate, in no way tying my hands," Harriman recalled. "But I was deeply worried that the President did not have a policy and had not decided how far he could go." Stopping overnight in Bermuda four days later on his way to London, Harriman recorded his concern in a note:

> All in all, I left feeling that the President had not faced what I considered to be the realities of the situation: namely, that there was a good chance Germany, without our help, could so cripple British shipping as to affect her ability to hold out. The President obviously hoped that he would not have to face an unpleasant decision. He seemed unwilling to lead public opinion or to force the issue but [he] hoped, without the background of reasoning, that our material aid would let the British do the job . . .
>
> Hopkins is the one man in official position who appears to be ready to force a decision . . .

Harriman's hope of getting the President to act decisively on the range of problems now assigned to him appeared to rest heavily upon his own ability to make a persuasive case for the British and then on Hopkins' influence with Roosevelt. He left New York on March 10, one day before the signing of the Lend-Lease Bill, on board a Pan-American Clipper. It was the first time Harriman had flown the Atlantic, although he had crossed by sea scores of times. "I felt very much the adventurer," he recalled. Among his ten fellow passengers were Anthony Drexel Biddle, the new American ambassador to the European governments-in-exile which had taken refuge in London, and a Swiss businessman who was trying to sell Oerlikon guns to both sides. The Clipper, a comfortable seaplane with a cruising speed of 145 miles an hour at 8,000 feet, offered the only practical connection between America and Europe in the early stages of the war. The first leg, the flight from New York to Bermuda, took about five hours. During the fuel stop Harriman discovered that the White House had neglected

to date the formal letter of authorization which he was to present to
Churchill on his arrival. His resourceful assistant, Robert P. Meiklejohn, scurried around and soon found a typewriter with approximately
the same typeface. Meiklejohn was careful to date the letter March 6,
1941, the day it had been handed to Harriman in Hopkins' office at
the White House. It read:

Dear Mr. Harriman:

Reposing special faith and confidence in you, I am asking
that you proceed at your early convenience to Great Britain,
there to act as my Special Representative, with the rank of
Minister, in regard to all matters relating to the facilitation of
material aid to the British Empire. In this capacity, you will
take all appropriate measures to expedite the provision of such
assistance by the United States.

You will, of course, communicate to this Government
any matters which may come to your attention in the performance of your mission which you may feel will serve best the
interests of the United States.

With all best wishes for the success of your mission, I am

Very sincerely yours,

Franklin D. Roosevelt

The second leg of the journey, from Bermuda to Horta in the
Azores, took fifteen hours, and the third, from Horta to Lisbon, five
additional hours. Transatlantic passengers enjoyed many of the comforts of sea travel. They could move freely about the Clipper, read or
play cards in the lounges, sit down to a table for their meals, and when
flying overnight, they were assigned roomy bunks—a far cry from
the crowded aisles and the plastic lunch trays of the contemporary jet
plane. The Clipper had the capacity to carry 21,500 pounds of payload
on flights up to 1,000 miles, from New York to Bermuda, for example.
But the weight of additional fuel needed for longer flights, such as the
2,000-mile leg from Bermuda to the Azores, made it necessary to
reduce the payload by 9,000 pounds. Pan Am, in short, could book
the Clipper up to its seating capacity of eighty passengers as far as
Bermuda but would carry less than half that number from Bermuda
to Europe. Bad weather in the Azores, where the Clipper had to land
in an open roadstead subject to heavy swells, sometimes caused delays
of a day or two in Bermuda. Occasionally, when the weather in the
Azores remained unfavorable for several days, the Clipper would fly
nonstop to Lisbon; then the need for additional fuel would reduce

the payload to only 5,500 pounds, little more than the weight of the mail on board. In these circumstances, most of the passengers would be left behind in Bermuda to await the next flight.

In Harriman's case the trip from New York to England took five days, three of them spent in neutral Lisbon waiting for a connecting KLM flight to Bristol. This flight, the only way to get to England in 1941, was constantly overbooked and Harriman fell victim to the rigors of protocol. Tony Biddle held the rank of ambassador; Harriman was merely a minister. So while Biddle left on an early flight, Harriman stayed in Portugal, fuming at the foolishness of officialdom. Lisbon in wartime had the reputation of a center of intrigue. Harriman was warned, for example, to be careful of his papers in the spy-ridden hotel at Estoril where he stayed with his party. He used the free time for a long talk with Colonel William J. Donovan, head of the Office of Strategic Services, who happened to be in Lisbon on his way to the Balkans and the Middle East, and a discussion with Sir Samuel Hoare, the British ambassador to Spain.

On March 15, the day he flew on to England, Harriman had what seemed to him an "eerie experience" in walking past a German plane, painted black except for a large white swastika, as he boarded the Dutch DC-3 at the Lisbon airport. Upon landing in Bristol, Harriman discovered to his great surprise that Commander C. R. Thompson, the Prime Minister's naval aide, was waiting with a special airplane to deliver him to Chequers.

"The Prime Minister welcomed me most warmly," Harriman recalled. "He remembered our first meeting, when I called on him at Cannes in 1927 to get his advice about Russia, and he talked about our meeting in New York two years later, when he was staying with Bernie Baruch at the time of the Wall Street crash. He freely admitted having caught the speculative fever of the time and lost the money he had just received from the publication of a new book.

"I was surprised to see how grateful Mrs. Churchill was for a small bag of tangerines I had brought her from Lisbon. Her unfeigned delight brought home to me the restrictions of the dreary British wartime diet, imposed by the sharp reduction of imports, even in the Prime Minister's house.

"After dinner Churchill took me aside and began to describe in considerable detail the problems of the war and what the United States might do to help. I forgot all about presenting my letter from Roosevelt. There was no need for formal introductions. As soon as I could I explained to the Prime Minister that Washington would need a lot more information about Britain's war plans and prospects if there was to be a large increase in assistance under the new Lend-Lease law. I warned him that the demands of our own Army and Navy were so

great, and the immediately available resources so pitifully limited, that
it would be a struggle unless our military chiefs were persuaded that
Britain could make better use of the matériel.

"My own usefulness in pleading Britain's case, I told him bluntly,
would depend entirely upon the extent of my knowledge and understanding of her position and needs. I was greatly reassured by his
response.

" 'You shall be informed,' Churchill said. 'We accept you as a
friend. Nothing will be kept from you.'

"During this, the first of many long talks I was to have with
Churchill, he laid out the brute facts of the 'Battle of the Atlantic,'
as he had recently named it."

Once again, as in the summer of 1940 when he had proclaimed
the decisive Battle of Britain in the air, Churchill's flair for the dramatic was at work, helping to focus public attention on a particular
arena of conflict. Hitler's U-boats, Churchill said, were sinking British
ships at an alarming rate, two to three times faster than British shipyards could build them. Nearly 10 percent of the bottoms in each
convoy were being sunk, with all their cargo, before they could reach
port. The tonnage lost was rising month by month: 320,000 tons in
January, 400,000 tons in February. The figure for March, Harriman
later learned, was 535,000 tons. Britain, in that period, was importing
about half its total food supply and virtually all its raw materials,
except coal. The stark facts needed no Churchillian oratory for em-
phasis: if the trend were not checked, and eventually reversed, there
would be no reason for Hitler to invade the British Isles. By cutting
the line of supply, he could strangle them.

The threat of a German invasion, Churchill said, seemed to have
diminished since the autumn of 1940; but the massing of barges in the
ports of France and the Low Countries suggested that this danger,
too, could not be dismissed. The shipping losses were so severe,
Churchill added, that he had felt compelled to risk the weakening of
Britain's coastal defenses by reassigning certain warships from home
waters to do battle with submarines and surface raiders along the
convoy routes.

"You must get in touch with the Admiralty," Churchill concluded. "I have arranged that you are to have an office there." Harriman himself could not spend much time in the Admiralty office. But
Commander Paul F. Lee, who had been assigned to the Harriman
Mission by Admiral Stark to handle naval and ship repair matters, used
it daily. Churchill also invited Harriman to attend the meetings of the
War Cabinet's Battle of the Atlantic Committee, an extraordinary
privilege for a foreigner. The committee met once a week, grappling

not only with the Royal Navy's frustrations in trying to keep the sea lanes open but also with the problems of building more merchantmen and keeping them in repair, with port facilities and turn-around rates—all matters that Harriman knew something about from his own shipbuilding experience in World War I and his shipping operations in the twenties. It was, moreover, a magnificent opportunity for Harriman, the Lend-Lease Expediter, to see for himself how the British coped with the most immediate threat to their existence, even more menacing than the German bombs that were dropping on Plymouth, Bristol or Coventry.

At one such meeting he heard Churchill accuse a British admiral of stealing manpower assigned to repair damaged merchant ships for new naval construction. The unhappy admiral defended himself somewhat lamely, saying he had given instructions that merchant ships were to have the highest priority. "You don't seem to have any greater success in having your orders carried out than I do," Churchill barked.

Harriman, who spent seven of his first eight weekends in England with the Churchills (and dined with the Prime Minister at least once a week in London), felt that he was being treated like a partner in the planning of that vast enterprise, the British war effort. It was a Churchillian gesture that clearly served British interest. But, as Harriman looked at it, his relationship with Churchill served American interests, and Roosevelt's, as well. The Prime Minister's warm-hearted welcome had the effect of opening doors to all the important ministries for Harriman and the carefully chosen staff of his small mission. During his first full week in London, for example, he had long discussions with Ronald H. Cross, Minister of Shipping; Sir Andrew Duncan, Minister of Supply; Lord Beaverbrook, Minister of Aircraft Production; Lord Woolton, Minister of Food; Hugh Dalton, Minister of Economic Warfare; Lord Reith, Minister of Works and Buildings; Oliver Lyttelton, President of the Board of Trade; and Brendan Bracken, who was soon to become Minister of Information.

"I was much gratified and relieved," Harriman recalled, "to find that each of the ministers talked freely with me about matters within his area of responsibility and gave me the most sensitive information. It was a great deal more than I had expected from my first talks with these men, most of whom I had not met before. We were still, after all, neutral. Evidently the word had gone out from the Prime Minister's office. I was somewhat embarrassed that I could not, in response to their questions, tell them exactly what help the United States was prepared to give. Their own plans, naturally, depended greatly on knowing in advance what raw materials, machine tools or finished weapons they could expect to receive from America. Fortunately I knew enough about the state of our mobilization program at home to answer at least some of their questions, although I had received no instructions.

"Beaverbrook, with his characteristic bluntness, hit me harder than the rest with a demand for aluminum, which was in short supply even in the United States. When I asked for more information to justify the demand, he turned part of his planning staff over to me and they worked out all the details—exactly how much aluminum Britain needed and why. The information was so detailed that when I sent it on to Hopkins, who was then in charge of Lend-Lease, he was able to promise the British larger quantities of aluminum than I had anticipated."

A few days after his first talk with Churchill at Chequers, Harriman received from A. V. Alexander, First Lord of the Admiralty, a formidable official document marked "Most Secret," analyzing the German submarine offensive and showing how hard pressed the British were to protect their inbound convoys. The German occupation of France and the Low Countries had forced the British to route all their shipping from across the seas to the north of Ireland; this made for a heavy concentration of shipping in what the Royal Navy called the Northwestern Approaches, a magnificent watery hunting ground for Hitler's U-boats and armed merchant raiders. The Admiralty estimated that as many as twenty U-boats were operating in the Northwestern Approaches, often in tandem with German airplanes overhead. The German battle cruisers *Scharnhorst* and *Gneisenau*, together with the cruiser *Hipper*, were prowling farther west and south in the Atlantic. These three vessels alone, during February and March, had sunk twenty-nine merchant ships.

To counter these attacks, the Royal Navy was forming convoys, protected by cruisers or battleships to beat off surface raiders, and fast escort vessels to deal with the U-boats. Of the fourteen battleships the British had in service, seven were on convoy escort, three were hunting surface raiders in other waters and only four were on fleet duty, three of these in the eastern Mediterranean. That left only one battleship to protect the home islands, a dangerously narrow margin of safety. Not one of the four British aircraft carriers was assigned to the Home Fleet. Of forty-five cruisers, only six were in home waters to fend off a possible invasion attempt by the Germans. As for the destroyer force, so recently augmented by fifty from the United States, it had been thinned in combat. The Admiralty was able to assign no more than four destroyers to each convoy, hardly enough to fight off wolfpacks of up to five German submarines operating against a single convoy. The arithmetic was thoroughly discouraging.[6]

As the toll of shipping, trained seamen and vital cargoes mounted tragically in the spring, Churchill's instinct led him to withhold the facts. In mid-April he ordered that weekly announcements of ships sunk should be discontinued; monthly communiqués were to be issued instead. Defending his action in the House of Commons, Churchill said,

> "I have no doubt there will be a howl, not only from the Germans, but from some well-meaning patriots of this Island. Let them howl. We have got to think of our sailors and merchant seamen, the lives of our countrymen and of the life of our country, now quivering in the balance of mortal peril."[7]

Harriman's instinct, to the contrary, was that the Prime Minister should be giving out more information, not less. It was their first disagreement. To make the frightening facts known, Churchill argued, would be to give aid and comfort to the enemy. Harriman's answer was that American opinion could not be expected to shift in the direction of more active involvement unless the full gravity of Britain's situation was understood. Admiral Land, for example, had already issued an overoptimistic statement on the British shipping outlook, misled (so Harriman felt) by Churchill's concealment of the facts. After a discussion in Washington with a British official, Sir Arthur Salter, on the increased tonnage—American and British—that would need to be built to offset convoy losses, Land and Rear Admiral Howard L. Vickery of the Maritime Commission had come away shocked and disbelieving. Land wrote to Roosevelt and Hopkins the next day: "If we do not watch our step, we shall find the White House en route to England with the Washington Monument as a steering oar."[8] Churchill, however, was adamant. Harriman argued the disclosure question with him, time and again, without yielding. "I accept your decision," he said to Churchill one evening, "but I must reserve the right to bring the matter up again at an early time." His willingness to debate issues of this kind evidently increased the Prime Minister's respect for Harriman.

There were disagreements also with Ambassador Winant over how much bad news President Roosevelt should be told. Churchill at times consulted both Americans before sending Roosevelt messages describing the gravity of Britain's situation and the urgent need for help. Winant tended to favor caution, the qualified opinion, the tentative statement of fact. Harriman, on the other hand, was for clear, blunt statements of the actual situation, no matter how distressing. One evening at Chequers, Churchill handed Winant a draft telegram for Roosevelt, having to do with the dismal statistics of shipping losses and the need for more convoy protection, including more direct involvement by the United States Navy. Winant responded, "Prime

Minister, I don't think you should disturb the President this way."
Harriman gave contrary advice: "If this is what you believe, then
you must send it."

Churchill's messages to Roosevelt were, of course, very much
his own. When Harriman on one occasion suggested a change that the
Prime Minister did not care for, he brushed it aside with some annoyance. Harriman stood his ground and Churchill said, "Well, I'll think
about it in the morning," closing the discussion. But Churchill asked
Harriman to his bedroom the next morning, and without mentioning
the discussion of the night before, handed him a new draft he had just
dictated, which incorporated the substance of Harriman's suggestion.

As far as his own messages to Roosevelt were concerned, Harriman believed it would be a disservice to shade the awkward facts. "My
idea was that I was serving the President," he remarked, "and that our
job was to amplify for him the desperate picture of Britain in that
late winter and spring of 1941—the effect of the bombing on British
production and the devastating effect of the submarines on British
supply lines."

The relationship between Harriman and Winant was both delicate
and difficult. Harriman possessed the powerful advantage of a direct
line to Roosevelt and Hopkins,* reinforced by his growing intimacy
with Churchill. Winant, however, was the American ambassador,
senior to Harriman in rank if not in responsibility. His closest official
relationship in London was with Anthony Eden, the Foreign Secretary. Here there was no conflict, as Harriman had little to do with
Eden or the Foreign Office. Churchill, however, was aware of
Winant's sensitivities. Winant had complained to Hopkins, who in
turn urged Churchill not to keep the ambassador at a distance. The
Prime Minister, accordingly, warned Harriman, "We'll have to be
more careful." Harriman was, in fact, scrupulous about showing
Winant his policy telegrams before he sent them to the President.
Harriman would ask, "Do you want to sign the message and say
'Harriman concurs,' or shall I sign it?" Winant's habitual reply was:
"You sign." The recorded responsibility was Harriman's.

THE HARRIMAN MISSION set up shop on the second floor of No. 3
Grosvenor Square in an apartment building adjoining the embassy,
which was then at No. 1. A door was broken through to connect the
Mission with the embassy. Writing home to an old friend, Bob Meiklejohn described the setting: "Mr. Harriman achieves a somewhat Mus-
solini-like effect—not at all to his liking—by reason of his office being a

* Through Navy channels, Harriman could send his cables directly to the
White House.

very large room that used to be the living room of a rather elegant flat."⁹ For want of a more resounding official title, the letterhead read OFFICE OF W. A. HARRIMAN. The available space, some 12,000 square feet, was more than Harriman needed for his own small staff, so he was able to offer office space to representatives sent from Washington by a variety of federal agencies, on condition that he be kept fully informed of their activities. In London, at least, he was determined to avoid interagency battles. Total chaos would have been the result if each of these special representatives had been free to deal individually with the British ministries.

Harriman kept his own staff lean, efficient, ferociously dedicated to work. The financial burden on the government was small. Harriman and Meiklejohn, his assistant on loan from the Union Pacific Railroad, cost the Treasury nothing. The initial staff of the Harriman Mission included another unpaid official, Colonel George Alan Green of Birmingham, Michigan, an Army Reserve officer on loan from the Yellow Truck & Coach Manufacturing Company, where he was a vice president; Edward P. Warner, then vice chairman of the Civil Aeronautics Board; and Russell T. Nichols, a statistician from the Office of Production Management. Harriman had recruited Commander Lee on loan from the Navy; Brigadier General Millard F. Harmon, an air officer, and Lieutenant Colonel James L. Hatcher, an engineer, from the Army; together with Harvey Klemmer and A. C. Spencer, from the Maritime Commission, to deal with shipping matters. William Dwight Whitney, an American then in London as a major in the Scotch Guards, joined the staff at the end of March as Harriman's executive assistant. Young William L. Batt, Jr., arrived in April to deal with food and agriculture. In June, Charles J. Hitch (a promising young economist who later became chancellor of the University of California) and Thomas A. Monroe, a vice president of the U.S. Lines, joined the Harriman Mission. By July of 1943, when the Mission's responsibilities had grown immeasurably, the Harriman staff counted all of thirty-six men. Of these, exactly nine were paid by the Mission. The salary range ran from $8,000 a year for Whitney to $4,000 for Hitch and Batt. All the rest were loaned by other government agencies.

CHURCHILL'S PRIVATE ESTIMATE of the military outlook—Harriman discovered during his second weekend at Chequers—was a good deal more somber than his public statements suggested. It was a time for holding action, he said, not bold new strokes. The first priority was industrial: greatly expanded arms production at home and in the United States. There were only two strategic imperatives—the British

Isles and the Suez Canal must be held at all cost. He was, in fact, stripping the defenses of Britain itself to sustain and strengthen General Archibald Wavell's forces in the Middle East and build up reserves in Egypt against the uncertain future. But the Prime Minister bluntly stated that he could see no prospect of victory until the United States came into the war. Hitler was massing troops in Bulgaria and Rumania for the assault on Greece and Yugoslavia, and Churchill would do what he could to help but that was not enough to be decisive. British intelligence had detected signs that Hitler might be preparing to attack Russia; Churchill had passed this warning on to Stalin, through Sir Stafford Cripps, the British ambassador in Moscow. But even a Russo-German war—if it came to that—might provide no more than a breathing spell for Great Britain. Churchill posed a series of hard questions: What if Hitler, having defeated the Greeks and swallowed up the rest of the Balkans, were to force the Turks to let his armies cross over into Asia Minor? Might he not then come to terms with Stalin? Or attack Russia in greater strength than he could now muster, overwhelm her quickly and then turn his full attention to North Africa or Britain?

As for the Far East, Churchill told Harriman that he would have to risk the loss of Singapore should the Japanese attack. In that event, he felt certain, the United States would enter the war and that would change everything. Then it would become possible, at long last, to think of eventual victory.

In March the Luftwaffe had turned its attention to the port cities of England and Scotland, raining high-explosive and fire bombs on the dock areas. The London newspapers called it "The Luftwaffe's Tour of the Ports." Churchill started dividing his weekends between Chequers and morale-lifting visits to the bombed cities. Harriman frequently accompanied him: "Churchill's idea of security was to rely on surprise. He never publicized his plans. He would travel by overnight train to a bombed city and then drive or walk through the streets, seemingly with no more than a few security men. At Swansea, I recall, he got out of his car and walked into the dock area. The dockers crowded round him and I am sure the security men accompanying him must have been concerned for his safety. But Churchill called out, 'Stand back, my man. Let the others see.' Then he put his square derby-like hat on the end of his cane and whirled it around for the crowd to see. The men pulled back and cheered the Prime Minister.

"When he made a speech, on trips like this one, he would introduce me as President Roosevelt's personal envoy. That was his way of letting the crowd know that America stood with them."

Through April and May the Prime Minister also visited Bristol, Dover, Plymouth and Cardiff. Harriman, who went along, recalled a contest of wills at Plymouth between Churchill and Lady Astor, who was determined to carry off Mrs. Churchill to a women's political meeting. "In war it is the Prime Minister who must make the vital decisions," Churchill said. "Clemmie comes with me." That ended the discussion.

Harriman vividly remembered a visit to Bristol on April 11. As chancellor of Bristol University, Churchill had agreed to award honorary degrees to Robert Gordon Menzies, the Prime Minister of Australia, together with Ambassador Winant and Dr. James Bryant Conant, the president of Harvard University. "I'd like to give you a degree, too," the Prime Minister said to Harriman, "but I know you're not interested in that kind of thing." Churchill's train was held up outside the city during the night while the Luftwaffe showered the city of Bristol and its docks with bombs. From the train, parked in a siding in open country, the Prime Minister and his party could see and hear the spectacular raid in progress.

The next morning the train pulled into the station and the Churchill party went to the hotel. The waiter who served breakfast had spent the night on the roof, putting out incendiary bombs. Moved by the scene of devastation, Harriman wrote President Roosevelt later that day:

> The P.M. inspected the damaged area, walking among the people and visiting the reception centers. A grim, determined people, but I talked to many of them. They wanted him to see they had no complaints and were ready for the next one . . .
>
> Winant's speech was simple and moving—the others also brief and fitting. No one had been to bed—the next building still smoldering.

The people of Bristol, apparently unaware that Churchill was there to present degrees at the University, believed the raid had brought him. Their enthusiasm ran high. As Churchill tramped the streets that afternoon, someone would shout, "Here's Winnie!" and people would tumble out of their houses to cheer. "There he is, dear old Winnie!" the women would shout. Harriman, believing he was out of earshot, remarked to General Ismay that Churchill seemed particularly popular with middle-aged women. The Prime Minister turned around brusquely and said, with mock severity: "Humph, not only with middle-aged women, with the young ones, too."

That evening, for the first time in Harriman's presence, Churchill showed deep emotion. They were alone as the train pulled out of the station and the last of the people he could wave to passed from sight. Churchill sank into his chair and picked up a newspaper to screen the tears in his eyes. "They have such confidence," he said. "It is a grave responsibility."

CHAPTER II

How to Be
"Something and Somebody"

T HE YEAR OF STORM that Churchill had foretold brought fresh
disasters in its wake. During the spring of 1941 Hitler's conquer-
ing armies swept into the Balkans, overwhelming Yugoslavia, Greece
and Crete. In the scorched wasteland of the Libyan Desert, his Afrika
Korps (under command of a brilliant young general named Erwin
Rommel) routed the British, driving them back into Egypt. The
British Isles were still under siege, battered from the air and pinched
for supplies owing to the success of the U-boat campaign in the
Northwestern Approaches.

It was a time of rising anxiety for Harriman, who feared that the
remarkable will to fight which Churchill had nurtured in the British
people might falter under the strain of continued losses and defeats.
He agreed with Churchill that victory was out of the question until
America entered the war; and he grew increasingly impatient with the
continued strength of isolationist sentiment in the United States, which
seemed to enforce half measures on President Roosevelt. Only in a
country at war, it seemed to Harriman, could Roosevelt impose the
production controls and priorities that would assure full mobilization.
As long as the half-war dragged on, the effort was bound to fall short.
Thus, less than a month after his arrival in London, Harriman was
pleading for more vigorous action and more direct American involvement. On April 10 he wrote to Roosevelt:

> England's strength is bleeding. In our own interest, I trust
> that our Navy can be directly employed before our partner is
> too weak.

Exactly two weeks later the President issued a directive authorizing the Navy to patrol the North Atlantic west of Iceland and to report the movements of German vessels. There was to be no shooting unless the Americans were shot at. Not until September 16 did the U.S. Navy extend its protection to Allied shipping as far as Iceland.

Harriman was relieved to discover, however, that Churchill and the men around him understood how difficult it was for Roosevelt to move the country more rapidly. Weighing his words with great care, Harriman again reported to the President on May 7:

> I find everyone here from the Prime Minister down deeply appreciative of the increasing aid that you are giving. It is natural that they hope for belligerent status but I am surprised how understanding all are of the psychology of the situation at home. It is because of what they went through themselves. There is both greater understanding of, and greater frankness about, their dependence on us for the final outcome.

From William C. Bullitt, the former ambassador to Russia and France, Harriman received a friendly but disappointing letter, dated April 29:

> The President is waiting for public opinion to lead and public opinion is waiting for a lead from the President. The people most concerned are now beginning to be fairly satisfied with the progress in the industrial field, which they attribute to an extraordinarily high level among the men below the top. . . . Nothing drastic will happen unless either the President leads or Hitler supplies an incident which public opinion will consider an affront to the national honor . . .
>
> Harry Hopkins is doing an excellent job within the limits imposed by his health and ways of work; but there has been no change in the President's working habits and, while he has never been wiser, weariness often prevents the dispatch of business with the speed that is requisite.

Harriman's grateful reply on May 21 (he was starved for news from home) betrayed his rising exasperation. With Bullitt he could be totally frank about his own state of mind:

> It is impossible for me to understand the ostrich-like attitude of America. Either we have an interest in the outcome of this war, or we have not. If not, why are we supplying England with the tools? If we have, why do we not realize that the situation could not be tougher and every day [that]

we delay direct participation—at least use of our Navy and Air Force—we are taking an extreme risk that either the war will be lost or the difficulty of winning it multiplied, for each week [that] we delay.

In a letter to Robert White, president of the Western Union Telegraph Company, Harriman was even more blunt:

We are going to have to come into the war some time, unless we are prepared to completely back water from the national policy we have adopted. The sooner we come in, the shorter the job will be.*

His weekends in the country with Churchill offered a welcome break from the daily grind of Grosvenor Square. But the Prime Minister brought with him to Chequers all the alarms of war, and Harriman shared the general agitation. On May 23, a Friday afternoon, he went to Chequers with the Prime Minister; Major General Sir Hastings Ismay, chief of staff to Churchill, who also was Minister of Defence; and Lieutenant General Sir Henry Pownall, Vice Chief of the Imperial General Staff. It was to be an anxious weekend. The battle for Crete was at its height; a major duel at sea was expected at any moment. The new German battleship *Bismarck*, the pride of Hitler's navy, had been spotted in the Bergen Fiord, together with the cruiser *Prinz Eugen*, on May 21. The following day a British reconnaissance plane, based in the Orkney Islands, had overflown the Norwegian coast through rain, fog and heavy ground fire only to discover that the German warships were gone. They had slipped out of Bergen twenty-four hours earlier and were headed for Denmark Strait, to the west of Iceland. Churchill had promptly alerted Roosevelt on Thursday evening:

We have reason to believe that a formidable Atlantic raid is intended. Should we fail to catch [the *Bismarck* and *Prinz Eugen*] going out, your Navy should surely be able to mark them down for us. *King George V, Prince of Wales, Hood, Repulse* and aircraft-carrier *Victorious*, with ancillary vessels, will be on their track. Give us the news and we will finish the job."[1]

Churchill and his guests spent a long, anxious evening waiting for word from the Admiralty. When none had come by two-thirty Saturday morning, they turned in. Harriman was jolted awake soon after seven o'clock by the sight of Churchill in a yellow sweater, covering a short nightshirt, his pink legs exposed. "Hell of a battle going on,"

* Harriman had been a director of the Western Union Company.

he said. "The *Hood* is sunk. Hell of a battle." Harriman asked about the *Prince of Wales*. "She's still at her," Churchill replied. The *Hood* was Britain's largest and fastest capital ship, a grievous loss at any time and most particularly at this moment of crisis in the Battle of the Atlantic. All but three of *Hood*'s company, more than 1,500 men, lost their lives when she exploded during an exchange of big guns with the *Bismarck*. The *Prince of Wales* continued the fight alone but she reluctantly broke off the action after receiving four hits from 15-inch shells. Churchill immersed himself in work for a few hours, reading telegrams and directing the hunt for the *Bismarck*. When he saw Harriman again about ten o'clock, the Prime Minister sounded more confident than he felt. "My American guest thought I was gay," Churchill remembered, "but it costs nothing to grin."[2]

"For three days," Harriman recalled, "Churchill concentrated his full attention on the chase, ordering out every available ship and aircraft in spite of generally foul weather." A few minutes after three in the morning on May 25, the pursuing ships lost contact with the *Bismarck*. Hope was beginning to fade when a Catalina flying boat of the RAF Coastal Command spotted the *Bismarck* steering for Brest at ten-thirty the following morning. That evening, Swordfish aircraft from the carrier *Ark Royal* attacked with torpedoes, scoring a lucky hit on her steering-gear compartment, which froze the rudder at 15 degrees port. Wallowing out of control, the *Bismarck* finally was dispatched on the morning of May 27. In the House of Commons the same day the Prime Minister was able to report that the loss of the *Hood* had been avenged.

Harriman returned to London deeply impressed by Churchill's leadership and drive. His own appreciation of British character and his solidarity with embattled Britain had not, however, been wholly formed during those first weeks in London. It could be traced back a long way, to the spring of 1912, when he was excused from classes at Yale for six weeks (an extraordinary concession in those less-lenient days) to see what he could learn at Oxford about how to win boat races.

A college junior, too light for the varsity eight, he had agreed to coach the freshman crew in the hope of restoring Yale's lackluster reputation on the river. Oxford was a mighty power in the rowing world then, with a style of its own that was greatly admired in New Haven. So Harriman sailed for England carrying two unaddressed letters of introduction from George Milburn, an American who had earned his blue at Oxford—one for Harcourt Gold, the stroke, and the other for G. S. MacLagan, the coxswain of his crew. Not knowing a better way to trace the two Oxonians, he called at Baring Brothers, who had been his father's London bankers, upon arrival in London. A Baring partner named Farrar took him to see George Rowe, a stockbroker and chairman of the Oxford graduate rowing committee, who in turn gave Harriman two letters. The first was addressed to Holland, then the Oxford coach, explaining Harriman's educational mission. The other was to the current coxswain of the varsity crew, a Magdalen College man, suggesting that Harriman be invited to the bump supper the same evening in celebration of Magdalen's having gained head-of-the-river standing, a considerable honor in the Oxford scheme of things.

Harriman took the train to Oxford, made his way in the rain to the varsity boathouse and asked to see Mr. Holland. After some time the captain of the crew came out, said that Holland was not there and asked what he could do for the young visitor from America. Harriman asked that he read the letter, which was unsealed. "We're going up the river in half an hour," the captain said after a long pause. "Take the tow path and you can watch." No one suggested that Harriman might come into the boathouse out of the rain. And no more words were spoken.

This less than cordial reception, rather typical of English university men of the day, was offset by the exuberant hospitality Harriman encountered at the Magdalen dinner. Champagne flowed freely and before the hilarious evening was out, Harriman had made a fast friend of the coxswain, whose name was Wells.

When the Oxford crew moved to Henley to prepare for the great boat race with Cambridge, Harriman moved, too. Through the good offices of George Rowe, he was put up at the Leander Club, where the Oxford team was staying. It was back to the tow path for Harriman, although at Henley he got a more elevated view of the training procedures by hiring a horse and following the Oxford boat from the riverbank. With characteristic attention to detail, a quality inherited from his father, Harriman meticulously recorded the measurements of the boat and the rigging of each crew member, as well as each man's strong points and rowing faults. He was not greatly troubled by the fact that the crew continued to treat him as an outsider. At mealtimes, Harriman sat by himself at a corner table while the crew occupied the center of the dining room. On Saturday night, however, he received an unexpected formal invitation from the captain: "Mr. Harriman, will you dine with us this evening?" The Saturday-evening break in the training routine allowed for a glass or two of champagne and that was enough to break the ice. Now an accepted member of the party, Harriman at last met Harcourt Gold, the great coach who was credited with developing the final rhythm and united power that made Oxford's rowing reputation. During the final stage of training at Putney on the Thames, Gold took him along in his launch for an intensive short course in the fine art of coaching.

In spite of his preoccupation with rowing, Harriman did not disdain the British political scene. "Yesterday suffragettes had broken shop windows in London," he recorded in his diary on March 2, 1912. "Great excitement. The coal situation is no better. Railroads are taking off many trains on Monday."

If he was not to overstay his leave of absence, Harriman found, he would have to sail home on the *Olympic*, five days before the Oxford-Cambridge boat race. The temptation to cable for permission to stay one week longer in England was powerful, but he resisted it. If his sense of obligation to honor the agreement with Dean Frederick Scheetz Jones had been somewhat less compelling, he would have sailed the following week on the *Titanic* (and this book in all probability would never have been written).

On his return to New Haven, Harriman took over the coaching of the freshman crew (Dean Acheson became a member) and began to apply the lessons he had learned at Oxford. Although he had been warned that it would take several years to teach the long, swinging stroke favored at Oxford, his freshman crew rowed a highly encouraging race with Harvard, losing by only a couple of feet. On the strength of that showing he was invited to coach the varsity crew in his senior year. But the older men, trained in a different stroke, did not take to the Oxford style as readily as the freshmen, and Yale again knew the taste of defeat. Resigning before he could be fired, Harriman told the rowing committee that Yale could not afford the time to let him learn the coaching trade. Instead, he recommended that Yale invite Guy Nickalls, a celebrated Oxford blue, to coach the varsity crew. He accepted and Yale's rowing fortunes brightened in short order. By 1915 its champion crew won every race it entered and left Harvard seven lengths behind in record time, proving to Harriman's satisfaction that the Oxford interlude had not been a total loss. As for the six hours a day he spent on the New Haven harbor during his junior and senior years with a rowing squad of some eighty aspirants, Harriman learned a great deal about handling men—teaching, selecting, criticizing and yet encouraging them. It was, he felt, a useful supplement to his more formal studies in history and economics.

While still a college senior, Harriman had been elected to the board of directors of the Union Pacific Railroad. His father, Edward Henry Harriman, had died in 1909, a few weeks before Averell entered Yale. E. H. Harriman had been described by an admiring French biographer as "le Napoléon des chemins de fer" and by President Theodore Roosevelt as "at least as undesirable a citizen" as

Eugene Victor Debs or William (Big Bill) Haywood, the most prominent radical leaders of the period. Edward Harriman had quit school at fourteen and gone to work as an office boy in Wall Street. His father, Orlando, was the grandson of William Harriman, a London stationer sympathetic to the cause of American independence who had settled in New Haven during the summer of 1797, where he soon became known as "the rich Englishman." But Orlando Harriman, a scholarly man who had been graduated with honors from Columbia University, chose the ministry instead of the business world.

Orlando's son, Edward, born in 1848, grew up in a succession of less-than-fashionable Episcopal parsonages, attending public school in Jersey City before his father sent him to the Trinity School in Manhattan. Two years at Trinity were enough for Ned Harriman, although he left at the head of his class. Over the protests of his father, he found a job in Wall Street at $5 a week. His progress there was swift and dazzling—from office boy to "pad-shover" to member of the New York Stock Exchange at the age of twenty-two. In later years, when his personal fortune was estimated at $70 million, E. H. Harriman was fond of saying, "My capital when I began was a pencil —and this," tapping his head. In those days before ticker tape, "pad-shovers" like Ned Harriman were sent to other brokers' offices to copy current stock quotations. Harriman was faster than his fellows and blessed with a precise memory for stock prices. In the summer of 1870 he borrowed $3,000 from an uncle to buy his seat on the Exchange. His brokerage office at the corner of Broad Street and Exchange Place prospered, thanks to the business of such mighty traders as August Belmont, Commodore Vanderbilt and Jay Gould.

In his thirty-first year, Harriman married Mary Williamson Averell, the daughter of an upstate banker and railroad man from Ogdensburg, whom he had met in New York while she was visiting relatives. They had six children, the first of whom, a boy, died in infancy. The Harrimans then had three daughters, Mary, Cornelia and Carol, followed by William Averell, who was born in 1891, and his brother, Edward Roland, in 1895. From childhood they were known as Averell and Roland.

With E. H. Harriman's success in Wall Street, he had started railroading in a small way, stimulated perhaps by his father-in-law's interest in a small northern New York road. The elder Harriman saw his first opportunity when he heard about a nondescript line, thirty-four miles long, known as the Lake Ontario Southern, which was badly managed and losing money. It ran between the little town of Stanley, New York, near Canandaigua, and Great Sodus Bay on Lake Ontario. He bought into the property in 1881, soon took it over, spent some money putting it in order and made a substantial profit in 1883 by selling out to the Pennsylvania Railroad. Some years afterward, Harriman explained his successful strategy:

> The property had great strategic value, which nobody seemed to recognize. I knew that if I put it into good physical condition, so it could handle and develop traffic, the Pennsylvania Railroad would jump at a chance to buy it, in order to get an outlet to the lake; and that the New York Central would be equally anxious to buy it, in order to keep its rival out.[3]

Over the next twenty-five years Harriman bought into and rebuilt bigger railroads. He gave up the brokerage business to become one of the dominant railroad men of the period. He first saw great opportunities in the Illinois Central. As its vice president and then acting president, he expanded its mileage by acquiring other connecting railroads and turned it into the great transportation link from the center of the country down the Mississippi Valley to New Orleans. When the Union Pacific fell into receivership in the early nineties, he joined with Kuhn, Loeb and Company to reorganize it. Under E. H. Harriman's driving leadership the Union Pacific became one of the most important and profitable railroad properties in the West. Backed by Jacob Schiff of Kuhn, Loeb, Harriman waged titanic battles with the elder J. P. Morgan and James J. Hill for control of other railroads. He made powerful friends and powerful enemies, of whom Teddy Roosevelt was far the most powerful.

His success was based on two principles: putting a good share of the profits back into the property to improve efficiency; and borrowing money when interest rates were low to expand his properties and to buy other railroads. Far ahead of his contemporaries, Harriman took a real interest in the welfare of his employees. As early as 1903, when such ideas were considered socialistic, he inaugurated a pension system and medical-care plan for the Union Pacific and Southern Pacific employees. Both plans were the first of their kind in the railroad industry. Harriman also was among the first to insist upon tough safety standards for the protection of both passengers and employees.

When Averell in later years joined Roosevelt's New Deal Administration, he was able to trace certain of the current ideas back to the beliefs of his Republican father. "My father once told me," he recalled, "that he had tried all his life to make everything with which he became associated a little better for his participation. Before he died, he told me that in our democracy if men of wealth did not use their money for the public welfare it would be taken from them. This was long before the income tax and high inheritance taxes. For my father, wealth carried with it a responsibility for the development of the country and improvement in the life of the people."

Before he had made his fortune in railroading, E. H. Harriman had started the Boys' Club in Tompkins Square to help keep the immigrant youngsters of the Lower East Side off the streets. From a small beginning, the Boys' Club had grown into a large organization with three clubhouses and a summer camp of its own. In the early days Harriman devoted one evening a week to working with the boys personally. The breadth of his interests was phenomenal. In 1899, for example, when Averell was not quite eight years old, his father decided that the family should spend the summer exploring the Alaskan coast. He needed a vacation; it had been a strenuous year. He enjoyed hunting and he was determined to get a Kodiak bear. The steamship service to Alaska was so intermittent that Harriman decided to charter a boat, with a crew of sixty-five, out of Seattle. He consulted scientists at the Smithsonian Institution and the Geological Survey, who showed great interest in joining the expedition.

When the Harrimans set out for Seattle by private train at the end of the school term, they were joined by twenty-five carefully selected scientists eager to study the flora and fauna of Alaska and to chart its geological formations. Among the scientists were John Burroughs, the renowned naturalist, and John Muir, the Scottish-born explorer and conservationist. Muir marveled at Harriman's ability to keep the expedition on track and each of the scientists happily pursuing his particular interest. "Scientific explorers," Muir wrote, "are not easily managed, and in large mixed lots are rather inflammable and explosive, especially when compressed on a ship. Nevertheless, he [Harriman] kept us all in smooth working order."[4]*

The expedition lasted two months, traveling 9,000 miles. Its published scientific findings ran to many volumes. Burroughs alone produced thirteen of them, with illustrations. Harriman got his bear. Mrs. Harriman, who was determined to set foot in Siberia, had that wish fulfilled. (It was, incidentally, Averell's first glimpse of Russia.†) And

---

* In a personal memoir, published privately in 1911, Muir added this tribute: "Of all the great builders—the famous doers of things in this world—none that I know of more ably and manfully did his appointed work than my friend Edward Henry Harriman . . . He fairly revelled in heavy dynamical work and went about it naturally and unweariedly like glaciers making landscapes, cutting canyons through ridges, carrying off hills, laying rails and bridges over lakes and rivers, mountains and plains, making the nation's ways straight and smooth and safe, bringing everybody nearer to one another. He seemed to regard the whole continent as his farm and all the people as partners . . ."

† Some forty-odd years after the expedition to Alaska, Stalin asked Averell Harriman when he had first visited Russia. Harriman replied, "The first time I

the map of Alaska since then has been marked by a glacier and a fiord bearing the Harriman name.

"On my trips with my father," Averell Harriman recalled, "I was always greatly impressed with the personal attention he gave to every detail, as well as his capacity for leadership in a crisis." At the time of the San Francisco earthquake and fire in 1906, for example, the elder Harriman raced across the country in his special train, making record time to Oakland. He mobilized the resources of the Southern Pacific Railroad to help restore orderly conditions of life for the victims and to care for the displaced. Both the Union Pacific and the Southern Pacific, which Harriman then controlled, shipped thousands of tons of government relief supplies without charge.

Shortly after the San Francisco disaster, the Colorado River broke its banks and started to flood the Salton Sink, threatening the Imperial Valley of Southern California. Harriman telegraphed President Roosevelt, offering his help and urging that the government close the break which was endangering the settlers and the rich farmlands of the entire valley. Roosevelt replied that the government could not act without congressional authority, and as Congress was not then in session, he proposed that the Southern Pacific undertake the job. Harriman agreed on the understanding that the government would share the burden as soon as congressional approval could be obtained. Closing the breach turned out to be an enormous task. Rock had to be quarried and shipped long distances over a period of several weeks, then dumped into the breach. The flood was not brought under control, however, until whole railroad cars loaded with rock were thrown into the 1,100-foot-wide crevasse in the riverbank at a cost to the railroad of more than $3 million. The Imperial Valley was saved, but Congress never did get around to repaying any part of the cost.

In the Harriman family, summers were often reserved for travel. During the summers of 1903 and 1904 the Harrimans and their children roamed through Europe in the newfangled automobile. By 1905 E. H. Harriman had conceived an idea worthy of Jules Verne, nothing less than a round-the-world transportation network. The Union Pacific had acquired control of the Southern Pacific, and with it, the ownership of the Pacific Mail Steamship Company, which operated to the Orient. Late that summer the Harrimans sailed for Japan in the hope of negotiating a deal for the reconstruction and operation of the South Manchurian Railroad, which Japan had wrested from Russia in the Russo-Japanese War of 1904–05. Harriman reckoned that if he could

---

came was in 1899 when I landed with my parents on the Siberian side of the Bering Sea and I did it without a passport." Stalin said, "Well, you couldn't do that now."

buy or lease the tracks of the South Manchurian line and then the Chinese Eastern (by arrangement with Czar Nicholas of Russia), his global network would be well on the way to fulfillment.

He was received with elaborate courtesy by the Japanese bankers and high officials of the court, including the Emperor. A preliminary memorandum of agreement, in fact, was negotiated with the Japanese government, in the absence of the Foreign Minister, Baron Komura, at Portsmouth, New Hampshire, where the peace treaty was negotiated. On Komura's return, however, the Harriman agreement was first deferred and then broken off, in part because a provision of the Portsmouth treaty barred any transfer of control over the railroad, except with the consent of the Chinese government, which was in no mood to grant further concessions to any foreigner. The terms of the Portsmouth settlement also had provoked a great popular outcry in Japan. There was rioting in the streets, tinged with anti-Americanism, because President Roosevelt had initiated the Portsmouth negotiations, which seemed to many Japanese a sell-out.

Averell, then thirteen years old, never forgot the explosive character of those Japanese demonstrations. The house of one government minister was burned to the ground, although he escaped by climbing over the back fence. Young Averell was thrilled at the sight of Japanese soldiers encamped on the lawn of the American legation compound to guard the minister, Lloyd Griscomb, and his guests, the Harriman family. Earlier than most Americans, Averell learned that the Japanese were not necessarily a submissive people.

From Japan the Harrimans moved on to Port Arthur and then to China without Averell, the family looking at the sights and E. H. Harriman, as ever, looking into business possibilities. Averell had to miss the sights of China because his powerful father had come up against an immovable object in the Reverend Endicott Peabody, headmaster of Groton School. Harriman had cabled Peabody a request that Averell be excused from classes for several weeks so that the family could complete its tour of the Orient. Peabody sternly refused: Averell would be back in Groton for the start of classes or he would be dropped from the school. Father Harriman, as resourceful as he was persuasive, concocted a plan to extend Averell's Far East travels by one week without forfeiting his place at Groton. He rerouted a Pacific Mail liner and persuaded the Secretary of State, William Howard Taft, who was then about to leave the Philippines, to sail home by way of Japan and Seattle, taking young Averell with him, rather than follow the regular steamer route through Honolulu to San Francisco. That meant a ten-day trip instead of the seventeen days normally required across the Pacific. Averell made it back to Groton in time, but the incident permanently affected his feelings about Groton and the headmaster. "I've always regretted missing the Port Arthur trip," he recalled. "My father's party were the first foreigners to visit the region since the end of hostilities, and of course I also had to miss the fascinating visit to China. Although I continued to be influenced by Dr. Peabody's high principles, the experience released me from the Groton rigidities and perhaps contributed to my becoming something of a nonconformist."

The last years of E. H. Harriman's life were shadowed by failing health and a bitter quarrel with Theodore Roosevelt, although these preoccupations did not interfere with his continued attention to business and the development of his children. Roland had joined Averell at Groton, and Edward Harriman worried about his younger son's grades. "Can you not do something to wake him up?" Harriman wrote to Averell on February 21, 1909, from San Antonio, where he was supervising the construction of a new railroad running down to Mazatlán, in Mexico. Averell's grades also came in for fatherly attention:

> Can you not "jack up" on the English? I know you can
> as well as some other subjects. It is very encouraging to have
> you so improved, and I am sure you will catch on and go on
> and on and be something and somebody.

To be "something and somebody" was Harriman's fondest wish for Averell, who in reply suggested that Groton was not without blame for his brother's problems. "It seems to me," he wrote, "that the whole Groton organization needs an awakening, the Masters one and all, as well as the scholars like Roland."

Averell stayed the course, however, and at the time of his graduation received a long letter from his father in praise of Groton's legendary headmaster: "I have written to Dr. Peabody of my gratification at your well-being and the good you have gotten from his influence . . . somehow I feel confident that you will hold fast to the principles he has instilled in you."

Edward Harriman also took time to stimulate his son's interest in public affairs. When Averell, for example, was preparing for a school debate on the merits of railroad regulation, his father spelled out his own views on the subject:

> Your question about the Interstate Commerce Commission
> covers so much ground that I can hardly answer it intelli-
> gently in the time given and amidst so many interruptions—
> The idea of the Commission itself, I think, is all right, at least
> their having some arm of the government to look after the
> regulation of the RR—You will see by the letter to Taft that

I there refer to my belief in regulation too, but that we ought to have protection as well.*

The trouble with the Comm. has been with its personnel and their ambition for more power, which they have succeeded in obtaining by agitation and neglect to enforce the original act creating them—They should be the most dignified and important body except the Supreme Court. Instead, they have acted independently as individuals and made announcements of their individual opinions before the subject had been considered by the Commission as a body. Most of its acts have been unobjectionable but their methods have been wrong—In fact so it has been with the outgoing Administration all through—So you see such a committee is not competent to judge and have control of the affairs of a railroad.

Affectionately,

Papa

Harriman's conflict with Theodore Roosevelt dated from 1904. The trouble had its origin in a meeting between them two weeks before Roosevelt's victorious election that November. TR had become alarmed over the campaign outlook in New York, his home state. Money was short and the State Committee had accused the Republican National Committee of holding back some $200,000 in promised campaign funds. The President sent for Harriman to see what could be done about raising more campaign funds in a hurry. Harriman returned to New York and promptly raised $250,000, putting up $50,000 of his own money, a considerable sum for that period.†

There is no dispute over the financial details. The $250,000 that Harriman raised was delivered to the Republican National Committee, which in turn sent $200,000 to the State Committee. The controversy started from Harriman's understanding that Roosevelt had agreed to appoint Chauncey Depew, then a Republican senator from New York, ambassador to France. This was considered a move toward party harmony, which Harriman had urged upon Roosevelt. With Depew out of the way in Paris, the road would be open for Joseph Choate, an upstate favorite, to run for the Senate. After the election was won,

* Harriman *père* enclosed a copy of a letter he had written to William Howard Taft, then President of the United States, outlining his views on railroad regulation.

† Bernard Baruch, a great admirer of E. H. Harriman, told Averell many years afterward that his father had commissioned Baruch to place bets on the outcome of the election and in this way won back the $50,000 he had contributed.

however, Roosevelt changed his mind. He told Harriman sometime in December that he did not think it necessary to send Depew to Paris. Harriman felt that the President had placed him in a false position by reneging on what he considered to have been a solid commitment. It was particularly embarrassing to Harriman, as he had gone to one of Depew's closest friends, Hamilton Twombly, for help in raising the money.

Harriman spoke to no one of his disappointment with Roosevelt. Although he wrote a personal letter to his old friend Sidney Webster, a retired New York lawyer, describing the circumstances, Webster honored his confidence. Feeling betrayed by the President, however, Harriman refused any further contribution to the party when he was approached two years later by James S. Sherman, a Republican fund-raiser, and by way of explaining his reasons, showed Sherman a copy of his letter to Webster.

Roosevelt evidently received a highly colored version of Harri-man's attitude from Sherman. But he kept silent until Joseph Pulitzer's New York *World* in 1907 bought and published a copy of the letter, which had been stolen from Harriman's files by a recently fired male secretary. The explosion that followed echoed around the world. Bitterly denying the story of his broken promise, Roosevelt denounced Harriman as "an undesirable citizen and an enemy of the Republic." He also consigned Harriman to the Ananias Club (a mythical fraternity, invented by the Washington press corps, whose large and growing membership included all those whom Roosevelt had branded as liars).

The new Interstate Commerce Commission soon launched an investigation of Harriman's railroad transactions, and the Department of Justice started antitrust action to break up the Union Pacific–Southern Pacific combination. Harriman believed that Roosevelt had instigated both actions as a means of retaliating for the exposure of the Depew affair. It was a trying period for the Harrimans. Mrs. Harri-man loyally supported her beleaguered husband, who in spite of failing health remained active in business. He spread his investments into insurance companies, and at the time of his death two years later, was making plans for a large merger of New York banks.

Averell Harriman felt that Roosevelt had done his father a great injustice, but the incident did not turn him against government regula-tion. He came to believe that there had been too much useless compe-tition in the period when E. H. Harriman and his titanic rival, James J. Hill, built parallel railroads in the Northwest that proved not to be in the public interest. As chairman of the Union Pacific board in the thirties, he agreed with Joseph B. Eastman, chairman of the Interstate Commerce Commission in the New Deal era, that the country could no longer afford what Eastman called "competitive waste." With

Eastman's acquiescence, Averell Harriman took the initiative in encouraging the presidents of the Western railroads to get together and work out cooperative arrangements to reduce the waste of resources. There was plenty of room for competition in other ways, he felt, such as in the quality of passenger service. He built the first streamlined passenger train at the trough of the Great Depression and developed the first great Western ski resort at Sun Valley, Idaho, in order to develop a new industry in the Union Pacific territory.

His father dead and Yale behind him, Averell had gone to work for the Union Pacific in the summer of 1913. Judge Robert S. Lovett, E. H. Harriman's successor as chairman of the road, arranged an intensive course of on-the-job instruction in all aspects of railroading. Averell studied train operation, track and shop maintenance, worked with the comptroller's office out of Omaha as part of a team investigating waste and incompetence within the system.* After two years of these activities, Judge Lovett promoted Averell Harriman to vice president in charge of purchases, with headquarters in New York. In the same year, 1915, he married Kitty Lanier Lawrance, the daughter of a New York banker, who bore him two daughters, Mary and Kathleen.

Judge Lovett evidently believed that the principal qualification of a purchasing agent was honesty. Harriman had learned, during his two years of knocking around the system, that honesty was not enough. The lack of uniform standards among different components of the system—all the way from the design of cars and locomotives to specifications for paint—led to colossal waste. There was, he conceded, some excuse for variations dictated by differences of climate or terrain. But the bewildering variety of products and materials purchased by the Union Pacific system owed at least as much to prejudice, to persistence of zealous salesmen, and to a limited extent, to corrupt practices. The suppliers, Harriman found, were not above collusive bidding in order to carve up the available business. An early experience of the sort occurred when the Union Pacific invited bids from the two principal locomotive manufacturers, American and Baldwin. While Baldwin was the low bidder on an order for freight locomotives,

---

* A contemporary newspaper account, reporting that "young Harriman is as averse to publicity as a mouse is to a cat," exposed the carefully concealed fact that he was working on the railroad:

William Averill [sic] Harriman, Yale '13, son of the late E. H. Harriman and director of half a dozen banks, vice president, railroad official and heir to $75,000,000, is spending the fall on a handcar along the line of the Union Pacific in Wyoming and Colorado, serving as a section hand in one of the railroads of which he is vice president. Attired in blue overalls, he is mixing with the section men and the ordinary day laborers along the line . . . At noon Harriman's dinner is taken from a tin bucket, and he eats it in company with his fellow laborers. To them he is simply "Bill" and a cub engineer, who doesn't know much about the business but is learning.

American offered the best price on passenger locomotives. Harriman did some quick calculations, analyzing both bids on a cost-per-pound basis, and sniffed collusion. There ought, he felt, to have been no significant difference between the two bids in the per-pound cost of construction. When a Baldwin vice president came to see him, Harriman said he had decided to place the whole order with a single concern. He offered a per-pound price that was somewhat below either bid. The startled Baldwin man protested that he had no authority to bid on passenger locomotives. So Harriman handed him the telephone to call Samuel Vauclain, Baldwin's president, who grudgingly accepted the offer on Harriman's terms. There were loud protests from American Locomotive and appeals to Judge Lovett, but the one-price order stood.

E. H. Harriman had left his entire fortune to his wife, who in turn gave a substantial sum to each of her children. Mrs. Harriman shared her husband's interest in the Bureau of Municipal Research and after his death contributed liberally to its support. The bureau, directed until 1920 by the American historian Charles A. Beard and after his resignation by Luther Gulick, had as its goal the raising of standards in local government and public administration. Impressed by the high quality of the young men from Oxford and Cambridge who chose to make careers as public servants in England, Mrs. Harriman dedicated herself to fostering a similar movement in the United States. She tried out her idea on Charles W. Eliot, the president of Harvard University, on Nicholas Murray Butler of Columbia and on Arthur T. Hadley of Yale. Why was it, she asked, that in America promising young men seemed to shun politics? And why didn't American universities do something about it by preparing their graduates for careers in public administration as they did for law and business? The answer of all three Ivy League presidents was that in America politics was no career for a gentleman. Mrs. Harriman, not easily discouraged, raised $250,000 and established a Training School for Public Service in New York. This pioneering effort, guided by Averell Harriman's determined mother, eventually became the nucleus of the Maxwell School of Citizenship and Public Affairs at Syracuse University. She gave generously to the American Symphony Orchestra and served for many years on the board of the American Red Cross, in which she was particularly active during World War I. Carrying out her husband's wish, she also gave 10,000 acres and $1,000,000 to help create Harriman State Park, now a section of the Palisades Interstate Park which adjoins Bear Mountain. For Averell Harriman, a member of the Palisades Park Commission since 1915, this was his introduction to the world of public service.

With the money settled upon him by his mother, Harriman also began to spread his interests and his capital into fields other than railroading. There was the shipbuilding venture in World War I, followed by a shipping enterprise. Among other operations, Harriman concluded a twenty-year partnership agreement with the Hamburg-American Line to compete for the rich transatlantic trade. He wound up the partnership in 1926 when it became plain that American passengers preferred foreign ships, chiefly because the Volstead Act prohibited the sale of alcoholic beverages on vessels flying the American flag.

Banking, however, was his principal interest. In 1920, recognizing that the United States had become an international creditor nation and that Wall Street was likely to become increasingly the postwar financial center of the world, he organized with several of his business friends the firm of W. A. Harriman & Co., an international investment house. Several years later he and Roland Harriman organized an international banking firm called Harriman Brothers & Co. (Both firms were merged in 1931 with the older house of Brown Brothers & Co. to create Brown Brothers Harriman & Co., today one of the last private banks of consequence in the country.* The Harriman brothers remained the closest of friends and business partners throughout their lives. When Averell left the business world to serve in the administrations of Roosevelt and Truman, Roland looked after their business interests and took Averell's place as board chairman of the Union Pacific.†

As an investment banker, Averell Harriman became deeply interested in European affairs. He crossed the Atlantic twice a year to look after the firm's financial interests in several countries, establishing close relations with the large merchant banks of London. Among the European investments his firm marketed in Wall Street was a large zinc and coal-mining property in Poland. To the extent that it was possible in that period of postwar economic instability, the Harriman firm tried to protect itself by financing enterprises that earned their own foreign exchange. One such transaction, financed by the Harriman firm, was a loan secured by the German government's foreign postal receipts

---

  * Robert A. Lovett, a partner of Brown Brothers, joined the Harrimans in the new firm. The son of Judge Lovett, E. H. Harriman's lawyer and successor as chairman of the Union Pacific, Robert Lovett played a major role in the Roosevelt and Truman administrations. He served as Secretary of Defense from 1951 to 1953.

  † Roland Harriman served for twenty-seven years as president and then as chairman of the American Red Cross, having been appointed by Truman and reappointed by four succeeding Presidents from Eisenhower through Nixon.

that made possible the extension of the German cable system to the Azores. Another loan was made to a German steel company, 40 percent of whose business was with foreign countries.

Long before Hitler became Chancellor, however, Harriman stopped dealing with Germany. The breakdown of German credit under the Weimar Republic ended further financial transactions.

In 1927, as the only American attending an executive committee meeting of the International Chamber of Commerce in Paris, he put a troubling question to a group of European bankers and industrialists at dinner one evening. Why, Harriman asked, was Europe in a state of economic stagnation at a time when the United States economy was steadily expanding? The unanimous reply of his European friends was that America had a truly continental economy, without barriers to free trade and free movement of people. Why, then, Harriman asked his influential European friends, did they not work toward lowering national barriers in Europe? There would be no breaking down of barriers between nations, the Europeans replied, so long as military security could not be assured through international arrangements. Each country would insist on the highest possible degree of autarchy; each would rely on its own resources as far as possible to support its armed forces with everything from heavy castings for heavy guns to brass buttons for uniforms. Harriman recalled those Paris conversations many years later when he made recommendations to President Roosevelt for American assistance in European recovery after World War II and, in the Truman years, when he directed the Marshall Plan in Europe and became involved in NATO planning.

His original interest in Russia was political, not economic. As a boy he had read the elder George Kennan on the czarist prison system and had been profoundly shocked by that experience. As a young man he was eager to see for himself what the Bolsheviks could accomplish in the way of transforming their vast and backward country. The Russian Revolution, Harriman felt, inescapably would affect the pattern of world affairs—for good or ill—throughout his own lifetime.

Having decided to do business with the Soviet Union, he joined with M. M. Warburg and Company of Hamburg in buying Russian bills at big discounts from German firms which had taken them in payment for manufactured goods. He found that the Russians made good on their financial commitments. In 1924, upon the urging of a business associate, the Harriman firm also undertook a concession from the Soviet government to exploit the manganese deposits at Tchiaturi, near Tiflis, in the Caucasus. This area had been the largest manganese producer in the world before the war. During the period of Lenin's New Economic Policy (NEP), foreign concessionaires were encouraged to help develop Russia's resources under contract for a period of twenty years. After that, the Russians estimated, they would be able to handle their own affairs. The company, Georgian Manganese, started operations in June of 1925 and was showing a satisfactory profit. However, reports that the Soviet government was considering another concession to a German firm, which might lead to overproduction of manganese, persuaded Harriman that he ought to have a personal look at Moscow and Tchiaturi. Before leaving, he called on Herbert Hoover, then Secretary of Commerce, for advice. Showing little or no interest, Hoover stiffly warned Harriman not to expect any help from the U.S. government if he got into personal trouble in the Soviet Union. The United States, of course, had not yet recognized the Soviet regime.

En route to Russia, Harriman visited a number of embassies in Europe, and in most cases, heard the conventional forecasts of the period that the Communist regime could not last longer than five years. He had found from previous experience that the five-year limit was extended year by year. The absurdity of this attitude struck Harriman when he arrived in Moscow in December 1926. The Bolsheviks had been in power for nine years and he saw no evidence to doubt that they would remain in power. After Lenin's death Stalin seemed the inevitable leader, although he was not yet in command. Leon Trotsky, with whom Harriman had a four-hour talk, appeared to be losing out. Trotsky, then chairman of the Concessions Committee of the Supreme Economic Council, listened courteously to Harriman's proposals for changes in the concession agreement, article by article, giving no sign of his own opinion. He asked questions about world markets, but gave no answers. When Harriman signaled that he had no further questions, Trotsky got up, bowed and left the room.[5] "His coldness," Harriman later concluded, "may have been due to his difficult situation at that time. He behaved as if our conversation was being overheard and he was taking no chances that his talk with me would add to his troubles." Harriman left Russia convinced that the days of the NEP, and of foreign concessions, were numbered and that the sooner Georgian Manganese could wind up its affairs in the Soviet Union, the better. As Harriman was one of the few important American businessmen to visit Moscow at that early period, he saw many of the leading commissars but not Stalin, who was said to be out of the city. All the commissars raised the subject of U.S. recognition. Speaking as a private citizen, Harriman explained that recognition was unlikely until Moscow stopped financing the Communist party in the United States and made compensation for American properties confiscated by the Soviet government.

His first glimpse of Moscow and Leningrad was filled with surprises. He found life freer than in years to come. The arts were particularly lively, with the new theater flourishing. He was able to meet writers, painters, musicians and assorted intellectuals without difficulty. The Stalin terror had not yet begun. Harriman talked at length with members of the foreign press corps such as Walter Duranty and H. R. Knickerbocker, learning more from these journalists, he believed, than "from any diplomat." Although he had a feeling that he was being watched, he was not greatly concerned. Conditions of life for the Russian people were, however, grim and getting grimmer. He would always remember the *bezprizornye* (homeless children orphaned in the civil war), dressed in rags, dirty-faced and hungry, roaming the frozen streets of Moscow to beg or steal a crust of bread. Harriman saw thousands more *bezprizornye* on his trip south to the mines of Tchiaturi.

He hired a private railroad car for the trip, as a proper capitalist doubtless was expected to do. The car, dating back to czarist times, was the most ornate he had seen anywhere; all scroll work, wood inlay and gilt. The trip to Tiflis took four days over a rough track at speeds never exceeding twenty-five miles an hour. Like earlier travelers to the Russian interior, he was fascinated by the crowds at all the railroad stations, waiting stolidly in bitter winter weather to go somewhere, all weighted down with bedding and pots and straw suitcases. He stopped off at Baku to see the oil development. At a meal in the hotel, there was no butter, but in its place, caviar was served without charge. He spent a day in Tiflis staying with the American Relief team, went to the opera, and was taken by Georgian officials to visit the so-called state wine library, which had once been the cellar of the Grand Duke Nicholas. The wines being impressively old and mellow—choice French and German vintages and real Napoleon brandy—the tasting went on for hours with predictable results.

At Tchiaturi, Harriman inspected the manganese mine and its new concentrating plant, talked with the American engineers in charge, and after a few days, left Russia on a Danish ore freighter, sailing through the Black Sea from Poti to Constantinople, a four-day trip. Constantinople seemed to him a most modern Western metropolis after the backward cities of the Caucasus.

On the way home in January 1927, Harriman stopped in Milan to discuss the financing of a hydroelectric power project with Italian bankers. Harriman pointed out to them that it would be difficult, if not impossible, to sell the bonds in New York if the Italian government carried out its proposal to revalue the lira. The Milan bankers, who opposed the revaluation, urged him to explain this to Mussolini, and Harriman readily agreed, since it was his custom to take every occasion to meet the important men of the day. He vividly recalls being ushered into an enormous room and walking its full length to meet the

Fascist dictator, who was standing at his desk at the far end. Harriman carried out his promise to explain the disastrous effect of revaluation on Italy's international borrowing and Mussolini then explained his policies. "Mr. Harriman, you don't understand," he said. "I must restore the pride of the Italian nation. The value of the lira must be respected."

When Harriman asked for his opinion of the Soviet Union, Mussolini replied that while he vigorously opposed Communism he found it profitable to carry on a moderate amount of carefully selected trade with Russia. Mussolini was just learning English and proudly insisted on speaking it. Thus the interview suffered.

From Rome, Harriman went to Cannes, where he arranged to meet Winston Churchill, then Chancellor of the Exchequer, for the first time. He wanted Churchill's opinion of Russia with a view to the recommendation he was planning to make to his associates that the manganese concession ought to be terminated. In later years Churchill would maintain that he had saved Harriman millions of dollars by advising him to get out of the Russian business.

On his return to New York, Harriman did recommend to his associates that they terminate the concession, even though it was still profitable. The negotiations took about a year to complete. The settlement finally agreed upon provided compensation for the company's improvements in Tchiaturi, which permitted repayment of the original investment with a small profit. Half the compensation was to be paid in five years and the balance in ten annual installments at 7 percent interest. The Soviet government, as in other financial transactions, lived up to its commitments. Harriman was satisfied: it had been a fascinating personal experience and the group got its money back with interest. All things considered, Harriman had reason to feel that he got out of the deal in better shape than other concessionaires who tried to hold on too long and lost heavily. His early experience in Russia, moreover, was to prove of great value when he later represented the United States in its wartime relations with the Soviet government.

"My observations at the time," Harriman recalled, "led me to conclude that the Bolshevik Revolution, in fact, was a reactionary development. The dictatorship of the proletariat, providing that the few should make decisions for the many, and that the individual must be the servant of the state, seemed to me a regressive development substantially at odds with the legitimate aspirations of mankind. That was my view in 1926. I have had no reason to change it since."

During this period Harriman's life was not concentrated entirely on business. He had many other interests. Having "grown up on a horse" long before the day of the automobile, on his father's large farm and woodland property at Arden, he took up polo. He claimed it was less time-consuming than golf. He could leave his office at four o'clock, drive out to the Meadowbrook Club on Long Island and play a full game of polo before dinner. A round of golf would have taken half the day. He enjoyed polo and was particularly gratified when in 1928 he was chosen to play for the United States against the Argentines, the best of the foreign teams at the time. The *Morning Telegraph* of September 30, 1928, reporting on the American team's 7–6 victory, made much of Harriman's contribution:

> While the victory was thoroughly a team victory, nevertheless it amounted to a personal triumph for W. Averell Harriman, the American No. 1, who played startlingly beautiful polo. He tallied four of his team's seven goals. He came out of the game not only a hero but established as a first-rate poloist.

Harriman saw no need to apologize for playing polo, or breeding Labrador retrievers that won field trial championships in the early thirties. He worked hard as a banker and railroad executive, harder than other men of great wealth, and he felt the need for hard, competitive recreation. Nor did he limit his social circle to business associates. "A lot of Wall Streeters in that period seemed to confine their interests mostly to business and to golf," he recalled. "I did not find that particularly stimulating."

Especially after his second marriage in 1930 to Marie Norton Whitney, Harriman developed a broad set of friends. Mrs. Harriman managed an art gallery in Manhattan, dealing in modern American and French paintings. Together the Harrimans enjoyed a wide acquaintance in the world of artists and writers.

Harriman's mother had given him the great house at Arden, built by his father, when he first married in 1915. His mother, however, lived in the main house until her death in 1931. Averell and his family lived in the east end. They stayed there even after his mother's death because Arden House seemed too big for comfort.*

It was Alexander Woollcott, the prototype of *The Man Who Came to Dinner*, by George S. Kaufman and Moss Hart, who with Marie Harriman concocted the idea that the house should be filled at least once a year. Fill it they did on long Thanksgiving weekends by inviting some forty of their friends up to Arden each year. The Heywood Brouns came, along with the Herbert Swopes, the Robert Sher-

---

* During World War II, Harriman loaned Arden House to the Navy as a recuperation center. After the war he gave the estate to Columbia University for use as a conference center. He worked out the arrangements with Dwight Eisenhower, then Columbia's president, on the understanding that Arden would house the American Assembly and serve as an extension of the university campus.

woods, the Bennett Cerfs, the William Paleys, the Ernest Hemingways, Helen Hayes and Charles MacArthur, the Donald Klopfers, Moss Hart, George S. Kaufman, George Backer, Harold Ross, S. N. Behrman, Ben Hecht, Rudolph Kommer, Alice Duer Miller, the Howard Dietzes, Harold and Alice Guinzberg, Neysa McMein and Jack Baragwanith, Alfred Duff Cooper and Lady Diana, to mention a few. They were a brilliant crew, an assortment of individualists who happened to enjoy being together with the Harrimans in that enormous mountain-top house in Harriman, New York, on Thanksgiving weekends before the war.

The organ room would be turned into a badminton court. The bowling alley, in great demand for after-dinner entertainment, was much frequented by Heywood Broun, who liked to bowl in his stockinged feet, often exposing a big toe through the hole in his socks. Croquet on the lawn kept Woollcott, Swope and others busy in the daytime. In the evenings the Harrimans and their guests devised group games, of which the Murder Game was the most popular. Each of the guests had to invent an alibi to avoid implication in an imaginary murder. Broun (who was leading the movement that gave birth to the American Newspaper Guild at the time) won the prize for the most ingenious alibi one evening by announcing that he had been out in the kitchen organizing the Harriman servants while the murder was committed.

IT WAS HIS ELDEST SISTER, Mary Harriman Rumsey, who encouraged Averell's late-blooming interest in politics. A young woman of extraordinary determination, she had insisted on attending Barnard College at a time when, as Harriman recalled, "my father wasn't sure that it was a good thing for girls to go to college." In 1901, together with Nathalie Henderson, she had founded the Junior League in order to interest the daughters of the well-to-do in helping the poor through the settlement-house movement. Ten years older than Averell, she carried forward her parents' concern for good government and good works, including the defense of the unsophisticated consumer against less-than-scrupulous merchants, long before such advocacy became fashionable. She became a power in the Women's Trade Union League and in the Community Councils of New York. Her example inspired other well-born young women, including Eleanor Roosevelt, to enter social work.

Averell, as a classmate of Eleanor's younger brother, Hall, had come to know the Roosevelts while at Groton. The orphaned Hall Roosevelt lived with his sister and brother-in-law in New York. He would come to the Harrimans' town house from time to time for a meal; Eleanor and Franklin, in turn, would invite young Averell to join them and Hall for an evening at the theater during the Christmas or Easter vacation. It was a pleasant relationship. But Harriman, even into his twenties and thirties, did not see in Franklin Roosevelt a great national leader. "He was president of the Greater New York Boy Scouts Council after the war," Harriman recalled, "and while I admired his interest in the Boy Scouts, he did not impress me as a man of great force or depth. His character matured and developed, I later realized, during his great battle with polio."

Still a Republican though inactive in politics, Harriman became a Democrat after voting for Alfred E. Smith in 1928. As a member of the Palisades Interstate Park Commission he had met Governor Smith and learned to admire him greatly. Harriman had lost confidence in the Republican party with "its isolationist tendencies and its reckless domestic policies" (as he later expressed it); he believed it was leading the country in the wrong direction.

Mary Rumsey, who shared her brother's disenchantment, had a great many intellectual friends, among them the Irish poet and painter George William Russell, who signed his poems "A.E." Averell Harriman was fascinated by Russell, a celebrated talker, when they met at Mrs. Rumsey's in the late twenties. Russell talked that evening about America's "planetary understanding." He said, "You Americans have a vision about this planet that no other nation has had. You will be the first nation to assume a planetary responsibility." A poet's fancy, perhaps, but Harriman never forgot A.E.'s words.

When Franklin Roosevelt became President in 1933, Mary Rumsey encouraged her brother to take an interest in the New Deal reforms and to lend a hand when asked. "The average Wall Streeter," Harriman recalled, "was utterly opposed to almost everything Roosevelt tried to do and wouldn't even go down to Washington to consult with the government on recovery measures. I couldn't understand their attitude. The country was in appalling condition. I was quite ready to accept Roosevelt's conception that our economy had become so complicated that you could not leave it to individuals. Getting the country back on the rails would take a mighty effort. We needed new ideas and I admired Roosevelt very greatly for his willingness to experiment."

When Harriman in 1933 agreed to serve on the Business Advisory Council, a blue-ribbon group created by Roosevelt to mobilize support for the recovery program, and later the same year became New York State Chairman of the National Recovery Administration, he found himself ostracized by many in Wall Street. "The hate-Roosevelt sentiment ran strong," he recalled. "When I walked down Wall Street, men I had known all my life crossed to the other side so they would not have to shake my hand."

Mary Rumsey, a considerable New Deal figure in her own right, had moved to Washington where she shared a house in Georgetown with her old friend Frances Perkins, the new Secretary of Labor. Consistent with her early advocacy of consumer rights, Mrs. Rumsey became chairman of the Consumers Advisory Board within the NRA. Like Averell, she saw no conflict between her espousal of the New Deal and her devotion to her late father. Speaking of E. H. Harriman in 1933, she said, "His period was a building age, when competition was the order of the day. Today the need is not for a competitive but for a cooperative economic system." Her death in a riding accident the following year left her brother to carry on the new family tradition of public service. In 1934 he became first a deputy administrator of the NRA and later its administrative officer, serving to the end of that organization's life seven months later, when the Supreme Court ruled it unconstitutional. The kernel of the NRA, Harriman felt, lay in two concepts that were perpetuated in other legislation—the minimum wage and the right of labor to organize unions.

For Harriman the NRA period had been an education. He learned more about American industry in a few months than he could possibly have absorbed in any other way. That experience of seeking to mobilize America's resources against the despair of the times was to prepare him for the task of mobilization in wartime.

CHAPTER III

"The British Can Hold Out but They Cannot Win Alone"

B Y THE SPRING OF 1941, six months before the United States declared war, the "common-law marriage" with Britain (as Robert E. Sherwood described it) had been consummated. The new Harriman Mission in London was hard at work on every kind of measure, short of war, to keep Britain afloat. If the Neutrality Act took some hard knocks in the process, Harriman for one was not perturbed. Britain found herself close to starvation that spring, closer than she had ever been before or was to be again. She had been paying dollars for all the airplanes, tanks, ships and machinery ordered in the United States, and the dollars were running short. Churchill later recalled:

> We had already sold $335,000,000 worth of American shares requisitioned for sterling from private owners in Britain. We had paid out over $4,500,000,000 in cash. We had only two thousand million left, the greater part in investments, many of which were not readily marketable. It was plain that we could not go on any longer in this way. Even if we divested ourselves of all our gold and foreign assets, we could not pay for half we had ordered, and the extension of the war made it necessary for us to have ten times as much.[1]

American public opinion warmly approved the Lend-Lease shipments initiated by the Harriman Mission. Vast quantities of cheese, canned pork and fish, dried milk, powdered eggs, flour and canned or dried vegetables started arriving on May 31, when Harriman and

Lord Woolton, the Food Minister, met the first ship at Tilbury Dock, London. The British people, while no doubt grateful for the food from America, were less than enthusiastic in the beginning. They preferred their own cheeses (sharper in flavor) and could not see much merit in those canned luncheon meats, provenance unknown, all of which came to be known generically as Spam. Perhaps exaggerating the problem, Harriman's daughter Kathleen, who joined him in May, wrote home to her sister Mary: "The great difficulty is re-educating the people. They prefer to go without, rather than change their feeding habits." At a later stage in the war, when Harriman was pressing the British to bake only dark bread because it demanded less imported wheat, and incidentally, might be more nutritious, the Minister of Labor Ernest Bevin snorted, "I won't have my coal miners get diarrhea from eating this foul stuff."

It was, however, a series of less widely advertised actions undertaken at the time that stretched the meaning of "neutrality" beyond recognition and would, if Congress had known the details, have raised a storm in Washington. One of Harriman's first suggestions was that the United States should by degrees take over the job of directly supplying General Wavell's forces in the Middle East. The effect would be to conserve equipment in the British Isles, where it was badly needed, and to reduce the risk of running the German blockade twice (from Britain to the Middle East and then, a second time, from the United States to Britain in order to replace the equipment sent from there to the Middle East). On April 11, after Wavell's forces had succeeded in driving a far larger Italian army out of Eritrea, Ethiopia and Somaliland, President Roosevelt issued an executive order declaring that the Red Sea and the Gulf of Aden were no longer combat zones. That made it possible for American merchantmen to begin supplying the Middle East theater directly, without the need to unload and transship in England. Harriman also worked out detailed arrangements with the Admiralty providing for the repair of damaged British warships in American yards, clearly an unneutral act. The first of these, the battleship *Malaya*, had been torpedoed in the Atlantic while in convoy service. She was followed by the aircraft carrier *Illustrious*, dive-bombed in the Sicilian Straits while escorting a convoy to Greece. Many more ships followed. Rather than wait until the crippled warships limped or were towed into Newport News, Virginia, Harriman's aide Commander Lee found out from the Admiralty what special parts were needed from Britain to put the wounded vessels back into service and had them sent ahead, so that little time was lost. Thanks to Harry Hopkins' influence with the President, other irregular arrangements were swiftly approved. The United States transferred to Britain two million tons of old world-war merchant ships being held in mothballs, to make up for the steady loss of tonnage in the North Atlantic. "That was Hopkins' work," Harriman recalled. "There wasn't a thing we suggested to which he didn't give serious thought."

The next major step toward near-involvement was Roosevelt's decision, communicated to Churchill on April 11, that the United States would extend its security zone and patrol areas more than halfway across the Atlantic to longitude west 26 degrees. The new directive left the British still solely responsible for their own convoy protection, but it authorized American ships and planes—based in Newfoundland, Greenland, Nova Scotia and the West Indies, as well as the United States—to patrol the vast ocean area and warn the British in time if they found German submarines or surface raiders lying in wait for a convoy. There was to be no shooting by the U.S. Navy unless the Germans shot first.

Roosevelt hesitated to publish his new directive lest he alarm the Congress and the country. He preferred to "let time bring out the existence of the new patrol area." On April 24, while studying a map in a *National Geographic* magazine with Hopkins, the President extended the patrol area by drawing a line along the 26th meridian, bending it sharply to take in all of Iceland. Harriman welcomed the patrol plan as a step in the right direction, although he was impatient to see the Navy in a more active convoy role. He had become involved in every aspect of the war effort—what the British people ate; why the British, who lived on a giant coal field, were so short of fuel that they had to import it from the United States (too many miners had been drafted into the army in the early call-up); how the first shipments of American aircraft were standing up in battle (the P-40 fighter, said Air Vice Marshal Graham Dawson to Harriman and General Millard F. Harmon, "is no goddam good").

General Arnold came to England in April to see for himself how the British were fighting the air war—their tactics, equipment and priorities. He was astonished at "the calm and peaceful manner in which everyone worked in Harriman's office," Arnold later wrote, and delighted when Harriman invited him to visit Churchill at Ditchley the following Saturday.

After lunching with the Prime Minister and Eduard Beneš, President of the Czechoslovak government-in-exile, Harriman and Arnold went along to an Army camp at Leamington, where a remnant of the Czechoslovak forces was in training. Reviewing the troops, Churchill sadly remarked, "Two thousand men—all that is left of an army of 1,500,000." Harriman was deeply moved by the experience. "This was the last of the Czech army," he recalled. "After the Nazi invasion they had found their way to England with the sole objective of rejoining the fight to liberate their country. Many of the men now serving in the ranks had been officers before Hitler occupied their country. The determination in the faces of those men was inspiring."

He also was greatly impressed with the British method of arriving at decisions. All important decisions were made in Churchill's War Cabinet, a coalition of the Conservative and Labor parties. This assured both tight coordination and parliamentary approval when necessary, a far cry from the Battle of Washington, where agencies fought one another for scarce materials and appropriations. In Britain, he soon discovered, the Chiefs of Staff had no direct access to Parliament, nor did they enjoy the mighty influence that America's military leaders could exert on Capitol Hill. The British Chiefs were simply advisers to the War Cabinet, which in turn represented the political leadership of the country. It was the politicians who ran the war— Churchill, Eden, Sir John Anderson, Sir Kingsley Wood and Lord Beaverbrook for the Conservatives; Attlee, Bevin and Arthur Greenwood for Labor—not the generals or admirals. In Washington, Harriman had seen interagency meetings degenerate into bitter conflict where little action could be taken at the end of long, heated and wearying discussions. In London he found decisions being taken promptly, above all when Churchill was presiding. Even in his absence, however, thanks in no small part to the high competence of the Cabinet Secretariat, agreement came more readily than in Washington. These young men, predominantly honors graduates of Oxford and Cambridge, had made a fine art of capturing consensus on paper, even after meetings in which there had been a powerful clash of opinion. The minutes they drafted, distilling sharp disputations into cool and neutral-sounding recommendations, were accepted in most cases without cavil or complaint. To Harriman this was a refreshing revelation.

At No. 3 Grosvenor Square, Harriman determined, there would be no guerrilla warfare, no matter what was happening in Washington. It was not an easy task. The bulk of his staff members had been assigned from other government departments; they were thoroughly familiar with the attitudes and policies of their superiors back home. They came from the Army, Navy and Army Air Force; from the Maritime Administration and the War Shipping Administration, the Office of Lend-Lease Administration, the Office of Production Management (later the War Production Board) and just about every other principality of power along the Potomac. In London, however, they reported through Harriman, who gave them wide latitude in carrying out their assigned business. He held a staff meeting once a week to coordinate the Mission's activities. But he kept informed, and in control, by not permitting any cable to be dispatched to Washington without his approval. For some of the Mission staff, not seeing the boss more often proved upsetting. Colonel Green, for example, came in one morning obviously unhappy. He complained that Harriman never, or hardly ever, saw him. "Why the hell should I see you?" Harriman said, laughing. "I see your telegrams. They're first-rate. I only call in men when I don't approve their messages. What is it you want to talk to me about?" The colonel acknowledged that he had nothing special in mind but feared Harriman had lost interest in what he was doing.

Harriman's unique method of tying loose ends together did not sit equally well with all the Washington potentates. Later in the war Harriman tangled with General Brehon B. Somervell, the tough commanding general of the Army Service Forces. Somervell had taken to questioning British requests for nickel, copper and other strategic materials already cleared by the Harriman Mission, frequently demanding separate verification from General J. C. Lee (known to the troops as "Jesus Christ"), who was in charge of supply for American troops in the European theater. Harriman objected to the frequent duplication of effort, stressing that he wanted no crossed wires. He promptly worked out with Lee a scheme of cooperation providing that either Lee's Army staff or the Harriman Mission—not both—would investigate particular British requests for raw materials. When the investigation was completed, joint telegrams (bearing his own signature along with Lee's) would go out, reporting the facts and recommending action by Washington. Lee suggested that it would be well for Harriman, who was about to leave for Washington, to see Somervell in person, as he was known to be arbitrary and suspicious.

On Harriman's arrival Somervell asked him to lunch at the Pentagon. Harriman strode into Somervell's office, took off his hat and plopped it on the general's desk.

SOMERVELL: What's the matter, Averell, you got a chip on your shoulder?

HARRIMAN: No, I haven't got a chip on my shoulder but I want to know whether you want to work with me or have a row.

SOMERVELL: What's on your mind?

Harriman explained the problem and the plan he had worked out with General Lee in London. After a moment's thought Somervell said he would agree, on one condition—that he receive copies of all Harriman telegrams having to do with industrial raw materials for the British. This Harriman readily accepted. "Let's go to lunch," Somervell said. That settled the matter and established a satisfactory working relationship that continued throughout the war.

KATHLEEN HARRIMAN, who had wangled a job with the London bureau of International News Service to be with her father, went down to Chequers with him the last weekend in May and wrote to her sister about her first glimpse of the Churchills:

> It's rather a shock meeting someone you've seen carica-
> tured so many times. The P.M. is much smaller than I expected
> and a lot less fat. He wears RAF blue jaeger one-piece suits
> (the only way to keep warm in that house), and looks rather
> like a kindly teddy bear.
>
> He expresses himself wonderfully—continually comes out
> with delightful statements. I'd expected an overpowering,
> rather terrifying man. He's quite the opposite: very gracious,
> has a wonderful smile and isn't at all hard to talk to. He's got
> the kind of eyes that look right through you . . .
>
> Mother [Mrs. Churchill] is a very sweet lady. She's given
> up her whole life to her husband and takes a back seat gra-
> ciously. Everyone in the family looks upon him as God and she's
> rather left out . . .

Kathleen Harriman also accompanied her father to the country home of Lord Beaverbrook, the mighty press baron who had just resigned as Minister of Aircraft Production to turn his attention to tanks as Minister of Supply:

> Our host looks like a cartoon out of *Punch:* small, baldish,
> big stomach and from there he tapers down to two very shiny
> yellow shoes. His idea of sport is to surround himself with
> intelligent men, then egg them on to argue and fight among
> themselves. Sitting at dinner while all this is going on makes
> New York seem very remote. Even his best friends are half-
> scared of him, because he's got a fearful temper and no one
> seems to know when it will break. On top of all this, he's kind,
> very kind, and is wonderful with children; for some reason,
> he doesn't seem to scare them . . . He and Averell got on
> beautifully.

As Churchill's confidence in Harriman grew, thanks to the quick action resulting from Harriman's recommendations to Washington for increased American assistance, he revealed his hopes and fears for the Middle East. Churchill's hopes, when they ran high, were unconquerable. He could foresee a mighty British offensive, linked to a massive defection of the Vichy French, that would sweep clean the entire coast of North Africa. At other times, however, gloomy introspections dominated Churchill's mind as, for example, after Rommel had taken charge of the Afrika Korps and whipped Wavell's forces in the

Western Desert. To Harriman the Prime Minister spoke his honest fears: Rommel might break through to Cairo and seize the Suez Canal; the Germans might launch an attack from Crete against the Free French in Syria; they could move through Turkey into Asia Minor; or through Spain, with Franco's cooperation, into North Africa. The Prime Minister had run great risks in his determination to hold the Suez Canal. Stripping the defenses of the home islands to strengthen Wavell's position, he had persuaded the War Cabinet to send two mechanized divisions to the Middle East in the summer of 1940, during the Battle of Britain. This was one of Churchill's most courageous decisions, Harriman believed, taken at a time when he could not be certain that Hitler would forgo an invasion attempt against the British Isles. The Prime Minister worried less about this possibility than certain of his advisers, of whom the most formidable pessimist was General Sir John Dill, Chief of the Imperial General Staff. On May 6 Dill had submitted a paper urging that no more tanks be sent to the Middle East lest Hitler, flushed by his successes in the Balkans, should now decide to strike across the Channel. He wrote, in part:

> The loss of Egypt would be a calamity which I do not regard as likely, and one which we would not accept without a most desperate fight; but it would not end the war. A successful invasion alone spells our final defeat. It is the United Kingdom therefore and not Egypt that is vital, and the defence of the United Kingdom must take first place.[2]

Churchill was astonished to receive Dill's paper. He rallied the War Cabinet, however, dismissing the general's warning with barely disguised contempt. "Many Governments I have seen would have wilted before so grave a pronouncement by the highest professional authority," he later wrote, "but I had no difficulty in convincing my political colleagues, and I was of course supported by the Chiefs of the Navy and the Air. My views therefore prevailed and the flow of reinforcement to the Middle East Command continued unabated."[3]

It was in late May that Churchill asked Harriman whether he would go to the Middle East to make an independent appraisal of the situation, to see for himself what America might do to shore up the British position, and report back to him personally. Harriman immediately agreed. "Do you always make decisions so quickly?" Churchill asked, with a show of astonishment. Harriman admitted that he did. "Of course, the President has to agree," Harriman added, "but he will, if you express your concern and interest." Accordingly, on June 3 Churchill cabled Roosevelt requesting that Harriman be sent to the Middle East and the President cabled his approval the following day. No envoy—least of all the envoy of a foreign government—could have hoped for a more resounding introduction than the directive Churchill sent ahead to Wavell in Cairo: "Mr. Harriman enjoys my complete confidence and is in the most intimate relations with the President and Mr. Harry Hopkins. No one can do more for you . . . I commend Mr. Harriman to your most attentive consideration. He will report both to his own government and to me as Minister of Defence."

Harriman wanted to see what arrangements the British had made to receive and assemble the airplanes, tanks and trucks being sent from America, to satisfy himself that the equipment was being used effectively and that the Red Sea ports now open to American shipping were prepared to handle the expected tonnage. He set out on June 9 from Poole in one of the original PBY flying boats which the British had purchased before the start of Lend-Lease, taking with him Robert Meiklejohn, Colonel Alan Green and Brigadier General Ralph Royce (an air officer newly assigned to the Mission).

In a letter to Hopkins, written the next day during the stopover in Lisbon, he again vented his impatience with American developments:

> It is awfully hard for me to understand what is going on in the mind of America from this distance. Recent polls seem to indicate that 80 per cent or 85 per cent of the people believe we are eventually going to be in the war, and over two-thirds that we should be in the war, if necessary to save Britain, but only a minority think we should go in now. My conclusion after three months in London is that England cannot win without our direct intervention, at least without our Navy and Air Force, and that every week America waits the difficulties of the job when we do come in will be multiplied. Are the facts being properly presented and interpreted to America? After all, the British stopped the Germans from daylight bombing by taking a toll of about 10 per cent. Why, then, is Washington so complacent over the Germans' taking a similar toll of merchant ships and their cargoes in the Battle of the Atlantic?

While in Lisbon, Harriman hoped to see Captain James Roosevelt, the President's son, who was just returning from the Middle East, in order to find out what he had learned and to enlist his support. When young Roosevelt did not appear, Harriman left a letter for him, dated June 11, which states his own convictions at the time:

> I have come to the conclusion that material aid is not enough. The British Navy is not large enough to deal with the world problems that it faces . . . I believe the British can hold

out for a long time, but they cannot win alone. The longer we
delay active participation, the greater will be the difficulties
that confront us . . . I do not believe that a real air offensive
on Germany can come without help from us, not only in the
bombers we have promised but in manpower as well.

Harriman left Lisbon the following day on a swing along the
West African coast: to Bathurst in Gambia, where he caught up with
James Roosevelt and talked at length with Lord Louis Mountbatten;
then on to Freetown in Sierra Leone; Takoradi and Accra in the Gold
Coast; and Lagos in Nigeria. He spent June 13 in Freetown, then an
assembly point for British convoys, looking over the port facilities with
a view to their later use by the U.S. Navy for ship repairs. At luncheon
in the mountainside home of a senior British officer, Harriman remarked on the small formal English garden at the front of the house,
in contrast to the luxuriant tropical growth of the surroundings. "We
try to bring a bit of England with us," his admirable host replied.

At Takoradi the British had established a highly secret aircraft-
assembly plant. Harriman watched the workmen as they put together
British Hurricane fighters and Blenheim bombers, American Tomahawks
and Marylands, from parts and subassemblies which had been crated
and delivered by sea. Takoradi had a capacity of 175 planes a month
but there were so few pilots available to ferry them across Africa to
Cairo that dozens of new planes were sitting in the sun unused.

The long journey across the African continent in a Lockheed
Lodestar, from Lagos to Cairo, was filled with hazards: short airstrips,
no navigation aids to speak of, treacherous weather and only the
sketchiest of weather information. "We could fly only in the daylight
hours—about five hundred miles a day," Harriman recalled. "These
appalling conditions may have accounted for the large number of
wrecked fighter planes we saw at each of the airstrips. The ferry pilots
—mostly Poles—were too few to handle the traffic, and many of them
had come down with malaria. At El Fasher in the Sudan we were put
up in a big tent in a blinding sandstorm. It was a great relief to arrive in
Khartoum and to spend the night in a comfortable room with that
rarest of luxuries, a private bath, at the Governor General's house."

Harriman and his party finally reached Cairo on June 19, having
traced the ferry route from Takoradi by way of Kano and Maiduguri
in Nigeria and across Lake Chad to El Fasher. He was impressed by
the quality of the British civil servants at these out-of-the-way posts,
but not with the efficiency of the air ferry service. One of Harriman's
first recommendations was that the ferry route should be taken over
by the United States.

In Cairo, Harriman put up at Air Marshal Arthur Tedder's house. When he called on Wavell the following day, the commander of the Middle East forces politely inquired what he could do for his American guest. "I am here to find out what the United States can do for you," Harriman replied. The serious talk had to wait, however, until after a luncheon party Wavell was giving for members of the Greek royal family. "I was genuinely shocked," Harriman recalled, "by the luxury and complacence of British life in Cairo, as compared to London. There was no blackout. Food appeared to be in ample supply. I confess that I did not at the first meeting recognize Wavell's great simplicity, warmth and courage." That recognition came upon closer acquaintance during a period of supreme travail for Wavell. With the loss of Crete and the failure of the British offensive in the Western Desert, Churchill decided to relieve Wavell of the Middle East Command, naming General Sir Claude Auchinleck, the commander in chief in India, to succeed him in Cairo.

Two weeks later Harriman called on Wavell again. "I was, of course, keen to meet Auchinleck, who had just arrived," Harriman recalled. "But I was a little embarrassed about how to do it. Wavell made it easy for me. His first words were: 'I am sure you will want to see General Auchinleck. He is waiting in the library to talk to you.' I then expressed to Wavell, in the name of the American people, our respect and gratitude for the masterful way in which he had destroyed the Italian armies in the Western Desert and in Eritrea against heavy odds. Tears came to his eyes and he said quietly, 'It was the men I commanded.' Wavell impressed me as one of the fine characters the British army was capable of producing, a man of real integrity and a true leader."

Wavell had remained popular with his troops, in spite of the defeats the British had suffered in the Middle East. They remembered his early successes against numerically superior Italian forces. Against the brilliant Rommel, however, Wavell's leadership qualities were undermined by his weakness in logistics and the general shortage of matériel, which Harriman made it his business to overcome. He caught a glimpse of Wavell's way with the troops during a trip to Asmara, in the colony of Eritrea. It was unbelievably hot in the midday sun when Wavell's plane stopped at Port Sudan to refuel. Everyone on board, Harriman included, ran for a shady spot, some crouching in the shadow of the wing. Not Wavell, however. He stood there in the full glare of the African sun, holding a stick with a horsetail brush at the end of it to wave off the flies, talking to the ground crew as it serviced his aircraft.

While Wavell went on to Addis Ababa, where he was to receive the Star of Solomon* from the Emperor Haile Selassie for his military achievements in driving the Italians out of Ethiopia, Harriman flew to Massawa, a former Italian port in Eritrea, in a tiny plane with the senior British air officer for that part of the world. He found the port choked with ships scuttled by the Italians. The wrecks would take many months to clear, as Harriman recognized, but Massawa seemed to him a potentially valuable naval base which could provide repair facilities—an important fallback in the event that Rommel broke through to the Suez Canal and deprived the Royal Navy of Alexandria.

"The climate," Harriman recalled, "was among the worst in the area, close to the mountains and without the faintest cooling breeze from the desert. The British working there all looked yellow. I recommended to Admiral Stark, the Chief of Naval Operations, that our Navy should clear the port, stressing that all the offices and quarters for the men must be air-conditioned. My recommendations were carried out." Harriman also suggested the development of an air base at Gura, near Asmara, which in time became a valuable link in the chain of airfields across the width of Africa for ferry deliveries to Iran and India.

HARRIMAN WAS IN CAIRO when Hitler launched his invasion of the Soviet Union on June 22. The news did not come as a surprise to him; Harriman knew that both the British and American governments had warned Stalin the Germans were preparing to attack. His own rough estimate was that whatever the outcome of Hitler's eastern offensive, it would give the United States and Britain a year to build up their military capability and to deal with the U-boat campaign. By that time, he felt, it would be too late for the Germans to invade the British Isles. The general belief among the soldiers and statesmen Harriman met was that Hitler's attack had been delayed some five or six weeks by the resistance of the Yugoslavs and the Greeks, supported by the British, during the spring campaign in the Balkans. "I vividly remember," Harriman said, "Churchill's comment when the decision was made to send British forces from the Middle East to reinforce the Greeks. He said, 'Britain can afford to lose a battle but not her honor.' "

Wavell, like his senior commanders, told Harriman that he believed the Russians were doomed. He gave them six weeks. At the end of that time, Wavell predicted in a conversation with Harriman, Hitler would offer to make peace with Great Britain and Churchill would refuse. He asked Harriman what America would do. Harriman explained that

---

* According to Harriman's recollection, Wavell was the third person to receive the Star of Solomon. The first two were King George VI and Haile Selassie himself.

Roosevelt would never make a deal with Hitler behind Britain's back. "He seemed surprised," Harriman noted at the time, "that President Roosevelt could control the declining of a German peace offer when it seemed so difficult for him to bring America into the war."[4]

The general pessimism of Wavell and his staff officers was fully shared in Washington. Henry Stimson, the Secretary of War, reported to President Roosevelt that there was "substantial unanimity" between General Marshall, the War Plans Division of the General Staff and himself on the consequences of the German attack:

1. Germany will be thoroughly occupied in beating Russia for a minimum of one month and a possible maximum of three months.

2. During this period Germany must give up or slack up on
    a. Any invasion of the British Isles.
    b. Any attempt to attack herself or prevent us from occupying Iceland.
    c. Her pressure on West Africa, Dakar and South America.
    d. Any attempt to envelop the British right flank in Egypt by way of Iraq, Syria or Persia.
    e. Probably her pressure in Libya and the Mediterranean.

To Stimson, the German invasion of Russia seemed "like an almost providential occurrence." The Russians, of course, would be defeated. But Hitler's demonstrated perfidy would allow Roosevelt to take the steps he needed to win the battle of the North Atlantic; that was the right way, Stimson said, to help Britain, to discourage Germany and to strengthen America's own defense.

In Cairo, during those last oppressive days of June 1941, the British generals talked gravely with Harriman about whether it would be wiser to withdraw up the Nile, or across the Canal to the east, if Rommel (far from easing the military pressure, as Stimson believed) were to step up his offensive and drive the British out of Egypt. General Auchinleck, who had arrived in Cairo on July 2, told Harriman the following day that he was for withdrawing to the east, to Basra in Iraq, where the British had a base. The importance of maintaining Britain's position in the region, come what may, seemed to him twofold: to maintain her prestige in the Moslem world and to hold a position from which she could take the offensive one day. Harriman had his own calculation. He, too, felt that if the Germans broke through to the Canal, the British should be prepared to fall back on Basra and the Persian Gulf but for different reasons: the Iranian oil fields and the great Abadan refinery were absolutely essential to the

British war effort; in addition, Iran provided a possible gateway for supplies to Russia.

On July 10 Wavell, who had been dispatched to India as commander in chief, proposed to the War Office that Iran must be made secure against German designs:

> It is essential to the defence of India that Germans should be cleared out of Iran now. . . . It is essential we join hands with Russia through Iran, and if the present Government is not willing to facilitate this it must be made to give way to one which will.[5]

London promptly issued an ultimatum to the Shah, demanding the expulsion of German agents and residents in Iran. His refusal led to the joint occupation of Iran by British and Russian forces toward the end of August. The oil fields, the Abadan refinery and the Persian Gulf were thus made safe. It was the first act of military cooperation between the British and their new allies in Moscow. Over the next four years, Iran was to be the funnel for delivery of some five million tons of war supplies, chiefly from the United States, to the Soviet Union.

On June 30 Churchill had sent Harriman an impatient message through the British ambassador in Cairo, Sir Miles Lampson:

> How are you getting on? I am most anxious to have at least a 500-word telegram from you. You can cable in perfect secrecy through embassy. Considerable changes are afoot in Middle East and I hope you will be in Cairo in the first week of July. I will see you have full and timely information. All good wishes.

Harriman's response was a series of telegrams to Churchill—and to Roosevelt—detailing his reactions to the military situation as he saw it and the "considerable changes" the Prime Minister had mentioned. Apart from the relief of Wavell, and his replacement by Auchinleck, these included the appointment of Oliver Lyttelton, who had been President of the Board of Trade, to represent the War Cabinet in the Middle East with the rank of Minister of State. He was to relieve Auchinleck (as Churchill explained to Roosevelt in a message dated July 4) of nonoperational functions such as relations with the Free French and the Emperor of Ethiopia, recently liberated from Italian military rule, together with propaganda, the administration of newly occupied territories, economic warfare and supplies from the United States. Harriman welcomed Lyttelton's appointment, though he did not believe it went far enough. The most crucial need, Harriman felt, was an effective unified military command. He came to this conclusion after a troubling series of talks with field commanders of the three services. Admiral of the Fleet Sir Andrew Cunningham, for example, took Harriman around the port of Alexandria in his launch and showed him, among other ships, a gunboat armed with heavy cannon. The admiral said he could have used the gunboat to blast Halfaya Pass from the sea in support of the ground forces during their recent unsuccessful attack. But he had not been told of the army's plans and the attacking troops were badly mauled and thrown back, in part for lack of fire power. The total lack of coordination was underlined during Harriman's visit to the Western Desert on July 2. "At luncheon with Beresford-Peirse, the army commander, I heard bitter complaints that the air force had not supported the advance of his troops," Harriman recalled. "After lunch I went to the headquarters of the air force commander, Air Commodore Collishaw. He considered the army's requests for air-ground cooperation unreasonable without greatly improved radio communications, which did not exist." In a memorandum dictated the same day, Harriman observed:

> Although their headquarters are only two miles apart, the relationships between the two men are on a formal basis and there is a mutual lack of confidence and mutual recrimination over the late disaster, the Battle of Sollum.

Harriman's host in Cairo, Air Marshal Tedder, confirmed the dangerous lack of military coordination. In a memorandum dated July 5, Harriman summarized Tedder's view:

> Neither the Army nor the Navy understands the use of the air. If [either one were] given control, the Air Force would be wasted. He [Tedder] was rarely told in time what the Army and Navy wanted to do. For example, the Army wanted supplies at Tobruk and the Navy agreed to provide ships but not until the last minute was the RAF told they needed fighter protection.

On July 6 Harriman flew to Baghdad and Basra in Iraq to see what might be done about strengthening the British position there in the event of a forced withdrawal east of Suez. As the British ambassador's overnight guest, he slept on the roof of the embassy residence, the only tolerably cool place affording some relief after the unbearable heat of the day. He found the port of Basra the best in the Middle East, with a daily capacity of 7,000 tons. Its chief drawback was the vulnerable eighty-five-mile channel leading to the Persian Gulf. Harriman pointed out that if the enemy broke through to within aircraft range of Basra, the channel could easily be mined. He recommended several improvements and precautionary measures, including the development of an alternative port farther south, and extension of the existing railroad from Baghdad to the northeast, across the flat desert, toward Syria. Never having traveled in that part of the world before, Harriman brought back vivid recollections of the filth of Basra, the many fascinations of Baghdad, and the boyish thrill he felt upon seeing the Tigris and Euphrates rivers from the air. On the way back, he also stopped in Jerusalem to talk with General Sir Henry Maitland Wilson, whose troops were then engaged in clearing the Vichy French out of Syria.

On July 10 Harriman set out for London in a Sunderland flying boat. With its cruising speed of 90 knots, the swanlike white Sunderland, designed for leisurely civilian travel in the service of Imperial Airways, was a sitting duck for German fighter planes. It was a long, slow flight from Alexandria to Malta at no more than 200 feet above the Mediterranean, the RAF's tactic for avoiding detection and reducing the risk of a diving attack by German fighters. "We had to approach Malta after dark and leave before dawn," Harriman recalled. "That restricted our visit to three hours, time enough for a conference with Air Vice Marshal Sir Hugh Lloyd, the air commander at Malta, and an air raid from the Luftwaffe, but not enough for sleep." At Gibraltar, the second stop, Harriman's plane was delayed for five days by foul weather. The commanding general, Lord Gort, helped Harriman pass the time by escorting him through the labyrinth of caves he was carving out of the celebrated rock against the day when the Germans might sweep down through Spain to besiege the fortress.

Impressed by the dangers and delays of his return trip from the Middle East, Harriman promptly succeeded in having several American B-24s assigned to the Mediterranean service. The new four-engine planes could fly from England to Gibraltar at high altitude and then over the Sahara to Cairo with far less risk to crew or passengers.

In his definitive report to Churchill, titled "Observations on Middle East," Harriman bore down hard on the essential need for a unified command:

> G.H.Q. [General Headquarters] does not appear to be well organized. As symptomatic of this, the telephone service is inexcusably bad and without a prearranged guide it is impossible to locate the rooms of even important officers. The organization appears to be top-heavy and in many cases not to be in close touch with field operations.
>
> A general staff of the three services is being developed, and daily meetings are taking place of the three C-in-C's or their representatives with the Ambassador present and Mr. Oliver Lyttelton presiding. A unified command, it is hoped, will thereby be brought about.

Unified command is essential and in my opinion cannot be attained to an effective degree unless one man is charged with responsibility for the defense of the Middle East. The functioning of a committee is too wasteful of the time of men who ought to be out in the field and the results of the deliberations of such a committee are too apt to be a compromise.

The report, delivered to Churchill on July 16, the day after he arrived in England, was taken up by the War Cabinet soon after, with Harriman present. Harriman's recommendations and observations covered every aspect of the struggle: the need for a definite commitment of American aid to the Middle East; the overall shortage of spare parts; poor road and rail transportation; the incredible waste of equipment the British troops had never been trained to use, and above all else, the need for a single commander with overall responsibility for the defense of the Middle East.

Harriman also reported that he had found the West African plane ferry route badly disorganized, and while he praised the Takoradi assembly plant, recommended that rather than expand it, the British should start another plant at Lagos, which was 300 miles closer to Cairo.

The Harriman mission to the Middle East, unlike many such flying surveys before and since, yielded a great many practical results. For example, Pan American Airways took over the African plane ferry route, recruiting civilian pilots to deliver combat planes from Natal, in Brazil, to British West Africa and then to Cairo; an American repair and supply depot was established at Decamere in Eritrea, some thirty miles south of Massawa; civilian mechanics from Douglas Aircraft were sent to the Middle East to instruct RAF ground crews in the maintenance of the new American planes; General Motors found ways, with Colonel Green's help, to strengthen the frame of its Canadian-built three-ton truck so that it would no longer bend, when fully loaded, as it carried men and supplies to the front over jolting desert tracks; the jerry can, a tough and durable gasoline container, was made standard equipment for all American as well as British army units after the Harriman Mission had investigated the problem of the flimsier cans then in use, which tended to leak or burst, spilling more than half the gasoline before it could reach the front.

The War Cabinet in London and the United States government acted promptly on his chief recommendations, leading to a massive buildup of war matériel and maintenance facilities during the year that followed. This methodical buildup, supervised by Auchinleck on the ground, made possible the successful offensive of the British Eighth Army some fifteen months later under the new leadership of Generals Harold Alexander and Bernard Law Montgomery. One typical outcome of Harriman's report was a request by Churchill "that wherever American equipment is shipped to British forces unfamiliar with the type, American personnel shall precede the arrival of the equipment and be available to instruct the British in use and maintenance." A fairly obvious point, perhaps, but one that had been overlooked until Harriman recommended it.

BACK IN ENGLAND, Harriman soon found Harry Hopkins on his doorstep. Hopkins had flown over to discuss arrangements for a face-to-face meeting between Roosevelt and Churchill at sea off the Argentia peninsula in Newfoundland in August. He brought news of Roosevelt's immediate concerns: first, that Hitler's latest invasion was bound—if the common-law partners agreed to help Russia—to reduce Britain's share of Lend-Lease supplies; second, that the American Chiefs of Staff (sharing Sir John Dill's concern) believed that Britain was making too many sacrifices to maintain what they believed to be an indefensible position in the Middle East; and third, that the defense of the United Kingdom and the Atlantic sea lanes ought to have first priority.

Harriman listened to all this with a heavy heart. But Churchill, reinforced by his own military chiefs, rose to the occasion. He made clear that he was determined to go on reinforcing the Middle East, no matter what the Americans felt. The Battle of the Atlantic was going better, he said, with the help of the United States Navy and he was confident that Britain could repel any invasion attempt. The First Sea Lord, Admiral of the Fleet Sir Dudley Pound, agreed, and so did Air Chief Marshal Sir Charles Portal. That left General Dill to speak for the army. When Churchill called on Dill to expound the reasons for staying in the Middle East, he ignored all the arguments to the contrary that he himself had been pressing upon the Prime Minister barely two months earlier, and stated the case with apparent conviction. It was a vivid illustration of Cabinet supremacy in British affairs. The Americans, Churchill felt, were even more impressed by the show of British solidarity than by the force of their arguments.

The strategy meeting at No. 10 Downing Street, held on July 24, could not, however, come to grips with the Russian enigma. Hitler's invasion was then in its fifth week, and the Red Army, in refutation of most Western forecasts, had not yet collapsed. But the pace of the German advance was terrifyingly swift as the Russians bought time with ground surrendered, and no one could say how long Stalin would hold out. Hopkins realized that the Churchill-Roosevelt meeting at sea—barely two weeks in the future—would be held in a vacuum without some knowledge of what was happening on the eastern front and of Stalin's plans. So he volunteered again (as he had volunteered some months earlier to visit Britain at war and establish personal contact with Churchill for the President). He would fly to Moscow and see Stalin himself, returning in time to join Churchill and Roosevelt at the Atlantic Conference in Placentia Bay, Newfoundland. Both leaders promptly agreed. Fortified with pills and burning determination, Hopkins flew off to Russia in an RAF flying boat from Invergordon, Scotland, on July 27, wearing a hat borrowed from Churchill. "When we saw him off," Harriman recalled, "his flight seemed as much of an adventure as a trip to the moon today." The parting message from Churchill to Stalin was: "Tell him that Britain has but one ambition today, but one desire—to crush Hitler. Tell him that he can depend upon us."

Harriman left for Washington three days later to report to Roosevelt and others concerned on his Middle East observations. He talked at length with Stimson, General Marshall, Admiral Stark, General Arnold and Robert Lovett and found them reluctant to consider any role for the U.S. Army in Africa that would go beyond supplying equipment to the British. When Harriman recommended that the United States support the British in West Africa more actively, Marshall replied that as Chief of Staff he had to make certain that the U.S. Army's first venture overseas would be completely successful. West Africa was the wrong place, he explained, because of the submarine danger in the South Atlantic and the possibility of a German attack from the north. Harriman, pained by the caution he encountered, recorded his unhappiness in a memorandum dated Washington, August 6:

> Britain and therefore America is on the defensive. Is the idea that we should wait until England is on the offensive and we can pick a nice plum which is safe because Germany is no longer dangerous? Is the idea that we should let England undertake all the difficult tasks and we take over only the fruit of their efforts? Is the role of our Army [to be limited] to such venturesome and dangerous tasks as relieving British troops from their occupation of Iceland?

Britain's needs in the Middle East and elsewhere were large. With Russia now fighting a desperate battle against the heavily favored Germans, painful choices would have to be made in Washington. Two active fronts would be competing for scarce resources with the needs of the growing armed forces of the United States.

Roosevelt's motives in offering help to Stalin have been variously interpreted by a variety of historians. He is said by some to have shown more sympathy for the Bolshevik experiment than most Americans. Others suggest that, confronted with a choice between Stalin's Communism and Hitler's Nazi doctrine, he looked upon Russia as the lesser evil and the less immediate threat. In Harriman's view, ideology had little or nothing to do with the President's decision to help the Russians. It was a simple matter of American self-interest, as Roosevelt saw it: he supported the Russians, as he had earlier supported the British, in the hope that whenever America entered the war (as he believed she inevitably would) it might not be necessary to send large ground forces into battle. "Roosevelt," Harriman believed, "was very much affected by World War I, which he had, of course, seen at close range. He had a horror of American troops landing again on the continent and becoming involved in the kind of warfare he had seen before—trench warfare with all its appalling losses. I believe he had in mind that if the great armies of Russia could stand up to the Germans, this might well make it possible for us to limit our participation largely to naval and air power. The overriding motivation of President Roosevelt in giving every bit of help that was possible was that he wanted to keep the Russians in the war. He wanted to err on the side of generosity, rather than skimping the aid we sent, even when some of us felt that particular Russian requests were not necessary or had not been justified."

Hopkins' visit to Moscow was necessarily brief. He saw nothing of the battlefront, nor indeed of the home front. His business was with Stalin alone. He had flown to Moscow to deliver a message of paramount importance—that "the President considered Hitler the enemy of mankind and that he therefore wished to aid the Soviet Union in its fight against Germany." Stalin's reply was that the Hitlerite leaders of Germany, having trampled on the minimum moral standard that should obtain among nations, represented an antisocial force in the world. "Therefore," he said to Hopkins, "our views coincide." At the very first meeting, Stalin got down to business, asking for 20,000 anti-aircraft guns (20 mm. to 37 mm. in caliber), large machine guns to defend the cities, and a million rifles; high-octane gasoline for the Red Air Force, and aluminum to build new airplanes. A much longer list of items, which had been presented in Washington on July 8 by the Soviet ambassador, Constantine A. Oumansky, ran to almost $2 billion worth of equipment, including 3,000 pursuit planes and 3,000 bombers.

In their second talk, on July 31, devoted largely to Stalin's own estimate of the war with Germany, Stalin said that he had not believed Hitler would attack when he did. The Red Army, in consequence, had not been able to mobilize its full strength. But he was confident that the Russians would hold Moscow, Kiev and Leningrad. When winter came, he said, the line would be stabilized "probably not more than 100 kilometers from where it is now." How the battle would go after that, he added, would depend heavily on how well he could equip the Red Army for the spring campaign. This was what Hopkins had hoped to hear, although he probably read more assurance into Stalin's words than the grim facts appeared to warrant. At any rate, Hopkins flew back to Scotland elated over his talks with Stalin, pleased by the dictator's bluntness and impressed by his grasp of the war in all its complexity. On August 1, before meeting Churchill at Scapa Flow for the trip to Placentia Bay, Hopkins cabled Roosevelt: "I feel ever so confident about this front . . . there is unbounded determination to win."

Harriman, meanwhile, having wound up his Washington consultations, was spending a few days at his home in Sands Point, Long Island, where in years past he had made a great name for himself as a croquet player. Churchill had said that he hoped to see Harriman at Argentia. When Harriman, in turn, told Roosevelt that Churchill thought he ought to go, Roosevelt grumbled that there would be too many people and not enough space for them all. But Harriman persisted, and at the last moment received word that he was to fly up from Boston with Sumner Welles, the Under Secretary of State.

Churchill arrived in full majesty, in the Royal Navy's latest battleship, H.M.S. *Prince of Wales*, a thoroughly exhausted Hopkins at his side. Only Harriman and Hopkins, the two Americans he knew most intimately, understood how anxious the Prime Minister was to ingratiate himself with Roosevelt. "I wonder if he will like me," Churchill had confided to Harriman. More than once, as the conference at sea unfolded, he betrayed a trace of anxiety that he might be pressing too hard by drawing Harriman aside to ask whether the President liked him. The first meeting took place on board the American battleship *Augusta*, an erect Roosevelt supported on the arm of his son Elliott welcoming Churchill with full honors. The Prime Minister's worries, it quickly turned out, were needless. In "a bit of a scrawl" addressed to Kathleen Harriman and Churchill's daughter-in-law, Pamela, who were back in London, Harriman wrote:

> By the time you get this, the rumors (which I have no doubt everyone accepted as true) will have been confirmed. The historic meeting of the great men and their staffs has taken place. It is to be seen whether the seeds sown will bloom . . . The P.M. has been in his best form. The President is intrigued and likes him enormously.[6]

The most publicized product of the meeting at sea was, of course, the Atlantic Charter, which was made public August 14. It pledged their two countries to a set of common principles: no aggrandizement, territorial or otherwise, for the United States and Britain; no territorial changes anywhere that did not accord with the freely expressed wishes of the people concerned; respect for the rights of all men to choose the form of government under which they would live; equal access to trade and raw materials for all states; full collaboration among nations to raise living standards and social security; a world at peace in which all men could live in safety and travel the seas without hindrance "after the final destruction of the Nazi tyranny"; the disarming of nations that threatened aggression outside their frontiers and the abandonment of the use of force in international relations generally.

Churchill had put in the phrase about "the final destruction of the Nazi tyranny" half expecting Roosevelt to balk, lest America's ostensible neutrality be compromised. Its inclusion, the Prime Minister later observed, "amounted to a challenge which in ordinary times would have implied warlike action."[7] But Roosevelt raised no objection. He had evidently decided that American public opinion was prepared to accept the essential logic of the aid program (which was about to be extended to Russia as well as Britain)—that the Nazi regime must be destroyed before the world could live in peace.

From Harriman's point of view the most important business of the Atlantic Conference was the decision to send a British-American mission to Moscow which would follow up on Hopkins' hurried and somewhat preliminary talks with Stalin. Churchill immediately named Lord Beaverbrook to be Britain's "high representative" in these negotiations with Stalin. Roosevelt, who at first had thought of sending Hopkins back, decided that his health could not stand another long journey so soon. The American representative had yet to be named when Harriman and Beaverbrook left Argentia together on August 13. Bad weather forced them to take a train as far as Gander, the new transatlantic airport in Newfoundland. From there they flew to Washington together in a B-24 bomber, Beaverbrook pointing out his birthplace and other landmarks as the big plane passed over New Brunswick, his native province.

Soon after reaching Washington, Harriman discovered that both Henry Morgenthau, the Secretary of the Treasury, and Frank Knox, the Secretary of the Navy, wanted to go to Russia with Beaverbrook. "I talked with each of them," he recalled, "and I had the impression that both expected to be named. It came as a great surprise to me, therefore, when Roosevelt asked me to go instead. I was, after all, junior to either Knox or Morgenthau. Perhaps Roosevelt felt that I could get along better with Beaverbrook."

Both Churchill and Roosevelt were aware that the defense production program would have to be expanded greatly. "Our resources, though immense, are limited," they had said in a joint message to Stalin, dated August 12, "and it must become a question as to where and when those resources can best be used to further, to the greatest extent, our common effort." Both understood that a considerable part of the

American defense output, now to be allocated to Russia, would have to come out of the share Britain had hoped to receive. A substantial increase in weapons production had to be set in motion if the needs of all three powers were to be met. Roosevelt, upon his return from Argentina, asked the Secretaries of War and the Navy to estimate for him the amounts of munitions that would be needed to win the war, no matter which country used them.

This was to become the Victory Program, proposed to the President by General Marshall. Roosevelt liked the idea of setting fixed production goals to supply all fronts in the long war ahead. He wanted, above all, to speed the task of industrial mobilization so that America would have a running start when she had to fight.

Harriman found the official Washington attitude toward Russia as a possible ally changing rapidly. The all but universal assumption that Hitler would win in a matter of weeks had given way to a new assessment, clearly expressed in the report of a Joint Army and Navy Board:

> *The maintenance of an active front in Russia* offers by far the best opportunity for a successful land offensive against Germany, because only Russia possesses adequate manpower, situated in favorable proximity to the center of German military power.[8]

Roosevelt's personal attitude could be seen in a letter to Secretary of War Stimson, dated August 30:

> I deem it to be of paramount importance for the safety and security of America that all reasonable munitions help be provided for Russia, not only immediately but as long as she continues to fight the Axis powers effectively. I am convinced that substantial and comprehensive commitments of such character must be made to Russia . . . at the proposed [Moscow] conference.[9]

There were a good many obstacles still to be cleared when Harriman left for London. The Russians were not yet eligible for Lend-Lease under existing law. They had to pay for their first orders, although Morgenthau had arranged a credit of $100 million to tide them over temporarily. It was not until October, after Harriman had returned from Russia, that Congress approved legislation which was broad enough in its language to make the Soviet Union eligible for Lend-Lease. There were arguments with the Army and the Navy—some of them fairly heated—over the long lists of items that might be offered to the Russians.

Harriman put his Moscow mission together with considerable care after consultation with Roosevelt and Hopkins. The President personally selected Admiral William Harrison Standley, former Chief of Naval Operations. The other members of the Harriman mission were Major General James H. Burns, an Army Ordnance officer close to Hopkins; Major General James H. Cheney, an Air Force officer then stationed in London; William L. Batt, Jr., of OPM, to deal with raw materials; and Colonel Philip R. Faymonville, who had spent several years in Moscow with the military attaché's office, as secretary. General Marshall also sent Lieutenant General Stanley D. Embick with the Harriman group, as far as London, to join in the Victory Program discussions.

Within two hours of their arrival in London on September 15, Beaverbrook insisted upon calling a meeting of the two delegations in the so-called big room of the War Cabinet. The Americans had scarcely been allowed to wash and change after the long flight. Now, before a roomful of British officers and officials from all the armed services, the Ministry of Supply and the Ministry of Aircraft Production, Beaverbrook pressed Harriman to declare what quantities of munitions and raw materials the United States was prepared to offer the Russians. Harriman, who felt that Beaverbrook was trying to force his hand, refused. He proposed instead that the large group divide itself into four working committees—one to deal in an orderly way with ground-force requirements, another with air, a third with naval matters, and a fourth with raw materials. Then views could be exchanged between British and American opposite numbers, and tentative figures put before the conference as a whole. Beaverbrook protested that there was no time for such refinements. He again asked Harriman to specify what amounts of materials the United States was ready to make available to the Russians. Beaverbrook would then decide in Moscow—or so Harriman understood him to say—how much the British would have to add. Harriman replied that the procedure Beaverbrook had just outlined would relieve the Americans of the necessity of going to Moscow. "Oh, no, no, no," the horrified Beaverbrook replied. "We must go together."

Beaverbrook had overplayed his hand. He had tried to dominate the proceedings at the outset, and Harriman saw no choice but to have it out with him. His American colleagues, bone-weary after flying all night from Anacostia, near Washington, to Stranraer in Scotland, and from there to Hendon Airport, outside London, were plainly delighted that their chairman had stood up to Beaverbrook.

Churchill was anything but delighted when he received a highly exaggerated account of the clash from his scientific adviser, Professor Frederick Lindemann (later Lord Cherwell). The Prime Minister immediately invited Harriman to dinner.

"I know you and Max [Beaverbrook] had a fight," he said. "I know how difficult he can be. But it's a vital matter. I depend on you." Harriman explained to the Prime Minister that his informant had perhaps overstated the facts in the case. Of course he would go to Moscow, he said, but perhaps it was just as well that the equal standing of the British and American delegations had been settled before they left London.

For the next six days, in fact, as Harriman had proposed, the British and American teams analyzed together the lists of weapons and materials that might be offered to the Russians. They also developed production goals for the Victory Program, which were accepted in both London and Washington.

Kathleen Harriman commented in a letter to her sister in New York:

> Lord Beaverbrook doesn't like to be contradicted, and he's inclined to be set in his ways and views about people . . . Dinner tonight [with Beaverbrook] was in rather sharp contrast to last night—with the P.M. One's a gentleman and the other is a ruffian. Ave, luckily, can talk both languages.

CHAPTER IV

Red Wolves
in the Kremlin

IT WAS NOT FOR LACK OF WARNING that Stalin had clung to the paper shield of his nonaggression treaty with Hitler until disaster was upon him and the Russian people. He had received literally dozens of intelligence reports, from foreign governments—including the United States and Great Britain—and from his own spy networks in Europe and Japan, making plain that Germany was about to attack the Soviet Union. He dismissed them all as provocations, cunningly designed to draw him into the war before he was ready. Stalin had convinced himself that Hitler would not strike without presenting an ultimatum. There was no ultimatum.[1]

One of the factors that led Stalin to override the repeated warnings of imminent German attack, Harriman believed, was the experience of Czar Nicholas in 1914. The Czar had been persuaded, against his personal inclinations, to mobilize his forces against Austria-Hungary and Germany in turn during the five-day period from July 25 to July 30, 1914. Although he sent a personal message to the Kaiser assuring his "good friend, Willy" that the mobilization was not intended as a hostile act, the German General Staff demanded counter-mobilization and war became inevitable. Harriman felt that Stalin, mindful of the Czar's experience, was determined to avoid provoking the Germans again.

Not until thirty minutes past midnight on June 22 did Stalin allow the Soviet Commissariat of Defense to order a state of combat readiness in the border regions. Even at that late hour, exactly three hours before the Wehrmacht attacked, his purpose was not clear. The late

Marshal Rodion Malinovsky, then a corps commander on the south-west frontier, recalled his own confusion upon receiving the order: "To our question requesting clarification—'Could we open fire if the enemy invaded our territory?'—the answer followed: 'Do not succumb to provocation and do not open fire.' "[2] Thus, one month after the invasion was launched, the German armies controlled great swatches of Soviet territory, in aggregate more than twice the area of France. Now, in September, as the Harriman-Beaverbrook mission prepared to leave London for Moscow, Stalin was counting on the Russian winter to slow the German advance. But half the territory of the Ukraine was in German hands. The enemy pounded at the gates of Leningrad. The Krivoi Rog basin, chief source of Russian iron ore, had been lost. The Russians had been forced to evacuate industrial plants producing aluminum, aircraft, trucks and tanks to safe locations behind the Ural Mountains wall. It would take seven to eight months before they could be back in production. The Soviet Union, in short, faced "a mortal menace," as Stalin wrote to Churchill on September 4, appealing for help from the West. He saw only one way out—the opening of a second front "somewhere in the Balkans or France," which could draw some thirty to forty enemy divisions away from the eastern front. He also asked for massive supplies of aluminum, airplanes and tanks from the West:

> Without these two forms of help the Soviet Union will either suffer defeat or be weakened to such an extent that it will lose for a long period any capacity to render assistance to its allies . . .
>
> I realise that this present message will cause dismay to Your Excellency. But what is one to do? Experience has taught me to look facts in the face, however unpleasant they are, and not to fear to express the truth however unwelcome it may be.[3]

Thunderstruck by Stalin's demand for a second front, no less than by the "air of menace" which Ivan M. Maisky, the Soviet ambassador in London, projected in delivering the message, Churchill was moved to honest anger. "Remember that only four months ago we in this Island did not know whether you were not coming in against us on the German side," he told Maisky. "Indeed, we thought it quite likely that you would." The Prime Minister added, "You of all people have no right to make reproaches to us."[4] The plain fact was that there could be no second front in 1941, even if the Russians had been in a stronger moral position to demand it. The British forces were spread too thin and were on the defensive everywhere. In spite of Operation Barbarossa (Hitler's code name for the invasion of Russia), there were still more German divisions in the west than British divisions in the British Isles. The weapons and equipment needed for a successful landing on the Continent did not exist. These were to come, in large part, from the Victory Program, which was just being blueprinted in London by the Harriman-Beaverbrook team.

In his reply to Stalin the same day, Churchill plainly ruled out British landings in France or the Balkans for 1941. "Action, however well-meant, leading only to costly fiascos would be no help to anyone but Hitler," he wrote.[5] He was prepared, however, to share generously with the Russians the new weapons and new materials promised from the United States, in full awareness that many of the items sent to Russia would have to be subtracted from Britain's own needs and that his military chiefs would feel "it was like flaying off pieces of their skin."[6]

The Prime Minister did not, moreover, see eye to eye with Beaverbrook on the proper attitude toward the Russians. Beaverbrook had made himself the great champion of aid to Russia in the War Cabinet.* This did not greatly trouble the Prime Minister as long as Beaverbrook was in London. But he could see trouble ahead once the mission reached Moscow. "Your function," Churchill wrote to Beaverbrook, "will be not only to aid in the forming of the plans to help Russia, but to make sure we are not bled white in the process; and even if you find yourself affected by the Russian atmosphere I shall be quite stiff about it here."[7] Harriman felt that Beaverbrook was disposed to hand over every conceivable American weapon or material to the Russians, without counting the cost to Britain. "When B. makes up his mind," Harriman wrote, "he oversimplifies the subject to the point of disregard of other considerations. He now claims that the P.M. [Prime Minister] underestimates Russia. I can see no indication of this and, in fact, share the P.M.'s views regarding the importance of Turkey and the Middle East. I am personally also less ready to strip England than either of them."[8]

Before leaving London, the two delegations, British and American, were received at Buckingham Palace by King George VI and Queen Elizabeth. "Our crowd was much impressed," Harriman wrote in a note remarking on the earnestness and sincerity of the royal family.

Five days later, their disagreements intact, Harriman and Beaverbrook left Scapa Flow for Archangel on board the 14,000-ton cruiser H.M.S. *London*. General "Hap" Arnold had assigned two B-24 bomb-

---

* Beaverbrook was notorious in England for adopting extreme though frequently popular positions. His biggest newspaper, the *Daily Express*, had decried the danger of war with Hitler until hostilities, in fact, were under way on September 1, 1939. Day after day it carried articles predicting that there would be no war in Europe.

ers to fly Harriman and his mission to Moscow, but when Beaverbrook insisted on traveling by sea, Harriman decided that he and all his senior colleagues should board the *London* instead. The B-24s flew directly to Moscow, carrying junior members of the American delegation and Ambassador Oumansky, as part of a cover plan designed to conceal the fact that Harriman and Beaverbrook were traveling by sea. The Royal Navy sent no escort vessels along, on the theory that the cruiser might make better time and attract less attention from German aircraft if she sailed alone. On September 23, the second day out, the *London* overheard a Berlin radio report that the British and American delegations had arrived safely in Moscow by air. Although the cover plan appeared to be working, the rest of the journey was never free from anxiety as the cruiser sailed far to the north, beyond Bear Island near Spitsbergen, always within range of the formidable German air force based in Norway.

On board the cruiser, Beaverbrook had given up bullying Harriman and turned on his British colleagues.* He appeared to enjoy telling them that they were coming along for the ride; he and Harriman would handle all the important negotiations with Stalin. "Max was just being sadistic," Harriman recalled. "In fact, there would be plenty of work for them when we reached Moscow and our two delegations split up into six committees with their Russian counterparts (aviation, army, navy, transportation, raw materials and medical supplies) to work up detailed lists of requirements. But I didn't let Beaverbrook's browbeating affect our relations. Our row in London had set the pattern. After that, Beaverbrook was careful not to start another one."

On the afternoon of September 27 the cruiser dropped anchor at the mouth of the Dvina River, and the two parties transferred to a Soviet destroyer for the twenty-mile run upriver to Archangel. The Soviet Foreign Minister, Vyacheslav M. Molotov, was on board and a typical Russian banquet had been spread. Predictable toasts to Allied unity, to the downfall of the Nazis, and of course, to victory, were offered by Molotov, Harriman and Beaverbrook. One Russian even raised his glass to the International Red Cross, by way of welcoming Allen Wardwell of the American Red Cross, whom Harriman had invited to join the party in London. Wardwell, a prominent New York lawyer and a close friend, had once represented Harriman in his negotiations with the Russians over the manganese concession.

The rest of the trip was accomplished in four Soviet airplanes of

---

* Beaverbrook's principal colleagues included Major General Hastings "Pug" Ismay, chief of staff to Churchill as Minister of Defence; Harold H. Balfour, Parliamentary Under Secretary of State for Air; and Major General G. N. Macready, Assistant Chief of the Imperial General Staff. The Prime Minister sent Sir Charles Wilson, his personal physician, to look after Beaverbrook's health.

the DC-3 type, flying in formation with a fighter escort for five hours, at altitudes that gave the passengers "a view of the autumn leaves falling off the trees, from about 100 to 800 feet above them," as Captain Balfour noted in his journal. The approach to Moscow was unnerving. Soviet anti-aircraft guns opened fire and the Soviet pilots had to dive low into a wood before landing for a guard-of-honor reception at the airport, with the Stars and Stripes, the Union Jack and the Red flag all snapping in the breeze. Harriman was welcomed by the American ambassador, Laurence A. Steinhardt, and taken to Spaso House, the embassy residence. This ornate, strangely elegant structure had belonged to a wealthy sugar merchant before the Revolution. Several windows had been broken by German bombs that fell nearby during the early raids on Moscow and, glass being hard to find, the windows had been blacked out with composition board. The bomb damage elsewhere in the city, however, struck Harriman as slight in comparison to London. The Russians attributed this to the prowess of their anti-aircraft gunners. Harriman's skeptical reaction was that the Germans could not have been trying very hard; they expected to occupy Moscow before long and they probably wanted it intact. Besides, their bombers were kept pretty busy in the west.

"I recognized that the Germans were a relatively few miles away and that we might have to evacuate," Harriman noted later. "You had the feeling of going into a war area. We could see the flash of the Russian anti-aircraft guns at night. There were other changes from the Moscow of 1926, of course: the opening up of wide avenues; the building of workers' apartment houses, which looked pretty shoddy; the fact that there were automobiles in the streets now, in place of horse-drawn droshkies." The people appeared more warmly dressed than on Harriman's first visit fifteen years earlier, but the clothing they wore was drab, an advance (in his words) "from raggedness to shoddiness."[9]

The Kremlin, its onion-shaped domes and towers clustered behind the crenelated wall, had been camouflaged to deceive the German bombers. A gigantic stage canvas had been hoisted in place over the high wall overlooking the Moscow River. From the far bank of the river, the solid wall looked like a row of houses with gabled roofs. A wooden house had been placed over Lenin's tomb in Red Square, and Lenin himself spirited away to a secret location.

Although Ambassador Steinhardt and the embassy staff were hospitable, certain of the Americans in Moscow appeared to look upon Harriman as an interloper and his mission as an exercise in futility. Some embassy men, the military attaché in particular, were convinced that Moscow would fall in a matter of weeks. The late Charles Thayer, then a young third secretary in the embassy, told Harriman that feeling against the Russians was still running strong in the diplomatic corps. "I myself, as the American on the team which discussed transportation, had a very futile feeling because we realized that absolutely nothing was going to be decided except at the top levels," Thayer recalled. "I knew Mr. Harriman was seeing Stalin every evening, but I did not know what was going on between Stalin, Harriman and Beaverbrook. The Embassy people were concerned lest too much be promised with not enough strings attached."[10]

Harriman and Beaverbrook were equally wary of Steinhardt and Sir Stafford Cripps, the British ambassador. Hopkins had cautioned Harriman, before he left for Moscow, to expect little help from Steinhardt because the ambassador was disliked by Stalin and the rest of the Soviet leadership. "Both Beaverbrook and I felt that Stalin would be franker with us if we didn't take the ambassadors along," Harriman recalled. "We knew that Stalin had no very high regard for either of them, so there was nothing to be gained by taking them."

Cripps, moreover, had infuriated Harriman by raising objections to the presence of Quentin Reynolds, an American journalist highly popular in Britain for his broadcasts during the Blitz, as a member of the U.S. delegation. Harriman had personally invited Reynolds to come along and handle press relations with the American correspondents in Moscow—on condition that he write nothing while a member of the mission. Cripps, however, had protested to Eden (in a coded telegram that was picked up by the cruiser carrying the mission to Archangel) that Reynolds had arrived in one of the B-24s without a visa (which was untrue), that he was reporting for Beaverbrook's *Daily Express* (also untrue at the time) and that his very presence would doom the mission to failure (which seemed to Harriman plain nonsense and none of the British ambassador's business). Harriman exploded when he saw the message on shipboard. H.M.S. *London* could receive messages sent between London and Moscow but was forbidden to transmit lest the Germans detect her location at sea, a circumstance that increased Harriman's fury against Cripps by forcing him to remain silent.

Beaverbrook had his own reasons for keeping Cripps at a distance. He was always ill at ease with teetotalers, he explained to Harriman, particularly Socialist teetotalers who were candidates for sainthood. Besides, he wanted to feel free to speak his mind with Stalin and then to make his own report to the War Cabinet, without prompting or contradiction. Thus neither Cripps nor Steinhardt took part in the meetings with Stalin, and both, of course, were chagrined to find themselves excluded.

Cripps, nevertheless, tried to be helpful in his fashion by preparing an eighteen-point memorandum as a guide for the greenhorns from

London on how to deal with the Russians. The flavor of that document comes through in this sample:

> The way in which all available resources are divided up must of course depend upon the plans which each country has for the campaign over the next year. In this respect, the Russian plan is known, to continue fighting the Germans offensively or defensively in every way possible along the whole of the front. The plans of the other two governments are not yet known to the Soviet Government. Owing to the fact that the U.S.A. is not an ally or a belligerent, the Soviet Government are certain to be unwilling to discuss with them strategic questions.

It was pretty elementary stuff, Harriman felt, and somewhat presumptuous of the British ambassador. In fact, Stalin showed no less willingness to discuss strategic questions with Harriman than with Beaverbrook, as their first session quickly established.

Their invitation to the Kremlin immediately upon arrival was, in itself, encouraging to both Harriman and Beaverbrook. At nine o'clock on the night of September 28, the two rolled up to the Kremlin gate together in an embassy car. "It was an eerie experience," Harriman recalled. "All of Moscow, of course, was blacked out. The Soviet guards, though obviously forewarned, threw the beam of their flashlight in our faces to make sure of our identity. Only then did they swing the heavy gate open." After a brief exchange in the dark between their chauffeur and the Kremlin guards, they were delivered to Stalin's office: a large room dominated by huge pictures of Lenin, Marx and Engels, an apparently unused desk at one end, and a table large enough to seat twenty persons near the wall that was farthest from the window. Stalin's greeting was correct but reserved. Molotov stood beside him, with Maxim Litvinov next in line.

"I was somewhat shocked by Litvinov's appearance," Harriman recalled. "His clothes and shoes were shoddy and, I remember, his waistcoat and trousers did not meet to cover the expanse of his shirt front. I had the impression that he had been in disfavor since the time he was thrown out and replaced as Foreign Minister by Molotov." The worldly former Commissar for Foreign Affairs, once the great champion of collective security at the League of Nations in Geneva, had been pushed aside when Stalin decided to appease Hitler. Both Harriman and Beaverbrook, having known Litvinov in better days, had confidence in him. It had been Beaverbrook's idea—to which Harriman had assented with some misgiving—that they should not bring their own interpreter from the British or American embassies, but rely on the Russians to supply one. Beaverbrook evidently believed that this gesture would be interpreted by Stalin as a mark of trust. The Russians, accordingly, had sent word that Oumansky, their ambassador to the United States, would interpret. Harriman objected to Oumansky, whom he did not trust. Thus, when the visitors asked for Litvinov instead, barely three hours before the meeting, the Russians had produced him in a hurry.

Stalin was shorter and broader than Harriman had imagined. He wore a heavy black mustache shot with gray, and a simple tunic without decorations, mottled brown in color. The marshal's uniform he later affected had yet to appear. He seldom looked Harriman or Beaverbrook in the eye, frequently addressing his remarks to Litvinov, who was interpreting. "I was impressed with Molotov's silence," Harriman recalled. "Stalin did all the talking. Occasionally, when he tried to put in a word, Stalin would brush him aside. Throughout our discussion I had the impression that Molotov was not in a secure position. I guessed this was because of the failure of the Molotov-Ribbentrop agreement.

"The first meeting was marked by considerable frankness on Stalin's part. He described the tactical situation in detail, making no effort to disguise the obvious fact that it was critical. Stalin stressed the vital importance of holding Moscow at all cost. Although he was prepared to go on fighting a defensive war from behind the Ural Mountains if necessary, he acknowledged that the loss of Moscow, the nerve center of all Soviet operations, would gravely handicap any offensive action in the future. Hitler had blundered, Stalin added, in attacking the Russians on three fronts. If he had concentrated his attack on Moscow, the city certainly would have fallen."

Stalin described the tragic cost of the surprise attack on June 22, disregarding his own miscalculations. "If Hitler had given us one more year," he said, "it would have been different." Both Harriman and Beaverbrook took reassurance from Stalin's determination to hold Moscow, an impression sharply at variance with that of the embassy staffs. In his review of the military situation, Stalin conceded to the German Luftwaffe an air superiority of three to two over the Russians. In tanks, he said, it was much greater, something like three or four to one. By his count, the enemy had 320 divisions on the ground, the Russians 280. The German infantry, he claimed, was weaker than his own. For that reason, the Germans had to maintain their preponderance in tanks. His greatest need, therefore, was to offset this advantage by getting more tanks from the West plus antitank guns, medium bombers, anti-aircraft guns, armor plate, fighter and reconnaissance planes, and—most immediately—4,000 tons of barbed wire a month.

Tanks were the decisive factor, Stalin said. He needed 2,500 a month, and of that number, 1,400 could be produced in the Soviet

Union. Although he needed 1,100 additional tanks, he would settle for 500 a month from the United States and Great Britain, rather than be accused of "asking for astronomical quantities."

Stalin also suggested to Beaverbrook that the British might send troops to help the Red Army in defending what was left of the Ukraine. Beaverbrook replied that a buildup of British divisions in Iran was under way (to block a possible German breakthrough to the Middle East in the event that the Russian front did collapse) and that some of these troops might perhaps be sent to the Caucasus. "There is no war in the Caucasus," Stalin replied, "but there is in the Ukraine." He made no comment, however, when Beaverbrook suggested that the Soviet and British general staffs might open strategic discussions.

Harriman raised the question of using Siberian airports to deliver American aircraft to the Soviet Union by way of Alaska. Stalin agreed that information about the airports in Siberia should be made available; but when Harriman mentioned that American crews might ferry the planes, Stalin objected that it was "too dangerous a route." He was being careful not to jeopardize his new neutrality treaty with Japan. Harriman also mentioned President Roosevelt's anxiety about Catholic opposition to aid for Russia in the United States. The President felt that American public opinion would be favorably affected by some official assurance that Section 124 of the Soviet Constitution meant what it said about guaranteeing freedom of conscience and of worship for all citizens. To this, Stalin replied that he did not know much about American public opinion, leaving the impression that this was a matter best discussed with underlings and of no interest to him. Harriman decided not to press the issue then, promising Stalin a memorandum later on.

It was past midnight when Harriman and Beaverbrook left the Kremlin "more than pleased," as Harriman noted, with their first talk. Beaverbrook was so buoyed up that he talked of settling the whole complicated negotiation in just one more session and going home. Harriman was in no hurry to wind up the talks. He had come a long way at the head of a high-powered American delegation to discover what Russia's actual needs were. He and Beaverbrook in fact had arranged to meet with Molotov the following morning in order to set up six tripartite committees, each of which would deal with a separate area of supply. Harriman pointed out to Beaverbrook that rather than grab at Stalin's shopping list and rush back to London, they ought to let their colleagues learn as much as possible from meeting with their Soviet counterparts.

When Beaverbrook and Harriman returned to the Kermlin at seven o'clock the next evening, September 29, they found Stalin in a wholly different temper; their initial satisfaction with the progress of the talks turned out to be somewhat premature. "The second evening," Harriman recalled, "was very rough going. Stalin gave the impression that he was much dissatisfied with what we were offering. He appeared to question our good faith. He seemed to suggest that we wanted to see the Soviet regime destroyed by Hitler; otherwise we would offer more help. He showed his suspicion in a very blunt way. Whether he was trying to trade, to smoke us out, or whether he had discussed our offer with his associates and they had said it was not enough, I do not know. But the fact that he was so very blunt made it possible for me in turn to be blunt without giving offense."

At one point Stalin turned to Harriman with a question: "Why is it that the United States can only give me 1,000 tons [a month] of armor-plate steel for tanks—a country with a production of over 50,000,000 tons?" Harriman replied that America actually had a capacity of 60,000,000 tons but the demand for armor plate was great and it would take time to increase the capacity for this type of special steel. Stalin brushed aside the explanation. "One only has to add alloys," he said. It was a deeply discouraging talk. At another point, Harriman recalled, Stalin coldly dismissed the efforts of the British and Americans to help the Russians. "The paucity of your offers clearly shows," he said, "that you want to see the Soviet Union defeated."

Only once during the two-hour review of Russian needs did Stalin show lively interest. That was when Harriman offered to supply 5,000 jeeps. Stalin accepted the offer, then asked for more. He brusquely rejected a parallel offer for armored cars. They were death traps, he said and he did not want any. Beaverbrook noted other signs of agitation. "Stalin was very restless," he reported to Churchill, "walking about and smoking continuously, and appeared to both of us to be under an intense strain." He also was rude. When Beaverbrook handed him a letter from Churchill, Stalin ripped open the envelope, barely glanced at it and left it lying on the table, unread, throughout the meeting. Later, as Beaverbrook and Harriman were preparing to leave, Molotov reminded Stalin of the unread letter. He pushed it back into the envelope and handed it to a clerk. Neither Beaverbrook nor Harriman could account for Stalin's surly, disagreeable mood. But so little had been settled that they asked for a third meeting, and Stalin, to their great relief, agreed.

Disheartened by Stalin's behavior, Beaverbrook betrayed a degree of alarm when he returned to the British embassy. He talked to Harriman about the damage to his political standing that would flow from the apparent failure of their mission to Moscow. A man of volatile temperament at the best of times, he was in a state of deep depression;

he could not bear the onus of failure. At Beaverbrook's suggestion, Harriman agreed to take the lead in their final meeting with Stalin on the evening of September 30.

"Max was rattled," Harriman recalled. "The account he sent back to London after that second, discouraging meeting was less than frank, I felt, and did not sufficiently emphasize the difficulty we had with Stalin. Beaverbrook was constantly thinking of his own reputation with his colleagues in the British government. It was for this reason, I suppose, that he asked me to present at the third meeting the combined list of weapons and materials that the British and American governments were prepared to supply. Then, if things did not go well, the fire would be directed at me."

The meeting started on a sober note as Harriman explained the importance of concluding the conference as quickly as possible "with expressions of satisfaction by all concerned." Stalin agreed, remarking that the Berlin radio was already issuing propaganda statements to the effect that the conference had failed. Methodically, point by point, they went over the list of seventy items the Russians had requested, while Harriman explained which of those items the United States and Great Britain were ready to supply, and in what quantities.

Stalin seemed satisfied with the offers, puffing on his pipe with unexpected serenity. He asked for more scout cars. Harriman said he would see what could be done. Stalin then added a new request, for 8,000 to 10,000 trucks a month. Demonstrating an unexpected grasp of detail, he explained that three-ton trucks were the most desirable because many Soviet bridges could not carry anything heavier, but that trucks of one and a half tons or two tons would do. Harriman responded that some trucks certainly would be made available, but that he would have to investigate further. This was a war of motors, Stalin remarked. It was impossible to have too many of them, and the side which had the largest number of motors was bound to win.

So they continued down the list, Stalin evidently making an effort (according to Harriman's notes) to sound "reasonable and not too exacting." When they got down to barbed wire, he said, "It is necessary for us to have immediately 10,000 to 15,000 tons." Harriman reminded Stalin that the Soviet list called for no more than 4,000 tons. "Well," Stalin said, "if it were possible for you to give us at once 8,000 tons, or two months' supply, that would be particularly helpful." So it went, all business now, Stalin raising few objections. Lord Beaverbrook, sensing the change of atmosphere, asked Stalin whether he was pleased with the offers of help. Stalin smiled and nodded.

At this point Litvinov, who had been laboring somewhat over the interpretation, forgot his humble role, and bounding from his chair, cried, "Now we shall win the war!" In this new, buoyant mood, the talk turned from trucks and barbed wire to larger questions. Harriman, for example, urged Stalin to establish a personal relationship with Roosevelt—as Churchill had—by writing to him directly on matters of high importance. Stalin replied that he had not until then presumed on the President's time but would be glad to do so. Beaverbrook suggested an invitation for Churchill to visit Moscow. "Will he come?" Stalin inquired, possibly having in mind Churchill's past enthusiasm for Allied intervention against the Bolsheviks. "He well might if you ask him," Beaverbrook said.

The talk flowed freely. Stalin asked Beaverbrook to explain the mysterious case of Rudolf Hess, Hitler's chief lieutenant, who had astounded the world when he dropped by parachute on the Duke of Hamilton's estate in Scotland some four months earlier. Beaverbrook told the story with relish: how Hess, holding a highly inflated opinion of the power of the British aristocracy, had hoped to persuade the duke and his friends to overthrow Churchill and establish a new government that would make peace with Germany. Then, according to the Hess plan, Germany (with British help) would attack Russia, to general applause from the populace.

There was talk about the desirability, and the difficulty, of bringing Turkey into the war on the Allied side. Stalin complained that Finland had now become a complete vassal of Germany. He asked that Britain frighten the Finns by threatening to declare war against them. As for the United States, he would be content if President Roosevelt threatened to break diplomatic relations with Finland. When Stalin proposed extending his military alliance with Britain into a postwar treaty and inquired about Allied peace aims, Beaverbrook replied that it would be enough to win the war. Harriman added that the Atlantic Charter constituted a program for peace to which the United States and Britain had already subscribed. To Harriman's embarrassment, Stalin then proposed that the results of the Moscow talks be recorded in a written agreement, to be signed before the two delegations left Moscow. Harriman had no authority to sign anything, and communications with Washington were so slow that he could not expect to get specific instructions in time. Making a virtue of necessity, he argued that a written agreement would be both unwise and unnecessary; he pointed out to Stalin that the aid agreements in force between the United States and Britain were wholly informal. Beaverbrook supported him, but when Stalin persisted, the two agreed to take up the matter with Molotov the following day.

Harriman brought up the question of China (the United States was sending a mission and providing arms to Chiang Kai-shek at the time). Stalin said that he, too, had sent airplanes and artillery to Chiang some months earlier for use against the Japanese. This seemed odd in view of Russia's recently concluded neutrality agreement with Japan, but Stalin insisted that there was no provision in it against sending arms to the Chinese. He wondered why Chiang had stopped fighting and had not requested more arms. As for the Japanese, Stalin asked why no effort was being made to detach them from the Germans. Japan was not Italy, Stalin said. She would not accept a position of servitude to Hitler; thus something could perhaps be done to drive a wedge between the two.

Harriman's report on the final talk concluded:

> The meeting broke up in the most friendly fashion possible. Stalin made no effort to conceal his enthusiasm. It was my impression that he was completely satisfied that Great Britain and America meant business . . . I left feeling that he had been frank with us and if we came through as had been promised, and if personal relations were maintained with Stalin, the suspicion that has existed between the Soviet Government and our two governments might well be eradicated. There can be no doubt that Stalin is the only man to deal with in foreign affairs. Dealing with others . . . was almost a waste of time.[11]

Beaverbrook's unquenchable exuberance carried him a long way beyond the plain facts. He made the discovery that Stalin was "a kindly man," one who "practically never shows any impatience at all."[12] Noting that their host had sent for tea and food at one stage in the long discussion, he attributed this traditional Russian courtesy to Stalin's "pleased excitement" over the happy outcome of the talks. Beaverbrook also recorded, without comment or interpretation, the fact that Stalin had the habit of "drawing numberless pictures of wolves on paper and filling in the background with red pencil" while he waited for the interpreter to catch up with him.[13] In his report to the War Cabinet the following day, Beaverbrook boasted:

> The plan of campaign laid down by Mr. Harriman and me had been carried out with precision. There had not been any hitch. The structure of it was simply this:
>
> 1. The story from Stalin of his military situation.
> 2. A niggardly and grudging account of available assistance.
> 3. A generous and bountiful list of available supplies, culminating in an enthusiastic acceptance.
>
> It was sunshine after rain.

In a message to Roosevelt, Harriman added a personal note to Beaverbrook's account, registering his own, more sober, view:

This paragraph about our plans for the three nights is written after the event. The facts are we had hoped to be able to finish our discussions with Stalin the second evening, as we were afraid he might not be willing to continue to meet with us personally, but his attitude and mood on this evening made it quite impossible. Whether Stalin was:

1. Concerned over military news, or,
2. Considered that he would get more if he was tough with us, or,
3. Was just moody over something he heard of the meetings of the committees of the conference, or some incident in his entourage, we have no way of knowing.

Beaverbrook's and my guess is that he had just heard something about the prospective German drive.

Before the evening's talk ended, Stalin had started a half-jocular discussion with Harriman and Beaverbrook which led to the early removal of Sir Stafford Cripps and Ambassador Steinhardt from Moscow, along with the recall from Washington of Ambassador Oumansky. At the outset, Stalin denounced Steinhardt as a defeatist, a rumormonger, a man chiefly interested in his personal safety. During the first six weeks of the German invasion, Stalin said, the American ambassador had twice become panicky and demanded that the embassy be evacuated to the Volga. Harriman loyally defended Steinhardt, arguing that the ambassador had done everything in his power during a difficult period to improve Soviet-American relations.* Stalin, who was not about to modify his opinion, then asked for Harriman's impression of Oumansky.

Rising to the opportunity with more frankness than Stalin may have bargained for, Harriman exposed his personal feelings about the Soviet ambassador in Washington. He said that Oumansky was zealous to a fault, that he talked too much and that he ran around the capital creating more irritation than good will. According to his own memorandum of the conversation, Harriman explained: "Oumansky in his enthusiasm went to too many people on supply questions and, when they compared notes, it led to irritation and no one felt responsibility

---

* Upon his return to Washington, Harriman suggested to Roosevelt that Steinhardt's usefulness in Moscow was at an end. The President appointed his old friend Admiral William Standley, former Chief of Naval Operations, to succeed Steinhardt in Moscow.

to help with his request. Hopkins was the President's assistant on supply questions and Oumansky should follow his guidance and work
with Hopkins' staff." (This piece of frankness soon had its effect. In
a matter of weeks, Stalin sent Litvinov to Washington and Oumansky
to Mexico.)

Stalin then turned the conversation to Beaverbrook, asking for his
opinion of Maisky. Beaverbrook extolled the virtues of the Soviet ambassador to the Court of St. James's, his only reservation being that
Maisky came on too strong at times. When Stalin inquired whether his
ambassador sometimes lectured members of the British government on
matters of Communist doctrine, Beaverbrook replied, "I never give
him a chance."

"What about our fellow?" Beaverbrook asked Stalin, barely concealing his personal distaste for Cripps. Stalin shrugged (a negative
reading, Harriman felt) and said, "Oh, he's all right," with marked
lack of enthusiasm. "The modified acceptance of Cripps," Beaverbrook
reported to Churchill, "led me to observe that there was nothing
wrong with him except that he was a bore. 'In that respect,' asked
Stalin, 'is he comparable to Maisky?' I answered, 'No, to Madame
Maisky.' Stalin liked the joke immensely."*

Harriman, who believed that personal relationships could influence
—even if they could not determine—the affairs of nations, came away
from the meeting with a conviction that Molotov was going to be
difficult. "Oumansky had been eliminated," he recalled, "and I had
the feeling, as I said to Roosevelt, that we ought to indicate to Stalin,
in various subtle ways, which of his people we liked to deal with and
to avoid building up those like Molotov who seemed antagonistic. I
felt that we should have pushed this while Stalin was anxious to get
on a basis of cooperation with us, during the war." His own distaste
for Molotov, born at their first encounter in 1941, increased upon
closer acquaintance over the years that followed. It was Harriman's
impression that as Molotov became more sure of his position he also
grew more overbearing and unpleasant. He found Molotov a man of
great energy, totally lacking in humor or flexibility, literal-minded and
less open to compromise than Stalin himself. "I remember reporting to
Roosevelt, when I returned, that we would have great difficulties with
the Soviets as long as Molotov was an important factor," Harriman
recalled. "I therefore regretted very much the President's decision to
invite Molotov to Washington in the spring of 1942. I thought it was
better not to build him up."†

* The wife of the Soviet ambassador was notorious in London as a tireless
chatterbox.
† In a long talk with Harriman in Moscow in 1959, Nikita Khrushchev
admitted that Molotov was extremely rigid. He told Harriman, "In the negotia-

HARRIMAN'S FIRST IMPRESSION of diplomatic life in Moscow was grim. "I would think that life for a diplomat in Moscow," he noted, "was about as close to prison as anything outside of bars. They see no one socially except the diplomatic corps . . . With so much going on in the world . . . it appears an intolerable existence for anyone with an active mind. The life would lead to the development of any tendencies toward pettiness." Cripps, for example, told Harriman that he did not think much of Steinhardt (an opinion he also had passed along to Harry Hopkins). The American ambassador, Cripps said, had no standing with the Russians. Steinhardt, for his part, told Harriman that Cripps was jealous of his own higher place in the pecking order of Moscow officialdom. "It all sounds like a girls' school," Harriman noted. "But it is a bad situation in view of the determined policy on the part of the British and American Governments to get on a basis of mutual confidence with the Soviets."

In spite of their early disagreements, Harriman developed a high regard for Cripps's intelligence as he came to know him better. Their relationship improved markedly during a long, intimate conversation on the night of October 3 when the two found themselves in agreement on the importance of settling Russia's territorial demands during the war without delay—for the sake of the peace to come. According to Harriman's notes, Cripps said:

> Russia would unquestionably want a Russian-dominated Balkans [after the war]. On what terms? What boundaries?
>
> He thought at the present time the Russians would be quite reasonable in their demands; but when victory came, particularly if her [Russia's] part was important in the ultimate success, the demands would be much greater and hard to meet.
>
> He commented that Winston was not interested in the peace and contended that he would resign, and let someone else make it, which was quite impossible.

As the two warmed to each other, Cripps explained to Harriman that he had become a teetotaler by way of protest against the heavy drinking in the House of Commons before the war. He had been particularly upset by the "most demoralizing" spectacle of rich Conservative members plying their working-class colleagues of the Labor party with alcohol. The conversation took place in the late evening at an American embassy party, with gypsy music, following a gala performance of *Swan Lake* at the Bolshoi Theater which had been

---

tions over Trieste, he was more Yugoslavian than Tito . . . If I had followed his advice in Vienna, there would have been no Austrian state treaty."

specially arranged in honor of the Beaverbrook and Harriman missions. At the ballet, Deputy Foreign Minister Andrei Vishinsky sat between Harriman and Beaverbrook. There was prolonged applause from the audience when they took their seats, followed by rapturous clapping for Ulanova and Sergeyev, the leading dancers.*

Harriman used the intermission opportunity to complain to Vishinsky that, as he had heard from other members of the delegation, the detailed talks in the working committees were not going well. The Soviet representatives in the committee on transportation, for example, had refused to answer any more questions or to attend any more meetings with their American and British counterparts. Nor had the Russians yet responded to his request that General Burns be permitted to visit the area of northern Iran, then under Russian control, in order to survey the proposed Lend-Lease supply route through the Persian Gulf. Vishinsky, supported by Oumansky, assured Harriman that there was nothing to worry about. He must not be disturbed, they said, by Russian officials who had yet to receive their instructions. This pattern of Soviet behavior was to become all too familiar to Harriman in the months ahead, more particularly when he became ambassador to the Soviet Union two years later. For the moment, however, he was a guest in Steinhardt's embassy under circumstances of considerable strain, although the ambassador remained gracious and helpful to the end. Harriman also was favorably impressed by two relatively junior members of the staff, the second secretary, Llewellyn E. Thompson, and Charles Thayer, the third secretary. "Thompson I rate very highly as to ability," Harriman recorded in a memorandum, also praising Thayer as an "energetic and resourceful youngster."†

ON OCTOBER 1 Harriman and Beaverbrook had met with their delegations to receive the reports of the six committees, some of them still in

* Harriman was to meet Sergeyev again in 1974 during a visit with his wife to the Kirov Ballet School in Leningrad. After being introduced to Sergeyev, then director of the Kirov Ballet, Harriman mentioned the special performance of *Swan Lake* in 1941 and the distress of the Bolshoi ballerinas that Ulanova should have been called to Moscow from the Leningrad company on that occasion. Sergeyev reminded Harriman that he had been Ulanova's partner that evening. With Leningrad under German siege at the time, he said, the company had been evacuated to a safe place behind the Urals. He still had the telegram, Sergeyev added, summoning Ulanova and himself to Moscow for the special performance. Harriman apologized for not having recognized the youthful Prince Siegfried whose dancing he had so greatly admired some thirty-three years earlier.

† Thompson rose rapidly in the Foreign Service after the war, serving twice as ambassador to the Soviet Union. During the Kennedy-Johnson years, when Thompson was the adviser on Soviet affairs to both Presidents in turn, he and Harriman became fast friends.

sketchy form, and then rushed off to see Molotov about the protocol the Russians wanted them to sign, by way of marking the successful outcome of the conference. They had agreed beforehand on two points: the commitment of the British and American governments was to "make available" the weapons and materials the Russians had requested, but they could not undertake the obligation of delivering them to Russian ports; and the lists would be reviewed if a new theater of war opened up.

Molotov raised no objection to the second point but he seemed troubled by the first, in view of the fact that the Soviet Union had no significant merchant fleet of its own. "Then you will not help us with transportation," he said. "Oh, no, no," Beaverbrook responded in his most reassuring tone. "We will help but we can't guarantee delivery." Molotov accepted that interpretation, the only time in Harriman's experience that he showed any willingness to make an immediate decision.

He kept pressing Harriman and Beaverbrook, however, to record their agreements in a formal protocol. Beaverbrook protested that a protocol was nothing more than a glorified memorandum, and made the point that no documents had been signed when the British worked out their initial Lend-Lease arrangements with the United States. But Molotov, under firm instructions from Stalin to get a signed protocol, persisted. "You [the British and the Americans] didn't have a conference," he said, rejecting the parallel. "A conference must terminate with a protocol."

Harriman's position was extremely awkward. He was still without specific instructions from Washington. Moreover, the Lend-Lease Act had not yet been amended to allow aid for Russia without payment. Litvinov, whose English was still somewhat rusty, had some difficulty in catching for Molotov the precise nuance that Harriman was trying to convey. Even with Thayer's help, Litvinov spent much of the meeting, which lasted some forty minutes, struggling with the idea that while the United States would "make available" certain war supplies to Russia, as agreed in the talks, it could not guarantee their safe delivery across the ocean. Molotov had trouble with the words "make available." He kept asking who would pay. Harriman carefully explained the legal situation again and again, without much help from an increasingly confused Litvinov. "I explained that England had worked out financial arrangements with the Soviet Government but that the American Government had not; and that all we were offering by these words was to allow the Soviet Government to buy and export the items that were listed," according to Harriman's notes dictated at the end of the meeting. At last Molotov said that he understood the point, and the protocol was approved for signing the next day.

Harriman had an easier time explaining the procedural and political intricacies of Lend-Lease to Anastas Mikoyan, the Commissar for Foreign Trade, after the signing of the document. Mikoyan asked Harriman whether Russia could expect Lend-Lease help. Harriman replied, stressing it was his personal opinion, that the Soviets would be declared eligible for Lend-Lease before the end of the year, probably in December, and that terms would have to be negotiated "on a friendly basis." He made the point that the British also had paid out large sums in cash before their Lend-Lease agreement was in effect.[*] The problem was more political than financial, Harriman explained, stressing the depth of feeling against aid to Soviet Russia among Roman Catholics and various ethnic groups, which required the President to move carefully. "The high officials of the Soviet Government must understand," Harriman said, "they must be willing to have confidence in the President's political judgment in America, and not allow certain difficulties regarding finance to lead to suspicion of his good intentions toward Russia." Mikoyan, for one, appeared to understand. "We have complete confidence in your good intentions because you have been so careful in your promises," he said. Harriman took this remark as an indication that Mikoyan had been fully informed of the hard going in the Kremlin negotiations with Stalin.

At dinner the same evening in the ornate Kremlin hall named for Catherine the Great, Stalin sat between Beaverbrook and Harriman, chatting amiably as if not a harsh word had been uttered during the negotiations. It was a lavish affair, Harriman's first glimpse of the vast gulf separating the rulers of the Soviet Union from the ruled. More than a hundred people had been invited: the whole of the Beaverbrook-Harriman mission, the air crews of the B-24 bombers which had delivered part of the delegation to Moscow, members of the British and American embassy staffs, and dozens of ranking Soviet officials. In his notes, Harriman described the menu and the scene:

> . . . endless hors d'oeuvres beginning with caviar and various forms of fish, cold suckling pig; then the dinner of hot soup, chicken and a game bird, with ice cream and cakes for dessert. There were various types of fruit, not available in the public markets, which had probably been flown from the Crimea.

In front of each man were a number of bottles containing

---

[*] After congressional action, Roosevelt was able to inform Stalin on October 30 that he had approved shipments under the Moscow Protocol up to the value of $1 billion. On November 7 he added the Soviet Union to the list of countries eligible for Lend-Lease assistance, formally declaring that "the defense of the Union of Soviet Socialist Republics is vital to the defense of the United States."

pepper vodka, red and white wine, a Russian brandy—and champagne brought in at the time of the sweet.

Stalin drank his first toast in pepper vodka, only part of the glass, then poured the balance of it out into one of his larger glasses, and for the rest of the meal drank red wine [from] this glass, filling it frequently. The glass was very small, about the size of a pony of brandy. When the champagne came he drank this out of the same glass. He put one of his other glasses [on top of] the champagne bottle in order, he said, to keep in the bubbles.

Harriman found the contrast between the Kremlin and 10 Downing Street startling. "Churchill," he recalled, "was always careful to conform to the British rations, whereas the tables of the Russian officials were groaning with all kinds of delectable foods and the people were hungry. This became increasingly apparent in 1942 and 1943. I thought it was disgusting."

Thirty-two toasts were proposed that evening in the Kremlin: to the valorous Soviet soldier and to all Allied fighting men, to victory over Hitlerite Germany, to the importance of engineers in winning a mechanized war, and among others, to the American B-24 pilots— Major A. L. Harvey and Lieutenant L. T. Reichers—for their nonstop flight of 3,200 land miles from Prestwick, Scotland, by a circuitous route carefully plotted to avoid German-occupied Norway. They had flown a long way north of North Cape, then to the east over Archangel and south into Moscow. It was the longest flight made till then by an Army plane carrying passengers, and a most hazardous one. At times, over Arctic waters, the temperature inside the two planes had dropped to twenty degrees below zero. Heavy ice formed on the wings and at no time could the pilots get any confirmation of their position from the Russian flight controllers on the ground. When Oumansky, who had been a passenger in one of the planes, toasted the American air crews, Stalin walked all the way around the long head table to the center of the room to clink glasses with the two pilots. Harriman noted that whenever Stalin liked the ring of a particular toast—as in the case of the American fliers—he would clap his hands before drinking. There was much clapping before the night was out.*

At the head table, in the pauses between toasts, Stalin talked at

---

* The two B-24s completed pioneering flights on their way home. Major Harvey flew back by way of Iran, India and across the Pacific, touching down in the Philippines, Wake Island and Hawaii. Lieutenant Reichers went via Teheran, Cairo, the West African ferry route to Bathurst and then across the South Atlantic to Natal, in Brazil, before he landed in Florida. The crews of both planes were decorated in April 1942 for their adventurous flights, which inaugurated a new age of long-distance aviation.

length with Beaverbrook and Harriman about the past follies of Great Britain. Neville Chamberlain, he said, had been a disaster for England, and for Russia. It was his impression, Stalin added, that Chamberlain and much of the Conservative party disliked and distrusted the Russians. Stalin defended his 1939 treaty with Hitler as a last resort that was forced upon him by Chamberlain's blundering hostility. He said that when the British had not consulted him at the time of Munich, it seemed clear that Chamberlain was trying to divert Hitler's aggressive ambitions to the east. Then, in the summer of 1939, when it might still have been possible to forestall Hitler—and avoid war—by quickly concluding a tripartite British-Russian-French mutual-defense pact, Chamberlain had blundered again by sending "a clerk" instead of a minister to negotiate with the Russians.* Thus, finding himself rebuffed by the West and fearful of standing alone against the Germans, Stalin explained, he had made his treaty with Hitler. When Hitler invaded Poland a few days later, and Stalin protested, Hitler invited him to move his own forces into eastern Poland.† He justified this action as a military necessity, designed to keep the Wehrmacht at a greater distance from the old Soviet frontier. He admitted, nevertheless, that the German attack had come as a devastating shock which, in spite of the buffer strip he had seized in 1939, had taken an enormous toll in Russian lives.

In response to a question from Harriman about the current military outlook, Stalin predicted that Leningrad would withstand the German attack and that the Crimean front would hold, thanks to the recent reinforcement of fresh troops from Odessa. The graver danger, he said, was in the Ukraine, where Marshal Semyen Budenny's troops were fighting in territory that was not altogether friendly to the Soviet regime. That gross understatement was Stalin's only acknowledgment of the real and widespread disaffection in the Ukraine, where German troops in fact were being welcomed as liberators in many towns and villages until the SS began shooting local leaders suspected of subversive action.

Before the long evening at the Kremlin was over (two motion pictures were shown after dinner), Stalin again taunted Beaverbrook

* The British negotiator was William Strang of the Foreign Office, hardly a clerk even in 1939, but not the major political figure that Stalin had expected. Churchill, in his memoirs, agreed that "the sending of so subordinate a figure gave actual offence." He pointed out that Eden had volunteered to go in place of Strang, but Chamberlain had refused the offer.

† This was Stalin's disingenuous version of what happened. The fate of eastern Poland, the Baltic States and parts of southeastern Europe had already been sealed at the time the nonaggression pact was signed in August 1939. The specifics were set down in a "Secret Additional Protocol," which did not come to light until after the war.

about opening a second front. "What is the good of having an army if it doesn't fight?" he said. "An army which does not fight will lose its spirit." In Britain's own interest, therefore, she ought to launch an immediate offensive against Germany on the Continent or in the Middle East. General Ismay did his best to explain to Stalin that the British army in fact was fighting hard in the Middle East but that an early invasion of France was out of the question. Patiently, Ismay went over the troop figures, and Stalin listened. But he was not persuaded. The British must realize, he said, that they could no longer depend upon their sea power. They would have to build their army and learn to fight on the ground, or they would be defeated.

Harriman felt it was a supremely tactless remark. Until June 22, 1941, Stalin had turned a deaf ear to the bombs bursting over Rotterdam or Coventry or Warsaw, while the British had been fighting since 1939—in France, Norway, Greece, the Middle East, in the desperate and decisive air battles over southern England and at sea in the North Atlantic. Now that Russian blood was being spilled, and his own power threatened, Stalin had discovered that the war Hitler forced on him would take a lot of winning and he wanted all the battlefield help he could get. That evening in the Kremlin seemed the wrong occasion to challenge his argument. Stalin's demand for military action was to be heard again and again in the months ahead.

WHILE IN MOSCOW, Harriman raised an issue with the Russians that was to bedevil Allied relationships for years to come—the issue of Poland. It started with the fact that when the Russians had invaded eastern Poland in 1939 they deported close to two million Polish citizens to the Soviet interior, chiefly to Siberia. Of this number, many officers had been imprisoned, among them General Wladyslaw Anders, who spent twenty months in Lubianka Prison. When Hitler attacked Russia, Moscow decided to establish diplomatic relations with the provisional Polish government headed by General Wladyslaw Sikorski, which had taken refuge in London. General Anders and others were promptly released and saluted by their jailers as new-found allies. Anders, in fact, was appointed commander in chief of the so-called Free Polish Army and set to work recruiting Polish combat divisions on Soviet soil. He urged Stalin to let him arm and train four to six Polish divisions so they could join the common battle against the Germans, but the Russians were showing a certain reluctance.

Harriman had been alerted to the problem by Sikorski in London, and had talked with Anders at the American embassy in Moscow before he raised the matter with Molotov. The Foreign Minister's reply was that the Russians could afford to arm only one Polish division, but that they would be glad to have the United States or Britain provide equipment for as many more divisions as the Poles cared to form. Harriman responded that the British were prepared to take the lead, provided the Polish units were moved to the Caucasus, where they could be supplied from Iran and be available to join the British forces there in resisting a possible German breakthrough to the south.

On October 25, 1941, exactly three weeks after Harriman left Moscow, word was received that the Soviet government would provide no more food for the Poles beyond the 44,000 then enrolled in military units, and that no arms would be supplied beyond the single division already organized. At the suggestion of President Roosevelt, Harriman sent a personal message to Stalin on November 7 renewing his proposal that (since the Russians could provide no more arms or supplies) the Polish troops be transferred to Iran, where they could be clothed and equipped by the British with American help. The new Polish divisions might then be returned to the Soviet Union to fight alongside the Red Army. Stalin evidently preferred not to let the Poles, whom he regarded as troublemakers, return as allies. He eventually allowed some 60,000 of them (with 30,000 women, children and elderly people) to leave for Iran. As Churchill informed Roosevelt on September 14, 1942, the Russians refused to permit any further recruitment on Soviet territory. The two and a half Polish divisions formed in the Middle East fought the rest of the war under British command in Italy and later in France.

ON THE NIGHT OF OCTOBER 2, as Beaverbrook and Harriman were sitting down to dinner together in the Hotel Nationale, where Beaverbrook was staying, air-raid sirens wailed all over Moscow. Both had been through so many raids in London that they were quite ready to stay in the hotel. But the management, on government orders, insisted that they go to the air-raid shelter in a nearby subway station. They were served dinner in high style by waiters from the Nationale in a room off the subway platform that apparently was reserved as an air-raid shelter for very important persons. After dinner, while waiting for the all-clear signal, they played cards. Harriman taught Beaverbrook to play rummy and Beaverbrook had a run of beginner's luck. He returned to the hotel after the raid, boasting that he simply could not lose a hand.

Before leaving Moscow, Beaverbrook had instructed a junior officer of the embassy, John Russell, to buy twenty-five pounds of caviar for him and Harriman. Beaverbrook's idea was to share this bounty with the wardrooms of the cruiser, where the party had been entertained on the outbound voyage, and with several London friends,

Churchill included. Unfortunately, Russell mentioned the caviar purchase to Philip Jordan, Moscow correspondent of the London *News Chronicle*, who promptly reported that the Prime Minister was about to receive a gift of twenty-five pounds of caviar. Other newspapers picked up the story and Churchill dashed off a blistering telegram to Beaverbrook. The very idea that large quantities of caviar were being imported for the Prime Minister's personal use in wartime had greatly embarrassed him. Beaverbrook, who was furious over Russell's indiscretion, gave him a tongue-lashing to remember. (Happily, the young diplomat's career suffered no lasting damage. In later years he served as ambassador to Ethiopia and Brazil and in several other important posts.)

The religious question, which Harriman had raised with Stalin on September 28, was regarded by Roosevelt as a matter of the highest domestic priority. The President, in fact, had chosen to declare at his Washington press conference on October 1 that freedom of worship was assured under Section 124 of the Soviet Constitution. In making known this hopeful interpretation, the President was clearly trying to disarm opponents of aid to Russia while at the same time nudging Stalin to confirm his statement.

Section 124 also guaranteed "freedom of antireligious propaganda," a point that Roosevelt in his concern with Roman Catholic sentiment at home saw no benefit in stressing. Having made no progress with Stalin, Harriman impressed upon Molotov, Oumansky and lesser Soviet officials the need, as Roosevelt saw it, of appeasing American opinion by some public gesture that would affirm freedom of worship. He received the most profuse assurances from Oumansky and an enigmatic nod from Molotov. On October 4, after the Harriman and Beaverbrook delegations had left Moscow, the Soviet government called a press conference to confirm Roosevelt's interpretation of Section 124. Commissar Solomon A. Lozovsky told foreign correspondents that the Soviet state did not meddle with religion. It was a private matter, he insisted, except that under the Soviet Constitution "freedom for any religion presupposes that the religion, church or community will not be used for the overthrow of the existing authority which is recognized in the country."

Harriman left Moscow expecting nothing more than lip service to the principle of freedom of worship. In a memorandum written on his return, he accurately predicted that "religious worship will be tolerated only under closest G.P.U. scrutiny with a view to keeping it under careful control like a fire which can be stamped out at any time, rather than allowed to burn freely with the dangers of uncontrolled conflagration." Harriman had talked at length with Father Leopold Braun, an American priest who was conducting services in the Catho-

lic chapel of the French embassy. Father Braun cited some easing of
the official Soviet attitude toward his congregation, estimated at 20,000.
He was the only priest authorized to conduct Roman Catholic services
in Moscow, and these, he said, were not being interfered with. Father
Braun attributed this improvement chiefly to Roosevelt's influence.
But his testimony about several cases of official harassment against his
communicants by the secret police tended to confirm Harriman's pessimistic outlook. Roosevelt, who had hoped for more solid assurances
than Harriman was able to bring back from Russia, was not satisfied.
"He made me feel that it was not enough and took me to task on my
return," Harriman recalled.

The homeward journey was disagreeable all the way. The Russian
DC-3 carrying the delegation chiefs from Moscow to Archangel
"bobbed like a cork in a storm," to the intense discomfort of the passengers. The same river boats which had brought the two parties up-
stream now carried them back the twenty-mile distance. Owing to
delays en route, the *London* had been forced by the tide to move out
past the bar at the entrance to the harbor. Thus the transfer had to be
carried out in two stages—from the Soviet river boat *Pearl of the
North* to the British minesweeper *Harrier*, and then, in extremely
rough water after dark, from the *Harrier* to the *London*, by a gang-
way that was "only intermittently in contact" with the deck, according to the diary of Harriman's faithful amanuensis, Bob Meiklejohn.
Harriman and the others managed to jump aboard the *London* as she
and the *Harrier* heaved up and down, seldom in phase. But Beaverbrook had to be tied and hauled across the angry water. "While Mr.
Harriman gave me his fur gloves, scarves and galoshes to protect me
from the Russian winter," Thayer recalled, "Beaverbrook, who had
lost one of his gloves, peeled poor Russell of all the fur clothing he
had. Only Mr. Harriman remained on the deck of the London to wave
goodbye to those of us who remained behind."[14]

On the way back to Scapa Flow, Harriman spent five days in bed
with acute sinusitis. The Prime Minister's doctor, Sir Charles Wilson
(later Lord Moran), came to see him each day, but being profoundly
skeptical of drugs, he administered chiefly advice. On the third day
out, burning with fever, the patient rudely asked to see the ship's doctor, who prescribed a dose of sulfanilamide.

Harriman was sufficiently recovered toward the end of the journey to ask General Ismay about the strategic outlook on the Russian
front. The general replied that in his opinion Moscow would hold
against the Germans for perhaps three weeks longer. Harriman noted:

> If there is one thing about the British staff, [it is that]
> they have been consistent since the first gun was fired—'three

weeks to Moscow.' It is still, three and a half months later, 'three weeks to Moscow.'[15]

Upon their return to England, Harriman and Beaverbrook went directly to Chequers to review with Churchill and Eden their impressions of Russia at war, based on their talks with Stalin. "As soon as we sat down to dinner," Harriman recalled, "Beaverbrook began to berate the Prime Minister. It was intolerable, he said, for Churchill to accuse him of embarrassing the government by importing illicit caviar from Russia. Churchill protested that he had made no such accusation. By way of changing the subject, I accused Eden of trying to run the American delegation when he and Cripps had objected to my bringing Quentin Reynolds to Moscow as my press officer. Eden attempted to shift the responsibility to Cripps.

"Beaverbrook, as always, enjoyed this kind of contretemps, and the argument raged through much of the dinner. Our telegrams, in fact, had been so detailed that there was little need to go over the ground again. The dinner, in any event, broke up in a good mood. Churchill told us that we had done an effective job and seemed greatly reassured by our reports of Stalin's determination to fight on. Churchill was not, however, so totally absorbed in affairs of state that he had forgotten the argument. Turning to Beaverbrook as we left the dining room, he said, 'Now, after all this talk, where is that caviar?' "

CHAPTER V

Pearl Harbor: "At Least There Is a Future Now"

Less than a week after Harriman and Beaverbrook had sailed for England, carrying Stalin's personal assurances that he would fight to the last to prevent the fall of Moscow, a creeping panic gripped the city. Hitler had launched a powerful new offensive, touted in his order of the day issued October 2 as "the last great decisive battle of this year."

The people of Moscow did not hear about the German offensive until October 8—and then only by careful indirection. The Soviet communiqué issued that day spoke of hard battles in progress near Vyazma, less than 150 miles from Moscow on the road to Smolensk. The news was shattering, in view of the fact that the Germans had last been reported in the vicinity of Smolensk, some 240 miles due west. The Wehrmacht, in short, had advanced some 90 miles closer to Moscow. On the following day, October 9, Hitler's press chief, Otto Dietrich, announced that "for all military purposes the Soviet Union is done for." The Germans were moving rapidly to envelop the Soviet capital. Orel, a city 220 miles to the south, and Kalinin, 100 miles to the northwest, also fell to the enemy, further confirmation for the drab crowds in Gorki Street that the new offensive was still unchecked and that Moscow itself might soon be under fire.

On October 15 Ambassador Steinhardt summoned the entire American embassy staff to Spaso House for a grim discussion of plans to evacuate the capital. Charles Thayer later described the scene for Harriman:

Probably for the first and only time in Russian history, no policemen were on the streets of Moscow; they had all been sent to the front where, it was believed, they constituted the only Russian defense forces. We had already commandeered food from Russian trucks, in preparing to evacuate. Hysteria reigned at Spaso . . .

[Major Ivan D.] Yeaton [the military attaché], who had always been the most drastic and fatalistic about impending doom, gave the Russians 36 hours more; [Colonel] Faymonville now had completely lost his nerve and gave them only five more hours before the Germans would arrive. While the debate was going on, a messenger arrived from Molotov, asking Steinhardt to come to him at the Kremlin within 20 minutes. He returned with orders for our evacuation to Kuibyshev.[1]

Steinhardt and Cripps had been called to the Kremlin together. Molotov told them they were to leave Moscow with the rest of the diplomatic corps by special train about eight or nine o'clock in the evening. Both ambassadors asked permission to stay behind in Moscow as long as Molotov and Stalin stayed. Molotov, however, was firm. They must leave the same evening, he said. He and Stalin would join them in Kuibyshev after a day or two. His manner calm and unruffled, as in the quieter past, Molotov assured them: "The fight for Moscow will continue and the fight to defeat Hitler will become more furious."

The special train Molotov had ordered made a nightmarish trip to Kuibyshev. There was no dining car and no drinking water, and it took five days and four nights to travel less than six hundred miles. The unhappy diplomats—tired, hungry and travel-stained—discovered upon reaching Kuibyshev that Stalin had never left Moscow. Molotov, however, kept his word. He explained to Steinhardt that the sudden decision to evacuate Moscow had been made after the Germans had broken through the Soviet defense line at Mozhaisk, some seventy miles to the west, on October 14. It then appeared to the Soviet leadership, he said, that the Nazi advance might not be checked.[2] Although the crisis passed with the coming of winter, most of the diplomatic corps was stranded in a dull provincial city on the Volga for many months to come.

Back in London, Churchill watched the Russian front closely. He was "satisfied the Russians would continue to fight no matter where the front might be," the Prime Minister said to Harriman on October 15, although he had not put out of his mind the thought that Hitler still might attempt an invasion of the British Isles. Harriman, who was about to leave for Washington, asked Churchill how he saw the war developing. "Well," the Prime Minister replied, "Hitler's revised plan undoubtedly is now—Poland, '39; France, '40; Russia, '41; England, '42, and, '43, maybe America."[3]

Harriman and the members of his Moscow mission flew home on October 16, set up offices in the State Department and went to work on their report to President Roosevelt. They submitted their detailed recommendations to the President on October 29 and saw him again the following day. Roosevelt promptly cabled Stalin that he had approved all the items specified in the Moscow Protocol and that shipments up to the value of $1 billion would be financed under the Lend-Lease Act, with no interest charged. The Soviets were to have ten years for repayment, beginning five years after the end of the war. Stalin's reply, dated November 4, was uncommonly gracious. "Your decision . . . ," Stalin wrote, "is accepted with sincere gratitude by the Soviet Government as unusually substantial aid in its difficult and great struggle against our common enemy, bloodthirsty Hitlerism." He also accepted Harriman's suggestion, which Roosevelt had renewed in his message of October 30, that the two should "establish direct personal contact whenever circumstances warrant."

American opinion, by and large, appeared to understand and approve aid to Russia. Harriman tried to help with a broadcast on the CBS radio network and with a public speech, confessing that he had gone to Moscow uneasy in his own mind about the wisdom of diverting large quantities of arms and materials to the Soviet Union. Many military experts, he recalled, were then predicting that Russia would collapse under Hitler's hammer blows, and besides, many Americans disliked the Soviet system. He had returned from Russia, Harriman said, fully persuaded that the Soviet Union would not collapse, that its fighting men and mechanics knew how to use the equipment they were getting from America, and that American self-interest demanded all-out aid to keep the Russians fighting. He went on:

> "Under these circumstances I am not concerned with the social or economic beliefs of those who are fighting Hitler. What does concern me is that the bitter experience of others and our own enlightened self-interest clearly dictate a course of action for us: that is to deliver every plane, every tank, every pound of material that we can possibly put into the hands of those who are fighting Nazism on their own soil, with their own men.
>
> "To put it bluntly, whatever it costs to keep this war away from our shores, that will be a small price to pay."

The time of ostensible neutrality in Washington was fast running out, in any event. Even as the President on October 9 requested from

Congress several amendments to the Neutrality Act which would permit American merchant ships to be armed and sent into the war zones, the Germans drew first blood in the Battle of the Atlantic. The U.S. destroyer *Kearney* was hit by a torpedo 350 miles southwest of Iceland. Although she managed to limp into Rejkjavik, eleven of her crew were killed. On October 30 a second destroyer, the *Reuben James*, was torpedoed and sunk with the loss of 115 men, including all the officers. Yet the isolationists remained strong. Hitler showed no inclination to declare war on the United States. And the broad American public refused to get any more excited about the sinking of a destroyer or two than it had over the loss of the *Lusitania* in 1915. When the Senate on November 7 approved the amendments to the Neutrality Act, the vote was 50 to 37. A week later the House adopted the amendments by an even closer vote of 212 to 194.

On October 20 Harriman had sent Churchill, through the British embassy, a "personal and secret" message on the puzzling state of American public opinion. It read, in part:

> The interventionists have increased in number and are more confident and aggressive. Many of the less violent isolationists have become reconciled to the inevitability of war. Some of the more violent isolationists like Lindbergh have been discredited in the public eye. Others are running to cover.
>
> And yet, with all this trend, it is not at all clear what or when something will happen to kick us into it.
>
> The news on Saturday of the torpedoing of the *Kearney* did not cause even a ripple. It seemed that the public had expected—and were thoroughly prepared for—such occurrences . . . As to opinion regarding Britain, people are wondering why you don't do something offensively. In my opinion it is important that more should be said about what you are doing—Constant pressure of the R.A.F. with attendant diversion of the Luftwaffe; your fighter squadrons in Russia; also constant comment on supplies to Russia . . .
>
> Shipments to Russia are moving fast. Production plans are on the increase. In all, my first impressions of the situation are bullish.

On his return to London on November 18, Harriman found Churchill and Eden preoccupied with a new problem—Stalin's pressure for a political agreement that would give Britain's blessing to the territorial changes he had engineered before the German invasion. Stalin was seeking the recognition of his new allies for Soviet claims to all the territories he had added to his domain during the brief term of his nonaggression pact with Hitler: the Baltic States, eastern Poland, a strip of Finnish territory, and (from Rumania) the regions of Bessarabia and Bukovina. He also had made clear to Harriman and Beaverbrook in Moscow, citing Finland as an example, that he wanted Russia's enemies to be treated as Britain's enemies. Churchill hesitated over Stalin's demands that Britain should declare war on Finland, Rumania and Hungary, although all three had joined in the German attack on Russia. The Prime Minister argued that it might be the wiser course to leave open any opportunity that might develop later to detach them from Germany. But Stalin insisted. There could be no mutual trust in the British-Soviet relationship, he said, without an explicit agreement on war aims and on plans for the postwar period. For this reason, Churchill decided to send Foreign Secretary Anthony Eden to Moscow in December, his primary assignment being to discuss war aims and the tentative shape of the peace settlement with Stalin.

On December 4 Secretary of State Cordell Hull learned for the first time that Eden was leaving for Moscow in three days. Ambassador Winant reported that Eden hoped to eradicate from Stalin's mind "certain suspicions" of British intent and to give him "as much satisfaction as possible, without entering into commitments." Hull was informed that Eden also had in mind persuading Stalin to reaffirm both his acceptance of the Atlantic Charter and a promise he had made in a speech on November 6 that the Soviet Union would not interfere in the internal affairs of other nations. The old Wilsonian's visceral abhorrence of secret territorial arrangements, secretly arrived at, while the war was far from being won and the United States was still technically at peace, shone through Hull's agitated response the next day. Instructing Winant to read the message to Eden, but not to leave a copy with him, Hull decried "any willingness to enter into commitments regarding specific terms of the postwar settlements" on the part of the British or Soviet governments. "Above all," he wrote, "there must be no secret accords."[4]

Harriman's personal view was opposed to Hull's. Nothing would be gained—and much might be lost, he felt—by refusing to negotiate Stalin's territorial demands until after the war was won. The border lands he claimed for Russia could easily be overrun once the tide of fighting had turned in favor of the Red Army, and it might well be too late then for negotiated settlements. But Hull was adamant. He wanted no more talk about concessions to Russia at a moment when the United States was risking war with Japan by its refusal to concede similar territorial claims presented by two special envoys from Tokyo, Kichisaburo Nomura and Saburo Kurusu, who were then in Washington. Already Hull had warned the Japanese that their persistence in a policy of "force and conquest" in the Far East could lead to a devastating war, a war that Japan was bound to lose (as Roosevelt had stressed to Nomura and Kurusu).

On Saturday, December 6, as Eden left London for Invergordon, Scotland, on the first leg of his sea voyage to Russia, Harriman cabled Hopkins in Washington:

> The President should be informed of Churchill's belief that in the event of aggression by the Japanese it would be the policy of the British to postpone taking any action—even though this delay might involve some military sacrifice—until the President has taken such action as, under the circumstances, he considers best. Then Churchill will act "not within the hour but within the minute." I am seeing him again tomorrow. Let me know if there is anything special you want me to ask.

As Kathleen Harriman's birthday fell on the weekend, she was asked to Chequers along with her father and Ambassador Winant. Her actual birthday was Sunday, but it was mistakenly celebrated Saturday evening at dinner. When the birthday cake was carried in, the Prime Minister offered an appropriate toast and gave Kathleen an autographed copy of his book *The River War*.

Mrs. Churchill was not feeling well the next evening, Sunday, December 7. As she did not come downstairs for dinner, Kathleen and Pamela Churchill were the only women present. General Ismay was there; also the Prime Minister's naval aide, Commander Thompson; his principal private secretary, John Martin; Winant and Harriman.

"The Prime Minister seemed tired and depressed," Harriman recalled. "He didn't have much to say throughout dinner and was immersed in his thoughts, with his head in his hands part of the time."

Near nine o'clock, Churchill's butler-valet, Sawyers, carried in a little flip-top radio that Harry Hopkins had given the Prime Minister for the nightly ritual of listening to the BBC news. The Prime Minister must have been a bit slow in opening the radio because the first headline item heard by his guests was about a tank battle in Libya, south of Tobruk. The British forces, Harriman recalled, were not doing too well.

After reading the headlines, the announcer turned to a more detailed summary of the day's happenings:

> "The news has just been given that Japanese aircraft have raided Pearl Harbor, the American naval base in Hawaii. The announcement of the attack was made in a brief statement by President Roosevelt. Naval and military targets on the

principal Hawaiian island of Oahu have also been attacked. No further details are yet available."*

"I was thoroughly startled," Harriman recalled, "and I repeated the words 'The Japanese have raided Pearl Harbor.' Tommy Thompson heard it differently. 'No, no,' he interrupted. 'He said Pearl River.' While Tommy and I argued the point, the announcer went on to other news about Hong Kong and Japanese troop concentrations in Indochina.

"The Prime Minister, recovering from his lethargy, slammed the top of the radio down and got up from his chair. At that moment Martin appeared at the door and said excitedly that the Admiralty was on the phone for the Prime Minister. Winant and I followed him out to his office. The Admiralty, of course, confirmed the news."

Churchill immediately put in a call to Roosevelt. When the President came on the line, Churchill said, "Mr. President, what's this about Japan?" Roosevelt replied, "It's quite true. They have attacked us at Pearl Harbor. We are all in the same boat now."[5] Roosevelt said that he would go to Congress for a declaration of war the next morning and Churchill responded that he would follow suit immediately in the House of Commons. The Prime Minister then handed the phone to Winant, who asked Roosevelt whether the Japanese planes had sunk any American warships. The President confirmed that ships had indeed been sunk, although he had as yet no precise count. Churchill, in his memoirs, later recorded: "My two American friends took the shock with admirable fortitude." For Harriman the plain fact that America, too, was now at war came as a great relief. "The inevitable had finally arrived," Harriman recalled. "We all knew the grim future that it held, but at least there was a future now. We both had realized that the British could not win the war alone. On the Russian front there was still a question whether the Red Army would hold out. At last we could see a prospect of winning."

Churchill's first impulse, after declaring war on Japan on December 8, was to meet again with Roosevelt. He sent the President a telegram the same day: "Now that we are, as you say, 'in the same boat,' would it not be wise for us to have another conference? We could review the whole war plan in the light of reality and new facts, as well as the problems of production and distribution. I feel that all these matters, some of which are causing me concern, can best be settled on the highest executive level."[6]

* A copy of the script read at nine o'clock that evening by Alvar Liddell, supplied to Harriman by the BBC, shows the hurried changes made at the last moment to accommodate the shocking news from Hawaii.

With Eden at that moment on his way to Russia, the Prime Minister saw an opportunity to bring Stalin and Roosevelt together into a three-way discussion of the fresh dangers and opportunities presented by the new, wider war in which the United States was now a full-fledged ally against Germany as well as Japan. On December 11, Hitler had declared war on the United States. Roosevelt promptly invited Churchill to Washington.

Two days before he sailed for the United States, however, the Prime Minister had the painful duty of informing the House of Commons that Japanese torpedo bombers, based in Saigon, had sunk the *Prince of Wales* and the *Repulse* in Malayan waters. The Royal Navy was left without a single capital ship in the Indian Ocean or the Pacific, and the Pacific Fleet of the United States had just been crippled at Pearl Harbor. Thus Japan in two strokes had achieved mastery of the vast ocean.

Churchill also had reason to worry that Lend-Lease supplies for Britain were bound to be sharply reduced by America's entry into the war, all the more so if the United States were to decide that Japan was now the main enemy—and shift the weight of its war effort to the Pacific. These matters were also on Harriman's mind when he accompanied Churchill to Washington. They sailed from Greenock, Scotland (with Beaverbrook, General Dill, Admiral Pound and Air Chief Marshal Portal) in the Royal Navy's newest battleship, *Duke of York*, for the Washington Conference known by its code name as Arcadia. It was a rough crossing, so rough that for the first three days the deck was off limits and the Prime Minister kept dosing himself with Mothersill's seasickness pills, over the protestations of his doctor, Sir Charles Wilson. Once he had recovered his sea legs, however, Churchill talked incessantly at mealtimes, even during movie showings in the evenings. Harriman recalled how greatly the Prime Minister enjoyed *The Sea Hawk*, a film in which Queen Elizabeth was shown refusing to provide ships for England's defense against the Spanish Armada. He found in the film a moral lesson for his own time. "You see," Churchill said to Harriman, "the British have always been the biggest damn fools in the world. They are too easygoing and niggardly to prepare [for war]. Then at the last minute they hurry around and scrape together and fight like hell. Good luck has pulled them through. If the good Lord once forgets them, they will be finished."[7]

Another evening, in the middle of a film, the Prime Minister leaned over and said to Harriman, "It is a sad business, the *Prince of Wales* and the *Repulse*. They could have harassed the enemy, always a threat, playing the second role to your big fleet. We made great sacrifices to send them [to the Far East]. They came in time. It is a cruel thing. Perhaps it was bad judgment. But I will never criticize a man who aims his arrow at the enemy. I will defend him."*

At times Churchill talked of strategic matters: "It is in the hands of the United States to make this a long or short war. If you defend each town on the Pacific with fighter aircraft it will be a long war—five years. If you will be courageous—let the raiders come; what does it matter?—then it can be finished in two years." He also talked with Harriman about the life he had led as a writer:

CHURCHILL: Worldly goods have never come my way. The most satisfactory thing would have been to have a series of windfalls come one's way, at proper intervals, when one had accumulated some debts or desires; not too much at a time, of course, just enough to set things right.
HARRIMAN: But then you would never have written your books.
CHURCHILL (*paraphrasing Samuel Johnson*): Only a fool writes for anything except money. I have done very well with my writing—250 to 300 pounds for two hours' work. Not bad, is it?
HARRIMAN: That's very good.
CHURCHILL: I have lived by the ink of my pen . . . (*Then, upon reconsidering the phrase*) . . . by the sweat of my pen.

The Prime Minister insisted upon telling stories about seasickness in nauseating detail to his mostly seasick companions, notably Sir John Dill, who turned green and left the table while Churchill chatted gaily about certain special-purpose buckets he had seen on the bridge of a destroyer. He particularly enjoyed telling the story of the passenger on an ocean liner who rushed up the companionway, heading for the nearest rail. The steward protested, "But, sir, you can't be sick here." To which the unfortunate passenger replied, "Oh, can't I?"

Harriman's personal notes of matters to be taken up in Washington with Roosevelt, Hopkins and others, dictated on shipboard, show the sweep of his own concerns after nine months in England.

1. IRELAND

    a. Obtain cooperation from Eire (Southern Ireland) for use of bases and airfields.
    b. Send 3 divisions to Ulster (Northern Ireland) to replace 3 British divisions.
    c. Send additional troops to defend Eire if necessary to get cooperation on (a)

* The officer Churchill defended was Vice Admiral Sir Tom Phillips, Commander of the Far East British Fleet, who lost his life on December 9 when torpedo-carrying Japanese planes intercepted the *Prince of Wales* and the *Repulse* after a gallant but vain attempt to interfere with the Japanese landings in Malaya.

d. Also air defense fighter protection in relation to the above.

Note: P.M. won't let Ulster down. Persuasion not force. "No good making enemies of friends in order to try to make friends of enemies."

2. BRITAIN

a. Supply tanks and machine guns, rifles, etc., anti-aircraft guns to defend airdromes, etc., in relation to strengthening defense of beaches, airdromes and otherwise defense of Britain against invasion.
b. A few squadrons of air to bomb Germany (particularly 4-engine), possibly to strengthen coastal patrol in connection with convoys.
c. Take over balance of job in Iceland freeing British troops, etc.

3. AFRICA AND MIDDLE EAST

a. Continue flow of aircraft and tanks to strengthen Middle East & Iran supply, and to India to develop Indian mechanized divisions.
b. Ferry bombers. Develop and run maintenance units for U.S. equipment.
c. Undertake strong Vichy policy with view obtaining cooperation for U.S. and British forces in North Africa.
d. Send expeditionary force to French North Africa in collaboration with British.

4. PORTUGUESE AND SPANISH ISLANDS (Azores)

a. Develop strong policy with view to take over in near future.

5. FAR EAST

a. Reinforce Singapore with air and 1 division.
b. Merge two fleets in Pacific for joint action to regain command of Pacific Ocean.
c. Strengthen Dutch air force Australia (?)
d. Strengthen China and Burma by supplies and air force.
e. Induce Russia to enter war vs Japan view to sap Jap strength but principally to bomb Japan.
f. Send bomb air force to Siberia to bomb Japan.

6. SHIPPING

Action which would reduce volume of imports (example: the more concentrated foods Britain gets, the less wheat is consumed. Concentrated foods are of less volume and tonnage).

Reduce wasteful forms—less canned fruits and more dried. Improve packing to reduce space and weight.

Reduce sharply U.S.A. civilian use to conform if need be to U.K. practices.

Coordination of buying of raw materials—chrome, manganese, nitrates, tungsten, tin, Argentine beef, etc., etc.

Increase shipbuilding, particularly of the most needed types, coordinating U.S.A. & U.K. programs.

Set up a permanent joint conference board which should have the right to obtain information as to programs and practices of each country including military. Duties would be to recommend action to Departments concerned to eliminate waste, to direct best joint use of available tonnage. If recommendations are not accepted to report to President & P.M.

SHIPPING

Shipping of all types is now and will probably continue to be the overall bottleneck—both cargo ships and transports. Therefore: ways and means of economizing on shipping should be given first consideration by:

a. Eliminating wasteful movements—
   Examples: steel from U.K. to Dominions, Colonies or fighting areas. It should *all* be shipped direct from U.S.A., thus reducing necessity of U.S.A. to U.K. imports.
   Plans should be made and carried out by which, as far as practicable, British forces in Middle East, etc., should be supplied from U.S.A. and Dominions, etc.

b. Joint reserve stocks including raw and finished supplies should be built up in U.S.A., Canada or elsewhere from which each country should draw in accordance with priority needs. Stocks should be stored with a view to economy in shipping.

c. Imports into both countries should be reviewed, having in mind cooperation.

Churchill arrived in Washington on December 22, flying up from Hampton Roads, Virginia, where he had left the *Duke of York*. He put up at the White House in a large bedroom across the hall from Hopkins' room, while Harriman went to the Mayflower Hotel. On Christmas Day, the President and the Prime Minister attended interdenominational services together at the Foundry Methodist Church. The day after Christmas (Boxing Day in England), the Prime Minister addressed a joint session of the House and Senate, remarking to the delight of his fellow legislators, "I cannot help reflecting that if my father had been American and my mother British, instead of the other way around, I might have got here on my own."

Hong Kong, the British Crown colony, had just capitulated to the Japanese, but Churchill took comfort from the Arcadia talks. At the first of twelve meetings between the American and British Chiefs of Staff, which took place in the Federal Reserve Building on Constitution Avenue on December 22, his fear that America might shift to an Asia-first strategy had quickly been dispelled. General George C. Marshall and Admiral Harold R. Stark for the United States presented a heartening two-paragraph summation of the basis for overall British-American strategy:

> 1. At the A-B [American-British] staff conversations in February, 1941, it was agreed that Germany was the predominant member of the Axis powers, and consequently the Atlantic and European theater was considered to be the decisive theater.
>
> 2. Much has happened since February last, but notwithstanding the entry of Japan into the war, our view remains that Germany is still the key to victory. Once Germany is defeated, the collapse of Italy and the defeat of Japan must follow.

That policy was to stand until the German surrender, in spite of objections from the Navy and other Pacific-first advocates.

The next major piece of Arcadia business was the formal establishment of a grand coalition of all the nations at war with Germany and Japan. The initial draft had been prepared by Roosevelt. He called it a Declaration of the Associated Powers. Roosevelt later struck out the words "Associated Powers" and wrote in "United Nations," a term he had just invented. There were a great many arguments over drafting details. The Soviet Union, for example, at first objected to any mention of "religious freedom" in the preamble but conceded the point at Roosevelt's insistence. Litvinov, the newly installed Soviet ambassador in Washington, persuaded Roosevelt and Churchill that his government, being at peace with Japan, could not sign a document

pledging itself to the defeat of "members or adherents of the Tripartite
Pact." The matter was adroitly resolved by making the text read
"those members of the tripartite pact . . . with which such government is at war." The War Cabinet in London cabled Churchill, insisting that the British Dominions must be listed in a group, immediately
behind Great Britain in the list of signatories. The British ambassador,
Lord Halifax, a former Viceroy of India, objected that it would be a
mistake to exclude that country, which had yet to be granted Dominion status. The War Cabinet yielded, and India was listed among the
signatories, along with Canada, Australia, New Zealand and the rest.
The final declaration was issued and signed on New Year's Day, 1942,
by the representatives of twenty-six countries, not including Free
France. "The declaration could not by itself win battles," Churchill
admitted, "but it set forth who we were and what we were fighting
for." The operative provisions read:

> 1. Each government pledges itself to employ its full resources,
> military or economic, against those members of the Tripartite
> Pact and its adherents with which such government is at war.

> 2. Each government pledges itself to cooperate with the gov-
> ernments signatory hereto, and not to make a seperate ar-
> mistice or peace with the enemies.

Not even the military decisions made at Arcadia could, by themselves, win battles for the Allies, but one important principle which
Harriman had been pressing since his survey trip to the Middle East
was established during the Washington talks—the principle of unified
command. General Marshall proposed the appointment of a single
commander for the new theater of war, to be known as ABDA
(American, British, Dutch, Australian), who would be responsible for
the vast, doomed area from the Bay of Bengal to Australasia. Marshall
pointed out that the Allied powers in World War I had waited until
1918, with the needless sacrifice of much "time, blood and treasure,"
before making the sensible decision to appoint Marshal Foch commander in chief of Allied forces in France. "I am convinced," Marshall said, "that there must be one man in command of the entire
theater—air, ground, and ships. We cannot manage by cooperation.
Human frailties are such that there would be emphatic unwillingness
to place portions of troops under another service. If we make a plan
for unified command now, it will solve nine-tenths of our troubles."[8]
The British needed a lot of persuading, the more so after Roosevelt
proposed that General Wavell, who was now in India, should become
the supreme commander of the ABDA theater. They preferred to see

an American officer saddled with the dreadful responsibility of defending a region in which the Japanese had shown themselves to be such formidable adversaries. But after a private meeting with General Marshall, Churchill agreed. The unfortunate Wavell never had a serious opportunity to pull his command together (the swift Japanese advances rapidly nullified his plans). But the principle of unified command had been established and was not again seriously challenged; it was to make possible the eventual appointment of General Dwight D. Eisenhower as supreme commander in Europe. Another Arcadia decision, of more immediate consequence, was the creation in Washington of a British-American Combined Chiefs of Staff Committee to direct Allied strategy under supervision of the President and the Prime Minister. Both Churchill and General Marshall considered this decision the most valuable and lasting result of the Arcadia conference.

The brunt of the Allied military effort in 1942 was to be directed at wearing down Germany's resistance by a greatly accelerated bombing offensive, naval blockade and continued generous assistance to the Russian armies. "It does not seem likely that in 1942 any large-scale land offensive against Germany, except on the Russian front, will be possible," the Chiefs of Staff agreed. "We must, however, be ready to take advantage of any opening that may result from the wearing-down process . . . In 1943 the way may be clear for a return to the Continent, across the Mediterranean, from Turkey into the Balkans, or by landings in Western Europe."

Even before the Arcadia meetings ended, Roosevelt had dispatched the first contingent of American GIs to Northern Ireland, permitting the British to withdraw their forces for service elsewhere. This operation, code-named Magnet, made sense to Stimson and Marshall, who were inclined to begin building up American troop strength in Europe preliminary to the full-scale invasion of the Continent they both favored. For psychological reasons, the arrival of the first GIs in Ulster was widely advertised through the press. The news served a dual purpose—to impress the Germans with America's resolve to fight in Europe and to reassure the British that they did not stand alone. The Arcadia planners also slated a landing in North Africa for as early as March 1942, provided the French authorities in Algeria and Morocco invited the operation or it became necessary to checkmate a German thrust into Spain. This operation, known first as Gymnast, then as Super-Gymnast, came finally to be known as Torch.

Harriman was not directly involved in the military deliberations. At Hopkins' suggestion he and Beaverbrook, who had presided together over the development of the Victory Program in London, were busy expanding the concept to fix new and seemingly astronomical production goals. The original Victory Program had been adopted,

though never made public, beforce America herself was plunged into
the conflict. Now these goals for victory in Europe had to be raised
to fight a war in the far Pacific at the same time. Beaverbrook and his
team of statisticians brought over from London played a vital role in
applying the lessons Britain had already learned, to speed the conversion of American industry. "We had all agreed," Harriman recalled,
"that it had taken the British too many years to get full war production, and Hopkins had the idea, I think with Roosevelt's full approval,
that this time could be shortened if we set our sights high at once.
Beaverbrook and his very able statisticians worked in the Mayflower
Hotel. I worked with them and out came the figures which were eventually accepted." Rounded off in a few cases by Roosevelt, the figures
speak for themselves:

ORIGINAL VICTORY PROGRAM ESTIMATES FOR 1942

Operational aircraft	28,600
Tanks	20,400
Anti-aircraft guns	6,300
Merchant ships (deadweight tons)	6,000,000
Anti-tank guns	7,000
Ground and tank machine guns	168,000
Airplane bombs (long tons)	84,000

NEW GOALS FIXED AFTER PEARL HARBOR

	For 1942	For 1943
Operational Aircraft	45,000	100,000
Tanks	45,000	75,000
Anti-aircraft guns	20,000	35,000
Merchant ships (deadweight tons)	8,000,000	10,000,000
Anti-tank guns	14,900	(expansion not fixed)
Ground and tank machine guns	500,000	(expansion not fixed)
Airplane bombs (long tons)	720,000	(expansion not fixed)

When announced by Roosevelt, the new production goals produced real consternation. No plan of comparable scale had been
dreamed of by Harriman's friends among the defense planners. It
seemed to many of them a blueprint too bold to be realized. Some
denounced the President's "numbers racket" so violently that Harriman could not bring himself to confess even to his old friend and
banking partner, Robert Lovett, that he had something to do with
setting the targets. The plain fact was that the goals of the Victory
Program, though causing at first some confusion and waste, were
achieved or surpassed, fulfilling Roosevelt's early prophecy that Amer-

ica would make herself "the arsenal of democracy." The task was so immense that civilian production had to be put aside in many industries until the war was over. The great automobile companies, for example, gave up building passenger cars until after the war, turning their assembly lines to the production of tanks, trucks, jeeps, bomber planes in spectacular numbers. Harriman himself never doubted that "Roosevelt's action forced the United States to more complete mobilization, more rapidly, than if we had allowed the production people to set their own goals."

CHURCHILL LEFT WASHINGTON on January 14 and flew from Norfolk to Bermuda, where his warship and its destroyer escorts were waiting. But on an impulse he decided to fly home the rest of the way. It was, for the time, a long and hazardous nonstop flight, but the news from Malaya (where the Japanese were threatening Singapore) was so dismaying that he was able to justify the risk to his aides and advisers. Harriman stayed behind for two weeks to recruit additional staff for his London mission and to follow up on several matters for which there had been no time at the Arcadia conference, such as British military requirements and the shipping bottleneck. He found that one effect of Pearl Harbor had been to reduce the number of ships carrying war supplies to Russia. Although 25 ships had sailed for Russia in December, the numbers had fallen off to 24 in January and (as he later learned) 19 in February. Harriman lobbied with every federal official concerned for a maximum effort to fulfill the commitments he had made to Stalin. On January 29, with Roosevelt's approval, he cabled Stalin:

> While in America during the last few weeks I have reviewed the program for the supply . . . of the Moscow protocol items. I am satisfied that the material will be made available substantially as promised . . .
>
> In spite of the disappointing results during the past four months I find all concerned endeavoring to ship what has been promised and to increase the quantities as soon as practicable.
>
> I find at the present time in the United States an everincreasing sympathy for and understanding of the people of the Soviet Union . . .

Eden's discussions in Moscow, concurrent with the Washington Conference, soon confirmed Cordell Hull's suspicion that Stalin wanted to redraw the map of Eastern Europe by secret covenant. In his very first talk with Eden, on December 16, Stalin had laid down his postwar demands: recognition of the Soviet frontiers as they had existed just before the German attack in June of 1941. This meant that the Baltic States, a strip of Finland and the Rumanian province of Bessarabia were to belong to the Soviet Union. The boundary with Poland was to be based on the so-called Curzon Line, drawn after the Paris Conference in 1919 as a temporary demarcation, which would award to Russia virtually all the territory of eastern Poland she had grabbed in September 1939. In addition, Stalin wanted Soviet air bases in Rumania and—as Molotov had intimated to Eden—air and naval bases in Finland as well. Molotov also mentioned pushing the Soviet frontier on the Baltic Sea all the way into East Prussia. Stalin pressed Eden to sign a secret protocol approving all these changes. He offered in return an oddly misconceived promise of Soviet support for the acquisition of British bases in France, Belgium, the Netherlands, Norway or Denmark. Churchill, in a message to the War Cabinet from shipboard, dated December 20, had swiftly rejected Stalin's claim. He pointed out that the territorial demands were in direct contradiction to the first, second and third articles of the Atlantic Charter, to which the Soviet Union had subscribed. "There can be no question whatever of our making such an agreement," he wrote, "secret or public, direct or implied, without prior agreement with the U.S."[9]

Eden, accordingly, turned aside the Soviet demands without passing judgment on them, giving as one of his reasons the British government's promise to the United States that it would not then enter into any territorial agreements. He left Russia on December 28, having promised Stalin that his demands would be discussed promptly with the United States and the British Dominions. The Soviet territorial demands, in short, had not been rejected, only deferred. More was to be heard of them before long, together with the problems of Lend-Lease supply (which continued to preoccupy Harriman) and the unappeased Russian pressure for a second front somewhere in the West.

Harriman set out for London on January 28 by Pan American Clipper. He reached Bermuda the same afternoon, stayed overnight and took off the next day for the Azores, only to have the seaplane turned back because heavy swells at Horta made a landing impossible. Back again in Bermuda on the third day, January 31, Harriman and his fellow passengers were told that the plane would have to leave without them because it had to fly directly to Lisbon this time and could safely carry only a State Department courier and some 1,795 kilograms of mail.* Harriman had grown progressively more exercised at the poor state of transatlantic air service ever since his assignment to London the year before. His investigation with the help of the British censor in Bermuda confirmed that most of the mail being flown

* The terms of Pan American's subsidy from the government gave first priority to mail.

across the ocean was low-priority stuff of the "how Aunt Bessie is progressing with her lumbago" variety, as Hopkins later described it. It seemed to Harriman intolerable that chit-chat of this kind should command a higher priority than people who had important work to do. Moved to indignant action, he warned the Pan American representative in Bermuda: "I don't have much power in Washington, but I have enough to see that you are fired if that plane leaves without me." Harriman also demanded that Adolph Foerster, a machine-tool expert who had just joined his staff, be cleared to fly on with him. Foerster was carrying with him drawings of the reduction gear for the new C-2 and C-3 merchant ships, and his mission was to find out in a hurry whether they could be built in the United Kingdom. If so, Harriman stressed, it would be possible to complete some thirty to thirty-five additional, sorely needed, merchantmen during 1942. After a telephone call to Juan Trippe in New York, Pan American agreed to leave part of the mail behind in order to make room for Harriman, Foerster and Meiklejohn. They finally reached London on February 2.

Before leaving Bermuda, Harriman had lost no time writing letters to Roosevelt and to Robert Lovett, Assistant Secretary of War for Air, recommending immediate measures to build more transport planes capable of flying the Atlantic nonstop and to create, with the British, a joint board that would finally crack the air-transport bottleneck. The time had come, he wrote Roosevelt, to supersede peacetime policies regarding commercial aviation with new directives better suited to the world-wide war in progress. Harriman's advocacy led in time to the establishment of direct transatlantic service by both the Royal Air Force and the U.S. Army Air Forces through their Ferry Commands, not without a great deal more Harriman pressure on Hopkins and other Washington officials.

Larger problems awaited him in London, including the discovery that Churchill—so commanding and indomitable in the eyes of his foreign allies—was in political trouble at home. Although the Prime Minister had promised his countrymen nothing but blood, toil, tears and sweat, many were beginning to lose confidence in his leadership. Parliament and the press were demanding what Churchill had yet to deliver—an end to defeats and disasters.

CHAPTER VI

No End of Defeats

THE STRAIN OF DEFEAT was beginning to tell when Harriman returned to London. Not that the British had suddenly grown weary of sacrifice—of air raids and blackouts, ration books and shortages. All these they had learned to endure with a certain amount of cheerful grumbling. It was the endless chain of defeats, Harriman felt, that stung the public in its pride.

A great deal had changed since Dunkirk, when the British stood alone, fired by Churchill's brave rhetoric and strangely uplifted by disaster fairly shared. Now they could count on powerful allies, the United States and Russia, and the tide of war was turning inexorably.

Yet public opinion in that third winter at war struck Harriman as embarrassed, unhappy, increasingly baffled. In the parliamentary corridors there was talk of a need for new blood in the War Cabinet, even suggestions that Churchill ought to let someone else run the war. Harold Nicolson has recorded the disenchantment of many Members of Parliament during that bleak winter. Churchill, they said, was not an organizer; he was a poor judge of men, too trusting in his relationship with Beaverbrook. He was running a one-man show as both Prime Minister and Minister of Defence, and one job or the other suffered.[1] It became evident to Harriman that Churchill himself was increasingly depressed by the monotony of defeat following defeat.

At the same time, public admiration for the Russian army and people ran high. They were killing Germans while Britain had yet to come to grips with the main enemy in Europe. Sir Stafford Cripps had come home from Moscow and was quick to receive more public credit than he could rightly have claimed for himself as the man who had made fighting allies of the Russians. Churchill bore him no grudge, and sensing the need to strengthen his administration, offered to put Cripps in charge of the Ministry of Supply. Cripps declined, insisting that he must be a member of the War Cabinet, the inner circle of top party leaders.

Strains also were becoming apparent within the alliance. The Russians kept agitating for a second front in the west and for British acquiescence in their seizure of the Baltic States. Roosevelt appeared to favor an early assault on the Continent, but he frowned on any territorial concessions in advance of the peace treaty. The fact that the United States now had its own war to fight in the Pacific, moreover, raised tensions and sharpened rivalries in Washington. Although the Arcadia conference had just confirmed Roosevelt's Europe-first strategy, American and Filipino troops were fighting a doomed, rear-guard action in the Philippines; the Prime Minister of Australia appealed for American protection; and Chiang Kai-shek clamored for help in China. The Dutch East Indies, Burma and Malaya all came under Japanese attack. Although Roosevelt refused to alter the fundamental strategic plan, events were forcing his hand, compelling him to revise allocations of men and materials. He sent 132,000 troops overseas during the first two and a half months of 1942, for example, but of these only 20,000 went to Iceland and Northern Ireland, as previously agreed. More than four times that number, some 90,000, were sent to the Pacific instead.[2]

Churchill had forced a vote of confidence in the House of Commons on January 29, taking full responsibility for the defeats overseas and failures at home. He won by the fantastic count of 464 to 1. But the need to shake up his War Cabinet could no longer be postponed. The biggest change involved the creation of a new Ministry of Production, to be headed by Lord Beaverbrook. But at the last moment Beaverbrook, suffering from asthma and uncharacteristically irresolute, changed his mind.

Harriman and Brendan Bracken, one of Churchill's staunchest supporters in the House, had spent a number of exhausting evenings with Beaverbrook in the bomb shelter where he slept. Torn between staying or quitting the government, Beaverbrook would rehash his interminable arguments with Churchill over how the government might be better organized and the war pushed through to victory. "There was no doubt in my mind," Harriman recalled, "that Max thought the Prime Minister was slipping. He appeared to believe that he might be called to succeed Churchill, although that was the last thing in the world I could see happening. In fact, as I listened to Beaverbrook my sympathy for Churchill grew steadily."

On the morning of February 9 Beaverbrook asked Harriman to

his office and said, "I am going over to see Churchill and tell him I am resigning." Harriman's surprisingly quick response was "Max, that is precisely what you should do."

Beaverbrook resigned that morning. In a personal message to Roosevelt on February 10, Harriman reported:

> Beaverbrook has quibbled and quarreled with the PM to the point where the PM will not tolerate it any longer. He feels Beaverbrook has been unjust and disloyal to seize this moment of all moments to make an issue. I believe Beaverbrook over-emphasizes the adverse effect on the Government of his resignation. The PM is confident that it will not be serious and, even if it were, there is nothing he can do about it.

On February 19 Churchill announced his reconstructed War Cabinet. Cripps became a member, after all, as Lord Privy Seal and Leader of the House. Oliver Lyttelton, recalled from Cairo, took the job intended for Beaverbrook as Minister of Production, though with somewhat reduced powers. Harriman recorded his impressions of the government crisis in a letter to Roosevelt dated March 6:

> Dear Mr. President:
>
> I have been worried about the Prime Minister—both his political status and his own spirits. He did not take well the criticism he found on his return from Washington. The criticism was not directed at him personally but against certain policies and against various individuals. Unfortunately, he bared his chest and assumed the blame for everything and everybody—politicians and soldiers alike. The natural effect of this was to turn the criticism against himself.
>
> He was forced, obviously reluctantly, to make changes, thus failing to get full credit. He has, however, quieted things for the present. His opponents have found that he has an Achilles heel and will undoubtedly attack again. It is curious how, when criticism starts, a coalition government suffers from lack of party loyalty and support.
>
> Although the British are keeping a stiff upper lip, the surrender of their troops at Singapore has shattered confidence to the core—[confidence] even in themselves but, more particularly, in their leaders. They don't intend to take it lying down and I am satisfied we will see the rebirth of greater determination. At the moment, however, they can't see the end to defeats.
>
> Unfortunately Singapore shook the Prime Minister him-

self to such an extent that he has not been able to stand up to this adversity with his old vigor.

A number of astute people, both friends and opponents, feel it is only a question of a few months before his Government falls. I cannot accept this view. He has been very tired but is better in the last day or two. I believe he will come back with renewed strength, particularly when the tone of the war improves.

There is no other man in sight to give the British the leadership Churchill does.

Cripps wears the hair shirt and wants everyone else to do the same. The British are prepared to make any sacrifice to get on with the war but are not interested in sacrifice for its own sake . . .

It was a season of unrelieved disaster for the British. On the night of February 11 the German battle cruisers *Scharnhorst* and *Gneisenau*, blockaded in the French port of Brest for almost a year, had slipped out to sea, run the Dover coastal batteries boldly in daylight, and with the help of the cruiser *Prinz Eugen*, made good their escape to Wilhelmshaven. Although the cruisers were attacked through the afternoon of February 12 by waves of British bombers, torpedo-carrying planes and destroyers, they reached home port the following day. Both ships, the British secret service later learned, had been damaged by mines sown from the air. The *Scharnhorst* was out of service for six months and the *Gneisenau* was not seen again in the war. But many Englishmen looked upon their escape as humiliating proof that Britain had now lost control even of the English Channel.

The fall of Singapore on February 15 was even more galling to the Prime Minister. He called it the largest capitulation in British history. The loss of Java and Burma followed, closing off the recently opened Burma Road, the only land route to China. Even the Battle of the Atlantic, which had turned more favorable to Britain in the last months of 1941, flared once again as the U-boat fleet of Admiral Karl Dönitz ranged up and down the East Coast of the United States and Canada almost at will. From Boston to Miami, the metropolitan centers of the Atlantic coast were still brilliantly lighted at night, sharply silhouetting the slow-moving merchant ships and tankers for the benefit of the German torpedo marksmen. It took three months of massacre offshore before the city lights were dimmed, over the protests of some resort operators that the tourist business would be ruined. The U.S. Navy, moreover, its resources thinned by the sudden demands of a two-ocean war, lacked the convoy experience the British had gained in the Northwestern Approaches. The heaviest losses were now being taken along the North American sea frontier, within 300 miles of the coastline. From January through July, more than three million tons of Allied shipping went to the bottom. It was not until midsummer that the U.S. Navy mastered the convoy technique. Only then did the toll of ships and seamen begin to drop.

HOPKINS, HIS FRAIL HEALTH undermined by overwork, had been forced to spend two weeks in the Naval Hospital at Bethesda, Maryland, during the period of maximum stress that followed the Arcadia conference. On March 7 Harriman wrote to him, adding to his own best wishes a tribute from Churchill: "Hopkins is worth more to us than any battleship." There could be no higher praise from a Former Naval Person, as Harriman pointed out. In the same letter, Harriman reported on the Prime Minister and his difficulties:

> Things are quiet now—for how long depends upon a number of things and perhaps most of all on the developments of the war. The Prime Minister hates the kind of rumpus he has had to go through and it has taken a lot out of him. He is better now.
>
> Much to my regret I must report that his hold on popular imagination has been somewhat weakened, but don't exaggerate this. So far the opposition comes largely from the House [of Commons] and Fleet Street. Whether he will regain his strength is impossible to predict. Aside from the situation here, I feel it would be tragic if he slipped, from an international viewpoint. He is the only Englishman who has the real confidence of people abroad.
>
> Cripps' star has risen high on the backs of the fighting Russian armies. It may hold but he lacks, I believe, an understanding of the British people. He is personally austere in his habits and wants the British people to wear the hair shirt for the sake of wearing it. They are ready to do anything they are asked to do provided they understand it is to get on with the war, but they don't want to make sacrifices for the sake of sacrifice. It has been proved workmen need entertainment and good food to keep up production for long periods.
>
> Cripps is a vegetarian, does not drink though he smokes a bit. His intimate friends tell me he thinks he is the Messiah. That sometimes carries people far in a crisis but I just can't feel he has the understanding of the British people to be their leader . . .

Harriman was pressing the British government harder than ever at the time to conserve shipping by accepting further massive cuts in its import program. His early successes in persuading the British to eat darker bread, reduce their overseas exports and accept the idea of direct shipments of American war matériel to the Middle East had released many bottoms for supplies to the Russian front and the new war in the Pacific. Imports in fact had been reduced from some 45 million tons in 1939–40 to 38 million in 1941. He now gave his determined support to Lord Leathers, who against all opposition was proposing to cut the import program back to 26 million tons for 1942, exclusive of petroleum. "I almost got my head bitten off," Harriman reported to Hopkins. But after much wrangling among the ministers, each "trying to get his part of the spoils increased," Churchill accepted the figure his Minister of War Transport had submitted.

Although Harriman felt justified in putting pressure on the British, he was far from satisfied that Americans were doing their bit. In the same long letter he prodded Hopkins for more information:

> It was all very well when the British were suitors for our favor to expect them to make the biggest sacrifices while we were living on the fat of the land. Now they look on us as partners and when we ask them to make sacrifices they expect us to do the same.
>
> When I am insisting, as I have been, that [British] imports must be reduced, it is not enough to say that everything possible is being done in America. The British must have the facts and figures to show this is true . . .
>
> It is hard, also, to maintain that we are short of tankers when they know that we have no rationing of petroleum products and so many tankers are being used to supply civilian use on the East and West coasts . . .
>
> There are a lot of things on the American end which are hard for the British to understand. On the other hand, having been in the war for two and a half years, they are not as inclined to be critical of us as we seem to be of them.

British policy in India was one such area of American criticism. India had become a major concern for Roosevelt, no less than Churchill, as the Japanese advanced steadily toward its frontiers. It was Roosevelt's opinion, shared by many Americans, that unless the Indians were promised early independence they would lack the incentive to resist the Japanese wholeheartedly. Churchill, for his part, felt that Roosevelt had little understanding of India's complexities and made no secret of his determination to play the hand without too much prompting from Washington. On February 26 Harriman received instructions to deliver a highly sensitive personal message from Roosevelt inquiring what steps Churchill proposed by way of conciliating the Indian leadership in order to generate more public enthusiasm for the war effort. Harriman remembered this as one of the most difficult assignments he handled for Roosevelt, in view of Churchill's aggrieved attitude. The approach was to be informal, Roosevelt directed, "since it isn't, strictly speaking, our business."

Roosevelt, nevertheless, was prodding Churchill (through Harriman) to promise the Indians their independence, a matter on which the Indian National Congress of Gandhi and Nehru was at sword's point with the Moslem League of Mohammed Ali Jinnah. Harriman carried out his instructions, pulling no punches. And the Prime Minister made it plain that he was less than grateful for the President's sudden interest in matters Indian. Harriman reported back to Washington the same day:

> The Prime Minister will not take any political steps which would alienate the Moslem population of over 100 million. About 75 per cent of the Indian troops and volunteers are Moslems. Of the balance less than half, or perhaps 12 per cent of the total, are in sympathy with the Congress group. The fighting people of India are from the northern provinces largely antagonistic to the Congress movement. The big populations of the low-lying provinces of the center and the south have not the vigor to fight anybody.
>
> Training and equipping, not manpower, is the problem in India. There are ample volunteers willing to fight.

The plain fact was that the prospect of an independent, predominantly Hindu state of India terrified millions of Moslems. For generations they had looked to the British for protection against the Hindu majority. If there were to be new constitutional arrangements, the answer for people like Jinnah was not one independent state but two—one predominantly Moslem, the other chiefly Hindu. These and other home truths about India's complex social-religious structure were conveyed to Roosevelt in a series of increasingly unhappy Churchill messages. Roosevelt, however, had taken it into his head that the Indian problem could be settled in much the same way that the American colonies had achieved their Federal Union. He wrote to Churchill on March 11, briefly surveying the progression from thirteen British colonies through thirteen sovereign states, tied together loosely by the Continental Congress and the Continental Army, to a Federal Republic based on the American Constitution.

Perhaps the analogy of some such method to the travails and problems of the United States from 1783 to 1789 might

give a new slant in India itself, and it might cause the people
there to forget hard feelings, to become more loyal to the
British Empire, and to stress the danger of Japanese domination,
together with the advantage of peaceful evolution as against
chaotic revolution.

Such a move is strictly in line with the world changes of
the past half-century and with the democratic processes of all
who are fighting Nazism. . . .[3]

On the subject of India there was, and could be, no meeting of
minds between Churchill, the unashamed conservator of Britain's empire, and Franklin Roosevelt, the champion of self-determination for
all. India remained a stubborn point of friction between them. Two
years after Roosevelt's death, with Churchill voted out of office, the
British Labor government offered the people of India a plan for
independence substantially different from the one Roosevelt had advanced in 1942. But in deference to the powerful Moslem feelings
Churchill had warned against, British India was divided into two
sovereign states—India and Pakistan—resulting in a colossal massacre.

More urgent questions of strategy were being fought out in
Washington during the late winter and early spring of 1942. Perhaps
the most forceful advocates of a cross-Channel assault on Hitler's
Fortress Europe were Stimson and Marshall. Their position, fairly stated
by a little-known staff officer in the War Plans Division named Dwight
Eisenhower, had the simplicity of a mathematical theorem: a straight
line was the shortest distance between two points.

"We've got to go to Europe and fight—and we've got to stop
wasting resources all over the world—and still worse—wasting time,"
Eisenhower wrote in a personal note to a fellow officer. "If we're to
keep Russia in, save the Middle East, India and Burma, we've got to
begin slugging with air at West Europe; to be followed by a land attack as soon as possible."[4] Only by concentrating on Germany first,
Eisenhower had argued before the Joint Chiefs of Staff on February
28, could the strength of Britain, Russia and the United States be
combined. (The Soviets were not at war with Japan.) He raised the
additional consideration that it would take three to four times as many
ships to transport and maintain an American force of given size in the
Pacific, in view of the longer distances and the fact that the sea lanes
to Britain had to be kept open in any case. In short, for reasons of
supply as well as strategy, plans for an assault in Europe must have
first priority.

The Joint Chiefs endorsed Eisenhower's staff recommendations on
March 16. Roosevelt gave his approval on April 1 and promptly sent
General Marshall to London with Hopkins to work out a schedule with

the British Chiefs and the War Cabinet. The plan they brought with them, code-named Roundup, looked toward an Allied landing in Europe on April 1, 1943. The United States would supply some thirty divisions and more than 3,000 combat planes; the British, eighteen divisions and 2,500 aircraft. Roundup was hinged to a contingency plan called Sledgehammer. This called for a smaller assault, in 1942, by about one-third the number of troops, if the Russians were facing imminent collapse (Stimson called it "a sacrifice for the common good"), or if events inside Germany seemed to offer an opportunity that warranted quick exploitation.* Operation Gymnast, or its variant, Super-Gymnast—the plan for a landing in North Africa approved at the Arcadia conference—had been shelved, its promise dimmed by the fresh defeats the British Eighth Army had suffered in Libya. The Combined Chiefs of Staff had concluded, in a unanimous memorandum dated March 3, that as a result of the British setback in eastern Libya, "far from cooperating, the Vichy French will continue to aid the Axis . . . until such time as the Axis is on the run."[5] Churchill wrote Roosevelt the following day: "The check which Auchinleck has received [in Libya] and the shipping stringency seem to impose obstinate and long delays."

Through Hopkins, Roosevelt made clear to Churchill that he was determined to see an offensive launched in Europe without delay. "Our men must fight" was the message Hopkins delivered. It was the surest way of blocking the daily pressures from Admiral Ernest J. King and General Douglas MacArthur to divert more forces to the Pacific. Churchill surprised both Hopkins and Marshall by his show of agreement. On April 12 he informed Roosevelt that the British Chiefs of Staff had approved the Roundup-Sledgehammer plan in principle.† The record is clear that Marshall and Hopkins left London believing that a firm decision had been made to invade the Continent no later than the summer of 1943, and conceivably as early as September 1942.

This "momentous proposal" was formally accepted by Churchill at a meeting of the War Cabinet's Defence Committee on April 14.

* In his "Biennial Report" for the year ended June 30, 1945, General Marshall distinguished sharply between the two operations: "In the discussions at this [London] conference a tentative target date for the cross-Channel operations, designated by the code name ROUNDUP, was set for the summer of 1943. However, the immediate necessity for an emergency plan was recognized. It was given the code name SLEDGEHAMMER and was to provide for a diversionary assault on the French coast at a much earlier date if such a desperate measure became necessary to lend a hand toward saving the situation on the Soviet front."

† Roundup, the code name for the cross-Channel invasion plan, eventually was changed to Overlord. The code name for the preliminary buildup of men and supplies in the British Isles was Bolero.

Ironically, Churchill and the American Chiefs of Staff had embraced the same proposal for different reasons: anxiety on the Prime Minister's part that unless he accepted the plan, the United States might direct its major military effort to the Pacific, and on the part of the Joint Chiefs, that the British would contrive to divert large forces to the Middle East and India.

Hopkins and Marshall had kept Harriman fully informed of their talks with Churchill and the British Chiefs of Staff. He was impressed by their optimism. Accompanied by Harriman and Hopkins, Marshall flew to Northern Ireland before returning to Washington in order to inspect the first GI contingent in the European theater. He explained to Harriman the great merits of Sledgehammer: it would draw German divisions away from the Russian front, easing the pressure on the Red Army. If the Soviets, on the other hand, could not stand up to the expected summer offensive of the Wehrmacht, it might then become possible to put ashore a larger-than-planned Allied force while the Germans were still preoccupied in the east.

Hopkins and Harriman were billeted at the country house of a retired army officer who lived in elegant discomfort not many miles from Ballyrena, the base General Marshall was visiting. Hopkins developed an immediate aversion for the place, resenting not only the lack of creature comforts but also his host, who upon closer acquaintance revealed himself as a great admirer of Adolf Hitler. Harriman had more lasting reasons to regret the visit. Soon after saying goodbye to Marshall and Hopkins, he became gravely ill. He was forced to spend three weeks in bed, feverish and at times delirious, with what the doctors believed to be a form of paratyphoid, probably traceable to drinking water from the Irishman's old well.

Before taking to his bed, Harriman had returned to London, seen Churchill and received a far less optimistic account of the understandings reached during the Marshall-Hopkins visit. The Prime Minister had agreed, he said, to begin the military planning for Roundup, but he had the gravest doubts about the wisdom of an assault on the coast of France in 1942. "Churchill told me that Sledgehammer was impossible, disastrous," Harriman recalled. "He was gravely concerned that the British, with their limited resources and the limited support we could at that time give them, would have another setback. He was fearful that the divisions they landed would be destroyed—and this would undermine Britain's ability to launch future operations. I believe that General Marshall may have overestimated the state of readiness of the twenty to thirty British divisions in the United Kingdom. My information was that they were not up to strength and were seriously under-equipped.

"I was going to jump on a plane and warn Roosevelt that there had been a serious misunderstanding. It was clearly impossible to explain this in a written message. But I had to go to bed and while I was out of action Churchill decided to go to Washington himself. So I left it to him."

Roosevelt, meanwhile, had come to believe that he could resolve some of the misunderstandings between Russia and the West by a face-to-face meeting with Stalin. The idea had surfaced in a conversation between Harriman and Ambassador Ivan Maisky in London on February 5. The Soviet ambassador, impressed by the wartime intimacy between the United States and Britain, asked how the Russians could go about establishing closer relationships with both Western powers. Harriman replied that the deepening intimacy of British-American official relationships was largely the result of the personal intimacy that Churchill and Roosevelt had established through their meetings. This discussion led naturally to the question of a Roosevelt-Stalin meeting. Maisky said he was quite sure that Stalin would welcome the opportunity if such a meeting could be arranged. He did not believe that Stalin could go far afield, suggesting that the Bering Strait might be a feasible meeting place. Harriman reported Maisky's view and Roosevelt liked the idea so well that on March 18 he wrote to Churchill: "I know you will not mind my being brutally frank when I tell you that I think I can personally handle Stalin better than either your Foreign Office or my State Department. Stalin hates the guts of all your top people. He thinks he likes me better and I hope he will continue to do so . . ." On April 11 Roosevelt had sent a message to Stalin regretting that a face-to-face meeting could not be set up in short order. He raised the possibility that if the war went "as well as we hope," the two might meet in the summer. In the meantime, he invited Molotov to visit Washington in Stalin's place:

I have in mind [a] very important military proposal involving the utilization of our armed forces in a manner to relieve your critical western front. This objective carries great weight with me. Therefore, I wish you would consider sending Mr. Molotov and a General upon whom you rely to Washington in the immediate future. Time is of the essence if we are to help in an important way.

. . . I need your advice before we determine with finality the strategic course of our common military action.

I have sent Hopkins to London relative to this proposal. The American people are thrilled by the magnificent fighting of your armed forces and we want to help you in the destruction of Hitler's armies and material more than we are doing now. . . .[6]

Roosevelt, evidently, had made up his mind that there would have to be early military action in the European theater. His message to Stalin was sent even as Hopkins and Marshall were still in London discussing the Roundup-Sledgehammer plan with Churchill and his generals. Stalin accepted the invitation for Molotov, who arranged to stop in London on his way, to work out final details of the British-Soviet treaty of alliance.

Ever since Eden's visit to Moscow in the winter, the proposed terms of that treaty had deeply disturbed both Secretary of State Hull and the Under Secretary, Sumner Welles. They saw in Stalin's insistence upon British recognition of his territorial conquests the first serious challenge to the Atlantic Charter. Eden, supported by Cripps and Lord Halifax, the British ambassador in Washington, argued that recognition of the boundaries Stalin claimed was a small price to pay for Soviet cooperation in the war, even if this meant that the peoples of Estonia, Latvia and Lithuania were forever consigned to Russian overlordship. True, the Atlantic Charter—to which the Soviet Union also had subscribed—expressly ruled out any territorial changes that did not accord with the freely expressed wishes of the people concerned. But, for the British, a readiness to yield on the frontier issue had somehow become the "acid test," in Cripps's words, of their new relationship with the Russians.

On March 30 Halifax had called on Welles to notify him that Britain was going ahead with the treaty, in spite of American objections. "Stalin states to Great Britain that his views governing British recognition of Russia's pre-1940 boundaries must be met before intimate relations can be established between the Soviet Union and Great Britain," Halifax reported. "Mr. Eden cannot incur the danger of antagonizing Stalin, and the British War Cabinet have consequently determined that they would agree to negotiate a treaty with Stalin which will recognize the 1940 frontiers of the Soviet Union, except for that portion which constituted the Polish-Russian frontier."[7] The United States would not be asked to subscribe to the treaty, Halifax added. All Britain asked of President Roosevelt was that he should try to understand the reasons for the treaty and not openly condemn it.

The Soviet Foreign Minister arrived in London on May 20 to start his talks with Eden. Molotov immediately pressed his maximum demands: British recognition of Soviet claims on eastern Poland and Rumania as well as the Baltic States. As soon as word of this reached Washington, Hull was moved to furious blocking action. Believing that such a treaty would be "a terrible blow to the whole cause of the United Nations," he drafted a message, which Ambassador Winant communicated to Eden, warning that the United States could not be counted upon to remain silent if the territorial clauses were included in the treaty about to be signed. To sharpen the point, he threatened to issue a separate American statement disavowing the whole business. "Our memorandum was so strong," Hull recalled in his memoirs, "that we were in some fear lest the President disapprove it. Mr. Roosevelt, however, quickly returned it with his O.K. . . ."[8]

The threat of an open break with the United States had its swift effect. At the first opportunity Eden told Molotov that the territorial clauses had better be left out of the treaty draft, and surprisingly, after a brief delay to consult the Kremlin, Molotov agreed. In retrospect it seems plain that the Russian leaders had another good reason for not then pressing their territorial claims: the more urgent need of a second front. By their reckoning, a timely concession on the terms of the treaty could avoid a profitless squabble with the Western Allies at a moment when the Germans had broken through in the eastern Crimea and halted the Soviet counteroffensive in the Ukraine. Conceivably it might hasten the day when the British and Americans would launch their great assault on the Continent. So Molotov and Eden signed the treaty on May 26. Ignoring territorial claims, the text pledged both governments to help each other in the common struggle against Hitler and his European allies. It barred a separate peace with Germany by either party, and looking ahead to the end of the war, united them in a twenty-year commitment to prevent Germany from again threatening the peace of Europe.

The outcome appeared to vindicate Roosevelt's judgment in one respect. He had sent word to Eden through Hopkins the previous month that the promise of a second front "should take the heat off Russia's diplomatic demands upon England."[9] He now had to face Molotov's demands for military action just as Churchill (to Harriman's certain knowledge) had made up his mind that a cross-Channel invasion in 1942 was out of the question. Molotov reached Washington on May 29 and was put up at the White House as Roosevelt's guest. At dinner that evening, he lost no time presenting his demands. He urged that the Western Allies "do something now, while the U.S.S.R. was still strong, to draw off an appreciable share of Hitler's forces from the Russian [front], thus modifying the balance and making it possible for the Red Army to come in with a decisive blow which would either crush his forces now or make certain his defeat within a reasonably short period." The goal of the Allied landing, Molotov said, should be to draw off some forty Axis divisions.[10]

The President brought Admiral King and General Marshall into the talks the following day and Molotov restated his second-front proposition, asking for a straight answer. According to the official record by Professor Samuel H. Cross of Harvard (who acted as the President's interpreter during these meetings), Roosevelt then asked Marshall, in Molotov's presence, whether "developments were clear enough so that we could say to Mr. Stalin that we were preparing a second front." Marshall replied "Yes." The President, accordingly, authorized Molotov to inform Stalin that "we expect the formation of a second front this year."[11] Whether Roosevelt necessarily had in mind a cross-Channel invasion, or the alternative of a landing in North Africa, is not clear from the notes of Professor Cross. Nor did Roosevelt say exactly where the Second Front offensive would be launched or when. His statement to Molotov thus fell short of a firm commitment. It was, at best, a declaration of intent and Molotov understood it that way, judging by his continued pressure for a more definite undertaking.

At their final session, on June 1, Roosevelt told Stalin's Foreign Minister that while the United States hoped and expected to open a second front in 1942, the preparations would go faster if the Russians agreed to reduce their Lend-Lease demands (from 4.1 million tons to 2 million tons), thus freeing a great many ships to speed the pre-invasion buildup of men and arms in the British Isles. After all, ships could not be in two places at once, and hence "every ton we could save out of 4,100,000 tons would be so much to the good," he said, adding that the Soviets could not "eat their cake and have it too." At this, Molotov bristled. His immediate retort to Roosevelt was that the second front would be stronger if the first front stood fast.

With a touch of bitterness he then inquired what would happen if the Soviets agreed to cut their Lend-Lease shipments and still there was no second front. Once again he pressed Roosevelt for a more conclusive answer that he could take back to London and Moscow:

> To this direct question the President answered that Mr. Molotov could say in London that, after all, the British were even now in personal consultation with our staff officers on questions of landing craft, food, etc. We expected to establish a second front. General Arnold would arrive next day from London, and with him Lord Mountbatten, [Air Chief] Marshal Portal, and General Little, with whom it was planned to arrive at an agreement on the creation of a second front. Mr. Molotov should also say in London that we could proceed toward its creation with the more speed if the Soviet Government would make it possible for us to put more ships into the English service.[12]

At Stalin's request, the Molotov visit to Washington had been kept secret. The President's guest had been identified only as "Mr. Brown." Although a number of White House correspondents had recognized him, the American press honored an official request for voluntary censorship. As the visit neared its end, however, an official announcement was being prepared in the State Department (which had taken no significant part in the talks), to be released after Molotov had returned to Moscow. Molotov objected to the State Department language, submitting a draft of his own which said, in part: "In the course of the conversations full understanding was reached with regard to the urgent tasks of creating a Second Front in Europe in 1942."[13] That single sentence was to be interpreted, misinterpreted and over-interpreted for many years to come. In accepting Molotov's version, Roosevelt provided employment for a whole generation of Cold War publicists and historians who solemnly argued its meaning in dozens of books and hundreds of articles. Hopkins noted at the time that General Marshall "felt that the sentence about the second front was too strong and urged that there be no reference to 1942." Roosevelt, however, when notified of Marshall's objection, told Hopkins that he wanted the sentence about the second front left in the public statement, which was duly issued on June 11, after British concurrence. Harriman's belief was that Roosevelt had been so deeply affected by the dark outlook on the eastern front, as Molotov sketched it, that he hoped to encourage the Russians to hold out by raising their expectations for Allied action in the west.

The British were more careful. While they agreed to issue the identical communiqué ("There could be no harm," Churchill later wrote, "in a public statement which might make the Germans apprehensive and consequently hold as many of their troops in the West as possible"), the Prime Minister personally handed Molotov on his way home an *aide-mémoire* making it clear that no promise or commitment was intended:

> We are making preparations for a landing on the Con-
> tinent in August or September, 1942. As already explained, the
> main limiting factor to the size of the landing-force is the
> availability of special landing-craft. Clearly however it would
> not further either the Russian cause or that of the Allies as a
> whole if, for the sake of action at any price, we embarked on
> some operation which ended in disaster and gave the enemy an
> opportunity for glorification at our discomfiture. It is impossi-
> ble to say in advance whether the situation will be such as to
> make this operation feasible when the time comes. *We can
> therefore give no promise in the matter,* but provided that it

appears sound and sensible we shall not hesitate to put our plans into effect.[14]

Molotov returned to Moscow seemingly gratified by the results of his mission to the West, and made a great deal of the public statement appearing to promise a second front in 1942. He ignored, in a speech before the Supreme Soviet on June 18, the private message from Churchill with its cautionary words "We can therefore give no promise in the matter." To Admiral Standley, the American ambassador, Molotov said the following day, "This could mean winning the war in 1942, certainly in 1943." The Soviet press and radio promptly spread the word throughout the country that Allied landings in the west were near. Standley was sufficiently concerned about the raising of false hopes to warn the Secretary of State, in a message dated June 22:

> In view of the manner in which the Soviet Government and people have accepted what would appear here to be a solemn obligation on the part of the United States and Great Britain to create a second front in 1942, I feel convinced that if such a front does not materialize quickly, and on a large scale, these people will be so deluded in their belief in our sincerity of purpose and will for concerted action that inestimable harm will be done to the cause of the United Nations.[15]

But Stalin and Molotov, in spite of their hopeful public statements, evidently understood that no firm pledge had been given. Stalin, for example, remarked to Standley on July 2 that wanting a second front and having one were two different matters; and when Molotov was reproached by the new British ambassador, Archibald Clark Kerr, for talking too freely about "Anglo-Saxon promises" at a diplomatic luncheon, he acknowledged that his remarks had been somewhat "subjective." He had heard in London, Molotov added, that there were real problems to be overcome before the second front could be opened.

ONE IMMEDIATE PROBLEM which greatly preoccupied Harriman during the spring and summer of 1942 was the ominous rising curve of ships lost on the Arctic supply route from Iceland around the North Cape to Murmansk and Archangel. The protocol that Harriman and Beaverbrook had signed in Moscow did not obligate the Western Allies to deliver the supplies to Russian ports, only to "give aid" in delivering them. But the Russians did not have enough ships of their own to carry more than a fraction of the matériel, so the traffic was entrusted chiefly to British, Norwegian, Canadian and American merchant ships. Only in the Pacific, where Soviet-flag ships could ply freely between the West Coast of North America and Vladivostok, thanks to Stalin's neutrality treaty with Japan, did the Russians take responsibility for their own deliveries. The Arctic route was shorter and more direct but it was also far more dangerous. The danger became acute in March 1942, after Hitler had greatly strengthened his naval units in Norwegian waters and turned loose the Luftwaffe to harass the convoys from bases in northern Norway. The German forces were formidable: the battleships *Tirpitz* and *Scheer*, the cruiser *Hipper*, several modern destroyers, 20 or more U-boats, 30 dive bombers, 150 long-range bombers and reconnaissance planes, some 70 fighter planes and a like number of coastal patrol aircraft. The Arctic convoys, as a result, were having to fight their way in and out again, being spotted and shadowed from the air and then attacked by submarines, surface ships and aircraft for days on end. The hazards multiplied in the spring and early summer as the long Arctic daylight exposed the slow processions of merchant ships to the enemy, and the ice pack forced the convoys to keep within range of German shore bases in Norway.[16]

Roosevelt as well as Hopkins and Harriman were all determined to maintain and increase the deliveries to Russia in spite of the dangers at sea. "I felt," Harriman recalled, "that we had a moral, though not a written, obligation to do everything we could to get the ships through. It was the British who, all through this period, however, bore the burden of running the convoys from the United Kingdom and Iceland, where our ships were collected, to the Russian ports." And in late April the British were beginning to find the burden of risk overwhelming. On April 20 the British officer in charge of the fourteenth convoy to Russia recommended to the Admiralty that further convoys be suspended during the months of virtually continuous daylight in the Arctic. The hazards were simply too great, he said. His own convoy of 23 ships had run into heavy pack ice north of Iceland, forcing 14 of the ships to turn back. One was sunk on the way. Thus only 8 ships of the original 23 reached their destination. Moreover, a major bottleneck was developing in Iceland as ships bound for Russia jammed the harbor waiting for onward convoys. Spurred by a directive from President Roosevelt on March 17 to the Lend-Lease Administration, the War Production Board and the War Shipping Administration that all supplies promised to Russia must be shipped without delay "regardless of all other considerations," 107 ships had been rushed to Iceland during March, April and May. At this point the British Naval Staff informed Churchill that the convoys to Russia would have to be cut back. Three convoys every two months was to be the limit, each convoy consisting of no more than 25 ships. The decision was a painful shock to Roosevelt. He cabled Churchill on April 27:

About the shipments to Russia. I am greatly disturbed by
your cable to Harry [Hopkins], because I fear not only the
political repercussions in Russia, but even more the fact that
our supplies will not reach them promptly. We have made
such a tremendous effort to get our supplies going that to have
them blocked except for the most compelling reasons seems to
me a serious mistake. I realize . . . that the matter is extremely
difficult . . . but I very much prefer that we do not seek at
this time any new understanding with Russia about the amount
of our supplies in view of the impending assault on their armies.
It seems to me that any word reaching Stalin at this time that
our supplies were stopping for any reason would have a most
unfortunate effect.

Stalin also appealed to Churchill in a message dated May 6. "I am
fully aware of the difficulties involved and of the sacrifices made by
Great Britain in this matter," he wrote. "I feel however incumbent
upon me to approach you with the request to take all possible measures
in order to ensure the arrival of all the above-mentioned materials
[backed up in Iceland] in the U.S.S.R. in the course of May, as this is
extremely important for our front."

Churchill's reply to both Stalin and Roosevelt was that the Royal
Navy could do no more. With Roosevelt he was more frank: "I beg
you not to press us beyond our judgment in this operation, which we
have studied most intently, and of which we have not yet been able to
measure the full strain. I can assure you, Mr. President, we are absolutely extended, and I could not press the Admiralty further." To
Stalin, Churchill replied in less bleak tones: "We shall continue to do
our utmost . . . We are throwing all our available resources into the
solution of this problem, have dangerously weakened our Atlantic
convoy escorts for this purpose, and, as you are no doubt aware, have
suffered severely." The Prime Minister appealed to Stalin for Soviet
naval and air support in fighting off the German raiders on the Arctic
approaches to Murmansk and Archangel. Stalin replied four days later
that he would do what little he could but that the Russian navy was
small and the air force all but totally committed to the great land
battles with the Wehrmacht.

Harriman undertook to break the Iceland bottleneck. He dispatched Alexander Kerr of the Mission staff to Rejkjavik to determine
which of the waiting vessels could be diverted to British ports and have
the most urgently needed cargoes reloaded in other ships. With the
help of the Soviet embassy in London, which decided the relative
priorities, much of the most urgently needed cargo was thus dispatched
directly to Russia in British convoys. There were not enough ships,

however, to carry all the off-loaded material, with the result, which Roosevelt had foreseen, that the hard-pressed Soviet government gave way to dark suspicions of Allied intent. The Russians accused the British of appropriating certain of "their" supplies. But the dismal climax was yet to come.

Convoy 17 sailed from Rejkjavik on June 28. In deference to Roosevelt's wishes, the British had agreed to take 35 merchant ships, 10 more than the limit of safety decreed by the Admiralty. The close-in escort included 6 destroyers, 4 corvettes, 7 trawlers, 2 submarines, 2 anti-aircraft ships and 3 lifesaving vessels. The covering force, which tended to operate many miles from the convoy, included the U.S. cruisers *Wichita* and *Tuscaloosa* and the battleship *Washington*, the British cruisers *London* and *Norfolk*, the battleship *Duke of York*, the aircraft carrier *Victorious* and 9 destroyers. Nine British and 4 Soviet submarines operated ahead of the convoy, making a formidable total of 53 escort vessels to protect 35 merchant ships.

Convoy 17 came under German air surveillance and attack on the third day out, July 1. The first ship was sunk on the morning of July 4, and by nightfall 3 more had been torpedoed. That evening Sir Dudley Pound, the First Sea Lord, sent signals to the convoy escort from London, ordering the cruisers to withdraw at high speed and the smaller vessels to scatter. His orders were based on a mistaken assumption that the *Tirpitz* (escorted by the *Scheer* and the *Hipper*) was about to attack the convoy. The German raiders, in fact, did not leave their Norwegian harbor until midday on July 5, knowing by the time they put to sea that the convoy had dispersed. That evening the *Tirpitz* and her escort were ordered back to port without joining the fight. No capital ships were needed to deal with the scattered, defenseless merchant ships. Easy prey for the U-boats and German aircraft overhead, 24 of the 35 were sunk, their crews for the most part perishing in the icy waters. Only 11, some heavily damaged, limped into Archangel. No more than 70,000 tons of cargo reached Russia out of the 200,000 tons which had started from Iceland.

The disaster prompted the British to suspend further Arctic convoys until the end of the summer. On July 16 Roosevelt reluctantly accepted this decision, agreeing that Churchill should explain the whole matter to Stalin, whose response was predictably bitter. He found the reasons for suspending the convoys "wholly unconvincing," contended the British were too fearful of risks and losses in wartime, and reopened the second-front issue with characteristic bluntness. The matter of relieving the Red Army by opening a new front in the west, he complained, "is not being treated with the seriousness it deserves." The Soviet government, he added, "cannot acquiesce in the postponement of a second front in Europe until 1943."

The cross-Channel invasion was even then being planned for 1943 at the earliest. Churchill and Harriman had flown to Washington separately in June. In a meeting at Hyde Park on June 20, the Prime Minister handed the President a note on the strategic situation in which his misgivings about a landing in France had taken firm shape:

> Arrangements are being made for a landing of six or eight divisions on the coast of Northern France early in September. However, the British Government do not favour an operation that [is] certain to lead to disaster, for this would not help the Russians whatever their plight, would compromise and expose to Nazi vengeance the French population involved, and would gravely delay the main operation in 1943. . . .
>
> No responsible British military authority has so far been able to make a plan for September, 1942, which has any chance of success unless the Germans become utterly demoralised, of which there is no likelihood. Have the American Staffs a plan? At what points would they strike? What landing-craft and shipping are available? Who is the officer prepared to command the enterprise? . . .
>
> . . . Ought we not to be preparing within the general structure of "Bolero" some other operation by which we may gain positions of advantage, and also directly and indirectly to take some of the weight off Russia? It is in this setting and on this background that the French Northwest Africa operation should be studied.[17]

If the Allies were to strike anywhere, in short, they should revive the old Gymnast plan. North Africa had a special appeal for the Prime Minister. In Harriman's words, "He always liked to go round the end rather than through the center." Churchill knew the price that Britain had paid in the mud of Passchendaele and the Somme during World War I. He talked to Harriman of the emotions he felt as he looked about him in the House of Commons "at the faces that are not there," the faces of men destined to lead Britain who had never returned from the Great War, as it was sometimes called. Roosevelt, too, had a visceral abhorrence of trench warfare. He nevertheless told Harriman at Hyde Park the same day that he was "going to insist on some action" but he was having a difficult time finding a place "where the soldiers thought they could fight." His great fear, Roosevelt said, was that if large numbers of American soldiers and equipment remained idle in the British Isles, it would become increasingly difficult for him to fend off demands for a Pacific-first strategy. This also was the reason that Gymnast (soon to be renamed Torch) appealed to Roosevelt as a substitute. Churchill had shrewdly sensed Roosevelt's mood. Stimson, who shared General Marshall's feeling that the North African landing would be a costly diversion, suspected that Churchill "had taken up Gymnast knowing full well, I am sure, that it was the President's great secret baby."[18] The strongest argument against Gymnast/Torch was that it would siphon off vast shipping tonnages to the Mediterranean, inevitably slowing the buildup in Britain, so the prospect for a successful European landing in 1943 would be jeopardized. But, strong as it was, the argument did not prevail.

On the morning of June 21 the President handed Churchill a slip of paper with the news that Tobruk had fallen and that 25,000 British troops had been taken prisoner. For thirty-three weeks, Tobruk had withstood the German siege. Now it had surrendered to a much smaller German force. The shock of one more defeat was to Churchill a staggering blow. He did not at first believe the news. But when it was confirmed, by telephone from London, he made no attempt to hide his pain from Roosevelt. "It was a bitter moment," Churchill recalled in his memoirs. "Defeat is one thing; disgrace is another." He had to be content for the moment with Roosevelt's instantaneous decision to send the British forces in the Middle East 300 brand-new Sherman tanks and 100 of the 105-mm. self-propelled guns that were just coming off the production lines. The fall of Tobruk was a terrible blow, pushing the Desert Army back to the positions of two years before at Mersa Matruh and giving fresh voice to Churchill's critics in the British press and Parliament.

Churchill, accompanied by Harriman, started back to London from Baltimore in deepest secrecy on June 25. On instructions from British security, Harriman slipped away from a dinner meeting of the Commerce Department's Business Advisory Council at the end of his speech, and made his way to Baltimore alone. Churchill had gone there separately, and together they boarded a Pan American Clipper which the British had recently acquired. After a few hours' sleep they landed in Botwood, Newfoundland. It was breakfast time, according to their own watches. But they were served "too sturdy a breakfast" for Harriman's taste—excellent lobster washed down with Scotch whiskey—at midday, local time. The Prime Minister, however, seemed to thrive on it, reinforcing his energies for the vote of censure that awaited him in the House of Commons.

A party government, Churchill later acknowledged, might well have been overturned by the same rush of intense public feeling that two years earlier had driven Neville Chamberlain from power. But the national coalition stood united and party discipline held firm. Again the vote of censure was defeated by a massive majority, 475 to 25.

GENERAL AUCHINLECK BELATEDLY took personal command of the Eighth Army, pulled back into Egypt as far as El Alamein, and after a short period of reorganizing his forces, counterattacked on July 2. Victory was out of the question, but he managed to stabilize the position and secure the Canal zone. Tobruk, of course, had raised fresh doubts in Washington about the wisdom of the proposed North African operation. Torch made strategic sense only if the Eighth Army could pull itself together and begin to drive westward along the rim of the Mediterranean, to join forces eventually with the American divisions that would be landed in Northwest Africa. That way the entire North African coastline could be cleared, from El Alamein to Casablanca. But Roosevelt, in his eagerness to see American soldiers come to grips with the German army before the year was out, was beginning to see great opportunities in the Mediterranean theater. Three weeks after Harriman had returned to London, the President shared his thoughts with Hopkins:

> . . . my main point is that I do not believe we can wait until 1943 to strike at Germany. If we cannot strike at SLEDGE-HAMMER, then we must take the second best—and that is not the Pacific. . . .
>
> If SLEDGEHAMMER cannot be launched then I wish a determination made . . . as to a specific and definite theatre where our ground and sea forces can operate against the German ground forces in 1942.
>
> The theatres to be considered are North Africa and the Middle East.[19]

On July 16, the day following Hopkins' conversation with the President, he flew once again to Britain with General Marshall and Admiral King to settle at last upon joint military plans for the rest of 1942. Marshall and King pressed their British colleagues loyally and hard for approval of Sledgehammer. They had turned the early plan for a "sacrificial" landing in France into a blueprint for seizing and holding the Cotentin Peninsula in Normandy, which looked (at least on paper) like a permanent gain. But the British were not persuaded that such an operation could be mounted with any hope of success in the two or three months that remained before the Channel turned wild and stormy. So it was that in order to break the stalemate Roosevelt agreed to invade North Africa, an operation he considered "second best," which was to take place no later than October 30.

Once again Marshall showed his confidence in Harriman by briefing him carefully on the progress of the military talks. The general, aware of Harriman's close personal relationships with both Roosevelt and Churchill, had long since made it his practice to keep this particular civilian fully informed. "Marshall gave me three reasons for the Torch decision," Harriman recalled. "First, it would relieve the Russian front by forcing the Germans to fight in North Africa. Second, by sending American troops into action, it would neutralize the Pacific-first pressures at home. And third, it was the only large military operation that seemed feasible at the time." In time Marshall came to see an additional virtue in Torch: it would give the raw GIs their first experience of combat under conditions far less difficult than those they would have faced in landing on the fortified coast of France.

At last the military agenda was set. Churchill, who was planning a trip to the Middle East, volunteered to go on to Moscow after his talks in Cairo. He proposed to break the news to Stalin personally that there would, after all, be no Second Front in France that year. It was a painful assignment, but he felt ready to brave Stalin's predictable wrath. When Harriman drove down to Chartwell, Churchill's country place, on the Friday evening after Hopkins, King and Marshall had returned to Washington, he found Churchill staying in the cottage rather than in the big house. Maisky, the Soviet ambassador, was just leaving when Harriman arrived. At dinner alone with Harriman that evening, Churchill said he was going to Moscow to tell Stalin the plain truth about the military situation. He proposed to make clear why there could be no Second Front in 1942, why he and Roosevelt had decided to invade North Africa instead. It was the only way, he felt, to put the suspicions of the recent past behind them and to establish a solid personal relationship of trust with Stalin.

Harriman worried over the prospect the rest of the weekend. The Russians knew, as Molotov had told him personally in June, that on the question of a Second Front in Europe the Western Allies were divided. Molotov had seen and heard enough during his visits to Washington and London to understand that Roosevelt and General Marshall were far more optimistic about the feasibility of a cross-Channel invasion than Churchill and the British Chiefs of Staff. All this would, of course, have been reported to Stalin. If no American went to Moscow with Churchill to vouch for the combined decision to abandon Sledgehammer and to invade North Africa, Stalin's suspicions might well be heightened, not allayed. "My concern," Harriman recalled, "was that Stalin would not believe a word of what Churchill was telling him. He would think that the British alone had blocked the Second Front."

On the morning of Tuesday, August 4, Harriman consulted Eden, telling him of his concern that Churchill should not go to Moscow unaccompanied by an American. "Hopkins would be best," Harriman said, "but if he is not available I am ready to go." Eden readily agreed, reproaching himself for not having thought of it. He sent a cable to Churchill, who was already in Cairo: "From the political point of view you may think there would be advantage in showing in this way that our two governments are in agreement in both political and military matters. Harriman's presence would give a three-party complexion to such discussions as he attends and this might be useful, not merely during the discussions themselves but also for public opinion in the USA."

Harriman cabled his suggestion to Roosevelt, reporting Eden's favorable reaction and stressing that his presence in Moscow would in no way harm "the personal and intimate nature" of the Stalin-Churchill talks. On the contrary, Harriman argued, his participation at this critical moment would help the alliance by showing the Russians that Britain and the United States stood together.

At first Roosevelt disapproved: "As I do not want anyone anywhere to have the slightest suspicion that you are acting as an observer, I hesitate to have you go. I know you would be useful but I think it wiser not to run any risks of misconstruction." The President evidently was concerned lest Churchill misinterpret Harriman's presence as betraying some lack of American trust. The Prime Minister, however, reacted as Harriman had expected. He cabled Roosevelt: "I should greatly like to have your aid and countenance in my talks with Joe. Would you be able to let Averell come with me? I feel that things would be easier if we all seemed to be together. I have a somewhat raw job." The President promptly reversed himself in a message that reached Harriman at seven-thirty in the evening on August 5: "Have wire from Former Naval Person saying he thinks you would be helpful. Will you therefore please leave as soon as possible for Moscow? I am sending the following wire to Stalin: 'I am asking Harriman to proceed to Moscow to be at the disposal of yourself and your visitor to help in any way possible.' "

That was the beginning and the end of Harriman's instructions from Roosevelt. His immediate problem was how to get to Cairo in time to catch up with Churchill. Harold Balfour, the Parliamentary Under Secretary of State for Air, who happened to be dining in Harriman's apartment that evening, picked up the telephone and issued orders to hold up the only available plane, a B-24 that was scheduled to leave from Cornwall at midnight with Charles de Gaulle on board. Fortunately, Harriman had talked earlier in the day with Air Chief Marshal Sir Charles Portal and with General Eisenhower. He knew the talks with Stalin were bound to concentrate on military planning, and General Marshall, just a few days earlier, had briefed him fully on the reasons for abandoning Sledgehammer in favor of Torch. Thus Harriman was not totally unprepared for the sudden mission to Moscow, thanks in large part to his close relationship with Marshall. At midnight Eden dropped in with Winant to say goodbye and at three-thirty in the morning of August 6, Harriman left London for Cairo, by way of Cornwall.

CHAPTER VII

To Moscow Again, with Churchill

THE DELAYED TAKEOFF for Cairo at eight-thirty in the morning displeased Harriman's traveling companion, General de Gaulle. Hardly an easy companion at the best of times, De Gaulle seemed particularly unbending that morning. He had been kept waiting overnight, at some cost to his dignity. The flight, moreover, ran additional dangers in daylight from Luftwaffe fighter planes based in German-occupied France. The Royal Air Force had adapted the bomber for transport service by installing two lines of benches with a narrow aisle between them, so narrow that men as tall as De Gaulle and Harriman, sitting face to face, were bound to lock knees together. For some twenty hours, then (not counting a stopover in Gibraltar), De Gaulle found himself forced into a degree of reluctant physical intimacy with Harriman, their knees interlocked as they sat in the converted bomber. Harriman's notes suggest no comparable interlocking of minds.

DE GAULLE: Things are not going well.

HARRIMAN: Yes.

DE GAULLE: The war is difficult.

HARRIMAN: Yes.

DE GAULLE: You [the United States] must do better.

HARRIMAN: Yes.

"De Gaulle is a dull companion," Harriman noted. "He never

loosened up. I confess I didn't try much." Both men had reason to be preoccupied. Harriman turned his thoughts to the forthcoming talks in Moscow with Churchill and Stalin. De Gaulle remained inscrutable. He had divined in a meeting with General Marshall in London on July 23 that there was to be no invasion of France in 1942. But De Gaulle had not been told of the projected landing in French North Africa. Roosevelt feared that Free French participation might endanger Operation Torch by provoking fierce resistance from troops loyal to the Vichy regime of Marshal Henri Philippe Pétain. Considering himself a friend of France ("about the best friend they have," as the President had written to Admiral William D. Leahy, his ambassador in Vichy), Roosevelt thought it more likely that the North African French would fire on the Cross of Lorraine than on the American flag. De Gaulle found Harriman's silence during the flight remarkable. He later wrote:

> Mr. Averell Harriman . . . was on the plane taking me to Cairo; this ordinarily frank and fluent diplomat seemed on this occasion to be nursing some weighty secret . . . these symptoms assured me that a major operation would soon be under way without us in the Mediterranean.[1]

Arriving in Egypt on August 7, Harriman found that Churchill would not be leaving for several days; he had important military business in the Middle East before flying on to Russia. The Prime Minister confided to Harriman that he had decided to replace General Auchinleck. General Sir Harold Alexander, who had made a great impression at Dunkirk and in Burma for his imperturbable competence, would succeed Auchinleck as commander in chief. Lieutenant General W. H. E. "Strafer" Gott, an experienced desert tactician much admired by the troops, was to take command of the Eighth Army in the field. The War Cabinet had just cabled its approval of these command changes from London when General Gott's plane was shot down as he was flying to see the Prime Minister in Cairo. Gott's death set the stage for the appointment of General Montgomery to serve under Alexander as commander of the Eighth Army.

Harriman used his time in Cairo to advantage. He had left London alone because the British were unable to bump more than one passenger from the plane assigned to De Gaulle. Seeing the value of a small staff to check on Lend-Lease developments and the Soviet war effort, Harriman set about recruiting one in Cairo. At the American embassy he ran into Loy Henderson, who had been chargé d'affaires in Moscow during the period of Stalin's great purges. Henderson was in Cairo on an inspection tour for the State Department, and when Harriman cabled for permission to take him along, the Department readily agreed. He also found Brigadier General Sidney P. Spalding, a

Lend-Lease officer who had been sent out from Washington to survey the Persian Gulf supply route, in Cairo. In addition, Harriman persuaded General Marshall, by telegram, to let him borrow Major General Russel L. Maxwell, commander of American supply forces in the Middle East. Marshall stipulated, however, that General Maxwell not be empowered to discuss strategic questions with the Russians. A converted B-24 bomber was assigned to fly the party to Moscow, although Harriman was to travel from Teheran with Churchill at the Prime Minister's invitation.

On August 8 Harriman had the satisfaction of visiting with Churchill four armored British brigades which were being trained to use General Grant and General Sherman tanks. The soldiers he met expressed great confidence in their new American equipment. After a sleepless night in the sweltering American embassy, Harriman flew on to Teheran ahead of the Prime Minister. He wanted to have a look at the Persian railroad, which had taken on new importance as a supply gateway to Russia since the suspension of the Arctic convoys. He found the British-built railroad running no more than four to five trains a day between the Persian Gulf and the Caspian Sea. The seldom-attained British objective was to move 3,300 tons of freight a day. After consulting with three American officers on the spot (one of whom had been a Santa Fe railroad engineer), Harriman determined that with better management and equipment, the daily volume could be raised to some 6,000 tons.

On the afternoon of August 11 he put this proposition to Churchill and the Chief of the Imperial General Staff, General Sir Alan Brooke, in a meeting at the British summer legation, an elaborate and beautiful tent some ten miles out of Teheran and 700 feet higher in elevation, where the diplomats could escape the heat of the capital. Harriman suggested that the U.S. Army should take over the running of the railroad. Both General Brooke and Churchill sounded dubious. Pointing out that the railroad was the main supply channel for the British forces in Iran, they worried about handing over control to the Americans. The matter was deferred until after the Moscow visit.[2]

The next morning Churchill and Harriman set out for Moscow, flying over the northern range of the Elburz Mountains and the eastern shore of the Caspian Sea to avoid the German armies driving toward Baku, then over Kuibyshev to the Soviet capital. Churchill's plane, another converted B-24, had not been sound-proofed and the noise inside was deafening. Although Churchill and Harriman sat side by side, normal conversation was ruled out by the roar of the engines. Instead they passed notes back and forth when one or the other had something to say. There was, therefore, no opportunity to discuss in advance of their arrival the part Harriman was to play in the conversations with Stalin. At midday the Prime Minister called for lunch. Commander Thompson produced a ham sandwich from the lunch basket prepared by the British legation kitchen in Teheran. Churchill demanded mustard. Thompson rummaged in the basket but there was no mustard. The Prime Minister was horrified. "Ten demerits!" he wrote. "You should know that no gentleman eats ham sandwiches without mustard."*

Churchill has recorded his conflicted thoughts upon the approach to Moscow, his first visit to "this sullen, sinister Bolshevik State I had once tried so hard to strangle at its birth . . ." He was determined to tell Stalin the blunt truth that there would be no second front in 1942 and to have it out with him face to face. "It was," Churchill reflected, "like carrying a large lump of ice to the North Pole."[3]

Less than three hours after their arrival, Churchill and Harriman met with Stalin at the Kremlin. Harriman found Stalin looking older and grayer than the year before, but no less vigorous. Their first talk of three hours and forty minutes went unexpectedly well, although the first two hours were somber enough as Churchill explained, "with the greatest frankness," in Harriman's view, why the Second Front could not be opened in 1942. To begin with, he said, time was running out. September was the last month in which the Channel seemed trustworthy and it would be impossible to mount an operation in the time remaining to draw off German divisions from the Russian front. The Allies, Churchill added, had only enough landing craft to put six divisions ashore in France, too few for a penetration deep enough to do the Russians any good. In 1943 they would have eight to ten times as many landing craft and a million American troops, compared with the two and a half U.S. divisions then in Britain. A great offensive was being planned for 1943. The Allies were prepared to throw twenty-seven American and twenty-one British divisions against the Germans in the west. Nearly half of these divisions would be armored. Churchill conceded that the plan he had outlined offered the Russians no help in 1942. Stalin frowned when the Prime Minister added that he thought it possible the German army in the west would be even stronger in 1943 than it was at the moment. Harriman's report, marked "Personal for the President Only," noted:

> Stalin took issue at every point with bluntness, almost to the point of insult, with such remarks as "You can't win wars if you aren't willing to take risks" and "You must not be so afraid of the Germans." This phase of the discussion ended by

* On the homeward flight, Churchill magnanimously erased all of Thompson's demerits when the lunch basket, packed this time by the Kremlin kitchen staff, was found to contain caviar and champagne.

Stalin stating abruptly, but with dignity, that he could not force action [by the Allies] but he did not agree with the arguments. He expressed the opinion, too, that grave difficulties confronted Roundup and showed little interest in it. So far there had been no agreement on any point and the atmosphere was tense.

The Prime Minister then described the bombing activity over Germany and his hopes for substantial increase with American participation. Here came the first agreement between the two men. Stalin took over the argument himself and said that homes as well as factories should be destroyed. The Prime Minister agreed that civil morale was a military objective, but the bombing of working men's houses came as a by-product of near-misses on factories. The tension began to ease and a certain understanding of common purpose began to grow. Between the two of them, they soon had destroyed most of the important industrial cities of Germany.

The Prime Minister, with great adroitness, took the occasion of the more friendly interchange to bring the discussion back to the Second Front. He explained the decision regarding Torch and its tactics, emphasizing the need for secrecy . . .

About this time the Prime Minister drew a picture of a crocodile and pointed out that it was as well to strike the belly as the snout.

At this point Stalin's interest quickened. He asked when Torch was scheduled to begin, adding that he would withdraw the question if Churchill found it embarrassing. Not at all, Churchill responded; the target date fixed by President Roosevelt was October 30.

Showing more interest all the time, Stalin wondered if the North African landing would not embroil the Western Allies in war with France and Spain. Churchill replied that the operation would be carried out under the American flag with British support, and that he expected only half-hearted resistance from the French. What about Spain? Stalin inquired. The Prime Minister did not believe that Spain would make war, and if she did, Germany would have to defend her. Churchill outlined his scenario: In September the British would defeat Rommel's forces in the Western Desert and at the end of October the Americans would land in North Africa, all the while tying down Hitler's forces in northern France by a series of invasion feints and ruses. His goal was to end the year in possession of all North Africa and from there to threaten the soft underbelly of Hitler's Europe, Churchill said, pointing to his crocodile, while at the same time whacking at the hard snout. Harriman added, "President Roosevelt, in spite

of his serious preoccupations in the Pacific, looks upon the European
theater of war as his principal concern. He will support it to the limit
of the resources at his disposal." Stalin, the former seminarian, exclaimed, "May God help this enterprise to succeed."

Stalin later asked if General de Gaulle had been told about Torch.
Churchill responded that when De Gaulle recently inquired about a
possible operation in North Africa, he personally had denied any such
intention. Stalin expressed doubt concerning the French attitude. Success was the only answer, Churchill said. If the Americans came to
liberate France, the French would not declare war. Harriman said that
he did not believe any Frenchman would see in Torch an effort by the
United States to annex French North Africa. The President, he said,
was well informed about conditions there. American agents in North
Africa had been reporting for some time that an overwhelming majority of the population would welcome an American landing.

Stalin expanded on his doubts. Although he felt it was "militarily
sound," he worried about the political soundness of Torch. If De
Gaulle was in charge, the French would support him, he predicted,
but if it was an American-British operation, the people might be an-
tagonized. Harriman argued that De Gaulle was not being repudiated,
but the plain fact was that he talked too much and many Frenchmen
in North Africa were suspicious of his political aspirations. Stalin responded that he himself was not in favor of De Gaulle; he thought it
important, however, to show that Torch was being undertaken in the
interest of France, not the United States. Churchill gave assurance that
from the beginning of Torch, it would be made clear that this was the
first step in the liberation of France. He felt certain that many Frenchmen would come over to the Allies. All at once, Stalin appeared to
grasp the merits of Torch. He saw in it four advantages: (1) It would
hit Rommel's Afrika Korps in the rear; (2) it would lead to fighting
between Frenchmen and Germans; (3) It would force Italy out of the
war; (4) it would keep Spain neutral by intimidating Franco. All told,
Stalin said, it was a good plan, though he would like to see it put on a
more solid political footing.

As the three gathered around the large globe in Stalin's office
before saying good night, Harriman traced a fifth argument for Torch:
by driving the enemy out of the Mediterranean, it would greatly improve the shipping situation for all the Allies by eliminating the war-
enforced long hauls around the Cape of Good Hope.

After the Kremlin meeting, Harriman rode with the Prime Minister back to his dacha a few miles outside the city. Both were delighted
with the talk. The Prime Minister, who was meeting Stalin for the
first time, felt it had been the most important conference of his long
life. He was pleased at Harriman's presence and thanked him for his

help in getting over some of the rough spots. "No Prime Minister," he said, "has been better supported by a representative of another country." Harriman readily agreed to the suggestion that Churchill should see Stalin alone the second evening, August 13.

Harriman was occupied with other business. He sent off his cables to Washington, called on Ambassador Standley at the American embassy and invited the American correspondents in for a drink in the evening. He had just started dinner about ten o'clock in the guesthouse provided by the Soviet government when Churchill telephoned to say that Stalin had insisted that Harriman take part in the second meeting as well; he wanted to go over the ground of the previous evening once again. Thus, at eleven-fifteen, Churchill and Harriman returned to the blacked-out Kremlin for what turned out to be an unexpectedly tough encounter with Stalin.

At the outset, Stalin handed each a memorandum which, he said, summed up the outcome of the August 12 conversation. It was a document bristling with recriminations. Recalling the Molotov visit to London in May, and the June communiqué on the prospect of a Second Front in 1942, the document argued that the Soviet Union had been left in the lurch by Churchill's refusal:

> It will be easily understood that the Soviet command built their plan of summer and autumn operations calculating on the creation of a second front in Europe in 1942.
>
> It is easy to grasp that the refusal of the Government of Great Britain to create a second front in 1942 inflicts a moral blow to the whole of Soviet public opinion, which calculates on the creation of a second front, and that it complicates the situation of the Red Army at the front and prejudices the plan of the Soviet command.
>
> I am not referring to the fact that the difficulties arising for the Red Army as the result of the refusal to create a second front in 1942 will undoubtedly have to deteriorate the military situation of England and all the remaining allies.
>
> It appears to me and my colleagues that the most favorable conditions exist in 1942 . . . inasmuch as almost all the forces of the German Army, and the best forces to boot, have been withdrawn to the Eastern front, leaving in Europe an inconsiderable number of forces and these of inferior quality. It is unknown whether the year of 1943 will offer conditions for the creation of a second front in Europe as favorable as 1942. We are of the opinion, therefore, that it is particularly in 1942 that the creation of a second front in Europe is possible and should be effected. I was, however, unfortunately unsuc-

cessful in convincing Mr. Prime Minister of Great Britain hereof, while Mr. Harriman, the representative of the President of the U.S.A., fully supported Mr. Prime Minister in the negotiations held in Moscow.

(signed) I. Stalin

Churchill and Harriman listened soberly to the translation. Then the Prime Minister, in a shrewd stroke, promised Stalin his answer in writing. The recriminations could wait. He said that he was bound to agree with Stalin's final sentence. It was correct that the British and American governments had reached the joint conclusion that there could be no second front, as Stalin defined it, in 1942. Harriman stressed that President Roosevelt was in agreement with the carefully considered Allied decision. The President, he added, was determined to use all available resources as early as possible in the most effective way for the United Nations, including the Soviet Union, and was ready for any sacrifice that promised a reasonable prospect of success.

If Harriman was talking about Torch, Stalin responded, that operation did not directly concern the Soviet Union. It was, from the military point of view, doubtless a correct operation but a matter of secondary importance compared with the Russian front. Churchill protested that Torch was a better operation than Sledgehammer. A premature landing in the West could only hurt the Allied cause and do great injury to next year's prospects for a full-scale invasion of the Continent. Stalin at last agreed that every blow against the Axis gave some relief. But he registered a fresh complaint: the Western Allies were falling behind on their promised deliveries of war supplies. Churchill explained the difficulty about the Arctic convoys, promising that they would be resumed in September. Stalin, however, dismissed the idea that enemy action had anything to do with the reduced deliveries. Britain and the United States, he charged, underrated the importance of the Russian front and gave him only leftovers. Brushing aside the explanations of Churchill and Harriman, Stalin called for greater sacrifices by the Western powers. The Russians, he said, were sacrificing 10,000 men a day and yet the Russian people did not complain. The problem, Stalin insisted, was not a lack of trust on the part of the Russians, but Britain's reluctance to fight, as the Russians were fighting, on the ground. Recalling Stalin's tactics a year earlier, Harriman slipped Churchill a note, recalling that Stalin had been equally rough with Beaverbrook and himself on the second night. The show of hostility, he cautioned, should not be taken too seriously. Churchill cabled to Attlee and the War Cabinet:

. . . he said a great many disagreeable things, especially about our being too much afraid of fighting the Germans; that if we tried it like the Russians we should find it not so bad; that we had broken our promises about "Sledgehammer"; that we had failed in delivering the supplies promised to Russia and only sent remnants after we had taken all we needed for ourselves. Apparently these complaints were addressed as much to the United States as to Britain.

I repulsed all his contentions squarely, but without taunts of any kind. I suppose he is not used to being contradicted repeatedly but he did not become at all angry, or even animated. . . .

On one occasion I said: "I pardon that remark only on account of the bravery of the Russian troops."[4]

Churchill appealed for the ring of comradeship in the Kremlin discussions. He knew what the Russians were going through—Britain had fought alone for a year. He had traveled a long way in the hope of receiving the hand of friendship. The democracies would show very soon by their deeds that they were neither sluggish nor cowardly. They were just as ready as the Russians to shed blood; he and Roosevelt would not hesitate to sacrifice 150,000 men on the shore of France if by that action they could be of real help to the Soviet Union. But no one would profit from such a foolish enterprise. It grieved him that the Russians did not think the Western Allies were doing their utmost in the common cause.

"It was one of the most brilliant statements I ever heard from Churchill," Harriman recalled. "Unfortunately, it was not recorded. It was a magnificent performance, all the more convincing because Churchill did not once reproach Stalin for his infamous treaty with Hitler.

"The Prime Minister never felt comfortable with interpreters. He would forget to stop for his words to be translated. This time he swept along until he noticed that his poor interpreter, Dunlop, had put down his pencil. Dunlop evidently found it impossible to keep pace with the Prime Minister. Churchill then pressed him to translate. Dunlop tried to recapture what the Prime Minister had said. But he stumbled over his notes. It was a difficult task at the best of times to find appropriate Russian words for Churchillian English. Churchill, who wanted to make certain that Stalin did not miss a single point, kept at him. 'Did you tell him this?' the Prime Minister demanded, punching Dunlop's arm. 'Did you tell him that?' "

Stalin at last intervened, smiling broadly. "Your words are of no importance," he said to Churchill. "What is important is your spirit."

With that remark the tension eased. Stalin had pressed Churchill to the edge of endurance. Now he appeared to recognize that nothing more could be accomplished by insulting accusations. At last he accepted the truth: there would be no Second Front in 1942. It was clear to Harriman that Stalin wanted the visit to end on a happier note. He then invited Churchill and Harriman to dine with him the next evening, August 14. The Prime Minister thanked him, adding that he proposed to leave Moscow at dawn on the fifteenth. At this point Stalin showed a trace of concern. Why leave so soon? he asked. Churchill agreed to stay an extra day if some good would come of it, and the talk turned to other matters.

Stalin then described a new Soviet weapon, a rocket-firing trench mortar which, he said, was devastating in its effect. He offered to stage a demonstration for the military experts in Churchill's party, and to turn over all the required information. What new weapons could the British offer in exchange? Churchill responded that Britain would give him everything, without bargaining, except for certain types of airborne radar equipment which, if they fell into enemy hands, would make the task of bombing Germany more difficult. Stalin agreed to have his military advisers meet the British generals, headed by General Brooke, to examine more fully the technical aspects of future operations, including Torch. Stalin still grumbled about the scrapping of Sledgehammer. When he said again that the Western Allies had not kept their promise, Churchill (now taking the offensive), responded, "I repudiate that statement. Every promise has been kept." He pointed to the memorandum he had given Molotov in London. Stalin made a kind of apology, saying there was no mistrust between the Allies, only a difference of view.

The Prime Minister raised the question of defending the Caucasus. This was a matter of prime concern to the British General Staff, which could not rid itself of the fear that the Germans might break through the mountain wall, drive to the oil fields of Iran and invade India. There had been anxious talk in London for months past that the Japanese, now in control of Burma, might join hands with the Germans in India. Such a scheme, as the Allies learned after the war, had actually been proposed to the Japanese by Joachim von Ribbentrop, Hitler's Foreign Minister. Stalin sent for a relief model of the Caucasus and carefully pointed out the passes to be defended. All were fortified, he said, and twenty-five Soviet divisions were available to stop the Germans north of the main mountain range. In two months, Stalin added, snow would block the passes. He also planned a great counteroffensive.

Stalin's lingering resentment flared briefly when Harriman raised once again, as he had the year before, the long-stalled plan to ferry American Lend-Lease planes into the Soviet Union by way of Alaska and Siberia. The Russians, after many months of delay, had agreed in June that such a ferry route should be opened, and Major General Follett Bradley of the Army Air Forces was then in Moscow trying to make the final arrangements. Stalin dismissed the whole matter curtly. "Wars are not won with plans," he grumbled.[5]

After leaving the Kremlin at midnight, Churchill, in a deeply depressed mood, kept Harriman up until three-thirty in the morning, analyzing Stalin's behavior. Their guess was that Stalin's fellow commissars in the Politburo possessed more power than the West commonly supposed. Perhaps Stalin had presented his *aide-mémoire* for their benefit. He would be able to show the Politburo that he had tried as hard as any man could to persuade the emissaries from the West that a Second Front must be opened in 1942—and that they had rebuffed him. "That night and all the next day," Harriman noted, "the P.M. was sunk. I kept telling him I was positive that things would be quite cordial when he got together with Stalin again, but he wouldn't believe it."

To Roosevelt, Harriman cabled a reassuring message:

> The technique used by Stalin last night resembled closely that used with Beaverbrook and myself in our second meeting last year. I cannot believe there is cause for concern and I confidently expect a clear-cut understanding before the Prime Minister leaves.

Just to keep the American record straight, Harriman also sent Stalin on August 14 a formal reply to his memorandum of the night before, reaffirming Churchill's statement that "no promise has been broken regarding the second front."

Whatever the reason, Harriman's prediction that the final talks would go better was quickly confirmed. In Harriman's view, the harshness of Stalin's hot-and-cold tactics could only be understood in relation to the plight of the Red Army at that moment of grave crisis. The Germans were advancing toward Stalingrad, and by all accounts, the battle was going badly for the defenders. Leningrad was still under German blockade after 350 days. Stalin could hardly be blamed for pressing the Western Allies to take action, any action, that would force the Germans to slacken their attack by drawing off some divisions to the west. "They were really desperate," Harriman recalled. "Stalin's roughness was an expression of their need for help. It was his way of trying to put all the heat he possibly could on Churchill. So he pressed as hard as he could until he realized that no amount of additional pressure would produce a second front in 1942. He had the wisdom to know that he could not let Churchill go back to London feeling there had been a breakdown."

Stalin's dinner for Churchill and Harriman, on the evening of August 14, seemed less gay and far more abstemious than the party for Harriman and Beaverbrook the previous year. Stalin ate a little cheese and a single potato, explaining to Harriman that he had dined earlier, and sipped his wine from a small vodka glass for the toasts. The mood was sober, hardly an occasion for great festivity. Members of the Soviet Defense Committee and a group of high officers from the General Staff were in attendance as Stalin toasted various commanders in turn. "He would walk down the table to see who was present," Harriman recorded in his notes. "Then he would come back [to his place at the head of the table], make his toast and walk towards the man and clink glasses. The only foreigner he toasted himself was the President of the United States. All the others Molotov toasted." Stalin appeared "entirely oblivious of the unpleasant discussions of the night before," Harriman reported to Roosevelt.

Between toasts, Harriman told Stalin that President Roosevelt hoped to meet him before long. Stalin responded that he shared the hope. "It is of great importance," he said. Harriman asked when he might be ready to meet the President and where. "In the winter I am not so preoccupied," Stalin replied. "Perhaps in the Far East, perhaps in Western Europe." Harriman explained that the President did not like to fly and that he probably would not wish to leave the United States until after the midterm congressional elections in November. "Perhaps Iceland," Stalin suggested, "in December." Iceland might be possible for the President, Harriman said, but for Stalin that would mean a long, possibly dangerous flight. The flight did not worry him, Stalin replied—he had good airplanes. When Harriman remarked that Americans did not want him to run too-great risks, out of concern for his *well-being*, his words apparently were mistranslated as "*good health*." Stalin responded, "My health is excellent. It is the President's health that should concern us."

Turning to the Far East, Harriman said that Roosevelt wanted to keep the Japanese so busy in the Pacific that they would not be tempted to invade Siberia. Stalin agreed that would be most helpful.

> I asked what else in the Pacific might be helpful. He answered, More airplanes. I asked where. He said in the Japanese Ocean. I explained that was impossible unless he opened up Siberia [for American bomber bases]. He stated positively: "Oh, no, go from Alaska." I explained that it was too far and he again said Alaska was close enough to bomb Japan with the B-24.
>
> I thought there was no need to argue and said, "It will be a great day when Soviet and U.S. planes go together and bomb

Japan." He showed enthusiasm and drank a toast to the bombing of Japan.[6]

Both Harriman and Churchill talked with Stalin about the possibility of sending Allied air squadrons to help in the defense of the Caucasus. Churchill had suggested sending twenty British squadrons after Rommel had been defeated in North Africa, or as many as forty with American participation. That would be a great help, Stalin acknowledged. Harriman then inquired whether Stalin would rather have just the planes or whole Allied squadrons. It made no difference, Stalin replied. He would accept either. Speaking to Harriman, out of Churchill's hearing, Stalin then renewed his complaints about the British:

> Stalin told me the British Navy had lost its initiative. There was no good reason to stop the convoys. The British Armies didn't fight either—Singapore, etc. The U.S. Navy fought with more courage and so did the Army at Bataan.
>
> The British Air Force was good, he admitted. He showed little respect for the British military effort but much hope in that of the U.S.[7]

During dinner, Stalin told a long story about a prewar visit to Moscow by Lady Astor and George Bernard Shaw in which Lady Astor had proposed that Stalin should invite David Lloyd George to visit the Soviet Union. Stalin had demurred, recalling that Lloyd George had been Prime Minister during the period of Western intervention against the Bolsheviks. "It was Churchill who misled him," Lady Astor said. Stalin replied that he preferred an outright enemy like Churchill to a pretended friend like Lloyd George. "Well, Churchill is finished," Lady Astor had said. Stalin disagreed. "If a great crisis comes," he recalled saying, "the English people might turn to the old war horse." At this point Churchill admitted that there was much truth in what Lady Astor had said about him. "You know, I was not friendly to you after the last war," he acknowledged. "Have you forgiven me?" Stalin replied, "All that is in the past. It is not for me to forgive. It is for God to forgive."

Churchill left the Kremlin at one-thirty in the morning, fearing that if he stayed much longer he would have to sit through a long propaganda film as well. Stalin walked Churchill to the door, explaining to Harriman that it was a courtesy he owed to a man four years older than himself. When Harriman in turn got up to leave a few minutes later, Stalin urged him to stay longer. But he went home to bed, pleading exhaustion and a stiff neck.

Some good had come of the visit, Harriman felt. Stalin had accepted Torch, together with the hard truth that he could expect no immediate diversion in Western Europe. In spite of his grumbling about Churchill's reluctance to fight the Germans on the ground, Stalin also appeared to have developed a certain admiration for the Prime Minister. "If Churchill had not possessed the courage to go to Moscow and the bluntness to explain to Stalin why the cross-Channel operation was impossible, I think it would have led to a very serious misunderstanding," Harriman reflected. "Stalin came to appreciate Churchill's qualities—in spite of his rough talk the second day—and showed he was anxious to continue the collaboration, not only in the war but after the war as well."

Their personal relationship was firmly cemented on August 15, Churchill's last evening in Moscow, when he called on Stalin alone to say goodbye. Stalin kept him talking all evening, in fact for seven hours. The Prime Minister acknowledged that some of the things he had said must have been painful to Stalin but he believed in plain speaking. He had traveled to Moscow "with the earnest wish for a personal understanding" and he hoped that Stalin shared his own feeling that progress had been made. Stalin responded that the visit had been of the utmost importance. "We have got to know each other," he said, "and we have understood one another. Obviously there are differences between us but differences are in the nature of things. The fact that the meeting has taken place, that personal contact has been established, means that the ground has been prepared for future agreement."

The talk flowed easily after that. Stalin led the way to his private apartment, a privilege extended to few visitors, and there introduced his daughter Svetlana to Churchill. Dinner was served by an elderly housekeeper after Molotov joined the party, and they sat up talking together until two-thirty. This time there were few reproaches. Stalin allowed that the North African landing would have a great indirect effect on the Russian front. If the operation succeeded, he asked, did the Allies then propose to occupy the South of France? Of course, Churchill replied, both France and Italy. Stalin volunteered a report that the Germans had broken through into the northern Caucasus in the south and toward Stalingrad and Voronezh in the east; but they had fallen short of their objectives and the Red Army would soon launch a great counteroffensive in two directions to cut them off. They also discussed the possibility of a Stalin-Roosevelt meeting, already raised by Harriman. Churchill said that he hoped to be present. Stalin agreed that a meeting must take place and that all three ought to be there. "We have no antagonistic interests," Churchill said. Stalin agreed.

From Churchill's vivid account to Harriman and the notes of the

new British interpreter, Major A. H. Birse, who had replaced the unfortunate Dunlop, it is clear that the meeting was extraordinarily cordial throughout. Stalin asked for more trucks from the West, even at
the cost of giving up tanks. The Red Army, he explained, was rapidly
motorizing its infantry divisions and it needed 20,000 to 25,000 trucks
a month. Churchill said the problem was not a shortage of trucks but
the difficulty of delivering them safely to Russia. Stalin again wondered if the Royal Navy could not have kept the convoys sailing
through the summer. "Has the British Navy no sense of glory?" he
asked. Churchill defended the suspension, insisting that he really knew
quite a lot about navies and the war at sea. "Meaning," said Stalin,
"that I know nothing." Churchill replied, "Russia is a land animal;
the British are sea animals." There was no sting in the words this time.

Both agreed it might make matters easier if the British and the
Russians were to join forces and capture the German bases in northern
Norway as well as Petsamo, in Finland. Churchill had long favored
such an operation, but as Stalin reminded him, the General Staffs had
once before disapproved the idea. Churchill warmed quickly to the
subject. Britain, he said, was ready to provide two specially trained
divisions. Stalin offered three. Churchill, seemingly on the spur of the
moment, supplied a code name (Jupiter) and said he would be in touch
with Stalin by telegram.

Before the long evening's talk was concluded, Churchill had invited Stalin to visit England if he was going all the way to Iceland to
meet Roosevelt. Stalin recalled that he had been to England in 1907
for a Socialist conference together with Lenin, Plekhanov, Gorki and
others. What about Trotsky? Churchill asked. Stalin replied that Trotsky had been there too but that he had left the conference a disappointed man because he represented nobody.

Churchill then recalled that in 1938, before Munich, he had drawn
up a plan for a League of the Three Great Democracies, as he tactfully
described them for Stalin's benefit: Great Britain, the United States
and the Soviet Union. Between them they could have stopped the fatal
drift to war, as there were no antagonistic interests to divide them.
Stalin said he always had hoped for some development of that nature
but it had proven impossible with Neville Chamberlain in Downing
Street. He cited the failure of the British-French-Russian talks in 1939,
saying it had been his impression that the Western powers wanted only
to warn Hitler and later come to terms with him. Churchill told Harriman the next morning that he could not help but agree that the British
and French delegations had no weight behind them. The Prime Minister reminded Stalin that he himself had been out of the government for
eleven years and that his warnings had gone unheeded.

Stalin acknowledged that for him the stresses of the war had not been so great as the strain of collectivizing Russian agriculture by brute force, once persuasion had failed. "It was fearful," he said. "Four years it lasted. It was absolutely necessary for Russia, if we were to avoid periodic famines . . ."[8]

Churchill, greatly pleased and relieved over his new intimacy with Stalin, joined Harriman at the airport before dawn. A bleary-eyed Molotov was there to see them off, together with a military band and guard of honor. The aircraft took off at five-twenty for Teheran en route to Cairo, its exhausted passengers feeling that the Moscow visit, which could so easily have turned into a disaster for the alliance, had raised the wartime relationship with Russia to a new plane of understanding and partnership. "The P.M.," Harriman noted, "has been all for Uncle Joe ever since."

Yet, for all the free discussion at the summit of Soviet power, Harriman could see that at lower elevations not much had changed. For example, he had tried almost daily since reaching Moscow to arrange a meeting with the senior Soviet general in command of the armored forces. He wanted a report for General Somervell on how the light and medium American tanks turned over to the Red Army were performing in battle. This was scarcely a matter of idle curiosity. The information was of vital importance, Harriman felt, because the Russians alone at this point in the war had experience fighting in American tanks whereas the U.S. Army had none. The Russians had taken their time over Harriman's request. Nothing was done until he mentioned the matter to Stalin upon leaving the Kremlin dinner the night before. At ten o'clock on his last evening in Moscow, the Russians did produce a General Lebidov, technical assistant to the senior tank general. Harriman took with him, to meet Lebidov, three American officers—General Maxwell, General Spalding and Faymonville, who was handling Lend-Lease matters in the U.S. Moscow embassy. Lebidov's comments on the shortcomings of the American equipment and his suggestions for correcting them impressed the visitors. He complained, for example, of fire hazards, urging the use of diesel instead of gasoline engines, fireproof paint and less rubber padding on the interior. The silhouette of the M-3 medium tank, Lebidov added, was too high, and its 75-mm. gun would be far more effective if it was mounted in a traversable turret. This modification was later built into the Sherman tank. The Russians, moreover, who liked to transport infantrymen on top of their tanks, found this difficult to do with the M-3. Its contours were too rounded, Lebidov said; also, its rubber tracks did not stand up as well as the metal tracks commonly used by the Red Army, especially in ice and snow. All this information was reported back to Washington, and certain of the Soviet observations were incorporated in later-model American tanks.

Before leaving Moscow, Harriman called on the Foreign Trade Commissar, Anastas Mikoyan, to discuss the flow of Lend-Lease supplies. Mikoyan, like Stalin, asked for more trucks, but unlike Stalin, showed no disposition to reduce tank deliveries in exchange. As for delivering the material, he said the Russians still preferred to have military supplies and raw materials shipped to Murmansk and Archangel. They would take what they could get through the Persian Gulf, Mikoyan said, but it was clear that he had no great faith in that avenue.

Harriman was convinced, however, that the time had come for the United States to take over the Persian railroad and thus increase the daily flow of supplies to Russia. The North Russian convoy route was simply too dangerous to rely upon. Accordingly, while Churchill flew on to Cairo on August 17, Harriman stayed behind in Teheran to survey the railroad more closely and see the young Shah.* In his notes, Harriman recorded his impressions:

> Inspected shops in a.m. and called on Shah in p.m. at his summer palace in foothills. He dressed in uniform of army—sickly yellow, talked for 2 hours. He much impressed with Churchill and says, "I have nothing to fear from Britain postwar. Churchill convinced me." Russia may be difficult. Wants U.S. to make sure Russian internal government is not aggressive! Wants to make friends with President (Churchill told him to). "How can I do it?" I said I would give message informally—but formal communication must go through Minister Dreyfus.†
>
> He wants Iran to fight, not humiliated as now. "Why can't we be allowed to defend ourselves as men should?" It would raise morale of his people. He doesn't like either British or Russians . . . Twenty-two years old, talks French fluently, understands English, loves skiing, educated in Switzerland. Wants U.S. interest postwar and treaty now—to agree to fight with United Nations, but he does not have power.

For the first time in his life, Harriman inspected a railroad from the air. He checked the grades and curves, the repair shops ("the worst mess I have ever seen") and the roundhouses, the barges and lighters used to unload oceangoing ships—all matters in which his ex-

---

* In 1941, when British and Russian troops occupied Iran, the pro-German Shah had to go into exile. He was succeeded by his son Mohammad Reza Pahlavi, Iran's present-day monarch.

† Louis G. Dreyfus, Jr., the American minister in Teheran, was Harriman's host in Iran.

perience of railroading until 1940 helped him to decide how the job could be better done.

On August 19 he flew on to Basra, Baghdad and Cairo. The following day Harriman put his proposal to Churchill, who was still noncommittal about the United States taking over the railroad. His military advisers, General Brooke chief among them, worried about giving up control in a theater of predominantly British responsibility.

Having heard Churchill say, "Anything worthwhile can be put on one side of a page," Harriman prepared a single-page memorandum overnight. It ran to seven brief paragraphs. Everyone agreed, he argued, that the capacity of the railroad should be increased to 6,000 tons, for the benefit of the British forces in Iran as well as the Russians. This would call for additional manpower and railroad equipment, which the United States could supply. Harriman therefore advised Churchill to cable Roosevelt in Washington, requesting an American takeover. Churchill read the memorandum quickly. "This seems like a good arrangement to me," he said. General Brooke raised his final objection that the British in Iran would then find themselves wholly dependent on the United States for supplies. The Prime Minister, having resolved his own doubts, responded, "In whose hands could we be better dependent?" That settled the matter.

When Harriman returned to Washington a week later, he submitted his detailed proposals to Generals Marshall and Somervell, who promptly recommended to Roosevelt that the United States take over the Persian Gulf supply route—the ports of Khorramshah and Bandarsharpur as well as the Trans-Iranian Railroad and, "second in importance," provide the men and trucks needed to increase the tonnage that could be carried north by road.

During his two weeks at home, Harriman met several times with W. M. Jeffers, president of the Union Pacific, to work out arrangements by which several American railroads and locomotive builders agreed to supply enough locomotives to begin diesel service promptly on the Persian railroad. Diesels were bound to be more efficient than coal-fired locomotives in the extreme heat of the desert and the excessively long tunnels through the mountains. They also made fewer demands on scarce water along the right of way. The President approved the plan in early October and Major General Donald H. Connolly, an engineer picked by Marshall, was put in charge of the Persian Gulf Service Command, under orders to get the job of expanding the tonnage accomplished in the shortest possible time. Railroad men were recruited from several American roads. More diesel locomotives were requisitioned. And by May 1943 the volume of supplies for Russia moving through Iran had increased two and a half times.

It was a signal achievement, as even the skeptical Russians came to acknowledge in time, all the more so as the North African invasion had been launched by the time General Connolly took over and shipping became extremely short. In 1944 Mikoyan gratefully confessed that his skepticism had been unwarranted. "It has been a great help to the front," he said to Harriman. "When the Americans undertake anything, it is done."

During his visit to Iran, Harriman had toured the Abadan refinery, then the largest producer of high-octane gasoline in the world. He was shocked to discover that this absolutely vital installation was guarded by no more than a half-dozen antiquated biplanes and a few obsolete anti-aircraft guns. "The Germans were driving toward the Caucasus, no more than eight hundred miles away," Harriman recalled. "As they approached within bombing range, I could foresee a disaster. When I reached Gander on the way home, I found a squadron of our most modern fighter aircraft had been stationed there, together with more anti-aircraft guns than I had seen anywhere in the United Kingdom during the Blitz. When I asked the purpose of all these elaborate defenses I was told there had been a report that Gander might come under attack by small aircraft launched from German submarines. It seemed to me a fantastic conception. But when I raised the matter with Lovett and General Arnold in Washington I could not jar them out of the defensive attitude that since Pearl Harbor had imbued American attitudes."

Harriman's experience of London and Moscow at war had left him ill prepared for the sight of buckets filled with sand and two pairs of asbestos gloves in the New York town house of his brother Roland, asbestos and steel for buckets being in short supply. On a visit to his own country house at Arden, the highest point south of the Catskill Mountains about forty miles from New York, he was astonished to find that the tower had been commandeered for the air defense of New York. Twenty-four hours a day, seven days a week, the Harriman neighbors took turns standing watch against the approach of German bombers. He pointed out that the British, who were a lot closer to the fighting, had learned to abandon air defense as soon as the tide of war removed a particular area from the threat of German attack. Not, however, in Orange County, New York.

"I found it impossible, without giving offense, to point out what seemed to me the utter absurdity of all these needless preparations," Harriman recalled. "Even close friends seemed to regard me as unduly pro-British in my attitudes. But I could not help feeling that our domestic priorities ought to be redirected."

CHAPTER VIII

"I Prefer a Comfortable Oasis to the Raft at Tilsit"

W HEN HARRIMAN REACHED WASHINGTON on August 29, the news from the Russian front was grim. Hitler's Sixth Army had broken through at the Don River and advanced to the steep west bank of the Volga, fighting its way across the northern suburbs of Stalingrad. The Germans had cut all access to the city from the east bank, except by barge or ferryboat. They were devastating Stalingrad, block by block, with ceaseless air attacks and concentrated artillery fire. A second panzer army had wheeled southwest into the foothills of the Caucasus, reaching for the oil fields along the Caspian coast which Hitler had so long coveted. As soon as Harriman arrived at the White House his old friend Robert E. Sherwood, the playwright who was directing the overseas branch of the Office of War Information, told him that Army intelligence had all but written off Stalingrad. "Averell gave a lucid analysis of the situation," Sherwood later recalled, "and then firmly predicted that Stalingrad would not fall, and that the battle could conceivably end in a major military disaster for the Germans."[1] Harriman's hopeful estimate was based on the information he had received from Stalin about a great Soviet counteroffensive that was about to be launched from two directions to cut off the Germans.

At a meeting on August 31 in the office of the Lend-Lease Administrator, Edward R. Stettinius, Harriman reported that he had found Stalin and everyone else he saw in Moscow "exactly as determined as ever." He added, "They are going to put up a hell of a fight for Stalingrad, as already shown. They won't give any guarantee about it, but have not given it up . . . Unquestionably the Germans were stronger than the Russians anticipated, and one of the surprises was the number of Hungarian, Rumanian and Central European troops— and the way they fought. The Germans seem to have been able to make even the Italians fight. This was different from last year." He urged Stettinius and his staff to redouble their efforts and make certain that the Russians got the trucks and raw materials they needed—aluminum, nickel and rubber at the top of the priority list.

"If you can get them 10,000 trucks a month," he said to Stettinius, "it will have a very material effect on the fighting power of the Russians this winter and next year. There is no question there will be a Russian front. The question is how effective it will be, and the whole course of the war depends on that. The thing that strikes me as fantastic is the unwillingness of the military here and in the U.K. to recognize this. I will say that to any of them direct, but do not wish to be quoted on it."

Remarking on the lengths to which the British government had gone in fulfilling its commitments to Russia, Harriman told Stettinius how the Russians in May had asked for spare parts to keep their Hurricane fighters flying. Although the British had none to offer at the time, the War Cabinet had ordered three or four Hurricanes dismantled and the parts shipped to Russia. "I can't quite see General Arnold [chief of the Army Air Forces] agreeing to ground some of his airplanes in a war theater to get the Russians some spare parts," Harriman said.

The President was at Shangri La (now Camp David) when Harriman landed in Washington. He drove up to the new presidential retreat in the Catoctin Mountains of Maryland with Sherwood and Judge Samuel Rosenman, who were helping Roosevelt to write his Labor Day speech. The President listened closely to Harriman's account of the latest talks with Stalin. He appeared to enjoy hearing all about Churchill's discomfiture in those long, reproach-filled sessions at the Kremlin. Harriman told how the Prime Minister, although he had left Moscow with his profound distaste for the Soviet system intact, was still absolutely determined to help the Russians. His point of view seemed to Harriman utterly realistic: Stalin would go on getting British support because he was the most powerful enemy of Britain's enemy. Churchill did not fully share Roosevelt's hopes that the wartime partnership could be extended into long-term understandings with the Soviet Union. The President, at least on public occasions, had been careful not to encourage the popular wartime belief that with the passage of time the American and Soviet systems increasingly would come to resemble one another. In private conversations, however, with such close associates as Harriman and Sumner Welles, Roosevelt sometimes talked of his hopes for a gradual blurring of differences between the two systems, the process that latter-day scholars have called convergence.

"Roosevelt's attitude," Harriman recalled, "was more an instinctive approach than a matter of fixed policy. Being a religious man himself, he felt that the atheist Communist system would not be able to suppress permanently the deeply religious tradition of the Russian people. In time, he felt, greater freedom was bound to evolve in the Soviet system.

"From the economic standpoint, he was in a sense a forerunner of the present-day convergence school. His New Deal revolution had expanded American ideas about the government's social responsibility; he confidently believed this trend would continue after his own time. In the Soviet Union, he saw the completely centralized state bureaucracy giving way to a degree of decentralization.

"In the international field, he looked upon Stalin's policy as combining an ideological drive to promote world Communism with more traditional aspects of Russian imperialism. I believe he felt that the revolutionary fervor would gradually recede after the war and that the self-interest of the Russian people increasingly would become the guide to Soviet policy.

"Above all, he believed that the intimacies the war had forced upon us could, and should, be used to establish the basis for postwar collaboration. He recognized that the appalling devastation of vast areas of Russia would call for an enormous effort at reconstruction—and he was disposed to offer generous American help. He had seen Russia rebuffed and isolated by the Western powers before the war, in the League of Nations and outside it. Roosevelt felt that must not be allowed to happen again. He was determined, by establishing a close personal relationship with Stalin in wartime, to build confidence among the Kremlin leaders that Russia, now an acknowledged major power, could trust the West.

"For my part, although I did not disagree with his basic approach, I was far less optimistic in terms of the time it would take. I also believed that it would be far more difficult than Roosevelt imagined to develop a real basis of mutual confidence with Stalin. However, I fully agreed with Roosevelt's basic objective of using the wartime relationship to attempt to develop postwar agreements.

"Churchill had a more pragmatic attitude. He, too, would have liked to build on the wartime intimacy to achieve postwar understandings. But his mind concentrated on the settlement of specific political problems and spheres of influence. He despised Communism and all its works. He turned pessimistic about the future earlier than Roosevelt. And he foresaw much greater difficulties at the end of the war."

Aid for Russia was Harriman's chief concern in Washington that September, whether by expanding the freight-carrying capacity of the Persian ports and railroad or by applying pressure to speed the shipments of aluminum, nickel, trucks, tanks, medical supplies and food. On the invitation of his old friend Allen Wardwell, he addressed a New York dinner on September 8, launching the Russian War Relief drive. "Every day," he said, "the Russian armies are destroying some of the strength of our enemies. Therefore battles on the Russian front have a direct bearing on the sacrifices we will have to make and on the length of the war itself." He described the wholesale transfer of Russian munitions factories from the path of the invading Germans to new locations behind the Ural Mountains. Harriman had seen the start of this evacuation a year earlier and it was now an accomplished fact. He told of factories in which each piece of machinery was tagged and numbered, fastened to the concrete floor by bolts and ready to be moved at a moment's notice. Key workers moved east with their machines, traveling in the same boxcar, ready to set up in safe new locations as soon as the long, hard journey was done. "In Russia," he said, "it is truly total war."

At Shangri La, Harriman had found Roosevelt preoccupied with the plans for Torch and not a little touchy about the possibility that Churchill might upset the arrangements. A sharp difference had developed between the British and American military staffs. The Americans wanted to land at Casablanca and not move deeper into the Mediterranean than Oran until the operation was secure. The British, worried about the surf on the Atlantic side, preferred to cancel the Casablanca landing and put British troops ashore at Algiers as well, deeper inside the Mediterranean. Churchill had cabled Roosevelt on August 27:

> An operation limited to Oran and Casablanca would not give the impression of strength and of widespread simultaneous attack on which we rely for the favourable effect on the French in North Africa. We are all convinced that Algiers is the key to the whole operation.[2]

Roosevelt, in his reply dated August 30, left Churchill in no doubt that he wanted a free American hand; the British were welcome to land at Algiers a week after the Americans had grounded their landing craft on the Atlantic, near Casablanca, and at Oran.

> I would even go so far as to say I am reasonably sure a simultaneous landing by British and Americans would result in full resistance by all French in Africa, whereas an initial American landing without British ground forces offers a real chance that there would be no French resistance, or only a

token resistance. I need a week, if possible, after we land to
consolidate the position for both of us . . .[3]

The President was so greatly concerned over the British attitude
that he instructed Harriman to see the Prime Minister as soon as he
returned to London and to make two things plain: Torch was to be
essentially an American operation and he wanted no last-minute
change of plan promoted by the British.

With all due deference, Harriman upon his return delivered the
message to Churchill, who accepted it, though with some reluctance.
"I am the President's loyal lieutenant," he conceded. Harriman cabled
Roosevelt on September 14 that the Prime Minister "understands fully
that he is to play second fiddle in all scores and then only as you
direct." The Prime Minister, nevertheless, managed to have his way,
in part through direct suggestions to Roosevelt and through his weekly
luncheon conversations in London with General Eisenhower, the
newly appointed Allied commander of Torch. British troops, as a result,
joined in the landing operation at Algiers on November 8, the same
day that the Americans went ashore at Oran and Casablanca.

The date had been fixed by Eisenhower, at some risk to the Democratic party. November 3 was Election Day and Roosevelt's prospects
of getting a cooperative Congress would have been a good deal
brighter if a successful North African invasion could have taken place
at the end of October, as originally planned. But when Roosevelt heard
that the military planners wanted eight more days to get the men and
matériel in place, he approved the postponement without a moment's
hesitation. It was, he said, a decision for the responsible commander,
not the Democratic National Committee.

As Churchill had suspected, the French forces drew no nice dis-
tinctions between the two "Anglo-Saxon" forces. They resisted both
when ordered to fight by commanders loyal to Pétain. Roosevelt's
belief that the French in North Africa would abandon Vichy upon
catching sight of the American flag turned out to be a romantic
illusion. The advance work of a team of American secret agents,
headed by Robert D. Murphy, had cultivated small pockets of support
among Frenchmen and Arabs. But the French officials in North Africa
were a mixed bag—royalists and republicans, Vichyites and Gaullists,
many of them bitterly anti-British. To pull them together proved an
impossible task.

Other official American calculations fell as wide of the mark.
Spain, happily, did not intervene. But Roosevelt's decision to place
the French forces in North Africa under the command of General
Henri Honoré Giraud, who had been smuggled out of France in a

submarine by Murphy's people, turned out to be a serious miscalculation. Giraud, a traditional soldier of France not blessed with political acumen or leadership talents, was soon revealed as the wrong man for the job. Harriman, who came to know Giraud in the months that followed, marked him down as "a damn fool" politically. "I have always thought it was tragic that the British should have picked De Gaulle and even more tragic that we picked Giraud," he recalled. "Of all the available Frenchmen, those two were bound to be the most troublesome."

When Eisenhower, in hopes of ending local resistance, made a deal with Pétain's former Vice Premier, Admiral Jean François Darlan, a great storm of criticism blew up in the United States and Britain. Liberal opinion in both countries looked upon the Darlan deal, for which Eisenhower took full responsibility, as the unseemly triumph of expediency over principle. Stalin, however, was not troubled by such liberal qualms. On December 13 he wrote to Roosevelt:

> In view of widespread rumors of all sorts with respect to the attitude of the U.S.S.R. to the question of making use of Darlan and figures like him, it might be useful to inform you that in my opinion and in the opinion of my colleagues the policy of Eisenhower with respect to Darlan, Boisson,* Giraud and others is absolutely correct. I consider it a great accomplishment that you succeeded in bringing Darlan and others into the orbit of the Allies against Hitler.[4]

Harriman had "very little patience" for the anguished liberals. "For once, I agreed fully with Uncle Joe," he later observed.

Although the details of great military actions are not the subject of this book, it becomes necessary to sketch briefly those events in the closing months of 1942 which were perceived by Churchill as marking "perhaps, the end of the beginning," and by Roosevelt as "the turning point in this war."

On the vast Russian front, where the largest battles were fought, the Germans (in spite of their massive air superiority, which made possible 3,000 sorties a day against Stalingrad compared with some 300 Russian sorties) fell short of victory. They found the Russians absolutely determined to fight for every house, cellar and heap of rubble. In the words of a German general, Stalingrad was the place in which "a meter now replaced a kilometer" as the measure of distance. Even

---

* Pierre Boisson, Governor General of French West Africa under the Vichy regime, brought over that territory, including the big base at Dakar, to the Allies on November 24, 1942.

as their defense perimeter kept steadily shrinking, the Russians fiercely defended every inch of ground. By the time General Friedrich Paulus ordered his Sixth Army into the final assault on the last Russian pockets of resistance on November 11, the Wehrmacht was dangerously extended and the great Soviet counterblow, which Stalin had promised Churchill and Harriman in August, was ready. Within a week the Paulus offensive had run out of steam. At that moment Marshal Georgi K. Zhukov launched his thunderous counteroffensive from the north and south of the ruined city. Four days later Paulus and 250,000 of his men found themselves encircled in the ruins of Stalingrad and forbidden to surrender by the orders of their Führer. For them the war was soon to be over.

In the Western Desert, General Montgomery's Eighth Army pushed off from El Alamein on the night of October 23, heavily reinforced since the disaster at Tobruk with two new divisions from Britain. Montgomery had more than a thousand tanks, nearly half of them Grant and Sherman tanks from the United States. The divided command problems that Harriman had seen for himself in 1941 had finally been overcome. General Alexander was the unquestioned commander in chief. General Montgomery, Air Marshal Tedder and Admiral Cunningham all worked together under Alexander's direction. On November 4 Montgomery broke the enemy's front and drove Rommel into full retreat. By Christmas the Eighth Army had advanced 1,200 miles across Libya and Cyrenaica into Tripolitania, taking tens of thousands of prisoners and destroying much of Rommel's armor as it rolled westward.

In French North Africa, as well, the Allies had achieved military success after some hard fighting, thanks in part to Darlan's decision to order the French troops at last to lay down their arms. With French Morocco and Algeria secure, the Allied forces now pushed into Tunisia, in the hope of swiftly clearing the entire North African coast. But Admiral Jean-Pierre Esteva, the French Resident-General in Tunisia, chose to obey Pétain, not Darlan.* The Germans, meanwhile, flew some 40,000 reinforcements across the Mediterranean and managed to stall the Allied advance.

Even in the far Pacific, the Americans had taken the offensive. The Marines landed in the Solomon Islands, and a month later, started pushing back the Japanese on New Guinea. On the night of November 12 the U.S. Navy engaged the Japanese in the naval battle of

---

* On Christmas Eve, Darlan was assassinated by Fernand Bonnier de la Chapelle, a young Frenchman who had taken part in the Algiers coup against Vichy. In his memoirs, Eisenhower's deputy, General Mark W. Clark, wrote of the Darlan killing: "He had served his purpose, and his death solved what could have been the very difficult problem of what to do with him in the future."5

Guadalcanal, described by Admiral King as "one of the most furious sea battles ever fought," and in the space of twenty-four minutes broke the last significant effort by the Japanese to dislodge the American forces from their positions in the Solomons.

THE TURNING OF THE TIDE PRESENTED a wholly new set of questions for the Allies. At long last, defeat in the war had been ruled out. But victory was yet to be won and agreement reached on the next steps along the road to Germany's final conquest. Already Stalin was pressing the United States and Britain to make good their promise of a Second Front in 1943. His total preoccupation with the splitting of Hitler's forces by an assault in Western Europe tinged even his admiring comments about the North African landings. In response to questions submitted by Henry Cassidy of the Associated Press, Stalin remarked on November 13: "The African campaign refutes again the skeptics who affirm that the Anglo-American leaders cannot organize a serious war campaign. No one but first-rate organizers could carry on such serious war operations as the successful landings in North Africa across the ocean, as the quick occupation of harbors and wide territories and as the smashing of the Italo-German armies being effected so masterfully." Stalin's meaning was plain: North Africa showed that the Western Allies were perfectly capable of mounting a similar assault across the beaches of Normandy or Brittany; all they lacked was the will to strike in the west.

The British Chiefs of Staff, however, favored assaults instead on Sardinia or Sicily, looking toward an eventual landing in the South of France. The American Chiefs had long since concluded that the massive buildup of shipping and matériel for the North African invasion would necessarily slow the preparations for a cross-Channel landing. To a man, they looked upon Sardinia and Sicily as operations which would further divert the Allies from coming to grips with the main enemy in the heart of Europe. Admiral King, moreover, could be counted upon to demand more men and ships for the Pacific theater if there was to be no European landing in 1943. General Marshall remained true to his conviction that a cross-Channel operation was the best answer. But when President Roosevelt on January 7 asked Marshall if the Joint Chiefs were agreed in advocating a direct assault on the Channel coast, the Army Chief of Staff replied candidly that "there was not a united front on that subject, particularly among the planners."[6]

Churchill appeared to swing between one alternative and the other. On November 9 he had remarked, in a memo to his Chiefs of Staff:

. . . "Torch" is no excuse for lying down during 1943, content with descents on Sicily and Sardinia and a few more operations like Dieppe* (which can hardly be taken as a pattern).
. . . If French North Africa is going to be made an excuse for locking up great forces on the defensive and calling it a "commitment," it would be better not to have gone there at all.

On the other hand, the Prime Minister favored "a strong pinning down of the enemy in Northern France and the Low Countries by continuous preparations to invade" but not, apparently, a real invasion. In the same document, he talked of attacking Italy or Southern France, of putting pressure on Turkey to bring her into the war on the side of the Allies and of operating overland with the Russians in the Balkans.[7]

The climate of indecision and divided counsels in high places prompted Roosevelt to suggest that the British and American Chiefs of Staff ought to sit down with their Soviet counterparts to work out agreed military plans for the new year ahead. Hopkins soon persuaded Roosevelt, basing his argument on his own and Harriman's experience of dealing with the Russians, that the big strategic questions could not be settled by soldiers alone. Without a face-to-face meeting of Roosevelt, Churchill and Stalin, Hopkins argued, free discussion among the soldiers would be impossible.

Harriman, who was about to leave London on November 1 for an important trip to Washington with Oliver Lyttelton, the British Minister of Production, had a lengthy talk with Field Marshal Jan Smuts in London on October 28. The South African Prime Minister had a message for Roosevelt. He told Harriman that Operation Torch, in his opinion, could have a decisive effect on the course of the war. It would hit the enemy from the south, where he was vulnerable, Smuts argued, whereas a cross-Channel operation was bound to play into Hitler's hands until Germany was substantially weakened. He urged the President, through Harriman, to concentrate America's resources on a knockout blow to be delivered in 1944.

The month that Harriman and Lyttelton spent in Washington together resulted in a set of far-reaching decisions, the most important of which carefully apportioned the resources of Great Britain and the United States for the last, long pull to victory. They met with the Combined Food Board, the Combined Raw Materials Board, the Com-

* The Dieppe landing had taken place on August 17, 1942. Canadian troops made up the bulk of the landing force, which suffered enormous casualties in the assault. Of 5,000 men from the Canadian 2nd Division, some 900 lost their lives and almost 2,000 were taken prisoner.

bined Production and Resources Board, and the Combined Shipping and Adjustment Board. Roosevelt accepted the scaled-down British import program of 27 million tons for 1943, including 10.5 million tons of food (less than half the 23-million-ton level of prewar allocations) and 16 million tons of raw and industrial materials.* Arrangements were concluded to have the United States replace British merchant shipping sunk by German U-boats, the Americans at this stage of the war having more new ships than they were capable of manning, while the British had more idle crews than ships.

"We finally carried out many of the decisions I had been fighting for over nearly two years on both sides of the Atlantic," Harriman recalled. "The Washington decisions in November of 1942 laid the foundation for the enormous buildup that made possible the Normandy landings in 1944. My one regret was that Lyttelton did not take up with Roosevelt and Hopkins the postwar situation that would result from the sacrifices the British were making for the common cause. I had been deeply involved in the effort to persuade the British that their traditional export program be abandoned during the war. This meant increasing their dependence upon the United States then, and in the immediate postwar period. While in Washington, I strongly urged Lyttelton to seek an understanding with Hopkins and the President that Lend-Lease would continue after the war, in order to give the British time to rebuild their exports. He agreed that such an understanding was essential, but for one reason or another, he failed to raise the question in Washington. I have no doubt that if he had taken my advice, he could have received a commitment that would have made our financial relations with the British a lot easier after the war."

At luncheon with Roosevelt on November 30, Harriman received a delicate diplomatic assignment. After inviting him to attend the approaching conference with Churchill and Stalin, the President said he wanted "no ringers" there; Cordell Hull was to be excluded. This meant, as a practical matter, that Harriman would have to persuade Churchill that Eden, Hull's counterpart, also must stay home.

"Hull was forceful, stubborn, difficult to handle," Harriman recalled. "He had some rigid ideas and Roosevelt felt he would be a nuisance at the conference. Hull used to complain whenever I saw him at this period that the President did not keep him informed. That was certainly true, but I felt it was undignified for him to talk so frankly to someone he did not know intimately. The President wanted to handle these matters alone. It was to be mainly a military conference. He did not feel the need of expert advisers from the State Department. He did not want to be under pressures with which he was

---

* These figures were for dry cargo, exclusive of petroleum products.

not in sympathy. Churchill, on the other hand, took the typically British view of having everybody come along."

Selling Churchill the idea that his own Foreign Secretary must be left behind for no better reason than that Roosevelt wanted to keep Hull at a distance proved a daunting task for Harriman. He met three times with Churchill before he could report back to Roosevelt, on December 7:

> I have been thoroughly beaten up but he [Churchill] finally understands that Anthony [Eden] cannot be viewed as a member of the War Cabinet, divorced for the moment from the Foreign Office, and he agrees to drop him out. He still wants one or two of the Joint Staff Secretariat . . . a couple of private secretaries to conduct his business and 24-hour shifts of cipher men, some of whom can be provided locally. Also he wants his Map Room. . . .

In spite of Churchill's reluctant agreement to leave Eden behind, there were still uncertainties about the meeting. Harriman cabled Hopkins as late as January 1, 1943:

> Will you tell me:
> (1) Does the Boss still want me to see that no ringers are in the party? You will recall my last day in Washington he asked me to do this.
> (2) Am I still included? You can well understand my concern as to the manner in which our decisions are put up to our gallant allies.

There could be no doubt that Roosevelt still wanted Harriman to join him at the conference. He had cabled Churchill on December 2 that in addition to the Chiefs of Staff, he proposed to bring Harriman and Hopkins "but no State Department representative." Only the place was still in question: "I should prefer a secure place south of Algiers or in or near Khartoum . . . I prefer a comfortable oasis to the raft at Tilsit."[8] * When, on December 14, Roosevelt proposed "a satisfactory and safe place" just south of Casablanca which had just been scouted by General Walter Bedell Smith, Churchill readily agreed. On January 4 the President cabled Churchill: "I hope you can bring Averell with you and I have asked him to go to see you. He can be very helpful."

* It was on a raft at Tilsit in the Neman River that Napoleon Bonaparte met with Czar Alexander I of Russia and the King of Prussia, Frederick William III, to conclude a pair of treaties on July 7-9, 1807. Prussia ceded to Napoleon all the lands between the Rhine and the Elbe. In a secret article, Alexander agreed to become Napoleon's ally against England if the British refused French terms for peace.

Churchill needed no persuading. He replied the following day that he would be "delighted to bring Averell."

Stalin, however, was unwilling to leave the Soviet Union with his winter offensive under way. "I must say that things are now so hot that it is impossible for me to absent myself for even a single day," he wrote. "The battle is developing on the Central Front as well as Stalingrad. At Stalingrad we have surrounded a large group of German armies and we hope to achieve their final liquidation."[9] * When Roosevelt offered to postpone the conference from January to March, Stalin again declined, saying that "affairs connected with the front" would require his constant presence in Moscow. Stalin also made it plain that for him the paramount question was still the Second Front in the west—and that required no further talk, only action.

Thus the hoped-for Big Three conference at Casablanca turned into one more Roosevelt-Churchill meeting. It can be argued that Stalin's participation would have strained the alliance severely. The plain fact was that the invasion of North Africa, as General Marshall and other American military leaders had foreseen, necessarily precluded the grand invasion of Western Europe that Stalin was demanding of his allies in 1943. Not until May was the unexpectedly dogged German resistance in Tunisia overcome, causing a slippage of five to six months in Allied plans. Stalin's refusal to attend, in effect, spared Roosevelt and Churchill the embarrassment of having to rebuff his demands face to face. Stalin, moreover, had become increasingly impatient with the various military alternatives offered by the Western Allies. When Roosevelt, on December 16, inquired why nothing had come of the offer made by Churchill and Harriman in August to send a British-American air force to help in the defense of the Caucasus, Stalin replied that he no longer needed that kind of help: "I shall be very grateful to you if you expedite the delivery of planes, especially fighter planes, without the personnel . . . The peculiar state of Soviet aviation is that we have more than enough fliers, but not enough planes."[10]

On the departure for Casablanca, Harriman found himself involved in an elaborate cover plan designed to screen the Prime Minister's movements. Both Roosevelt and Churchill took boyish delight— as Harriman had long since learned—in the business of concealing their identities and their destinations on trips such as this one. They had carefully arranged that the President should travel under the *nom de guerre* Admiral Q. The Prime Minister chose to be known as Air Commodore Frankland. Casablanca was assigned the code name Symbol. And Harriman was to be the decoy for Churchill's departure from

* The German capitulation at Stalingrad took place on January 31, 1943.

England. To maintain secrecy, Churchill's RAF plane had been booked in the name of Harriman, who told the senior members of his staff that he was flying to Algeria for a few days to look into Lend-Lease matters there.

He had been instructed to drive up from London to a military airfield near Oxford, bringing with him two "stooges" equipped with suitcases to give the impression that they were going along. For these roles, Harriman had chosen Winthrop Brown, his senior assistant, and Robert Meiklejohn of his London staff. Arriving at the airport around ten o'clock in the evening on January 12, they were fitted with parachutes and taken to the officers' club for late supper, where they talked freely about their trip to Algiers. (Harriman had sent his driver back to London so he would not see Churchill arriving.) Their bags were loaded in Churchill's converted B-24 bomber, *The Commando;* Harriman and his decoys then climbed aboard to wait for the signal of Churchill's arrival—a bang on the side of the fuselage. When it came, about midnight, Brown's and Meiklejohn's bags were quickly removed. At this point a junior officer raced up to the air commodore in charge of all the mystifying arrangements to announce, "The party is arriving." The air commodore snapped, "Hell, haven't I eyes? I have seen them coming for two miles." Anyone with normal eyesight could see in the distance a convoy of limousines, led by one car with the brightest headlights Harriman had ever seen—in spite of the blackout. The convoy rolled up to the plane at high speed, sirens blaring, and the Prime Minister climbed out, thinly disguised in the uniform of an air commodore. At which, the genuine air commodore remarked to Harriman: "Good God, the only mistake they made was that they didn't put it in the local newspaper! No one could make that much noise except the Prime Minister."

Churchill's insouciant attitude toward the mystifications of security men was still at work when his plane touched down at Medouina Airport near Casablanca nine hours later. As the Prime Minister, conspicuous in his blue RAF uniform, stepped down from the plane, he noticed a second plane coming in to land. Told that his Chiefs of Staff were on board, Churchill insisted on waiting for them. He stood on the tarmac for several minutes, puffing his cigar in full view, to the dismay of all his security men, who were under strict orders to keep the visit to Morocco secret. When General Ismay stepped down from the plane he was horrified to see Churchill standing there. "Any fool can see that is an air commodore disguised as the Prime Minister," he remarked.

Roosevelt arrived on the evening of January 14, having been en route from Washington for five days. All told, the President (who did not care for flying) had spent forty-eight hours in the air and almost thirty-six hours in a special train to cover a distance that takes ten hours in a modern jet plane. In spite of his long journey Roosevelt was in high spirits, relishing the drama of his secret flight to Africa and his brief release from the daily cares of Washington.

The setting for the Casablanca Conference was the Hotel Anfa, on a hill overlooking the southern outskirts of the Moroccan city. The U.S. Army had taken over the hotel and its adjoining villas, girdling the grounds with barbed wire and a heavy guard, including airplanes and artillery. President Roosevelt occupied a spacious villa known as Dar es Saada. Churchill's Villa Mirador was about fifty yards away. Harriman shared a third villa with Roosevelt's special representative in North Africa, Robert Murphy, and Harold Macmillan, the British Minister Resident newly assigned to Allied Force Headquarters in North Africa.

Although his military chiefs had vetoed a presidential visit to the front, Roosevelt hugely enjoyed an excursion by automobile from Casablanca to Rabat, where he reviewed the 9th Infantry Division. Harriman, Hopkins, Murphy, Admiral Ross T. McIntire and Major General George S. Patton, Jr., went with him. As the troop review began, the protective zeal of the Secret Service aroused some hard feeling, chiefly among the senior officers present. "The Secret Service insisted," Harriman recalled, "that Tommy guns be trained on the troops from the President's car. Some officers interpreted this super-fluous display of force as showing a lack of confidence in their men. But for the soldiers it was a tremendous event; their thrilled reaction to the President was to me very moving." Roosevelt himself found the sight of so many young Americans in good health and spirits, well equipped and ready to fight, a tonic for his soul. He lunched in the open air with the 20,000 troops (boiled ham, sweet potatoes and fruit salad) while an Army band played "Chattanooga Choo-Choo," "Deep in the Heart of Texas" and the "Naughty Marietta" waltz. Afterward Roosevelt told reporters, "It was a darn good lunch. We had to move the band because it was a very windy day, from leeward to windward, so we could hear the music."

It was at Anfa that the Combined Chiefs of Staff set the Allied military agenda for the year ahead, under the close supervision of Roosevelt and Churchill. With marked reluctance the American Chiefs of Staff yielded to the arguments of their British counterparts that it would be impossible to launch a cross-Channel invasion during 1943 in sufficient strength to make much difference to the Russians. Harriman had been surprised when Churchill assured Stalin in Moscow that the invasion of Europe would take place in 1943. He felt that the American military planners at Casablanca were still far too optimistic about the number of landing craft and army divisions, properly equipped and trained, that the British could contribute. "Even in Moscow back in August I was skeptical of their ability—or ours, for that matter—to launch a successful attack in 1943 if we got diverted in North Africa. I knew too much about the shipping bottleneck to believe it was possible."

In a meeting with Roosevelt on January 16, Admiral King grumbled that the British "do not seem to have an overall plan" for winning the war. But, for lack of an agreed alternative, he and Marshall went along with the Mediterranean strategy of General Brooke and the Prime Minister.[11] The main military decisions taken at Casablanca were these:

- To invade Sicily (Operation Husky) in July or, if possible, in June. General Eisenhower would be in supreme command, with Sir Harold Alexander as his deputy. The decision to strike at Sicily, rather than Sardinia, produced a substantial argument. Lord Louis Mountbatten strongly advocated the Sardinia-first strategy even after Sicily had been decided upon.* But Churchill put his weight behind Operation Husky in the hope that it would knock Italy out of the war, forcing the Germans to tie down a great many divisions in the defense of the Italian peninsula and the Balkans.

- To accelerate the strategic bomber offensive against Germany. After a talk with Major General Ira C. Eaker at Casablanca, Churchill withdrew his long-standing objection to daylight bombing by the American Air Forces based in Britain. Thereafter the Royal Air Force was to bomb Germany by night—and Eaker's Eighth Air Force by day—in a thunderous offensive designed to wear down German resistance.

- To go on supplying Russia with food, industrial raw materials and weapons of war in fulfillment of all American and British obligations.

- To intensify the war at sea and from the air against Hitler's U-boats, reaffirming the principle that the security of sea

---

* The argument for Operation Brimstone (the invasion of Sardinia), as expressed by Mountbatten to Harriman and Hopkins, was that it could be done quickly and that it would provide a major base for Allied bombers, with fighter escort, to devastate the major industrial and transportation centers of Italy. "Husky is much more difficult and can only come later," Mountbatten told Harriman. "He talked to Harry and me at length," Harriman wrote in his Casablanca notes, "and although it is dead now he hopes it may be revived if things don't move fast enough for Husky."

communications to Britain must remain the first charge upon Allied resources.

* To continue the American troop buildup in the British Isles (938,000 men by December 31) for the eventual invasion of France. A new joint command (COSSAC, acronym for Chief of Staff to the Supreme Allied Commander) was created to begin immediate planning for this climactic operation, later known as Overlord.

The Combined Chiefs gave less detailed attention to the war in the Pacific, the British conceding that this was a theater of more direct concern to the Americans. At luncheon with Harriman on January 14, Churchill had said to General Marshall, "You must educate me about the Pacific war while you are here. We must stay on long enough this time to come to a conclusion everywhere." Harriman's notes show that Marshall stressed the importance of sending more planes to Brigadier General Claire L. Chennault's China Air Task Force so that the systematic bombing of Japan could begin, instead of fighting from "ant hill to ant hill." The British Chiefs of Staff, however, fearing that new American offensives in the Pacific would draw off Allied resources needed to win the war in Europe, resisted the demands of Admiral King and General Marshall for more strenuous efforts against Japan in 1943. Only after a warning from Marshall that "a situation might arise in the Pacific at any time that would necessitate the United States regretfully withdrawing from the commitments in the European theater"[12] did the British Chiefs agree to a number of carefully limited operations: more transport planes to fly supplies into China over the Himalayas from India; more combat planes for Chennault; an overland campaign late in the year to reopen the Burma Road and advances against the Japanese base at Rabaul, on New Britain, together with moves toward Truk and Guam, by American and Australian troops.

The key to all these military decisions was shipping, still the most stubborn of all the shortages confronting the planners. Even at the end of 1942, losses of Allied shipping had exceeded new construction by about one million tons. It was a two-ocean war now, and the island-hopping strategy of General MacArthur in the South Pacific imposed a constant drain on the common shipping pool. Shipload after shipload of essential supplies was being sent to the Pacific without regard to unloading facilities, which did not exist in many of the islands. As a result, Harriman recalled, "The Pacific became a morass for our shipping. Valuable ships sat offshore month after month without being unloaded or, at best, without being released because only the immediately usable cargo had been unloaded. The misuse of our shipping in the Pacific made our job in Europe that much more difficult."

At Casablanca, Harriman and Lord Leathers, the British Minister of War Transport, spent many long hours with General Somervell working out the intricate calculus of tonnages required to keep Britain and Russia supplied, while at the same time providing enough ships to move hundreds of thousands of American soldiers—and their combat equipment—overseas for future operations. One of the most potent arguments in favor of invading Sicily, in fact, was that the troops to be used were for the most part already in the Mediterranean and likely to have nothing better to do after the final clearing of Tunisia. Operation Husky, based on North Africa, made no impossible demands on Allied shipping, while an assault on the Channel coast of France, in Harriman's view, was out of the question. On January 20, during a discussion of aid to Russia, Somervell pointed out to the Combined Chiefs that if the Allies were able to cut their shipping losses from 2.6 percent a month in 1942 to 2 percent in 1943, they would be able to deliver 500,000 additional troops, with their supplies and equipment, to England. If the loss rate could be further reduced by one tenth of a percentage point that would mean a further addition of 50,000 troops.[13]

In his notes on the conference, Harriman recorded that after initial disagreements, Somervell and Leathers had come to understand one another through their work together at Casablanca. But Somervell, he noted, "still wants to raid the British import program." Harriman added:

> President and P.M. are much pleased with meeting, although both are disappointed by slowness of new moves. So am I. I am convinced earlier steps could have been taken—perhaps Brimstone instead of Husky. Meeting has given mutual understanding of each side's problems: Pacific by British—Burma, China; also submarine warfare by King and Arnold—agreement to attack U-boat [problem] and cover convoys, etc. A most important result.

Harriman saw Churchill every day, whether for a meal or a hand of bezique. He also attended several of the meetings in Roosevelt's villa at which the American Chiefs reported to the President on their talks with the British Chiefs of Staff. He was impressed by the personality differences between General Marshall and Admiral King:

> Marshall is almost completely objective. King, crafty, always. Taking care of his war, namely Pacific.
> Both always try to blame British for [postponement of] Channel crossing. I got the feeling they understand difficulties

thoroughly, but now and later will put blame on British for no action.

Arnold is impatient with slowness of Army build-up in Mediterranean and blames British for slow shipments. But I got the feeling that there was, for the first time, real willingness to be fully frank and work together with mutual confidence.

While the Combined Chiefs of Staff were meeting twice a day at Casablanca to hammer out joint strategic plans, Roosevelt and Churchill invested much of their time in a far more difficult joint effort to bring Giraud and De Gaulle together. General Giraud, who had been named High Commissioner after Darlan's death, was frankly delighted when Murphy and Macmillan, in a meeting in Algiers on January 12, invited him to Casablanca. He was confident that he could work matters out with De Gaulle, Giraud said, making the point that before the war, De Gaulle had "after all, served as a colonel under my orders." De Gaulle, who was in London, refused the invitation. If Roosevelt wished to see him, De Gaulle would go to Washington but he would not meet with Giraud, as Frenchman to Frenchman, on French territory in an atmosphere dominated by the British-American high command. Giraud arrived in Casablanca on January 17, calling on Roosevelt the same afternoon. The President told him it would be a splendid thing if he and De Gaulle could handle the military situation for Africa together, and with a leading civilian, form a "Committee for the Liberation of France." Giraud responded with enthusiasm, saying he was certain that he and General de Gaulle could work out some military arrangement.[14]

The arrangement Giraud had in mind was not one calculated to please De Gaulle. Count André Poniatowski, Giraud's civilian aide, explained to Harriman and Hopkins on January 19 that the general would insist on being "top dog," with De Gaulle in a secondary role. When Poniatowski, a Harriman relative by marriage, pressed his chief's claim to the leadership of France, Hopkins cautioned him that "the President stuck by his position that sovereignty rested exclusively with the French people, and that he would recognize no one, not even Giraud, as representing France."[15]

Giraud, nevertheless, impressed both Roosevelt and Churchill favorably. "During the week that he was at Casablanca," Harriman noted, "he did not make a misstep." Even Hopkins liked Giraud. "I know he is a Royalist and is probably a right-winger in all his economic views," Hopkins noted on January 19, "but I have a feeling that he is willing to fight."[16]

De Gaulle, meanwhile, sulked in London, telling Eden that he refused to meet Giraud under the auspices of Churchill and Roosevelt, who might press him to compromise. The Prime Minister, his patience at an end, finally sent word back through Eden that if De Gaulle persisted in his refusal, the British government would insist that he be replaced as the head of the French Liberation Committee in London. "If with your eyes open you reject this unique opportunity," Churchill wrote to De Gaulle, "we shall endeavour to get on as well as we can without you."[17]

De Gaulle finally arrived in Casablanca on January 22. At first he refused to call on Giraud, relenting only after a stern talk with Churchill in which the Prime Minister again threatened to break with him. The match Roosevelt and Churchill had insisted upon—Giraud being cast, in the President's words, as the eager bridegroom and De Gaulle as the unwilling bride—was never consummated. Harriman wrote at the time:

> Each Frenchman offered the other the privilege of serving under him. De Gaulle said: "You will be Foch, I, Clemenceau." Giraud offered a War Committee of three, himself as head, De Gaulle to handle his present colonies and [the third man] to be selected [for] North Africa. The War Committee to have general direction of all policies.
>
> The British, as a compromise, were pressing for a dual-headed regime. I always considered it cockeyed, attaining only the immediate objective of outward unity . . . but troubles and discord would multiply afterward.
>
> The President insists on unified recognition of any set-up, [the] fundamental purpose to fight and rule the territories and colonies [of France] till after the war, when the French people must choose their own government . . .
>
> The thing that became more and more obvious was that the personal hatreds which had developed from the events and fights of the last two and a half years between the followers of both camps were such that no immediate marriage was possible or wise.

The outcome, as Harriman had anticipated, was not a marriage at all but an agreement to try to negotiate a matrimonial contract later on. Under Roosevelt's forceful pressure, De Gaulle and Giraud shook hands stiffly on January 24 before a party of photographers and war correspondents just summoned from Algiers. The photograph, published around the world, was memorably misleading. For the careful newspaper reader there was more truth in the joint Giraud–De Gaulle communiqué, issued after Casablanca:

> We have seen each other. We have discussed. We have

affirmed our complete agreement that the goal to be reached is the liberation of France and the triumph of human liberty by the total defeat of the enemy. That goal will be achieved by the union in the war of all Frenchmen fighting side by side with their allies.

De Gaulle and Giraud, in short, had agreed that Germany must be defeated before France could again be free and that union between their forces, if attainable, would be a useful step in that direction. It is hard to see how they could have said less in the circumstances. Giraud came away from Casablanca the apparent victor. The Allies had acknowledged him as commander in chief, with "the right and duty of preserving all French interests under the military, economic, financial and moral plan." They had promised to rebuild and re-equip his army in North Africa with "the most modern material." De Gaulle, on the other hand, had demonstrated that he was his own man and, by his lights, the true champion of French national interest, even at the cost of infuriating his most powerful allies.

"Churchill and Roosevelt in fact had agreed that De Gaulle should be eliminated before the liberation of France," Harriman recalled. "But they never could agree on the timing. I have no doubt that if De Gaulle had persisted in his refusal to come to Casablanca, that would have been the end for him. It's true that Roosevelt, on the whole, was keener than Churchill to get rid of De Gaulle. But even Churchill had once before considered putting him under house arrest for insubordination, and at the time of Casablanca he was thoroughly fed up.

"We certainly made a bad bet on Giraud, just as the British did on De Gaulle. It was a pity that no other Frenchman appeared who had the courage of De Gaulle but who was something less of an egotist."

The spectacle of De Gaulle stiffly offering his hand to Giraud, in the smiling presence of Roosevelt and Churchill, was not, however, destined to remain the grand climax of Casablanca. The President created a bigger sensation a few minutes later when he announced in a joint press conference with Churchill that the Allies would enforce a policy of "unconditional surrender" upon the Axis powers. Some fifty war correspondents, sitting cross-legged on the lawn behind the presidential villa, heard Roosevelt report on the decisions of the conference and then add, as if on the spur of the moment:

"Another point. I think we have all had it in our hearts and heads before, but I don't think that it has ever been put down on paper by the Prime Minister and myself, and that is the determination that peace can come to the world only by the total elimination of German and Japanese war power.

"Some of you Britishers know the old story—we had a General called U. S. Grant. His name was Ulysses Simpson Grant but in my (and the Prime Minister's) early days he was called 'Unconditional Surrender' Grant. The elimination of German, Japanese and Italian war power means the unconditional surrender by Germany, Italy and Japan. That means a reasonable assurance of future world peace. It does not mean the destruction of the population of Germany, Italy or Japan, but it does mean the destruction of the philosophies in those countries which are based on conquest and the subjugation of other people."[18]

Churchill has recorded, with admirable British understatement, that he listened to all this "with some feeling of surprise."[19] But speaking privately with Harriman the same evening at bezique, the Prime Minister registered hotter emotions. "He was in high dudgeon," Harriman recalled. "He was offended that Roosevelt should have made such a momentous announcement without prior consultation and I am sure he did not like the manner of it. I had seen him unhappy with Roosevelt more than once, but this time he was more deeply offended than before. I also had the impression that he feared it might make the Germans fight all the harder." When Harriman the next morning told Roosevelt of Churchill's dismay, the President explained:

. . . what he had in mind was paralleled by the surrender of General Lee to General Grant. General Lee stated that, before surrendering, it was necessary to have certain things settled, such as the rights of the officers to their horses, which were their own property. Grant stated his terms were unconditional surrender. Lee accepted. Lee then asked about the horses. Grant replied that the decision was that the officers should retain their horses: "They will need them for the spring plowing."

Roosevelt's recollection of Civil War history, however, was somewhat muddled. Grant in fact had made his name synonymous with "unconditional surrender" two years earlier, in 1863. He was speaking not to Robert E. Lee at Appomattox Court House, but to General Simon Buckner, his classmate and friend at West Point, then the Confederate commander at Fort Donelson. Buckner had asked for terms and Grant replied, "No terms except an unconditional and immediate surrender can be accepted. I propose to move immediately upon your works." The talk of horses and of spring plowing came in 1865 with Lee's surrender. Although Roosevelt never wavered on the principle of unconditional surrender, it seemed clear that he meant to show comparable generosity to the German people after their leaders had capitulated. "I am sure he had this in mind," Harriman recalled. "It was fundamental to his thinking. Yet in the months that followed he failed to clarify his meaning, to my eternal regret."

Harriman felt the President's announcement was a mistake, prompted by his understandable determination to rule out any bargaining with the Axis powers. Other public men, no less determined than the President himself to see the Axis powers totally defeated, warned that Roosevelt's announced insistence on unconditional surrender was likely to stiffen the resistance of the Germans, Japanese and Italians and thus prolong the war.

Roosevelt later told Hopkins that the idea of talking about unconditional surrender had just "popped into" his mind. "We had so much trouble getting those two French generals together," he said, "that I thought to myself that this was as difficult as arranging the meeting of Grant and Lee—and then suddenly the press conference was on . . ."[20] It is clear from the notes prepared for the President's use at the press conference that he may not have been speaking off the cuff, although there is no proof that he read them carefully. The notes, dated January 22–23, read, in pertinent part:

> The President and the Prime Minister, after a complete survey of the world war situation, are more than ever determined that peace can come to the world only by a total elimination of German and Japanese war power.
>
> This involves the simple formula of placing the objectives of this war in terms of an unconditional surrender by Germany, Italy and Japan. Unconditional surrender by them means a reasonable assurance of world peace, for generations . . .[21]

There can be no question that the idea had been in the President's mind for some time. A government subcommittee in Washington, headed by the career diplomat Norman H. Davis, had agreed on May 6, 1942, some eight months before Casablanca, "to begin its discussion of the armistice period with the assumption that unconditional surrender will be exacted of the principal defeated states. The view was expressed that it might prove desirable to negotiate an armistice with Italy in order to pull her out of the war, but that nothing short of unconditional surrender could be accepted in the case of Germany and Japan."[22] Davis, moreover, had informed the President of his subcommittee's views. Before leaving Washington, Roosevelt also had discussed unconditional surrender with the Joint Chiefs of Staff at a meeting in the White House on January 7. Nor is there any ground for doubting that the President had raised the matter with Churchill at Casablanca. At a meeting with Roosevelt and the Combined Chiefs of Staff on January 18, the Prime Minister proposed the release of a public statement "to the effect that the United Nations are resolved to pursue the war to the bitter end, neither party relaxing in its efforts until the unconditional surrender of Germany and Japan has been achieved."[23] Two days later Churchill asked the War Cabinet for its views, reporting that he and Roosevelt believed that Italy ought to be excluded from the unconditional surrender requirement in order to speed its internal collapse. The reply from London by Attlee and Eden, dated January 21, raised no objection to announcing a policy of unconditional surrender. The War Cabinet was unanimous, however, in the view that Italy should be included: "Knowledge of all rough stuff coming to them is surely more likely to have desired effect on Italian morale."[24]

Churchill's genuine surprise and dismay, it would appear, had less to do with the principle of unconditional surrender than with the fact that Roosevelt had proclaimed it on his own. The two had, of course, discussed it. But the Prime Minister evidently believed that the matter had been dropped after he and Roosevelt had carefully reviewed the text of their joint statement, to be issued at the close of the conference, which made no mention of unconditional surrender. Once the words were uttered, however, the Prime Minister felt compelled to go along. To admit any divergence between himself and Roosevelt at that moment, Churchill felt, would be damaging to the common war effort.

Roosevelt's motives are perhaps best understood in the light of his other preoccupations at the time of Casablanca. Harriman believed that one purpose in the President's mind was to offset the suspicions the Darlan deal had created by ruling out in advance any dealings with the enemy. Concerned over Stalin's absence, the President also felt a need to reassure the Kremlin that the Western Allies would make no separate peace with Hitler. He had told the Chiefs of Staff on January 7 that he proposed to send General Marshall to Moscow after the conference "for the purpose of giving impetus to Russian morale."* He wanted Stalin to know, Roosevelt said, "that the United Nations were to continue on until they reach Berlin, and that their only terms would be unconditional surrender."[25] Apart from these considerations, the President told Harriman that he was determined not to repeat Woodrow Wilson's tragic mistake in proclaiming his Fourteen Points and starting a discussion of peace terms with the enemy before the surrender. Roosevelt wanted to rule out any compromise with Nazism, bargaining over terms, or cries of deception from the Germans after the war.

* Stalin declined Roosevelt's offer to send Marshall to Moscow. A visit at the time, he said, would serve no useful purpose.

Churchill might have argued the case man to man, but Roosevelt gave him no opportunity. As soon as the press conference was over, the two were off to Marrakesh with Hopkins and Harriman, the Prime Minister's son Randolph, Hopkins' son Robert, Admiral McIntire and an entourage of aides. It was a four-hour drive of 150 miles through the desert, the dusty road lined with American soldiers standing at attention while fighter planes swept overhead. The British had prepared a picnic lunch of hard-boiled eggs, sandwiches and mince pies to eat along the way. At dinner that evening in the extraordinarily beautiful Moorish house of Mrs. Moses Taylor, then occupied by Kenneth Pendar, one of Murphy's special agents, there were speeches, songs and toasts. Pendar took the head of the table, seating Roosevelt on his right and Churchill on his left. Harriman sat beside Roosevelt, and Hopkins next to Churchill.

It was the President's habit to shift gears conversationally when he preferred not to discuss weighty matters. This time he expounded to Pendar and Harriman his views about independence for Morocco on the Philippine pattern. He talked of compulsory education, of fighting disease through immunization and of birth control. "Occasionally," Harriman noted, "the P.M. interjected a pessimistic—and realistic—note. He doesn't like the new ideas but accepts them as inevitable."

Here again, as in their disagreements over India, Roosevelt and Churchill did not march to the same drumbeat. The Prime Minister made no secret of his determination to preserve the British Empire, although he knew that would be difficult. Roosevelt enjoyed thinking aloud on the tremendous changes he saw ahead—the end of colonial empires and the rise of newly independent nations across the sweep of Africa and Asia. "I felt his objectives were right," Harriman said. "I think he had a belief that his prestige, both personally and as President of the United States, was so great that he could influence the trend. He recognized the rise of nationalism among the colonial peoples. He also recognized that Churchill was pretty much a nineteenth-century colonialist. So he said some of these things partly to jar Churchill but also from a fundamental belief that the old order could not last. All this was surely in Churchill's mind when he later said that he had not become Prime Minister to preside over the liquidation of the British Empire."

Throughout this, their final evening together, Churchill kept looking for an opportunity to talk privately with Roosevelt. But the seating arrangement, to Churchill's great annoyance, made a tête-à-tête impossible. "Roosevelt rather liked the idea," Harriman recalled, "that he did not have to go through with this talk. He always enjoyed other people's discomfort. I think it is fair to say that it never bothered him very much when other people were unhappy."

Before turning in, long past midnight, Hopkins and Harriman went back to work drafting joint messages for Stalin and Chiang Kai-shek on the Casablanca decisions. Hopkins drafted; Harriman edited the drafts; and Roosevelt and Churchill went over them, line by line, suggesting small changes before the cables were dispatched to Moscow and Chungking.

Churchill was still in bed at seven forty-five the next morning when Roosevelt looked in to say goodbye. The Prime Minister insisted on riding to the airport with the President, after stepping into his bedroom slippers and zipping up his siren suit. As he watched Roosevelt being carried into the plane and comfortably settled for the long flight home by way of West Africa and across the South Atlantic to the bulge of Brazil, Churchill reflected on the hazards of flying great distances in wartime. "I always regarded them," he later wrote, "as dangerous excursions."[26]

Harriman saw how dangerous such excursions could be, at the end of his return flight to Britain on January 29, after a change of planes in Casablanca, a stop in Algiers to discuss shipping and supply problems, and a weather delay at Gibraltar. The lead plane, carrying Harriman and Ismay, had just landed safely at Lyneham Airport in Wiltshire when the second plane, a B-24 carrying other members of the British staff, crashed as it came in to land. Brigadier Vivian Dykes, Joint Secretary of the Combined Chiefs of Staff, and Brigadier Guy M. Stewart, Director of Plans for the British War Office, were killed and a third officer seriously injured.

The Casablanca decisions to invade Sicily and step up the bomber offensive against Germany came as a bitter disappointment to Stalin and his generals. He complained to Churchill and Roosevelt that far from drawing off German divisions to the west by the operation in North Africa, the Western Allies had slackened the pace of their attack in Tunisia, allowing Hitler to transfer twenty-seven divisions to the Russian front. Roosevelt replied that he regretted the delays in North Africa, even as Stalin did, and that he fully understood "the importance of a major effort on the Continent of Europe at the earliest practicable date." But he could not fix a date certain.

CHAPTER IX

Interlude at Sea

THE UNITED STATES HAD BEEN at war more than a year before the Army Air Forces struck their first direct blow against Germany. Not until January 27, 1943, three days after the conclusion of the Casablanca Conference, was General Eaker able to send out his B-17 Flying Fortresses and B-24 Liberators from their new bases in East Anglia, without fighter escorts, to bomb the port of Wilhelmshaven and other objectives in northern Germany. Although three bombers were lost that day, the promised round-the-clock air offensive had started. For Eaker—as well as Harriman—it marked the culmination of a long struggle.

From the beginning Churchill and his air marshals had taken a jaundiced view of the American plan to bomb Germany by day. Having smashed the Luftwaffe's daylight-bombing offensive early in the war, the British were reluctant to believe that the Americans could succeed where the Germans had failed. Being short of bombers themselves, they argued that their experienced RAF crews ought to have first call on the new planes coming off the American assembly lines. Roosevelt, however, backed his ranking air generals—Arnold, Carl Spaatz and Eaker—in their insistence upon creating an American air force in Britain, with American air crews flying American bombers under American command. A sharp, sometimes angry, argument flared between the Allied air forces. The Americans were determined to prove that daylight bombing could be more accurate and, over the long haul, far more effective than the so-called saturation bombing practiced after dark by the RAF. The British, from Churchill down, predicted that if the Americans persisted in this folly, the B-17 losses from German interceptors would be appalling—as they were in the beginning, before long-range fighters became available to escort them deep into Germany.

Although Churchill had assured Eaker at Casablanca that he no longer would oppose daylight bombing, the Prime Minister had not been wholly converted, and the RAF took a lot more persuading. On April 22 Harriman wrote hopefully to Robert Lovett in Washington:

> There is complete acceptance of the fact that bombing is our only present offensive direct on Germany and, together with the blockade and the destruction of the German forces in Africa, the principal aid we are giving in weakening the German strength on the Russian front . . . It is recognized that the bombing is an essential prelude to our occupation of the Continent . . .
>
> To keep England going and before an offensive on the Continent is safe to undertake, the submarine must be got under control and the Bay [of Biscay] offensive is considered to have possibilities of being effective. The immediate need, however, of striking at Germany by our bombing offensive must not be sacrificed.
>
> The Prime Minister is constantly critical of the British services for what he calls "combing their tails to sharpen their teeth" and there is here suspicion of wasteful use of resources by Washington in continuing defensive programs when the character of the war has so changed that they are no longer necessary . . .
>
> For instance, we are all wondering here about the amount of effort that is going into defense of the United States and elsewhere against improbable air attack, the construction of bases that cannot be effective in this war, and in other directions that do not look as if they are going to contribute to early, energetic prosecution of the defeat of the Axis. The atmosphere here is now concentration of resources for the offensive.
>
> There is no doubt, however, that the British view the crossing of the Channel as a greater problem than, I gather, we do. Perhaps it is because they have placed too much reliance on [the Channel] as a defense when they were weak—or perhaps they are right.
>
> . . . The Prime Minister, in spite of early advices to the contrary and his own prejudice, has accepted the effectiveness of daylight bombing without reservation. This has been a tough job but Ira [Eaker] has finally done it. This goes, too, for the Air Staff—and [Air Chief Marshal] Harris, of course. If there are a few people down the line who have not learned the gospel, don't let it worry you. I hope we can get increasing

public expression by the top people here to lay for all time the ghost of the past when there was skepticism.

On the top side, I can assure you, the British, although slow to accept new things . . . are ready to be shown and to reverse their previous judgments. Our Air Force and our equipment are winning increasing respect.

The bombing of German cities, power stations, railway yards, factories and shipyards—by day and by night—had become a matter of the highest priority in the spring of 1943. The U.S. Eighth Air Force, however, was fast outgrowing its airfields in the south of England. The building of new airfields—and the expansion of old ones—called for more manpower than the British felt they could spare. Colonel George A. Lincoln, a staff officer sent over from Washington to make certain that the airfields were ready in time, found himself blocked at every turn. He went to see Harriman in near-desperation, seeking help. After listening to Lincoln's story, Harriman called in his labor adviser, Sam Berger, and asked him what could be done to help the Eighth Air Force. Berger replied that the Ministry of Labor and National Service was proposing to draft some 65,000 construction workers for the armed services. Harriman might request that the British defer the call-up of construction workers. It would be a complicated undertaking, Berger cautioned, requiring a Cabinet decision because several ministries were involved. The next morning Harriman went to see Churchill.

"I asked him whether he wanted to see our air force in England," Harriman recalled. " 'Of course,' he said. 'Why do you ask?' I told him that he would have to reverse the call-up decision, and after a while, he agreed. The Prime Minister took it up with his Cabinet, and over the strong opposition of the armed services, it was agreed. After that I was the most unpopular man in London for a time. But the construction workers were assigned and the airfields were built on time."

However, the relentless squeeze on Allied shipping remained the Harriman Mission's most active concern during the spring of 1943. General Somervell's calculations at Casablanca began to look overoptimistic as the battle for Tunisia dragged into the spring, pre-empting ships needed elsewhere and threatening the whole British import program, including the meager rations of the people. As a result the Prime Minister had actually given orders to curtail current production of several types of weapons and ammunition, a calculated risk that in Harriman's view cut stocks in the United Kingdom to the point of danger. When Harriman cabled Hopkins in late March, pressing for the transfer of more American ships to Britain under Lend-Lease in order to make full use of available British crews, he received a discouraging reply: the shipbuilding program in the United States had fallen behind schedule in January and February; military requirements for all fronts exceeded the total tonnage available. Hopkins saw no prospect of assigning more ships to carry industrial raw materials and food to Britain. On April 1, with great misgiving, the British government cut the individual weekly meat ration from 1 shilling, 2 pence (28 cents' worth) to 1 shilling (24 cents).

German U-boats, surface raiders and aircraft at the same time kept up their devastating attacks on the northern convoys. Having consistently failed to provide air cover for the merchant ships as they approached Soviet territory, Stalin also dismissed British suggestions that RAF units be stationed at Murmansk or Archangel, pleading a lack of adequate accommodations in those Arctic ports. Harriman cabled Hopkins on February 28:

> Understand British are determined to be firm with Russians on need to establish British air units in North Russia if convoys are to continue. Unless some new aspect develops with which I am not familiar, I hope that we will support them. I believe nothing is gained with the Russians by letting them kick us around when we are on sound ground.

But no amount of Allied firmness could persuade Stalin that his own interests would be served by allowing British flying boats and their crews to operate from Soviet bases. His dark suspicion of foreigners on Soviet soil ran deeper than ever now that the second front in France had been further postponed by the Casablanca decisions. The ultimate blow fell when Roosevelt reluctantly accepted Churchill's decision to cut Allied shipping losses by once again suspending all northern convoys to Russia until September 1943. "I shudder to think," the Prime Minister said to Harriman at dinner on March 30, "what Stalin's reaction will be."

His predictably bitter reaction was to accuse the Western Allies of weakening the Red Army by their "catastrophic diminution of supplies of arms and war materials." The ships already loaded for Russia contained more than 650 fighter planes—375 British Hurricanes, and 285 Bell Airacobras and Kitty Hawks from the United States. Harriman was so determined to see this commitment honored that he cabled Hopkins, proposing that the American planes be shipped back to the United States and flown from there, by way of Alaska, to Siberia. Churchill put his mind to other ways of delivering the Hurricanes—for example, by shipping them to Africa, having the planes uncrated there and then flown to Russia by way of Iraq and Iran. "With the President's approval," he cabled Stalin on April 4, "Mr. Harriman is collaborating with us in making the plan. I hope to telegraph to you next week giving you our concrete proposals. I am determined that you shall have the aircraft as soon as it is humanly possible to get them to you." But word came back from Hopkins on April 14, ruling out flight deliveries by way of Alaska or Iran. The reason: an acute shortage of ferry pilots. Harriman wrote to Churchill the same day:

Dear Prime Minister,

In spite of the early encouragement that I had from Harry, I have received today a definite cable from him stating that we have not a sufficient supply of trained ferry pilots to accomplish flight delivery of the Russian airplanes to Persia. He therefore advises me that the only feasible method of delivering these planes will be by ship.

I am in touch with the Minister of War Transport [Lord Leathers], but have not worked out any plan pending advice from the Admiralty on the feasibility of using the Mediterranean.

Yours sincerely,

Averell

Churchill's response, written on the margin of the letter, was: "Mr. Harriman. We must send them somehow." The two canceled convoys, each of thirty merchant ships, were to have sailed in March and May. Rather than let sixty sorely needed ships sit idle for months, Harriman insisted (with Washington's prompt approval) that they be unloaded in British ports. The tanks and airplanes were stored in Britain until they could be safely shipped through the Mediterranean to the Persian Gulf. Harriman turned over other items in short supply, such as foodstuffs and TNT, to the British government on the understanding that these would be replaced by direct shipments to Russia from the United States, whether across the Pacific to Vladivostok or through Iran. Stalin protested vigorously, and the Soviet embassy in London dragged its feet about transferring title to the British. But when Harriman told Ambassador Maisky that he would begin unloading the ships in seventy-two hours—with or without Soviet approval—Moscow agreed in forty-eight hours. "I had no doubt in my mind that they would be suspicious," Harriman recalled. "But I got along much better with the Russians after that. The reputation I had established with them for fulfilling past commitments must have helped."

Stalin's suspicions were not always so predictable. His dismissal of the British-American offer to help bolster his front with air support, followed in January by his refusal to receive General Marshall in Moscow, had not been understood in Washington and London. Harriman explored the reasons behind Stalin's behavior at one of his periodic luncheons with Maisky and reported back to Hopkins on February 14:

> Maisky . . . indicated Stalin had misunderstood the President's offer to send U.S. bomber groups to Siberia as indicating desire on our part to embroil them with Japan at a time when their information indicated no imminent prospect of Japanese attack. It was for this reason Stalin answered so curtly regarding Marshall's proposed visit, requesting definition of his reasons for coming.
>
> I told Maisky it was my personal view that this type of over-suspicion and the character of the reply was not repeat not the way to further Soviet interest.

In spite of Stalin's bitter recriminations over the canceled convoys, his paramount interest in the defeat of Hitler led him to salute his Western allies whenever they struck a hard blow against Germany from the air. On March 29, for example, he cabled Churchill: "I congratulate the British Air Force on the new, big and successful bombing of Berlin." Again, on April 12: "We are delighted that you are not giving respite to Hitler. To your strong and successful bombing of the big German cities we add now our air raids on the German industrial centers of East Prussia." These encouraging messages addressed to Churchill and Roosevelt were not, of course, made public in the Soviet Union. On the contrary, the people were being told little or nothing about Western contributions to the eventual defeat of Germany. Thoroughly exasperated by this Russian attitude, Admiral Standley held a press conference in Moscow on March 8, 1943, at which he registered his concern that the Soviet press and radio, under direct government control, gave the people no inkling of the magnitude and character of Lend-Lease aid from the United States and Britain. Harriman soon reported to Hopkins:

> I find my British and American friends, seniors and juniors, secretly pleased that Admiral Standley spoke out in Moscow even if it was indiscreet.
>
> There is growing feeling here that we are building up trouble for the future by allowing the Russians to kick us around, as evidenced for example by Maisky's series of public Second Front talks and private discussions with American newspapermen regarding inadequacy of American military and supply aid.

Maisky in London and Litvinov in Washington were busy at the same time agitating public opinion to demand a great ground offensive in the west. Roosevelt became increasingly annoyed—as Harriman learned during one of his visits to Washington—with Litvinov's second-front zeal. At the President's request, Harriman agreed to have a stern talk with the Soviet ambassador. "The President told me I could quote him as roughly as I wanted to, even to the point of saying we might ask for his recall," Harriman noted. "The President, I assume, preferred to have me do it instead of asking the State Department to raise the matter officially. I lunched with Litvinov alone at the Soviet embassy. I was very blunt with him and explained how upset the President was. I didn't go so far as to say that the President would ask for his recall, but I said if he continued that way he would get into serious difficulties with the President.

"Up to that point, Litvinov had been ebullient. I have never seen a man collapse so completely. His attitude showed that he was in a rather tenuous position with Stalin and he must have feared for his life in the event that his Washington mission ended in disgrace. Litvinov was falling between two stools: the more faithfully he carried out the instructions he was getting from Molotov, the more trouble he was in with Roosevelt." (When Litvinov was recalled to Moscow in August 1943, his British-born wife stayed behind in Washington for a time, confiding to friends that she feared she might never see her husband again. However, Litvinov and Maisky—whom Stalin recalled from London at about the same time—were both appointed Vice Commissars in the Ministry of Foreign Affairs, only to drop into obscurity after the war. Litvinov was succeeded in Washington by that most durable of Soviet ambassadors, Andrei A. Gromyko, then a diplomatic *Wunderkind* in his mid-thirties.)

THE SPRING OF 1943 was a bitter season for the alliance. With suspicion rising in Moscow as the Arctic convoys were again suspended and the second front once more postponed, the spring thaws also brought to the surface the new-old problem of Poland, which was to bedevil the Roosevelt-Churchill-Stalin relationship until the President died and the Prime Minister lost power in 1945. On April 13 the German government announced with great fanfare the discovery of mass graves in the forest of Katyn, near Smolensk, an area then occupied by Hitler's troops. The Germans accused the Soviet government of having murdered several thousand Polish officers who were known to have been interned by the Russians after their invasion of eastern Poland in September 1939. On April 16 the Polish government in London issued a public appeal to the International Red Cross, requesting an impartial on-the-spot investigation of the Katyn murders. "We have become accustomed to the lies of German propaganda and

we understand the purpose behind its latest revelations," the Polish
statement said. "In view, however, of abundant and detailed German
information concerning the discovery of the bodies of many thousands
of Polish officers near Smolensk, and the categorical statement that
they were murdered by the Soviet authorities in the spring of 1940,
the necessity has arisen that the mass graves should be investigated and
the facts alleged verified by the competent international body . . ."[1]

On April 21 Stalin notified Churchill and Roosevelt that he was
going to break relations with Premier Sikorski's regime for acting on
an "infamous Fascist slander." It merely proved, Stalin said, what he
had long suspected: that the London Poles were not only hostile to
Russia but under Nazi influence. Both Churchill and Roosevelt appealed to Stalin. The Prime Minister conceded that even if the Polish
government had been foolish to act on German accusations, this was no
time for quarrels in the alliance. "We have got to beat Hitler," he
pleaded. But the Moscow radio confirmed the break two days later.

Harriman, who was about to return to the United States, called on
Sikorski on May 1. "I asked him bluntly why the message had been sent
to the International Red Cross," he recalled. "I put it to him that
whether the German accusations turned out to be true or false, the
Polish statement was bound to have a disastrous effect in Moscow. He
asked me to tell the President that he recognized it had been a great
mistake for his Defense Ministry to issue the statement. He had been
in bed at the time running a high fever, Sikorski said. He assured me
that even though he believed the Russians were responsible for the
Katyn massacre, he would try to disregard his personal feelings and
go as far as he decently could to patch things up with Stalin. But it
would be difficult to persuade his Cabinet, because of such actions as
the Soviet government's refusal to allow the families of thousands of
Polish soldiers to leave Russia. His last word to me was that he feared
a Soviet takeover of all the smaller states of Eastern Europe if the
Russians persisted in their breach of relations with the Polish government in London."

The Soviets, in fact, had unveiled a shadowy "Union of Polish
Patriots" in Moscow, which promptly denounced the London Poles.
The emergence of this new group foreshadowed an eventual Communist challenge to the government-in-exile, already on the defensive
for its Katyn accusations. A graver blow followed with the death that
summer of General Sikorski in an airplane accident at Gibraltar.
Sikorski was, in Harriman's view, the only effective national leader in
the exile regime. He alone could keep its quarrelsome factions and
personalities working together, Harriman felt, and he alone had demonstrated a capacity for dealing with Stalin. Sikorski's successor, Stanislaw Mikolajczyk, took office on July 14. Mikolajczyk, representing

the Polish Peasant party, inherited the heartbreaking responsibility of leadership at the worst possible moment. Although he impressed Harriman as a decent, able man of moderately liberal views, Mikolajczyk plainly lacked Sikorski's authority for the struggle ahead, not only with the Russians and their Polish Communist protégés in Moscow but also with those of his own Cabinet colleagues who equated any concession to the Soviet Union with national dishonor.

AT THE HEIGHT OF THE FUROR over Poland on April 29, Churchill decided the time had come for another visit to Washington, his third such trip since the United States entered the war. The Prime Minister at first had invited Hopkins and General Marshall to meet with him and General Brooke in North Africa. He wanted to make certain there would be no great delays in launching the Sicily landing. Churchill had told Harriman, as early as March 28, that he feared a delay would give the Germans an opportunity to reinforce Sicily and thus make the invasion all the more hazardous. The Prime Minister also had in mind deciding then and there—with Hopkins and Marshall—where the Allies should strike next. Hopkins sent back word, however, that the President preferred to put off the next Anglo-American strategy meeting until the Tunisian situation had clarified. Hopkins, meanwhile, had suggested to Harriman that he return to Washington for consultations. Since Lord Beaverbrook, no longer a member of the British government, was also on his way to the United States, the two were planning to travel together. At the last moment the Prime Minister decided to make the trip himself, inviting Harriman and Beaverbrook to travel with him on board the blue-ribbon passenger liner *Queen Mary*, which had been converted to a troop transport. She was then in the Clyde, loading some 5,000 German prisoners of war from North Africa for internment in the United States. The two principal decks were quickly sealed off from the rest of the ship and restored to some semblance of prewar comfort for the Prime Minister and his party.

To confuse the enemy, notices in the Dutch language had been posted around the ship, with the aim of starting rumors that Queen Wilhelmina of the Netherlands—not Churchill—was traveling to America. In addition, a number of ramps suitable for wheelchairs had been constructed along the passageways to spread the equally false rumor that President Roosevelt would be sailing to England on the return voyage. "The more tales, the more safety," Churchill used to say. Having installed his indispensable map room on board, together with his staff of cipher clerks, secretaries and military aides, the Prime Minister was able to keep in constant touch with his Cabinet and with the war.

At luncheon the first day out, according to Harriman's notes of the voyage, Beaverbrook suggested that the Prime Minister ought to drive through the streets of New York—and be recognized by the populace—when the *Queen Mary* docked. Brendan Bracken, the British Minister of Information, would like that, Beaverbrook said. When Harriman countered that the Secret Service would not like it at all, Churchill growled, "One can always do what one wants to if it takes people by surprise. There is not time for plotters to develop their nefarious plans." Churchill liked the idea so well that he talked of cabling Roosevelt about the arrangements Beaverbrook had proposed. The Prime Minister would be put ashore in a small boat at the Battery and ride uptown (so Beaverbrook imagined the route) along Broadway and down Fifth Avenue to Pennsylvania Station. That evening, as they played cards together after dinner, Harriman pointed out to Churchill that Beaverbrook's idea of Manhattan geography was pretty foggy and that the notion of suddenly surfacing the Prime Minister in the streets of New York was potentially dangerous, even absurd. The Prime Minister changed the subject.

Churchill, who loved to gamble for modest stakes, used to say that while it might seem undignified for His Majesty's First Minister to play cards with subordinates, it was entirely appropriate for him to play with "the President's personal envoy," as he liked to describe Harriman. They most frequently played bezique, a two-handed game calling for the use of six packs, each of thirty-two cards, all shuffled together. As Churchill's stubby fingers made the task of shuffling all those cards a slow business, he and Harriman had some of their most interesting conversations while the Prime Minister was thus engaged. Harriman's notes for May 6 suggest the sweep of their card-table talks:

> He talked a lot during bezique and afterward, when we went alone to the War Room, about the amount of effort that was being put into protecting this ship. He spoke of the tremendous courage and risks of the merchant seamen. He didn't like the idea that he personally was given all the protection but explained that everything in war was relative and the value of the party to the war* as against the individual lives was the

---

* The Prime Minister's party on board the *Queen Mary* included Admiral of the Fleet Sir Dudley Pound, the First Sea Lord; Admiral Sir James Somerville, Commander in Chief, Eastern Fleet; General Sir Alan Brooke, Chief of the Imperial General Staff; General Archibald P. Wavell, Commander in Chief, India; Air Chief Marshal Sir Charles Portal, Chief of Air Staff; Air Marshal Sir Richard Peirse, Air Officer Commanding, India; Lord Leathers, Minister of War Transport; Lord Cherwell, the Prime Minister's scientific adviser; Lord Beaverbrook; and Lieutenant General Sir Hastings Ismay, chief of staff to the Minister of Defence. Sir William Beveridge, author of the new British social security plan, was also on board, with Lady Beveridge.

basis for it. He spoke about the losses of the British merchant seamen—21,000 out of perhaps 100,000—[which were] relatively much greater than the losses of the armed services. He went over the map of the Atlantic again and the location of the submarines, the convoys and their escorts. He said: "I think perhaps it is time for us to attempt to get the Portuguese to give us use of the Azores. Will the President support me? It will save perhaps 1,000,000 tons of shipping." We had just had sad news that thirteen ships had been torpedoed out of one [convoy] of fifty-odd ships, eleven of them already sunk. "It is sad to think of these convoys, the ships and their priceless cargoes. It is all delaying the end of the war." I said I understood the Portuguese had at last finished their airfield on one of the islands which, although short, was useful for reconnaissance aircraft. He said, "But we can use [the Azores] for seaplanes." I explained (which he had not seemed to grasp) the difficulties with swells at Horta for regular operation. As I have been consistently an Azores advocate for many months, I naturally expressed the hope that he would press the matter. . . .

Harriman, who had detected some backsliding from the Prime Minister's endorsement of daylight bombing by the Eighth Air Force (owing to particularly heavy losses in a recent raid on Bremen), cautioned the Prime Minister against disparaging the American air tactics in his Washington conversations. He explained that advocates of the Pacific strategy were already pressing for the diversion of new B-17s to that theater; they were arguing that since the British had no enthusiasm for the American air effort in Europe, the bombers could be better used in the Pacific:

I said that the anti-British and anti-Atlantic group were always ready to explain how wise the British were when it was [in] their interest to do so. This seemed to amuse him and later on in the evening, he said: "Don't worry, I won't express my views about bombing; but it is a tragedy that your brave men are taking such risks in order to prove a theory when they could be more effectively employed—and with less risk." I explained that . . . they were doing better with a small force than they had ever thought they could and that, to do daylight bombing justice, it had always been maintained by the advocates that at least 500 bombers were needed. He said, "You really believe it!" I said, "I do, until the defense tactics of the Germans change."

Churchill acknowledged that the .50-caliber guns of the Flying Fortresses had proven highly effective against German fighters. But he complained that the American air force, by its commitment to daylight bombing, had put itself at the mercy of the weather; too many missions were being canceled for lack of clear skies. Harriman did not press the argument further, relieved that Churchill had promised not to raise it in Washington.

The following evening at dinner, however, Churchill reopened the discussion. He argued that the destruction of German industry would have been much farther along if the Eighth Air Force had bombed by night, as the Lancasters of the RAF Bomber Command were doing with great success. To Churchill's apparent surprise, Air Chief Marshal Portal stood up for the American policy. Harriman noted:

> I again told the Prime Minister that if he wanted to assure the allocation of American bombers to the Pacific Theater there was no better way than for him to make in Washington, even to the President, the statement he had just made.
>
> Something that I don't fully understand has set his mind that daylight bombing will not be effective—the combination of weather and the great losses which he is sure will be suffered. He evidently has not seen the overall figures of average losses. The Bremen raid was much in his mind—16 [bombers lost] out of 80. Portal and I tried to explain the special circumstances of this raid: the fact that [a German] reconnaissance plane accidentally picked them up over the North Sea and that the German fighter force was in the air over the target . . . We spent a good deal of time on the subject. The Prime Minister talked about what a similar number of Lancasters would have done. I continued to ask him to keep his mind open until the middle of the summer, when the American Air Force would have enough planes to try out their tactics in accordance with plan. The PM got the idea that I was somewhat offended . . . and said that he never minded when I was critical of the British and we must be able to talk things over frankly. I feel the argument made no impression on his judgment [although] he again said he would not discuss the subject in Washington.

Churchill was in holiday spirits throughout the voyage. He did not appear greatly perturbed when on the second evening out, the night duty officer in the improvised war room pointed out that a German submarine, heading west from the French port of Brest, seemed likely to cross the *Queen Mary*'s course about fifteen miles ahead of the great liner. Churchill assured Harriman: "Pound says we are just as likely to ram the submarine as it is to see us first." He then disclosed that he had arranged for a machine gun to be fixed in his own lifeboat.

CHURCHILL: I won't be captured. The finest way to die is in the excitement of fighting the enemy. (*Then, after a moment's thought*) It might not be so nice if one were in the water and they tried to pick me up.

HARRIMAN: Prime Minister, this is all very disquieting to me. I thought you told me that the worst a torpedo could do to this ship, because of its compartments, was to knock out one engine room, leaving sufficient power to steam at twenty knots.

CHURCHILL: Ah, but they might put two torpedoes in us. You must come with me in the boat and see the fun.

The following day, May 7, word reached Churchill's floating command post that Tunis and Bizerte had fallen to the Allies, closing off the last ports for German reinforcements from Italy. At last the Battle for Tunisia had been won, clearing the entire North African coast for the Allies. Harriman noted that the Prime Minister, showing "the human consideration that is typical of him," had shared the great news with three Royal Marines standing guard outside the war room. "There is good news," the Prime Minister said. "Have you heard it? Our troops are in Tunis." Having lost the Tunisian ports, Churchill predicted, the Germans would be unable to evacuate any appreciable number of their troops. Beaverbrook wanted to see a large bag of prisoners taken because, he said, Stalin would never believe that the British and American forces had killed so many Germans. In fact, 250,000 Axis soldiers were taken prisoner with the final collapse of their positions on May 13. Churchill sent word to London that church bells were to ring out the victory all over the United Kingdom, although he was not there to hear their joyous clang.

As he played a few hands of bezique with Harriman that evening, the Prime Minister said, "These are momentous events. Surely America will respond." His apparent concern was that after the proposed landing in Sicily the American military planners would insist upon returning troops and equipment to Britain for the invasion of France, instead of exploiting the new opportunities that he, for one, saw in the Mediterranean. Churchill was still for whacking the underbelly of the crocodile he had sketched for Stalin and Harriman nine months earlier, whacking it promptly and hard in 1943. But he had reason to worry—as Harriman had reminded him in their shipboard discussions of daylight bombing by the American air force in Britain—that many influential Americans wanted to see more troops and more resources committed to the war against Japan. As the Prime Minister advised Stalin in a cable dated May 10, he was on his way to Washington "to settle the further stroke after 'Husky' [the landing in Sicily] and also to discourage undue bias towards the Pacific . . ."[2]

A cable from Stalin had reached Churchill on shipboard, taking the British government to task for allowing the Polish government in London to launch an "anti-Soviet smear campaign" over the Katyn disclosures. ". . . it would have been only natural," Stalin wrote, "to dissuade one ally from striking a blow at another, particularly if the blow helped the common enemy. That, at any rate, is how I see the duty of an ally."[3] When Churchill showed the Stalin message to Harriman and Beaverbrook, the latter pronounced Stalin right, opening what seemed to Harriman a tirade against the Poles. Harriman's notes, dated May 7, make plain his own disapproval of Beaverbrook's views:

> Beaverbrook is for the appeasement policy toward Russia, to which I am dead opposed. I feel strongly that we must be friendly and frank but firm when they behave in a manner which is incompatible with our ideas. Otherwise we are storing up trouble for the future. I am also convinced that Stalin will have greater confidence and respect for us, as an ally in the war and postwar. These views I have held and expressed for at least 18 months.
>
> Beaverbrook is still an isolationist . . . and doesn't give a hoot in hell for the small nations. He would turn over Eastern Europe to Russia without regard to future consequences, the Atlantic Charter, etc.

Beaverbrook, who was in a somewhat equivocal position with respect to Churchill at the time, had seemed sulky at the beginning of the voyage. The Prime Minister put his hand on Beaverbrook's knee one day and softly said, "You don't talk any more." Beaverbrook later complained to Harriman, "I don't talk because the P.M. talks all the time." As the great champion of a second front in the west, Beaverbrook had disapproved of the North African campaign, dismissing it as a colossal blunder which had done nothing to speed the defeat of Germany. His personal ambitions, as Harriman noted, also had been frustrated:

> At the time he left the government and for some time thereafter [he] felt that the days of Churchill's Government were numbered and that there was a possibility, if he got out, that he would be called [to replace Churchill]. He believed, I think, that the situation would get so bad the public would call for him. Still, he personally made no public move to injure

Churchill at any time. He based his hopes largely on the demand of the people for a man who would be sympathetic
to Russia and had shown aggressive tendencies.

The hidden tension kept surfacing throughout the crossing. At
one point Beaverbrook ventured to disagree with the Prime Minister's
method of drafting, editing and redrafting cables. "A message is always better if you leave the flow as it comes out," he said. "If you
work over it, it loses its quality." This led to a discussion of good
writing and bad. Churchill sent for a copy of Fowler's *Modern English
Usage* and read aloud, with histrionic effect, certain passages on the
supposed wickedness of splitting infinitives and the use of "very"
instead of "much."* Beaverbrook alone gave the impression of being
bored by the Prime Minister's performance. "All that matters," he said,
"is that you make yourself understood." Churchill grunted, gazing at
Beaverbrook like an indulgent father whose small son had just said
something rude at a dinner party. That evening the Prime Minister
cajoled Beaverbrook into singing for the company some Presbyterian
hymns he had learned as a child in New Brunswick. Harriman found
it "an extraordinary performance," Beaverbrook being somewhat tone-
deaf. "He sang exactly as one would have thought he did when a boy
of twelve, shouting out the words without regard to note."

Churchill's admiration for Beaverbrook, in spite of their frequent
disagreements, had long impressed Harriman. Although Beaverbrook
had left the government in 1942, the Prime Minister still consulted him
steadily on matters involving the Russians. On May 8, for example,
Churchill read to Beaverbrook and Harriman a draft reply to Stalin's
cable complaining about the London Poles. When Beaverbrook objected that it was "too lengthy and protested too much," the Prime
Minister handed over the draft, saying, "Well, you rewrite it."
Churchill's attitude, Harriman felt, was tinged with gratitude for Beaver-

* The reader is left to imagine how Churchill delivered such lines from
Fowler as these: " 'The English-speaking world may be divided into (1) those who
neither know nor care what a split infinitive is; (2) those who do not know, but
care very much; (3) those who know and condemn; (4) those who know and
approve; and (5) those who know and distinguish . . .
" 'To the second class, those who do not know but do care, who would as
soon be caught putting their knives in their mouths as splitting an infinitive but
have only hazy notions of what constitutes that deplorable breach of etiquette,
this article is chiefly addressed. These people betray by their practice that their
aversion to the split infinitive springs not from instinctive good taste, but from
tame acceptance of the misinterpreted opinion of others; for they will subject
their sentences to the queerest distortions, all to escape imaginary split infinitives.
"To really understand" is a s.i.; "to really be understood" is a s.i.; "to be really understood" is not one; the havoc that is played with much well-intentioned writing
by failure to grasp that distinction is incredible.' "

brook's show of loyalty after resigning from the War Cabinet. The Prime Minister called him "my foul-weather friend." When Beaverbrook arranged to install a motion-picture projector at Chequers, together with a revolving supply of the latest films, the Prime Minister had said to Harriman, "Max knows how to do these things. I do not."

It seemed to Harriman an oddly naïve comment, rooted in Churchill's unworldly attitude toward money. One of the things the Prime Minister most admired about Beaverbrook was the fact that, born poor in a Presbyterian parsonage in Canada, he had made himself a millionaire by the age of thirty. Churchill, on the other hand, for all the advantages he was born to, had no talent for making money and regretted it. As he was shuffling the cards for another hand of bezique that evening, Churchill remarked, "It is a shame to have such a man out of the government; and yet he attacked many ministers so ferociously while in the government that he has created great bitterness against himself. I hope to find a way." Then, peering quizzically at Harriman, Churchill added, "You know, Max would like to come back."*

Harriman's notes of the conversation show that in spite of their disagreement over Russia he, too, would have liked to see Beaverbrook back in the government:

> I personally have great respect for Beaverbrook's drive and basic shrewdness. He is a bit theatrical in manner, appearing to make decisions with great rapidity. I saw him so intimately that I know these decisions were based on considerable study and prior discussion with members of his staff.
>
> Since Beaverbrook left the Government there is no one who has the aggressiveness to get things done in the same manner and I would personally welcome his return. He would make my job much easier.
>
> He is domineering—with somewhat the qualities of a bully —but when a man stands up to him he is apt to respect him rather than resent the incident.

During one of their shipboard conversations, Beaverbrook told Harriman that while he sometimes regretted being out of the government, he would refuse an appointment as ambassador to the United States, if it were offered, adding that he had no interest in rejoining the Cabinet. Harriman's impression was that Beaverbrook, in fact, would "jump at the chance" to rejoin the government if the circumstances were right—that is, if Churchill were to resign. "He always

---

* On September 28 Beaverbrook rejoined the government, but not the War Cabinet, as Lord Privy Seal.

shows the conflict within himself," Harriman noted, "of personal loyalty to Churchill and personal ambition to take an important part in the Government if the Prime Minister were out of it." During the same conversation Beaverbrook offered Harriman some remarkable unsolicited advice about his own future, suggesting that Harriman capitalize on his current prominence by running for the United States Senate:

> He explained the thing to do was to pick out a state where the election would be safe, taking up my residence and arranging it in advance.
> A curiously impractical point of view, based on British practice. Arizona or Idaho were the states of his selection. I didn't tell him that I had no political ambition and that my only interest was to do what little I could in connection with the war. He simply would not believe it.
> My only comment was that I was an adventurer in government affairs and was going to make decisions as they came along.
> "Ah, you make a grave mistake," he said. "A Senator is very powerful. You could have a great influence in the peace conference if you establish your position now. You have more intimate knowledge and understanding than anyone in the Senate. The politically powerful men in the United States have been Senators. You must have your own position, based on election, not a position calling for appointment by others."

"Running for the Senate was the last thing in the world I had in mind at the time," Harriman recalled. "I was working hard to see the war won and I expected to go back to private life as soon as it was over. But Max had a way of projecting his own ambitions to his friends and he was, I suppose, being kind in his fashion to forecast a splendid political career for me."

After dinner the three played poker, British style. Harriman and Beaverbrook had agreed beforehand that they would try not to win at the expense of Churchill, who played poker badly. But Beaverbrook, forgetting the agreement, played to win.

> This is typical of Beaverbrook's relationship with the Prime Minister [Harriman noted]. The PM considers that Beaverbrook can do a lot of things which he cannot, such as building up his successful newspapers, financial acquisitiveness, successful gambling, etc., and he does not understand what is back of them. Beaverbrook realizes this and never gives himself away. Winning from the PM at poker is an essential part of

their relationship . . . I came out one chip to the good, which
I considered a most successful and skillful performance.

Churchill, his spirits uplifted by the victory in Tunisia, had never
appeared more thoroughly relaxed. It was the eve of his third anniversary as Prime Minister and he had cause to reflect on the desperate
gamble he had taken in August of 1940 by dispatching to Egypt a
cruiser tank battalion, an infantry tank battalion and a light tank regi-
ment, the only fully equipped armored units Britain possessed, at a
time when the home islands were under direct threat of invasion. The
Tunisian victory, Harriman felt, really began with that daring decision
to reinforce the Middle East almost three years earlier.

ON MAY 11 THE *Queen Mary* anchored off Staten Island and Hopkins
came aboard to welcome the Prime Minister, escorting him and the
rest of the party to Washington by train for a two-week conference
code-named Trident. It was the largest strategy meeting since the
beginning of the war and the first in which field commanders from
the Far East took part. Churchill had brought Wavell from India.
Roosevelt had summoned General Joseph W. Stilwell and Chennault
from China, both determined to press for a bigger, bolder effort
against Japan, but each pushing his own plan.
    Harriman talked with both Stilwell and Chennault in Washington.
"I felt Chennault's idea of hitting Japan from air bases in China made
more sense than Stilwell's idea of getting American troops tied down
indefinitely in Burma," he recalled. Chennault, in fact, got more satisfaction than Stilwell from the Trident decisions, thanks to the backing
of Generalissimo Chiang Kai-shek. Chiang strongly endorsed Chennault's demand that all air transport into China for the next three
months be earmarked for aviation gasoline, and that decision was approved. Stilwell, who was pressing for more American infantry divisions to begin rolling back the Japanese in Burma, did not get them.
    As for operations in the Pacific, General MacArthur and Admiral
Chester Nimitz were authorized to step up the pace of their campaign
in the South Pacific, including the seizure of the Marshall and Caroline
islands, together with the positions the Japanese were still holding in
the Solomons, the Bismarck Archipelago and New Guinea. American
troops having landed on Attu Island in the Aleutians on May 11, Trident authorized a second landing on the island of Kiska to complete
the expulsion of the Japanese from the Aleutians.
    Roosevelt refused, however, to divert the main Allied effort from
Europe, insisting on the major invasion of France for which Stalin had
been clamoring since 1941. The target date for this operation, now

renamed Overlord, was fixed for May 1, 1944. The Combined Chiefs of Staff agreed that the initial assault force was to be made up of nine divisions, two of them airborne. Twenty more divisions were to be ready to move in as soon as the bridgehead had been secured. The task of assembling an invasion force of this size in the British Isles would call for the transfer of four American and three British divisions from the Mediterranean after November 1, precisely as Churchill had foretold with some anxiety in his shipboard conversations with Harriman.

The Prime Minister's hope of striking across the Adriatic into the Balkans as soon as Italy was knocked out of the war had to be deferred. Eisenhower got the go-ahead signal to plan other operations beyond the invasion of Sicily, just in case more military pressure was needed to knock Italy out of the war. But these plans would be subject to later review and approval by the Combined Chiefs. In short, no firm decision was made to follow up the conquest of Sicily with an invasion of at least the heel and toe of the Italian boot, a matter of bitter disappointment to Churchill.

Trident also approved a plan Harriman had advocated since his first trip to Washington with Churchill in December 1941—a plan to seize the Azores. Happily, the Allies did not have to fight for them. The War Cabinet in London insisted that the matter of establishing Allied air bases in the Azores should be negotiated with the Portuguese government, and the negotiations, in fact, succeeded without armed pressure after five months.

The combined British-American bomber offensive against Germany was to be heavily increased, building up in four phases to reach its peak in April 1944, a month before the Allies landed on the coast of northern France. Churchill kept his promise, made to Harriman on shipboard, not to question or disparage the daylight-bombing efforts of General Eaker's Eighth Air Force.

Trident was the first of the wartime conferences to be marked by a mood of genuine confidence that the war, at least in Europe, was on the way to being won. The hard-won Allied victory in Tunisia, soon to be followed by the landing in Sicily, and the turning of the tide of battle in Russia had wrought a remarkable change in outlook. For the first time the Chiefs of Staff were able to report that sufficient manpower and matériel had been provided for all contemplated operations.

At the end of the conference Churchill flew to North Africa with General Marshall for talks with Eisenhower while Harriman stayed behind in Washington. He discovered that far from facing the chronic shortfall of years past, the United States had built more Sherman tanks than its own forces, or those of the Allies, could use. The Russians had cut back and then eliminated their requests for Shermans—no surprise to Harriman in light of his conversation with General Lebidov in Moscow the past summer. And the British, having built up their own tank production, were reluctant to accept 4,000 additional Shermans they had pleaded for in November. Suddenly the Allies were confronted with an embarrassing overproduction of tanks. The United States, in particular, had built a number of tank factories in great haste and at high cost, which had been widely advertised as one of the signal wartime achievements of the Roosevelt Administration. Now it faced the prospect of having to shut down or greatly reduce production. Harriman succeeded in persuading a most reluctant Churchill to accept 2,000 more Shermans in 1944—at the cost of cutting back British production by 200 tanks in 1943 and by 800 more in 1944. After his return to London, Churchill agreed when pressed by Harriman to accept 1,000 additional Shermans but extracted in exchange a promise that the United States would speed delivery of special-purpose machine tools to build Meteor engines for Britain's new Cromwell tank program.

The shipbuilding lag also had eased to the point where Roosevelt on May 28 approved Harriman's suggestion of late March that more ships should be transferred to Britain. The United States had so greatly expanded its merchant fleet that it was now short of crews, while the British, their merchant fleet reduced by sinkings, had some 10,000 more seamen and officers than they could find ships for. "I am directing the War Shipping Administration," Roosevelt wrote to Churchill, "under appropriate bareboat charter, to transfer to your flag for temporary wartime use during each of the next ten months a minimum of fifteen ships. I have furthermore suggested to them that this be increased to twenty [a month]."

Yet relations with Russia showed no sign of improvement. Roosevelt at this point revived his plan for a personal meeting with Stalin. The President sent Joseph E. Davies, his former ambassador in Moscow, on a brief trip in May to put the proposition before Stalin. According to Davies, Stalin half promised, after many long hours of sparring, to meet the President about July 15. But on June 11, as soon as he heard about the Trident decision putting off the cross-Channel invasion until the spring of 1944, Stalin sent identical messages to Roosevelt and Churchill, bitterly listing their previous assurances that the invasion of France was in prospect for the autumn of 1943.

> Your decision creates exceptional difficulties for the Soviet Union . . . and leaves the Soviet Army, which is fighting not only for its country but also for its Allies, to do the job alone . . . against an enemy that is still very strong and formidable. . . . [The Soviet Government] cannot align itself with this

decision, which . . . may gravely affect the subsequent course of the war.[4]

Churchill's reply, dated June 19, was intended to mollify Stalin. It had the opposite effect. He wrote:

> I quite understand your disappointment but . . . it would be no help to Russia if we threw away a hundred thousand men in a disastrous cross-Channel attack . . . The best way for us to help you is by winning battles and not by losing them.[5]

Stalin responded with a message of surpassing bitterness, repeating once again in considerable detail the various second-front assurances he had received earlier and closing with a clear accusation of bad faith against the Western Allies:

> You say that you "quite understand" my disappointment. I must tell you that the point here is not just the disappointment of the Soviet Government, but the preservation of its confidence in its Allies, a confidence which is being subjected to severe stress. One should not forget that it is a question of saving millions of lives in the occupied areas of Western Europe and Russia and of reducing the enormous sacrifices of the Soviet armies, compared with which the sacrifices of the Anglo-American armies are insignificant.[6]

Stalin's mood can be gauged by his lack of response to a request from Roosevelt, in advance of the first air raid on the Rumanian oil fields at Ploesti, that damaged American bombers be allowed to make emergency landings in southern Russia instead of having to fight their way back across Europe. Stalin did not give his reluctant approval until a week after the first Ploesti attack had been made, with disastrous results. Virtually all the American bombers were lost or their crews interned after forced landings in Turkey.*

It was at this low point in the history of the alliance that Roosevelt asked Harriman whether he would accept the post of ambassador to the Soviet Union. The need to replace Admiral Standley had become apparent after the ambassador's outburst in March, when he accused the Soviet government of keeping its people in ignorance of the massive aid they were receiving from the United States. It was not the first time that Harriman had been offered the Moscow embassy. Hopkins had raised the matter in 1941, when Harriman returned from the joint mission to Moscow with Beaverbrook. "Harry and I agreed that Stein-

---

* The first effective attack on Ploesti was carried out many weeks later, on August 1, 1943. Of the 178 B-24s assigned to the mission, 54 were lost.

hardt ought to be replaced," Harriman recalled. "But I did not want to leave London. I had just seen what a hopelessly restricted life the foreign diplomats led in Moscow, the way they were fenced in. I was also thoroughly enjoying my relationships with Churchill and the British. I felt I was accomplishing a great deal there in connection with the war and I recognized that in Moscow I would be at the end of the line, probably losing such value as I had in London." So Harriman had declined, suggesting to Roosevelt that he send Admiral Standley, who had been personally selected by the President as the naval member of the Harriman mission to Moscow in 1941.

Harriman respected Standley, had been impressed by his vigorous ideas on how the war could be won, and believed that as a military man —and a personal friend of Roosevelt—he could be effective in Washington as well as in Moscow. But now that Standley was to be replaced, in any event, Harriman discussed the Moscow assignment at length with both Roosevelt and Hopkins during his frequent visits to the White House, including a dinner with the President on June 17, four days before his own departure for London. Roosevelt stressed the importance he attached to the establishment of closer personal relations with Stalin. Harriman promised to consider the proposition carefully and to send word back when he had made up his mind.

In the late evening of June 21, Harriman left the British Overseas Airways base in Baltimore with Beaverbrook and twenty-five other passengers, including General William Donovan of the Office of Strategic Services and Roy Howard of the United Press, on board the Boeing flying boat *Bangor*. The route—Baltimore to Botwood in Newfoundland, Foynes in Ireland and then to Poole, England—had been set up following Harriman's recommendations for improved transatlantic service two years earlier. Allowing for the six-hour time difference between Baltimore and London, and the rail journey up to London from Poole, Harriman made excellent time. He was back in London at five-fifteen in the evening on June 23.

CHAPTER X

Farewell to London

"There seems a real danger," Beaverbrook wrote to Hopkins, before flying back to London with Harriman, "that we shall go on indefinitely sewing the last button on the last gaiter, and the risk is increased by the undoubted fact that a real Second Front will always entail big risks, always remain the most difficult operation in military warfare. But if we are not prepared to accept the risks, face the difficulties, suffer the casualties, then let us concentrate at once exclusively on the production of heavy bombers and think in terms of 1950."[1]

Beaverbrook's heavy irony might better have been addressed to Churchill, who continued to harbor gloomy thoughts about the appalling danger of a cross-Channel invasion. The Prime Minister had flown to Algiers after the Trident conference, taking General Marshall with him, and had all but persuaded Eisenhower (in spite of Marshall's misgivings) that the next step after Sicily should be a plan to invade southern Italy across the Straits of Messina. The heel of the Italian boot had a special appeal for Churchill. He saw it as the means to his chosen end, a comparatively low-cost assault on the Balkans.[2] Harriman, who was seeing the Prime Minister almost daily at this period, observed that "he always had his eyes on the Balkans." The idea of striking across the Adriatic at what he called the "soft underbelly" of Hitler's Europe, rather than at the "hard snout," appeared to him the surer road to victory. The American Chiefs of Staff, on the other hand, kept insisting that the knockout blow could only be delivered across the Channel. They looked upon any proposed thrust into Yugoslavia or Greece as a wasteful diversion, confirming their belief that in this world war as in the first, Churchill had a weakness for "eccentric operations." But even now that he was committed to a cross-Channel landing in the spring of 1944, Churchill remained fearful. "He saw extreme dangers in it," Harriman recalled. "Nothing of the type had ever been undertaken before; the difficulties loomed large. Yet much of the criticism then being directed at Churchill seemed to me unjust. For more than two years I had watched him driving his generals to larger, bolder actions. One Sunday at Chequers, after a specially convened staff meeting, Ismay and I were walking down the hall to our bedrooms. It was two o'clock in the morning. As we approached my door the general shook his head and said. 'Churchill is the greatest military genius in history. He can use one division on three fronts at the same time.'

"There were two aspects to the difference of opinion between the British and the American military. One was the actual capability of the British army to land on the heavily fortified coast of France, which General Marshall in my judgment overestimated. The second was the inherent difficulty of such an operation, which the British in some ways understood better than the Americans. There could be no doubt, however, that Churchill was looking for the end run, while Marshall and Stimson were determined on the direct plunge."

Harriman had returned to London on June 23 with another difficult assignment from Roosevelt. He was to deliver the message that the President proposed to meet privately with Stalin prior to any formal conference of the Big Three. The objective, as expressed by Secretary of State Hull, was "to talk Mr. Stalin out of his shell, so to speak, away from his aloofness, secretiveness and suspiciousness until he broadens his views, visualizes a more practical international cooperation in the future, and indicates Russia's intentions both in the East and in the West."[3] Roosevelt felt the need to establish a personal relationship with Stalin, as Churchill had managed to do on the visit with Harriman in August. He saw no reason for the Prime Minister to take offense if he, too, could arrange to talk with Stalin face to face. Moreover, Roosevelt believed that he would get along better with Stalin in Churchill's absence. The Prime Minister, after all, was an unabashed imperialist who had marked himself as an enemy of the Bolshevik regime by openly advocating Allied intervention to choke off the Revolution in 1918. Roosevelt felt that he was under no such handicap in addressing Stalin. Harriman delivered the oral message from Roosevelt the same evening and promptly reported back:

> Max [Beaverbrook] and I arrived late Wednesday afternoon after two nights on the plane with little sleep to find an invitation to dine with the Prime Minister that evening. Max was tired and would have preferred to go to bed. He was not,

therefore, in too good a mood. The dinner, which included Mrs. Churchill and Kathleen, was argumentative and some of the fundamental disagreements between the two men came out. This type of argument with Max always upsets the Prime Minister.

Max left at midnight. I stayed to give the Prime Minister alone your several messages. The talk, which started with the proposed [Roosevelt-Stalin] meeting, developed into a two-hour discussion of every subject—from de Gaulle to China to India to Poland, etc., coming back throughout the talk to Russia and the question of the meeting.

I have never had a better opportunity to be direct and frank and, as he has since been more friendly than ever, it is obvious that he has accepted the sincerity of my statements even though he did not always agree with them. He firmly believes a three-cornered meeting is in the interests of the war but he admitted that his viewpoint is colored by considerations of the reaction in Great Britain. My main argument was based on the long view as against the immediate—(1) the value of the intimate understanding that in all probability would result from a tête-à-tête, impossible with three persons, and (2) the great importance of the favorable reaction of the American people to it and to your participation . . . I explained the difference in the public reaction in the United States to a personal meeting of two as compared with a three-cornered meeting on British soil in which it would appear that he, Churchill, had been the broker in the transaction.

There is no doubt in my mind as to his sincere desire and determination to back you up in anything that you finally decide to do and, although I must emphasize his disappointment if he is not present, I am satisfied he would accept it in good part and that it would, in the long run, improve rather than adversely affect your relations with him.

Harriman left Downing Street for Grosvenor Square in the small hours of the new day believing that he had won Churchill's grudging acquiescence. But the Prime Minister, upon further reflection, decided he had to oppose the Roosevelt-Stalin meeting. There is evidence that he worried about the reaction of the British public; his critics would surely make the point that he and Britain were being passed over. Moreover, the troubled relationship with Stalin had taken an angry turn. Reproaches and recriminations over the Second Front were flying between Moscow and London. Thus Churchill, losing no time, addressed a personal message to Roosevelt the next morning:

I consider that a tripartite meeting at Scapa Flow or anywhere else on the globe that can be agreed not only of us
three but also of the staffs, who will come together for the
first time, would be one of the milestones of history. If this is
lost, much is lost.

You must excuse me expressing myself with all the frankness that our friendship and the gravity of the issue warrant. I
do not underrate the use that enemy propaganda would make
of a meeting between the heads of Soviet Russia and the United
States at this juncture with the British Commonwealth and
Empire excluded. It would be serious and vexatious, and many
would be bewildered and alarmed thereby. My journey to
Moscow with Averell in August 1942 was on altogether a
lower level, and at a stage in the war when we had only to
explain why no second front. Nevertheless, whatever you decide I shall sustain to the best of my ability here.[4]

The discussion continued for several days as Harriman dined again
with Churchill. At Chequers, that weekend of June 26–27, the Prime
Minister explained to Harriman his belief that Stalin's unrelenting pressure for a Second Front in 1943 sprang from his designs on the Balkans.
What better way to keep the Western Allies from landing in the
Balkans than to tie them down in a long and costly battle for Western
Europe? Harriman, on the other hand, inclined to Roosevelt's views
that Stalin's reproach-filled cables were designed, among other things,
to satisfy his Kremlin colleagues and his military staff that he was
sparing no effort to bring the Western armies into battle against the
main force of the Wehrmacht.

In a letter to Roosevelt, dated July 5, Harriman warmly endorsed
the idea of a face-to-face meeting with Stalin. Having no faith in Joe
Davies, who had tried and failed to arrange a meeting, he offered to
fly to Moscow himself. The letter makes clear that Harriman was still
of two minds about accepting the Moscow embassy:

As you know, I am a confirmed optimist in our relations
with Russia because of my conviction that Stalin wants, if ob-
tainable, a firm understanding with you and America more
than anything else—after the destruction of Hitler. He sees
Russia's reconstruction and security more soundly based on it
than on any alternative. He is a man of simple purposes and,
although he may use devious means in attempting to accomplish
them, he does not deviate from his long-run objectives.

The situation is today in the making and we have much at

stake. If you don't get a follow-up on the Davies letter,* you may want to consider sending me to Moscow soon (assuming that you think I am the man to go).

I have thought a good deal about it since you talked with me and have some definite views as to how this situation might be handled. If you consider sending me, I would respectfully suggest that you recall me to Washington and give me an opportunity to put my ideas before you. You could then decide whether I should go. Real accomplishment by an Ambassador in Moscow is a gamble, with the odds against success, but the stakes are great both for the war in Europe and in the Pacific —and after.

I would know within a couple of months in Moscow whether I could be of value and would ask that, if I have not been able to do a job, I could then return or be fired.

I am so keen about the work you have given me in London, which I feel is of increasing value as the time for the offensive approaches, that I would like to go back to it if I cannot do a real job in Moscow. I am sure I can be of more use to you and the war in London than to remain in Moscow as a glorified communications officer.

Harriman was anything but eager to leave London. He had been happy and productive there, establishing the most intimate relationships with Churchill and the members of his government during the long, dark period of defeats and disasters. But now that victory was in prospect, his work in London had undergone a total transformation. In little more than two years the Allies had largely overcome their desperate scarcity—of aircraft, tanks, guns, and above all else, shipping. Although Roosevelt's great Arsenal of Democracy had taken many frustrating months to tool up, once geared to full production for war it had rolled out astonishing quantities of ships, weapons and military equipment. Now the Harriman Mission was trying to persuade the British to import more equipment which had been overproduced in the United States, such as medium tanks and aerial bombs.

Harriman knew and shared Roosevelt's concern about building a solid relationship with Stalin. The need to coordinate and synchronize military operations, he felt, was bound to become urgent as the Western Allies made good their landing in France and started their

* Davies on his return from Moscow had delivered to the President a letter from Stalin, dated May 26, 1943, agreeing that a meeting of the two was "necessary and that it should not be postponed," but declining to fix a date in view of the uncertain battlefront situation.

advance on Germany while the Red Army pushed westward to meet them. Another large question for the whole alliance, still unanswered, was whether—and when—the Soviet Union would enter the war against Japan.

"We had learned in the Pacific how fiercely the Japanese could fight," Harriman recalled. "I, for one, never doubted from what Stalin had said that he would come into the war against Japan. In fact, I believed that we could not keep him out, even if we wanted to, once Hitler had been defeated. But there was a real question whether he would come in early enough to help in the defeat of Japan. So, all things considered, it looked as if the job in Moscow would be of more critical importance than the job I was doing in London at that stage of the war.

"A large number of important people in the West, including the Prime Minister and the President, as well as some lesser lights, had the idea that they knew how to get along with Stalin. I confess that I was not entirely immune to that infectious idea. Having been to Moscow in 1941 and again in 1942, having been through those tough talks with Stalin, and having come out of those tough sessions with some sort of agreement, I was quite hopeful of accomplishing significant results. I felt I would be able to capitalize on my experience there. So when Roosevelt finally asked me to go, in August, I accepted."

Concerning Britain's part in the war against Japan, Churchill moved to erase any lingering doubts in a speech at the London Guildhall on June 30. After the defeat of Germany and Italy, he said, "Every man, every ship and every airplane in the King's service that can be moved to the Pacific will be sent there, and there maintained in action by the people of the British Commonwealth and Empire in priorities for as many flaming years as are needed to make the Japanese in their turn submit or bite the dust."

By midsummer of 1943, events were in the saddle, rapidly overtaking the Allied strategists. On July 10 a combined force of American, British and Canadian troops landed on the southern coast of Sicily, and in a hard campaign lasting thirty-eight days, completed its conquest of the island. On July 19, 521 planes of the United States Ninth Air Force in North Africa attacked the railway yards in Rome. Benito Mussolini, first of the Fascist dictators, was meeting with Hitler at the Villa Feltre, near Rimini, when he heard the news. He rushed back to find his regime of twenty-one years in danger. Six days later Mussolini was overthrown and arrested on the orders of Marshal Pietro Badoglio, who had been appointed by King Victor Emmanuel to form a new Cabinet. On the eastern front, Hitler had opened his grand summer offensive against the Kursk salient, between Belgorod and Orel, on July 5. The Russians, having concentrated heavy tank forces in the area through the winter and spring, were ready for the attack. After a furious tank battle, the largest ever fought, the Red Army broke the German advance and on July 15 announced the first in a series of victories, culminating in the recapture of Belgorod and Orel on August 4–5. By August 10 the Wehrmacht was in retreat along a front 300 miles wide.

All these developments raised immediate questions about operations to follow. Roosevelt continued to press for his tête-à-tête with Stalin before any meeting of the Big Three, and Churchill had now abandoned his efforts to block it.[5] But Stalin again cabled the President on August 8 that he would have to stay at home and tend to his "primary duty—the direction of action at the front."[6] He apologized for the lapse of twenty-three days between Roosevelt's last message and his reply, explaining that he had just returned from the front. "I have no doubt that you take into account our military position and will understand the delay of the answer," Stalin wrote.

By the time his reply was received, Churchill was once again crossing the Atlantic for a meeting with Roosevelt—this time at Quebec. Harriman had received a message from Roosevelt on July 31 reading: "Hope you can come with the Colonel." Thus on August 5, with Harriman and his daughter Kathleen on board, the *Queen Mary* sailed from Greenock, Scotland, for Halifax. The Prime Minister, accompanied by his wife, his daughter Mary and an official party of 238 persons, was traveling in the guise of Colonel Warden, a *nom de guerre* that paid its respects to his honorific position as Warden of the Cinque Ports. Once again Harriman dined with the Prime Minister every evening and had occasion to plumb his thoughts at the card table. "I found Churchill still worried that the Americans, in their preoccupation with the climactic assault on the French Coast, would insist upon withdrawing troops and landing craft from the Mediterranean, effectively vetoing the operations he had in mind for Italy," Harriman recalled. "The Prime Minister readily acknowledged the need to relieve the military pressures on the Russians, but he argued that the line of the Po River in Italy was as good a position as any from which to fight the Germans. If the Allies pressed their advantage now, he said, the Italians might turn on the Germans and the Balkans might collapse as well. Churchill also talked of the need to improve relations with Stalin, possibly by sending Beaverbrook on a special mission to Moscow, although nothing came of that idea."

After docking at Halifax on the evening of August 9, Churchill and his considerable company boarded two special trains of the Canadian National Railroad for the overnight trip to Quebec. The following afternoon he took up residence in the Citadel, the historic fortress dominating the steep cliffside scaled by General Wolfe and his Redcoats in surprising Montcalm on the Plains of Abraham. As the

American delegation had not yet left Washington, and Roosevelt was at Hyde Park, Harriman flew to New York with Kathleen to spend a few days with his family. He also had a chance to confer with Hopkins before joining the President and Churchill at Hyde Park for preliminary talks. The Prime Minister got there the long way around from Quebec because he wanted to show his daughter Niagara Falls. At dinner with the Roosevelts on August 14, Churchill launched into a discussion of his hopes that the "fraternal relationship" between the United States and Britain would be perpetuated in peacetime. He liked the idea of a loose association much better than a formal treaty, Churchill said, an association flexible enough to adjust itself to historical developments.* The First Lady, as Harriman's notes make clear, was not enchanted with the idea:

> Mrs. Roosevelt seemed fearful this might be misunderstood by other nations and weaken the U.N. concept. The PM did not agree, arguing that "any hope of the U.N. would be in the leadership given by the intimacy of the U.S. and Britain in working out misunderstanding with the Russians—and the Chinese too," he conceded, "if they become a nation."
>
> I was interested in the purity of Mrs. R's idealism. On the way to Quebec that night on the train, the PM expressed the highest admiration for Mrs. Roosevelt—"a spirit of steel and a heart of gold."

The Quebec Conference, code-named Quadrant, gave primary attention to detailed military plans for the proposed landing in France. Although Churchill assured Roosevelt and the American Chiefs of Staff that his long-standing objections to the cross-Channel operation had now been removed, he found many of the Americans still skeptical. After a talk with Churchill on August 16, Harriman noted: "He does not fully understand the suspicion that exists on the American side regarding the British determination to cross the Channel." The plain fact was that Churchill himself had contributed mightily to these American suspicions by dwelling at length on the hazards of Operation Overlord. As late as mid-July he had alarmed Secretary of War Stimson, then on a visit to London, by saying that "he would not have an easy moment"—even if the Allies put 50,000 men ashore on the Channel coast of France—because the Germans "could rush up sufficient forces to drive them back into the sea." The Prime Minister talked of seeing the Channel filled with "the corpses of defeated allies." When Stimson

* Churchill expanded on this idea, to the point of advocating a common citizenship, in a speech at Harvard University on September 6, when he received an honorary degree.

squarely charged him with still opposing the operation, the Prime Minister conceded that if he were commander in chief, he would not go ahead with Overlord. But, he said, having given his pledge "he would go through with it loyally."[7] Hopkins made certain that Roosevelt read Stimson's memorandum of the conversation with Churchill before leaving for Quebec. The Secretary of War was so dismayed that he wrote to the President, arguing that no British general could be trusted to command the invasion force because he was bound to be infected by the negative attitudes of both Churchill and General Brooke. "Though they have rendered lip service to the operation," Stimson wrote in his second memorandum, dated August 10, "their hearts are not in it." Stimson urged the President to appoint General Marshall supreme commander in Europe, adding: "We cannot afford to begin the most dangerous operation of the war under halfhearted leadership which will invite failure or, at least, disappointing results."[8]

Churchill had promised the job to General Brooke, but at Quebec he surprised Roosevelt by proposing that an American be appointed instead. The Prime Minister recognized that after the initial assault, which called for roughly equal numbers of British and American troops, the Americans would greatly outnumber the British forces on the ground in France. Both Stimson and Roosevelt were grateful for Churchill's change of heart and the matter was settled on that basis. For the moment, however, Roosevelt left in abeyance the name of the American commander.

On August 20, while the Combined Chiefs continued their talks at Quebec, the President, the Prime Minister and Mrs. Churchill went with Hopkins and Harriman on a fishing trip to Grand Lac de l'Epaule in Laurentide Park, some forty miles from the city. Harriman jotted down his impressions:

> A most delightful setting. A large log cabin kept for the Governor General, etc. Caught a lot of tiny little trout which were delicious eating at lunch. The Prime Minister and the President had a discussion of the Pacific war after lunch. (Harry went to sleep.)

The two had differed, at their meeting with the Combined Chiefs on August 19, in a discussion of long-term plans for the defeat of Japan. Churchill proposed the seizure of the tip of Sumatra, together with operations in northern Burma. Roosevelt said he doubted there were sufficient resources to do both. He favored concentrating all available resources in a campaign to reopen the Burma Road, "which represented the shortest line through China to Japan."[9] The argument, as recorded by Harriman, continued after lunch in the Governor General's cabin:

> The Prime Minister was arguing for "S"[umatra] which, I gathered, did not particularly appeal to the President. The Prime Minister was enthusiastic over this conception. As a matter of fact it is impossible because the shipping is not available. The President was more interested in "B"[urma]. The President used most of the glasses and salt cellars on the table, making a V-shaped diagram to describe the Japanese position in the . . . quadrant from Western China to the South Pacific, indicating the advantages of striking from either side, thereby capturing the sustaining glasses, and the disadvantage of trying to remove the outer ones [like Sumatra] one by one. It was not too serious but a pleasant relaxation.

The argument, in short, ran parallel to their disputations over striking across the Channel or in the Mediterranean. Roosevelt once again favored the straight-line approach, Churchill the end run.

In the afternoon, while fishing on the lake, Harriman talked alone with Hopkins about their respective personal plans. Hopkins, who had considered running for the Senate from Iowa and had even thought about the presidency, told Harriman that he no longer had any political ambitions. He looked forward to a quiet life after the war with freedom to write. This would mean getting a job that offered him a reasonable income and the time he needed for his writing. They also talked about relations with Russia, weighing the pros and cons of Harriman's going to Moscow as ambassador. Hopkins had been impressed by the argument of the Joint Chiefs of Staff that Russia was bound to be the dominant power in Europe after the war. He believed that winning her friendship was vitally important for the United States, not only for its effect in Europe but even more urgently as a means of hastening the defeat of Japan by bringing the Soviet Union into the Pacific war as a fighting ally.

Harriman's thought had been running in much the same direction. He accepted the military argument that the paramount objective of American policy must be to bring Russia into the war against Japan at the right moment. But he suffered no illusions about the dimensions of the task he would be taking on. He knew from his long talks with Stalin in 1941 and 1942 the great weight of suspicion to be overcome.

Stalin's suspicions that the Western Allies were being less than candid with him flared once again during the Quebec Conference. Roosevelt and Churchill had kept him informed of several peace feelers put out by the new Badoglio regime in Italy, including the latest approach to Sir Samuel Hoare, the British ambassador in Madrid, by Brigadier General Giuseppe Castellano. On August 19 they had cabled Stalin from Quebec, advising him that two Allied representatives, armed with specific instructions concerning surrender terms, were being sent from General Eisenhower's headquarters to meet with Castellano in Lisbon.*

The message, unfortunately, had been sent in sections, reaching Moscow incomplete and somewhat garbled. The British ambassador in Moscow, Sir Archibald Clark Kerr, delivered the less-than-complete text, promising a more accurate one in a day or two. But Stalin, sniffing conspiracy or collusion, pronounced the situation intolerable. The Soviet government, he complained, was not being kept informed of the Anglo-American negotiations with the Italians; "long passages" had been dropped from the message he received and the time was past due for Russia to be treated as an active partner by the Western powers. Stalin wrote:

> Until now the matter stood as follows: The United States and Great Britain made agreements but the Soviet Union received information about the results of the agreements between the two countries just as a passive third observer. I have to tell you that it is impossible to tolerate such situation any longer.[10]

He demanded that a military-political commission of the three powers be established at once and that it set up shop in Sicily "with the purpose of considering the questions concerning the negotiations with the different governments dissociating themselves from Germany."

Churchill has written that Roosevelt was much offended by the tone of Stalin's message. Harriman's notes of a dinner at Quebec on August 24 show that the Prime Minister was even more upset:

> The President came into the room first, after some of us had already arrived, saying: "We are both mad." He referred to the Prime Minister's, and his, annoyance over the most recent cable from Uncle Joe. His anger took the form of making him gayer than usual, both before and after dinner. The PM, however, arrived with a scowl and never really got out of his ill humor all evening—up to 3 A.M. when I left.
>
> I asked the President if he recalled the sentence in a cable that went to Joe from the PM in which he said: "I am entirely unmoved by your statement." I said the Prime Minister had shown me this cable and asked for comments. My only comment had been [to ask] him whether this statement was entirely

---

* The emissaries were Lieutenant General Walter Bedell Smith, Eisenhower's chief of staff, and Brigadier Kenneth W. D. Strong, a British officer who was G-2 on Eisenhower's staff.

accurate. The President roared with laughter and, much to my embarrassment, proceeded to tell the story to the PM when he came in. Needless to say, it not only fell flat but bounced in my direction. With a scowl, he said, "Impudence."

Eden and [Sir Alexander] Cadogan came in after dinner and got a chance to read the cable. As it was a bit garbled, and badly translated and paraphrased, I could not find that it was one about which to be irritated.

In recent days one has been worried about the Russians playing a lone hand. This cable rather rudely suggested that [Stalin] should have greater participation in certain directions. The Prime Minister and President were particularly annoyed because they had attempted to keep him fully informed. But one can't be annoyed with Stalin for being aloof and then be dismayed with him because he rudely joins the party. Pug Ismay and Anthony [Eden] shared this view . . . But the Prime Minister would not have any of it. After dinner, when we were alone, he said he foresaw "bloody consequences in the future," using "bloody" in the literal sense. "Stalin is an unnatural man. There will be grave troubles." He ticked off Anthony when [he] suggested it was not so bad, saying, "There is no need for you to attempt to smooth it over in the Foreign Office manner."

Toward the end of the Quebec Conference, Stalin nevertheless agreed to a meeting of the Big Three foreign ministers, preliminary to his first encounter with Roosevelt and Churchill, which had been proposed for the end of the year. Stalin, moreover, raised no objection to the Italian surrender terms, nor to Eisenhower's acceptance of the surrender in behalf of all three Allies on September 8. The next morning a task force commanded by General Mark W. Clark landed at Salerno, south of Naples. Although Italy had left the war officially, Hitler had determined that the war would not leave Italy. Rushing in reinforcements, the Germans quickly seized control of Rome and made certain that the Allies would have to fight their way up the Italian boot at the highest possible cost per mile.

WITH THE END of the Quebec Conference on August 24, Harriman returned to Washington and in a few days the matter of his going to Moscow was settled. He talked at length several times with Roosevelt about the challenge of working out a postwar settlement with the Russians. At luncheon with the President on September 2, the discussion turned to such territorial questions as the incorporation of the Baltic States into the Soviet Union, and Stalin's demands for territory at the expense of Poland and Rumania. Roosevelt, who had not taken issue with Hull in his refusal to consider any territorial changes until the war was won, told Harriman that he proposed to negotiate these matters with Stalin personally. Although the Russians obviously had the power to take what they wanted, the President said, he hoped to dissuade Stalin from unilateral action.

"He had the idea that he could explain to Stalin," Harriman recalled, "the world reaction he could expect from decent behavior on the part of the Russians, as opposed to the violent antagonism they would encounter if they seized certain territories. Roosevelt had several trading points in mind: first, the benefits to the Soviet Union that would flow from Stalin's cooperation with the United States and Britain; second, the need for restraint in order for the Soviet Union to be seated as an equal among the Great Powers at the council tables; and third, the promise of American support for measures to strengthen Russia's security such as the internationalization of access to the Baltic. The President told me he was willing to help in the postwar reconstruction of Russia. He also talked of internationalizing the Persian Railroad after the war to give the Soviet Union assured access to the Persian Gulf."

Roosevelt added that he hoped to persuade Stalin to grant the populations of the Baltic States the right to approve or disapprove any territorial changes through plebiscites, to be held within two or three years after reoccupation by the Russians. Any individual, moreover, who chose not to live under Soviet rule should be assured the right to emigrate. "Roosevelt probably had in mind the international implications of agreeing to a plebiscite, which would give a color of decency to the operation," Harriman has said in retrospect. "But he did not seem to realize that once the Russians occupied a territory, the plebiscite would almost certainly go their way."

Roosevelt also talked to Harriman that day about the treatment of Germany in defeat, a subject of deep concern to Stalin. "It was very much in Roosevelt's mind—as I know it was in Stalin's—that Germany would have to be controlled so that she could not again become a military threat to her neighbors," Harriman recalled. "He mentioned that postwar Germany ought to be denied all aircraft and that no German should be allowed to learn to fly. The President talked of breaking Germany up into three, four or five states."

Harriman's notes show that Roosevelt had no intention of stationing large American forces in Europe after the war, whether to help keep the peace or to occupy Germany:

He does not want to take direct military responsibility for Europe, only supplementary. It should be USSR, British and French (?) job. Occupation of Germany: through to Berlin. Perhaps not a big force. Three-party or four-party (if French are then admitted). Military commission to control. Small areas of occupation by army of each country.

Roosevelt also discussed the future of France with Harriman in considerable detail. "The President was very much opposed to the idea of imposing a government on the French, which he saw as the effect of backing De Gaulle. The people of France, he said, must be allowed to choose their own government. He had an elaborate theory that as the Allies liberated areas of France, the local people should be encouraged to select their own representatives from the villages, towns and cities; and when all of France was free, the representatives of these local governments should get together and constitute a national government. He felt that instead of imposing De Gaulle from the top down, the French ought to have an opportunity to develop their government from the grass roots up. It was an interesting theory, going back, as Roosevelt so often did, to the New England town meeting. But so far as I know it was never seriously discussed."

HAVING NOW ACCEPTED the Moscow assignment, Harriman spent the rest of his time in Washington in consultations on the future of the London mission and the staffing of his embassy. His own early experience in Moscow, and his anticipation of the need for direct military consultations with the Russians, led Harriman to urge the establishment of an American military mission in the Soviet Union, a step the British had taken earlier. Under Standley there had been a good deal of friction between the military and naval attachés, frequently involving Brigadier General Faymonville, who was in charge of Lend-Lease matters. Harriman felt that the British system, with one senior officer in command of the mission, would be more effective. Roosevelt quickly approved the idea, referring Harriman to Marshall and King for more detailed consideration. They, in turn, agreed that the head of the mission should be an Army officer who would report to Harriman in Moscow and to General Marshall in Washington. Harriman asked for either of two experienced staff officers, Major General John R. Deane or Brigadier General Albert C. Wedemeyer. Both had impressed him as men who understood the political implications behind the movements of armies. General Marshall told Harriman that Wedemeyer, then the chief Army planner, was being assigned to the staff of Lord Louis Mountbatten in the new Southeast Asia Command, which had just been created at Quebec. Harriman was delighted to get Russ Deane, who had been secretary to the Combined Chiefs of Staff. "One lesson I had learned early in my government career," he recalled, "was that I would be the prisoner of the people who worked for me. I was determined to choose the best men available and General Deane certainly met that test."

Although Harriman had decided to defer any changes in the embassy staff until he could judge for himself which of the men already there should be retained, he had taken some soundings at the State Department. The two most promising Russian specialists, he made up his mind, were Charles E. "Chip" Bohlen and George F. Kennan. "That sounds obvious today," Harriman recalled, "but this was long before either of them had made his reputation." Both were fluent in the Russian language, knowledgeable about the Soviet system, and both had served in Moscow before the war under Ambassador Bullitt.*

Settling the future of the London mission was a more intricate business. Its great strength had been the informal nature of its mandate and structure. Harriman himself had represented and negotiated for virtually all the federal agencies. When Roosevelt and Churchill, in early 1942, had created the Munitions Assignment Board, the Combined Shipping Adjustment Board and the Combined Raw Materials Board, Harriman represented the United States at the London end in all three. Recognizing that the time for ad hoc arrangements of this kind had passed, Harriman was anxious to see the London mission placed on a proper, formal footing before leaving his post. It was essential, he felt, to avoid the creation of overlapping and conflicting authorities, which could turn the mission after his departure into a new arena for the bureaucratic battle of Washington.

After talks with Roosevelt and with Leo T. Crowley, who had just been appointed head of the newly formed Office of Foreign Economic Administration, Harriman worked out a satisfactory arrangement and the President agreed to put it in writing. The mission, which had carried Harriman's name since 1941, would be renamed the Mission for Economic Affairs. All its activities would be continued and Harriman's deputy, Philip D. Reed, would succeed him.

Before he left Washington on October 3, both Hopkins and

---

* At the Teheran Conference in late November, Harriman asked Roosevelt and Hopkins to assign Bohlen to Moscow as counselor of the embassy. The State Department refused, contending that as a Class IV officer he lacked sufficient seniority for the post. Kennan, a Class II officer, had just been assigned to London after serving as chargé d'affaires in Lisbon. Harriman insisted upon Kennan and got him, although he had to wait until July before the transfer was accomplished.

Marshall had second thoughts about letting Harriman go to Moscow. Hopkins talked to him about succeeding Sumner Welles, who was about to retire as Under Secretary of State. Harriman replied that he preferred to remain overseas. Marshall had suggested several weeks earlier that Harriman might remain in Washington as Secretary to the Cabinet, taking over many of Hopkins' duties in view of his failing health. Again, Harriman declined. He was committed to Moscow, he said, asking Marshall not to raise the matter with the President.[11]

The President sent Harriman's nomination to the Senate on October 1. His appointment as ambassador to the Soviet Union was confirmed by unanimous vote on October 7, three days after his return to London to wind up his affairs there.

THE FOREIGN MINISTERS CONFERENCE, agreed to at Quebec, was scheduled to open in Moscow on October 18. When Secretary of State Hull informed the President that his doctors would not let him travel, Roosevelt suggested to Harriman that he should represent the United States in the talks with Eden and Molotov. That would be a mistake, Harriman responded. If Hull could not go, then Sumner Welles ought to take his place. He pointed out that the Russians were much impressed by rank and that as an ambassador he ought to be a member of the delegation, not its chief. The President readily agreed and called Welles at Bar Harbor, Maine. Although Welles showed no great eagerness for the Moscow assignment, Roosevelt persisted. Hull would just "mess things up," he said to Harriman; besides, it would be a fine thing if their fellow Grotonian were to round out his long career with an historic assignment like the Foreign Ministers Conference. But Roosevelt had not reckoned with the furious antagonism of Cordell Hull. For years past—as the Secretary of State had been complaining to Harriman—the President had failed to consult him on major decisions of foreign policy, going around him to deal with Welles instead.

Hull was almost seventy-two years old and in poor health, but when he heard that Welles might go to Moscow in his place, his long-suppressed rage boiled over. Although he had never been in an airplane, he went to the White House and told Roosevelt that "wherever the conference might be held—anywhere between here and Chungking—I would be there myself."[12] So Hull set out from Washington on October 7 while Harriman was saying his farewells in London.

He wrote to his fellow directors of the Union Pacific Railroad and the Illinois Central, offering his resignation. "I have accepted this diplomatic assignment as a service to my country which, in time of war, I am in duty bound to perform," he explained. "I do not look upon public office as my career. When I am free again to attend to my own affairs, I shall expect to renew my active participation . . ." The Union Pacific board decided to grant Harriman an indefinite leave of absence as chairman rather than accept his resignation.

On October 11 he took the oath as ambassador to the Soviet Union in a brief ceremony at the American embassy in London, and two days later left for Moscow with his daughter Kathleen by way of Algiers, Cairo and Teheran. In Algiers they stayed with Eisenhower, and Harriman got his views on the military outlook. He also talked with both De Gaulle and Giraud, finding them yoked together in a quarrelsome partnership as joint heads of the French Committee of National Liberation. Giraud, the commander in chief, had just landed a force of 15,000 French troops in Corsica, and with the help of the resistance movement, had liberated the island from German occupation. At luncheon on October 14 with Giraud, several members of his staff and Kathleen, Harriman congratulated the general on his success in Corsica. Giraud, who had been slow to perceive that De Gaulle was winning the upper hand in the French Committee at his expense, talked at length about his political difficulties with the Gaullists. "It is difficult," he complained, "to fight one's enemies while also fighting one's friends." He told Harriman that after the defeat of Hilter, the Western Allies (France included) must join forces and drive the Russians back behind their own frontiers. This view seemed to Harriman so preposterous that he did not press Giraud for a more detailed explanation.

De Gaulle, when Harriman saw him alone at noon the following day, outlined a totally different vision of France's place in the postwar scheme of things. He spoke of France and Russia as the only two powerful countries in Europe, after the collapse of Germany. The British, after all, would retire to their islands and the Americans would go home across the Atlantic. Thus the future of Europe, as he saw it, would be determined by France and Russia working together. "We cannot depend upon the help of Great Britain and the United States," De Gaulle said, "and therefore French policy should be tied to Soviet policy." He would not, of course, allow the Russians to interfere in French domestic affairs, De Gaulle added. Although he described the French Communists as "most earnest in their resistance to the Germans," he assured Harriman that they would never be able to control French political life. Harriman noted a certain ambiguity in De Gaulle's attitude:

> What he said about Soviet Russia could be taken both favorably and unfavorably. My impression was that he went so far that he made it clear he intended to use Soviet influence to promote his political fortunes within France and might well

play at some time a Soviet policy against us. This, however, is an impression and perhaps goes too far.

For Kathleen the visit to Algiers was a delight, although the Eisenhower villa seemed to her "the least sumptuous" building that "General Ike" might have chosen. In a letter to Mary, written from Moscow at the end of the trip, she told of the false start the Harrimans had made in setting out to lunch with Giraud:

> By mistake, we were driven in great state to General Catroux's villa and almost got ourselves invited to lunch, before we realized it was the wrong joint. Giraud was genial at lunch.
> I paid a call on Bogomolov, ex-Soviet equivalent to Tony Biddle in London, [now] accredited to the French. He gave me an hour & a half lecture on how to get on with the Russians —that was what he called it; actually it was just a talk on The Great Democracy.
> Waking up in Algiers the next morning, I thought for an instant I was back in NYC. The toots in the harbor were very Hudson River–tugboatlike.

Before Harriman's departure for Cairo and Teheran, where he was to meet Secretary of State Hull, he also called on Alexander Bogomolov, the newly appointed Soviet representative to the French Committee of National Liberation whom he had known in London as the ambassador to the governments-in-exile. He was shocked to find the Russian mission installed at the Aletti Hotel in one small room that served as sleeping quarters, sitting room and office. Bogomolov, recently arrived from Moscow, predicted that Harriman would find the Soviet authorities eager for cooperation. The reason, he said, was the improved war situation. Harriman asked whether increased Lend-Lease deliveries had anything to do with the new atmosphere. "They have marked them carefully," Bogomolov replied. The ambassador was generally optimistic. He said the Soviet government was going to insist upon friendly regimes in the neighboring countries of Eastern Europe, but would claim no territories beyond Russia's historic boundaries. Even the Polish question could be readily settled, he said, if there was a Polish government that wanted friendly relations. He assured Harriman that the Russian leadership had no desire to Sovietize its neighboring states. The Kremlin would insist only that its neighbors be friendly, Bogomolov said, and this did not preclude equally friendly relations with Britain and the United States.

After this talk Harriman went to see General Eisenhower and insisted that the Soviet ambassador be assigned better quarters. "I thought we ought to treat him with greater dignity," Harriman recalled. Eisenhower quickly set aside a comfortable villa for Bogomolov and his staff. Harriman's helpful attitude was not wholly altruistic. Knowing something about the housing difficulties the American embassy was having in Moscow, he hoped for a *quid pro quo.* "I thought that if I helped Bogomolov, they would do something for me in Moscow," he acknowledged. "But I found no gratitude in Moscow, not at least in the form of better living quarters for the embassy staff. I learned very early how much truth there was in an expression I heard from all the old Russian hands: 'You can't bank good will in Moscow.' "

CHAPTER XI

"I Have Come as a Friend"

T<small>HE</small> H<small>ARRIMANS</small>, father and daughter, reached Moscow in the late afternoon of October 18, 1943, riding with Secretary of State Hull and his party in a glistening new C-54 transport plane. On the way up from Teheran, Kathleen Harriman had her first glimpse of the wartime entente at work.

> Shortly after we got going [she wrote to her sister Mary in New York] I got a formal note from Hull's pilot (the best in the A.T.C.) that the pleasure of my company, etc., etc., was requested up front. Eventually I went and discovered that, courtesy of the Soviet Gov't., we'd taken on a Soviet radio operator and navigator. There was slight argument as to how and where we should fly, and my presence in the chair between the pilot and copilot kept the Russians just that much farther away from those who were doing the flying. The Russians wanted us to fly high and Doctor's orders were to fly at all times at the lowest possible altitude as it isn't good for the Secretary to fly high. There wasn't much argument as no one spoke any known language in common. The U.S. pilot flew the way he wanted and it always took the Russians a little time to discover what he was up to. However, by the time we neared Stalingrad all tension & difficulties ceased & in sign language the Battle of Stalingrad was fought out for us. By the time we reached Moscow we were all fast friends.

Molotov, Vishinsky, Maisky and Litvinov had turned out in the biting cold to great the Secretary of State and the new American ambassador at the airport. General Deane was filled with admiration for the shining helmets, snow-white gloves and ramrod postures of the Russian honor guard. A military band played "The Internationale" and then "The Star-Spangled Banner," in a version the Americans found stirring though faintly alien. Molotov spoke a few words of welcome into a microphone and Hull responded. Then the party was loaded into a procession of limousines for the five-mile ride to Spaso House, which was to be the Harriman residence for the next two years and three months. Its shabby elegance was familiar enough to Harriman but a new experience for Kathleen:

> We live in a sort of slum area of cobblestoned streets about five minutes by car from the Red Square, Kremlin & two hotels for foreigners. Our garden consists of some leafless shrubs and a couple of dead trees. (Averell brought his axe so he'll be able to occupy his muscles cutting the latter down.) But, to get back to the house, in general there is Regency—with plenty of gold & black & damask. Walls are white (dirty and plaster in very bad condition) & the designs are chiefly white sunflowers. The ceilings vary—either just moldings or painted women and fish and things or both.
>
> The house gets entered unpretentiously at the side into the vestibule—Monstrosity No. 1. This has great marble columns and it's generally so dark you can't even decide whether a Russian, a Chinese or a Finn let you in. Up a small flight of stairs you then get confronted, or at least find yourself in, Monstrosity No. 2, the Reception Room. This has huge Doric columns (white stone) and a chandelier to end all chandeliers that hangs down from the roof of the house. The ceiling is domed and fluted. Under your feet is a Bill Bullitt (so the rumor goes) creation in the form of a seasick green & yellow & pink & brown carpet. ("Beautiful," the chargé d'affaires calls it.) Halfway up to the roof the columns end and a gallery starts. The bedrooms are off this. For the moment I live at one end of the gallery and Averell the other. Due to the conference we are apt to meet once or twice a day, usually at mealtimes, when he sits at one end of the table & I'm half a mile away at the other. Think how cosy dining *à deux* will be!

The Foreign Ministers Conference, the first in what was to become a long series, had been proposed by Stalin as a preliminary to his much-postponed first meeting with Roosevelt and Churchill. Hull spent sixteen days with the Harrimans in Spaso House, meeting almost every afternoon with Eden and Molotov. He had brought from Washington the draft of a Declaration on General Security, which he was determined to see accepted and signed not only by the Soviet

Union, the United Kingdom and the United States but also by China, whose Foreign Minister had not been invited to Moscow. The declaration was adopted with surprising ease, but Hull had to expend much of his influence in persuading the Russians to let the Chinese ambassador, Foo Ping-sheung, sign the document in behalf of Chiang Kai-shek.

China's admission to the ranks of the Great Powers had assumed overwhelming importance in Hull's mind, as it had in Roosevelt's. The British government did not share this emotional commitment to Chiang Kai-shek's China. "As to China, I cannot regard the Chungking Government as representing a great world Power," Churchill had written to Eden in a minute dated October 21, 1942. "Certainly there would be a faggot vote on the side of the United States in any attempt to liquidate the British overseas Empire."[1] Eden nevertheless loyally supported Hull. It took a week to bring Molotov around, after Hull had warned him in a private conversation that China's exclusion could have "the most terrific repercussions" not only in the Pacific but on public opinion in the United States. The United States might be forced, Hull said, to make "all sorts of readjustments . . . for the purpose of keeping properly stabilized the political and military situation in the Pacific."[2] This was a plain hint that some part of the aid now being sent to Russia might be diverted to Chiang unless China was allowed to sign the four-power declaration, and Molotov backed down.

From Harriman's point of view, Hull's concentration on the declaration and China was a mistake. "He used all of his influence," the Ambassador recalled, "to get China accepted as the fourth Great Power. I thought he would have been better advised also to apply his considerable leverage with the Russians in attempting to work out agreements to safeguard the independence of Poland and other nations in Eastern and Central Europe, whose liberation was foreseen in a matter of months." Eden stood alone, however, in raising that issue. Molotov, predictably, contended that it was too early to talk about Eastern Europe, and Hull, in spite of Harriman's urgings, was not greatly interested. One day in Moscow when Harriman stressed the cardinal importance of pressing Molotov to talk about Poland, the Secretary of State responded, "I don't want to deal with these piddling little things. We must deal with the main issues."

And the main issue, as Hull saw it, was his own four-power declaration, a document breathing assurances that the Great Powers would behave with perfect decorum after the war was won. The preamble bound the four powers to continue the war until all their enemies "laid down their arms on the basis of unconditional surrender." This was the first time the Soviet Union had formally endorsed Roosevelt's policy. For the rest, the declaration provided that the Allies would:

- Work together to maintain peace and security, as they had fought together in the war.
- Act together "in all matters relating to the surrender and disarmament" of their common enemies.
- Take all necessary measures to guard against enemy violations of the surrender terms.
- Agree on the necessity of establishing at the earliest practicable date an international organization for the maintenance of world peace and security that would be "open to membership by all nations, large and small."
- Consult together and when necessary with other members of the United Nations "with a view to joint action on behalf of the community of nations" until the new system of general security was in being.
- Confer on a general agreement that would regulate armaments in the postwar period.

One further provision in Hull's original text pledged the four powers not to "employ their military forces within the territories of other states except for the purposes envisaged in this Declaration and after *joint consultation and agreement.*" Molotov objected vigorously. He made plain that the Soviet Union was not about to give the Western Allies veto power over its troop movements into neighboring countries, like Poland and Czechoslovakia, which were in the path of the advancing Red Army. Molotov was willing to *consult* but not to wait for Allied *agreement.* Hull dropped that requirement, agreeing that the injunction against sending military forces into the territories of other states should not come into force until *after the defeat of the enemy.* He had accepted, on second thought, the Soviet argument that the effect of his original draft might be to interfere with military operations. Much the same argument had been made, of course, by the British and Americans in fending off earlier Soviet demands for joint consultation and agreement in the case of Italy.

Just as the Secretary of State had come to Moscow with his mind fixed on getting a four-power declaration of principles, so Molotov had placed only a single item on the agenda—"Consideration of Measures to Shorten the Duration of the War against Germany and Her Allies in Europe." In plain English, this meant the Second Front. The Russians were asking for final, definite assurances that the Western Allies, in fact, would launch their invasion of France in the spring. Hull refused to discuss military matters. He had decided that if Molotov insisted on such

SPECIAL ENVOY

a discussion, Harriman and General Deane should speak for the United States. Accordingly, on October 19 Harriman alerted the senior officers of his new military mission—General Deane, Brigadier General Hoyt S. Vandenberg of the Army Air Forces and Commodore C. E. Olsen of the Navy—to prepare themselves. Recalling that "we had led the Russians to believe that action would be forthcoming on the second front," he told the military men:

> . . . we should take time to give the Russians the full military picture—submarines, the Mediterranean, bombing, the Pacific—how we use our resources and why, when the Mediterranean opened, [why] the tentative promise made to develop an offensive from England at an earlier date was impossible of fulfillment . . .

> He stated that the bomber offensive and the Pacific are two factors which the Russians don't fully appreciate.

Meeting the same morning with Deane, Ambassador Clark Kerr of Britain and General Ismay, Harriman again stressed that the Russians this time must get a full picture of the Allied war effort on all fronts. The war in the Pacific, he pointed out, is "one of the reasons why there are relatively fewer American troops in the European theater." Clark Kerr preferred to avoid a Second Front discussion. With more than a trace of unhappiness, he observed that "the ambassadors would have a long period to build up the house that had been knocked down" after Eden and Hull had left Moscow. Ismay in turn argued that the very term "second front" was misleading. He could show, he said, that the Allied campaign in Italy had drawn off German forces from the Russian front, and for that matter, "there was also a third front in the air." But Harriman cautioned Ismay against trying to score debating points. "It would not be helpful," he said, "to get into an argument as to what the second front meant."

Harriman's advice prevailed. At the meeting with the Russians, Deane and Ismay laid out the broad picture and were able to assure Molotov that the cross-Channel invasion would certainly be undertaken in 1944. They described the military plan for Operation Overlord in some detail, stressing the importance of the combined bomber offensive in softening the German defenses, continued military pressure in Italy, a secondary landing in the South of France, and all the intricacies of supplying the invasion force over the Channel beaches. This time the Russians appeared satisfied that the Western Allies meant business, as Harriman reported to the President on October 21:

> Mr. Hull has stood the trip well under the careful eye of his capable physician. He's conserving his strength in every

way for the business of the conference. The days have been
bright and crisp, the finest New England November football
weather. Molotov and our Soviet hosts have been extremely
hospitable and friendly. Yesterday's conference considered the
only point on the Soviet agenda, namely the war and the
second front . . . both officers [Deane and Ismay] did an
extremely competent job in outlining and explaining our plans
and showed willingness to answer freely any and all questions.
Deane was precise in defining the conditions which must be
precedent to their fulfillment . . . he appeared to satisfy and
win the confidence of the Soviet delegates.[3]

General Deane, who had braced himself for a tougher reception
from the Russians, then put forward, with Harriman's approval, three
American proposals for speeding the conclusion of the war: (1) that
the Soviet Union make available bases on its territory so that American
bombers could land, refuel, reload and shuttle back to their home bases
in the Mediterranean, hitting German targets as they came and went;
(2) that the Russians and Americans should exchange weather information and, for this purpose, improve their signal communications;
and (3) that more frequent transport flights be organized between the
Soviet Union and the West.

The Russians, who were not authorized to discuss anything but
the second front, gave no reply. Two days later Molotov announced
to the conference that the Soviet government had accepted General
Deane's proposals "in principle." Hull thanked Molotov, suggesting
that the details should be worked out at once between the Soviet
General Staff and the American military mission. Deane later wrote: "I,
of course, was elated—less than a week in the Soviet Union and three
major objectives achieved."[4] But it was not until February 1944 that
the Russians agreed to begin conversations on the shuttle-bombing plan,
only after continuous pressure on Stalin by Harriman and Roosevelt.
The experience taught Deane two important lessons that Harriman had
learned earlier: First, that subordinate officials in the Soviet Union did
not dare respond to any foreign proposal without consulting the
highest authority, generally Stalin himself, and second, that approval
"in principle" meant little or nothing.

Between sessions of the conference, Harriman started on the
round of official calls expected of a new ambassador. Molotov received
him on October 21 with more cordiality than Harriman had expected.

"I am glad you have come to the conference," Molotov said. "We
have found you a very tough man to deal with."

"I have come as a friend," Harriman replied.

"Oh, I know that," said Molotov. "I intended my remarks to be complimentary."

The Russians had observed, Molotov added, the intimacy of Harriman's relationships with the British, and they wondered whether there was any reason why Russians and Americans could not develop the same kind of relationship. Harriman responded that he would welcome it, pointing out that his relations with the British were on a basis of frankness and close personal acquaintance. He would like the opportunity to get to know Molotov, his fellow commissars and the military leaders as well as he knew their British counterparts. Harriman assured Molotov that in spite of acknowledged differences between the United States and the Soviet Union there were many points of common interest, and that the intimate American tie with Britain in no way argued against the possibility of developing a similar intimacy with the Russians.

Still curious about the British-American entente, Molotov asked whether it was based on a treaty. "None whatsoever," Harriman replied. There was, however, a clear understanding between the two peoples and their governments that they would fight the war to a conclusion side by side, both in Europe and in the Far East. This was made possible, Harriman explained, by the intimate relations between Roosevelt and Churchill, culminating in the appointment of a single supreme commander, under whom British and American troops fought as one force. Molotov sounded enthusiastic, but he volunteered nothing about Stalin's joining in the Roosevelt-Churchill intimacy.

The President and the Prime Minister, who were planning another joint strategy conference in Cairo in November, had offered to travel as far east as Basra, in Iraq, to meet Stalin. But the Soviet leader insisted that his command responsibilities would not allow him to go farther afield than Teheran. If Basra was to be the meeting place, Stalin said, he would have to send Molotov in his place. Harriman asked Molotov bluntly whether security of communications was the only reason for Stalin's insistence upon Teheran. The Foreign Minister said it was. The telephone and telegraph lines linking Moscow to Teheran were controlled and policed by Soviet troops, he said. Only there could Stalin be assured of secure communications to the General Staff in Moscow. Harriman explained that Roosevelt, too, had communications problems. With Congress in session, he had to be certain that bills could reach him in time to be signed or vetoed within the prescribed ten-day period. The President hesitated to go as far as Teheran because uncertain late-autumn weather there might delay his courier planes, conceivably allowing a bill he would otherwise have vetoed to become law without his signature.

Although Harriman had patiently laid out the President's legislative problem to Molotov, the Russian would not budge. Let the

President come to Teheran, Molotov suggested, and send his state papers back to Basra—a distance of 700 miles—by road or rail. Harriman countered with an equally impractical suggestion that the Russians should string their own telephone lines from Teheran to Basra so that Stalin could keep in touch with his marshals while conferring with Roosevelt and Churchill.

When Hull and Harriman called on Stalin on October 25, the outlook for an early meeting appeared to darken further. Stalin talked of postponing the meeting until the spring, when military operations on the Soviet front would be suspended by the thaw. The only alternative was for Roosevelt and Churchill to meet him at Teheran. He stressed that his position "was not based on stubbornness or considerations of prestige." The opportunity to defeat the Germans decisively was at hand, Stalin said, "an opportunity which might only occur once in fifty years," and he dare not be out of touch with the General Staff. Hull agreed that "military considerations came first."[5]

He left the Kremlin persuaded that Stalin was stalling. Harriman disagreed. "The Secretary made a splendid presentation from his viewpoint," he wrote in a memorandum the same day, "but did not, in my opinion, bring out the importance of the meeting to the war effort as being essential in the initiation of certain of our strategic plans . . . I attempted to offset these omissions in my talk with Molotov later in the afternoon. For my part I am convinced that Stalin wants to meet the President, but the prosecution of the war looms supreme in his mind and to some extent he is influenced by the insistent demands of his associates not to be out of intimate touch."

The stalemate was not broken until November 7, after Hull's departure, when Harriman cabled Roosevelt stressing the "supreme importance" of an early meeting with Stalin even if that meant going to Teheran. The Ambassador had taken the precaution of asking Deane and General Vandenberg to investigate the vagaries of Teheran weather and had found that they were grossly exaggerated. In fact, only two scheduled November flights between Cairo and Teheran had been seriously delayed in 1941 and 1942. Harriman proposed that Churchill and Roosevelt could fly up to Teheran from Cairo without undue risk and meet Stalin there: "You might plan to remain in Teheran 36 hours, which would give reasonable opportunity for two 3-cornered meetings and for you to see U.J. ["Uncle Joe," code name for Stalin] alone as well."[6] The following day Roosevelt sent a cheerful message to Stalin:

You will be glad to know that I have worked out a method so that if I get word that a bill requiring my veto has been passed by the Congress and forwarded to me, I will fly to Tunis to meet it and then return to the Conference. Therefore, I have decided to go to Teheran and this makes me especially happy.

As I have told you, I regard it as of vital importance that you and Mr. Churchill and I should meet. The psychology of the present excellent feeling demands it even if meeting should last only two days . . .

The whole world is watching for this meeting of the three of us . . .[7]

The "excellent feeling" Roosevelt cited was the product of the Foreign Ministers Conference. Molotov had delighted Hull by approving his four-power declaration. The foreign ministers also had agreed to create a European Advisory Commission, sitting in London, which was to study and recommend policies for the administration of former enemy countries. But Hull's reluctance to take up territorial problems, reinforcing Molotov's insistence that the question of Poland was for the Soviet government alone to settle, cut short the discussion of that issue. Eden briefly urged the Russians to re-establish diplomatic relations with the Polish government in London. But Hull failed to support him. Molotov dismissed the matter, saying that of course the Soviet Union wanted to see an independent Poland after the war, but it would have to be a friendly Poland and the London Poles were distinctly unfriendly.

Litvinov sounded far less circumspect, and more candid, in a discussion of the Polish question with Eden and Harriman at the British embassy on October 28. Harriman recorded his after-dinner comments in a memorandum:

Litvinov started with a torrent of abuse against the Poles, the gist of it being that they would have to learn to live within their ethnographical boundaries as a small nation and give up the idea that they were a great power. They were arrogant people without the ability or power to carry out their extreme nationalism. They had absurdly thought they could beat the Germans alone. All through the period when Litvinov was at Geneva they blocked everything of a constructive nature and played with the Germans. He mentioned also their hostility to Czechoslovakia during the Munich period.

They were historically antagonistic to Russia and had always created trouble for the peaceful Russians. They had to be taught a lesson or they would continue to be trouble-makers. It was unreasonable to consider the interests of a small nation like the Poles when they opposed the interests of 180 million Russians. The interests of the Poles would have to give way to those of the Russians when they conflicted.

Litvinov talked as if he were antagonistic not only to the

Government in exile in London but to the Poles in general. He said that, fortunately for us, Molotov did not feel as extremely as he did. He said the Poles were the most difficult people in the world and then corrected himself, and said, "next to the Japs." I turned to Eden and said laughingly, "Anthony, if you can't do some business with Litvinov over the Poles, perhaps I can do some business with him over the Japs."

Alert to any sign that the Russians might enter the war against Japan, Harriman had already reported to Roosevelt on October 27: ". . . a number of indications have been given us that the Soviet Government is disposed to cooperate in the Pacific after the collapse of Germany, to some extent at least. They no longer appear to fear Japan and I have a feeling that after the termination of hostilities in Europe they want the Pacific war ended as soon as possible." The signs kept cropping up in seemingly offhand remarks by Molotov and other high officials. For example, at a Kremlin dinner closing the conference, Molotov told Eden and Harriman that they were going to see a Soviet film, produced in 1938, describing the Japanese penetration into Siberia during the Revolution. "I am shocked to think that you would do this," Eden said, in mock horror. "It doesn't seem to me that it is appropriate for a neutral."

I commented that I thought it was entirely appropriate and applauded it [Harriman wrote in a personal note]. I then asked my interpreter to ask Mr. Molotov whether I might propose a toast (Eden not listening). I said I would thoroughly understand it if Mr. Molotov did not care to join me. I then proposed a toast to the day when we would be fighting together against the Japs. Mr. Molotov's immediate response was, "Why not? Gladly! The time will come." I said, "Do dna" (bottoms up) and he finished his glass.

Stalin told Hull at dinner the same evening that Russia would "get in and help to defeat the enemy in the Far East" after Germany had collapsed.[8] In his memoirs, Hull has recorded his delight and astonishment over this intimation.

The Secretary of State felt that "great things had been accomplished." He was particularly pleased that the Russians "never once raised the question that had disturbed us the previous year; namely, the settlement at this time of postwar frontiers."[9] In Harriman's judgment, the Secretary of State failed to grasp the essential point: Molotov had no reason to raise the Polish question because he regarded the matter as settled. The Soviet Union had said over and over again that it was claiming permanent title to those areas of eastern Poland overrun by the Red Army in 1939. Although the London Poles had bitterly protested the illegality and injustice of such Soviet demands, neither the British nor the American government had officially disputed the claim. "Piddling little things," Hull had called the boundary issues. When rebuffed this way by the Secretary of State, Harriman offered his support to Eden. "Anthony," he said, "if you will make it an issue with Hull to press the Russians on Poland, I'll support you." But Eden let the matter drop. Hull seemed enormously relieved that the boundary question—to him a "Pandora's box of infinite trouble"—had been left unopened. As for Molotov, Harriman feared that he perhaps misread Hull's silence as acquiescence. The storm over Poland had merely been postponed.

Eden tried valiantly to interest Hull and Molotov in a number of measures broadly designed to forestall the division of postwar Europe into separate spheres of influence. One proposal would have encouraged the smaller countries of Central and Eastern Europe to form federations "in order to increase their mutual welfare by the establishment of institutions on a wider scale then each can separately maintain." Eden pointed out to Hull and Harriman that the breakup of the Austro-Hungarian Empire after World War I had created in the heart of Europe a belt of small, weak countries which could only find stability and prosperity by pooling their resources. His own experience of Europe in the twenties led Harriman to agree fully with Eden. When this proposal came before the foreign ministers on October 26, however, Hull expressed no opinion. He was there, he said, to agree on general principles; the details could come later. Molotov vigorously opposed the idea, after offering the conference his personal "guarantee that there was no disposition on the part of the Soviet Government to divide Europe into . . . separate zones."[10] Besides, he argued, premature discussion could hurt the interests of the smaller countries and of European stability. To Harriman's regret, no action was taken at Moscow or later on the Eden proposal; although the foreign ministers made one decision of critical importance—that Austria, a potentially vital element in any Central European federation, should be treated as a victim of Hitlerite aggression rather than as a willing accomplice, subject to liberation instead of conquest by the Allies. Behind Molotov's refusal to discuss the federation issue, Harriman saw the first trace of a design for Soviet hegemony. "I gained the impression," he recalled, "that Stalin wanted a pulverized Europe in which there would be no strong countries except for the Soviet Union. It seemed to me that the Russians were determined to control the smaller countries and thought they could do so more easily if they remained apart." This Harriman insight was to receive a degree of confirmation at Teheran and its most striking illustration soon after the war, when Stalin denounced and effectively blocked a tentative effort by Marshal Tito of Yugoslavia and Georgi Dimitrov of Bulgaria, both veteran Communist leaders, to form a Balkan federation.

A second Eden proposal, which would have pledged each of the Great Powers not to make treaties with smaller powers except after consultation and agreement with the other two, also got short shrift. This was an issue that the British and Soviet governments had been discussing off and on ever since Molotov's visit to London in June 1942. Eden had the impression, he said, that they were in accord "as to the undesirability of their concluding any agreements during the war with small states relating to the postwar period and thus avoid[ing] any scramble for special relations with small powers."[11]

Lurking behind these generalities was the specific case of Czechoslovakia. Dr. Eduard Beneš, President of the Czechoslovak government-in-exile in London, had agreed with the Russians on the terms of a treaty governing postwar relations between the two countries, and as Molotov was fully aware, the British government had raised objections when Beneš proposed a trip to Moscow for the purpose of signing it. Here again the issue was debated by Eden and Molotov, Hull taking no significant part in the discussions because, he explained, he was not familiar with the details. As the restiveness of the American delegation grew steadily during this essentially bilateral discussion, Eden slipped a note to Hull explaining his purpose: "I am sorry to take your time, but behind all this is a big issue: two camps in Europe or one."[12] Harriman felt that the British hostility to the Soviet-Czechoslovak treaty was unrealistic, as he made plain in a series of penciled notes he exchanged at the conference table with James Clement Dunn, Hull's political adviser.

> I hope we can stay out of the argument over this question [Harriman wrote to Dunn]. I personally am not in full sympathy with the position Mr. Eden has taken over the last months & I feel it needs more study before we commit ourselves.
>
> I have felt that there was something to be said for the Soviets to work out a treaty with Czechoslovakia, as a pattern of the kind of relations they hoped to have with the Poles & other Eastern European states.

Dunn scribbled his agreement on the same sheet of paper:

> I must say that without very much information as to the British position I have not been able to understand what objection there would be to the Soviets and Czechs negotiating openly and frankly. Particularly as the Soviets are always expressing suspicion as to a possible "Cordon Sanitaire."

Eden, on the other hand, had told Beneš in London that he firmly opposed the treaty, in part because the effect of concluding it at a time when the Soviets refused to have any dealings with the Polish government would be to isolate the Poles. He also had warned Beneš that in signing the treaty he might give the appearance of placing Czechoslovakia in the Soviet camp. But Beneš had persisted, explaining that his government had less cause to fear Communism than the Poles because the social and economic structure of Czechoslovakia was in better balance than Poland's. The people of Czechoslovakia understood, he said, that for them Communism would be a step backward, not forward. Besides, the Russians had assured him that they wanted to see the independence of Czechoslovakia fully restored and had promised not to interfere in its domestic affairs. Beneš had told Harriman in London that having dealt successfully with Stalin before the war, he felt he could get along with him after the war.

Without fully subscribing to Beneš' hopeful view of the future, Harriman had nevertheless welcomed the treaty negotiations. "The Russians," he later explained, "would undoubtedly occupy most of Czechoslovakia in driving back the Germans. The Czechs had a division or more fighting with the Red Army. And it seemed to me the wisest thing for Beneš to try to work out a permanent relationship with the Soviet Union before the Red Army got control of Czechoslovakia, so that Beneš' government could be established and recognized. I felt it was better to face that problem as early as possible, believing that there was a better chance of working out a satisfactory understanding *before* the Red Army got in, rather than afterward."

Eden, at any rate, withdrew his objections to the Soviet-Czechoslovak treaty at the conference table after Molotov had read aloud a statement to the effect that in the case of agreements touching on "the direct security of their boundaries, and of the corresponding states bordering on them, as for example, the U.S.S.R. and Czechoslovakia" there could be no question of requiring prior consultation and agreement with Britain. (Beneš came to Moscow and signed the treaty on December 12, 1943, some six weeks after the conclusion of the conference.)

Stalin's dinner for the departing delegates on October 30 impressed Harriman as "more genuine, genial and intimate" than others he had attended in 1941 and 1942. "Stalin appeared to enjoy himself as much as anyone else," Harriman reported to Roosevelt. For Hull, who was nearing the end of his public career, the evening could not have been more gratifying. He sat at Stalin's right hand during dinner, chatting about the success of the conference and the prospect for postwar cooperation among the Allies. When Stalin said that the Soviet Union was determined not to follow an isolationist policy after the war, Hull "emphasized the soundness of that view by again pointing out that isolation has almost ruined my country and his."[13]

Before leading his guests into an adjoining room to see the inevitable motion picture, Stalin remarked to his guests that he hoped they had not come to Moscow with the idea that the Soviets were going to make a separate peace with Hitler. Such rumors, in fact, had been circulating in the West, but Eden protested that he never had entertained such a notion. Hull remarked that "any person who knows the Russian people and their relation to Germany in this war knows that they are incapable of making a peace with Germany."*

Stalin also told a story dating back to the time of his nonaggression treaty with Hitler, when Molotov was in Berlin for talks with the German Foreign Minister, Joachim von Ribbentrop. Ribbentrop had rushed him to an air-raid shelter when British bombers attacked the city. As they sat underground together, sirens screaming overhead, Molotov inquired about the strength of the British. Ribbentrop assured him that Britain was finished. At which, Molotov put a second question: "Why, then, are we sitting in this shelter?"

Eden assured Stalin that his confidence in Molotov was not diminished by the Soviet Foreign Minister's past associations. Stalin, who appeared to enjoy ridiculing Molotov before foreign visitors, responded that his Foreign Minister was really responsible for Neville Chamberlain's behavior in the Munich crisis, although "not 100 per cent."

BEFORE HULL'S DEPARTURE for Washington on November 13, which was delayed three days by poor flying weather, Harriman handed him a memorandum setting down several recommendations for the future. "We have an unfortunate record of offering more than we have been able to carry out," Harriman wrote. "These offers have been made in good faith, and with the usual qualifications. We have carried them out to the best of our ability and at real sacrifice. On the other hand, a better policy, I believe, would be to make our offers conservatively and attempt to do a little more than has been indicated."

Harriman also urged the Secretary of State to keep the Moscow

* Stalin's somewhat puzzling remark turned out to be a calculated indiscretion. On November 12 Molotov told Harriman that a German businessman named Edgar Klaus had been in touch with the Soviet embassy in Stockholm about the middle of October. According to Molotov, Klaus claimed to represent a group of German industrialists, headed by a man named Kleist, which was in close touch with Ribbentrop. The group ostensibly was interested in negotiating a separate peace with the Soviet Union, having concluded that Germany could not win the war. Molotov assured Harriman that the Soviets had rejected the overture.

embassy better informed about current developments in Washington than it had been in Admiral Standley's time. "I am sure you will agree that the mission—diplomatic, military and supply—can be used to greater advantage than in the past," Harriman wrote. He added that "it might be well for the mission here to inform the Soviet Government of favorable decisions and thereby create the atmosphere that the mission has some standing and influence at home." Even when the decisions were unfavorable, Harriman argued, there was some advantage in having the Moscow mission explain the matter and satisfy the Soviet government "as to the sincerity of our intentions." Sound diplomatic practice, Harriman felt, called for the American embassy in Moscow to inform the Soviet government of important decisions rather than have them transmitted through the Soviet embassy in Washington.

On November 5, as Roosevelt was preparing for his journey to Cairo and Teheran, Harriman sent him a long message summing up his own thoughts on what the Moscow conference had achieved, and failed to achieve. While Hull had flown home in a mood of euphoria, Harriman felt that he should put his own doubts and concerns before the President in advance of the meeting with Stalin at Teheran. He wrote:

> Now that I have had a chance to take a long breath, I thought you would want from me a review of the more important impressions of the Soviet attitude we got in and outside of the conference room. Certain of the doubts which some people have had regarding Soviet intentions are now laid to rest. On the other hand, the character of certain real difficulties that exist have been more sharply defined.
>
> The Soviet Government, before they agreed to the conference, had evidently decided that they would take a shot at working together with the British and ourselves in dealing with war and postwar problems. On the whole the Soviets are delighted with the way the conference went, and it has strengthened their tentative decision. It was interesting to watch how Molotov expanded as the days passed. As he began to realize that we had not come with a united front against him, and were ready to expose frankly our preliminary thoughts, he showed increasing enjoyment in being a full member with the British and ourselves. Before the conference, I doubt if they had any intention of allowing the inclusion of China as an original signatory of the Four-Nation Declaration. Their acceptance of China is a clear indication that they are genuinely satisfied with the way things went and are ready to make important concessions to further the new intimacy. On the

other hand, it cannot be assumed that this policy is already so set that we can take liberties with them . . .

The Soviets accepted the explanation of our military plans but our whole permanent relations depend in a large measure on their satisfaction in the future with our military operations. It is impossible to overemphasize the importance they place strategically on the initiation of the so-called Second Front next spring. An invitation to the next military conference is, I believe, essential if the seeds sown at this conference are to germinate. It is clear they never like to be faced with Anglo-American decisions already taken . . .

Their attitude toward Germany, as revealed at the conference, is fundamentally satisfactory. There is, of course, no doubt that they are bent on the complete destruction of Hitler and Nazism. They are ready to deal with Germany on the basis of three-way responsibility . . .

Harriman had nothing but praise for the Secretary of State. "His dignity and determination and sincerity," he wrote to Roosevelt, "in presenting our attitude toward the preservation of world peace . . . profoundly impressed the Soviet officials. I cannot overemphasize the important contribution his presence made toward the favorable outcome of the conference." At the same time, the Harriman message raised warning flags on two issues that proved to be crucial: Germany and Poland. With regard to the Soviet attitude on Germany, he warned the President:

Our difficulties with [the Russians], if any, will be that their present intent toward Germany is tougher than we have in mind, particularly in regard to the magnitude of reparations. Their measure of Germany's capacity to pay reparations in goods and services appears to be based on the concept that the Germans are not entitled to a postwar standard of living higher than [that of] the Russians.

With regard to Russia's territorial demands on Poland, Harriman saw deep trouble ahead:

Although Soviet territorial questions were never raised at the conference, it can only be inferred that the Soviet government expects to stand firmly on the position they have already taken in regard to their 1941 frontiers. I believe they have the impression that this has been tacitly accepted by the British, and the fact that we did not bring up the issue may have given them the impression that we would not raise serious objections in the future.

The problem of Poland is even tougher than we believed. They regard the present Polish government in exile as hostile and therefore completely unacceptable to them . . . They gave us no indication during the conference that they were interested in the extension of the Soviet system. I take this with some reservation, particularly if it proves to be the only way they can get the kind of relationships they demand from their western border states. They are determined to have no semblance of the old Cordon Sanitaire concept in Eastern Europe. Molotov told me that the relations they expect to establish with the border countries did not preclude equally friendly relationships with the British and ourselves. In the conference, however, it was indicated that, although they would keep us informed, they would take unilateral action in respect to those countries in the establishment of relations satisfactory to themselves. It is my feeling that their rigid attitude may well be tempered in proportion to their increasing confidence in their relations with the British and ourselves in the establishment of overall world security.

On November 3 Harriman sent a briefer message to Churchill, tempering his hopeful account with a dose of caution:

Long strides forward have been made by the conference but if it is not wisely followed up, we can get knocked back on our heels.

The war is still uppermost in the minds of the Soviets, regardless of their increasing interest in the postwar world. Therefore, their inclusion in the next military conference, and the manner in which they are dealt with, are of inestimable importance.

I endorse enthusiastically your word "prodigious" in reference to the conference's success. We cannot, however, assume too much. The essential quality [in] our relations with the Russians is still patience and forbearance. These, I am afraid, are not my long suit. Archie [Clark Kerr] can perhaps [supply] enough for us both.

In a bread-and-butter note to Eisenhower, Harriman wrote on November 11: "It seems the Soviets have made up their minds to play ball with us and I am confident, to a point, at least, that Russ Deane and his mission are going to be able to get on a reasonable basis with them."

But Soviet confidence in the Western Allies, Harriman learned, was a sometime thing. Official attitudes tended to swing unpredictably from cordiality to sour suspicion without apparent explanation. Three days after Hull left Moscow, flushed with confidence in Soviet good will, Molotov complained to Harriman that the Allies were not keeping their promises. He recalled that Eden, at the Kremlin dinner on October 30, had expressed the hope that Kiev and Rome would soon be taken by the Allies. Now it was November 6. Kiev, indeed, had been liberated, but not Rome. On the Italian front there was so little activity that the Germans, he said, had been able to transfer several divisions to the eastern front and the Soviet marshals were greatly dissatisfied with this development. Molotov shared their dissatisfaction, he said, because "the matter was not one of narrow military character only, but also one of political significance." He went on with great earnestness, Harriman reported, to question some figures Eden had left with Stalin concerning the number of German divisions fighting in Italy. Eden evidently had told Stalin that according to British estimates, the Germans had six armored divisions in the front line. But the Soviet staff had now discovered that the Germans had only 200 tanks in all of central and southern Italy. This seemed to the Soviet military authorities an inexplicable discrepancy, suggesting that the Germans were actually much weaker than the Allies had pretended and the time was past due for an Anglo-American offensive; instead, the fighting had been allowed to slacken.

Harriman replied that he would, of course, communicate Molotov's complaint to the authorities in Washington. He reminded Molotov that it was precisely to avoid such misunderstandings over military information that General Deane and his military mission had been sent to Moscow, suggesting that Deane needed to be in closer contact with the Soviet General Staff. Deane's initial meetings with Marshal Klementy Voroshilov, then Deputy Commissar of Defense, and General Alexei E. Antonov of the General Staff, turned out as frosty as the Moscow winter. But when the military mission received from Washington careful intelligence estimates of German strength in Italy, by way of refuting the Soviet accusations, Deane's Russian counterparts seemed to have lost interest.

Kathleen Harriman, meanwhile, was getting to know the Foreign Service and sharing her discoveries by letter with her sister Mary and Mrs. Harriman in New York:

> The number one attitude . . . is that Ambassadors are a necessary evil of our Foreign Service set-up.
> An Ambassador should be treated kindly and handled with the best of care, sort of like a great-grandfather or baby sister . . . Ambassadors are told what to do and, most particularly, what not to do. Can you imagine Averell under this type of

system? Or the consternation and bewilderment of the Foreign Service men at his complete failure after a month to fall into line?

Attitude number two deals with reports and cables. These are lengthy and usually manage to say nothing at all of importance. (If you don't say anything, you don't get blamed for perhaps creating an impression which at some future date will be proven false) . . .

Since they are boring to read and extremely pompous, no one reads them, except Averell, who reads them only to tear up. Now he spends most of his time redrafting cables. But filed away in his own notes he's kept a few beauts . . .

In the evenings, when we're not out dining with outsiders, we have a gay old time at dinner. In fact, the conversation has improved no end. Even the deadest, most straight-laced State Department guy made a mildly funny crack at Averell tonight. That we considered a major victory . . .

After dinner, one bunch play something called bottle billiards, very seriously, and the game lasts well on till midnight. Averell and I adjourn upstairs, maybe with a boarder or two. We converse a bit, then Averell and I settle down to the serious business of making me into a good bezique player. After that, Averell goes to bed and I study Russian. Incidentally, Russians call me "Gaspadeena Garriman." It sounds like an old man clearing his throat.

On November 9, Harriman inaugurated a series of weekly meetings at which each member of the embassy "was encouraged to bring up any subject which he considered of interest to the rest of the staff." After reporting on the Foreign Ministers Conference (he said it "went far beyond his expectations"), the Ambassador outlined his approach to the Russians: "We want to show them that (1) we are for the war first; (2) we accept them as equals, and (3) we have an intense interest in their reconstruction." Pointing out that "Lend-Lease was strictly a wartime measure," Harriman stressed the need, in his personal opinion, for American postwar credits to the Soviet Union. He mentioned helping the Russians with their railroads, coal mining, agricultural equipment and seed for their first crops.

In a conversation on November 5 with Anastas Mikoyan, the Commissar for Foreign Trade, Harriman had suggested that "it was perhaps not too soon to give some preliminary consideration to the Soviet needs for reconstruction of its economy after the war." Mikoyan said he would be glad to discuss postwar assistance. Other things being equal, he added, the Russians preferred American equipment to British or German equipment because of its high quality. But Soviet orders would depend on credit terms and American prices, which seemed to him high. He also mentioned that Hopkins already had opened discussions on the subject with a member of the Soviet purchasing mission in Washington. This was news to Harriman.

He promptly cabled Hopkins and Edward R. Stettinius, the new Under Secretary of State, that it was "somewhat embarrassing" to learn from Mikoyan that discussions of postwar assistance had been started in Washington. "It is my belief that we [in Moscow] are in a better position to find out what the Soviets really want and the kinds of arrangements that would be most satisfactory to both governments . . . As we are dealing here with the authoritative policy-making Soviet officials, I believe that a better deal from our standpoint can be made in Moscow."

Stettinius, in reply, promised to keep Harriman informed in the future. He added: "Harry, with whom I have discussed the question of talks with Soviet officials on American participation in postwar reconstruction, does not know of any discussions on this matter." It was not Hopkins but Donald Nelson, chairman of the War Production Board, who had discussed postwar assistance with Stalin during his visit to Moscow in October, Stettinius said. Nelson's suggestion that a committee of businessmen initiate the discussions did not sit well with Harriman, who cabled Stettinius on November 16:

> I am not certain whether I have made it clear that the Soviet Government regards this question of reconstruction as, next to the war, the most important political as well as economic problem with which it is confronted. An important and integral part of our diplomatic dealings with the Soviet Government is our participation in reconstruction and therefore, in my judgment, it is essential that the negotiations be handled not by a new independent agency or group but under the direction of those dealing with our overall relations with the Soviet Union.

Harriman's early initiative in planning for the end of the war coincided with a period of rising public confidence among the Russians. They spoke of 1943, the year about to end, as *perelom*, the turning point. The great battles at Stalingrad and Kursk had changed everything. Although the Germans still held most of the western Ukraine, Byelorussia to the north and the Baltic area, the Red Army had won back some two thirds of the territory occupied by the Germans in 1941 and 1942. The Foreign Ministers Conference, moreover, had been publicly pronounced a success by Stalin himself and he was about to meet Roosevelt and Churchill at Teheran. In his speech of November

7, marking the anniversary of the 1917 Revolution, Stalin even praised the contribution of the Western Allies, making specific mention of the victorious campaigns in the Mediterranean, the bomber offensive against Germany and "the regular supplies of armaments and raw materials that we are receiving from our Allies." Although the fighting in Italy was not yet the Second Front, he said, the real Second Front was "now not so far away." It was time, in short, for a great celebration.

On the evening of November 7, Molotov gave a lavish reception for the diplomatic corps, the biggest of the war, at the Spiridonovka Palace. For the first time, Molotov and other Foreign Ministry officials wore their splendid new dress uniforms, cut in the military style and stiff with gold braid. The guests had been invited to wear white tie and tails. As none of the Americans, Harriman included, had thought to carry such paraphernalia to wartime Moscow, they turned out in dark suits. Sir Archibald Clark Kerr had borrowed a stiff shirt from the neutral Swedes and scraped together what looked like someone else's dress suit. He wore his medals and a great red and blue sash. "Archie managed not to look insignificant next to a Russian," Kathleen Harriman wrote to her sister, "but he was the only one not to." The Russian officials seemed as proud of their new regalia, she noted, "as a little boy all dressed up in his new Christmas-present fireman's suit." Molotov at one point asked Miss Harriman why she alone had failed to compliment him on his uniform. Could it be that she didn't like it?

There was a great outpouring of Soviet wives whom the diplomatic corps had never before seen. Prominent Russian writers, artists and musicians, including the composer Dimitri Shostakovich in full evening dress, mingled with the foreigners. It was as if the Russian elite had been commanded to make up in a single night for the studied boycott of foreigners that for so many years past had been the iron rule of Moscow. Harriman caused a small stir when he spotted the Japanese ambassador sitting in an inner room reserved for select guests and refused to cross the threshold. The Russians bustled the Japanese out of the room and kept him surrounded by Foreign Ministry men the rest of the evening. Molotov, who was feeling no pain, created a major incident that evening by walking up to the Swedish ambassador and telling him that the Soviet government did not like neutrals. As a result the Swede was recalled from Moscow.

It was the last of Molotov's drunken parties. Harriman and Clark Kerr had been singled out for special attention. The point of the exercise, they soon discovered, was for the Russians to drink the American and British ambassadors under the table. Harriman had become the special responsibility of Mikoyan and Colonel General A. S. Scherbakov, chief of the Main Political Administration of the Red

Army. It was "pretty tough going," as he reported to Roosevelt the next day, "with the toasts we were expected to drink both collectively and individually." Kathleen sent a more graphic account to her sister in New York:

> Mikoyan is famous for his ability to put any guy under the table, so I guess that's why he was picked. He and Averell drank bottoms-up after bottoms-up in toasts to all the obvious things—in vodka . . .
>
> As time went on, I suddenly realized Averell was getting a worried look on his face—scared, I guess, I'd not be able to keep up the pace. It's hard to cheat at toast-drinking, as you have to turn your glass upside down at the end of it and the drops of liquor that fall out are, according to Russian custom, drops of misfortune [that] you wish on the person you are drinking with . . .
>
> Then, along about midnight, the British Ambassador rose to his feet for a toast with some difficulty . . . After that I turned to Averell and said, "Let's get the hell out of here . . ." So after one long last toast to Stalin, Churchill and the President, Averell and I gathered ourselves up and marched solemnly out down the long hallway and stairs to the car . . .
>
> Averell did himself proud, because the one thing the Soviets apparently appreciate is a guy who'll drink with them and be able to keep pace and not show any effect. All the Moscow Americans were very pleased.

CHAPTER XII

Teheran—"Friends in Fact, in Spirit and in Purpose"

O N THE MORNING of November 18, 1943, Harriman set out for
Cairo with General Deane and with Charles Bohlen, who had
remained briefly in Moscow after serving as Hull's interpreter at the
Foreign Ministers Conference. The Ambassador had invited Clark Kerr
and General G. LeQ. Martel, head of the British military mission, to
travel with him in the converted B-24 bomber assigned to him for the
duration of the war. With permission from the Soviet and Turkish
governments, Harriman planned a through-flight to Egypt, refueling
in Baghdad if necessary. When a faulty engine forced the pilot to
make an emergency landing at Stalingrad, Harriman found himself on
an open field under dismal skies, not a building in sight. Even the repair shops and operations office had been dug into the frozen ground.
The airport reception was as chilly as the weather. When Harriman
tried to stretch his legs by walking away from the plane, an armed
guard forced him back. Told that engine repairs would take the rest
of the day, Harriman was feeling pretty dismal himself when a procession of battered automobiles, evidently captured from the recent
German invaders, rolled up. The mayor of Stalingrad had arrived
with a reception committee to welcome his unexpected guests.

The party was delivered over icy roads pocked with shell holes
to the only intact building on the city's broken skyline. This turned
out to be the party headquarters of Stalingrad. Luncheon was served
(black bread, cheese and sausage, washed down with vodka by the
tumbler). Then the mayor proudly showed the guests the architectural
plans for a new city, to be built on the ruins of the old, and took them

on a tour of the battlefield. They saw the towering monument already erected on the banks of the Volga in memory of the Stalingrad dead, and they poked through the cellar headquarters in which Field Marshal Paulus had surrendered.

The two generals—Deane and Martel—had never before seen total devastation on the Stalingrad scale. As far as the eye could scan, streets and squares, houses and shops had been erased in the house-to-house fighting. Nothing remained but a desert of broken brick and rubble, the survivors huddling in cellars or tar-paper shanties. The city fathers of Stalingrad nevertheless unearthed enough food and drink, including champagne, for a dinner that lasted from late afternoon till well past midnight. Toasts were raised, in Russian and English, as if at a Kremlin banquet. But this was a highly informal party, producing a flow of songs, war stories and dances that no official entertainment could rival. Waitresses set down their trays to dance. Bohlen, recalling his bachelor days as a junior officer in the American embassy, was moved to sing Russian popular songs of the thirties. Harriman found himself weighed down with gifts—German pistols, watches and sabers—all trophies of the Stalingrad battle. The Ambassador was "in an expansive mood," General Deane has recalled. "This was evidenced by his asking me to sing. It was getting late and I was dead tired. I sang 'Show Me the Way to Go Home.' Sir Archibald Clark Kerr told me he had never heard the song rendered with such feeling."[1]

When the party flew on to Cairo the next day, passing over the oil fields of Baku, which Harriman noted had been vastly expanded since 1927, the two ambassadors sent back to earth a radio message, addressed to the mayor and the district chief, praising the "happy chance" which had forced them to spend a day and night in Stalingrad.

The conference at Cairo had been planned on short notice. Until the last moment neither Roosevelt nor Churchill could say with assurance whether the Russians would be there. Harriman had strongly urged Roosevelt to invite Molotov and a representative of the Soviet General Staff to join the Cairo talks, pointing out that the Russians disliked being confronted "with Anglo-American decisions already taken." On November 5 Harriman had cabled the President:

> If [the Russians] are asked to the conference, they will expect to participate during the consultative stage. It is obvious that this will be to some extent a nuisance and time-consuming, but from the long view it will be, in my judgment, well worthwhile.
>
> It is important to invite Molotov as well as the military staff. His position as second to Stalin is more apparent than on my previous visits.

A subsequent brief meeting with Stalin himself is still of
the highest importance and I feel that every effort should be
continued to find a way to bring this about.

Accordingly, Roosevelt sent a message to Stalin on November 9
inviting Molotov and a General Staff officer to Cairo. Churchill was
aghast. His purpose in going to Cairo was to make certain that he and
Roosevelt were in broad agreement before they flew on to Teheran
for their meeting with Stalin. "H.M.G. [His Majesty's Government]
cannot abandon their rights to full and frank discussions with you and
your officers about the vital business of our intermingled armies," he
protested. "A Soviet observer cannot possibly be admitted to the intimate conversations which our own Chiefs of Staff must have and his
exclusion may easily cause offence."[2] As soon as Stalin heard, however,
that Roosevelt also had invited Chiang Kai-shek to Cairo, he sent word
that Molotov would not be coming. Still formally neutral with respect
to the war in the Pacific, Stalin refused to take part in a conference
that would draw plans for the defeat of Japan. Little more than three
weeks had passed since all four powers had signed their joint declaration of postwar aims, owing to Hull's relentless exertions in behalf of
China. Now they were planning two separate conferences: the Chinese
would go to Cairo without the Russians, and the Russians to Teheran
without the Chinese.

On the morning of November 24, upon the invitation of General
Marshall, Harriman met with the Joint Chiefs of Staff at the Mena
House Hotel, in the shadow of the Great Pyramid at Giza, to report
on the current attitude of the Russians. The minutes show that Harri-
man urged the military chiefs to be open-minded in their meetings at
Teheran with the Soviet General Staff representatives:

> He [Harriman] thought it would be unfortunate if the
> Soviet representatives were given the impression that the U.S.
> and British Chiefs of Staff were arriving at the conference
> with anything approximating a cut-and-dried plan. He felt
> that the attitude of the Combined Chiefs of Staff should be
> characterized by perfect frankness and a willingness to weigh
> thoughtfully any proposals made by the Soviets. They do not
> like *faits accomplis* and will appreciate being consulted in con-
> nection with the plans of the U.S. and the British.

As for the Second Front, Harriman reported, Stalin now appeared confident that it would be opened in the spring and had said as much to
the Russian people. He appealed for frankness:

> It has been difficult for the Russians to understand why
> two nations of the strength of the United States and Great

Britain have been unable to contain more German forces than they have. [Harriman] suggested that in the coming conference, the Chiefs of Staff adopt an attitude of patience and afford the Soviet representatives ample opportunity to ask questions. Our experience with them has already proved that a frank and sympathetic explanation goes far toward removing suspicion.

Ambassador Harriman thought that the Soviets had every intention of joining the U.S. and the British in the war against Japan as soon as the Germans had capitulated. They fear, however, a premature break with Japan and place great value on the substantial amount of supplies which they are now receiving through Vladivostok . . . He hoped that the question of Russian participation in the Japanese war would be raised either by the President or by the Chiefs of Staff [at Teheran] and indicated that it would be well to point out and to emphasize any advantages which the Soviets would receive from such participation . . . He said that the Soviets are blunt themselves and understand bluntness. He had no fear of any basic misunderstanding or any break with them as a result of the coming Conference.[3]

The same morning, Harriman took Andrei Vishinsky, Russia's newly designated representative on the Allied Advisory Council for the Mediterranean, to see the President. Roosevelt tried out on Vishinsky his notion that "immature nations" like Morocco should be placed under trusteeship by the great powers. He also told Vishinsky, in considerable detail, about his lack of confidence in De Gaulle. Vishinsky did a lot of nodding in reply without showing his hand. He was, Harriman noted, "obviously much impressed with the President's frankness but somewhat surprised that the President felt so seriously about De Gaulle."

Vishinsky had been more forthcoming in a private conversation with Harriman while they waited to see the President. In response to the Ambassador's questions, the Russian left no doubt that the Soviet Union wanted to get rid of King Victor Emmanuel in Italy and that it now regarded Marshal Tito as the leader of effective Yugoslav resistance to the Germans. At this period Moscow still recognized the legitimacy of King Peter and the Yugoslav exile government in London, which had designated General Draza Mihailovic as its Minister of War.* When Harriman remarked that in his judgment the time had

---

* The young King and his government had fled to England after the German invasion in 1941, leaving two separate resistance movements (the Chetniks of General Mihailovic, and Tito's Partisans), to fight a civil war for postwar supremacy.

come for the Allies to tell Mihailovic, the Chetnik leader, to "fish, cut bait or go ashore," Vishinsky heartily agreed. He added, according to Harriman's notes, that "from his point of view, up to the present Mihailovic had not only not been helpful in the prosecution of the war but had been harmful." General Eisenhower, who met with the Combined Chiefs of Staff on November 26, had reached much the same conclusion. He reported that he was sending arms and equipment, captured from the Germans in North Africa and Sicily, to the Yugoslav guerrillas and that "all possible equipment should be sent to Tito since Mihailovic's forces were of relatively little value."[4] *

The presence of Generalissimo and Madame Chiang inevitably led the Cairo Conference to consider in detail military problems affecting the war in China and Burma. Churchill's interest in the Pacific war was, of course, more limited than Roosevelt's. The President looked upon Operation Anakim (a plan discussed at Cairo for driving the Japanese out of Burma) as a means of reopening the overland supply route to China and thus sustaining the Chinese front against Japan. Churchill, on the other hand, lacking Roosevelt's emotional commitment to China, had a simpler motive: to win back Burma, together with Singapore, Hong Kong and other imperial outposts, thereby avenging a long series of humiliating British defeats. Churchill continued to believe that sea power was the primary means of defeating Japan, by cutting her lines of communication and blockading the home islands. This strategic view was shared by Admiral King. But General Stilwell, supported by Marshall, had persuaded Roosevelt that the Japanese would have to be beaten on the Asian mainland, a task to which Chiang's armies could make a large contribution if they were better trained, equipped and led.

The plan to reopen the Burma Road, which was expanded and approved at Cairo, appeared to satisfy Chiang. He started back to Chungking on November 28 believing, just as Roosevelt had hoped, that China's demands were being met at long last. The Generalissimo's reluctance to begin a major offensive with Chinese troops in northern Burma unless the British at the same time moved by sea and air in the south had prompted promises of cooperation from Churchill. Chiang's close friend General Chennault cautioned Harriman at breakfast on

---

* In May 1943 an Allied military mission, headed by Brigadier Fitzroy Maclean, had parachuted into Yugoslavia and had been warmly received by Tito's Partisans. Major Linn M. Farish, an American officer detailed by the Office of Strategic Services, came back to report that Tito's Partisans "have always fought the Germans and are doing so now," while Mihailovic had turned to fighting "with the Germans and Italians" against Tito's forces. At the Teheran Conference, Roosevelt gave Stalin a copy of Major Farish's report.

November 23 that the Allies were probably biting off more than they could chew. According to Harriman's notes, Chennault said, "He thought the whole Burma plan was headed for disaster, that it was an attempt to cut in on a very strongly defended Japanese position without enough stuff to do the job . . . that a lot of confidence was being placed on what the Chinese would do but that they would not fight outside Chinese soil and that they would stop when they hit any strong opposition." The Burma campaign would only become feasible, Chennault added, after his Fourteenth Air Force had been able to disrupt and destroy Japanese communications, a job that would call for many more late-model planes than he was getting from the United States.

To Harriman's great surprise, Chennault also said that he was "not at all averse to the idea of concentrating our energies on the destruction of Germany, if we can get Russian support against Japan, and not diffuse our efforts by a weak and dangerous attack on Burma."

The rise of the Chinese Communists, already a formidable fighting force in the war against Japan, worried Chiang at Cairo. Harriman drafted a memorandum for Roosevelt, dated November 23, titled "Comments on Reports that the Generalissimo Is Deeply Concerned Over the Soviet Government's Attitude Toward His Regime and Its Intention to Support the Chinese Communists":

> In Moscow there are definite indications that the Soviet Government:
>
> 1) In the post-war period wants peace within China and a strong central government,
>
> 2) Recognizes that this objective can be obtained only through the Generalissimo,
>
> 3) Will insist on a more liberal policy based on democratic principles and improvement in social conditions,
>
> 4) Desires some solution of the Chinese Communist problem either by the Generalissimo's acceptance of them as an independent political party or by bringing them into the Government in some manner,
>
> 5) Does not have ambitions in respect to Chinese territory in general. This view is supported by their recent withdrawal from the Province of Sinkiang. The recognition of Outer Mongolia's independence was for military protection against the Japanese advance. There is no indication yet as to the Soviet Government's attitude regarding the question of a warm-water port, although it would be consistent for them to agree to the independence of Korea under some type of trust-

eeship in which the four great powers would participate. The
Chinese Ambassador in Moscow has expressed opinions along
these lines.

As events developed in 1944–45, it became even more evident to Harriman that far from being Soviet puppets, Mao Tse-tung's forces were
fighting their way to eventual power substantially on their own, and
frequently in defiance of Stalin's advice.

TALK OF CHINA FADED as soon as the President and his party left Cairo
in the early morning of November 27 for Teheran. During the six-
and-a-half-hour flight in the President's plane, Harriman talked at
length with Hopkins about the possibility of American postwar assistance to the Soviet Union in repairing its war-shattered economy. He
motioned to Roosevelt that this was a matter Stalin might raise at
Teheran.*

In a two-page document titled "Notes for the Impending Conference," which Harriman had written for the President before leaving
Cairo, he urged "complete frankness" with Stalin in the discussions of
Allied strategy at Teheran. "The pressure on the Soviet leaders for a
quick conclusion of the war," he wrote, "cannot be overemphasized.
Whether it is because they are fearful of the letting down . . . of the
morale of the Russian people, or of the loss of confidence in [their]
leaders, cannot be judged." The document carried a blunt warning
from Harriman that the fate of Poland would "probably go by default" unless Roosevelt raised the matter at Teheran.

At the President's request, there was no military salute or official
welcome to mark his arrival in Iran. Even the young Shah had been
discouraged from meeting Roosevelt at the airport—in the interest of
presidential security. The President went directly to the American
legation in an Army limousine, having politely declined the Shah's
offer to put him up in one of the royal palaces. Stalin had sent Roosevelt a message in Cairo offering to have him stay in the Soviet diplomatic compound, in order to avoid driving through the narrow,
crowded streets of Teheran to and from the American legation. But
Roosevelt, trusting his own security arrangements, seemed content to
stay at the legation, about a mile away.

When Harriman called on Molotov at six o'clock that evening to
discuss conference arrangements, he delivered Roosevelt's regrets. He
explained to Molotov that the President "thought it would create

---

* Neither Stalin nor any other Russian mentioned postwar aid at the Teheran
Conference. But Roosevelt authorized Harriman to discuss the possibility with
Molotov after they had returned to Moscow.

some feeling on the part of the British should he go to one place rather than the other." Molotov replied that the rooms set aside for the President were not going to be used in any event. They would be available if Roosevelt were to change his mind "or if difficulties arose."

After talking with Stalin in an adjoining room, Molotov approved the arrangements Harriman had proposed in Roosevelt's behalf: all the meetings the following day would take place at the American legation. Stalin would call on the President at three in the afternoon; the two would meet an hour later with Churchill and the military chiefs, and there would be a dinner at seven-thirty for Stalin and Churchill, together with Molotov, Eden, Clark Kerr, Harriman, Hopkins and Bohlen.

The only ripple of disagreement came when Molotov asked for a draft agenda and the names of the American delegation. Harriman drew the line at these formalities. "I gave him the names of the Chiefs of Staff, Admiral Leahy and Mr. Hopkins," he noted, "but explained that there was no American delegation. The President considered that the meeting was a personal one between him, Marshal Stalin and Churchill with their respective advisers." As for the agenda, Harriman said, the President had none to offer. He wanted to start with the strategic plans for the defeat of Germany. After that he would be ready to discuss any political topic that Stalin or Churchill cared to raise. Molotov had expected a more formal conference but, as Harriman noted, "he made no specific objection."

Clark Kerr, however, had seen Molotov later that evening and "caved in on the idea of delegations and agenda." When Harriman arrived at the British legation, after dining with Roosevelt, he found Clark Kerr and the Foreign Secretary "scurrying around trying to suggest an agenda." Eden showed Harriman a letter they had prepared for Molotov to the effect that "the British delegation" was submitting an agenda listing several topics, including the operations of the Allied commission for Italy. Harriman told Eden that Roosevelt had not traveled all the way to Teheran to get into that kind of detail. "After a lot of argument which was none too civil, Eden agreed to drop it out," Harriman recorded, "but he left in the word 'delegation.' I realized that we were all very tired, having been up since 3:30 in the morning, and therefore thought it better for me to clear out."

Harriman had just returned to General Connolly's house, where he was staying, when the Soviet embassy called to say that Molotov wanted to see him again, with Clark Kerr. It was past midnight when the two ambassadors arrived. Molotov told them he had received bad news. German agents in Teheran had learned of Roosevelt's presence in the city and were planning a "demonstration." This would create a scandal, Molotov added, a most unfortunate scandal for the Allies, which was bound to be exploited by the Nazi propaganda machine. Harriman pressed Molotov to explain what he meant. Molotov said that there might be an assassination attempt which, even if it failed, would certainly lead to shooting and might result in the killing of innocent bystanders. "I pressed him within the limits of civility for details," Harriman noted, "but nothing of importance was forthcoming."

At Harriman's request, Molotov showed him through a separate building inside the Soviet compound, already prepared for the President, which included a bathroom newly installed for his convenience. Although the furnishings were overelaborate and ugly, the quarters looked comfortable enough. Without expressing his own opinion as to the truthfulness of Molotov's story, Harriman sought out Michael F. Reilly, chief of the Secret Service, and General Connolly, commanding general of the Persian Gulf Service Command, to discuss the Russian offer. Both agreed to recommend that the President should move into the Russian compound.

"The next morning we went up to the Legation," Harriman noted, "and talked to Hopkins, who brought in everybody—'Pa' Watson, Admiral [Ross] McIntire and Admiral [Wilson] Brown. All at once agreed that the President should move, except Admiral Brown who took a high-handed attitude. He said that it was Stalin who suggested Teheran and why was he objecting now to security? While we were in discussion, Hopkins disappeared to see the President, who readily agreed and was delighted with the prospect."

Roosevelt moved to the Soviet compound the same afternoon, with Hopkins and Admiral Leahy, after Harriman had seen Molotov again. They arranged that a dozen of Reilly's Secret Service men—and as many American soldiers as he wanted—should be allowed inside the Soviet compound to guard the President. The guard around the American legation remained in place to maintain the fiction that the President was still there.

Harriman, in fact, never believed Molotov's story about an assassination plot. On his return to Moscow he pressed the Soviet Foreign Minister for the truth: "I said that I had a question to ask him, which he could feel free not to answer if he didn't wish to: namely, whether the plot in Teheran had been a German plot or a Molotov-Harriman plot? Molotov said that they knew there were German agents in Teheran but they had no information about a specific plot to attempt the life of any of the three men in Teheran; Marshal Stalin thought it would be safer if the President stayed at the Soviet Embassy." Stalin's show of solicitude for Roosevelt, in short, may well have masked a certain concern about his own safety, as well as Churchill's. He was anxious to avoid the needless risk of driving through the streets to meet with Roosevelt at the American legation when all three could live in the same sealed area (the walled compounds of the Soviet embassy and the British legation stood back to back, separated only by a narrow alley), under the protection of British and Soviet troops.

The long-awaited first tête-à-tête between Roosevelt and Stalin took place at three o'clock on November 28, to Churchill's apparent chagrin. The Prime Minister had asked to see Roosevelt that morning or at luncheon, in order to settle beforehand on the military matters they would discuss with Stalin at the first plenary session, scheduled for four o'clock. But Roosevelt was adamant: he wanted to see Stalin first and to see him alone except for the two interpreters, Bohlen and V. N. Pavlov. The President had reason to suspect that Churchill would press him to support a British plan to capture Rhodes and open the Dardanelles, even if this meant a delay of one or two months in the cross-Channel invasion. The American Chiefs of Staff felt the operation would be unwise, and the President, according to Harriman's notes, "did not want to be pinned down" by Churchill. So as soon as Stalin and Roosevelt sat down together, Harriman (forewarned by General Ismay that storm signals were flying in the British legation) walked over to see for himself "whether there was any need to calm the waters." He found Churchill in a grumbling but whimsical mood.

> He said that he was glad to obey orders; that he had a right to be chairman of the meeting because of his age, because his name began with C and because of the historic importance of the British Empire which he represented. He waived all these claims but he would insist on one thing, which was that he should be allowed to give a dinner party on the 30th, which was his 69th birthday . . . He said that he would get thoroughly drunk and be prepared to leave the following day.

The Stalin-Roosevelt encounter, meanwhile, was going famously. Roosevelt had raised with Stalin the possibility that some portion of the merchant shipping fleets of the United States and Britain, which at the end of the war were bound to exceed peacetime needs, should be turned over to the Russians. That would be a fine thing, Stalin replied, not only for the Soviet Union but also for the United States and Britain because the Western powers could get a plentiful supply of raw materials in exchange. They briefly discussed China and the thorny personality of Charles de Gaulle. The trouble with De Gaulle, Stalin said, was that he behaved as if he were the head of a great state when in fact he had little power and was out of touch with "the real France," a country which was busily helping the Germans and would have to be punished for it after the war. The President agreed, remarking that no Frenchman over forty years old and, more particularly, no Frenchman who had taken part in the Vichy regime, should be allowed to hold public office.

Stalin added that he did not propose to have the Allies shed blood in order to restore Indochina to French colonial rule. Roosevelt said that he agreed 100 percent, remarking that after a century of French rule the peoples of Indochina were worse off than ever before. He proposed a United Nations trusteeship for Indochina, which would prepare the peoples for independence within a definite period, perhaps twenty to thirty years, just as the United States had prepared the Philippines to govern themselves.

Both agreed that the matter of India's future should not be raised at Teheran because it was, as Stalin observed, a sore point with Churchill. At some future date, the President said, he would like to talk with Stalin further about India. The best solution, he felt, would be "reform from the bottom, somewhat on the Soviet line." Stalin replied that "reform from the bottom would mean revolution." India was a complicated society, he remarked, "with different levels of culture and the absence of relationship [between] the castes."

"I thought Stalin showed rather more sophistication than Roosevelt in the discussion of India," Harriman recalled. "I found it interesting that Stalin should have understood the complexities of Indian society. In my own talks with him, I was struck time and again by the extent of his knowledge of other countries, which I found remarkable in view of the fact that he had done so little traveling."

THE FIRST PLENARY SESSION concentrated chiefly on military plans. Although the Anglo-American Combined Chiefs of Staff were there in force, Stalin had left his military staff at home, bringing only Marshal Voroshilov. "I thought this extraordinary," Harriman recalled. "Voroshilov was one of Stalin's old stooges, incompetent but not dangerous. It seemed to me at the time that Stalin may not have wanted the military leaders to hear what he might say to Roosevelt and Churchill; that he preferred to control the discussion personally until he saw how the land lay with his allies."

Roosevelt, who presided, opened the discussion with a report on his plans for defeating Japan. Stalin welcomed the successes of his American ally in the Pacific. It was a matter of regret that his own armies could not join the battle, he said, because they were too deeply engaged in Europe. But once Germany was defeated, he proposed to multiply his forces in Siberia threefold and to play his part in the final defeat of Japan.

Turning to Europe, Roosevelt reaffirmed the Quebec decision to mount the cross-Channel invasion in May. The Channel, he remarked, was such "a disagreeable body of water" that amphibious operations earlier in the new year would be unsafe. To this, Churchill interposed that the British "had every reason to be thankful that the English Channel was such a disagreeable body of water."

Roosevelt then asked Stalin whether he favored more intensive Allied operations in Italy, in the Aegean Sea if Turkey could be brought into the war, or across the Adriatic, as a means of easing the short-term pressures on the Red Army by forcing the Germans to withdraw divisions from the eastern front. No, Stalin replied, the best move still was to invade France. Italy did not seem to him the right place from which to attack Germany because the Alps stood in the way, as the famous Russian soldier Suvorov had discovered in his time.* Turkey's entry into the war doubtless would help the Allied cause and open the way to the Balkans but, as he repeated several times, he doubted that the neutral Turks could be brought into the war. The way to get at the heart of Germany, Stalin insisted, was through France.

It was Roosevelt, not Churchill, who raised the specific question of a thrust across the Adriatic from Italy to link up with Tito's Partisans in Yugoslavia, and then a drive northeastward into Rumania in conjunction with the Soviet advance westward from Odessa. Stalin replied that it seemed to him unwise to scatter the Allied effort. He argued for treating Overlord as the main operation. If there was to be a diversionary operation, let it be hinged to Overlord, Stalin said; for example, by shifting Allied troops after the liberation of Rome to mount a landing in the South of France. This would help to ensure the success of the cross-Channel operation in the north.

To Harriman's distress, both General Marshall and General Arnold missed the first plenary session because nobody in the President's personal entourage had remembered to alert them. As a result, the Army and Air Force Chiefs had disappeared into the mountains near Teheran on a sightseeing tour. After that, Harriman took personal responsibility for the organization of the President's party. "I saw Molotov daily," Harriman recorded in a note on the conference, "and made with him the arrangements for the day in accordance with the President's wishes, and conveyed to the President Molotov's messages from Stalin. During the period, Molotov became more and more frank and friendly (particularly as he found things working out so favorably and informally). I used to give him some tidbits every day about the President's reaction

---

* In the autumn of 1799 a Russian army under Field Marshal Alexander Suvorov tried to cross the Swiss Alps from south to north and suffered a disastrous defeat.

to the events of the day before (of no particular political importance but indicating the President's satisfaction)." Day by day it became increasingly apparent to Harriman that the Russians were enjoying the unaccustomed informality of their new relationship with the Western leaders.

At Teheran, Stalin and Hopkins met for the first time since 1941. Harriman watched with satisfaction as Stalin, upon entering the conference, spotted Hopkins across the room and walked over to greet him warmly. It was not Stalin's habit to take the initiative this way; as a rule he waited for people to approach him. "Stalin showed Hopkins a degree of personal consideration which I had never seen him show anyone else except Roosevelt and Churchill," Harriman recalled. "I believe that Stalin's feelings for Hopkins went back to July 1941. Hopkins was the first Western visitor to Moscow after the German attack, when things were going pretty badly. Stalin evidently saw in Hopkins a man who, in spite of ill health, had made that long, exhausting and hazardous journey to bring help. It was an example of courage and determination that impressed Stalin deeply. He had not forgotten."

Harriman attended a dinner the same evening at Roosevelt's villa in the Soviet compound when Stalin again spoke out with great bitterness against the French. The entire French ruling class, he said, was rotten to the core. Having handed over their country to Hitler, the French now were actively helping the common enemy, and in Stalin's view, they deserved no consideration from the Allies. It would be unjust and positively dangerous to leave them in possession of their former empire, Stalin insisted. When Churchill protested that he could not conceive of the civilized world without a flourishing France, Stalin's response was contemptuous:

> . . . France could be a charming and pleasant country but could not be allowed to play any important role in the immediate postwar world. He characterized de Gaulle as a representative of a symbolic and not a real France, but one who nevertheless acted as though he was the head of a great power. He appeared to attach little importance to de Gaulle as a real factor in political or other matters.[5]

As for the Germans, including the German working class, Stalin saw no hope of reforming them. He told of visiting Leipzig in 1907 when some two hundred German workers failed to appear at an important rally because, Stalin said, there was no controller on the railway platform to punch their tickets on arrival. Without properly punched tickets, these stalwart representatives of the German working class were too timid to leave the station. There was, as he saw it, no hope of changing a popular mentality so totally obedient to authority.

Stalin, nevertheless, questioned the wisdom of demanding unconditional surrender from the Germans without defining the precise terms to be imposed upon them:

> He felt that to leave the principle of unconditional surrender unclarified merely served to unite the German people, whereas to draw up specific terms, no matter how harsh, and to tell the German people that this was what they would have to accept, would, in his opinion, hasten the day of German capitulation.[6]

Harriman was pleased to hear Stalin raise the question. "I had sounded out Molotov before leaving Moscow about the Soviet reaction to unconditional surrender," Harriman recalled. "He indicated that Stalin had some reservations about it, that it might make the Germans fight harder. I suggested that Stalin might want to raise the question with the President, which he did. But Roosevelt—unfortunately, in my view—never followed up Stalin's suggestion that he clarify his meaning. I felt it was a mistake, although I fully understood and agreed with Roosevelt's determination to avoid repeating the mistake of Woodrow Wilson in announcing his Fourteen Points."

After dinner the President retired to his bedroom but the rest stayed on. Churchill tried to draw out Stalin on the Polish question. It was in defense of Poland, Churchill said, that Britain had gone to war, and while he was not wedded to any specific frontier arrangement, the British government was certainly committed to the restoration of a strong, independent Poland after the war. Stalin replied that he did not feel it was necessary or desirable to discuss the Polish question then and there. He said only that the Soviet Union favored pushing Poland's frontier with Germany westward to the Oder River in compensation for the loss of her eastern territories. The Poles, in short, were to receive German lands in the west to which they had long claimed title. Stalin was determined to keep the lands up to the Curzon Line, which the Red Army had overrun in 1939, as he had long since informed the Western Allies. Churchill raised no objection. "He said that, as far as he was concerned, he would like to see Poland moved westward in the same manner as soldiers at drill execute the drill 'left close' and illustrated his point with three matches representing the Soviet Union, Poland and Germany."[7] Churchill proposed that the Big Three should try to work out an understanding on the Polish frontier question, but Stalin demurred. It would be necessary to look into the matter further, he said.

When Stalin called on Roosevelt again the following afternoon, the President asked that he give his personal support to the shuttle-bombing plan which Harriman and General Deane had put forward during the Moscow conference, the proposal accepted in principle a month earlier by Molotov, which the Soviet General Staff appeared in no great hurry to discuss. Roosevelt handed Stalin a memorandum Harriman had given him outlining the shuttle-bombing project and proposing an exchange of weather information, together with brief additional memoranda looking to the day when Russia would enter the war against Japan, which called for the use of Soviet bases in the Far East by the U.S. Air Forces and Navy. "The subject first came up in my talks with General Arnold before leaving Washington," Harriman recalled. "It was a matter of particular interest to Arnold, who hoped that the shuttle-bombing project would become the forerunner to joint operations against Japan from the Maritime Provinces. In presenting the memoranda to Stalin, Roosevelt stressed the importance of getting started on secret planning so that one day the U.S. Air Forces could bomb Japan from bases on Soviet territory in the Far East and our Navy could operate, jointly with the Russians, from Soviet port facilities in the North Pacific." Stalin promised to study the documents. On December 1, however, he told Roosevelt that he had not been able to find the time. He assured the President that he would take up the matter with Harriman after their return to Moscow.

For the rest, Roosevelt and Stalin talked in global terms about how the hard-won peace could be kept by the Great Powers. The President put forward his concept of a world assembly of some thirty-five or forty member states. The assembly would have an executive committee composed of the Soviet Union, the United States, Britain and China, together with two additional European countries, plus one state from South America, one from the Near East, one from the Far East, and one British Dominion. The executive committee, as he saw it, would deal with nonmilitary questions such as food and agriculture, health, labor and economic questions.

The President then outlined a third component of his proposed world organization which he called the Four Policemen. This body, consisting of Russia, the United States, Britain and China, would have real power to deal immediately with any threat to peace or sudden emergency. Had the old League of Nations possessed such power to act in defense of peace, he said, it could have closed the Suez Canal and thus prevented Mussolini's conquest of Ethiopia.

Stalin had his doubts. He thought that some European countries might well resent dictation by the Great Powers, above all by China. He preferred to see two separate commissions, one for Europe and the other for the Far East. The United States, Stalin added, should be a member of the European commission.

Roosevelt, in reponse, expressed doubt that Congress would ever agree to American participation in an exclusively European peace-keeping commission which might be able to force the dispatch of United States forces to Europe. When Stalin pointed out that the logic of the Four Policemen proposal also might compel the sending of American troops to Europe, Roosevelt said the United States would send only ships and planes. It would be up to the Russians and the British, he said, to provide land armies in the event of a future threat to peace on the Continent. Roosevelt went on to say "that if the Japanese had not attacked the United States, he doubted very much if it would have been possible to send any American forces to Europe."[8]

Stalin remained dubious about the elevation of China to Great Power standing. The President replied that the reason he had insisted upon China's participation in the four-power declaration at Moscow was not that he failed to recognize China's present weakness. He was thinking ahead, Roosevelt said. China, after all, was a nation of 400 million people and he thought it better to have them as friends than as a potential source of trouble.

At the second plenary session, which followed the Stalin-Roosevelt conversation of November 29, General Brooke (for the British) and Marshall (for the Americans) reported on the planning for Operation Overlord. Stalin then bluntly inquired who would command Overlord. Roosevelt responded that the commander had not yet been picked. Churchill added that while a British general had been responsible for the planning, his government was willing to see an American placed in overall command. Stalin replied that nothing would come of the operation unless one man was made responsible not only for the preliminary planning but also for its execution. The Russians, he said, were not asking for a voice in the selection; it was just that they wanted to know who the commander would be and to see him appointed as soon as possible. "Stalin made it plain," Harriman recalled, "that until the supreme commander was appointed he could not take seriously the promise of a cross-Channel invasion. For him the appointment was a specific assurance that the invasion would take place."

The man both Roosevelt and Churchill had in mind was, of course, General Marshall. Stalin, too, had come to believe that Marshall would be appointed. Stimson, Hopkins and Harriman were all totally devoted to Marshall. They considered him the one soldier pre-eminently qualified to command what all agreed was likely to prove the most difficult operation in the history of warfare. The new supreme commander, moreover, would have his headquarters in London, and the feeling in the White House was that Marshall alone, with his granite integrity, was equipped to resist any eleventh-hour maneuvers by Churchill and General Brooke to delay or divert the cross-Channel operation.

Marshall, of course, had been informed of his prospective new command and Mrs. Marshall had quietly started to move their personal belongings out of the Chief of Staff's residence at Fort Myer, Virginia, when the storm broke. Both Admiral King and General Arnold objected to the appointment on the ground that Marshall could not be spared from his position as the acknowledged leader of the Joint Chiefs. King saw nothing but confusion resulting from the preconceived plan to have Marshall wear two hats—as Chief of Staff and European commander—while Eisenhower was recalled from the Mediterranean to serve as the Army's Acting Chief of Staff. Eisenhower, moreover, was not on the best of terms with General MacArthur and there were dark predictions of serious trouble ahead if he were to replace Marshall.

Some of the high-level muttering had found its way into the newspapers, and by the time of the Cairo-Teheran conferences, the Marshall appointment had become distinctly moot. Roosevelt would have to reflect further before he could answer Stalin's question. Harriman saw no real alternative to Marshall. "He was the towering personality in all the British-American military discussions," Harriman recalled. "General Marshall had the respect and confidence of the Prime Minister and the British Chiefs of Staff as no other American had. I had seen a good deal of Eisenhower in London and I liked him. But compared to Marshall, Eisenhower seemed to me inexperienced and personally insecure. I was profoundly aware of the inter-Allied difficulties that Overlord would encounter and I felt we should put the first team in the field. For example, I cannot believe that the deep feeling which arose between Montgomery and [General Omar] Bradley would not have been avoided with Marshall as supreme commander. I know that General Marshall wanted more than anything else to command this historic military action, and I have no doubt that Roosevelt would have appointed him if he had given the slightest indication of his personal desires. But he left the decision entirely to the President. It was the most selfless thing any man could do—and I still feel, as I felt at the time, that the campaign in Europe would have been concluded more swiftly if Marshall had been in command."

Apart from the choice of a supreme commander, the timing of Overlord had yet to be decided. Stalin was pressing for the month of May, with Roosevelt's full assent. Churchill was not prepared, however, to abandon all hope of further operations in the Mediterranean, leaving surplus British forces in the Middle East to "stand idle" for six months. Harriman knew how deeply Churchill felt about his proposed campaign in the Greek islands. "He talked to me about it before I went to Moscow in October," Harriman recalled. "He had just been turned down by Roosevelt and he was in one of his rare depressed moods. He complained bitterly that they weren't going to let him have even a few of his own British battalions in the eastern Mediterranean to do what he considered important."

At Teheran, Churchill tried again. He talked of keeping the enemy busy by capturing Rhodes, then starving out the other Greek islands and reopening the Dardanelles. If Turkey agreed to enter the war, Churchill argued, these operations could be carried out with comparatively few troops. But it would be necessary to keep in the Mediterranean some sixty-eight landing craft needed for the cross-Channel invasion, which could force a delay of a month or two in that operation. He was, therefore, reluctant to give Stalin his unalterable commitment that Overlord would be scheduled for May. The conference record shows that Stalin, after listening to Churchill's arguments and dismissing the proposed operations in the eastern Mediterranean as "really only diversions," resorted to frontal attack:

> Marshal Stalin then said he wished to ask Mr. Churchill an indiscreet question, namely, do the British really believe in Overlord or are they only saying so to reassure the Russians?
>
> The Prime Minister replied that if the conditions set forth at Moscow were present it was the duty of the British Government to hurl every scrap of strength across the Channel.[9]

At dinner in the Soviet embassy that evening, Harriman recalled, Stalin kept needling Churchill without mercy. Several times through the evening he plainly implied that the Prime Minister, nursing some secret affection for the Germans, wanted a soft peace. The Soviet Union, Stalin said, would insist upon strong, effective measures to keep the Germans under control after the war. If these were not agreed to and strictly enforced, Germany was bound to rise up again in a matter of fifteen or twenty years and plunge Europe into another devastating war. To make sure this did not happen, he proposed that at least 50,000 German officers should be physically liquidated. In addition, the victorious Allies must hold all the important strategic points in Europe so that if the Germans dared to assert themselves they could be stopped at once.

Harriman felt that Stalin's fear of a resurgent Germany was entirely genuine. "He had spoken to me on several occasions of his concern that history would repeat itself, that there would be a revival of German militarism after the war—unless we took steps to prevent it," Harriman recalled. "Stalin never lost his respect for German superiority in organization and production, even though he was able to reorganize the Red Army and inflict a massive defeat on Hitler. I am satisfied that his concern was real, not an expression of his negotiating tactics, as in the case of certain other statements he made."

But Churchill was horrified at the suggestion of liquidating

50,000 German officers. "The British Parliament and people will never tolerate mass executions," he thundered. "Even if in war passion they allowed them to begin, they would turn violently against those responsible after the first butchery had taken place. The Soviets must be under no delusion on this point."[10]

At this moment, in a heavy-handed effort to break the tension, Roosevelt interposed that he did not favor shooting 50,000 Germans, only 49,000. The Prime Minister was not amused. In his wrath, Churchill also scorched the proposal for Great Power control of strategic points, which Roosevelt had already endorsed. Britain, he said, would hold fast to her own territories and bases and no one would take them away from her without going to war. He mentioned Singapore and Hong Kong in particular. The Prime Minister allowed the possibility that some parts of the British Empire might be granted eventual independence but insisted that "this would be done entirely by Great Britain herself, in accordance with her own moral precepts."[11]

Recognizing that he had pushed Churchill too far, Stalin turned abruptly to praising the British. They had fought well in the war, he acknowledged, and he personally would like to see the British Empire expanded, particularly in the area around Gibraltar. He suggested that Britain and the United States should install what he described as "more suitable governments" in Spain and Portugal, remarking that Franco, the Spanish dictator, was certainly no friend to the Western powers. But when Churchill tried to draw him out on Russia's territorial ambition, Stalin replied: "There is no need to speak at the present time about any Soviet desires; but when the time comes, we will speak."

NOVEMBER 30, Churchill's sixty-ninth birthday, marked the high point of the Teheran Conference. Both Roosevelt and Churchill met privately with Stalin in the forenoon while the Combined Chiefs of Staff wrote out their military recommendations. Roosevelt read them to Stalin before the Big Three sat down to luncheon: "We will launch Overlord during May, in conjunction with a supporting operation against the South of France on the largest scale that is permitted by the landing craft available at that time." Stalin, who had waited two years to hear those words, showed great satisfaction. He promised that the Red Army would open a series of offensives on the eastern front at the same time to prevent any shift of German divisions to the west. Russia would demonstrate by her actions the high value she placed on the Allied decision to invade France. Stalin asked when the commander would be named and the President replied "in three or four days," after he and the Prime Minister had returned to Cairo.

In response to a question from Churchill, Stalin said he had read and thoroughly approved the Cairo communiqué on the Far East, which Harriman and Clark Kerr had presented to Molotov a few days earlier. It was right, Stalin said, that Korea should be independent, as agreed at Cairo. As for the other Cairo decisions—that Manchuria, Formosa and the Pescadores islands should be returned to China after the defeat of Japan—these, too, were right. But, he added, the Chinese must be made to fight the Japanese, something they had not done so far.

The talk turned to the sheer size of the Soviet land mass. Stalin frankly admitted that Hitler would probably have defeated the Red Army but for the advantage of depth that their vast territory gave the Russians. Churchill volunteered the suggestion that so large a land mass deserved access to warm-water ports. It was, he said, a matter that could be settled agreeably as between friends. Although he had not raised the subject, Stalin responded by asking Churchill whether Britain was now prepared to relax the provisions of the Montreux Convention so that Russian ships could pass freely through the Dardanelles. Churchill assured him that Britain hoped to see Russian ships, both naval and merchant, sailing all the seas. Lord Curzon had other ideas, Stalin rejoined. True enough, said Churchill, but that was in the days when Russia and Britain did not see eye to eye. Stalin conceded that Russia, too, had changed since Curzon's time. He welcomed Roosevelt's suggestion that the Kiel Canal should be placed under international control as part of a larger scheme to form a free zone based on the old Hanseatic cities of Bremen, Hamburg and Lübeck. This would open the Baltic to ships of all nations.

Encouraged by the attitude of Roosevelt and Churchill, Stalin then inquired what his allies were prepared to do for Russia in the Far East. Vladivostok, he pointed out, was not wholly ice-free and could be closed by the Japanese through their control of the Tsushima Straits. Roosevelt liked the idea of a free port also in the Far East, mentioning Dairen as a possibility. The Chinese, Stalin warned, would not care for such a scheme. Roosevelt replied that the Chinese might like the idea better if Dairen became a free port under international guaranty. The important thing, Churchill said, was that Russia's legitimate needs should be satisfied because the Great Powers, if they were to lead the world into an era of peace, would have to behave like rich men who demanded nothing from their neighbors.

Molotov, Eden and Hopkins, lunching together separately, had embarked on a discussion of the so-called "strong points," or strategic bases, to be taken from Germany and Japan. Molotov argued that France ought not to escape without punishment for her willing collaboration with the enemy. She ought to be stripped of such bases as

Bizerte and Dakar; let them be placed under American or British control, he suggested. Eden objected mildly: perhaps the French could be made to see the need for a voluntary contribution to the peace-keeping task by putting these bases under control of the United Nations—that way French pride would not be hurt. Molotov agreed that Eden's way of arranging matters might be preferable but he could not contain his bitter hostility to France. Unlike Belgium and the Netherlands, which could not have been expected to withstand the Germans, he said, France was not small or weak. The French had made no real effort to defend themselves, preferring to collaborate with the Germans, and they must pay the price.

Hopkins said that the United States, feeling no immediate postwar threat from Germany, would leave the question of strong points in Europe to the Russians and the British. The United States proposed to establish bases only in the Far East, against Japan. Hopkins added that America would seek naval and air bases in the Philippines, even after the Islands had been granted their independence, and on Formosa as well. Neither Molotov nor Eden raised the slightest objection.

Churchill's birthday dinner at the British legation surpassed all others in cordiality. "As the President had not come with a birthday present for the Prime Minister," Harriman recalled, "he asked if I could get one for him. I immediately went over to see my friend Joseph M. Upton, a curator at the Metropolitan Museum of Art in New York, who was then stationed in Teheran. He let me have at cost a twelfth-century Kashan bowl from his personal collection. The President was delighted with it. My own gift was an eighteenth-century print on cloth of warriors on horseback with lions in the background. I felt it was entirely appropriate for the oldest warrior of the three, and Churchill seemed greatly amused by it."

In an exuberant mood, the Prime Minister toasted Roosevelt and Stalin in turn. He extolled the President for his lifelong devotion to the cause of the weak and the helpless, describing him as a man who by his courage and foresight in the dark days of 1933 had prevented a revolutionary upheaval in the United States. As for Stalin, he would be ranked with the great heroes of Russian history and had earned the title "Stalin the Great."

Stalin responded that the honors being heaped upon him truly belonged to the Russian people. In the service of such a people, he said, it was easy to be a leader. It was true that the Red Army had fought the Germans with great heroism, but the Russian people would have tolerated nothing less.[12] "The men of the Red Army had to be braver to turn back than to face the enemy," was the way Stalin put it, according to Harriman's notes.

Edward Henry Harriman, described by a French journal as the Napoleon of railroad men, with his sons, Averell (left) and Roland (right).

ROUGHING IT, *on a pack trip from E. H. Harriman's Pelican Bay Camp in the Klamath Lake district of Oregon, August 1908. Left to right: guide, Roland, Dr. William G. Lyle, E. H. Harriman and Averell.*

Mary Williamson Averell Harriman, a determined woman who felt that public administration ought to be a fit career for gentlemen, established the Training School for Public Service in New York after being rebuffed by the presidents of Harvard, Yale and Columbia.

INTERNATIONAL POLO PLAYER. *Averell Harriman (left) during a practice in preparation for the 1928 match against Argentina. He scored four of the U.S. team's seven goals in the 7–6 victory on September 30, 1928.*

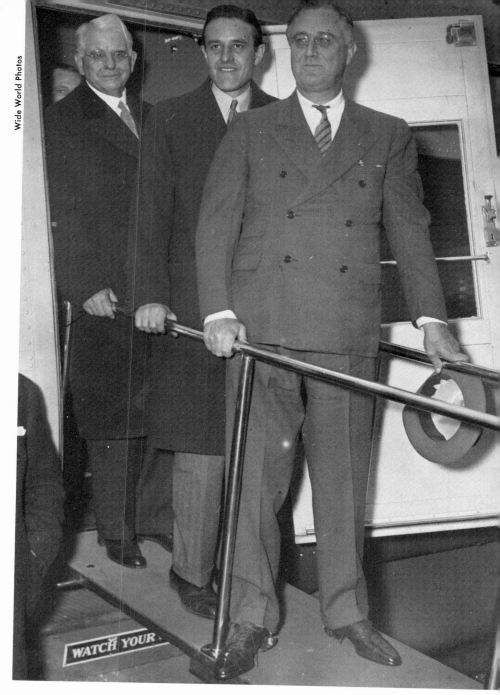

FIRST OF THE STREAMLINERS. *Harriman escorts President Franklin D. Roosevelt through the Union Pacific's first streamlined train at Union Station in Washington. Carl Gray, former president of the railroad, stands behind Harriman.*

STANDING UP FOR A FRIEND. *Harriman and his friend Harry Hopkins at Des Moines, Iowa, in February 1939. At Hopkins' request, Harriman accompanied him to Iowa for his first major speech as Secretary of Commerce. Harriman's presence was designed to reassure Iowans that Hopkins was no woolly-headed New Dealer but a sound thinker on good terms with captains of industry.*

SURVEYING THE MIDDLE EAST THEATER FOR CHURCHILL. *Harriman in Cairo, June 1941, with the Prime Minister's son, Captain Randolph Churchill (center), and Air Marshal Tedder of the RAF.*

INTERLUDE AT SEA. *General George Catlett Marshall and Harriman at prayer services on board H.M.S.* Prince of Wales *in Argentia Bay, Newfoundland, 1941. Of all America's military leaders, Harriman held Marshall in the highest regard. The general, in turn, kept Harriman fully informed of military plans and estimates throughout the war.*

FIRST WARTIME MISSION TO MOSCOW. *Hats off for the national anthems, Harriman and Lord Beaverbrook arrive in the Soviet capital to open Lend-Lease negotiations with Stalin, September 1941. Sir Stafford Cripps, the British ambassador, stands to the right of saluting Soviet naval officer. The American ambassador, Laurence Steinhardt, stands behind Harriman, and Andrei Vishinsky, Deputy Foreign Minister, at the far right (hat over his chest).*

After three extremely difficult negotiating sessions with Stalin, filled with reproaches against the British for not fighting harder, Harriman signs the first Lend-Lease Protocol for the United States. Left to right: Lord Beaverbrook, V. M. Molotov, Steinhardt (behind Harriman), Admiral W. H. Standley, who later succeeded Steinhardt as ambassador to Russia, and young Charles Thayer of the embassy staff.

Kathleen Harriman and Brendan Bracken, British Minister of Information, welcome Harriman at Euston Station on his return from Russia with Beaverbrook.

COMING DOWN TO EARTH

*Cartoon by David Low reproduced in program of dinner on
October 13, 1941, honoring Beaverbrook, Harriman and their
delegations on their return to London.*

*Less than a year later Harriman arrives in Moscow again, this
time with Churchill, to break the news that there will be no
Second Front in the West. It was a bleak encounter, like carrying ice to the North Pole, according to Churchill.*

At the end of the reproaches, Stalin agreed that the proposed
Allied landings in North Africa (Operation Torch) make military sense. He and Molotov smile on Churchill and Harriman
during Kremlin negotiating session.

Cartoonist Low in the London Evening Standard assesses the
Churchill-Harriman mission as a success.

NOW FOR SOME TEAMWORK, JOE

THE AMERICAN TEAM AT CASABLANCA, *January 1943, following the successful landings in North Africa. Roosevelt is flanked by General Marshall and Admiral King. Back row: Hopkins, General H. H. Arnold, General Brehon Somervell and Harriman.*

Kathleen Harriman after giving up her job with Newsweek *in London to accompany her father to Moscow, where she worked for the Office of War Information.*

BACK TO MOSCOW AS AMBASSADOR. *Harriman, accompanied by General John R. Deane, head of the new military mission to the Soviet Union, following formal presentation of his credentials to President Kalinin, October 1943.*

THE BIG THREE AT TEHERAN. *Standing behind them, left to right: Hopkins, Molotov, Harriman, Sarah Churchill, Eden.*

PRELUDE TO TEHERAN. *Roosevelt and Churchill confer in Cairo with Chiang Kai-shek and Madame Chiang before flying to Teheran for the first Big Three conference with Stalin. Standing behind the President and the Prime Minister, left to right: Sir Alexander Cadogan, Permanent Under Secretary of State for Foreign Affairs; Anthony Eden, British Foreign Secretary; Laurence Steinhardt (in hat), American ambassador to Turkey; John G. Winant, American ambassador to Great Britain; Harold Macmillan, British Minister in North Africa; Dr. Wang Chung-hui, Secretary General of the Supreme National Defense Council of China; R. G. Casey, British Minister of State, Middle East; Lord Killearn, British ambassador to Egypt; Major Desmond Morton, assistant to Churchill; Averell Harriman; Lewis W. Douglas; Lord Leathers, Minister of War Transport; John J. McCloy; and Harry Hopkins.*

Eden and Harriman at Luqa Airport, Malta, on January 29, 1945, before the Yalta Conference.

FINAL REUNION AT YALTA. *Roosevelt's haggard looks alarmed both Churchill and Harriman. He was dead ten weeks later. Rear row, left to right: Eden, Secretary of State Edward R. Stettinius, Cadogan, Molotov and Harriman.*

Stalin and Molotov at Yalta, with Harriman in the middle.

VICTORY CELEBRATION ON THE LENIN MAUSOLEUM, *August 12, 1945. Eisenhower received a hero's welcome on his visit to Moscow. Left to right: Marshal Georgi K. Zhukov, General Eisenhower, with Stalin and Harriman review the parade from a platform on top of Lenin's tomb.*

*A Stalin-Harriman tête-à-tête during the five-hour parade.
The chairs at the back of the platform looked "mighty inviting"
to Harriman after the first two hours. But as Stalin remained
on his feet, the Ambassador did not dare sit down.*

*Harriman at the Potsdam Conference with, left to right, an
unidentified GI, his devoted assistant, Bob Meiklejohn (in
naval uniform), and Ambassador Edwin W. Pauley, U.S.
reparations commissioner.*

The new Secretary of State, James F. Byrnes, visited Moscow in December 1945. Harriman found him stiff and unwilling to listen.

With the new President, Harry Truman, he developed a warm and enduring relationship.

On his way home from Moscow, Harriman visited General Mac-Arthur in Tokyo to brief him on Russia's postwar foreign policy.

As postwar ambassador to Great Britain, Harriman addresses a cloth-cap audience at the traditional miners' gala in Durham. Lord Beaverbrook accused him of mixing in British politics. The Conservatives decided not to make an issue of it after Harriman pointed out that they would do him "a world of good" with Labor party.

"Hopkins made one of the wittiest after-dinner speeches I ever heard, in tribute to Churchill," Harriman recalled. "Unfortunately it has not been fully recorded. He undertook the formidable task of teasing Churchill without offending him. After long study, Harry said, he had made a great discovery—that 'the provisions of the British Constitution and the powers of the War Cabinet are just whatever Winston Churchill wants them to be at any given moment.' His toast might not have been so well received had it come from someone Churchill valued less highly. In any event, the Prime Minister joined in the laughter with the rest of us. Hopkins' relationship with Churchill was so deeply rooted in mutual respect and warm affection that he could say pointed things, in his uniquely humorous way, without arousing the Prime Minister's resentment."

Harriman recognized the sting of truth in Hopkins' teasing. In his London years, he had seen the Prime Minister shoulder full responsibility for setbacks and disasters time and again. Yet when he preferred to avoid a commitment, Churchill would speak of his limited authority under Britain's unwritten constitution and the need to consult the Cabinet, or even the Parliament.

Churchill had just raised his glass for the concluding toast when Stalin requested the privilege of proposing one more toast—to the President and people of the United States:

I want to tell you, from the Russian point of view, what the President and the United States have done to win the war. The most important things in this war are machines. The United States has proven that it can turn out from 8,000 to 10,000 airplanes per month. Russia can only turn out, at most, 3,000 airplanes a month. England turns out 3,000 to 3,500, which are principally heavy bombers. The United States, therefore, is a country of machines.

Without the use of those machines, through Lend-Lease, we would lose this war.

This generous tribute prompted Roosevelt to ask for the last word. He talked about the diversity of political complexions around the banquet table which, he said, reminded him of the rainbow, to Americans "a symbol of good fortune and of hope." The President continued:

We have differing customs and philosophies and ways of life. Each of us works out our scheme of things according to the desires and ideas of our own peoples.

But we have proved here at Teheran that the varying

ideals of our nations can come together in a harmonious whole, moving unitedly for the common good of ourselves and of the world.

So as we leave this historic gathering, we can see in the sky, for the first time, that traditional symbol of hope, the rainbow.

On that high note the dinner ended. Throughout the conference Harriman had been impressed by the respect Stalin had shown for Roosevelt. "When the President spoke," he recalled, "Stalin listened closely with deference, whereas he did not hesitate to interrupt or stick a knife into Churchill whenever he had the chance. I felt at the time that Stalin's attitude was motivated not only by the greater power of the United States but also by his understanding that Roosevelt represented something entirely new; his New Deal was reforming capitalism to meet the needs and desires of the 'working class.' There was nothing about that in Communist doctrine."

Harriman's personal notes on Churchill's birthday dinner record his own assessment of the conference:

> It was clear that those present had a sense . . . that historic understanding had been reached and this conception was brought out in the statements and speeches; but back of that was the feeling that basic friendship had been established, which there was every reason to believe would endure.
>
> This strong feeling of optimism appeared to be based on the realization that if the three nations went forward together there was real hope for a better future, and that their most vital interest dictated such a policy.

With the military decisions out of the way, the Big Three turned the following day to the more treacherous terrain of politics. At three-twenty, following a luncheon devoted for the most part to an inconclusive discussion of ways to get Finland out of the war and to bring Turkey in, Roosevelt with Harriman met Stalin and Molotov for their final tête-à-tête. The President explained that he had asked Stalin to come and see him for a frank discussion of American politics. He did not wish to run again in 1944, the President said, but if the war was still in progress, he might have to run. There were between six and seven million Polish-American voters, he added, and he did not wish to lose their votes. For that reason, although he personally agreed with Stalin's views on shifting the Polish border with the Soviet Union to the west, and the border with Germany as far west as the Oder River, he could not "publicly take part in any such arrangement at the present time," nor even the following winter. Stalin replied that he now understood the President's position.[13]

Roosevelt went on to say that he also had to think about American voters of Lithuanian, Latvian or Estonian origin. He was fully aware, the President said, that the three Baltic republics had belonged to Russia in the past and had once again been incorporated into the Soviet Union in 1940. He did not, he added with a smile, intend to go to war with the Soviet Union when the Red Army reoccupied these areas. It was important, however, to satisfy public opinion in the United States and the world at large that the Baltic peoples had exercised the right of self-determination. "He personally was confident that the people would vote to join the Soviet Union," Roosevelt said, but there must be "some expression of the will of the people."

Stalin replied that the Baltic States had not been autonomous under the last Czar, who had been an ally of Great Britain and the United States. Yet no one had then raised the question of public opinion and he did not understand why it was being raised now. The truth of the matter, Roosevelt said, was that the public did not understand these matters. Then let them be informed, Stalin suggested; it was time for some propaganda work to be done. He added that there would be lots of opportunities for the will of the Baltic peoples to be expressed, in accordance with the Soviet Constitution. But any form of "international control" was excluded. Roosevelt observed that a public declaration with regard to future elections would be helpful to him personally. Stalin made no promises, repeating that there would be plenty of opportunities later on for the Baltic peoples to express their will.

"Roosevelt's primary political objective at Teheran," Harriman recalled, "was to get Stalin's agreement for the establishment of the United Nations at the end of the war. The President had outlined his rough design for the proposed world organization at his second private meeting with Stalin, on November 29. He took tremendous encouragement from Stalin's statement on December 1 that after thinking it over, he had come to agree with Roosevelt that the organization should be world-wide, not regional."

The rest of the dialogue, however, left Harriman with a profound sense of misgiving. He had no patience with the idea of leaving the boundaries to be settled after the election. The crucial flaw in Roosevelt's approach, as he saw it, was that once the Red Army had taken physical possession of Poland and other neighboring countries, it might well be too late for a negotiated settlement. But the President was looking at the practical politics of the Polish question. He knew that any compromise on the eastern boundary would almost certainly be rejected by the Polish government-in-exile, which in turn could raise a great outcry among the Polish-American voters in Buffalo, Detroit, Chicago and other centers across the country. Having alienated many traditionally Democratic Italian voters by his stab-in-the-back speech, he did not want to borrow trouble with the Poles as well. The 1944 election was fast approaching and he preferred to postpone the Polish outcry until after the votes were counted, leaving Churchill to take the lead meanwhile.

When the Polish issue came up again at the final meeting of the Big Three the same evening, Roosevelt urged Stalin to reopen diplomatic relations with the Polish government in London. Predictably, Stalin objected. He accused the London Poles of maintaining close connections with the Germans, and their "agents" inside Poland of killing partisans.

Although Stalin did not commit himself, he responded to the pleas of Roosevelt and Churchill in his fashion by conceding that he might agree to negotiate with the Polish government-in-exile if it agreed to cooperate with the partisans and sever all connections with German agents.

With regard to territorial claims, Stalin said that he proposed to take the northern part of East Prussia from Germany, including the ports of Tilsit and Königsberg. If the Soviet Union could have this swatch of territory, running along the left bank of the Neman River, he would then be prepared to accept the Curzon Line as the frontier between Russia and Poland. During this discussion he marked the boundaries of his territorial ambitions in red pencil on a map prepared in the State Department. Churchill had indicated earlier that he would carry Stalin's terms back to the Polish government in London. If the London Poles refused to negotiate the boundary question, Churchill said, "then Great Britain would be through with them and certainly would not oppose the Soviet Government under any condition at the peace table."[14]

Falling in with the mood, so conducive to drawing lines across the map of Europe, Roosevelt talked of dividing Germany into five separate states:

1. Prussia, which should be "rendered as small and weak as possible."
2. Hanover and Northwest Germany.
3. Saxony and the Leipzig area.
4. Hesse-Darmstadt, Hesse-Kassel and the area south of the Rhine.
5. Bavaria, Baden and Württemberg.

The Ruhr and the Saar basin, Germany's chief coal and steel

regions, would be placed under United Nations control. An international regime also should be devised for the area of the Kiel Canal and the city of Hamburg.

"He had mentioned his idea to me long before Teheran," Harriman recalled. "Roosevelt had studied in Germany and felt that he was particularly knowledgeable on the subject. I did not think much of the idea that Germany ought to be split up. It was not really a plan and it seemed to me too drastic; I felt that German nationalism was so strong that it would bring the divided states together again. It was another case of Roosevelt dreaming aloud."

Churchill appeared dumbfounded by the audacity of Roosevelt's suggestion. It seemed to him, if he might borrow an American expression, that "the President has 'said a mouthful.' "[15] His own plan was less sweeping. He agreed that Prussia should be detached from Germany. As for the South German regions, he would detach Bavaria, Baden and Württemberg and make them part of a Confederation of the Danube. Stalin, showing his fear of a strong Germany, did not think much of either idea, though he said that of the two he preferred Roosevelt's. The trouble with fitting any part of Germany into a larger confederation, he said, was that this would merely encourage the German elements to take control and re-create a great national state. Besides, he saw little difference between one part of Germany and another. All Germans, with the possible exception of the Austrians, fought like the devil.

The Prime Minister said he did not wish to be quoted as opposing the dismemberment of Germany. In his judgment, however, the separate German states would sooner or later come together into one nation. The main thing, he said, was to keep the Germans divided, if only for fifty years. Stalin acknowledged that whatever the Allies decreed, there would always be a strong urge on the part of the Germans to unite. For this reason, the task of the victorious powers would be to make certain they possessed the strength to defeat the Germans if they should ever again embark on the path of war.

Even as Eden had tested the ground for a Central European confederation at Moscow a month earlier and found Molotov unwilling to consider it, Churchill pressed the idea upon Stalin, with the same result. Stalin made clear that he would not allow Rumania or Hungary to federate with any remnants of Hitler's broken Reich.

Was the Soviet Union insisting, Churchill asked Stalin directly, on a Europe of small, separate and weak states? No, Stalin replied. He wanted to see a weak Germany, not a weak Europe. Poland, he said, would be a strong state; also France and Italy.

No one remarked on the striking contradiction between Stalin's earlier denunciation of Poland as a country too big for its breeches and France as "rotten to the core" and their sudden elevation to the rank of Europe's most powerful states. After all, Churchill observed, the discussion at Teheran amounted to no more than a preliminary survey of a vast historical problem. Stalin agreed that it was certainly very preliminary.

A declaration on Iran also was signed at the last possible moment. This brief document, committing the three powers to respect the "independence, sovereignty and territorial integrity of Iran," was dealt with casually at Teheran, although it assumed considerable importance in the first postwar crisis over Azerbaijan. Recognizing Iran's assistance to the Allied cause "by facilitating the transport of supplies from overseas to the Soviet Union,"/ the declaration also pledged the great powers to help the Shah's government economically at the end of the war. Although the draft had been approved in principle, Harriman found on the last night of the Teheran Conference that it had not been signed. He showed the only existing draft, in English, to Stalin and asked him whether he wanted it translated into Russian. "Stalin asked Pavlov to translate it for him verbally," Harriman recorded, in a memorandum for the White House, "and in my presence and Mr. Bohlen's said that he approved the Declaration and that, in view of the shortness of time, it was not necessary to have a Russian text. I then asked Stalin to sign the Declaration. He said he would do so after the President. I then took the Declaration to the President, who signed it. Thereupon Stalin signed it forthwith."

Before Roosevelt and Churchill flew back to Cairo to decide, among other matters, who should command the cross-Channel invasion, they joined Stalin in signing a three-power declaration, published around the world on December 6. It was a brave document, filled with ringing words about working together in peace as well as war:

> We recognize fully the supreme responsibility resting upon us and all the United Nations to make a peace which will command the good will of the overwhelming mass of the peoples of the world, and banish the scourge and terror of war for many generations. . . . We shall seek the cooperation and the active participation of all nations, large and small, whose peoples in heart and mind are dedicated, as are our own peoples, to the elimination of tyranny and slavery, oppression and intolerance. We will welcome them, as they may choose to come, into a world family of democratic nations . . . Emerging from these cordial conferences, we look with confidence to the day when all peoples of the world may live free lives, untouched by tyranny, and according to their varying desires and their own consciences. We came here with hope and de-

termination. We leave here, friends in fact, in spirit and in purpose.

The declaration, Harriman felt, was an astonishing statement for Stalin to have signed. "Later on I began to realize that his ideas of tyranny were quite different from ours," he recalled. "He believed in killing the few for the benefit, as he saw it, of the many. Tyranny for him did not exist in the Soviet Union. It was capitalism exploiting the downtrodden. At the time, however, I was puzzled that he and Molotov should have fought so hard over some bit of innocuous language and raised no objection to other language that seemed to me far more important."

Neither Roosevelt nor Churchill was blind to the continuance of terror and tyranny in the Soviet Union. For Churchill, the matter had probably been settled on June 22, 1941, the day Hitler invaded Russia. "If Hitler invaded Hell," he said that day to his private secretary, J. C. Colville, "I would make at least a favourable reference to the Devil in the House of Commons." Writing about Teheran seven years later, Churchill explained that he and Roosevelt saw no decent alternative: "It would not have been right at Teheran for the Western democracies to found their plans upon suspicions of the Russian attitude in the hour of triumph and when all her dangers were removed."[16] Roosevelt, too, understood the expediency of welcoming Stalin as an ally against Hitler. But he hoped and believed that tyranny would not forever endure in Russia. He continued to believe that the Russians, as a deeply religious people, were bound to stand up against the atheist ideology of Soviet Communism and its repressions.

Harriman's view, though less hopeful than Roosevelt's, was that the Teheran Conference had laid to rest "the feeling that existed among the Russians that we were not doing enough, and the doubts that existed as to our real intentions." At a staff conference in the embassy on December 8, after his return to Moscow, he acknowledged that the three-power declaration "sounds like generalities. But there is meaning in every sentence." He noted that Stalin had seldom spoken of "the Soviet government" at Teheran. More often it was "we Russians" or just "Russia." Stalin even made a joke about the prospect of world revolution. "We won't worry about that," he said to Roosevelt and Churchill. "We have found it is not so easy to set up a Communist society."

CHAPTER XIII

"The History of War Has Never Witnessed Such a Grandiose Operation"

Hᴵᴳʜ ᴛᴵᴅᴇ ꜰᴏʀ ᴛʜᴇ ᴛʀᴏᴜʙʟᴇᴅ ᴀʟʟᴵᴀɴᴄᴇ followed in the wake of Teheran. Roosevelt set the tone in a message to Stalin sent from Cairo on December 3: "I consider that the conference was a great success and I am sure that it was an historic event in the assurance not only of our ability to wage war together but to work in the utmost harmony for the peace to come." Stalin responded in the same confident vein: "Now it is assured that our people will act together jointly and in friendship both at the present time and after the completion of the war." Both leaders expressed the hope that they would meet again before long.

Roosevelt had sent a second message the same day, thanking Stalin for his "thoughtfulness and hospitality" in putting up the presidential party at the Soviet embassy in Teheran. Through an unexplained quirk of wartime communications, this bread-and-butter note did not reach Moscow until two weeks later in the form of a sealed letter, which Harriman had to deliver unopened to Stalin on December 18. The Ambassador registered his annoyance with Washington and made certain that it did not happen again. "I am glad," Stalin promptly replied, "that Fate gave me an opportunity to render you a service in Teheran. I also attach great importance to the conversations there which touched on such essential questions as the hastening of our common victory and the establishment of a lasting peace among the nations."

Any last, lingering doubt in Stalin's mind about the validity of the Roosevelt-Churchill commitment to cross the Channel had been effectively dispelled by a one-sentence presidential message that Harriman delivered to Molotov on December 7, the second anniversary of Pearl Harbor: "The immediate appointment of General Eisenhower to the command of Overlord has been decided upon." Stalin had said bluntly at Teheran that he could not consider the Overlord promise as binding until a supreme commander had been appointed. Now Roosevelt had kept his word. "When I received the message for Stalin," Harriman recalled, "I was somewhat concerned. I feared that he would misinterpret the naming of Eisenhower instead of Marshall as a sign that we were downgrading the operation, and that we might be in for a revival of the recriminations so recently laid to rest about our determination to go ahead with Overlord in the spring. I was so concerned, in fact, that when I delivered the message to Molotov I asked him how soon we could have Stalin's reaction. He said, 'I will telephone to him,' which he did in my presence. To my great relief, Molotov reported an immediate, affirmative reaction. Stalin remarked that Eisenhower was a general experienced in directing large forces and amphibious operations. A few days later he cabled Roosevelt: 'I welcome the appointment of General Eisenhower. I wish him success in the preparation and carrying out of the impending operations.' "

Marshall himself accepted the President's decision with characteristic grace. Roosevelt had pressed him to say whether he preferred to command the European invasion or to remain in Washington as Chief of Staff. But Marshall had refused to make a choice, saying the issue was too important for personal feelings to be considered and that he would accept the President's decision without question, either way. So the President had decided to keep Marshall in Washington.

The embassy, in its constant review of the Moscow press and radio, detected an almost "revolutionary change" of attitude toward the Western Allies in the afterglow of Teheran. Showing a wholly new respect for the United States and Britain, the Soviet press was citing the "historic decisions" of Teheran almost daily. The purpose of this campaign was no doubt to encourage in the war-weary populace a belief that the alliance, now on a solid footing, would make short work of Hitler's armies.

All over the Soviet Union, factory workers were summoned to meetings for the purpose of whipping up public enthusiasm. The Yugoslav ambassador described to Harriman on December 10 how

this was done in one Moscow factory, according to the testimony of a
workman he had met:

> Every brigade in the factory had been called together and
> a "political" had explained the [Teheran] declaration and its
> significance. The workers had been encouraged to ask ques-
> tions and when one questioned the importance that the speaker
> had attached to the declaration, by saying, "But we have heard
> all this before!," another workman said: "But this time Stalin
> himself left Russia to attend the conference and that means
> this is the real thing."

Incidents of this kind left little room for doubt in Harriman's
mind that the Russian people in the mass had not lost their faith in
Stalin's infallibility. A new party line, he felt, was emerging from
these factory meetings: "This is what Stalin has done for you. Now
what are you going to contribute, by way of increasing production, to
bring about the final victory?" Kathleen Harriman, in her winter walks
through the Moscow streets, noticed other signs of morale-building.

> There's a lot of superficial bomb-damage repair work go-
> ing on day and night [she wrote to Mary in New York].
> Camouflage is being taken off, etc., which in view of the sup-
> posed shortage of materials and labor at first seems strange.
> But it's apparently just part of the general "victory is in
> sight" program to bolster up morale. In London the wear and
> tear of the war was fairly visible, but here it's unmistakable.
> There are no petty luxuries—not that there ever were—but
> money buys nothing as there's nothing to buy at "reasonable"
> prices. Cigarettes, bought in non-government stores, cost about
> 35 cents a piece. (That's just an example.)
>   Now I'm just beginning to realize that the good old
> Russian communiqués that deal in impersonal heroics and huge
> numbers of dead, missing and wounded mean something very
> personal here in the way of friends and family. When you get
> down to it, despite the teachings that the state comes first,
> the Russian still is a human being and the government treats
> him as such—and so the reason for the periodic fireworks when
> a new victory is announced and the dressing-up of the bombed
> buildings.

During her walks Kathleen absorbed many of the homely sights
and smells that a career diplomat might have missed: the mysterious
Moscow system, for example, of distributing cabbages and firewood.
Approximately once a month, she noticed, a truckload of wood or

cabbages would be dumped in the street outside a large apartment house. People would come out and carry in what appeared to be their share, though how the sharing was determined or by whom, she could not discover.

The Russians impressed her at times as a people of monumental patience. Outside a food store they would stand in line for hours, some even sitting down on the icy pavement in stolid acceptance of the necessity to wait their turn. But when minutes were at stake, rather than hours, as after a performance at the theater or the ballet, "not even a two-ton truck" could halt the wild scramble for hats and coats at the check room.

> It's an impersonal town [she observed in one of her letters home]. People in the streets seem divorced from one another. Perhaps it's the wideness of the streets that makes it so, and makes all the scurrying figures seem so dwarfed. Every house I've been to I've asked, "Who are your neighbors?" No one knows. We know only that on our right live some NKVD boys. Behind us is a crowded apartment house, but faces never appear in the windows, washing is never hung out to dry. Walking in the streets, people look down at the ground rather than up. (That may be because it's so damned slippery. They stare at my galoshes and I stare back at their huge, shapeless *valenki* [felt boots]).

Some ten days after Harriman's return from Teheran, Dr. Eduard Beneš, President of Czechoslovakia, arrived in Moscow to sign his new treaty of friendship with the Russians. In the course of two long talks with Harriman, who had known him well in London, Beneš told how thrilled he was at his warm reception by Stalin and how bright were his hopes for the future of Czechoslovakia, based on what seemed to him a fundamental change in Soviet attitudes. Beneš had last visited Moscow in 1935 and he found the Russians transformed. His near-rapturous impressions are recorded in Harriman's telegrams:

> . . . modesty and calm have taken the place of the previous aggressiveness and excitability of the Soviets. Their feeling that their leadership of the Russian people is now secure is, in Benes' view, the basis of this self-confidence. At last, the revolution is accomplished. For war and for peace, Soviet Russia is strong and consolidated. There has emerged a vigorous nationalism, linked with Russia's past—Russia for Russians, and not a base for international revolution. The bolshevizing of other countries had been replaced as an objective by the determination to participate as a powerful nation in world affairs.

Great satisfaction in the new relationships with the United
States and Great Britain was expressed to Benes by Stalin, who
had been much impressed with the President and who felt that
complete agreement on all questions, not of course in detail
but in approach, had been reached with him at Teheran. . . .

Stalin felt more sympathetic to Roosevelt than to Churchill, Beneš
told Harriman, but he was determined to build a triangular relationship
with both Britain and the United States. He was equally determined
to create a three-cornered relationship with Czechoslovakia and Poland
as a barrier against any future *Drang nach Osten* by a resurgent Germany. For this purpose, so essential to the peace of Europe, Poland
would be asked to subscribe to the Soviet-Czechoslovak treaty.

Beneš insisted that the new treaty would in no way interfere with
or diminish Czechoslovakia's independence. On the contrary, his country would be perfectly free to maintain its long-standing relationships
with the United States and Britain. He saw no threat of Soviet domination, Beneš said, comparing his new relationship with Russia to
Roosevelt's Good Neighbor policy in the Western Hemisphere.

It was a point of pride with Beneš that the Russians over the years
had talked more frankly with him than with other foreign statesmen.
This time they had openly discussed their troubles with Poland. Before flying to Moscow, Beneš had met with Premier Stanislaw Mikolajczyk in London, finding him suspicious that the Russians were determined to bolshevize Poland and then incorporate her into the Soviet
Union. Stalin's response, when Beneš had explained Mikolajczyk's
fears, was to rise up abruptly in his chair and exclaim, "What fools
these people are!"

Stalin had questioned Beneš closely about individual members of
the Polish government in London. He seemed surprised to hear that
Mikolajczyk was peasant-born, not a member of the landowning class.
Beneš acknowledged that there were some men in the Polish government whom he considered reactionary and anti-Soviet, such as General
Kazimierz Sosnkowski, commander in chief of the Polish armed forces,
but Mikolajczyk was not one of them. Would it be possible, Stalin
asked, to create a new Polish government based on the democratic
elements and divorced from the reactionaries? Beneš did not think so.
Such a government, he said, would be too weak to govern Poland.

When Harriman asked Beneš to forecast the course of events inside Poland, he replied that perhaps the only possibility was to wait
until the Red Army drove out the Germans; at that time a representative government capable of dealing with the Soviets would arise. He
expressed confidence that the Red Army would enter Poland under

instructions to win the good will of the people and that the Soviet government would not attempt to bolshevize the country.

Harriman now outlined his own, more pessimistic, view of the future. What if the Polish people did not, in fact, welcome the Red Army? He mentioned the possibility of "conflicts from the Polish side, especially if the Government in London encouraged them; and that, in any case, the assistance of the Polish underground would not be had by the Red Army." Beneš acknowledged the validity of Harriman's concern.

But after a further meeting with Stalin, Beneš talked hopefully of a possible rapprochement between the Russians and the London Poles —if Mikolajczyk and the other "democratic elements" could get rid of the "irreconcilable reactionaries" and sincerely seek to work with the Soviet Union. "Beneš said to me at our second meeting on December 20: 'There need be no fear among the Poles that the Soviets intend to dominate Polish internal policies or to Sovietize Poland,'" Harriman recorded. "Stalin, in fact, had offered to modify his original frontier demands as part of the package. The Poles could keep Bialystok in the north and Przemysl in the south. Beneš showed me a map of the new boundaries Stalin had in mind for Poland." The boundary "appeared to follow the Curzon Line to the east, included East Prussia except for Königsberg and the area north, and bounded by the Oder on the west."

Mikolajczyk, in short, was being asked (through Beneš) to reconstruct his government and accept the new frontiers, much as Stalin had drawn them in red pencil at Teheran; the Russians would then be prepared to make the same kind of treaty with him that they had just signed with Beneš, Stalin said.

Regarding the future of his own country, Beneš had few qualms or doubts. Stalin had assured him, he said to Harriman, that the Soviet Union would respect Czechoslovakia's frontiers as they had existed before the Munich accord; that is, before Hitler grabbed the Sudetenland and Poland helped itself to Teschen. Beneš also had reached an understanding with several leaders of the Czechoslovak Communist party living in Moscow on terms for reconstructing his government. The Communists were to receive one fifth of the places in that new government and Beneš was confident that this arrangement would be workable. "In his many talks with different Soviet officials," Harriman reported, "Beneš said it had been frequently repeated that the Soviet Government desired stability and strong representative governments [on its frontiers] and had no desire to foster a Communist revolution in Czechoslovakia or, in fact, in any other European country."

While Beneš has been criticized, with the benefit of hindsight, for placing too much trust in the assurances he received from Stalin then and later, it must be remembered that he negotiated the treaty in the belief that he was serving the genuine interests of both countries. The Russians, he felt, had every right to seek assurances that they would not again be threatened by unfriendly neighbors. The Czechoslovaks, believing that they had been sold out in 1938 by the British and French at Munich, felt that they could never again rely solely, or even chiefly, on the Western powers for protection. The Red Army soon would be moving into Czechoslovak territory in pursuit of the weakened Wehrmacht, leaving Stalin free to dominate the country if he chose to do so. And unlike the London Poles, Beneš was determined to work out a friendly arrangement with his powerful neighbors before the opportunity slipped from his hands. He left Moscow determined to "urge the Poles as their friend to decide at once to negotiate with Moscow and to accept Stalin's offer."[1]

Harriman later recorded that his own view of Soviet intentions toward Poland and other neighboring countries could not help but be affected for a time by Beneš' optimism. His attitude of the period can be seen in the transcript of a meeting with American correspondents at Spaso House on January 19, 1944. William H. Lawrence of the *New York Times* asked how the Polish problem might be resolved and Harriman replied:

> 1. That the Soviets don't trust the Polish Government in London at all and, from their standpoint, I think they are reasonable in this distrust.
>
> 2. On the Polish side, they have a definite suspicion, which I don't think is well founded, that the Soviets are desirous of communizing Poland, or setting up a puppet government, or making it a part of the Soviet Union. The Soviets have enough racial indigestion without adding this problem to their own.
>
> Basically, I believe the Soviets are anxious to have a solution of the problems of their border countries which will lead to as much harmony as possible with Poland. I think they have made up their minds that they can't find such a relationship with this group in London.

He did not suppose, Harriman added, that one American in ten thousand had heard of the Curzon Line or had the faintest idea whether it represented a fair boundary between the Soviet Union and Poland. The Curzon Line seemed to him a less-than-perfect solution, but it was "rather closer to being a natural ethnographic division than any other line that has been talked about."

Harriman told the reporters that in his judgment, the boundary question would be less difficult to overcome than the burden of suspicion, rooted in centuries of Polish-Russian conflict, that weighed so heavily on both sides. He added:

> I don't know what the Poles in Poland think. We know very well what the Polish Government in London thinks. It is predominantly a group of aristocrats, looking to the Americans and the British to restore their position and landed properties and the feudalistic system of the period before and after the last war. They have a basic suspicion of the Soviets and don't like communism, which latter opinion I share with them. They think the only future of Poland lies in Great Britain and the United States fighting Russia to protect Poland. I don't see that we have any interest in getting back to that kind of thing.

In the months to come, the terrible complications of the Polish question were to receive a great deal of attention from Harriman. But the Ambassador's first priority in the weeks after Teheran was to persuade Stalin and Molotov that the time had come for a serious attempt at joint military planning. Stalin himself had promised Roosevelt at Teheran that he would take up such matters as the shuttle-bombing plan with Harriman soon after their return to Moscow. On January 9, however, Harriman reported back to Washington that for all the surface cordiality shown by Molotov and other high officials, he and General Deane were getting a "complete runaround." He was not inclined to attribute the lack of action to Soviet ill will but to "the bottlenecking of all decisions in the Kremlin and [the] fact that the spirit of Teheran has not percolated to lower echelons." If the stalling continued, he would insist upon taking up the matter with Stalin. "Unless we blast this open now," Harriman cabled to Washington, "and I believe it can be done by a firm but still friendly approach, a pattern will be set in our relations with the Soviets which will result in our getting a minimum of value out of the cooperation agreed to at Teheran, except on the highest strategic level, in the war and in fact in our postwar relationships as well."

General Deane was called over to the Soviet General Staff the following day and managed to settle a dozen minor matters. But the Russians told him they were not yet ready to take up the major military proposals which Roosevelt had put before Stalin at Teheran. Harriman found this discouraging. He cabled Washington: "We still have a fight ahead to get the cooperation to which we are entitled."

The hot-and-cold pattern showed itself in large matters and small. In late December, Brigadier General William J. Donovan, director of the Office of Strategic Services, visited Moscow. He had been authorized to establish an OSS mission in Moscow, if the Russians would agree, and to offer them in exchange an opportunity to set up a Soviet intelligence liaison mission in Washington. On Christmas Day, Harriman took Donovan to see Molotov, who made it plain that the Russians, impressed by Donovan's intelligence operations, were prepared for prompt, serious discussions, even though Stalin was out of the city.

In exactly two days Donovan (accompanied by Deane, with Bohlen as interpreter) found himself being escorted into a gloomy building few Muscovites entered voluntarily, the Commissariat of Internal Affairs, headquarters of the NKVD. Donovan had been invited in for a confidential talk with Lieutenant General P. N. Fitin, described as the chief of the External Intelligence Service, and Major General A. P. Ossipov, who was introduced as the head of the section that conducted subversive activities in enemy countries. Both officers—Fitin wearing an army uniform with blue piping to denote his special duties, and Ossipov, a civilian suit—received Donovan cordially. He outlined the structure and functions of the OSS. Then the Russians questioned him about the particular methods of spying, American style. They were interested in how the Americans introduced their agents into enemy territory, how these men were trained and what special equipment they carried. The shop talk among spymasters went briskly. Although the Russians volunteered no information about their own methods, Donovan succeeded in piquing their interest by describing some of the special equipment the OSS had developed, including suitcase radios and plastic explosives. He then repeated the offer he had made to Molotov: the OSS was prepared to exchange intelligence with its counterpart organization in Moscow if the Russians were agreeable. In that event, he suggested, he would designate an American liaison officer to serve as a member of General Deane's military mission in Moscow and would welcome the appointment of a Soviet officer to maintain liaison with the OSS in Washington.

General Fitin responded warmly, offering an example of the kind of situation in which liaison officers could be helpful. Suppose, he said, that Soviet agents were preparing to sabotage an important industrial installation or a railroad in Germany. It would then be most desirable to inform the American government in advance so that it could avoid unwitting interference with the Soviet plan.

There was one tense moment when Fitin asked Donovan whether his sole purpose in coming to Moscow was to offer cooperation or whether he had something else in mind. With icy indignation, Donovan replied that he had no other intentions.

Before the end of the meeting, an agreement had been worked out: Donovan would send back Colonel John H. F. Haskell, who had accompanied him to Moscow, and Fitin would assign Colonel A. G. Grauer to Washington. General Deane, who had been hoping for just such an opportunity, suggested that until the exchange of liaison officers was accomplished, a communications channel should be established between himself and Fitin or Ossipov so that important information could be passed along in both directions. He was delighted when Fitin gave him a telephone number he might call—a considerable breakthrough, as Deane saw it, in his long, frustrating battle with the Soviet bureaucracy, which still guarded telephone numbers as if they were military secrets. "It was my first telephone number in Russia," he later wrote, "and I felt that I had achieved a tremendous victory."[2]

The arrangements went forward swiftly after that first meeting at NKVD headquarters. Molotov assured Harriman on New Year's Eve that the exchange of intelligence officers would certainly be approved at the Soviet end because, he said, it was such a sensible move. Colonel Grauer and a staff of six assistants were all set to leave for Washington. His American counterpart, Colonel Haskell, had already drawn an organization chart for the staff of nineteen he would bring to Moscow. General Fitin even called on Donovan at the embassy, an unheard-of event.

His business accomplished, Donovan prepared to leave Moscow in triumph on board Harriman's converted B-24, known as *Becky*. The OSS chief was trying to get to the Mediterranean in a hurry and Harriman had offered the use of his four-engine plane, which could fly as far as Teheran nonstop. The two-engine Russian version of the DC-3 then in use often took two days or more in the winter, because the daylight hours were short and it had to land for refueling at Stalingrad, Astrakhan or Baku. To Donovan's consternation, the Russians would not let him take off, insisting that the plane was for the exclusive use of the Ambassador. Just to make sure that *Becky* did not get off the ground, the Russians refused to give the pilot any weather reports.

A test of wills followed. Donovan boasted to Harriman and Bohlen that as a former mayor of Rochester, New York, he knew better than any diplomat how to deal with recalcitrant Slavs. He would be firm, insist upon his rights as an Allied officer, and the Russians would necessarily give way. Harriman had his doubts but agreed to try the Donovan approach. Every morning for eleven days in succession, the Harrimans, Bohlen and General Deane would get up at six o'clock and drive Donovan out to the airport. Eleven mornings in a row they sat around until the Russians announced that they could not clear *Becky* for takeoff, ostensibly because the weather was unfavorable. Not until the twelfth morning was the impasse broken, after Harriman had made a personal appeal to Molotov. Donovan reached Teheran in six hours and fifty minutes; a Russian plane that left Moscow the same morning took three days. But the Soviets, arguing that no other ambassador kept a personal plane in Moscow, refused to allow *Becky* to return until an understanding as to her future use had been worked out. After the Donovan brouhaha, the plane remained in Cairo and was flown into the Soviet Union only when Harriman or General Deane had to leave the country or return from abroad.

Then, as if to add American insult to Russian injury, General Donovan's deal with the NKVD was abruptly nullified by the President himself. On March 15, to Harriman's astonishment, he received a message from Roosevelt: "Please inform the Marshal when you have an opportunity that for purely domestic political reasons which he will understand it is not appropriate—just now—to exchange these missions." Roosevelt had in mind his little talk with Stalin at Teheran about the constraints imposed by the approaching presidential election. Dismayed at what seemed to him the fumbling of an opportunity to break down Soviet resistance in other fields, Harriman appealed for reconsideration:

> We have penetrated here for the first time one intelligence branch of the Soviet Government and I am certain this will be the opening wedge to far greater intimacy in other branches, if pursued. I cannot express too strongly my conviction that our relations with the Soviet Government in other directions will be adversely affected if we close the door on this branch of the Soviet Government after they had shown cooperative spirit and good faith.
>
> In regard to shuttle bombing, we are making very satisfactory progress with the Soviet Air Staff . . . Since we are now asking that over 1,000 men be permitted to enter the Soviet Union in connection with our air operations, I do not know how I can explain satisfactorily to Molotov or Stalin why these few Soviet officials should not be allowed to enter the United States.

But the President barred any reconsideration. He was confident that Stalin would understand, Roosevelt replied on March 29, that the exchange of intelligence missions was being postponed only because the timing was wrong. Roosevelt had been persuaded that the overt presence in Washington of an NKVD mission, above all in a presidential election year, could prove a political embarrassment. Harriman and Deane were deeply disappointed. The exchange plan, after all, had been proposed by the Joint Chiefs of Staff in Washington, not by the Russians, and authorized by the President. They argued that the Russians doubtless had long since planted innumerable agents in their large purchasing mission, and there were hundreds of Soviet inspectors in defense plants all over the United States. What possible added harm could there be in a small liaison mission that would operate openly, trading official information with the OSS? "It seemed to me the height of stupidity," Harriman recalled, "since we were dealing with a small group of marked men who would have had to be particularly circumspect in their behavior. I later learned that J. Edgar Hoover and Admiral Leahy had been chiefly responsible for changing the President's mind."

Harriman had long since become accustomed to the minor pinpricks and unexplained postponements of life with Soviet officialdom. In January 1944, however, the Moscow press executed a 180-degree turn. Its treatment of the British and Americans, so mild and benevolent just a few weeks earlier, turned harsh. The most plausible explanation was that the NKVD or party zealots had warned Stalin against letting the post-Teheran euphoria go too far, lest some Russians relax their revolutionary vigilance against Western influence. The abrupt chill started with the publication in *Pravda* of a patently false dispatch from Cairo to the effect that "two leading British personalities," both unnamed, had been discussing a separate peace with Ribbentrop "in a coastal town of the Iberian Peninsula."

This unmistakable warning that the British were not people to be trusted by honest citizens of the Soviet Union was followed by an unprovoked and savage attack in *Pravda* on Wendell Willkie, who had visited the Soviet Union in 1942 as the personal representative of President Roosevelt. On October 5, 1942, *Life* magazine had published an account of Willkie's conversations with Stalin, in which he had raised some questions about the Russian attitude toward the Baltic States, Poland, Finland and the Balkans. Although Willkie's article had appeared fifteen months earlier, the *Pravda* writer, David Zaslavsky, dredged it up to make the point that the postwar development of Eastern Europe was going to be determined by the Soviet Union, without prompting or prodding from the West. "It is high time it was understood," he wrote, "that the question of the Baltic States is an internal Soviet matter which is none of Mr. Willkie's business . . . As for Poland and Finland, not to mention the Balkan countries, the Soviet Union will manage to thrash things out with them, without any assistance from Mr. Willkie."*

Two days after the so-called Cairo Rumor was printed, *Pravda* published a denial from the British Foreign Office. To the experienced reader-between-the-lines of the Soviet press, this meant a repudiation. But the attack on Willkie, plainly suggesting that the Russians were staking out a sphere of influence in Eastern Europe, seemed to fore-

---

* Willkie found the *Pravda* affair incomprehensible in view of his record as a supporter of aid to Russia. When Stalin heard of Willkie's reaction from Clark Kerr, he suggested sending a cable to this effect: "I like you but I don't want you to be President."

shadow serious disagreements within the alliance. Molotov had already dismissed, in a meeting with Harriman on January 18, Hull's offer of American good offices to help resolve the Russo-Polish dispute. The Kremlin also had published a statement stipulating that the eastern frontier of Poland must follow the Curzon Line while, at the same time, refusing to discuss this or any other matter with the Polish government in London. All these signs of trouble ahead were in Harriman's mind when, on January 20, he wrote to Churchill: "The Russian bear is demanding much and yet biting the hands that are feeding him." The Prime Minister, who had just returned to London from a period of convalescence in Marrakech after a bout with pneumonia, cabled back: "I agree with your political comment but he is biting others at the same time too."

The Russians, indeed, were biting the Germans ferociously. In January they finally broke the 900-day siege of Leningrad but only after a million men, women and children—one-third the city's population—had perished of starvation, disease and exposure. The successful Soviet offensive sent the Germans into full retreat along the Baltic front. In February and March, troops of the Second Ukrainian Front under Marshal Ivan S. Koniev encircled several German divisions in the Korsun salient on the Dnieper River and broke through into Rumania after forcing the Bug, the Dniester and the Prut rivers. All along the front the Germans were falling back to the borderlands, fighting stubbornly, counterattacking and then again retreating.

On January 30, with the shuttle-bombing plan still in limbo, Harriman asked to see Stalin. He was invited to the Kremlin on February 2, finding Stalin ready at last to listen and to act. The Ambassador presented his case: "Daylight bombing can penetrate more deeply into Germany if American bombers from the United Kingdom and Italy are permitted to land regularly in the Soviet Union." Harriman made the additional point that the loss of planes and crews could be greatly reduced if, after bombing targets deep inside Germany, the Americans did not have to fight their way back, often in a crippled condition, through swarms of German interceptors.

Stalin asked Harriman how many planes would be involved. One to three flights of 120 planes at a time, the Ambassador replied. Would the Russians have to supply fuel? No—fuel, bombs and spare parts would be supplied by the United States. What about ground crews? Would Americans or Russians be used to service the planes? Harriman replied that a number of Americans would have to be brought in, men who were specialists in servicing the B-17 and B-24 bombers. If the Russians could supply ground personnel to work under the supervision of American specialists, that would be an excellent arrangement.

To Harriman's great relief, Stalin at last approved the shuttle-bombing plan. "We favor it," he said, adding that the effect would be to make the Germans "feel the Allied blows more." To begin the operation, code-named Frantic, Stalin offered to provide airfields on Soviet territory for 150 to 200 heavy bombers. He also agreed that two American photoreconnaissance planes each day—one from Italy and the second from England—would be allowed to land on Soviet airfields. The pilots would photograph German targets as they flew in and out, Harriman explained, and they would gladly give special attention to any areas of particular interest to the Red Army.

Stalin's grasp of detail once again amazed Harriman. He put questions about the octane rating of the fuel needed for the American bombers, about air-to-ground communications and the language barriers to be overcome if American pilots and Russian air controllers were to work together. When it came to choosing airfields for the photoreconnaissance planes, Stalin suggested one near Veliki Luki and another at Kotli, west of Leningrad.

Once Stalin had approved the plan, the Russians made a prodigious effort. Suddenly General Deane was getting all the official cooperation he needed. In the space of four months, three airfields were completed in the Ukraine; their runways, hangars and service facilities made ready to accommodate the American bombers, and all the manpower needed for Frantic, both Russian and American, in place. At one stroke, which only Stalin could deliver, everything that needed doing was done.

Harriman found Stalin as yet unwilling to make commitments regarding air bases in the Maritime Provinces for the final air offensive against Japan. Stalin said he was still fearful of provoking a Japanese attack before his forces in the Far East were re-equipped and reinforced. He talked of transferring four infantry corps of twenty to twenty-two divisions to the Far East, but that could not be done, he said, until German resistance in the west had begun to falter. "As soon as these forces are transferred," Stalin said to Harriman, "the Soviet Government will cease to fear Japanese provocation and may even provoke the Japanese itself. It is too weak to do so now, however, as such action might result in the loss of the coastal positions. Consequently there is no immediate possibility of cooperation in that theater; it can only materialize later." Harriman reported to Roosevelt:

> He told me categorically (after I had explained in detail the importance of our knowing at the earliest moment what facilities could be made available) that facilities would be provided to base 300 U.S. heavy bombers in addition to Russian bombers, and agreed to have the Chief of their Far Eastern Air Forces come to Moscow shortly to discuss the location of

suitable bases with Deane. I explained that General Arnold had contemplated the basing of as many as 1,000 bombers in this area. Stalin replied: "Then we must build new bases. We will see what is possible."

Stalin also agreed to exchange intelligence regarding Japan with the United States, although the information available in Moscow was, he said, "not rich." By way of inaugurating this exchange, he passed along three interesting bits of information, adding up to the conclusion that the Japanese leaders were getting "very scared." According to Harriman's report of the conversation, Stalin told him: "At a recent official Japanese function in Tokyo (where the Soviets do not have a military attaché), a Russian lieutenant colonel (one of the Soviet agents) was approached by the Chief of the Japanese General Staff, Sugiyama, who expressed a desire to meet Marshal Stalin. Sugiyama said the Germans meant nothing to the Japanese and that their treaty with Germany was only a scrap of paper. Stalin said of course he would not see the man and that no answer had been given, adding, 'Let them go to the devil.' He considered it significant, as a further indication of their fear, that such a high-ranking officer would approach a junior officer on such a subject."

Another straw in the wind, Stalin said, was the sudden willingness of the Japanese to sell the Russians their oil and coal concessions in the northern part of Sakhalin Island. The sale had been provided for in a secret exchange of letters at the time when the Russians and the Japanese signed their nonaggression treaty in April 1941. It was to have been completed by October of that year but the Japanese had stalled for more than two years. Now they were eager to conclude the bargain, Stalin said, and he read this as another sign of nervousness in Tokyo. (Vishinsky later told Harriman that the Russians had concluded the deal, paying "a small sum for a large property.")

Stalin also volunteered the information that according to Soviet intelligence reports, "the Japanese may be preparing to withdraw from their outer line of defense running through Indonesia. He said that they are now reported to be building a new inner defense line and to be evacuating plants and machinery to Japan and Manchuria. They may suddenly begin to retreat." Harriman asked Stalin where the new defense line would run. He was not sure of the details, Stalin replied, but he believed it would run "through Shanghai, the Shantung Peninsula, Manchuria and around the Japanese Islands." The Japanese, he added, would not engage their main forces to defend their outer perimeter but would withdraw to the inner line "which was more convenient and easier to defend."

Harriman left the Kremlin feeling that, all things considered,

Stalin "could not have been more friendly" or cooperative, as he reported to Roosevelt the same evening. The new cordiality showed itself in many ways. The Soviets decided, for example, to present the Order of Suvorov, their highest military decoration, to Generals Marshall and Eisenhower.

In a conversation with Harriman on February 10, Anastas Mikoyan made a point of praising American accomplishments in developing the Persian Gulf supply route. Admitting that their performance had overcome his own skepticism and surpassed all expectations, he spoke of decorations for General Connolly and for certain civilians who had made substantial contributions, including Hopkins, Harriman himself, and William L. Batt, vice chairman of the War Production Board. Harriman explained that there were policies and regulations against accepting such awards from a foreign government. But he recommended to Hull that Connolly and certain of the men under his command be authorized to accept the honors. Accordingly, on April 15 Moscow announced that the Order of Suvorov, Second Class, had been awarded to General Connolly, and lesser Soviet orders to thirty-three men of his Persian Gulf Command, for "transporting munitions supplies and foodstuffs to the Soviet Union, which have provided great assistance to the Red Army in the struggle with the German Fascist invaders."

Even the ice-locked social front thawed somewhat in the new climate of Allied cordiality. The Harrimans found that a limited circle of Soviet celebrities—film directors and musicians, ballet stars and actors, a painter or two and the historical novelist–playwright Alexei Tolstoy—had now been authorized to accept invitations to the American embassy. Tolstoy came frequently to showings of American films arranged by the Harrimans. He would stay till well past midnight, drinking rather freely as he savored the new sociability with characteristic gusto.

"I remember Tolstoy telling me," Harriman recalled, "that he had fled to Paris in the early Revolutionary days, but then his longing for Russia got the better of him and he returned. He said that he got along with the authorities because he wrote within the prescribed limits. In the historical field he found enough leeway to write without offending party sensibilities. He told me that during the war the rules had changed. Up to the war, he said, Soviet history had started with the Revolution. Now, in order to stimulate patriotism, the Revolution had become part of the sweep of Russian history. All this was an expression of Stalin's concern for morale. The people were taught that they were fighting for the motherland, not the party. Tolstoy was a Russian patriot above all, a distant cousin of Count Leo Tolstoy, and his anti-German fervor became a powerful asset to the regime. My discussions with him gave me some insight into Stalin's character and the Soviet system. He once told me, 'To understand the Kremlin today you must understand the Kremlin of Ivan the Terrible and Peter the Great.' Terror in the Kremlin did not begin with Stalin, nor was it the Communist party that initiated the suspicion of foreigners and foreign ideas. (Years later Khrushchev said to me, 'Like Peter the Great, Stalin fought barbarism with barbarism'—and then added, 'He was a great man.') All things considered, Tolstoy was one of the most interesting and genial of our new intellectual friends."

It was Tolstoy who invited the Harrimans to their only non-official Russian dinner party at his dacha about a half-hour's drive from Moscow. It was "quite an event," Kathleen Harriman wrote home:

> Shostakovich and his wife were there, a very nice theater director, an architect and another couple.
>
> We were invited at five o'clock and, after cocktails, sat down to a two-hour dinner. The hors d'oeuvres alone, in quantity, were equal to a big meal by our standards. And after them came a special meat-and-cabbage pastry, soup, fish, and finally a huge roast pork with vegetables and, finally, ice cream. There was an abundance of wines and toasts throughout the meal and afterwards we adjourned upstairs for a slight breather with coffee and brandy. The breather over, we returned downstairs for tea, fruit, and candy . . . quite some hospitality.
>
> Shostakovich turned out to look about 21 years old (he's over 30), with very heavy glasses and more concentrated nervousness than I've ever seen in any man. He continually wiped his face, rattled his fingers or squinted his eyes.
>
> Shostakovich drank considerably during dinner and then decided he didn't feel like playing for us after dinner (something I don't blame him for in the least) but finally he did— part of a concerto and [a setting of] a children's poem. He seemed a nice guy but very definitely the introverted-genius type . . . a couple of times he suddenly got up and went and sat alone on the stairs, for no particular reason that I could see. Quite the opposite, Tolstoy revels in exhibitionism. In his own house, he's at his best, being able to talk as much and as long as he wants . . . After dinner, Tolstoy spent his time sitting or lying on his stomach, expounding on any subject that happened into his mind. He's really a very loveable sort. He prides himself [on] being "the most glorious drunk" in Russia and he certainly is a very pleasant one.

As the Harrimans settled into the Moscow scene, Kathleen discovered a snowy slope in the Lenin Hills, close to the city, where she could ski during the lunch hour once or twice a week. Her father would join her on occasional Sundays. These outings created problems for the NKVD detail assigned to the Ambassador, which was supposed to keep him in sight at all times. "When I ski myself," the Ambassador wrote to his wife Marie in New York, "I am attended by one of my NKVD guards on skis. Unfortunately for him, he is not too skillful and he has considerable difficulty keeping me in sight. I am getting quite fond of my 'boys,' twelve of them in three shifts of four at a time."

Harriman's pleasure in physical activity was a source of unending amazement to ordinary Russians. When he started to shovel snow one Sunday at the embassy dacha, the horrified caretaker said he could not understand how anyone, much less an ambassador, would shovel snow just for the exercise. As for Kathleen, her skiing soon caught the attention of Moscow. Invited to race in the women's slalom championship of the Russian Republic, she finished third behind two Red Army instructors. *Vechernaya Moskva,* the evening paper, reported on February 21: "The daughter of the American Ambassador in the Soviet Union, Mr. Harriman, participated in the competition *hors de concours.* In the results she was only behind two participants in the championship, Rodionova and Speronskaya."

Kathleen, who had been a correspondent for International News Service and then for *Newsweek* in London, worked in Moscow with the playwright Samuel Spewack, for about three months the Office of War Information chief in the Soviet Union. After Spewack's departure, Kathleen handled OWI affairs herself. On January 15, at the Ambassador's request, she was included in a large group of Western correspondents going by train to Smolensk for a grisly guided tour of the mass graves in the Katyn Forest nearby. The point of the exercise was to persuade the foreign press that the Polish corpses unearthed there had been shot and buried by the Germans in the late summer or autumn of 1941 and not, as the Germans had charged, in the spring of 1940 by the Russians. The correspondents were shown seven mass graves and then watched a number of autopsies being conducted by Russian doctors. In spite of the cold, the stench was overpowering. In the autopsy tent, Russian doctors in white aprons and rubber gloves exhibited slices of brain or liver on dinner plates, exclaiming over the "freshness" of the tissues—as if to clinch the argument that the Poles had been killed in 1941 by the Germans, not in 1940. Fortunately, Kathleen had a cold that day, so she was less bothered than others by the stench.

Many of the correspondents were impressed by the fact that in all but a few cases, the exhumed bodies showed a single bullet hole at the base of the skull, a typically German technique, the Russians said.

Moreover, most of the corpses appeared to be of enlisted men, not officers, as the Germans had claimed in announcing their discovery of the graves the year before. They wore no badges of rank on their uniforms.

Kathleen Harriman, in a letter to Pamela Churchill several days after the visit to Katyn, described how the Russians pulled seemingly incriminating documents from the pockets of the dead Poles. "While I was watching," she wrote, "they found a letter dated the summer of 1941, which is damned good evidence." But there were discrepancies enough to raise troubling questions. Some of the dead, for example, had newspapers and letters in their pockets dated March and April 1940, including an April 11 copy of *Izvestia*. These bits of evidence squarely conflicted with the Soviet contention that the Poles had not been murdered until after the German invasion of June 1941.

The Russians had appointed a "Special Commission to Establish and Investigate the Circumstances of the Shooting by the German Fascist Invaders of Captive Polish Officers in the Katyn Woods." The evidence it heard that day impressed Miss Harriman as "minute in detail and, by American standards, petty," but the Western newsmen were not permitted to question directly any of the five witnesses. Much of that testimony sounded glib, as if carefully rehearsed; when questioned, several of the witnesses hesitated or stumbled. The correspondents recognized that they had no choice but to report what the Russians had shown them, without attempting to pass judgment. They were hardly qualified to decide, after looking at a slice of tissue, whether it had come from a body two-and-a-half or three-and-a-half years dead. But the methodical horror of the deed seemed to stamp it as more German than Russian, even if the evidence of the time was still confused and contradictory.

Upon her return to Moscow, Miss Harriman reported: "We were expected to accept the statements of the high-ranking Soviet officials as true, because they said it was true. Despite this it is my opinion that the Poles were murdered by the Germans." John Melby of the embassy staff, who accompanied Miss Harriman, also was troubled by the nature of the evidence. He reported: "It is apparent that the evidence in the Russian case is incomplete in several respects, that it is badly put together and that the show was put on for the benefit of the correspondents without opportunity for independent investigation or verification. On balance, however, and despite the loopholes, the Russian case in convincing."

CERTAINTIES CAME HARD in Moscow, then and later. The inner workings—and true motives—of the regime were always screened from

public view. The most brilliant of embassy analysts found themselves
hard pressed for a plausible explanation when Molotov, in a speech on
February 1 before the Supreme Soviet, announced a government plan
to reorganize the Commissariats of Foreign Affairs and Defense. The
Union of Soviet Socialist Republics had decided that its constituent
republics now were free to "enter into direct relations with foreign
states" and create separate military formations within the all-Union
Army.

The first impulse of some diplomats and journalists in Moscow was
to read the constitutional changes as evidence of a cunning design to
push out the frontiers of the Soviet Union by turning Poland, for
example, into an autonomous Republic of the Soviet Union, with its
own Ministry of Foreign Affairs and of Defense by way of sugar-
coating the bitter pill. Harriman's reaction was both more cautious and
more accurate. In one of his regular sessions with the American press
corps on February 4, he speculated that among other things the Russians probably wanted more than one vote in the United Nations. He
said of the changes:

> I am not sure that they fully understand how they will
> use it. It is not unusual for the Soviets to have two weapons to
> shoot one bird when it is convenient to do so, and particularly
> when it is inconvenient for the bird. The idea, undoubtedly,
> is to strengthen, not weaken, Russia as a world power. They
> will want more votes in international conferences. I think they
> believe we dominate the Latin-American countries. Control
> of important issues will be from Moscow.

To a question from Richard E. Lauterbach of *Life* ("Does this make
it easier for other countries to join the Soviet Union?") Harriman
replied:

> I have never found any indication of a Soviet interest in
> annexing Finland or Poland. They have a problem of assimila-
> tion already . . .
> If it had not been for the Teheran Conference, and the
> statements made then, this move might have caused consider-
> ably more concern. They won't go back on the Teheran deci-
> sions. They have given advance notice of the territory they
> want—Bessarabia, the Baltic states, part of Poland. They guar-
> anteed the territorial integrity of Iran.

The answers were characteristic of Harriman's way with the press.
He betrayed no secrets. But he was prepared to speculate, when hard
facts were not available, and to steer the correspondents away from
rash conclusions of their own.

In a telegram to the Secretary of State, dated February 6, Harriman developed his analysis in greater detail, making the point, with past experience as guide, that even if certain of the Republics were encouraged to set up their own Commissariat of Defense and of Foreign Affairs, these would certainly be directed and dominated from Moscow. The real instruments of power, he pointed out, would remain the Communist party and the NKVD. But Republican Commissariats might be useful to Moscow in working out certain border disputes with neighboring countries. The Ukrainian Republic, for example, which might be assigned nominal responsibility for the new border arrangements with Poland and Czechoslovakia, could be expected to put forward more ambitious national claims than the USSR itself and thus increase Moscow's leverage in the bargaining.

Some semblance of autonomy might have its value also in the case of the Baltic States, Harriman reasoned, by making their incorporation into the Soviet Union seem less unpalatable to world opinion, and to the local populations. There was, finally, the matter of claiming more votes in world organizations. The argument for Great Power parity had already been made in the periodical *War and the Working Class*. This was based on the argument that Britain enjoyed more than one vote thanks to such Commonwealth countries as Canada and Australia, while the United States could count on the support of Latin America. Harriman's analysis concluded:

> We have no indication, at least for the immediate future, that the constitutional changes have an imperialistic motivation by making it more attractive for new states to join the Union, except in the case of the Baltic States and possibly Outer Mongolia. It is to be doubted whether the Soviet Union at present desires to increase its racial indigestion by adding to its own problems the difficulties of absorbing the Poles and the Finns . . .

> In spite of our difficulties over Poland and some other matters, I have found in my talk with Stalin and many conversations with Molotov since Teheran no diminution in the desire of the Soviet Government for development of the closest relationship with the British and with us and in international cooperation. My impressions are given encouraging support by Benes' reports.

The defense reorganization was more easily explained. Harriman pointed out that the Russians had never wholly solved the problem of drafting certain national or racial groups into the army. Differences of language and custom could be more easily accommodated in special units based on the specific Republic rather than on the Soviet Union as a whole. "The growing political strength of the Red Army may also be of concern," Harriman added, having in mind the rising prestige and popularity of such Red Army commanders as Marshal Zhukov. "The Army's influence after the war would tend to be minimized by the partial decentralization of the army and thereby the injection of [its] political influence at a lower level."

As the weeks passed, however, without clarification of the Soviet government's intent, Harriman admitted in a message to Washington that the motivation behind these changes was still "puzzling." One thing was absolutely clear: the westward advance of the Red Army into Rumania and Czechoslovakia in the spring of 1944 meant that the Soviet Union would be dealing from strength vis-à-vis its neighbors and its allies. In the same telegram, dated February 20, he pressed the State Department to define its attitude toward the countries of Eastern Europe:

> Have there been developed any ideas as to what will follow upon the completion of the work of UNRRA and what helping hand are we prepared to give in the later reconstruction period to those countries?
>
> Is the development of sound economic conditions under a democratic form of government within those countries of sufficient interest to the United States to justify a program being developed now, through which it might be hoped that there might result politically stable conditions? Information regarding any of the Department's preliminary thinking on these questions would be helpful.

There is no record of a response to Harriman's suggestion that postwar planning ought to be accelerated. General Ismay wrote to Harriman on March 17 that in London also the problems of the beckoning peace were not getting the attention they deserved:

> Superimposed on all the worries about how to win the war in the shortest possible time are the worries about how to win the peace, and thereafter how to organize the British Commonwealth, Europe and the world. Committees considering these various aspects have sprung up like mushrooms, but the problems are so nebulous and complicated as to be almost insoluble. Moreover, so far as the fighting services are concerned, all the better brains are required to deal with our immediate affairs, and the postwar problems have perforce to be left to the lesser lights, who are long past their best.

Ismay also mentioned his disappointment over General Mark Clark's slowness to exploit the Anzio landing.

It looked from this end, once the initial landing had been completely successful, that Rome and a few thousand German prisoners would be ours in a very short time. But, as the Prime Minister put it in his usual graphic language—"The wildcat which we had intended to throw ashore became a stranded whale"; indeed it was touch and go whether the whale would not be pushed back into its natural element . . . It is always very easy to ride a race from the grandstand, but it certainly looked to us, sitting in comfortable armchairs, that our initial success was not exploited at the speed and with the fury that the situation demanded.

The Red Army, meanwhile, was pressing its advance westward. On April 2 Moscow announced the crossing of the Prut River, adding that the river line "represents the state border between the USSR and Rumania." The significance of this announcement was plain: all of Bessarabia and the former Austrian province of Bukovina, seized by the Red Army in June 1940, were already being treated as Soviet territory. Stalin had made no secret of his intention to restore the western boundaries of the Soviet Union as they had existed—for exactly one year—before the German invasion of June 22, 1941. Although the Western Allies had refused to endorse his claim during the Anglo-Soviet treaty negotiations in the winter of 1941–42, and the Rumanians had never been consulted, he was now enforcing his will. Bessarabia, part of the Russian Empire from 1812 until the end of World War I, had been awarded to Rumania by the Treaty of Versailles. Bukovina had never belonged to Russia until annexed by Stalin in 1940. Harriman noted the new assertiveness in a report to the State Department, dated April 20:

Soviet diplomacy is becoming increasingly active and positive. The pattern of these developments is consistent with the basic policies previously outlined by Soviet officials but in some cases is startling in its aggressiveness, determination and readiness to take independent action. That the Soviet Union intends to play an important part in world affairs, commensurate with its power and with the sacrifices it has made toward winning the war, is increasingly clear . . . Nothing indicates that the Soviet Union does not value the relations [it has] attained with the British and with us. On the other hand, it is obvious that they are unwilling to compromise certain basic principles which, they believe, are essential to Soviet interests and security.

The Western boundaries established in 1940, with the exception of the compromise Curzon Line for the boundary with Poland, are considered fixed and irrevocable from Finland to the Black Sea.

As far as European countries beyond the Red Army's reach were concerned, the clearest clue to Stalin's intentions had been the dissolution of the Communist International in May 1943, an event widely and eagerly misinterpreted in the West.* The announcement—signed by Klement Gottwald of Czechoslovakia, Georgi Dimitrov of Bulgaria, Wilhelm Pieck of Germany, Maurice Thorez of France, Palmiro Togliatti of Italy, Ana Pauker of Rumania and Matyas Rakosi of Hungary, among others—proclaimed a new line: "Whereas in the Axis countries it is important for the working class to strive to overthrow the government, in the United Nations countries it is, on the contrary, the duty of the working class to support the governments' war effort." The end of the Comintern at once gave rise to great expectations in the West. Joseph E. Davies, always the wishful thinker, was among the first to read it as a sign that the Russians now intended "to cooperate with, and not to stir up trouble for, their neighbors, with whom they are pledged to cooperate to win the war and the peace." Representative Martin E. Dies of Texas regretted that with the Comintern laid to rest, his House Committee on Un-American Activities might have nothing more to investigate.

For Harriman, the plain fact was that the Comintern had become an embarrassment to Stalin in his wartime alliance with the two predominant capitalist powers, and new methods were in order. "I thought at the time that it was an important action," Harriman recalled. "Stalin was giving the Communist parties around the world a freer hand to participate in the political life of their own countries, to form popular fronts and to build up their influence through constitutional rather than revolutionary means. The Communist parties in both Italy and France were very strong, and my own guess is that, but for the Marshall Plan, they would have succeeded in taking power after the war."

In many European countries the old order had been largely discredited in defeat. This popular feeling, sharpened by the brutalities of Nazi occupation, had given rise to new national resistance movements embracing a broad spectrum of political groups from far right to far left. Communist parties in France, Italy, Yugoslavia, Greece and other countries were already taking a leading role in this underground struggle against the Germans, building popular support in the process. Their opportunities to work in coalition with other anti-Fascist groups

* The Comintern (Third International) had been established by Lenin in 1919 as the vehicle for spreading revolutionary propaganda and to unite Communist groups of various countries.

were bound to be enhanced by the dissolution of the Comintern. Less and less would they hear the taunt that all Communists marched to Moscow's beat.

Far from weakening the Communist movement in Western Europe, the end of the Comintern had the effect of strengthening the national parties. Josip Broz Tito, once a Comintern official known at the Lux Hotel in Moscow as Comrade Walter, had shown the way in Yugoslavia. Creating a Partisan army, based on the remnants of the small Yugoslav Communist party, he had raised the flag of national resistance to the German occupation, undercutting the Serbian royalist forces of General Mihailovic. By the end of 1943, Tito had won the admiring support of the Western Allies and completed the groundwork for his postwar regime by establishing a provisional government behind German lines.

Palmiro Togliatti, a far more important Comintern figure than Tito, who had lived in Moscow under the name of Mario Ercoli, returned to Italy in March 1944, after eighteen years in exile. He at once took command of the Italian party, pressing for the abdication of Victor Emmanuel and the formation of a new all-party government.

With Communist parties now operating openly, the Soviet government developed a sudden concern for political and civil liberties in newly liberated countries far from its own borders. It would insist that Italian Communists, for example, enjoy "full opportunity for political expression," as Harriman emphasized in his April 20 report, while denying this right for any but authorized Communist views in the Soviet Union.

HARRIMAN'S MODERATELY HOPEFUL ATTITUDE endured a number of setbacks during the spring of 1944. His pressures for a more effective exchange of weather information, and for improved air transportation, yielded no response. The Russians, obedient to their inbred suspicion of foreigners, were still showing enormous reluctance to let American pilots fly over Soviet territory. In addition, Harriman and General Deane were becoming progressively more exasperated by the consistent refusal of Soviet officials to justify their requests for more Lend-Lease assistance in terms of need. From the beginning of the program in 1941, President Roosevelt had directed that Soviet aid requests be processed without insisting that the Russians explain how they proposed to use the equipment and materials they were receiving. Harriman and Deane found that much of the industrial equipment was being misused (a complete tire factory, for example, shipped from Detroit in 1943, was not yet in production when the war ended). When they learned that the Russians had requested 100 fighter planes a month beyond the number already agreed to, Harriman cabled Hopkins:

> In view of our estimates of the reduced German air strength on the Russian front, the fact that the Soviets are at present nowhere subjected to strategic bombing by the Germans, and the fact that the Soviets do not engage in strategic bombing requiring fighter support, there is in this case an element of doubt as to the Soviet need for additional fighters. In consideration of this, it may be that their present production plus our shipments already agreed to will suffice. However, if they furnish even a general analysis of their situation it might well show that there is justification for the request . . .
>
> Molotov immediately uses the word "reciprocity" whenever I talk to him on any of our requests. The Soviets evidently consider the Lend-Lease allocations made in Washington to be contributions to the Red Army in recognition of their offensive and apparently they do not consider themselves called upon to do anything that would be helpful to our forces in return. To get a trading atmosphere into our negotiations over mutual assistance in the war is, as you know, most distasteful to me; but trading seems to be the language the Soviets understand, and once commitments have been made in Washington we don't find them at all impressed by any obligation on their part to reciprocate.
>
> It is quite clear that we will not get from the Soviets the kind of assistance which, as Allies, they can and should give to our forces, unless you support the Military Mission at this stage.

But Harriman's effort to persuade Hopkins and Roosevelt that the time had come to evaluate the Soviet requests more carefully made no immediate impression, not even after General Marshall had endorsed the idea. Harriman and Deane kept insisting on more information at their end, and their efforts were undercut in many cases by the President's Protocol Committee in Washington. The Russians consequently did not hesitate to ask for industrial equipment on a rising scale in 1944 and 1945, even though much of it would take two years or more to produce and could hardly be expected to play any part in the winning of the war.

The matter had yet to be resolved when Harriman left Moscow toward the end of April for consultations in Washington and London. Meeting with his former staff in London on May 4, the Ambassador made known his disenchantment with the Hopkins policy:

The Protocol Committee had resisted our intention to ask
the Soviets to allow us to analyze the use they make of our
supplies. We thought we could break it down (i.e. the Soviet
resistance to giving us any information); but the Protocol
Committee has the idea that the way to get along with the
Russians is to do everything they ask. This is not the way to
get along. They are tough and [they] expect us to be tough.

Harriman gave the Russians high marks, however, for their efficiency in unloading 12,000 tons of Lend-Lease cargo a day during a
four-day visit he had just paid to Murmansk. Although he found the
Arctic port half destroyed, he was impressed by the "great job" the
Russian dock workers were doing. Pointing out that the people of
Murmansk received extra rations, he remarked: "Russia is the land
of privilege for those who are considered to have done most for the
war effort." The Ambassador had gone to Murmansk to take part in
the ceremonial transfer of the cruiser U.S.S. *Milwaukee* to the Soviet
navy. He was received with great cordiality and was pleased to see
American seamen getting along well with their Soviet counterparts.
For several days Americans stood the port watch on board the *Milwaukee* while Russians took over the starboard watch in a symbolic
expression of Allied comradeship. Harriman was pleased to note that
not a single Russian had mentioned the Second Front to him. When he
visited the Soviet naval base at Polyarnoe, the admiral of the Northern
Fleet invited him into the war room, much as a British admiral might
have done, to point out the disposition of his ships.

When Harriman passed through London on his way to Washington, preparations for the cross-Channel invasion were all but complete.
He saw General Eisenhower twice, on May 2 and May 4. "I found
him grown in stature since my last talks, confident and determined,
but realizing fully the difficulties of his task," Harriman recorded in
a memorandum of his London conversations. "He explained the beach
obstacles that had been erected by Rommel and the difficulties of over-
coming them." Considerations of moon and tide might dictate a slight
delay in the schedule for D-Day, Eisenhower said. Harriman assured
him that if the matter was fully explained to the Russians, they would
understand and accept the change of schedule. When Harriman mentioned Stalin's promise at Teheran to launch a great new offensive on
the eastern front in conjunction with Operation Overlord and stressed
the need for coordination, Eisenhower showed no sign of concern.
"He did not think it important to attempt to get from the Red Army
staff their plans for an offensive paralleling Overlord," according to
Harriman's notes. "But after our troops were established on the Conti-

nent there would be need for intimate liaison." Harriman suggested that General Deane and his British counterpart, General Montagu B. Burrows, be allowed to handle the arrangements in Moscow, and Eisenhower readily agreed.

Before flying on to Washington, Harriman also talked at length with Churchill. He found the Prime Minister still oppressed by "the dangers and disasters that could flow from Operation Overlord if the landings should fail." Even at this late date, the first week of May 1944, Churchill was torn by doubt. "He told me," Harriman recalled, "that if Overlord failed, the United States would have lost a battle, but for the British it would mean the end of their military capability."

In Washington, Harriman found the President looking ahead to the November election. "When I saw Roosevelt on May 17," Harriman recalled, "he gave me a number of messages for Stalin. I was to explain to him that the President could not take an active interest in the Polish question until after the election. The Curzon Line with modifications seemed to him reasonable as a basis for settlement, although he was still puzzled about Lwow. Mikolajczyk was coming to the United States in June on condition that he make no public speeches while in the country. The President would urge Mikolajczyk to drop General Sosnkowski from his Cabinet, with one or two others who were resisting a settlement with the Russians. He was still hopeful of finding a satisfactory solution to the Polish problem; Stalin could help by giving the Poles a break and carefully avoiding any step that would embroil the issue in the heat of the presidential campaign.

"The President also wanted to be helpful in getting Finland out of the war. He would welcome any suggestions from Stalin or Molotov but had no particular ideas of his own.

"I was to tell Stalin that Chiang Kai-shek was the only man who could hold China together and for that reason his government should not be undermined. If China broke apart and civil war flared up, effective resistance to the Japanese invaders would end. The President hoped that Stalin would be patient in working out a solution between Chiang and the Chinese Communists.

"The next meeting of the Big Three might have to be called on short notice as the Allied forces converged on Germany from east and west. The President thought Alaska would be a feasible meeting place, up to the middle of September."

Stopping in London again on the return flight, Harriman found Churchill "much better in spirit and physically than he was when I saw him several weeks ago . . . Although conscious of the risks, he is confident and determined and is throwing the full strength of his energies back of them. He speaks with respect and enthusiasm of Eisenhower and the other United States officers on the team. Due largely to Stalin's recent civil messages, the sun is shining again on the Soviet horizon."

On the Polish horizon, however, dark clouds were gathering. During a two-hour luncheon conversation with Harriman on May 29, Beneš reported that although Mikolajczyk had been persuaded to seek an early settlement with the Russians, he had failed to carry the Polish Cabinet with him. "Mikolajczyk and those who conform to his views feel that the London Government will lose all standing with the Polish people unless a settlement is effected promptly," Harriman noted. "The opposition, however, has become more firm in [rejecting] the proposed settlement of the boundary question. It is Benes' belief that at some stage a definite break between the two groups will take place."

In the first days of June, however, much of the Allied bickering and frustration was briefly forgotten in the rush of great events. Harriman and Kathleen flew back to Moscow by way of the Mediterranean and Teheran. They arrived on June 1 to find General Deane waiting at the airport. He was off for the Ukraine the same day, to welcome the first shuttle-bombing flight from Italy. Harriman decided to go along, and Kathleen, after some cajoling, persuaded her father that she should go too. The Russians had outdone themselves in getting the bases ready. When the Harrimans and Deane arrived at Poltava the same evening to a round of cheers from the American ground staff and assembled correspondents, they found a hospital ready to treat the injured, wreckage disposal trucks lined up to move any damaged aircraft off the runway, the Soviet anti-aircraft system already alerted to the route the American bombers would follow from their target—Debrecen in Hungary—into their new Russian bases at Poltava, Mirgorod and Piryatin.

Operation Frantic, belying its code name, was ticking like a fine Swiss watch. The Russians—for all their initial obfuscation—had thought of everything to make the inaugural flight a resounding success: a USO-type concert for the servicemen, both Russian and American; champagne flowing freely; a suite for the Harrimans, with curtains on the windows and huge jars of dahlias and irises on the tables; and a late supper at which the bottoms-up rule was mercifully waived. Kathleen and her father were particularly grateful for the last favor, having been up since four-thirty in the morning and having flown all day—from Teheran to Moscow and on to Poltava with only a brief pause on the ground.

The morning of June 2 was a time for last-minute fretting over small details. GI mechanics explained to their Soviet counterparts in pidgin Russian, using as many hand signals as words, how Flying Fortresses were serviced. Kathleen toured the hospital tents, finding them "complete and trim as a doll's house." General Deane waited for a radio message that the flight, headed personally by General Eaker, had left Italy. When it came at twelve-thirty, the vigil started, all eyes straining to the west. Kathleen relived the tension in a letter to her sister:

> We were driving out to the field when the first bombers appeared as specks off the horizon. It looked like thousands. Then the first squadron was overhead with its welcome roar. Jesus, but it was exciting—more so than anything I ever saw in England. Ave said he'd never before been so thrilled by anything, and I'm damn sure I haven't. Ave was in the back seat with General Perminov [Major General A. R. Perminov commanded the Russian base] and I was in front, driving a low-slung Buick cross country after a jeep. The General was every bit as excited as we, only being Russian he showed it. He bubbled over with joy and apparently threw his arms around Ave to kiss him when he restrained [himself] and instead let out a few Russian equivalents of the cowboy hoot.
>
> The first Fort landed and taxied over to us and out stepped our ex-host from Naples [General Eaker]; and there, standing informally in the rain, while bombers continued to circle and circle and land, one after the other, we had a very impressive spontaneous ceremony. [Eaker] presented Perminov with the Legion of Merit and read the citation. In return, he and I were given huge bouquets of flowers (the Russian custom when a general enters a town victorious). Russ [Deane] made a short radio speech, Ave having refused on the ground that this was a military show, hence Russ's ...
>
> Most of all the Russians were impressed by our bombers being in formation after a long bombing mission. Apparently theirs never are, and they appreciated the skill of our pilots— the skill of our bombardiers, too, after they saw the photos of the damage done to the targets. So, all in all, the shuttle bombing has made a great impression on them and it's certainly a big step forward, proving that Goddamit we all can do a job of work together.

Kathleen's youthful enthusiasm was fully shared by her elders. As the silvery planes dropped from the dark sky, landing one a minute until all seventy-three were down, Americans and Russians shared the feeling that here at last was true Allied cooperation. The first mission had been highly successful, the German airfield at Debrecen completely destroyed with all its planes, hangars and shops.

On June 4, Rome fell to the Allies and Stalin hailed this "grand victory" in a message to Churchill the following day. When the Allied

Expeditionary Force of American, British and Canadian divisions made good its landing in France on the morning of June 6, Moscow was awash in boozy good feeling. Edward Page, second secretary of the American embassy, who was dining out that evening in a newly opened restaurant, found himself being toasted and embraced all night long by Russians he had never met. Kathleen had some OWI business the same afternoon with the Soviet cultural relations office concerning an exhibit of American photographs. The only business done was to kill two bottles of cherry brandy in midafternoon on the great occasion of the Second Front.

When Harriman called on Stalin to deliver the President's several messages on June 10, he took along a map showing exactly where the Allied troops had landed in Normandy and the depth of their bridgeheads. This was a different Stalin, unstinting in his praise for the achievements of the Allied armies in France as Harriman described the landings. The Ambassador pointed out that they had been "less difficult than originally feared." The Allied troops had succeeded in destroying Rommel's underwater obstacles by going ashore at low tide. Although bad weather had slowed the second phase of the operation, more troops and supplies were being landed every day. "Taking the good news with the bad," Harriman said, "events were moving satisfactorily."

Stalin was filled with admiration. "We are going along a good road," he said. He spoke of "the vast scale of the operations with entire armies being landed" in France, adding that "he believed it was sufficient to seize eight kilometers in depth and then build up."

It was Stalin's turn this time to explain that the Soviet summer offensive had been delayed, in spite of his assurance to Roosevelt and Churchill at Teheran that he would try to launch it in coordination with the Normandy invasion. A smaller offensive had been launched that very day against the Finns on the Karelian Peninsula, north of Leningrad. "They are a serious, stubborn, blunt people and sense must be hammered into them," Stalin said. In ten or fifteen days another offensive would be launched elsewhere. But the general offensive against the Germans would not be at its "full force" until July, because the clearing of the Crimea had taken longer than expected.

Oblivious to the bitter recriminations of the past, and his own accusations at the time of the Churchill-Harriman visit in 1942 that the British were too cowardly to fight, Stalin at last acknowledged the tremendous achievement of Allied arms in successfully crossing the Channel. He said to Harriman:

"The history of war has never witnessed such a grandiose operation. Napoleon himself never attempted it. Hitler envisaged it but he was a fool for never having attempted it."

CHAPTER XIV

Poland, the Touchstone

Again the Poles," Stalin growled. "Is that the most important question?" Those troublesome Poles, he complained to Harriman, kept him so busy that he had no time for military matters.

The date was March 3, 1944. Harriman, who had requested the Kremlin meeting on instructions from Roosevelt, replied that he too would prefer to discuss military questions, but Poland had become a pressing problem. He promised to be brief. It was not a question of time, Stalin said. The Russians had taken their position and would not recede from it: "Isn't it clear? We stand for the Curzon Line." The trouble was that the Polish government in London (he called it "the émigré government") took the Russians for fools. It was now demanding Wilno as well as Lwow. Happily, the people of Poland, who were not the same as the London émigrés, would take a different attitude. He was certain they would welcome the Red Army as liberators.

Harriman did not doubt that Stalin believed this would happen. Only later, when he learned that his troops were widely regarded as foreign invaders, did Stalin find it necessary—in Harriman's view—to impose rigid controls on Poland and Rumania. For the moment, Harriman's task was to persuade Stalin and Molotov that they should resume discussions with the Poles in London and try to negotiate a settlement instead of imposing one by brute force. It was hard going.

Roosevelt feared, Harriman said, that if the problem was not soon resolved, there would be civil war in Poland. Stalin saw no such danger. "War with whom?" he asked. "Between whom? Where?" Mikolajczyk had no troops in Poland. What about the underground force known as the Home Army? Harriman inquired. Stalin grudgingly acknowledged that the London government might have "a few agents" in Poland, but the underground, he insisted, was not large.

Harriman asked what kind of solution Stalin could envisage. He replied, "While the Red Army is liberating Poland, Mikolajczyk will go on repeating his platitudes. By the time Poland is liberated, Mikolajczyk's Government will have changed, or another government will have emerged in Poland."

Roosevelt was concerned, Harriman said, lest a new regime, formed on the basis of the Soviet proposals, should turn out to be "a hand-picked government with no popular movement behind it." Denying any such intention, Stalin nevertheless proceeded to rule out the return from exile of Polish landlords—"Polish Tories," as he called them. "Poland," he said, "needs democrats who will look after the interests of the people, not Tory landlords." Stalin added that he did not believe Churchill (a British Tory, after all) could persuade the London Poles to reshape their government and modify its policies; he was sure that Roosevelt agreed with him on the need for a democratic government in Poland.

Stalin assured Harriman, however, that he would take no immediate action on the Polish matter. The time was not ripe, he said. When Harriman remarked that there were some good men in the London government, Stalin replied, "Good people can be found everywhere, even among the Bushmen."

Not for the first time, Harriman mentioned the President's worries over public opinion in the United States. Stalin responded that he had to be "concerned about public opinion in the Soviet Union." Harriman remarked, "You know how to handle your public opinion," to which Stalin replied, "There have been three revolutions in a generation." Molotov, who had been silent through most of the interview, added without smiling, "In Russia there is an *active* public opinion which overthrows governments." When they spoke of three revolutions, Stalin and Molotov meant the uprising of 1905, the Kerensky revolution of February 1917, and the Bolshevik Revolution the following autumn. Stalin, the revolutionist, was always alert to the possibility of a new revolution, which would have to be stamped out before it got started.

Harriman's bleak interview with Stalin on March 3 was the second in a long series on the intractable Polish problem. He had gone to Moscow as ambassador in 1943 with another set of priorities in mind, military cooperation first among them. But in the months that followed Teheran, Poland was to use up much of his energy and patience. There was no end, he recalled, "of indignities and disagreeable incidents unrelated to political issues." The Russians, for example, had two broadcasting stations in the vicinity of Moscow whose location was important to American pilots in order to triangulate their approach

to the Soviet capital. In spite of repeated requests, the Russians refused to disclose to the embassy more than the one well-known location. The issue disappeared when an American pilot flew over the
second transmitter accidentally and marked the location.

"We were treated as potential enemies," Harriman recalled. "Our
Russian staff—servants, office staff and chauffeurs—had their food-ration
cards taken away because they worked for the American embassy.
Kathleen had to feed them all after that, but our supplies ran short at
times when a convoy was delayed or our shipments sunk. Then we
would send someone out of Moscow to buy potatoes and cabbages from
a collective farm."

It was the Soviet attitude toward Poland, however, that was to
shake Harriman's hopes for Soviet-American cooperation more profoundly than the daily frustrations of Soviet secrecy, inefficiency and
general high-handedness as they affected Lend-Lease negotiations,
joint military planning, such homely matters as potatoes, cabbages or
the issuance of exit visas to Russian women who had been unpatriotic
enough to marry American citizens. Yet Harriman continued to believe, long after George Kennan had given way to these frustrations,
that each small victory at the expense of the Soviet bureaucracy was
worth the fight; limited agreements were better than none. He accepted even minor concessions in the belief that small steps forward
could lead to longer strides toward cooperation once the enveloping
suspicion, as much traditional Russian as Communist, had been
pierced.

But Poland was to become the touchstone of Soviet behavior in
the postwar world, the first test of Stalin's attitude toward his less
powerful neighbors. It was to raise troubling questions in Harriman's
mind about differing war aims within the alliance and about the differing meanings attached to such simple words as "friendly" or "democratic." His role at this period surpassed the conventional bounds of
ambassadorial duty. His personal convictions, which he did not hesitate to make clear in communications to the President and the State
Department, were often at variance with his instructions from Washington. During his first days in Moscow, Harriman had come to believe that all the earnest talk about a free, independent Poland was
likely to become academic once the Red Army occupied the country.
Cordell Hull was not disposed to listen when Harriman urged upon
him the supreme importance of pressing the London Poles to come to
terms with the Kremlin before it was too late. Roosevelt, looking
ahead to the 1944 election and the predictable wrath of the Polish
voters, had pleaded with Stalin to give the Poles "a break," and above
all, not to jeopardize his own re-election prospects by unilateral action.

Washington treated Poland as a British problem in the first instance, one that Churchill alone might be able to solve by pressing the London Poles to reorganize their government.

Churchill and Eden had talked sternly to Mikolajczyk after Teheran, pressing him to "accept the so-called Curzon Line (prolonged through eastern Galicia) as a basis for negotiations with the Soviet Government." The Prime Minister reported to Stalin and to Roosevelt:

> I said that although we had gone to war for the sake of Poland, we had not gone to war for any particular frontier line but for the existence of a strong, free, independent Poland, which Marshal Stalin had also declared himself supporting. Moreover, although Great Britain would have fought on in any case for years until something happened to Germany, the liberation of Poland from the German grip is being achieved mainly by the enormous sacrifices and achievements of the Russian armies. Therefore Russia and her Allies had a right to ask that Poland should be guided to a large extent about the frontiers of the territory she would have . . .
>
> I advised them to accept the Curzon Line as a basis for discussion. I spoke of the compensation which Poland would receive in the North and in the West. In the North there would be East Prussia; but here I did not mention the point about Koenigsberg. In the West they would be free and aided to occupy Germany up to the line of the Oder. I told them it was their duty to accept this task and guard the frontier against German aggression towards the East . . . in this task they would need a friendly Russia behind them and would, I presumed, be sustained by the guarantee of the Three Great Powers against further German attack.[1]

Churchill appeared to draw the line, however, at forcing the Poles to reconstruct their government by a purge of the so-called reactionaries. "Do you not agree," he wrote to Stalin, "that to advocate changes within a foreign government comes near to that interference with internal sovereignty to which you and I have expressed ourselves as opposed?" Stalin did not, of course, agree.

> I think you realize [he replied on February 4] that we cannot re-establish relations with the present Polish Government. Indeed, what would be the use of re-establishing relations with it when we are not at all certain that tomorrow we shall not be compelled to sever those relations again on account of another fascist provocation on its part, such as the "Katyn Affair"?[2]

Nor had Stalin's offer of territorial compensation at Germany's expense reconciled the Polish government to the loss of territory in the east. The Poles had seen their country partitioned in 1939 between Germany and Russia, and they looked to the Western powers to restore it. For them, the Soviet effort to annex one third of Poland looked like another cynical repartition, the evil fruit of the Hitler-Stalin pact of 1939. The Russians, understandably, had a different perspective. Poland was the foreign invader's route to Moscow (a point Stalin had made repeatedly to Harriman), not a country like any other. Both Napoleon and Hitler had marched into Russia across the Polish plain and Stalin, believing in defense in depth, was determined that it should not happen again. The Russian leadership had not forgotten or forgiven the prewar Polish government's refusal to let Soviet troops traverse Polish territory, even in the hypothetical event of their joining the British and French against the Germans. Nor had it forgotten the humiliations inflicted upon the young Red Army in 1920 by the Polish forces of Marshal Jozef Pilsudski. In taking back the strip of territory they had lost to Pilsudski after World War I and briefly reoccupied in 1939, they proposed to fix a new boundary close to the Curzon Line, itself the product of an unsuccessful earlier British effort to mediate between Poles and Russians in December 1919 and January 1920.

At the Paris Peace Conference in 1919 the Allies had decided to reconstitute a Polish state out of the wreckage of the old Austro-Hungarian, German and Czarist empires—a decision that raised serious questions about the undefined eastern frontier. In December 1919 the Supreme Council of the Allied Powers suggested a line that roughly followed the ethnic divisions of Eastern Europe: Poles living to the west of the line, White Russians to the east. The proposed new boundary would run from the East Prussian frontier in the north to the edge of eastern Galicia in the south. No effort was made at the time to push the boundary line through eastern Galicia. That fragment of Austro-Hungary, with its major city Lwow, was supposed to become a League of Nations mandated territory under Polish administration.

Neither the Polish nor the Soviet governments, however, would accept the proposals of the Peace Conference. In the spring of 1920 the new Polish republic, encouraged by the French (who hoped to build up Poland as an ally against both the Germans to the west and the Bolshevik Russians to the east), struck against the Soviet Union. Despite early successes in the field, the Polish offensive collapsed and soon the Red Army was pushing deep into Poland. For a time, in the summer of 1920, it appeared that Poland might be bolshevized at the point of a Russian bayonet. The Poles then appealed to the Allies and, as a condition of mediation, accepted a British proposal that they withdraw to the suggested boundary of December 1919. The British terms, though, were unclear about who would control Lwow. This proposed armistice line, bearing the signature of Lord Curzon, the British Foreign Secretary, was dispatched to the Soviets on July 11, 1920. But the Soviets rejected it, continuing their advance toward Warsaw and East Prussia until they outran their supply lines. At this point the Poles, with French assistance, counterattacked and by autumn they were advancing into Russian territory.

Lenin's new Bolshevik regime—increasingly aware that the Russian people had been totally exhausted by three years of intervention and civil war, famine and economic disruption—agreed to negotiate in the winter of 1921. The result was the Treaty of Riga, which ceded to Poland a large area east of the Curzon Line, including a 150-mile-wide belt of White Russian and Ukrainian territory. It was this belt of contested land—earlier administered by czarist Russia and Austria-Hungary—that the Soviets had reoccupied in 1939, part of Stalin's price for the nonaggression treaty with Hitler.

At Teheran, after Roosevelt had made clear to Stalin that he could take no public position on the Polish dispute, Churchill had tried to draw out Stalin on the details of a frontier settlement. There was no quarrel between them on the Curzon Line, only some debate about its application to Lwow. In fact, the Curzon note of 1920 had left the future of Lwow and Galicia in limbo. Stalin returned to Moscow having accepted the Curzon Line, but insisting that Lwow must be Russian. Churchill had agreed to the Curzon Line, with Polish territorial compensation in the west, but deferred the fate of Lwow for future negotiations. Beneš, meanwhile, assured Churchill (as he had earlier assured Harriman in Moscow) that Stalin would be willing to resume relations with the London Poles, but only if they purged the anti-Soviet elements from their government and accepted the Curzon Line.

On January 6, 1944, as the Red Army was about to crash into the disputed territory, the Polish government in London issued a declaration ignoring the whole issue of new boundaries. It promised military cooperation by the underground Home Army on condition that the Soviet Union resumed diplomatic relations with the London government. Five days later, Harriman and Clark Kerr were called to the Kremlin after midnight to be handed a reply by Molotov, who explained that "as everyone else is talking about Poland it would be wrong for us to remain silent." The Soviet response gave the London Poles no quarter. It accused them of "not infrequently" playing into the hands of the Nazis, while the Union of Polish Patriots and the Soviet-sponsored Polish Army Corps under Major General Zygmunt Berling were already "operating hand in hand with the Red Army on the front against the Germans." The "emigrant Polish Government," by contrast, had shown itself "incapable of organizing the active struggle against the German invaders," the Soviet government contended.

Finding Molotov "most anxious and hopeful" for Washington's reaction, Harriman sent a message the same day pleading for a more active American role behind the scenes:

> I recognize that we should not become directly involved in attempting to negotiate this question between the two Governments. On the other hand, I cannot help but be impressed by the chaotic conditions adversely affecting our vital war interests that will probably result as Soviet troops penetrate Polish territory unless relations are re-established promptly between the two Governments.
>
> It would seem that the Poles can make a better deal now than if they wait, living as they appear to be in the hope that we and the British will eventually pull their chestnuts out of the fire.
>
> If it is clear, and I believe it is, that we will not be able to aid the Poles substantially more than we already have in the boundary dispute, are we not in fairness called upon to make plain the limitations of the help that we can give them and the fact that, in their own interest, the present moment is propitious for them to negotiate the re-establishment of relations with the Soviets?

Mikolajczyk, meanwhile, had approached Hull through his ambassador to Washington, apparently in the hope of strengthening his own hand against Churchill through a reaffirmation of the American policy of opposing territorial settlements before the end of the war. Hull's noncommittal response was that the Administration's policy against wartime settlements did not rule out negotiated agreements by mutual consent. Hull, in short, was neither as frank with the Poles as Harriman would have wished, nor as totally opposed to negotiations as Mikolajczyk may have hoped. Thus Roosevelt and Hull left the main responsibility to Churchill and Eden, even though the proposals they kept pressing on the London Poles would have raised a storm across the United States had they been made public.

When Harriman saw Molotov again on January 18, the Soviet Foreign Minister for the first time gave some indication of the Cabinet changes the Russians wanted to see before they would deal with the Poles in London. The London government must be reconstructed, Molotov said, to include Poles now living in England, the United States and the Soviet Union. These must be "honest men" who were "not tainted with fascism; men with a friendly attitude toward the

Soviet Union." As possible members of the new government he volunteered the names of Dr. Oskar Lange, a Polish economist who was then teaching at the University of Chicago; Father Stanislaus Orlemanski, an obscure priest of an obscure Catholic parish in Springfield, Massachusetts; and Leo Krzcki, a trade-union leader who was then national chairman of the American Slav Congress. Mikolajczyk could remain, Molotov added, though he had doubts about the Polish Foreign Minister, Tadeusz Romer.

On January 21 Harriman sent another telegram to Washington suggesting that in his opinion, the Soviets would recognize a reconstituted London government under Mikolajczyk if it was ready to accept the Curzon Line as "a basis for the boundary negotiations." It was his impression that the Russians would not insist on a total purge; Mikolajczyk could pass muster "by eliminating the irreconcilably anti-Soviet members and bringing in at least one Polish leader from the United States, one now in Russia, and perhaps one from Poland." Harriman sounded a prophetic warning:

> Unless the Polish group in London proceeds along the above line, I believe the Soviets will foster and recognize some type of Committee of Liberation. Then one of two alternatives would face us:
> (1) Continued recognition of the Polish Government in London, the practical effect of which would be to give the Russians a free hand to do what they wish in Poland, at least until after the hostilities are terminated.
> (2) Insistence on our being given representation in setting up administrative machinery within Poland similar to what has been given to the Russians in Italy by us. Withdrawal of recognition from the Polish Government in London would be one consequence of this course.

That painful choice could only be averted, Harriman argued, by quickly persuading the London Poles to reconstruct their government and negotiate with the Russians before the Red Army crossed the Curzon Line. This would require "the strongest pressure" that Churchill and Eden could bring to bear. "I would not feel qualified," Harriman added, "to say how far the American Government should go." He asked Hull for his reaction and "any information as to the line of thinking you have in mind."

All the Ambassador got in return was a request from Hull that he should see Molotov and go back over the old ground, warning the Russians again that their unilateral actions in the case of Poland ran the risk of alienating American public opinion. Believing this approach to be fruitless, Harriman sent the Secretary of State his own capsule version of Molotov's predictable responses: that the Soviets "perceive no reason why Poland should be liberated through the efforts of the Red Army so that there may be placed in power a group which has shown a basically antagonistic attitude toward the Soviet Union"; that the Curzon Line "has had the sanction of the British Government and no recorded objection from the United States Government"; and that the Soviets would allow the people of Poland to select a government of their own choosing. "I make no attempt to argue the Soviet case," Harriman wrote on January 24, "but I want to put before you as clearly as I can what I am satisfied is, and will be, the attitude of the Soviets." In order to be useful at the Moscow end, Harriman added, he needed clear answers to a number of policy questions:

- Was the United States prepared to accept as "reasonably warranted" the Soviet position that the present Polish government was so unalterably hostile as to justify Moscow's refusal to deal with it?
- If so, was Washington ready to say as much to the Russians, the British and the Poles, and to decide "how far are we ready to involve ourselves in negotiations" on reconstructing the London government?
- If not, would the United States be prepared to claim in Poland the same rights to participate in occupation policy-making as it had granted the Russians in Italy?

Until Washington defined its policy and was ready to present specific suggestions, Harriman concluded, it would not be in an effective position to argue against any unilateral Soviet action. But Hull and Roosevelt were not prepared to take hard, unpopular decisions.

When Harriman saw Stalin again on February 2, he took the occasion to express the President's hope that some way might be found to settle the Polish dispute. In reply, Stalin reached for a bulging briefcase on his table, pulled out a six-month-old copy of *Niepodloglosc*, an underground paper printed in Wilno, and thrust it angrily in front of the Ambassador. The headline, in Polish, read: "HITLER AND STALIN —Two FACES OF THE SAME EVIL." It was difficult to deal with people who could publish such a paper, Stalin said. The Poles in London might be able to fool Mr. Eden but now they had shown their true character.

When Harriman, nevertheless, stressed the high importance of reaching a Polish settlement, Stalin said he would be glad if relations with the Polish government could be improved. He was convinced, however, that it could not be done so long as people like General Sosnkowski and Stanislaw Kot, the former ambassador to the Soviet Union, remained in the government. "These people would have to be removed before the Soviet Government could deal with the Polish Government in London," Stalin said. The Poles liked to think, he added, that "Russians were good fighters but fools. They thought they could let the Russians carry the burden of the fighting and then step in at the end to share the spoils. But the Poles would find out who were the fools."

Clark Kerr reported that Stalin sounded slightly less negative later the same evening, when he in turn called at the Kremlin. In response to a series of written questions, Stalin promised that Poles living east of the Curzon Line would be permitted to migrate westward and that democratic elections would be allowed in Poland after the liberation. It was Clark Kerr's impression, Harriman reported, that "although Stalin manifested a firm determination not to establish relations with a government he could not trust, he indicated no desire to 'hand-pick' a new Polish Government."

Churchill continued to press the London Poles for concessions to reality. In a meeting at Chequers on February 6 he warned Mikolajczyk and Romer that "the Curzon Line was the best that the Poles could expect and all that he would ask the British people to demand on their behalf." If they persisted in their present course, Churchill added, they would lose everything "while the Russian steamroller moved over Poland, a Communist government was set up in Warsaw and the present Polish Government was left powerless to do anything but make its protests to the world at large."[3]

Mikolajczyk, however, rejected the Curzon Line in the name of the underground leaders inside Poland as well as his own government. He had gone a long way toward meeting the Russian demands, he said, by agreeing to negotiate all questions, including frontier changes. He had issued orders to the underground movement to enter into friendly contact with the Russians. But he could not announce, the Polish Premier said, "that he would accept the Curzon Line and give away Wilno and Lwow." To do so would only undermine his government's authority with the Polish people. On February 22 Churchill told the House of Commons: "I cannot feel that the Russian demand for a re-assurance about her Western frontiers goes beyond the limits of what is reasonable or just." His statement failed to sway Mikolajczyk's government, nor did it satisfy Stalin. When Clark Kerr saw Stalin on the last day of February, trying once again to discover whether the Kremlin would yield an inch on its demands, he found that "no argument was of any avail." It was, the British ambassador reported, "not a pleasant talk."

Harriman's second talk with Stalin on March 3 went no better. "Again the Poles," Stalin had said, in a mood of aggravated annoyance with the exile government. Harriman had come away with no encouragement other than Stalin's promise to take no immediate action because, as he said, the time was not ripe.

IN THE DAYS THAT FOLLOWED, Harriman put his mind to various ways of breaking the deadlock. With Clark Kerr's advice and agreement, he drafted a proposal that would get around the Soviet refusal to deal directly with the London Poles. The Western Allies could, on the one hand, take their cue from Stalin's statement that the time was not ripe for action on Poland and resign themselves to a period of "watchful waiting." The great disadvantage of this course, he pointed out in a draft never sent on to Washington, was that the Red Army, meanwhile, would move into Poland, leaving the Soviets free to do as they pleased. He felt that the Russians in time were likely to surface a new Polish regime of their own, led by Communists who had sat out the war in Moscow, and extend to it the recognition they had denied the London government. The cost of waiting, in short, would be high: "The solution to the Polish question would be a completely Soviet one."

The second course, which Harriman clearly preferred, was to try for agreement between the British, the Americans and the Russians on a set of ultimate objectives for Poland. The three powers would commit themselves to the restoration of a strong, independent Poland and to assuring the Polish people's right to freely select a broadly representative government of their own after the war. The Soviets would be authorized to administer the disputed territory east of the Curzon Line, leaving the final frontier settlement to be concluded after the war. As for the liberated areas west of the Curzon Line, an Advisory Council representing all three powers could be set up to consult with the Soviet military authorities on "questions of a political character," to make certain that the long-suffering population received relief assistance and to promote conditions which would permit the early transfer of governmental responsibility to Polish bodies.

The second course had its advantages, Harriman argued. It would restore faith in the agreements of Moscow and Teheran, demonstrating that the Big Three were searching together for an honest solution; moreover, the participation of Western representatives might "operate as an automatic restraint upon Soviet excesses." He conceded the disadvantages as well: the danger that by participating in the proposed commission, the United States and Britain would find themselves obliged to underwrite "at least tacitly" whatever the Soviets did on Polish territory—either that or contemplate a serious breach in the alliance. He also foresaw an undermining of the London government's authority, which could sharpen disunity among Poles overseas and damage morale among Polish servicemen fighting with the British.

"I knew that only the British government could bring about the changes that I believed to be essential in the composition and attitude of the Polish government-in-exile," Harriman recalled. "For that reason I kept urging Clark Kerr to send vigorous telegrams to his government. The reason I did not send some of the messages I dictated late at night to Meiklejohn was that when I read them again in the morning I felt they might do more harm than good. I knew I couldn't influence Hull. I had to reach the President and Hopkins. And I kept coming back to the realization that the main effort would have to be made in London, not Washington."

Churchill was still pressing Mikolajczyk hard in the spring of 1944 and being reproached by Stalin for not pressing harder. Increasingly exasperated, Churchill notified Stalin on March 21 that he proposed to make a statement in the House of Commons suggesting that all territorial changes be postponed for the duration of the war. "Of course, you are free to make any speech in the House of Commons— this is your affair," Stalin wrote back. "But if you make such a speech I shall consider that you have committed an act of injustice and un-friendliness toward the Soviet Union."[4]

As Harriman in Moscow thought about these unhappy developments he became more convinced than ever that the territorial dispute would, in the end, prove less of an obstacle than the determined anti-Soviet character of the London government. Torn between his long-standing view that nothing would be gained by appeasement of Stalin and a desire to understand the Soviet position, he set down his thoughts in a memorandum on March 24:

> I realize that the Polish situation does not look the same to me as it does in Washington, but I do not consider that my view is entirely colored by the Moscow atmosphere. I knew Sikorski intimately, had a number of long talks with him and have seen a number of the Poles, both important and lower rank, in London and elsewhere. The majority of them, with the exception of Sikorski, are mainly committed to a policy of fear of and antagonism to the Soviet Government. There is no doubt in my mind that the policies of the [Polish] Government are dominated by the officer group who are convinced that a war with Soviet Russia is inevitable.
>
> Sikorski himself, shortly before he was killed, when I asked him why he could not consolidate his Government on a policy which he favored of working with the Soviet Union,

said to me: "This is impossible for me to accomplish at the present time. The only constituents I have now are the Army."

Stalin is convinced that there is no hope for a friendly neighbor in Poland under the leadership of the controlling group in London, and he is unwilling to have the Red Army re-establish them in power. I believe he is basically right. In spite of the conjectures to the contrary, there is no evidence that he is unwilling to allow an independent Poland to emerge.

Harriman's disagreements with Churchill had been few during the London years. Now he felt that the Prime Minister was mistaken in threatening to withhold recognition of territorial changes until after the war. Although Churchill, in fact, did not make the speech which in prospect had so greatly alarmed Stalin, Harriman found him filled with bitterness when he dined at 10 Downing Street on May 2 on his way to Washington for consultations with Roosevelt.

Churchill arrived late and visibly tired at the end of a long Cabinet meeting. He asked some perfunctory questions about life in Moscow and did not appear to be much interested in Harriman's answers. But the vigor and the passion came flooding back when Harriman raised the Polish question. The Prime Minister argued that he had done a great service for Stalin as well as the London Poles. With great effort he had persuaded the Poles to accept the Curzon Line as a temporary demarcation for administrative purposes, leaving the final determination to the peace conference. He had committed the British government to support the westward expansion of Poland's frontiers at the expense of Germany. And all he got in exchange, he said, was "insults from Stalin—a barbarian."

Harriman quietly took issue with Churchill, explaining his belief that the Soviet government worried less over the boundary issue than over the composition of the Polish government and its political attitudes. "I explained that Mikolajczyk was not unacceptable to the Soviets as an individual, nor were others coming from the Polish democratic parties, but that Stalin was convinced that the group in London were under the domination of Sosnkowski and the military, who saw in the future only war with the Soviet Union," Harriman noted in his memorandum on the dinner conversation with Churchill.

The Prime Minister made no promises to reconsider his position. But as Harriman was leaving he showed signs of a new mood. He asked Harriman to tell Stalin "how earnestly he had tried to find a solution, how much progress he had made and how hurt he was that Stalin had not believed in his good intentions."

Two days later, at a garden party for the visiting prime ministers of the British Dominions, Churchill sent for Harriman and reopened the subject. "He made me listen to a fifteen-minute fight talk," Harriman remembered, "on how badly the British had been treated by the Soviet government beginning with the Ribbentrop treaty, during the period when Britain stood alone, the insults that had been hurled at him by Stalin consistently, and his determination that the Soviets should not destroy freedom in Poland, for which country Britain had gone to war. He asked that I present this attitude to the President and asked for the President's support in this policy 'even if only after he is re-elected to office.'"

Harriman had encountered the same attitude of sour disenchantment in a talk with Eden on May 3. There was a serious question, Eden said, whether Britain could ever again work with the Soviets. Harriman argued the contrary proposition: that by patience, understanding and readiness to be firm on matters of principle, the Western Allies could still develop "reasonably satisfactory relationships" with the Russians. "For example," he said, "we should have dealt with the political side of the Polish question at Moscow and Teheran. The fact that we did not register opposition to the Soviet Government's unwillingness to deal with the Poles in London had been accepted by the Soviets as acquiescence, even though [it was] understood to be reluctant. The Soviets' own policy was to react violently against any statement of ours, and they expected us to do the same. This technique of theirs is one that we should bear in mind at all times and not allow ourselves to drift into difficulties as a result of indecision. On the other hand, we should attempt to understand their basic objectives and not make issues where we are not on firm ground."

Harriman, in short, was thoroughly aware of the sharp swing in official British opinion when he looked up Lord Beaverbrook. He found his old friend in improved health and far less vehement than in his War Cabinet days, "fussing with civilian aviation and watching developments" from the sidelines. Beaverbrook announced with dramatic effect that everyone in the British government except himself was anti-Russian now. His own view was that the Soviets ought to have a free hand in Eastern Europe but should be excluded from Allied councils in Italy and Western Europe generally. "In other words," Harriman noted, "he believes in spheres of interest."

On his way back from Washington, Harriman stopped again in London to find that Churchill's rage against Stalin had blown itself out. "Due largely to Stalin's recent civil messages," he reported to Roosevelt on May 29, "the sun is shining again on the Soviet horizon." Something more substantial than a change in Stalin's tone had affected the Prime Minister, as he soon explained. During Harriman's absence in Washington he had tried his hand at a sphere-of-interest arrangement with the Russians, and it appeared to be working. The British had agreed to keep hands off Rumania while the fighting there continued, Churchill said, and the Russians in turn were willing to leave the British a free hand in Greece. Already the Greek Communists were being more cooperative, to the point of indicating that they would join rather than oppose a new coalition government of all the main resistance groups and political parties, then being organized in Cairo, with George Papandreou as Prime Minister. The Soviets were being so cooperative about Greece, Churchill added, that he was now hopeful of resolving even the Polish problem.*

Back in Moscow, Harriman assured Molotov on June 3 that the President would urge Mikolajczyk, who was about to visit the United States, to drop Sosnkowski and his followers from the Polish Cabinet. The President, he said, considered it of paramount importance that permanent, friendly relations be established between the Soviet Union and Poland; for that reason Mikolajczyk would have to reconstruct his government. Roosevelt remembered Stalin's reassurance at Teheran that Poland's independence would be respected, Harriman added. With the election five months off, the President "thought it best to keep quiet on the Polish question," as he had explained to Stalin at Teheran, and he had insisted that Mikolajczyk make no public speeches during his American visit. "It was a time to keep barking dogs quiet," Harriman said. The Soviets could be helpful by not airing the question for a time.

Molotov inquired whether there had been any change in the President's views on the Polish question since he had discussed it with Stalin at Teheran. No, Harriman replied, adding that the President was confident that Stalin too would stand by his statements at Teheran. Molotov put several questions about American reactions to the Moscow visit of Father Orlemanski and Professor Lange, whom the Soviets had put forward as possible candidates for a reconstructed Polish government, at which Harriman remarked that neither had an "especially large" following in the United States.

When Harriman saw Stalin on June 10, there was more talk of the Normandy landing than of Poland. He raised the subject with the appearance of hesitation, saying that he knew Stalin did not like to

---

* Churchill's enthusiasm was running ahead of events. The possibility of a temporary sphere-of-interest arrangement had been mentioned to the Soviet ambassador, Fedor T. Gusev, on May 5 by Eden. On May 18 Gusev informed the British Foreign Office that his government favored the idea but would like to know whether Washington had any objection. Hull objected strongly. Thus it was not until mid-July, following repeated appeals from Churchill to Roosevelt, that the United States gave its lukewarm assent to a three-month trial period. Stalin let the proposal drag and Churchill, sensing fresh Russian encouragement to the Communist resistance group in Greece, did not press the matter for several months.

talk about the Poles. "Why not?" Stalin responded in obvious good humor. Harriman had never seen Stalin in a more agreeable mood. The success of the Second Front doubtless affected his attitude, although he was cordial even in discussing Poland. Stalin expressed gratitude for the President's reaffirmation of his statements at Teheran, adding that he fully realized how difficult it was for the President to speak out during the election campaign. He also undertook to keep Roosevelt informed of any new development in Polish-Soviet relations. Harriman remarked that the President was puzzled about the status of Lwow but believed it was a matter to be worked out between Russians and Poles.

The unanswered question was "Which Poles?" While Mikolajczyk was in Washington seeing Roosevelt, Stalin had been meeting in Moscow with a delegation from the so-called Polish National Council, a body of uncertain origin recently formed inside Poland. Stalin urged Harriman to talk with them. These, he said, were "living people," not émigrés, and they would have a great deal to tell him regarding conditions in Poland. Harriman agreed to meet the delegation unofficially the following day. The principal spokesman for the group turned out to be Edward Boleslaw Osubka-Morawski, who described himself as a Catholic, an economist and a member of the Polish Socialist party. He had changed his name four times during the German occupation, he said, and was now Vice President of the Polish National Council. The others were a Colonel Turski, the only acknowledged Communist in the group; a former Lodz industrialist called Hanecki; and a young man who called himself Hardy. He had been a student in Warsaw before the war, he said, an active partisan and a member of the Peasant party, although his wing of the party had broken away from Mikolajczyk's leadership.

Osubka-Morawski, who did most of the talking, denounced Sosnkowski and his "reactionary Fascist clique" at length, insisting they had no real support in Poland except for an underground force of perhaps 30,000 men. He appealed for arms from the United States for what he described as the "People's Army." Questioned by Harriman about the Council's position on frontiers, he said that it hoped Poland would be able to keep Lwow and the Galician oil fields, but he personally saw little prospect of holding Wilno "because of its geographic position." The Council, he added, was trying to be practical. It recognized the great power of the Soviet Union and felt the chance of getting a reasonable settlement from the Russians was bound to increase if its own demands were reasonable. He acknowledged that the National Council was "in agreement on fundamentals" with the Union of Polish Patriots in Moscow but insisted there had been no contact between the two organizations before his visit to the Soviet Union.

Harriman found it curious that Osubka-Morawski and the London

Poles appeared to feel much the same way about keeping Lwow and the Galician oil fields. "It seemed to me at the time," he recalled, "that if the best of the London Poles had gotten together with the National Council people, they could at least have saved Lwow and the oil fields."

When Harriman asked his visitors what the outcome of a present-day election in Poland might be, Osubka-Morawski replied that Mikolajczyk's Peasant party would run ahead of the others. It was axiomatic, however, that after the war the large estates would have to be broken up, the land distributed to the peasants and the principal industries placed under national control.

Mikolajczyk, meanwhile, had met four times with President Roosevelt in the week of June 7–14. The President told him, among other things, that Lwow ought rightfully to belong to Poland and that he should avoid "any final or definite settlement of the frontiers now." Roosevelt added that "it might be desirable to find an opportunity to bring some changes in your cabinet in order to make an understanding with the Russians possible."[5] Roosevelt stressed, however, that the Poles would have to negotiate their own settlement with Stalin. He urged Mikolajczyk to fly to Moscow without delay for a "man to man" discussion with the Soviet leader. Mikolajczyk agreed to go if invited, as he was, after both Churchill and Roosevelt intervened with Stalin.

A four-day visit to Soviet Central Asia with Vice President Henry Wallace offered Harriman a welcome break from his Polish preoccupations in mid-June. Wallace had undertaken a brief, enthusiastic study of Russian in preparation for his trip. But Roosevelt did not want Wallace to talk with Stalin. At the President's direction, Wallace flew from Alaska across Siberia to Tashkent and Alma Ata, then on to China. "The President was perfectly willing for Wallace to see Chiang Kai-shek," Harriman recalled. "Indeed, he thought that the Vice President's liberal influence might do some good with Chiang. But he was taking no chances of confusing Stalin about American policy."

On June 14 Harriman flew to Tashkent, accompanied by Tommy Thompson; the Chinese ambassador to the Soviet Union, Foo Ping-sheung; and the Mexican ambassador, Luis Quintanilla, a personal friend of Wallace's. He met Wallace there and together they visited several agricultural experiment stations, where Soviet scientists were trying to develop improved strains of cotton, potatoes and melons. Wallace, who had made a considerable fortune as a developer of hybrid corn, was in his element. "All his life, Wallace had been trying to get American farmers to accept science," Harriman reported on his return to Moscow. "In the Soviet Union he saw scientific methods being forced on the farmers, and it was heaven for him. Here he found capable agricultural scientists with the authority to compel farmers to follow their orders."

Throughout the trip Wallace was totally absorbed in matters agricultural. Harriman and Thompson took more interest in the social and political attitudes of a region normally closed to foreign diplomats. They found the people refreshingly hospitable, the fruits displayed in local markets both succulent and abundant, and the evidence of economic uplift in what had been an isolated, backward region compelling. They discovered, among other things, that few of the Uzbek population (whose devotion to Moscow was not being taken for granted in the Kremlin) had seen service in the Red Army at the beginning of the war. As the fighting raged on, however, and the casualties multiplied, the Uzbeks were called to combat like other Soviet citizens and suffered heavy losses in the Battle of Stalingrad.

Wallace got to deliver a short speech in Russian, Harriman noting that the crowd in the Tashkent theater "managed to understand" him. The American guests also were treated to the first performance of Bizet's *Carmen* in the Uzbek language. Thompson dryly observed in his report to Washington that "fortunately for the guests, only one act of the opera was given."

Harriman returned to Moscow on June 19 and was soon again absorbed in Polish problems. Two days later he warned the State Department that the London Poles were about to be outflanked. The Ambassador's "best guess" was that with the Red Army now rolling into Poland proper, the Russians "in consultation, no doubt, with the Polish National Council" would install local administrations in the liberated areas. "Mikolajczyk and certain other representatives of the democratic parties of the London Government will then be asked by the Polish National Council to return to Poland and associate themselves in the formation of a government," he predicted. "Individuals of the Union of Polish Patriots in Moscow, and perhaps Dr. Lange and one or two other Poles in the United States, will be similarly invited. A government will be formed, based on the 1921 constitution and repudiating the constitution of 1935, regardless of who accepts these invitations."*

Moscow would promptly recognize the new government, having

---

* The Polish Constitution of 1921 established the new state as a parliamentary democracy. By the late twenties, however, power reverted to the military, General Pilsudski and his colonels. In 1935 the Pilsudski regime instituted a frankly authoritarian constitution more nearly in step with the rise of Fascist regimes elsewhere in Europe. Overwhelming power was now concentrated in the President, and Parliament lost effective control. Civil liberties were restricted, and the rights of political organizations curtailed.

Poland, the Touchstone

333

made certain that "real influence in Polish affairs will be exercised by the Soviet Government," and would then call upon London and Washington to follow suit. "We will [then] be faced with a *fait accompli*," Harriman wrote, "and with the difficult decision as to what will be our relations with the Polish Government in London and our attitude toward the new government in Poland."

That forecast was confirmed the following evening, July 22. Radio Moscow announced, from liberated territory, the formation of a Polish Committee for National Liberation, which was to serve as the executive authority of the Polish National Council (four of whose members had so recently and so modestly called upon Harriman to plead for American arms). The Committee's mission was anything but modest: "to direct the fight of the people for liberation, to achieve independence, and to rebuild the Polish state." The announcement had been issued from Chelm, the first large town liberated by the Red Army on territory that was Polish beyond dispute. The Committee moved on to Lublin after a few days and came to be known as the Lublin Committee. The Russians, moreover, had already signed an agreement with the Chelm-Lublin Committee, assigning to it "full responsibility in matters of civil government" behind the Red Army's lines.

The Polish government-in-exile in short, was suddenly confronted with a rival Polish regime, bearing out Harriman's early warnings to Roosevelt and Hull; a rival already established on Polish soil and enjoying full support from the Russians. Exactly six weeks earlier Stalin had assured Roosevelt, through Harriman, that he would keep him informed of any new Polish developments. As he explained to Harriman on another occasion, he never broke a promise but sometimes he changed his mind.

When Mikolajczyk at last reached Moscow and asked for a meeting with Stalin, Molotov replied that he had better see the Lublin representatives. They were, Molotov said, better informed than Stalin about conditions in Poland. The Polish Premier insisted. He had, after all, been invited to Moscow by Stalin, however grudgingly. Molotov told him on July 31 that he would try to arrange a meeting with Stalin in three days. He added that the Red Army was only ten kilometers from Warsaw. The next day Warsaw rose up in arms against the Germans.

"Warsaw will be free any day," Mikolajczyk said to Stalin, when they finally met on August 3. "God grant that it be so," Stalin replied. But he went on to sneer at the underground army: "What kind of army is it—without artillery, tanks, air force? They do not even have enough hand weapons. In modern war this is nothing . . . I hear that the Polish Government instructed these units to chase the Germans out of Warsaw. I don't understand how they can do it. They don't have sufficient strength for that."

Mikolajczyk asked Stalin whether he would help the Warsaw uprising by supplying arms. "We will not permit any action behind our lines," he said. "For this reason you have to reach an understanding with the Lublin Committee. We are supporting them. If you don't do it, then nothing will come out of our talk. We cannot tolerate two governments."[6]

The scene was being played out much as Harriman had prophesied on January 21. Washington had chosen the course of sitting tight to await developments. Feeling powerless to alter the course of events inside Poland, it watched with rising alarm as the Russians installed their friends in power. Only the Russians were by reason of geography in a position to liberate Poland. And as Stalin said to Tito in 1945, "Whoever occupies a territory also imposes on it his own social system. Everyone imposes his own system as far as his army can reach. It cannot be otherwise."[7]

Harriman continued to believe, however, that in Poland it might have been otherwise—if the British government, backed strongly by the United States, had pressed the Polish government-in-exile to swallow the Curzon Line and get rid of its bitter-end generals like Sosnkowski. It was, he felt, the only hope (a slender hope, admittedly) of preventing a wholly Russian solution to the Polish question.

CHAPTER XV

Warsaw—The
Doomed Uprising

THE WESTWARD SWEEP of the summer offensive had carried the Red
Army across the Curzon Line on July 18, 1944. The Russians captured Lublin on July 23. They took Brest-Litovsk on July 26. Three days
later the right flank of Marshal Rokossovsky's First White Russian
Front, having advanced 300 miles in little more than a month, reached
the east bank of the river Vistula, opposite Warsaw.

Harriman recalled the race to the west, as described by General
Deane after a visit to the front: "Suddenly everything was going forward. When a truck broke down, the Russians would commandeer a
team of horses or of oxen, reload as much of the stuff as the wagons
could hold and move on. The Germans had broken. Their divisions
had been obliterated by death or by capture. There was nothing to
stop the Russians—until they hit the Vistula."

The people of Warsaw and the underground army had waited
almost five terrible years for this moment. Now they were determined
that Poles should free their own capital. At eight-fifteen in the evening
on July 29 they had listened to a broadcast from Moscow, on the
so-called Kosciusko Station, in which the Union of Polish Patriots
summoned the population to turn the city into a battlefield:

> "For Warsaw, which did not yield but fought on, the
> hour of action has now arrived. The Germans will no doubt
> try to defend themselves in Warsaw, and add new destruction
> and more thousands of victims. Our houses and parks, our
> bridges and railway stations, our factories and our public
> buildings will be turned into defense positions. They will

expose the city to ruin and its inhabitants to death . . . It is therefore a hundred times more necessary than ever to remember that in the flood of Hitlerite destruction all is lost that is not saved by active effort; that by direct, active struggle in the streets of Warsaw, in its houses, factories and stores, we not only hasten the moment of final liberation but also save the nation's prosperity and the lives of our brethren.

Poles, the time of liberation is at hand: Poles, to arms! There is not a moment to lose!"[1]

The broadcast could only have been made with the Soviet government's specific authorization. General Tadeusz Bor-Komorowski, commander in chief of the Home Army, had already received instructions from the London government to proclaim a general insurrection "at a moment to be chosen by you." When the leaders of the underground met secretly in Warsaw on July 31 there could be no question that they would respond. They had intercepted a coded radio message from the commander of the Fourth German Panzer Army ordering his units to withdraw westward across the Vistula. In the streets of Warsaw, the Nazis were rounding up men and boys to build fortifications. To remain in hiding at this moment would only have confirmed Stalin's taunts that the Home Army existed chiefly in Mikolajczyk's imagination, or that it collaborated willingly with the Nazis. So the doomed uprising began at five o'clock in the afternoon on August 1, even as Mikolajczyk was waiting in Moscow to plead his case with Stalin.

General Bor had mustered 35,000 to 40,000 Poles equipped with only light weapons and meagerly supplied with ammunition, food and medicine. It was a grotesquely unequal contest. Bor had not sent word to the Russians on the far bank of the river that the Battle of Warsaw was beginning, nor had he heard from them. Although the Red Army represented the only hope of quick, substantial relief for his desperate street fighters, he directed his appeals to London.

The Russians did not move that day, or the next. The Moscow radio made no mention of the fighting inside the Polish capital. Nothing more was heard from the Union of Polish Patriots or its radio station. The people of Warsaw, even as they listened for the reassuring boom of Russian guns from the direction of Praga, an industrial suburb on the east bank of the Vistula, were left to face the Germans alone.

Almost four weeks earlier Harriman had reported to Washington that the Red Army might by-pass Warsaw. He based this forecast on a July 5 conversation with Molotov in which the Soviet Foreign Minister had told him that the Russian high command intended the armies in Byelorussia to strike toward Königsberg in East Prussia and then push southwest into northern Poland, going around Warsaw. Molotov had added that the liberation of the capital would probably be left to Polish partisans and troops under command of General Berling, whose army corps was being held in reserve for that purpose. "It is my belief," Harriman reported on July 21, "that Warsaw may very well be bypassed by the Red Army and that Berling's army, with the cooperation of the partisans, will take the city, if not wholly then at least in appearance, after communications are cut from the west and provided it is not too difficult."

In the pell-mell rush westward, however, the strategic plan outlined by Molotov had been modified. To begin with, the drive toward Königsberg faltered in early August and the push through East Prussia into northern Poland did not materialize. As a result, the German divisions committed to the defense of Warsaw continued to enjoy uninterrupted communications to the west. As for the river crossing, Harriman came to believe that although a frontal assault had been contemplated, the Red Army soon discovered that more weapons and equipment were needed before it could hope to overpower the reinforced German defenses on the west bank. The initial reason for the halt on the Vistula, in Harriman's view, was less political than military: "I think Stalin would have crossed the Vistula without any thought of how it would affect the London Poles—if he felt strong enough to overcome the German defenses. Military considerations were overriding with him. But the Germans brought in three more divisions to reinforce the garrison troops already in or near Warsaw. The Red Army had advanced so far and so fast that it had run far ahead of its supplies. The Russians had no boats or bridges ready. It was all improvisation. They discovered that getting across the Vistula, five to six hundred yards wide at Warsaw, would take a lot more stuff than they had, and Stalin was unwilling to admit it.

"But once the Poles had risen up against the Germans, prematurely as he saw it, he dealt with the whole matter as a provocation. He refused to help. Nor would he permit the British or ourselves to resupply them. He wanted it understood that the Poles had risen up on their own and if the Germans had disposed of them, that was not his responsibility. I'm convinced that he was not the slightest bit distressed to see them killed off. These were the Poles, loyal to the London government-in-exile, who stood in the way of his Lublin Committee. He thought of them as enemies of the Soviet Union, as indeed many of their leaders were. If the Germans should now get rid of them, they would not be a thorn in his side later on."

Churchill's repeated appeals for help in behalf of the Warsaw insurgents had no effect except to sharpen Stalin's rage against the Poles for their effrontery. "I think that the information given to you by the Poles," he wrote on August 5, "is greatly exaggerated and unreliable . . . The Home Army consists of a few detachments miscalled divisions. They have neither guns, aircraft nor tanks. I cannot imagine detachments like those taking Warsaw, which the Germans are defending with four armoured divisions, including the Hermann Goering Division."[2]

The battle for Warsaw meanwhile was turning inexorably in favor of the Germans, who sent Tiger tanks into the streets against the insurgents. They soon drove an armored wedge across the city to the west bank of the Vistula, splitting General Bor's irregulars into two isolated sectors. Although RAF planes dropped supplies on the nights of August 4 and August 8, having flown all the way from Italy in darkness, their efforts proved, in Churchill's words, "both forlorn and inadequate."

In Moscow, Mikolajczyk had agreed under Stalin's pressure to talk with five representatives of the Lublin Committee: Boleslaw Bierut, Osubka-Morawski, Andrzej Witos, Wanda Wassiliewska and General Michal Rola-Zymierski. He met with them on August 6 and 7, sparring over the allocation of Cabinet seats between the London and Lublin regimes in a new Polish government. Mikolajczyk, who kept Harriman and Clark Kerr closely informed throughout the talks, had been offered the post of Premier in the proposed new government, but Lublin was demanding fourteen out of eighteen places for its own people. Harriman urged Mikolajczyk not to return to London but to ask his "more reasonable" Cabinet colleagues to join him in Moscow, lest he lose his opportunity to influence the situation. Mikolajczyk refused, saying that he would have to consult the Cabinet as a whole.

On August 10, the day Mikolajczyk flew back to London, Harriman reported: "He believes that the Committee for Liberation has found that they are not getting the full support of the Polish people and that they realize that they cannot set up competent governmental machinery without the cooperation of himself and the leaders in his government. This situation gives him confidence that some arrangements can be worked out through which all factions can unite. He has, however, not been able to agree with the Committee on a plan."

Harriman found Mikolajczyk greatly impressed with Bierut, chairman of the Polish National Council, who dominated his Lublin colleagues throughout the discussions. Mikolajczyk "respects Bierut but fears him," Harriman reported. Bierut's personal and political past was a mystery. He talked sensibly, Mikolajczyk felt, about social and economic programs for the future. But when Mikolajczyk stressed the importance of bringing leaders of the established Polish parties into the new government, Bierut betrayed a certain lack of patience. "Parties are a thing of the past," he said, adding that he and his Lublin colleagues spoke for the "Polish masses." Mikolajczyk told Harriman that he feared Bierut's goal was a Communist Poland. The Premier's suspicions were further aroused when Rola-Zymierski, in a private talk, urged him not to return to London but to go back to Poland with the Lublin delegation. "If you don't, *they* will take control and it will be too late," the general said. "They" clearly meant the Polish Communists. Again Mikolajczyk refused.

He nevertheless left Moscow more hopeful than he had arrived. Stalin at last had promised help for the Warsaw insurgents. He had assured Mikolajczyk at their final meeting, on August 9, that a Soviet communications officer would be dropped into Warsaw by parachute to establish direct radio communications with General Bor's headquarters. Then supplies could be air-dropped to the Poles by prior arrangement.

Nothing more was heard of Stalin's promise until Harriman sent a letter to Molotov on August 14 asking immediate approval for a shuttle mission of American bombers from England which would drop arms to the Warsaw insurgents, bomb German airfields nearby and then land in the Ukraine. The next morning he received a written reply from Vishinsky to the effect that the Soviet government "could not go along" with the project because the Warsaw uprising was "a purely adventuristic affair to which the Soviet Government could not lend its hand."

Harriman and Clark Kerr requested an immediate meeting with Molotov. They were received on the afternoon of August 15 by Vishinsky, in Molotov's unexplained absence. Reminding Vishinsky of Stalin's promise to Mikolajczyk, the two ambassadors warned that Moscow's refusal to help General Bor, compounded by its refusal to let American bombers drop supplies into Warsaw, was bound to have serious repercussions in London and Washington. Even if the rising had been premature, Poles in the streets of Warsaw were killing Germans—and being killed. Like Tito's Partisans in Yugoslavia and the underground in France, the Poles were having to fight without tanks or aircraft but this should not be held against them. On the contrary, the ambassadors insisted, simple humanity and the interests of the common cause demanded emergency relief for Warsaw. "It was the toughest talk I ever had with a Soviet official," Harriman recalled. Vishinsky stood his ground doggedly. As Harriman reported to Washington:

> Vishinsky clung to the statements made in his letter and to the view that the outbreak in Warsaw was not worthy of assistance, that it was an ill-advised but not a serious matter, and that the future course of the war would not at all be in-

fluenced by it. He said that there were no reasons why the position of the Soviet Government should be reconsidered.

Harriman pointed out that the United States was not asking for Soviet participation in the contemplated airdrop. It was difficult to understand, he argued, how the Russians could possibly object to an American effort to assist the Poles. The very fact that the planes would be landing at Soviet bases, Vishinsky replied, would amount to Soviet participation, and as he had said before, Moscow refused to encourage any "adventuristic actions" which at a later stage might be turned against it. When Harriman pressed him to explain these dark hints, Vishinsky mentioned articles critical of the Soviet attitude which had been published in the Western press. That kind of thing showed all too clearly, he said, what the Warsaw uprising was all about. Upon returning to Spaso House, Harriman sent the President a further message:

> . . . I am for the first time since coming to Moscow gravely concerned by the attitude of the Soviet Government.
> If the position of the Soviet Government is correctly reflected by Vishinsky, its refusal is based on ruthless political considerations—not on denial that resistance exists nor on operational difficulties.

The following evening Harriman and Clark Kerr were called back to receive from Vishinsky the Kremlin's definite reply: "The Soviet Government cannot, of course, object to English or American aircraft dropping arms in the region of Warsaw, since this is an American and British affair. But they decidedly object to American or British aircraft, after dropping arms in the region of Warsaw, landing on Soviet territory, since the Soviet Government does not wish to associate itself directly or indirectly with the adventure in Warsaw."

Faced with Vishinsky's stony refusals, Harriman urged the President to intervene directly with Stalin. "Anything in the nature of a threat should be carefully avoided," he advised Roosevelt, in spite of Stalin's increasingly blunt language in recent messages. But he stressed the fundamental right of the Warsaw insurgents—and their vital need—for Allied assistance in fighting the Germans. Suggesting one line of argument that Washington could make, Harriman wrote: "I personally feel that Marshal Stalin should be made to understand that, if the Soviet Government continues such a policy, the belief of the American public in the chances of success of postwar cooperation and of world security organization would be profoundly shaken."

When Harriman and Clark Kerr insisted upon seeing Molotov, he received them on August 17 for another barren dialogue. The ambassadors pressed him to explain why Stalin had not kept his promise to Mikolajczyk (made just eight days earlier). Molotov mentioned certain Western newspaper articles and broadcasts condemning the Soviet Union for its refusal to help the Warsaw uprising. All this, he said, was the work of the London Poles and nothing could be done to save them—or the street fighters of Warsaw—from their own folly. Harriman reminded Molotov of the Moscow broadcasts calling on the Poles to rise up against the Germans. He had not heard of such broadcasts, the Foreign Minister replied.

It was futile to reason with Molotov as he was obviously following the line of his instructions [Harriman cabled to Roosevelt and Hull]. Our various difficulties with the Soviet Government have, as you know, been dealt with by me in a spirit of consistent optimism and patience. I am led to the opinion, from my recent conversations with Vishinsky and particularly with Molotov this evening, that these men are bloated with power and that they expect they can force acceptance of their decisions without question upon us and all countries.

In the same conversation Molotov also warned Harriman that with the winter season approaching, the Soviet air force proposed to take back the three air-shuttle bases in the Ukraine which had been turned over to the Americans with such resounding fanfare at the beginning of the summer. This threat failed to intimidate the Ambassador. He protested that the airfields had been made available not for the summer season alone but for the duration of the war. Molotov dismissed the argument, contending that the fields were seldom used; only one flight a month was planned for the winter months. Harriman reminded him that the shuttle-bombing had been interrupted by a German air attack on the Poltava base during the night of June 21–22, resulting in the destruction of fifty Flying Fortresses on the ground. It had taken some time to overcome the effects of this misfortune. But the program had been highly successful in permitting the Army Air Forces to strike important targets that could not otherwise have been reached deep inside Germany and the occupied countries of Central Europe. Harriman insisted on an opportunity to discuss the matter of shuttle bases more fully another time. He reminded Molotov, with deliberate aggressiveness, that the United States had been most patient in the face of repeated Soviet delays with regard to joint military planning. The Ambassador had in mind Stalin's unfulfilled promise, made in June, to arrange for talks on the use of Soviet air bases in the Far East against Japan. Molotov assured Harriman that in spite of these delays he need have no concern about the outcome.

Washington, however, took Molotov's threat more seriously than Harriman, showing real apprehension that too much aggressiveness in behalf of the Warsaw insurgents might jeopardize the prospect of further Soviet military collaboration. The State Department informed Harriman on August 19 that it might be well to ease off, bearing in mind "the importance of the continuance and smooth functioning of the shuttle bombing arrangements which should not in any way be allowed to be imperiled by this [Warsaw] question." The British, with no air bases to worry about, might feel free to go on trying to force a degree of Soviet cooperation in sending help to the Polish underground. But "there is a tendency on the part of the British to go considerably farther than the President is prepared to go," the Department advised Harriman. "Since the Soviet Government is not attempting to prevent our independent actions in this matter we feel, although sharing your views as to the character and motives of the Soviet attitude, that as a result of your representations our chief purpose has already been achieved."

Harriman found the Washington attitude hard to understand. The Russians, after all, were still refusing to help the Poles directly, still barring effective British or American arms drops. "I find it difficult to see how it can be considered that 'our chief purpose has already been achieved,'" he cabled Washington on August 21, "although I realize that the peculiar conditions in Moscow do not always lead to clarity of thinking. Even though it may not bring immediately apparent results, I feel strongly that the Russians should be made to realize our dissatisfaction with their behavior. I plan, of course, to take no further steps here, but I hope that our attitude can be conveyed to Gromyko." Whatever Washington's "chief purpose" might be, Harriman could not see that anything constructive had been achieved by seeming to back down. On August 19 he had warned Roosevelt and Hull: "I also believe, in our long-term relations with the Russians, that we should impress our views on them as firmly as possible and show our displeasure whenever they take action of which we strongly disapprove. Only by such procedure would I have confidence that we can find common ground eventually." In a letter the same week to General Eaker, he did not conceal his outrage over the "dirty business" of the Soviet attitude toward the Warsaw uprising. "I realize," he wrote, "it is essential that we make every effort to find a way to work with them and, in spite of disagreements, I am still hopeful. But one thing is certain, that when they depart from common decency we have got to make them realize it."

Kathleen, returning from a trip to Italy at this period, found her father "beginning to show the strain." She wrote to her sister: "He feels lousy and can't do anything about resting up. Thank God I'm not the American Ambassador to Russia." Meiklejohn told Kathleen that the Ambassador had been working as late as two o'clock in the morning throughout the Warsaw crisis and on one occasion until six-thirty. Harriman himself, in a letter to his brother Roland, admitted that his work was "extremely strenuous," owing to the Kremlin's preference for late hours. "It is not unusual," he wrote, "to have a conference beginning anywhere from ten o'clock to two o'clock in the morning and lasting some hours. And then afterward there are always cables to send to get information to Washington by the following morning." He added:

> The Soviets are all much concerned lest Roosevelt be defeated. They are highly suspicious of Dewey and the "reactionary and isolationist" elements around him. If there were a Gallup Poll for Russia the score would be 99% for Roosevelt, 1% who didn't know and zero for Dewey. Everywhere they seem to understand there is an important election taking place which will vitally affect them and their relations with the United States.

Stalin's concern for Roosevelt's re-election found no reflection, however, in his brusque rejection of a joint appeal from the President and Churchill dated August 20. "We hope that you will drop immediate supplies and munitions to the patriot Poles of Warsaw," they wrote, "or will you agree to help our planes in doing it very quickly?"[3] Stalin's reply, dated August 22, ignored the request that relief planes be allowed to land behind Soviet lines. Instead he railed against the "handful of power-seeking criminals" who had persuaded the gullible population of Warsaw to throw itself into a battle it could never hope to win against German guns, armor and aircraft. All this had accomplished, Stalin said, was to aggravate the military situation. Now the Red Army was having to fight off German counterattacks on the east bank of the Vistula before it could resume the offensive and liberate Warsaw "for the Poles."[4]

Harriman's faith in the possibility of cooperation with Stalin was badly shaken. His state of mind can be seen in the draft of a telegram for Roosevelt and Hull, dated August 25, which on second thought he decided not to send:

> It is impossible to overlook the fact that the Soviets have constantly demanded active resistance movements in all occupied countries, no matter what the cost to the population, and during the latter days of July specifically allowed the Union of Polish Patriots to urge uprisings in Warsaw. Stalin's present position completely ignores these previous policies and his

constant criticism of the underground movement loyal to the London Government for its inactivity in resistance.

I can only draw the conclusion that this action [was taken out of] ruthless political considerations in order that the underground may get no credit for the liberation of Warsaw and that its leaders be killed by the Germans or give an excuse for their arrest when the Red Army enters Warsaw. Under these circumstances it is difficult for me to see how a peaceful or acceptable solution can be found to the Polish problem.

Torn between frustration and hope, Harriman added: "In spite of my concern I am still optimistic that we can lead the Russians to a change of attitude." His optimism depended heavily on a change of attitude in Washington, as Harriman emphasized in a personal letter to Hopkins on September 10, suggesting that he return home and report to the President "at the earliest convenient time and place." With the end of the war in sight, he wrote, the Russian relationship had taken a "startling turn":

> I have been conscious since early in the year of a division among Stalin's advisers on the question of cooperation with us. It is now my feeling that those who oppose the kind of co-operation we expect have recently been getting their way and the policy appears to be crystallizing to force us and the British to accept all Soviet policies, backed by the strength and prestige of the Red Army.
>
> Demands on us are becoming insistent. You have seen a part of it in the negotiations over financial terms of the [Lend-Lease] Protocol in Washington. We have other examples here. The general attitude seems to be that it is our obligation to help Russia and accept her policies because she has won the war for us.
>
> I am convinced that we can divert this trend but only if we materially change our policy toward the Soviet Government. I have evidence that they have misinterpreted our generous attitude toward them as a sign of weakness, and acceptance of their policies. Time has come when we must make clear what we expect of them as the price of our goodwill. Unless we take issue with the present policy there is every indication the Soviet Union will become a world bully wherever their interests are involved. This policy will reach into China and the Pacific as well when they can turn their attention in that direction. No written agreements can be of any value unless they are carried out in a spirit of give and take, and recognition of the interests of other people.

I am disappointed but not discouraged. The job of getting the Soviet Government to play a decent role in international affairs is, however, going to be more difficult than we had hoped. The favorable factors are still the same. Ninety per cent of the Russian people want friendship with us and it is much to the interest of the Soviet Government to develop it. It is our problem to strengthen the hand of those around Stalin who want to play the game along our lines and to show Stalin that the advice of the counselors of a tough policy is leading him into difficulties . . . I am not going to propose any drastic action but a firm but friendly *quid pro quo* attitude.

Hopkins replied on September 12 that while he and the President were disposed to listen, it would be a mistake for the Ambassador to leave Moscow at that moment. He advised Harriman to wait for "a green light" from Washington.

The Secretary of State, meanwhile, had developed his own anxieties about future relationships with the Russians. Hull till then had not been overly concerned with Soviet behavior in Poland. What troubled him more was Russia's position on voting procedures in the Security Council of the proposed United Nations organization. In the Dumbarton Oaks Conference, which had begun on August 21, Ambassador Gromyko had insisted that Russia (and the other great powers) must have the widest possible veto powers, including the right to block consideration of disputes in which they were directly involved. "I have begun to wonder," Hull wrote in a personal message to Harriman dated September 18, "whether Stalin and the Kremlin have determined to reverse their policy of cooperation with their Western Allies apparently decided upon at Moscow and Teheran and to pursue a contrary course. In deciding how to meet this change in Russian attitude, I should greatly value the benefit of your estimate of the present trend of Soviet policy."

In a long, analytical reply on September 20, Harriman wrote that he did not believe the Kremlin was reversing its policy. Recent events perhaps were now revealing what that policy goal had been all along —to establish a Russian sphere of influence extending through Eastern Europe and the Balkans:

I believe the Soviets consider that we accepted at Moscow their position that although they would keep us informed they had the right to settle their problems with their western neighbors unilaterally. Then, too, words have a different connotation to the Soviets than they have to us. When they speak of insisting on "friendly governments" in their neighboring

countries, they have in mind something quite different from
what we would mean. With Czechoslovakia they have insisted
upon a military alliance. Although they guaranteed Czechoslovakia non-interference in internal affairs, they insisted that
Benes should agree to give a prominent position in his national
government to the Communist party. As they appear satisfied
with the attitude of Benes' Government, these were the only
conditions imposed.

In the case of Poland, however, where there is not the
same political stability and where greater suspicion of Soviet
good intents exists, they are insisting on a hand-picked government which will ensure Soviet domination. It is too early to
judge how far this policy will be carried in other neighboring
countries or how far they will insist in the future on subservi-
ence to the Moscow will. In terms that we could understand, I
believe that it is their intention to have a positive sphere of
influence over their western neighbors . . . It is also too early
to judge how far they expect to extend Soviet practices in
these states on such questions as secret police (thereby eliminating personal freedom), control of the press and controlled
education. It can be argued that American interests need not
be concerned over the affairs of this area. What frightens me,
however, is that when a country begins to extend its influence
by strong-arm methods beyond its borders under the guise
of security it is difficult to see how a line can be drawn. If the
policy is accepted that the Soviet Union has a right to penetrate her immediate neighbors for security, penetration of the
next immediate neighbors becomes at a certain time equally
logical . . .

At the present time I believe they certainly expect us to
give them a free hand with their western neighbors. They are
therefore most suspicious that this policy will be affected if
they agree to refrain from voting on disputes in which the
Soviet Government is involved.

The answer, Harriman argued, was an American foreign policy that
took "a definite interest" in solving the problems of each country as
they arose instead of giving the Russians a free hand. This would lead
to some unpleasant situations, but if the United States was sufficiently
insistent on holding the Soviets to decent standards of behavior, the
Kremlin would accede.

When we oppose them we must be certain that we are
right, and be clear in advance how far we are ready to go. In
minor matters, the registering of our objection may be suffi-

cient . . . When it comes to matters of greater importance, we should make it plain that their failure to conform to our concepts will affect our willingness to cooperate with them, for example, in material assistance for reconstruction. They should be made promptly to feel specific results from our displeasure. Lastly, on matters that are vital to us and on which we can find no compromise (as I understand, from what you say, is the case in connection with the voting of the four powers) I believe we should make them understand, patiently but firmly, that we cannot accept their point of view and that we are prepared to take the consequences if they adhere to their position. In such cases, I am satisfied that in the last analysis Stalin will back down.* We have seen him reverse his decision in connection with aid to the insurgents in Warsaw.

Stalin's reversal, unfortunately, had not come until September 9, and by that late date the Germans had overpowered much of the Warsaw resistance. Mikolajczyk heard the news from Clement Attlee the following day, Churchill having left London for a second conference with Roosevelt at Quebec. The Kremlin at long last had yielded to the Prime Minister's appeals, Attlee said, agreeing that Allied planes could land on Soviet airfields "provided that a plan of such operations will be submitted to the Soviet authorities and will be agreed upon."[5]

Beginning on the night of September 13, Soviet planes tried to drop food to the people of Warsaw. Five days later, after a delay caused by weather, the Americans sent over a large group of bombers which dropped supplies from high altitude and then landed behind Soviet lines. The Soviet air force also reappeared over the city, bombing German airfields nearby. But the airdropped supplies, for the most part, fell in territory controlled by the Germans. And Rokossovsky's army, after completing its occupation of the Praga suburb on September 15, still made no effort to cross the river.

General Berling, a Polish officer under Russian orders, begged for permission to attempt a crossing with four infantry battalions of Polish troops. He was ferried across the Vistula and managed to hold a shallow bridgehead on the west bank for a few hours but his plan to link up with the beleaguered underground fighters failed.

When Harriman and Clark Kerr saw Stalin together on September 23, he belatedly acknowledged that the fighters of Warsaw had good

---

* Stalin, in fact, softened his hard-line position on voting procedures in the United Nations Security Council during the Yalta Conference. He finally accepted the U.S. position on this point when Hopkins and Harriman saw him together in June 1945.

reason, after all, to rise up against the Germans and for the first time showed a degree of sympathy. With disarming frankness, Stalin admitted that he had misjudged the motives of the Warsaw insurgents:

> He stated that it was now understood why the insurgency had started prematurely. The Germans had threatened to deport all the male population from Warsaw upon the approach of the Red Army. It thus became necessary for the men to rise up and fight—they had no other choice as they were faced with death either way. As a result most of the population of Warsaw went underground and started resistance.

When Harriman asked how the battle for Warsaw was progressing, Stalin defended the Red Army's failure to storm the river. He spoke of the Vistula as a "tremendous obstacle":

> It was impossible to get tanks across the river because of continual heavy German shelling, and it was difficult to carry on operations without tanks. Even medium tanks could not be ferried across the river because of German vigilance. The Russian plan was to encircle the city and to cut the German communications so that the Nazis would find themselves in a "mousetrap." They could not take Warsaw by a frontal attack because of the advantageous position of the Germans.
>
> I inquired whether contact had been made with the resistance groups in Warsaw. Marshal Stalin replied that some infantry battalions had been ferried across the Vistula to support the resistance groups. These were Polish troops—four infantry battalions—and they had been transferred on General Berling's insistence against the better judgment of the Red Army. They had suffered great losses and they would have to be withdrawn.
>
> I inquired whether fighting was still going on in Warsaw. Marshal Stalin replied that after Praga had been taken the Russians got a clearer picture of the Warsaw situation. The insurgents were still fighting in four different isolated parts of the city. They were attempting to defend themselves but they had no offensive ability. They had beaten off some German attacks but could not emerge from their positions of hiding. They had no artillery and were equipped only with rifles and pistols. The Russians had dropped mortars, tommy guns, food and medicinal supplies and the Red Army was in contact with the groups both by radio and by men who got back and forth by swimming the river. It was now clear, he continued, that

little of the supplies dropped by the American and British planes had actually gotten to the Poles. Most of these supplies had been scattered by the wind, in some cases up to 30 kilometers away.

Harriman found Stalin's extraordinary admission hard to explain. "Perhaps Molotov had never fully or accurately reported Clark Kerr's or my representations," he later remarked. "Stalin may have been misinformed by his NKVD. To me, nothing could excuse his outrageous denial of help for so very long. But the episode again underlined the importance of getting to Stalin directly on matters of importance."

It was too late, in any event, for last-minute heroics. After sixty-two days of front-line battle, the exhausted Warsaw insurgents laid down their arms on October 2. Roughly one quarter of the city's population, nearly 250,000 men, women and children, had been killed or wounded in the fighting. Of the underground army's 40,000 members, 15,000 were dead. The Germans also had paid a heavy price in spite of their enormous military superiority—10,000 dead, 9,000 wounded and some 7,000 missing. (Three months were to pass before the Red Army entered Warsaw. It found the entire city in ruins, so bitter had been the hand-to-hand fighting. The broken streets were still littered with unburied bodies.)

The memory of Warsaw's martyrdom was to scar the relationship between Russians and Poles, including Communist Poles, for all the years to come. Just as virtually all Poles to this day, regardless of personal ideology, share the common Western belief that the Russians were responsible for the massacre of the Katyn Forest.

THE POLISH AGONY had preoccupied Churchill and Roosevelt throughout August and much of September. Now they met a second time at Quebec to lay their plans for the final defeat of Germany. During the nine months since Teheran, the military outlook had been totally transformed. Hitler's downfall was now assured; Allied armies were converging on German territory from west and east. No one could say with assurance whether the war would end in a matter of weeks or months, but the end was so palpably near that detailed decisions could not be postponed much longer. On September 23 Harriman and Clark Kerr put before Stalin the decisions reached at Quebec:

> 1. NORTHWEST EUROPE—Our intention is to press on with all speed to destroy the German armed forces and penetrate into the heart of Germany. The best opportunity to defeat the enemy in the west lies in striking at the Ruhr and the Saar since the enemy will concentrate there the remainder of his

available forces in the defense of these essential areas. The northern line of approach clearly has advantages over the southern and it is essential that before bad weather sets in we should open up the northern ports, particularly Rotterdam and Antwerp. It is on the left, therefore, that our main effort will be exerted.

    2. ITALY—Our present operations in Italy will result in either: (a) The forces of Kesselring will be routed, in which event it should be possible to undertake a rapid regrouping and a pursuit toward the Ljubljana Gap; or (b) Kesselring will succeed in effecting an orderly retreat, in which event we may have to be content this year with the clearing of the plains of Lombardy. The progress of the battle will determine our future action. Plans are being prepared for an amphibious operation to be carried out if the situation so demands on the Istrian peninsula.

    3. THE BALKANS—We will continue operations of our air forces and commando-type operations.

    4. JAPAN—With the ultimate objective of invading the Japanese homeland we have agreed on further operations to intensify in all theaters the offensive against the Japanese.

    5. Plans were agreed upon for the prompt transfer of power after the collapse of Germany to the Pacific theater.

ROOSEVELT

CHURCHILL

Stalin responded warmly to this information. Commenting on the success of Allied operations in France, he said to Harriman and Clark Kerr, "They are most bold and daring. Great risks have been taken in driving wedges into the German lines. But no success can be attained without risks. The operations in the west have never been equaled here." Once again, as at the time of the Normandy landings, he paid an ungrudging tribute to his allies.

He also showed great satisfaction over the plan to capture the Ruhr and Saar. Before long, he said, the Red Army would take Katowice and Upper Silesia. Then Hitler would have lost his coal and much of his basic industry—in the east as well as the west. When Clark Kerr mentioned that the Allies also were contemplating operations in Greece before long, Stalin responded, "Good! It is high time!"

Harriman then reopened the question of joint military planning for the final stages of the war against Japan. In a message to Roosevelt, marked "For the eyes of the President only," Harriman reported:

    In discussing the Pacific war I explained that the plans referred to in your message covered the use of British and

American resources. Stalin inquired whether we wished to bring Japan to her knees without Russian assistance or whether you wished, as you suggested in Teheran, Russian participation. The British Ambassador and I both assured him that Russian participation was desired but that no plans could be made for the use of Soviet resources until Marshal Stalin was ready to initiate discussions. He then stated that there was no change in his attitude as he had expressed it to you at Teheran. Russia is ready to participate in the war against Japan after Germany is defeated . . .

He was somewhat surprised that after the assurances he had given at Teheran we were not taking into account in our planning the participation of Russia and he appeared anxious to know specifically what role we would want Russia to play. He gave every indication of being ready and willing to co-operate but did not want to be an uninvited participant. It seems clear that we will get greater cooperation from him if we will suggest the operations that we would like the Russians to undertake, rather than wait their proposals. Because of this new aspect General Deane is cabling the Joint Chiefs of Staff for more detailed instructions than he has previously received.

I strongly recommend that we follow the course Stalin has indicated and that General Deane be authorized to discuss with the Red Army staff, in broad outline at least, our Pacific strategy and to propose the full measure of Russian participation desired.

Stalin showed no immediate interest, however, in discussing arrangements for the use of Soviet air bases in the Maritime Provinces by the American Air Forces, a matter he had promised to deal with months before. "That is not the most important question," he said to Harriman, adding that the Russians would have to move some twenty-five to thirty divisions to the Far East before they could play their part against the Japanese.

Stalin was more forthcoming when Harriman asked for permission to send 500 trucks with GI drivers across Soviet territory by way of Teheran and Alma Ata all the way to China for use there by the American air force. General Deane and Harriman had been pressing this request upon subordinate Soviet officials for many months without result. "Stalin agreed readily," Harriman reported, "and appeared not to have known before of our request. He even offered to supply trucks from Russia if they were needed quickly, to be replaced at a later date."

Encouraged by Stalin's reaction, Harriman then reopened another subject which had been waiting for a Soviet decision—the need to coordinate military operations now that Allied armies were converging on Germany from two directions. He proposed that a tripartite military committee be established in Moscow for this purpose. Stalin preferred to call it a commission. Committees, he said, existed to make decisions, and this body, after all, would be purely consultative. Harriman offered to accept any title that suited Stalin. The important thing, he said, was to get the machinery set up. Stalin inquired who the members would be, and when Harriman nominated General Deane to represent the United States he seemed well satisfied, until Clark Kerr added that Lieutenant General M. B. Burrows, Deane's counterpart in Moscow, would be the British member. There Stalin unexpectedly drew the line.

"The Soviet military people," he said, "are reluctant to deal with General Burrows. It is apparent that General Burrows has no respect for the Russian military and this feeling is vice versa." The British ambassador did his best to defend Burrows, but Stalin was not to be swayed. Marshal A. M. Vasilievsky and other senior officers of the Red Army had told him, Stalin said, that General Burrows considered them "savages." Accordingly, they would refuse to work with Burrows, whom they, in turn, considered altogether too arrogant. On a trip to the front in July, General Burrows evidently had got off on the wrong foot with Vasilievsky, the Red Army's Chief of Staff. General Deane at first attributed their misunderstanding to Burrows' unconscious air of superiority. It later developed, however, that the Russians had planted listening devices in each room of the British military mission, which was housed in the former Czechoslovak legation, and must have overheard private comments by General Burrows that were distinctly uncomplimentary to the Red Army. (After Burrows had left Moscow, an American technician sent by Harriman to look over the British mission dug out thirty "bugs," all of them linked to a listening post across the street.) Harriman asked Stalin how the Russians felt about General Deane. He was greatly reassured by Stalin's reply—that his generals held Deane in the highest respect. To Harriman, this statement implied that the NKVD had not succeeded in tapping Deane's office.

Before leaving Stalin, Harriman on instructions from the President reopened the question of the next Big Three meeting. Roosevelt, he said, was thinking about November, after the election, and since it was too late in the year for Alaska, he proposed a meeting somewhere in the Mediterranean. Such a meeting would, of course, be most desirable, Stalin said, but he feared that his doctors would not allow him to travel. Old age was creeping up on him, he complained. In years past he could shake off an attack of the grippe in two or three days but now it seemed to take a week or two. Harriman praised the healing effect of the Mediterranean sun. But his doctors insisted, Stalin said, "that any change of climate would have a bad effect." He offered to send Molotov, who had his complete confidence. To this, Molotov remarked that he could never replace Marshal Stalin. "You are too modest," Stalin replied, favoring his first deputy with a kindly glance. Harriman assured Stalin that while the President was always glad to see Molotov, he hoped there would be second thoughts in the Kremlin. Conceivably the doctors would change their minds or Stalin perhaps would change his doctors. This humorous suggestion led Stalin to observe that if he had faithfully followed the advice of his doctors, he would long since have been in his grave. Doctors were always too cautious, he said. Healthy people could fly wherever they liked. Churchill, for example, that "desperate fellow," was forever flying around the world, Stalin said, with obvious admiration. So the time and place of the next Big Three meeting were deferred temporarily.

Churchill, however, was not disposed to wait until the American election was out of the way and Stalin had his doctors' permission to travel again. Believing that events were fast outrunning the agreements reached at Teheran, and encouraged by Stalin's cordiality toward Harriman and Clark Kerr, the Prime Minister decided to go to Moscow himself. The Russian armies had rolled over most of the Baltic region. They had occupied Bulgaria and Rumania while advancing into Hungary and Yugoslavia. Now they stood on the frontiers of Turkey and Greece, raising in Churchill's mind definite anxieties over the future of southeastern Europe. (The Prime Minister, as early as May 4, had put the question to Eden: "Are we going to acquiesce in the Communization of the Balkans and perhaps of Italy?") The fate of Poland was uppermost in Churchill's mind. In a matter of days or weeks the Red Army could be expected to cross the Vistula and sweep westward across the Polish plain. What then? By a timely discussion of all these matters with Stalin, Churchill hoped to work out agreements that would safeguard the national independence of Poland and Greece. To Roosevelt, Churchill wrote on September 29:

> The two great objects we have in mind would be, firstly, to clinch his [Stalin's] coming in against Japan, and, secondly, to try to effect an amicable settlement with Poland. There are other points too concerning Yugoslavia and Greece which we would also discuss. . . . Averell's assistance would of course be welcomed by us, or perhaps you could send Stettinius or Marshall. I feel certain that personal contact is essential.[6]

The President's lukewarm reply the following day suggested that

Washington did not welcome the idea of a Churchill-Stalin tête-à-tête concerning the Far East. "It is my opinion," the President wrote, "that Stalin is at the present time sensitive about any doubt as to his intention to help us in the Orient. At your request I will direct Harriman to give you any assistance that you may desire. It does not appear practical or advantageous for me to be represented by Stettinius or Marshall." Hopkins had become particularly concerned lest Churchill enter into agreements with Stalin that would appear to commit the United States, even though it took no part in the Moscow conference. On October 4 he persuaded Roosevelt to send a message to Stalin, through Harriman, making clear that the Prime Minister was not authorized to speak for the United States:

> I am sure you understand that in this global war there is literally no question, military or political, in which the United States is not interested. I am firmly convinced that the three of us, and only the three of us, can find the solution of the questions still unresolved. In this sense, while appreciating Mr. Churchill's desire for the meeting, I prefer to regard your forthcoming talks with the Prime Minister as preliminary to a meeting of the three of us, which can take place any time after the elections here as far as I am concerned.
>
> I am suggesting under the circumstances, if you and the Prime Minister approve, that my Ambassador in Moscow be present at your coming conference as an observer for me. Mr. Harriman naturally would not be in position to commit this Government in respect to the important matters which very naturally will be discussed by you and Mr. Churchill.

The President expanded on his misgivings in a covering message to Harriman:

> Quite frankly, I can tell you, but only for you and not to be communicated under any circumstances to the British or the Russians, that I would have preferred very much to have the next conference between the three of us for the very reasons stated to Marshal Stalin. My hope is that this bilateral conference should be nothing more than a preliminary exploration by the British and Russians, leading up to a full-dress meeting between the three of us. Therefore you should bear in mind that there are no subjects of discussion that I can anticipate between Marshal Stalin and the Prime Minister in which I will not be greatly interested. Consequently it is of importance that Mr. Hull and I have complete freedom of action when

this conference is over. Immediately upon the conclusion of the discussions I will expect you to come home. During the talks you will naturally keep me and Mr. Hull fully and currently advised.

While the message was on its way, on the evening of October 4, Harriman had visited Stalin to present him with a portrait bust of the President by Jo Davidson.* The gift marked the third anniversary of the signing of the first Lend-Lease protocol providing wartime assistance to the Soviet Union, which Harriman had negotiated in 1941. Stalin, appearing deeply touched, kept his eyes fixed on the bust through the greater part of his conversation with Harriman. "He thought it was not only an excellent likeness but a fine work of art," Harriman reported. At one point in the conversation Stalin got up from the conference table on which the bust was resting to survey the room. He decided the Roosevelt bust ought to sit on a pedestal about a foot and a half higher than the tabletop; again that astonishing attention to detail.

Harriman took the occasion to assure Stalin that there had never been a doubt in the President's mind regarding eventual Soviet participation in the war against Japan. Roosevelt was much pleased to learn, Harriman added, that the planning talks would start in just a few days. Stalin volunteered that since their last conversation he in fact had instructed General Shevchenko, the commander of Far Eastern Ground Forces, and General Zhegelev, head of the Far Eastern Air Forces, to return to Moscow for planning talks with General Deane.

Upon returning from the Kremlin, Harriman found the message from Roosevelt directing him to participate in the Churchill-Stalin talks as an observer. "I accepted it," Harriman recalled, "but I was quite unhappy with the President's attitude. So far as Poland, at least, was concerned, I felt that Hopkins and the President should have encouraged Churchill to go ahead and settle the matter with Stalin, if he could. The clock was ticking and I felt the opportunity slipping away. Hopkins, I suspect, was too much out of it—his health being what it was—to realize how vitally important it was." The following day Harriman wrote the President:

> Your instructions are clearly understood. There is one subject on which I had hoped a definite understanding with Stalin might be reached by the Prime Minister, namely the Polish situation. It seems clear that a solution becomes more

---

* Having accepted a gift of two horses from Stalin, Harriman felt it proper to present him in return with a gift of equivalent value.

difficult the longer the situation drifts. I assume you will have no objection if the Prime Minister can work something out with Stalin, provided you are not involved or committed at this time to any line of policy.

Stalin, who received the President's message on October 5, was just as puzzled by it. In Harriman's view, the President's implied warning that any agreements worked out in Moscow would not bind or commit the United States may have diminished Stalin's interest in reaching decisions with Churchill. Stalin, at any rate, showed a degree of discomfiture in his own response, dated October 9:

> I am somewhat embarrassed by your message of October 5. I had supposed that Mr. Churchill was coming to Moscow in accordance with agreement reached with you at Quebec. However, it happens that this supposition of mine does not appear to correspond to reality. I do not know with what questions Mr. Churchill and Mr. Eden are coming to Moscow. I have so far not been informed . . .

The Prime Minister and Eden arrived in Moscow the same afternoon. Before calling on Stalin that evening, Churchill told Harriman of his disappointment that Roosevelt had refused to authorize American participation. Churchill promised, however, to keep Harriman fully informed and to see that he was invited to the larger meetings.

Harriman, accordingly, did not attend the first Churchill-Stalin session at which the Prime Minister, after swiftly arranging that Mikolajczyk should be invited back to Moscow, put his notorious spheres-of-influence proposal on the table.* It took several days before Churchill told Harriman the full story, much as he later recounted it in his history of the war:

> The moment was apt for business, so I said, "Let us settle about our affairs in the Balkans. Your armies are in Rumania and Bulgaria. We have interests, missions, and agents there. Don't let us get at cross-purposes in small ways. So far as Britain and Russia are concerned, how would it do for you to have ninety per cent predominance in Rumania, for us to have ninety per cent of the say in Greece, and go fifty-fifty about Yugoslavia?"

Churchill records that while his words were being translated he wrote out the percentages on a half-sheet of paper, adding a 50-50 split for

---

* In his own account of the meeting, Churchill erroneously listed Harriman among the participants. Harriman's calendar and his messages to Roosevelt leave no room for doubt that the Ambassador was otherwise occupied.

Hungary and conceding to the Russians a 75-25 predominance in Bulgaria.

> I pushed this across to Stalin, who had by then heard the translation. There was a slight pause. Then he took his blue pencil and made a large tick upon it, and passed it back to us. It was all settled in no more time than it takes to set down. . . .
>
> After this there was a long silence. The pencilled paper lay in the center of the table. At length I said, "Might it not be thought rather cynical if it seemed we had disposed of these issues, so fateful to millions of people, in such an offhand manner? Let us burn the paper." "No, you keep it," said Stalin.[7]

The same guilty impulse that prompted Churchill to suggest burning the paper a few minutes after writing down the percentages doubtless led him not to tell Harriman of his strange bargain with Stalin, except in bits and pieces, spaced over several days. On October 10, for example, unaware that the question had been decided, Harriman reported to Roosevelt: "On matters in the Balkans, Churchill and Eden will try to work out some sort of spheres of influence with the Russians, the British to have a free hand in Greece and the Russians in Rumania and perhaps other countries. The British will attempt to retrieve a position of equal influence in Yugoslavia. They can probably succeed in the former but I am doubtful about the latter objective." In a joint message to Roosevelt the same day, Churchill and Stalin said no more than: "We have to consider the best way of reaching an agreed policy about the Balkan countries including Hungary and Turkey."

At lunch that day Harriman learned that in the first draft of the message to Roosevelt, Churchill had included the phrase "having regard to our varying duties toward them." Stalin had suggested that the phrase should be deleted because it so clearly implied a sphere-of-influence arrangement. Upon hearing this, Harriman told Stalin that the President would be glad the phrase had been eliminated because he had so carefully stressed the importance of having all major questions decided by the Big Three. "Stalin said he was glad to hear this," Harriman reported to Roosevelt, "and, reaching behind the Prime Minister's back, shook my hand."

On October 11 Churchill put his intentions somewhat more directly in a message to Roosevelt:

> It is absolutely necessary we should try to get a common mind about the Balkans, so that we may prevent civil war

breaking out in several countries when probably you and I would be in sympathy with one side and U.J. [Stalin] with the other. I shall keep you informed of all this, and nothing will be settled except preliminary agreements between Britain and Russia, subject to further discussion and melting-down with you. On this basis I am sure you will not mind our trying to have a full meeting of minds with the Russians.[8]

But Harriman did not learn that percentages had been committed to paper until midmorning on October 12, when he called on the Prime Minister at the guesthouse provided for him by the Soviet government.

"I vividly recall Churchill's being in bed, where it was his custom to dictate letters and memoranda," Harriman later wrote. "He read me a letter he had drafted for Stalin, giving his interpretation of the percentages agreed to at their first meeting three days earlier. I told him that I was certain both Roosevelt and Hull would repudiate the letter, if it was sent. At this point Eden came into the bedroom and Churchill said to him: 'Anthony, Averell doesn't think that we should send this letter to Stalin.' The letter was never sent and I believe that my warning to Churchill persuaded him not to go ahead with it.*

"I don't understand now, and I do not believe I understood at the time, just what Churchill thought he was accomplishing by these percentages. I know that he wanted a free hand in Greece, with the support of the United States, and that he wanted to have a hand in the development of the new Yugoslav Government, combining the government-in-exile in England with Tito and his group. Churchill certainly knew that President Roosevelt insisted on keeping a free hand and wanted any decisions deferred until the three could meet together. The interesting thing is that when they did meet, at Yalta, the question of percentages was never again raised."

Poland, however, was too serious a problem to be dealt with in this summary fashion. Britain felt a moral commitment to the government-in-exile and Stalin held the high cards, through the Red Army and the Lublin Committee on the ground. Churchill had persuaded Mikolajczyk ("under dire threats," as he confessed to Hopkins in a message from Moscow dated October 12) to try again to work out a form of national coalition with the Lublin Poles. The threats continued when Mikolajczyk, accompanied by Foreign Minister Tadeusz Romer and Professor Stanislaw Grabski, reached the Soviet capital on

---

* In *Triumph and Tragedy*, Volume VI of Churchill's *The Second World War*, the Prime Minister published his undelivered letter "only as an authentic account of my thoughts" (page 231). He wrote: "In the end I did not send this letter, deeming it wiser to let well alone."

October 12. He had dismissed General Sosnkowski on September 30, as part of a Cabinet reshuffle designed to make his government more acceptable by getting rid of die-hard anti-Russian elements. But Mikolajczyk came with little or no authority to negotiate. He was bound by the terms of a Cabinet memorandum stipulating that the new postwar Poland must have as much territory as before the war, including "in the east the main centers of Polish cultural life and the sources of raw materials." The memorandum also proposed equal representation in the new government for five political parties: four that belonged to the London government-in-exile and the Communist party, which controlled the Lublin Committee.

At Mikolajczyk's first meeting with Stalin and Churchill, which Harriman attended as an observer, he at once found himself under powerful pressure from both the British and the Russians to accept the Curzon Line. When Mikolajczyk balked, Churchill sternly reminded him that the British government was committed to support the Curzon Line, adding in Stalin's presence that this was a poor time for the London Poles and the British government to separate. "I cannot decide this problem," Mikolajczyk pleaded, "for the decision lies with the Polish nation; you would form a very bad opinion of me were I to agree to ceding 40 per cent of the territory of Poland and five million Poles." Stalin interrupted to deny that there were so many Poles in the disputed territory. Most of the people who lived there, he said, were Ukrainians and White Russians. Churchill held out the promise of territorial compensation in the west. "On this basis," he said, "there would be a great Poland; not the same one as was established at Versailles, but still a real home where the Polish people could live in security and prosperity."[9]

Molotov interjected that at the Teheran Conference even Roosevelt had agreed that the Curzon Line was the right boundary between Poland and Russia but that he did not at the time consider it advisable to make his position public. Mikolajczyk showed surprise and shock at this statement. Harriman reported the contretemps to Roosevelt on October 14:

> Molotov did not refer to me for confirmation and I decided it would only make matters worse if I, being present as an observer, had attempted to correct his statement. I talked to Churchill about Molotov's statement afterwards at dinner. He recalls as clearly as I do that although you showed interest in hearing the views of Stalin and Churchill [on] the boundary question, you had expressed no opinion on it one way or the other at Teheran. I intend to tell Molotov privately at the next opportunity that I am sure you will wish that your name

not [be] brought into the discussions again in regard to the boundary question.

The London Poles bitterly criticized Harriman for not having spoken up at once in refutation of Molotov. On October 16 Mikolajczyk handed the Ambassador a letter pointing to the discrepancy between Molotov's version and the assurances which he personally had received from Roosevelt in June to the effect that only Stalin and Churchill had accepted the Curzon Line at Teheran. Harriman explained to Mikolajczyk that the President's remarks had been misinterpreted by the Russians, but he made no serious effort to defend himself.

Upon close examination a day or two later, the record of what Roosevelt actually said at Teheran proved somewhat ambiguous. Harriman could find no trace in Bohlen's minutes, made in the tripartite sessions with Stalin and Churchill, of any Roosevelt statement endorsing the Curzon Line. He found in the minutes of Roosevelt's last private talk with Stalin on December 1, 1943, however, this statement: "He [the President] said personally he agreed with the view of Marshall Stalin as to the necessity of the restoration of the Polish state but would like to see the eastern border moved further to the west and the western border moved even to the Oder River." Roosevelt later explained that he meant to tell Stalin he accepted the general idea of shifting Poland's frontiers to the west, but did not intend specific approval of the Curzon Line.

Harriman, after studying the Teheran record, wrote a memorandum marked "To be shown to no one except Mr. Hopkins," suggesting that the President's meaning might have been warped in translation. Certainly, the language of the official minutes was sufficiently imprecise to permit more than one interpretation, though it was not clear whether Roosevelt had been careless with words or Bohlen, the interpreter and notetaker, had missed a nuance. Harriman also remembered that during his visit to Washington in May, the President had said to him that the Curzon Line seemed a reasonable basis for settling the eastern boundary of Poland, but that he was puzzled over the proper solution for Lwow. This message he had delivered to Stalin in June, as instructed by the President, another consideration that made it awkward for Harriman to dispute Molotov's assertion.

Churchill, who had long since accepted the Curzon Line, stepped up the pressure on Mikolajczyk day by day. "We are not going to wreck the peace of Europe because of quarrels between Poles," he threatened. "Unless you accept the frontier you are out of business forever. The Russians will sweep through your country and your people will be liquidated. You are on the verge of annihilation."[10]

In calmer moments, Churchill recognized that Mikolajczyk and Romer sincerely wanted to work out a compromise with the Russians. He understood that most of their Cabinet colleagues in London would certainly refuse to endorse larger concessions to Moscow and Lublin. The arithmetic of Polish politics in exile was stacked too heavily against them. Nor did Bierut make matters easier by now demanding two-thirds to three-quarters of the seats in the reconstructed Polish government for Lublin, since Mikolajczyk was to become Premier. Churchill tried to help by telling Stalin bluntly after a Kremlin dinner that unless Mikolajczyk received half the places, in addition to his own, the Western world would never accept the new regime's *bona fides* as an independent government. Stalin at first said the 50-50 split might be acceptable but quickly corrected himself to a lower figure. Harriman felt that with sufficient time and effort the matter could be worked out. He warned Romer that it would be a mistake for Mikolajczyk to rush back to London, as he reported to Washington on October 16:

> I told Romer that I would not discuss with him at all the question of the boundary but on the question of getting together with the Lublin Poles I personally felt that he would never again have as good an opportunity as now, on account of the presence of the Prime Minister and Mr. Eden. As much depended on the details of how the relationships could be worked out, I felt that the Prime Minister and Mr. Eden could be of great assistance to him. If he went home, he would find that the relationship between the Poles in Lublin and Moscow would become more and more cemented, bitterness within Poland would be accentuated and nothing but difficulties could be looked forward to. My impression is that Romer sees much more clearly than Mikolajczyk the need for an early solution.

But Mikolajczyk, thoroughly disheartened, insisted on returning to London, leaving the issue unresolved. He and Bierut agreed to meet again in Moscow after Mikolajczyk had a chance to consult his recalcitrant Cabinet colleagues. He assured Harriman before leaving that he and Romer would try to persuade them they must accept the Curzon Line.

Poland apart, the Churchill-Stalin talks produced a hopeful glow within the alliance. Harriman noted in his dispatches the extraordinary courtesies shown to Churchill by Stalin. He went to dinner at the British embassy, for example, an event without precedent which Harriman attended, and in a toast to the absent President made a point of praising the indispensable contribution of the United States to the winning of the war. There was a time, Stalin said in his toast, when Great Britain and Russia between them could handle the affairs of Europe. Together they had defeated Napoleon. They had fought the Germans together in World War I. But in World War II, Britain and Russia could not have prevailed over Germany. He doubted, Stalin said, whether Germany could have been defeated without the full weight of the United States on the side of the Allies.

Stalin also went to the Bolshoi Theater with Churchill, where they were received with thunderous cheers and handclapping. Kathleen Harriman described the scene in a letter to Pamela Churchill:

> Ave and I were invited to sit in the royal box. The P.M. arrived late, with U.J. coming in some minutes afterward, so the audience didn't realize they were there till the lights went on after the first act. A cheer went up (something I've never seen happen here) and U.J. ducked out so that the P.M. could have all the applause for himself, which was a very nice gesture. But the P.M. sent Vishinsky out to get U.J. back and they stood together while the applause went on for many minutes. It was most, most impressive, the sound like a cloudburst on a tin roof. It came from below and above on all sides and the people down in the audience said they were thrilled at seeing the two men standing together. Perhaps this may sound odd to you but that night was the first time probably that most of the audience had seen either man. Stalin hasn't been to the theater since the war started and for him to go with a foreigner was even more amazing.
>
> Between the acts, we went in to a sit-down dinner at which Molotov presided: about 12 of us, all of which was very exciting for me. There were toasts to everyone and Stalin was very amusing when Moly [Molotov] got up and raised his glass to Stalin with a short, conventional phrase about "our great leader." Stalin, after he'd drunk, came back with, "I thought he was going to say something new about me."

Kathleen, prompted by her father, offered a toast to the Soviet artists who had done so much to maintain public morale during the war. Stalin responded with a toast to Miss Harriman, remarking that her presence in Moscow during the difficult war years had helped to raise morale among the Russians. When someone spoke of the Big Three as the Holy Trinity, Stalin said, "If that is so, Churchill must be the Holy Ghost. He flies around so much."

At one of the entertainments for Churchill, Litvinov asked General Deane whether it was true, as reported in *Look* magazine, that

Harriman had a fortune of $100 million. Deane confessed that he did not know. To which Litvinov responded with another question: "How can a man with a hundred million dollars look so sad?"

Perhaps the most significant business transacted during the Churchill visit was handled by Harriman and General Deane, with the Prime Minister's loyal support. This was to discuss Russia's eventual contribution to the defeat of Japan. The American war in the Pacific had been going well. A succession of brilliant naval victories had dangerously weakened the Japanese at sea. Their long supply lines were under constant attack and more than half their merchant fleet had been sunk. But the British and American Joint Chiefs were agreed that before victory could be won, the large, still powerful Japanese armies in China, Manchuria and the home islands would have to be smashed on the ground. In this final campaign, they reckoned, the Russians could decisively assist the Chinese and American forces.

The visit of Churchill and General Sir Alan Brooke, Chief of the Imperial General Staff, gave Harriman his long-awaited opportunity to break the disheartening cycle of Soviet evasions. He suggested to Churchill that since the war in the Far East was chiefly an American responsibility, the British ought to step aside when the matter came up, letting the Americans take the lead in the discussions with Stalin and his generals. The Prime Minister readily agreed.

Accordingly, at the first meeting on October 14, after General Brooke had outlined the plans and prospects on the western front in Europe, General Deane reviewed the progress of the Pacific fighting from the time of Pearl Harbor through the battles of the Coral Sea and Midway, the imminent landing in the Philippines and the plans to invade Japan itself. In behalf of the American Chiefs, he then put three questions to Stalin:

1. How long after the defeat of Germany may we expect Soviet-Japanese hostilities to commence?

2. How much time will be required to build up the Soviet forces in the Far East to the point where they can initiate an offensive?

3. How much of the capacity of the Trans-Siberian railroad can be devoted to the buildup and support of an American strategic air force?

"Young man," Churchill said to Deane, "I admired your nerve in asking Stalin those last three questions. I have no idea that you will get an answer, but there was certainly no harm in asking."[11] The next evening, surprisingly, Stalin came back with his answers:

It would take three months after the defeat of Hitler, he said, before the Red Army could take the offensive against Japan. A reserve of two to three months' supply would have to be stockpiled in Siberia before operations could begin because the Trans-Siberian Railroad could not fully support the sixty Red Army divisions—twice the number already there—needed to launch and sustain a big offensive. Accordingly, while bases in the Maritime Provinces would be made available to the American air force, it would have to be supplied across the Pacific. The United States Navy also was welcome to use the port of Petropavlovsk.

In response to a question from Harriman, Stalin firmly promised to take the offensive against Japan three months after the defeat of Germany if two conditions were met: the United States would have to help build up the enormous supply stockpile in Siberia, and "certain political aspects" of Russia's participation would have to be clarified. "The Russians would have to know what they were fighting for," Stalin said. "They had certain claims against Japan." At Teheran on November 30, 1943, Stalin had inquired what his allies were prepared to do for Russia in the Far East, making the point that Vladivostok was not a wholly ice-free port. Roosevelt had mentioned the possibility of turning Dairen into a free port and Churchill had said that Russia's legitimate needs should certainly be satisfied. The fact that Stalin was now asking for both supplies and territory did not visibly disturb the President or the Joint Chiefs when Harriman's report of the conversation reached Washington. Stalin had promised to fight the Japanese armies, not only in Manchuria but also in North China, and Washington seemed well satisfied with the bargain.

There was little disposition in Washington to pick quarrels with the Russians. Before flying home in late October to tell the President and Hopkins of his concern that with victory in Europe assured the Soviets were becoming difficult partners, Harriman received a letter from his old friend James Forrestal, the Secretary of the Navy, who despite the bitterness he later developed still reflected the hopeful domestic mood:

> Dumbarton Oaks I think has done well, although it is not a finished job by a long shot. I think there is general agreement that England, Russia and ourselves have got to play together; it will need patience and tolerance on the part of all hands to accomplish that—the strains and tensions will increase the farther we get from danger. These are obvious bromides, but I find it is a good thing to keep saying them to oneself because, as you and I found in the 20s, it is easy for success to pry the best friends apart.
>
> There is great admiration here for the Russians and, I think, an honest desire, even on the part of so-called "cap-

italist quarters," to find an accommodation with them. Some of the Russians' enthusiastic friends, however, hinder rather than help the result we are after. Which, as I see it, is a realistic, common-sense awareness that together the three of us can secure world peace for a good many years, but that if we drift apart another war will come in due course.

CHAPTER XVI

Molotov's "Unconventional Request" for Postwar Credits

RETURNING FROM MOSCOW in late October, Harriman found Washington in the grip of fourth-term election fever. At luncheon on October 24 in the sun room of the White House with his daughter, Anna, and Harriman, Roosevelt predicted a close race, although he hoped for a moderate majority in the Electoral College. "Whether he believed it or not I was not able to judge," Harriman observed in his notes on that first conversation. "The President," he thought, "looked well but very much thinner than when I had seen him in May and therefore the lines in his face made him look considerably older. He was, however, vigorous and determined in spirit."

Until the election was over, Roosevelt said, he felt "helpless to do anything constructive" about the Polish question. Harriman noted that the President "consistently shows very little interest in Eastern European matters except as they affect sentiment in America." In other respects the Ambassador found Roosevelt a good listener. "The President could not have been more cordial," he noted. "He listened to what I had to say, which of course I made brief and direct. He did not, as he sometimes does, spend a lot of time talking about his general ideas and past experiences. The lunch started at about 1:15 and I heard afterward that he ruined his afternoon appointments by remaining at lunch until three o'clock."

Harriman asked permission to make a radio speech in support of the President's re-election, and Roosevelt agreed that it would be useful. So the Ambassador bought fifteen minutes of air time on the

National Broadcasting Company network at his own expense, and on the evening of November 3, urged his countrymen to vote once more for Roosevelt:

> "If the people of this country fail to re-elect Roosevelt, doubt and suspicion of our intent cannot fail to be engendered.
>
> "Regardless of what Dewey's real objectives may now be, regardless of whether he now realizes the President has been right, his past views are well known. It is also well known abroad that he is supported by our isolationist groups. If Dewey is elected our leadership in the world cannot help but be impaired, for some time at least. There is no time to rebuild confidence. The solution of problems cannot wait. Never in the history of the world has a nation had so great an opportunity to play such a vital role in affecting the course of history, in giving leadership to the fulfillment of the hopes and aims of the peoples of the world for peace and security.
>
> "Never in the history of the world has one man—Roosevelt —had the confidence of the peoples of so many nations and of their leaders. This confidence is, for us in the United States, an invaluable asset in obtaining decisions which will further our interests and build the kind of world in which we want to live. This confidence we can ill afford to lose at this critical and formative time."

The fact that a serving ambassador should have felt free to campaign openly for his President may today seem remarkable. "To me it seemed far more honest to let people know how I felt," Harriman recalled, "than to pretend that I had lost all political emotions upon accepting a government position. Today ambassadors are supposed to be nonpolitical—and of course they are not." No less remarkable in hindsight was the fact that Harriman could buy access to a nationwide audience for $5,000. The heavy hand of television had yet to inflate the cost of campaigning.

Harriman saw the President again when he returned from voting and receiving the returns at Hyde Park. Roosevelt won by less than a landslide but respectably enough with 432 electoral votes out of 531.

Looking "somewhat tired but quite relaxed," Roosevelt was full of election talk. Harriman's notes indicate that the President had developed an uncharacteristic hostility toward his Republican opponent, Thomas E. Dewey:

> He told me that he had never been so bitter about any opponent as Dewey as the campaign developed because of Dewey's dirty tactics. He said he had become much more determined to win as a result.

He expressed the hope that Dewey would no longer be an important Republican leader and that the country would be in safe hands if the leadership of the Republican party went to such a man as Saltonstall or Stassen, both of whom he respected greatly. I drew the inference, though he in no sense said so, that he considered the next President would probably be a Republican.

The President's interest in Leverett Saltonstall, a Boston aristocrat just elected to the Senate whose background and Groton-Harvard schooling was of a piece with his own, seemed to Harriman wholly predictable. Roosevelt saw in Harold Stassen, the youthful governor of Minnesota, a progressive Midwestern Republican like Henry Wallace and Harold Ickes, both members of his original Cabinet, who could be expected to lead the party in a new direction after the war. (It seemed obvious to Harriman that Roosevelt recalled Stassen from wartime service as a naval commander on Admiral Halsey's staff in the Pacific and appointed him to the United States delegation to the founding session of the United Nations in the hope of advancing his political career.)

In mid-conversation Roosevelt's grandson Curtis Dall wandered into the room with his dog, a Labrador retriever. The President chatted briefly with the boy, who then wandered off again to play in the garden. Harriman noted that Roosevelt, accustomed to such interruptions, showed real affection for the boy and the dog.

Harriman had three more talks with Roosevelt—on November 10, 17 and 18—before he returned to Europe. They discussed Stalin's proposal that the next Big Three conference be held in the Black Sea area. The President did not at first think much of that idea. The Navy felt it would be unsafe for a battleship to go through the Dardanelles, he said, because so many mines had been sown in those waters. Nor was he willing to fly to Odessa or the Crimea because both Churchill's physician, Lord Moran, and his own Admiral McIntire feared that all kinds of diseases were rampant in that part of the world, "from dysentery to bubonic plague." Harriman assured him that the Crimea was entirely suitable. The weather would be mild and the President in any case would be bringing his own food, as well as his Filipino messboys.

Unpersuaded, Roosevelt then suggested that Stalin might meet him in Jerusalem. Harriman quickly discounted this notion by pointing out that since the Soviet government had taken an anti-Zionist position in order to win support in the Arab world, it would hardly welcome a meeting in Palestine, the center of that historic controversy. The President offered the alternative of a meeting in Italy or Sicily in the last days of January or early February. By that time, he said, Stalin could perhaps travel by rail all the way from Moscow to the Dalmatian coast of Yugoslavia and there board an American warship for the final leg of his journey across the Adriatic Sea.

The President told Harriman that he had promised Churchill he would visit England briefly while in Europe. "He would not address Parliament but simply drive through the streets, have a meal perhaps with the King and meet with Churchill and his Cabinet," Harriman noted.

Harriman still found it difficult to capture the President's attention for a serious talk about the problems of Poland or Eastern Europe generally. In one of their conversations after the election Roosevelt indicated that "he wanted to have a lot to say about the settlement in the Pacific, but that he considered the European questions were so impossible that he wanted to stay out of them as far as practicable, except for the problems involving Germany." Harriman warned the President that the Polish situation was growing progressively worse and that unless a settlement was reached promptly, the United States was bound to confront some unpleasant choices. But only one aspect of the Polish puzzle seemed to intrigue Roosevelt—the fate of Lwow. According to Harriman's notes:

> The President developed the fantastic idea that Stalin might agree to have the city, which was a Polish island in a sea of Ukrainian peasants, governed by an international committee, leaving it for future plebiscites to decide the outcome. I tried to tell him that it was impossible to have a Polish, capitalistic city in a Ukrainian, socialist countryside. The President saw no problem with that. He said the peasants could come into Lwow and sell their produce to the Poles for roubles. I tried to explain that in the Soviet Union the government took most of the farm produce anyway and that, even if there were no political difficulties, the distribution system he had in mind would not work. I carried it as far as I could until he became annoyed that I was unwilling to dream with him.

When Roosevelt was in a mood for dreaming aloud or romancing (as Harriman sometimes called it), it was wise not to take his flights of the imagination too seriously. This was Roosevelt's way, Harriman had long ago decided, of not then facing up to a definite position.

Roosevelt also talked of personally arbitrating the Russian-Polish boundary dispute or the Russo-Finnish settlement and handing down a decision within a year of the armistice. "He has no conception," Harriman noted, "of the determination of the Russians to settle matters in which they consider that they have a vital interest in their own manner, on their own terms. They will never leave them to the President or anyone else to arbitrate. The President still feels he can persuade Stalin to alter his point of view on many matters that, I am satisfied, Stalin will never agree to."

During their final talk on Poland, Roosevelt for the first time appeared to accept Harriman's argument that Stalin would insist upon a definitive settlement of the Polish boundary without delay instead of leaving it to a plebiscite, as the President at first suggested, or to arbitration in the distant future. The President told Harriman he would not object to the Curzon Line "if the Poles, Russians and British got together on it." But he instructed the Ambassador to explain to Stalin that it would be a fine gesture toward peace and understanding with the new Poland if he could agree to give up Lwow.

"I have tried to impress on the President that our principal interest in Eastern Europe is to see that the Soviets do not set up puppet governments under the Soviet system of government of a few picked men supported by the secret police." Harriman recorded in his notes on the Washington visit. "I do not believe that I have convinced the President of the importance of a vigilant, firm policy in dealing with the political aspects in various Eastern European countries when the problems arise. The Department, however, is fully alive to this necessity unless we wish to turn Eastern and Central Europe over to complete Soviet influence if not domination."

Roosevelt showed more concern and a surer grasp of reality in discussing the Far East. When Harriman on November 10 described Stalin's plan to split the Japanese armies in China and Manchuria by driving all the way to Peking and Kalgan, the President responded with a troubling question: "If the Russians go in, will they ever go out?" It was a question he had not raised in the case of Eastern Europe, perhaps because he knew the answer and felt powerless to affect it.

In China he saw reason for hope, explaining to Harriman that Major General Patrick J. Hurley, an Oklahoma Republican then on a presidential mission to China, had made good progress in his efforts to promote an agreement between the government of Chiang Kai-shek and Mao Tse-tung's Communist forces in Yenan. Under Secretary of State Stettinius, who sat in on the early part of this talk with Roosevelt, raised the question of a successor to Ambassador Clarence E. Gauss, who was about to come home from Chungking. Several names were mentioned, including that of Donald Nelson. Harriman told the President that Nelson would be the wrong choice because of his "egotistical approach to every question and his unwillingness to cooperate with other people." (To his own regret just a few months later, Harriman "put in an oar for General Hurley because of my conviction that he was completely loyal to the President in carrying out his missions and had a shrewd Irish skill in negotiation.") The Ambassador was surprised to find that Stettinius had no recommendations of his own "but put the matter up only for the President's consideration."

On November 17 Harriman gave the President his own impressions of the China tangle, as seen from Moscow:

> I explained why I thought Stalin was so anxious to have a settlement between the Generalissimo and the Communists, namely, so that when he started his offensive against Japan the Communists would protect his right flank. I thought Stalin would cooperate in bringing pressure on the Communists to accept any reasonable deal that the Generalissimo might offer prior to the opening of the Russian campaign.
>
> If, however, a settlement was not reached, I was very fearful that we would have a situation somewhat similar to the Tito situation in Yugoslavia. If the Russians got into China and Manchuria they would back, I thought, the so-called Communist leadership and the terms to the Generalissimo would be very much stiffer. Thus we would have a situation on our hands perhaps impossible of satisfactory solution.

Roosevelt then authorized the Ambassador to ask Stalin "what sort of political agreement he wished before the entry of Russia into the war against Japan." Harriman remarked that he expected no great surprises. Stalin had made clear at Teheran that he wanted to abrogate the Treaty of Portsmouth, imposed upon Czarist Russia after her defeat by Japan in 1905. The use of Manchurian ports and railroads by the Russians would have to be worked out. There might well be difficulties regarding Korea. "Certainly, however," Harriman added, "the overall political question of China was the one which I thought would give us the greatest difficulty as between us and the Russians."

Harriman's luncheon conversation with Roosevelt that day lasted only forty minutes. The President had forgotten that a press conference was scheduled for the early afternoon and he was not dressed for it. "But I have never had a more satisfactory talk," Harriman recorded. "The President kept his mind on the subjects and came to clear-cut decisions."

Before leaving Washington, Harriman lunched again with the President and Hopkins on November 18 to discuss the latest request from Stalin for a two-to-three-month supply stockpile in Siberia. The quantities were impressively large: 860,410 tons of dry cargo and 206,000 tons of liquid cargo, enough to supply a force of 1,500,000 men; 3,000 tanks; 75,000 motor vehicles; 5,000 airplanes. All this had to be delivered across the Pacific by June 30, 1945. Although shipping was still in short supply, Harriman urged that additional ships be made available somehow, stressing that if they were not, Stalin might delay joining the war against Japan. Roosevelt promised to do all he could. "The defeat of Japan without the aid of Russia," he said, "would be extremely difficult and costly and we should do everything to support Stalin's plans, but that Eisenhower must be supported now with all the help that could be furnished."

The President was in a gossipy mood. He told Harriman that he had urged Churchill to proclaim the return of Hong Kong to Chinese rule. Roosevelt, for his part, had promised to persuade Chiang Kai-shek to issue an immediate statement hailing the British action as the most generous in the history of the world, and offering in return to declare Hong Kong for all times a free port under joint British and Chinese control. The Prime Minister, who was not amused, had replied, "I will not give away the British Empire."

With Secretary of State Cordell Hull about to retire, Hopkins and Harriman also discussed the matter of his successor. "Hopkins told me that Wallace wanted the job," Harriman recorded. "But we agreed that Wallace would bring out all the visionary ideas of the President, exaggerate them and get them out in the press, which the President never does. The President does a lot of dreaming but when it comes down to hard decisions his judgment is good and tough." Hopkins said that he was using all his influence to see James F. Byrnes appointed in Hull's place. "I heartily endorsed that," Harriman noted.

He also urged upon both Hopkins and Stettinius the necessity of "briefing the President thoroughly on the subjects that would come up for discussion at the meeting of the Big Three." If the President "did not make up his mind on exactly what he wanted" to accomplish at the conference, Harriman warned, Stalin and Churchill would "get what they wanted and the President would not sufficiently understand what they were after to block it." Both Hopkins and Stettinius agreed that Harriman should join the presidential party several days before the meeting to prepare Roosevelt for his talks with Stalin. The President also told Harriman that he expected him to attend the conference.

On his way back to Moscow, Harriman stopped in London at Roosevelt's request to discuss with Churchill the Polish situation and what the British might do about releasing ships in order to build up the supply stockpile the Russians needed in preparation for their entry into the war against Japan. He also delivered a message from Roosevelt to Mikolajczyk. The letter, in response to a set of questions delivered by the Polish ambassador in Washington, Jan Ciechanowski, spelled out the official United States attitude: support for a strong, free, independent Polish state; the promise of assistance for postwar reconstruction; approval of the transfer of minority populations to and from the territory of Poland in connection with the drawing of new frontiers. But on the point that was crucial for Mikolajczyk—an American guarantee of the new frontiers—Roosevelt's reply was bound to disappoint the Poles:

> In so far as the United States guarantee of any specific frontiers is concerned, I am sure you will understand that this Government, in accordance with its traditional policy, cannot give a guarantee for any specific frontiers. As you know, the United States Government is working for the establishment of a world security organization through which the United States, together with the other member states, will assume responsibility for general security which, of course, includes the inviolability of agreed frontiers.

When Harriman delivered the letter on November 22, he told Mikolajczyk that Roosevelt had instructed him to ask Stalin if he would leave Lwow and the Galician oil fields to Poland. Mikolajczyk replied that he saw no point in such intervention, "since he could not obtain the consent of his associates to any boundary settlement now, even if Stalin would agree to the inclusion of Lwow within Poland." For all but his own Peasant party, Mikolajczyk said, even Lwow was not enough. This attitude, he told Harriman, coupled with the unceasing pressure of Great Britain and America's noncommittal attitude, left him no alternative but to resign. On November 24, in fact, he resigned. His successor, Tomasz Arciszewski, was an old Socialist who had fought the Russians in Czarist times and the Germans in World War II until he was smuggled out of Poland in June 1944. Harriman concluded that with the withdrawal of Mikolajczyk and his party, the London Poles would soon be by-passed. Whatever influence the government-in-exile had once been able to exercise was virtually at an end. On December 31, 1944, the Lublin Committee announced that it had become the Provisional Government of Poland. Then, without consulting the British or American governments, the Soviet Union on January 5 recognized the new regime.

From London, Harriman flew on to liberated Paris, shivering in the late-autumn cold for lack of coal, and from there to Eisenhower's advance headquarters, east of Rheims. This was the famous *manoir* on the golf course, which then looked more like an unmowed hayfield. The *manoir* turned out to be a fairly modest house, large enough to accommodate the Supreme Commander's small staff with a few rooms to spare. Eisenhower himself lived in an elaborate trailer, which was divided into an office and a bedroom. Eisenhower had his personal aide, Brigadier James Gault of the British army, his map room, a number of junior officers to handle his communications, and his personal driver, Kay Summersby. Harriman saw "no reason in the world" for Eisenhower to be off in a field with his little entourage, dozens of miles from his headquarters at Versailles and not appreciably closer to the front. It was Harriman's theory that Bedell Smith, a most loyal and effective chief of staff, probably believed that he could accomplish more with Eisenhower out of the way. The Supreme Commander, of course, was in constant communication on all important decisions. For the rest, Harriman felt, Bedell Smith was in charge of Supreme Headquarters.

At the time of Harriman's visit, the Allied advance was bogged down by flood waters. Eisenhower urged Harriman to spend a day in the field with General Patton's Third Army so that he might explain the situation to Stalin upon his return to Moscow. He found Patton's troops knee-deep in mud and water. The Saar River had overflowed its banks, flooding the countryside. Tanks could not move forward except on the hard-surfaced roads, which were under German artillery fire.

"I had a very interesting day with Patton," Harriman recalled. "At one divisional headquarters he gave the commanding general and his staff unshirted hell for not driving ahead faster. Patton was in one of his toughest moods. In spite of all the mud and the water Patton's cavalrymen's boots were a mirror. He wore his three stars on his helmet and on his car, which was against regulations. But he also showed me that he had an extraordinary understanding of men. At the next divisional headquarters, he applied his talent for leadership to a commander whose exhausted troops, having suffered heavy casualties, were expecting to be relieved. 'If you can make it to the top of that hill,' Patton said, 'it will make a hell of a difference to the unit that takes over from you. I know you've had a tough time, and I know it's a lot to ask of your men, but if you can do it, it'll make a lot of difference.' It was an amazing experience, seeing how he put the fighting spirit back into those men, knowing exactly when to give them hell and when to encourage them instead.

"I got back late and Eisenhower was absolutely furious. He had warned me to get home before dark and he blasted Brigadier Gault who had been escorting me. I took the blame, saying that even if I had not returned in time, I at least had done the job he asked me to do. I had seen the conditions in the field and now I would be able to give the Russians a more accurate picture.

"That night we had a long talk and Eisenhower for the first time mentioned his presidential aspirations. This was late November 1944. The Battle of the Bulge was just a few weeks in the future. He said that some of his friends had come to him and said that he ought to be President. He seemed torn between becoming President and playing the role of an elder statesman after the war. I found his naïveté astounding. He was, of course, in many ways a great political general. He knew how to compromise and he somehow kept soldiers from a number of nations working together. But he didn't have the faintest knowledge of what was going on in the United States. Although I liked Ike personally I did not feel that he was qualified to be President."

A FEW DAYS AFTER HARRIMAN'S RETURN to Moscow, Charles de Gaulle arrived with his Foreign Minister, Georges Bidault. De Gaulle, characteristically, had gone to Moscow without consulting the British or American governments. He was trying hard to get along with the large French Communist party, which was then enjoying a new respectability thanks to its prominent role in the resistance. It was Stalin, not De Gaulle, who informed Churchill and Roosevelt that the French were proposing a treaty of alliance and mutual assistance with the Soviet Union, similar to the Anglo-Soviet treaty of 1942. "We can hardly object," he wrote to Roosevelt on December 2, "but I should like to know your views on this subject." Stalin added that De Gaulle would probably suggest extending the eastern border of France to the left bank of the Rhine. He carefully pointed out that this proposal might conflict with a scheme, then being studied by the Allies, to establish a Rhenish-Westphalian province under international control. This was one occasion when Stalin asked for the opinions of Roosevelt and Churchill before acting. Neither one objected to the proposed treaty. Both argued, however, that the frontier change should be deferred until after the German collapse—and Stalin agreed.

De Gaulle's stock had risen sharply since the liberation of Paris. His Provisional Government had been recognized by the United States, Britain and the Soviet Union in late October. All three powers had sent ambassadors to Paris. The new French administration was getting along well with Eisenhower's Allied headquarters, and normal civilian life was being restored in the liberated regions of France in spite of the shortages of coal and industrial raw materials which made that first winter in freedom so wretchedly disappointing for the French people.

Stalin's attitude toward De Gaulle had changed abruptly, Harriman observed, showing no trace of the bitter hostility he had ventilated at Teheran. There was no more ridicule, no suggestion that France must be made to pay for her collaboration with the Germans, no further talk about stripping away her colonies. Instead De Gaulle was received in Moscow with all the honors due an Allied head of state.

In the late afternoon of December 5, Bidault asked Harriman to the French embassy and outlined to him the terms of the proposed treaty. One clause would have accorded recognition to the Lublin regime as the Provisional Government of Poland. Harriman asked Bidault whether he was consulting or informing the United States government. Bidault replied that it was a case of informing Washington. Harriman decided to see De Gaulle personally rather than discuss the treaty further with Bidault. He called on De Gaulle the next morning, and in the course of a long talk, raised the thorny question of Polish recognition. It was, of course, a matter for France to decide, Harriman said, but as a friend he felt that he should indicate what a powerful adverse reaction De Gaulle could expect from the government and people of the United States. De Gaulle responded that he had made no commitment, although Stalin was making a great point of French recognition for Lublin, and would discuss the matter again with him. "Later the same afternoon, at a reception," Harriman remembered, "he called me aside to tell me that since our talk he had made it plain to Stalin that he would take no action on Poland without consulting us and the British."

Stalin's effort to squeeze an immediate advantage for the Lublin Poles out of the French desire for a treaty to hold the Germans in check after the war did not sit well with De Gaulle. "Soviet policy," he said to Harriman on December 6, "would make for great fear among the small nations of Europe." Reverting to a theme he had expounded to Harriman some fourteen months earlier in Algiers, De Gaulle said that with Germany out of the picture, the smaller nations would have to rally around France if they were to prevent Soviet domination of Europe. Britain, after all, was an island country with imperial entanglements, and the United States, so far across the ocean, had her own interests outside the Continent. France, in short, would necessarily assume the leadership of Europe.

Harriman made no comment on the larger vision De Gaulle unfolded in Moscow that December day. But he expressed doubt that the Russians intended to absorb Poland or other neighboring states into the Soviet Union. It was more likely that the Russians would set out to dominate these countries, he said, in order to assure their own security through a belt of what Stalin euphemistically called "friendly neighbors."

Turning then to domestic affairs, De Gaulle said the French Communist party took its orders from Moscow. Although its leaders had now "abandoned revolutionary tactics," they were "always creating difficulties and trouble" in France by pressing radical social programs. De Gaulle told Harriman that he believed Moscow's chief interest in the Communist party was to use it as a tool for advancing its own foreign policy rather than to convert the French to Communism.

De Gaulle was prepared to leave Moscow without his treaty, and Harriman noted clear signs of tension at Stalin's pre-departure banquet for the French leader on December 9:

> De Gaulle took his place glumly on Stalin's right with Bidault across the table on Molotov's right. I was assigned my usual place on such occasions on Stalin's left. I asked Stalin how he was getting along with the general. He replied that he had found him "an awkward and stubborn man." In spite of De Gaulle's coldness, Stalin was determined that the evening would be gay. "They must drink more wine and then everything will straighten out," he said, as he started the toasts. First came flowery but perfunctory toasts to the French guests [by Molotov]. [Stalin] became pointedly profuse in his toasts to President Roosevelt, as the great leader for peace as for war, and to Churchill, whom he called "my collaborator in this war, a man of indestructible fighting spirit." Then rudely disregarding his guest of honor, he toasted a succession of Russians in turn, praising their contributions to the war effort.

When coffee and brandy were served in an adjoining room after dinner, Harriman found himself sitting beside De Gaulle, who was in a mood to provoke the Russians. "Pointing to Bulganin as he moved toward us," Harriman recalled, "De Gaulle asked me, 'Isn't that the man who killed so many Russian generals?' It was said loudly enough for Pavlov, the interpreter, to hear. Molotov, meanwhile, had hustled Bidault to a separate table where they began a heated argument. Molotov evidently was still insisting upon recognition for the Lublin Poles and Bidault was refusing. At this point Stalin called out to Bulganin: 'Bring the machine guns. Let's liquidate the diplomats.'

"This clumsy attempt at humor left De Gaulle unmoved. We adjourned to the private theater and sat through one film. When Stalin asked us to stay for a second, De Gaulle stiffly declined the invitation and walked out. Stalin asked me to stay, which I did. Several times during the second film Molotov walked up to talk with Stalin. When the film at last had run its course at two o'clock, I felt it was time for me to leave. General Deane remained and later reported to me that Stalin spent the rest of the night drinking champagne and making conversation with the generals while Molotov and Bidault wrestled with their treaty. They were so absorbed in their conversation that when I walked through the room on my way out they barely raised their heads to say good night."

The denouement, as related to Harriman the next day by the French minister, Roger Garreau, came after Molotov had accepted a minor compromise: the French would send an army major to Lublin but they would withhold diplomatic recognition. Stalin then invited De Gaulle back to the Kremlin in the small hours of the morning. "A bizarre incident occurred when De Gaulle arrived," Harriman recalled. "Stalin handed him the original draft of the treaty to sign. He appealed to De Gaulle for French support of the Lublin Committee, emphasizing the necessity of having a Poland that was completely friendly to the Soviet Union, in order to avoid the threat of a resurgent Germany after the war. France, as a continental country, Stalin contended, should understand the requirement more clearly than Great Britain or the United States. De Gaulle was furious at having been called from his bed to listen to the same argument all over again. 'France has been insulted,' he said, and started to stalk out of the room. Stalin then calmly asked Molotov for the new draft, oblivious to his own crude, last-minute effort to break down De Gaulle's resistance. After De Gaulle had satisfied himself that the new draft conformed to his previous offer, the treaty was signed at six-thirty A.M. with all due ceremony and he left for Paris a few hours later."

De Gaulle's firmness with Stalin greatly increased Harriman's respect for the French leader. "He must have been gratified by the results," Harriman recalled. "The treaty meant a great deal to him politically in France. He also must have felt that his success with Stalin would add to his stature with the British and ourselves."

When a few weeks later De Gaulle learned that the Big Three were planning to meet again, without inviting his participation, he notified Moscow, Washington and London through their respective ambassadors that France "could not consider itself bound" by any decisions they might take in his absence.[1]

ALLIED HOPES of ending the war by the end of 1944, meanwhile, had been frustrated in the east as well as the west. When Harriman called on Stalin December 14 to explain how flooding rivers and early cold had disrupted Eisenhower's plans of reaching the Rhine before winter set in, the Red Army was massing in central Poland for its own delayed offensive. Harriman said that Eisenhower and Marshall, being eager to plan further operations in concert with the Russians, were anxious to learn of developments on the eastern front. He explained that Eisenhower had the choice of throwing in his reserves gradually or quickly and that he could make his decision more readily if he knew what the Russians were planning. "His wish will be met," Stalin said.

He promised to provide this information after conferring with his military staff, in about a week. Bad weather was affecting the Red Army's operations, Stalin added. It had been a curious winter till then—bitter cold in Moscow but strangely warm in Poland and in the Baltic region. Fog, moreover, had deprived the Russians of their big superiority, which was not in manpower, Stalin said, but in artillery and planes, both requiring good visibility. So the Red Army also was having to wait for better weather.

At this point Stalin made the surprising suggestion that five or six Allied divisions might be transferred from the Italian front to Dalmatia for an advance on Zagreb, the capital of Croatia, and then join forces with the Red Army in southeastern Austria. The German forces in northern Italy would find themselves in a most difficult situation, Stalin said, outflanked and forced to withdraw or be captured. He added that the Russians would be able to advance as far as Vienna and that it would be desirable if eight to ten divisions of British and American troops joined up on the Russians' left. Harriman replied that Churchill had long advocated just this Balkan strategy, but staff studies had shown that a major amphibious operation on the scale proposed would require several weeks of special training, and besides, winter weather in the upper Adriatic tended to be foul. Stalin explained that he was not suggesting the assault across Yugoslavia must take place in the winter. It seemed to him an attractive operation for the spring. Harriman promised to present Stalin's views to the Chiefs of Staff, and General Deane promptly sent an account of their conversation back to the Pentagon.

Harriman also drew Stalin out, as instructed by Roosevelt, on his political demands in the Far East, as mentioned without elaboration in their last conversation.

> After bringing out a map from the next room [Harriman reported to Roosevelt], the Marshal said that Lower Sakhalin and the Kurile Islands should be returned to Russia. The approaches to Vladivostok are now controlled by the Japanese, he explained. He considered that the U.S.S.R. is entitled to protection for its communications to this important port and remarked that "all outlets to the Pacific Ocean are now held or blocked by the enemy." He stated, drawing a line around the southern part of the Liaotung Peninsula including Dairen and Port Arthur, that Russia again wished to lease these ports and the area surrounding them.
>
> I said my recollection was that at Teheran you and he had discussed this question and that, if my memory served me right, it was in fact you who had initiated the question of the

Soviet Union's need of access to a warm-water port in the
Pacific. On the other hand, I said I thought that what you had
in mind was not the lease of this area by the U.S.S.R. but
rather an international free port . . . which was more in line
with present-day concepts of how best to deal with international questions of this character. "This can be discussed," the
Marshal stated.

In addition, Stalin told Harriman that the Soviets would want to
lease the Russian-built railway lines from Dairen to Harbin, and from
there northwest to Manchuli and eastward to Vladivostok. He had no
intention, Stalin said in response to a question from Harriman, of interfering with Chinese sovereignty in Manchuria. Regarding this
assurance, Harriman showed considerable skepticism. "Of course there
is no doubt," he wrote to Roosevelt, "that Soviet influence in Manchuria will be great, what with the control of the railroad operations
and with the probability of Soviet troops to protect the railroad."
Harriman suggested that "it might be useful" to get more information
concerning Stalin's demands in the Far East before the Big Three
conference. But he received no follow-up instructions. The possibility that Stalin might take the President's silence for assent was
not, by all the available evidence, taken seriously in Washington. The
Soviet Union would not, in any case, be entering the war against Japan
until three months after the defeat of Germany, and the Wehrmacht,
in December of 1944, had just launched a powerful counteroffensive in
the Ardennes, which brought home to the Allies that the end of the
war in Europe was not yet in sight.
     The fact that certain of the German divisions used in the Battle
of the Bulge had recently been transferred from the eastern front,
then comparatively quiet, led Eisenhower to request more urgently
than before the information about Soviet campaign plans which Stalin
had promised Harriman but had so far failed to deliver. Roosevelt sent
Stalin a message on December 23 pressing him "in view of the emergency" to receive a senior staff officer from Eisenhower's headquarters
and to tell him directly when the Soviet offensive could be expected.
Stalin promptly agreed and Eisenhower sent his deputy, the British
Air Chief Marshal Arthur Tedder, to Moscow. By the time Tedder
and his party arrived in Russia on January 15, having been delayed en
route by bad weather, Churchill had prodded Stalin for a preliminary
answer. The reply was that the Red Army had been waiting for clear
weather (as Stalin had said to Harriman a month earlier), but that in
view of Eisenhower's difficulties in the west he now proposed to begin
a large offensive along the central front "not later than the second
half of January," regardless of the weather.

That operation, in fact, had already started when Tedder saw Stalin on his first day in Moscow. Stalin said the Red Army had concentrated a force of 150 to 160 divisions for a drive of two months or more, with the ultimate objective of reaching the Oder River. Stalin and Tedder exchanged information on a variety of subjects: the poor state of German reserves, the Luftwaffe's lack of trained pilots, and the timing of spring operations on both fronts, when the Russians would be trying to cross the Oder and the Western Allies to cross the Rhine for the final assault on Berlin.

"We have no treaty but we are comrades," Stalin said at the end of their discussion. "It is proper and also sound, selfish policy that we should help each other in times of difficulty. It would be foolish for me to stand aside and let the Germans annihilate you; they would only turn back on me when you were disposed of. Similarly it is to your interest to do everything possible to keep the Germans from annihilating me."

Although the Tedder visit was generally accounted a success, General Deane felt there was a better way to deal with Stalin on military matters. In an "Eyes only" message to General Marshall, dated January 17, he disclosed that Tedder (like other first-time visitors) had imagined that Stalin would talk more freely if he went to the Kremlin alone. Harriman at once had stepped out of the picture, although he had insisted on Deane's participation.

I felt that it was a great mistake to exclude Harriman from the conference and gave Tedder my reasons [Deane reported]. Harriman has constituted our only direct contact with Stalin on all military matters. He had seen Stalin more than any other Britisher or American. He could have been invaluable in pressing the discussion and clarifying points in question . . . Experience in dealing with the Soviets is invaluable and yet at this conference our most experienced individual was left out.

. . . The big point at issue in the conference was the timing of operations this spring. As an observer I felt that the possibilities were not probed deep enough, nor the conclusions reached sufficiently precise and clear-cut. This was because of the natural inhibition that all visitors have in pinning Stalin down. Had Harriman been there, I am sure that the subject would have been explored in greater detail. I believe this because Harriman is persistent and tenacious and has passed the stage of having inhibitions when talking to Stalin.

General Deane was growing steadily more discouraged over the waning prospect of setting up joint military talks with the Soviet

General Staff to plan for combined operations in the Pacific. In the absence of Soviet cooperation he decided to simulate the problems that were bound to confront the Russians and their American ally in the final stage of the war against Japan through a series of in-house war games. Deane's primary purpose was to establish how large a force the Russians would need and particularly the size of the supply buildup required to support it, in view of the limited capacity of the Trans-Siberian Railroad.

With Harriman's enthusiastic support, Deane transformed the ballroom of Spaso House into a kind of war college. Partitions were thrown up to divide the ballroom into separate cubicles for the staff sections of two contending armies, one Japanese, the other Russian. The walls of each cubicle were covered with detail maps of the Far Eastern theater. Colonel James C. Crockett, like General Deane a former instructor at Fort Leavenworth, took charge of the war games, dividing the fifty officers assigned to the Moscow mission into two camps. Colonel Moses W. Pettigrew, who played the role of supreme commander of the Japanese armed forces, came to be known thereafter as "Tojo."

"I doubt," General Deane has written, "if any more incongruous situation developed during the war than that of the American military and naval representation in Moscow resorting to schoolroom war games in order to get some conception of the situation which might confront the Soviet forces."[2] Deane never doubted that the NKVD must have had a pretty shrewd idea of what was happening in the ballroom of the embassy residence. A number of Soviet citizens worked in the building, and certain of them were bound to report what they saw and heard to the secret police. If the Russians were somewhat mystified by these goings on, they said nothing to Harriman or Deane. Each of the five set problems was played out in the ballroom before the Ambassador; Rear Admiral Clarence E. Olsen, who headed the Navy division of the U.S. mission; Brigadier General William E. Crist, head of the Army division; Major General Spalding of the Lend-Lease division; and Deane himself.

Although the war games had to be based on some fairly arbitrary assumptions, they helped to convince Harriman and Deane that there was not much hope of setting up an American strategic air force in the Maritime Provinces. They also came to believe that while the Russians would certainly require a reserve stockpile of supplies in Siberia before entering the war against Japan, it would no longer be absolutely necessary to keep open a Pacific supply route from the West Coast of the United States to support the Red Army in the Far East. Each of these conclusions in fact was vindicated by later developments.

In a final, fruitless attempt to start joint planning with the Russians, the Pentagon sent a team of four officers, headed by Brigadier General Frank N. Roberts, to Moscow in December.* The team spent four months in Russia, meeting only twice with its reluctant Soviet counterparts, before concluding that further efforts to initiate joint planning would be a waste of time.

By the time the Soviet Union entered the war against Japan, an American air force in Siberia would have been of negligible value in any case. The B-29 fleet had all the bases it needed to force Japan's surrender. As for the Pacific supply route, it presented no problems because Japanese power at sea had been all but eliminated.

The new Russian winter offensive, meanwhile, pushed westward across Poland. Eisenhower recovered his lost initiative in the Ardennes. And preparations for the Big Three conference became the first order of business in Moscow. Roosevelt at last yielded to Stalin's refusal to leave the Soviet Union and on December 27 sent word to Harriman that he was prepared to meet Stalin and Churchill at Yalta in the Crimea. The President would sail across the Atlantic into the Mediterranean as far as Malta, flying from there to the Crimea. The decision prompted Churchill's high-spirited New Year's Day message: "No more let us falter! From Malta to Yalta! Let nobody alter!"

Roosevelt was to stay at the Livadia Palace, formerly the summer palace of Czar Nicholas II, about one and a half miles outside the town of Yalta. After the Revolution it had been turned into a rest home for tubercular patients. During the German occupation of the Crimea, the building had been used (and stripped of virtually all its original furnishings) by the German high command. Nothing remained but two paintings in the bedroom reserved for the President. All the rest had to be shipped from Moscow. "Because of the looting of furniture in the Crimea," Harriman cabled Admiral Leahy in Washington, "it is going to be quite an undertaking for the Russians to make all the arrangements."

Although Roosevelt had planned to limit his party to thirty-five persons, including the Joint Chiefs of Staff, Secret Service men and servants, he brought ten times that number, and the British delegation was equally large. General Deane, in his methodical way, arranged to have an Army finance officer on the spot to exchange dollars for roubles at the diplomatic rate. He also set up an infirmary and a bar.

The embassy staff wrote a seven-page guide to the Crimea, tracing its history from the early Taurians, who lived in the Yaila mountains

---

* General Roberts, the senior Army member of the Joint Staff Planners in Washington, was accompanied by Brigadier General William L. Ritchie, Captain Houston L. Maples of the Navy, and Colonel Frank A. Bogart, then a member of the Planning Division of General Somervell's staff.

along the Black Sea coast, through the Scythian kingdom, founded in the second century B.C., and the rule of the Tartar khans, until it became a province of Russia in 1783. The anonymous author even reminded members of the American delegation that Anton Chekhov had spent the last four years of his life in a small villa above Yalta, which was now a museum tended by the playwright's sister and open to visitors.

Kathleen Harriman, in the role of hostess for her father, saw to the room assignments and the general housekeeping. While the Ambassador, well aware from his Teheran experience how disorganized a Roosevelt delegation could be, took upon himself the job of scheduling, record keeping and coordinating the work of the conference on the American side. All these complicated preparations were in full swing when Harriman was invited to call on Molotov on the night of January 3, 1945, to receive in writing an amazing and oddly conceived proposal:

> Having in mind the repeated statements of American public figures concerning the desirability of receiving extensive large Soviet orders for the postwar and transition period, the Soviet Government considers it possible to place orders on the basis of long-term credits to the amount of six billion dollars.

This credit, to be repaid in thirty years at an annual interest rate of 2 percent, would also cover orders for railroad cars and locomotives, steel rails, trucks and industrial equipment placed under Lend-Lease but not delivered before the end of the war. The United States, moreover, was to grant the Soviet Union a 20 percent discount on all orders placed before the end of the war.

"As a banker," Harriman recalled, "I've had many requests for loans but Molotov's was the strangest request I have ever received. The extraordinary thing was when he started by saying that in consideration of the vast unemployment and the economic dislocation the United States would have at the end of the war, the Soviet Union was ready to be a good friend and help us out by placing orders for six billion dollars' worth of goods and commodities. There would be no payments for the first nine years. Beginning in the tenth year, they would repay the interest and capital in annual installments. I could recall no similar transaction in which the prospective borrower had specified all the terms before the potential lender could get a word in."

Harriman told Molotov that he could make no general comment on the Soviet proposal but would at once report it to Washington. He explained that the Administration had no statutory authority to deal with any but wartime Lend-Lease requests. The Lend-Lease authorization would necessarily expire with the termination of hostilities, and new congressional authority would have to be voted for postwar reconstruction assistance. As for the Lend-Lease part of the transaction, Harriman added, Molotov knew that "we had been trying for months to come to an agreement with the Soviet Government with respect to financing those requests which we had received from them for industrial equipment under the fourth protocol.* I pointed out that the interest rate we had offered was two and three-eighths, not two and a quarter percent."

Molotov agreed that the Lend-Lease aspect should be settled promptly, adding that he had instructed Ambassador Gromyko in Washington to do so. But a great deal more than Lend-Lease was at stake. "The future development of Soviet-American relations, he said, must have certain vistas [Molotov used the Russian word "prospects"] before it and must rest on a solid economic basis," Harriman reported.

On January 6, having recovered from his surprise over Molotov's approach, Harriman sent his reactions to Washington in a long message, quoted here in pertinent part:

> One. I feel we should entirely disregard the unconventional character of the document and the unreasonableness of its terms and chalk it up to ignorance of normal business procedures and the strange ideas of the Russians on how to get the best trade. From our experience it has become increasingly my impression that Mikoyan had not divorced himself from his Armenian background. He starts negotiations on the basis of "twice as much for half the price" and then gives in, bit by bit, expecting in the process to wear us out.
>
> Two. Molotov made it very plain that the Soviet Government placed high importance on a large postwar credit as a basis for the development of "Soviet-American relations." From his statement, I sensed that the development of our friendly relations would depend upon a generous credit. It is, of course, my very strong and earnest opinion that the question of the credit should be tied into our overall diplomatic relations with the Soviet Union and, at the appropriate time, the Russians should be given to understand that our willingness to cooperate wholeheartedly with them in their vast reconstruction problems will depend upon their behavior in international matters . . .
>
> Five. It is my basic conviction that we should do everything

---

* The Fourth Protocol had been held up many months because for the first time the Russians were requesting long-term industrial equipment to be used in postwar reconstruction, and the terms had not yet been accepted in Moscow.

we can to assist the Soviet Union through credits in developing a sound economy. I feel strongly that the sooner the Soviet
Union can develop a decent life for its people the more toler-
ant they will become. One has to live in Russia a considerable
period of time to appreciate fully the unbelievably low standards which prevail among the Russian people and the extent
to which this affects their outlook . . .

Six. I believe that the United States Government should
retain control of any credits granted in order that political
advantages may be retained and that we may be satisfied the
equipment purchased is for purposes that meet our general
approval.

Harriman was unaware at the time that Henry Morgenthau,
Secretary of the Treasury, had sent the President on January 10 a
plan for an even larger credit on terms more generous than those the
Russians themselves were requesting. Instead of $6 billion over thirty
years at 2¼ percent as requested by Molotov, Morgenthau had suggested a $10 billion loan, at 2 percent interest, to be repaid over thirty-
five years. A week later Morgenthau called on Edward R. Stettinius,
the new Secretary of State, with Harry Dexter White of the Treasury
staff to explain his views. Morgenthau said that his purpose was to
"reassure the Soviet Government of our determination to cooperate
with them and break down any suspicions the Soviet authorities might
have in regard to our future action."[3] As for the terms of the Lend-
Lease Protocol, Morgenthau regretted that nine months had passed
without an agreement because of a tendency in the State Department
to "bargain and bicker" with the Russians. The time had come, he
argued, to make a "clear-cut, very favorable proposal which would be
considered by the Soviet Government as a concrete gesture of our
good will." What he had in mind, he said, was to offer the Soviet
Union the same amount of credit as previously planned, but without
charging interest. On the other hand, the Russians should be denied
any discount from cost prices.

Dean Acheson, then Assistant Secretary of State, reminded Morgenthau that in early 1944 his own Treasury Department had vetoed
a proposal for an interest-free loan to the Russians, contending that the
United States must never offer long-term credits at a lower rate of
interest than the U.S. government itself had to pay in order to borrow
money. Within a few days the Treasury withdrew its proposal for a
no-interest loan under Section 3C of the Lend-Lease Act.

As for the postwar credit, Assistant Secretary of State Will
Clayton notified Harriman on January 27 that the President was keenly

interested in the idea but that nothing more was to be done until he could take it up personally with Stalin at Yalta.

Not content to let the matter drift, Harriman urged Molotov to make certain that Stalin discussed the postwar credit proposal with Roosevelt when they were together. He also urged the President to take it up with Stalin. But neither side, as the historical record confirms, raised the question at Yalta. It must be accounted an odd omission in view of the apparent conviction on both sides that the hope of friendly postwar relations between the United States and Russia would, in Harriman's words, "depend upon a generous credit."

CHAPTER XVII

Yalta—"In Better Health, FDR Might Have Held Out Longer, but I Can't Believe that It Would Have Made a Great Difference"

Franklin had high hopes that at this conference he could make real progress in strengthening the personal relationship between himself and Marshal Stalin . . . He knew that negotiation invariably involved some give and take, but he was a good bargainer and a good poker player, and he loved the game of negotiation. I am sure that even at the Yalta conference, the necessity of matching his wits against other people's stimulated him and kept him alert and interested, no matter how weary he may at times have been.

—Eleanor Roosevelt,
This I Remember

Roosevelt had less than ten weeks to live when he reached Malta on Friday morning, February 2, 1945. His worn, wasted look alarmed both Churchill and Harriman. "I was terribly shocked at the change since our talks in Washington, after the November election," Harriman recalled. "The signs of deterioration seemed to me unmistakable." The Prime Minister watched with trepidation the following day as the President in his wheelchair was lowered to the ground from his new plane, *The Sacred Cow*, at Saki Airport in the Crimea. To him, Roosevelt looked "frail and ill."[1]

Rumors that the President was in failing health had been circulating even before the 1944 campaign. Although the White House dismissed such talk as politically inspired, Roosevelt had been suffering from abnormally high blood pressure since 1937. Not even Mrs. Roosevelt knew that since the spring of 1944 her husband was being treated for an enlarged heart and congestive heart failure.* Admiral McIntire, the President's doctor, saw to it that the truth about Roosevelt's condition was kept from the country and from the Roosevelt family as well.

After the President's death, however, a tidal wave of rumor swept the country. Critics of the Yalta decisions kept raising the question whether Roosevelt had been physically and mentally competent at the time of the conference. As late as August 17, 1951, in a statement he submitted to the Joint Senate Committee on Armed Services and Foreign Relations at the request of Senator Brien McMahon of Connecticut, Harriman testified:

> Unquestionably, he was not in good health and the long conferences tired him. Nevertheless, for many months he had given much thought to the matters to be discussed and, in consultation with many officials of the Government, he had blocked out definite objectives which he had clearly in mind. He came to Yalta determined to do his utmost to achieve these objectives and he carried on the negotiations to this end with his usual skill and perception.

"I stated under oath what I felt at the time," Harriman remarked, following the belated publication of Dr. Bruenn's clinical notes. "What I want to add now is that I felt his last election campaign took a lot out of him. He didn't get up as early in the morning after that. He seemed to tire when conversations wore on too long. I used to say that Roosevelt had a Dutch jaw—and when that Dutch jaw was set you couldn't move him. At Yalta, I believe, he didn't have the strength to

* The diagnosis was made by Dr. Howard G. Bruenn, a New York heart specialist then serving in the U.S. Navy who attended the President almost daily during the last year of his life. Dr. Bruenn's article, "Clinical Notes on the Illness and Death of President Franklin D. Roosevelt," was published in the *Annals of Internal Medicine* (1970), pages 579–91. "I have often wondered," Dr. Bruenn wrote, "what turn the subsequent course of history might have taken if the modern methods for the control of hypertension had been available."

be quite as stubborn as he liked to be. I suppose that if FDR had been in better health, he might have held out longer and got his way on a number of detailed points. But I can't believe that it would have made a great difference on, say, the Polish question. At the time of Yalta, the Red Army was in full control of the country and no amount of careful drafting could have changed that. If Stalin was determined to have his way, he was bound to bend or break the agreements, even if they had been sewn up more tightly."

Ironically, the ailing Roosevelt had decided to travel all the way to the Crimea—4,883 miles by sea from Newport News, Virginia, to Malta, and then 1,375 miles by air from Luqa Airfield, Malta, to the snowy runway at Saki—because Stalin, on the advice of *his* doctors, refused to leave the Soviet Union. The President had first proposed that Stalin meet him in Scotland, then in Malta or Athens or Cyprus, only to have each of his suggestions politely rejected. Determined to settle the paramount questions and thus to clear the ground for a new structure of power in the postwar world, Roosevelt overruled the objections of his own advisers. "All of the President's close advisers were opposed to his going to Russia," Hopkins wrote in a memorandum on the genesis of Yalta; "most did not like or trust the Russians anyway and could not understand why the President of the United States should cart himself all over the world to meet Stalin."[2] Even Hopkins, however, who saw no chance of persuading Stalin to go anywhere but the Crimea, must have developed second thoughts when he flew to Europe ahead of the presidential party. From London, he cabled Roosevelt on January 24:

> Churchill . . . says that if we had spent ten years on research we could not have found a worse place in the world than MAGNETO [the code name for Yalta] but that he feels that he can survive it by bringing an adequate supply of whiskey. He claims it is good for typhus and deadly on lice which thrive in those parts . . .[3]

The President's careful regard for Stalin's suspicions led him to spend less than a full day at Malta, where the British and American Chiefs of Staff had been meeting since January 30. Churchill, Eden, Stettinius, Hopkins and Harriman met him there, but the President, as usual, showed little interest in detailed strategy talks on the diplomatic side. He did not want to feed Soviet suspicions that the British and Americans would be operating in concert at Yalta. Roosevelt held fast to his belief that he personally could accomplish more in man-to-man talks with Stalin than Churchill, the State Department or the British Foreign Office. Once installed at the Livadia Palace, he put off seeing Churchill alone until the fifth day of the conference. Harriman, who talked with Churchill almost every day, felt that this was a matter of Rooseveltian tactics, not a studied slight to the Prime Minister. The President still believed that Stalin would prove more tractable if the Western powers did not appear to be acting in unison. In his private meetings with Stalin, Roosevelt talked openly about his differences with Churchill, and on more than one occasion, poked a little fun at the Prime Minister for his old-fashioned attachment to the Empire. Eden, in his memoirs, complained: "The President, mistakenly as I believe, moved out of step with us, influenced by his conviction that he could get better results with Stalin direct than could the three countries negotiating together."[4]

Twenty American Skymasters and five British Yorks transported the official party of some 700 British and Americans from Malta. The planes took off at ten-minute intervals through the night of February 2. Each aircraft followed the same flight plan at constant air speed: three and a half hours due east, a 90-degree turn to avoid Cyprus (still under German occupation) as far as the coast of Greece, then over the Aegean Sea to the Dardanelles and across the Black Sea to the Crimea, each plane executing another 90-degree turn at the Soviet radio transmitter near Saki to identify itself as friendly.

The Sacred Cow, escorted by five P-38 fighters (a sixth had been forced to turn back to Athens because of engine trouble), swept in to land at ten minutes past noon, bumping the full length of the short concrete-block runway before it stopped. The President remained on board until Churchill's plane came in about twenty minutes later. Lowered to the ground by a special lift mechanism, the President then took his place in a Lend-Lease jeep to review the Soviet honor guard, with Churchill walking beside him, after a Red Army band had played "The Star-Spangled Banner," "God Save the King" and the "Internationale" in turn.

The drive to Yalta took almost five hours. Russian soldiers, many of them stocky young women, stood guard along the entire eighty-mile route, snapping each car a succession of smart salutes as it passed. The countryside, sparsely populated, bore the scars of heavy fighting —gutted buildings, charred tanks and wrecked German railway cars in crazy disarray. Roosevelt, traveling in the lead car with his daughter, Anna Boettiger, marked the sights of war with rising bitterness against the Germans. "I'm more bloodthirsty than a year ago," he said to Stalin the following day.

Kathleen Harriman, as hostess for her father, received the President on his arrival at the Livadia Palace at six o'clock. "Well, I've at last had my wish and met the President," she wrote to her sister Mary in New York. "It seems sort of odd it would be in Russia. He's absolutely charming, easy to talk to, with a lovely sense of humor. He's in fine form, very happy about accommodations and all set for the best." Three times in her letters home, and to Pamela Churchill in London, Kathleen mentioned how genial and relaxed FDR appeared.

Livadia, built for Czar Nicholas in 1911 of white Inkerman granite, stands 150 feet above the Black Sea shore, commanding a spectacular view of mountains and sea. The President was quartered in a suite of three rooms, possessing the only private bathroom in the palace. Hopkins had a bedroom to himself just a few feet from the President's room. But his health at the time of Yalta was so precarious that he left his bed only once a day to attend the full-dress meetings. Under orders from Admiral McIntire, Hopkins attended none of the big dinners. When Harriman and other members of the delegation needed to consult him, they went to Hopkins' room.

The rest of the American delegation lived upstairs and in two nearby houses. All the bedrooms had been whitewashed and hastily refurbished to replace the looted furniture, paintings, doorknobs, even plumbing fixtures. The Soviet government had commandeered cooks, waiters, maids and housekeepers from three Moscow hotels and sent them down by train—a seemingly endless journey, also experienced by the Harrimans. Kathleen's account of the trip down to Yalta, drawn from her heavily censored letters home, are vivid with detailed observations of Russia at war:

> To start at the beginning, we trained down here, despairing of ever being able to get flying weather. A long affair —three days and three nights—most of the time spent standing in bombed-out stations . . . Ave was well escorted, all his boys [security guards]—three compartments full. A female Pullman porter made beds and, every hour or so, walked down the passage cleaning up the dirt—a wonderful procedure. She'd spray water through her teeth on the carpet to dampen it, and then sweep. Made an intriguing sound . . .
>
> My God, but this country has a job on its hands, just cleaning up.
>
> The Ukrainian peasants seem far more prosperous than those around Moscow. Their cottages are painted, with thatched roofs and quite picturesque. Some stations had vendors. At one we bought four fresh eggs (cheap at $4) and made a nice punch—canned milk, bourbon and butter.
>
> The train at last dumped us in Simferopol [at] midafternoon. The delegation of Soviets wanted us to spend the night as the mountain pass was too "dangerous" for night driving. Ave was adamant so we went off—a snow storm, winding

roads but good drivers (one car got stuck) and arrived in Yalta [in] about 3½ hours.

Two days after the Harrimans' arrival, the Ambassador had flown off to Italy and from there to Malta for the preliminary meetings with the British, leaving Kathleen in charge of the housekeeping details. She wrote home on February 1:

> I never quite realized that so many things could go wrong so many ways. It's lucky that Averell isn't here to fret . . . The rugs for the President's suite have been changed four times. Each time all the furniture had to be moved out—and it's big and heavy and Victorian. The Soviets just couldn't make up their minds which oriental colors looked best . . . Washing facilities are practically nil (Mrs. Boettiger and I [will] share a small room opposite the one complete bathroom). Only full generals and admirals and chiefs of state get rooms to themselves. The rest are packed like patients in a ward . . . All the Moscow hotels have been stripped . . . to look after us. I wonder what the poor folk in Moscow are doing. Beside that, the country nearby is being scoured for such things as shaving mirrors, coat hangers and wash bowls. I guess they are just being "requisitioned" out of homes. We've found one ashtray that advertises a china factory, "by appointment to" five Tsars!

Kathleen and General Deane assigned the former imperial bedchamber on the second floor to General Marshall. Admiral King occupied what once had been the Czarina's boudoir and took a lot of ribbing for it. Churchill and his party were installed in the Vorontsov Villa, some twelve miles down the coast, and the Russians at the Villa Koreis, about six miles from Livadia.

STALIN DID NOT REACH YALTA until the morning of February 4. He called on Roosevelt the same afternoon, an hour before the first plenary session. It was at their first private meeting, which Harriman had arranged with Molotov the night before, that Roosevelt pronounced himself more bloodthirsty than at Teheran in 1943. Stalin told him that the destruction he had seen in the Crimea was as nothing compared with the havoc the Germans had wrought in the Ukraine; there they had done it with method and calculation.

Roosevelt said that coming over on the *Quincy*, he had made a few bets as to whether the Russians would get to Berlin before the

U.S. Army liberated Manila.* Stalin replied that he was certain the Americans would take Manila before the Red Army got to Berlin because very heavy fighting was going on along the line of the Oder. Although the Russians had established five or six bridgeheads on the west bank of the Oder, not much more than forty miles east of Berlin, he said, they were meeting with fierce German resistance.

(Oddly, Stalin had told Churchill a different story when they met an hour earlier: ". . . that the Oder was no longer an obstacle, as the Red Army had several bridgeheads across it and the Germans were using untrained, badly led and ill-equipped Volkssturm for its defence. . . . on the whole their front was broken and they were merely trying to patch up the gaps.")[5]

One of the Soviet marshals, Vassili I. Chuikov, has since argued in his memoirs that "Berlin could have been taken as early as February."[6] Chuikov contended that Stalin, at the time of Yalta, called a halt in operations on the Oder and by telephone ordered Marshal Zhukov, commander of the First White Russian Front, to divert "as many forces as possible" north to Pomerania in order to crush Himmler's Army Group Vistula. Marshal Zhukov defended the decision in his own memoir, published in 1965. "It would have been the purest adventurism to undertake a decisive assault on Berlin," Zhukov wrote, pointing out that the Red Army had advanced so far, so fast in reaching the Oder (500 kilometers in twenty days) that it had outrun its supply lines, the air force had not been able to shift its tactical squadrons to forward bases and there was "serious danger" of a German counterblow from eastern Pomerania against the flank and the rear of the advancing Russians, had they pressed on toward Berlin.[7]

As for the western front, Roosevelt told Stalin on February 4 that General Eisenhower did not expect to cross the Rhine until March because the current was strong and floating ice was bound to make pontoon operations difficult. Thus the decisive assault on Germany, from east and west, was deferred until the spring.

Roosevelt and Stalin then exchanged impressions about the exasperating obstinacies of Charles de Gaulle. They agreed that he was being somewhat unrealistic in demanding full rights alongside the British, Russians and Americans, when the French had done so little fighting. Roosevelt said he was going to be indiscreet by telling Stalin something that he would not wish to say in front of Churchill—that the British, in their peculiar way, wanted to "have their cake and eat it, too." They had been trying for two years, he said, to build up France artificially into a strong power.

Before moving into the ballroom for the first plenary session,

---

* MacArthur's troops entered Manila the following day.

Stalin asked Roosevelt whether he thought the French should have a zone of occupation in Germany. The President replied that "it was not a bad idea" but if it were done it would be "only out of kindness." Both Stalin and Molotov agreed that kindness was the only possible reason for giving France a zone.

At Stalin's suggestion, Roosevelt then opened the plenary session. He was honored to have the first word, the President said, and to express the deep appreciation of all the Americans at Yalta for Marshal Stalin's splendid hospitality. "We understand each other much better now," he added, and the talks could be conducted informally with each man speaking his mind "frankly and freely." Although the Yalta Conference was bound to range over the map of the whole world, Roosevelt said, at the first session the Big Three ought to concentrate on military matters and "the most important front of all, the Eastern front." General Alexei Antonov then read a lengthy paper prepared by the Soviet General Staff describing in considerable detail the Soviet offensive of early January. This was followed by a report from General Marshall on the military situation in Western Europe.

Roosevelt believed that Stalin would talk more frankly about military matters if the number of civilians in the conference room was held to a minimum. Accordingly, he did not invite James F. Byrnes, Director of the Office of War Mobilization, to attend the first part of the session. He expected Byrnes to join in the political discussions afterward. But the military talks went on for a long time and Byrnes was kept waiting behind a closed door. In a fit of temper the "assistant President" refused to attend Roosevelt's dinner that evening for Stalin and Churchill, to which he had been invited. As soon as Harriman heard what had happened, he went to find Byrnes. "Anna Roosevelt was with him, trying to quiet him down," Harriman recalled. "But Byrnes kept storming that he had never been so insulted in his life and that he was going to order a plane to take him home. I tried, at first, to reason with him, and when that didn't work I told him, 'If you go home, you'll be a busted man. The American people will look on you as a man who has behaved badly.' I stalked out of the room and he finally appeared at dinner. This was an extreme case of conference fever—as I used to call it—of everyone wanting to go to every meeting because it made them feel important. Byrnes and I were to have our differences later on, when he became Secretary of State, but my lack of respect for him was born at Yalta."

At dinner that first evening in the Livadia Palace, with Roosevelt as host, Stalin opened the subject of great-power responsibilities and rights, as against those of the smaller nations. It was ridiculous to suggest, he said, that little Albania should have an equal voice with the great powers, which had won the war together. He never would agree that any action of the Big Three powers should be submitted to the judgment of the little ones. Churchill challenged this remark. There was no question of the small powers dictating to the great ones, he said, but greatness carried with it a moral responsibility to exercise power with moderation and respect for the rights of weaker nations. "The eagle," Churchill said, "should permit the small birds to sing and care not wherefor they sang."

When the Prime Minister offered a toast to the proletarian masses of the world, possibly by way of placating Stalin, the talk turned to the rights of people to govern themselves and get rid of leaders who no longer enjoyed their support. Churchill made the point that although he was constantly being "beaten up" as a reactionary, he happened to be the only leader present who could be thrown out of office at any time by his people, adding that he personally gloried in that danger. Stalin remarked that Churchill seemed to be afraid of elections. Not at all, the Prime Minister replied. Far from fearing them, he was proud of the right enjoyed by the British people to change governments whenever they saw fit.

A great cloud of myth and misinformation has obscured the true shape of the Yalta decisions for three decades now. With the benefit of hindsight, certain right-wing critics have traced back to Yalta many of America's postwar difficulties with the Soviet Union, the origins of the Cold War itself, and even the victory of Mao Tse-tung's Communist armies in China. Harriman, who was at Roosevelt's side during most of the crucial Yalta negotiations, stands by his 1951 testimony:

> The discussions at Yalta and the understandings reached there were an integral part of our negotiations with the Soviet Union throughout the war to bring the desperate struggle to a victorious and early conclusion and to find a way in which the United States, Great Britain and the U.S.S.R. could live together in peace. The postwar problems have resulted not from the understandings reached at Yalta but from the fact that Stalin failed to carry out those understandings and from aggressive actions by the Kremlin.

The Yalta discussions covered a wide range of topics: final plans for concerting the defeat and occupation of Germany, and the terms and circumstances for Soviet participation in the war against Japan. These essentially military decisions are best understood in light of the actual battlefield situation that first week of February 1945. Although General MacArthur had just entered Manila, the bloody battles of Iwo Jima and Okinawa were yet to be fought. It would be more than five months before the first experimental explosion of the atomic bomb at Alamagordo, New Mexico. The Joint Chiefs of Staff had not taken the bomb into account in their calculations of the military pressures needed to break Japan's resistance. (Harriman recalls that even five months later, at Potsdam, Admiral Leahy was offering bets that the bomb would not work.) The Chiefs of Staff, just before Yalta, had estimated that it would take eighteen months after the German surrender to defeat Japan. Far from visualizing Japan's quick collapse, they were planning to invade the home islands in the winter of 1945–46. And in the event that the European war was prolonged, necessarily postponing the redeployment of troops to the Pacific, they contemplated postponing that invasion until "well into 1946."[8]

Anxious to reduce American casualties from what General Marshall conceived as a bitter-end campaign to invade and occupy the industrial heart of Japan through the Tokyo Plain, the Joint Chiefs looked to the Russians for help. In a memorandum to the President, dated January 23, 1945, they declared:

> Russia's entry at as early a date as possible consistent with her ability to engage in offensive operations is necessary to provide maximum assistance to our Pacific operations. The United States will provide maximum support possible without interfering with our main effort against Japan. The objectives of Russia's military effort against Japan in the Far East should be the defeat of the Japanese forces in Manchuria, air operations against Japan proper in collaboration with United States Air Forces based in eastern Siberia, and maximum interference with Japanese sea traffic between Japan and the mainland of Asia.[9]

Stalin, understandably, had his own set of objectives in the Far East. He had outlined his terms to Harriman in December, claiming the return to Russia of the lower half of Sakhalin Island and the Kuriles. He wanted leases on the ports of Dairen and Port Arthur as well as the railroads in Manchuria built and operated by the Russians in Czarist times under contract with the Chinese. He also had asked for recognition of the status quo in Outer Mongolia, promising that the Soviet Union would not interfere with China's sovereignty over Manchuria. On February 8, at Yalta, Stalin took up his demands with Roosevelt. Secretary of State Stettinius had no part in these discussions. The President asked Harriman alone to join him, Bohlen sitting in as the interpreter. Stalin, who brought Molotov and his own interpreter, V. N. Pavlov, to the meeting, said he would like to discuss the political conditions under which the Soviet Union would enter the war against Japan, as he had explained them to Harriman earlier.

Roosevelt saw no difficulty about the return of South Sakhalin or the transfer of the Kurile Islands. As for Dairen, he had suggested at

Teheran that the Soviet Union ought to have access to a warm-water
port at the end of the South Manchurian Railroad. But he could not
speak for Chiang Kai-shek. Perhaps, rather than ask the Chinese for an
outright lease, Dairen could become a free port under an international
commission. That was the method he preferred, Roosevelt said, not
only in Dairen but also in Hong Kong. As for the Manchurian railroads, instead of leasing them he would like to see them operated
jointly by the Russians and the Chinese.

Stalin pressed harder. Unless his conditions were met, he said, it
would be difficult for the Soviet peoples to understand why Russia
was going to war with Japan. They clearly understood the war against
Germany, which had threatened the very existence of the Soviet
Union, but they would not understand why Russia should attack the
Japanese. If his political conditions were met, however, the matter
could be more easily explained to the people—and the Supreme Soviet
—in terms of "the national interest involved."[10] Roosevelt stressed that
he had not had an opportunity to discuss the matter with Chiang. It
was difficult to speak frankly with the Chinese, he said, because anything said to them in confidence was known round the world, Tokyo
included, in twenty-four hours.

There was no rush about talking to the Chinese, Stalin said, but
he did want his proposals put in writing and agreed to by Roosevelt
and Churchill before the conference ended. Turning then to internal
conditions in China, Stalin said he could not understand why the united
front against the Japanese invaders had broken down. The time had
come, he said, for Chiang to take the leadership, uniting his Kuomintang
forces with Mao's Communists in a common front against Japan.

On February 10, at Molotov's request, Harriman called at the
Villa Koreis to receive and discuss the first draft in English of Stalin's
political conditions for entering the war against Japan. He explained
to the Soviet Foreign Minister that Roosevelt would have to ask for
three amendments. Stalin had agreed two days earlier, Harriman
pointed out, that Port Arthur and Dairen should be free ports and that
the Manchurian railroads should be operated by a joint Russian-Chi-
nese commission. He also felt certain that the President would not wish
to settle these matters without Chiang's concurrence. All three changes
would have to be incorporated in the Russian draft.

Returning to Livadia, Harriman showed the President Molotov's
draft together with the amendments he was suggesting. Roosevelt
promptly approved the changes and Harriman resubmitted them to
Molotov. The matter was settled after the formal conference session
later that day. Stalin told Roosevelt that he agreed it would be more
appropriate for the Manchurian railroads to be operated by a joint
commission. He accepted the requirement for Chiang's concurrence,

adding that he wanted Chinese concurrence also on the status quo in Outer Mongolia. He was entirely willing to have Dairen a free port under international control, Stalin added, but Port Arthur was going to be used as a Soviet naval base, and for this a lease arrangement would be required. Roosevelt accepted this change, taking upon himself the responsibility for consulting Chiang Kai-shek as soon as Stalin notified him that the time was ripe.

Harriman was unhappy with the final Soviet text, submitted for signing by Roosevelt, Churchill and Stalin on February 11. Without prior discussion, the Russians had written into the sections concerning Manchurian ports and railroads a provision that "the pre-eminent interests of the Soviet Union shall be safeguarded." Harriman disliked the term "pre-eminent interests" and said as much to Roosevelt. But the President was not disposed to fuss over words. They meant nothing more, he said, than that the Russians had a larger interest in the area than the British or the Americans. This seemed to him true, and he was not disposed to argue over two words. Harriman also questioned a paragraph stipulating that the territorial claims of the Soviet Union in the Far East "shall be unquestionably fulfilled after Japan has been defeated." It was just language, Roosevelt replied. Here again he was not going to quarrel with Stalin.

Roosevelt felt other matters were more important, the establishment of the United Nations, for example. "He was trying like the dickens," Harriman recalled, "to get Stalin to be more cooperative in other areas that he cared about, the United Nations and Poland. He didn't want to use up whatever trading positions he had and he may have been trying to save his strength. Perhaps it was a combination of the two. Roosevelt never was much of a stickler for language. Even at Teheran, when his health was better, he didn't haggle with Stalin over language. It was my impression that as long as he could put his own interpretation on the language, he didn't much care what interpretations other people put on it."

Nor did the Joint Chiefs of Staff raise the slightest objection when Harriman showed each of them the draft agreement. He hoped that they would question one detail or another so that he could take it back to Roosevelt and persuade him to get the language changed. But Marshall, King and Leahy all approved the draft. Even Admiral Leahy, who later wrote that he believed Japan could be defeated without Russian participation, remarked to Harriman, "This makes the trip worthwhile." In his memoirs Leahy wrote: "No one was more surprised than I to see these conditions agreed to at Yalta labeled as some horrendous concessions made by Roosevelt to an enemy."[11]

The admiral carried the signed agreement back to Washington and locked it in the President's personal safe. It was not mentioned in the protocol of the Yalta Conference. When Stettinius in a private conversation at Yalta asked the President whether there was some aspect of the Far East negotiations that the State Department ought to know about, the reply was that Harriman alone had handled the matter, which was primarily military in any case, and that it had best remain that way.[12] Roosevelt, it would seem, had not a great deal more confidence in the State Department than in the Chiang Kai-shek entourage at Chungking, when it came to keeping secrets. The most important reason for secrecy, of course, was the plain fact that Russia remained at peace with Japan and ostensibly neutral. Stalin had promised Roosevelt he would shift some twenty-five divisions to the Far East as soon as they could be spared from the European front, and he had reason to fear a pre-emptive attack by the Japanese against this thinly defended area if word of his intention to declare war leaked out before those divisions were in place.

The crucial agreement, so far as the Joint Chiefs were concerned, was Stalin's commitment to join the war against Japan within two or three months after the German surrender. The Soviet Union also undertook to conclude an alliance with Chiang Kai-shek, to assist the Chinese in driving out the Japanese invaders and to respect China's "full sovereignty" in Manchuria. Stalin contended that he was asking, in return, little more than the restoration of rights and territories wrested from Imperial Russia by the Japanese in 1904. This was not strictly true of the Kurile Islands, which in fact had been peaceably transferred to Japan in 1875 by the terms of a Treaty of Commerce and Navigation with Russia. But Roosevelt dismissed Harriman's reservations on this point before signing the agreement. The Kuriles seemed to him a minor matter, measured against the larger benefits of a Russian helping hand against Japan.

Harriman, in spite of his reservations, felt the Far Eastern agreement was undermined less by Stalin's duplicity than by Chiang's weakness. "The agreement in no way weakened him," Harriman said. "Stalin recognized Chiang as the head of the government of China. The formal agreement negotiated with Stalin by Foreign Minister T. V. Soong in July of 1945 promised to respect continuing Chinese sovereignty in Manchuria. If Chiang had been strong enough at home to hold up his end, the outcome might well have been different. In my judgment it was Chiang's inherent weakness that gave the Chinese Communists their opportunity."

For Churchill the problems of winning the war in the Far East were "remote and secondary."[13] Although he signed the agreement, he had taken no part in the negotiations. His chief concern was to prevent the domination of Europe by the Soviet Union. He fought Stalin hard (Roosevelt as well, at times) to ensure a respectable postwar role for

France, to block the dismemberment of Germany and to guarantee the Polish people the right to govern themselves.

How to treat the people of Germany in defeat, a question already discussed but not decided at Teheran, consumed many hours at Yalta. Stalin insisted at the second plenary meeting on February 5 that Germany must be dismembered and forced to pay reparations. Churchill showed no enthusiasm. He talked of separating Prussia, "the tap root of all evil," from the rest of the country and he suggested that another, South German, state might be created with Vienna as its capital. But there were so many details to be settled—what about the Ruhr and the Saarland, for example?—that time would run out. The matter should be left to a group of experienced statesmen to work out later on, he argued, fighting for delay. Roosevelt agreed that further study was in order. At Hopkins' suggestion, the President as chairman referred the problem to the foreign ministers, charging them to report back within twenty-four hours. Both Roosevelt and Stalin favored telling the Germans what was in store for them by adding the word "dismemberment" to the articles of surrender, already drafted by the European Advisory Commission in London, which had agreed on "the complete disarmament and demilitarization of Germany." Churchill warned that the Germans might fight all the harder if they were told their country was to be dismembered. "We should not make this public," he pleaded. When the foreign ministers met the following day, Molotov pressed for more far-reaching language. But in the end he and Stalin accepted the single word "dismemberment."

Churchill then took the lead in advocating a zone of occupation for France, together with French participation in the Allied control machinery for Germany. Stalin need not concern himself with the details, he said. The French zone would be carved out of the zones already assigned to Britain and the United States. But Stalin persisted. If the French were to have a zone, would not other, smaller countries want a slice of German territory? Churchill dismissed the question. He was speaking only of the French, he said, and their participation was essential to keeping the peace after the war was won. It was problematical, Churchill added, how long the United States would keep its occupation forces in Europe and Britain could not, standing alone, bear the weight of an attack by a resurgent Germany in the future.

At this point Roosevelt volunteered that he did not believe American troops would stay on in Europe much longer than two years after the German surrender. Although he felt that Congress and the country would support "any reasonable measures designed to safeguard the future peace . . . he did not believe that this would extend to the maintenance of an appreciable American force in Europe."[14] The President's immediate confirmation of Churchill's surmise clinched the argument. Stalin said he now fully understood the need for a strong France, conveniently recalling that he had recently signed a treaty of alliance with De Gaulle in Moscow. Let the French have their zone, Roosevelt added, and Stalin dropped the matter, shifting his ground to the control machinery for Germany. The French had opened the gate to the enemy, he said, and the Allied Control Council for Germany should be run by those who had made the greatest sacrifices for victory; that is, the Big Three powers.

Here, too, Churchill had his way eventually, although Stalin and Molotov did not yield until several days later. Roosevelt's position had been ambiguous. He agreed with Churchill that the French should have a zone but he also sided with Stalin in trying to keep them off the Allied Control Council. The President's conversion can be traced to a series of private discussions with Hopkins and Harriman in advance of the seventh formal meeting, on February 10. Before announcing that he had changed his mind, Roosevelt sent Harriman to inform Stalin privately that he now favored a seat for France on the Control Council. Stalin replied that this being the President's considered position, he would go along with it. Accordingly, when the matter of French participation came up on February 10, it was promptly settled. The record reads:

> The President then said that he had changed his mind in regard to the question of the French participation in the Control Commission. He now agreed with the views of the Prime Minister that it would be impossible to give France an area to administer in Germany unless they were members of the Control Commission. He said he thought it would be easier to deal with the French if they were on the Commission than if they were not.
>
> Marshal Stalin said he had no objection and that he agreed to this.
>
> The Prime Minister suggested that there should be a joint telegram sent to De Gaulle informing him of these decisions to which there was general agreement.[15] *

* The telegram was delivered to De Gaulle on February 12. Although there is no record of his immediate response, it is clear that the French President was not mollified. Two days later Roosevelt received word from Jefferson Caffery, the American ambassador in Paris, that De Gaulle had changed his mind about meeting the President on his way home. Georges Bidault, the French Foreign Minister, told Caffery that De Gaulle had decided it was not convenient for him to see Roosevelt in Algiers, as arranged earlier. "I have been doing everything to make him go," Bidault said, "but he has changed his mind and you don't know how stubborn he is."[16]

The issue of exacting reparations from Germany was placed on the agenda of the February 5 meeting by Stalin. He asked Ivan M. Maisky, now Deputy Commissar for Foreign Affairs, to present the Russian plan. It called for reparations in kind rather than in money, a form of economic disarmament in which 80 percent of Germany's heavy industrial equipment was to be removed within a two-year period after the surrender, by way of compensating her victims for the devastation they had suffered. Reparations out of current production would continue for ten years. Aircraft factories, synthetic-fuel installations and other specialized plants useful only for military purposes would be totally eliminated. No amount of reparations, Maisky said, could adequately compensate the nations Hitler had attacked for their material losses. But the Russians had worked out a system of indices, assigning priorities to the victim countries in accordance with their contribution to the winning of the war and the severity of their losses. As for the Soviet Union, it was asking a total of $10 billion.

The figure, Churchill protested, was fantastic. In the last war, he recalled, all the Allies together had taken only £2 billion in reparations from Germany, and the Weimar Republic would not have been able to pay even this amount but for loans from the United States. He recognized that Russia had suffered more at the hands of Hitler than any other power, Churchill said, but the British too had suffered. They had sold off the bulk of their overseas assets to pay for the war, in spite of Lend-Lease, and would bear a heavier economic burden than any other country in the peace to follow. Yet he was inclined to doubt that it was feasible to demand large reparations for Britain.

Roosevelt played the mediator. The United States, he said, wanted no large reparations for itself. Having loaned money to Germany after the last war, it would not this time repeat the mistake. The United States also had allowed German owners to reclaim their sequestered properties in America after the war. This time he would ask Congress to pass legislation barring the return of such German assets. But if the Germans were not allowed to earn their way, they would necessarily become a burden on the rest of the world. Certainly, the President added, the German standard of living should be no higher than that of the Russians and he would support Soviet claims for reparations, but not to the point of creating mass starvation in Germany.

At the foreign ministers' meeting on February 7, Molotov submitted to Eden and Stettinius an overall estimate of $20 billion in reparations for all Allied countries, claiming 50 percent of the total for the Soviet Union. Maisky contended that $20 billion was not a large sum. Starting with an estimate of $125 billion for Germany's prewar wealth, and acknowledging that it had been reduced to some $75 billion by the cost of the war, he submitted that it was feasible to transfer 30 percent of a highly industrialized country's wealth, or as much as $22 billion to $23 billion, without inflicting gross hardship on the people. Eden and Stettinius made no comment on Maisky's arithmetic, asking for time to study the matter more carefully.

On February 9 Stettinius put forward an American reparations proposal, accepting the Russian approach that those countries which had borne the heaviest burden of war and suffered the heaviest losses were to have first priority. An Allied Reparations Commission would be set up in Moscow to study the overall amount of reparations, taking into consideration the Soviet Union's suggested total of $20 billion. Molotov seemed delighted. He asked only that the foreign ministers specify the Soviet Union was to receive half the total amount, or $10 billion. Stettinius agreed, but Eden opposed fixing any amount before the Reparations Commission had carried out its study. Harriman personally agreed with the British that it would be a mistake to mention any specific figure.

When the matter came before the Big Three the following day, Stalin taunted Churchill to say so frankly if the British felt the Russians should receive no reparations. The Prime Minister would not rise to the bait. Instead he read a telegram from the War Cabinet in London stating that the figure of $20 billion was too high, far beyond Germany's ability to pay. In the end, the Allies agreed to disagree. The final protocol recorded the American and Soviet delegations as agreeing that:

> The Moscow Reparations Commission should take in its initial studies as a basis for discussion the suggestion of the Soviet Government that the total sum of the reparation . . . should be 20 billion dollars and that 50% of it should go to the Union of Socialist Republics.

As for the British delegation, it was recorded as opposing any mention of figures until the Reparations Commission had studied the question.

It was Hopkins who had suggested this way out of the deadlock in a note he scribbled to Roosevelt during the final Yalta meeting:

> Mr. President,
>
> The Russians have given in so much at this conference that I don't think we should let them down. Let the British disagree if they want to—and continue their disagreement at Moscow. Simply say it is all referred to the Reparations Commission with the minutes to show the British disagree about any mention of the 10 billion.
>
> Harry[17]

After Roosevelt's death, the Russians were to claim that at Yalta he had supported their demand for $10 billion in reparations. They based this claim on the fact that he had agreed the Soviet figures should be taken "as a basis for discussion" in the "initial studies" of the Reparations Commission. Harriman felt, then and thereafter, that Roosevelt meant no more than what he said. It was one more case of the President, in Harriman's words, putting "his own interpretation on the language" and not troubling himself about the interpretations other people might put on the same words later.

"Stalin was most insistent that they mention the figure," Harriman recalled. "And Roosevelt gave in on that because, he said, 'This is just a basis for discussion. They have mentioned a figure and we're no worse off recording that they mentioned it.' The principle of the Russians getting fifty percent was not objected to, and the Russians certainly had every right to consider it a reasonable figure. That fifty percent was to plague us at Potsdam."

THE FATE OF POLAND, unlike the new reparations issue, had been largely decided before Roosevelt and Churchill took up the subject with Stalin at Yalta. Events were in the saddle. Stalin's troops had occupied the country. His Lublin allies were issuing decrees and seeing them carried out. If the legitimacy of the Lublin regime was still being questioned in the West, its rival was far away in London and its authority was being steadily augmented by the here-and-now presence of the Russians. It would have taken a great deal more leverage than Roosevelt and Churchill in fact possessed, or could reasonably be expected to apply, in order to alter the situation fundamentally.

Harriman understood clearly that the arrangements negotiated at Yalta could, at best, be expected to moderate the new order in Poland. Short of going to war with Russia, a prospect rejected by all but the most fanatical of the London Poles, he saw no way of undoing the Soviet Union's predominant position. "Stalin wanted weak neighbors," Harriman recalled. "He wanted to dominate them, to make certain they would never again serve as a pathway for German aggression against Russia. It is less clear to me that he was determined to communize them, at least in the beginning. He was, I think, surprised and hurt when the Red Army was not welcomed in all the neighboring countries as an army of liberation. In Poland and Rumania he discovered that the people were very antagonistic—and they have maintained those antagonisms to this day. I think he must have become more and more convinced that the only way to assure himself of friendly neighbors was to promote the establishment of Communist governments beholden to him. But it didn't happen all at once and there were exceptions—Finland, for example, Czechoslovakia and Hungary in the early days.

"Many of the things Stalin said were, of course, inconsistent. At one time he said to me that the Soviet system was not exportable. Yet, as we know, he exported it. I have often asked myself what he meant by 'the Soviet system.' Perhaps he had in mind the fact that Russia is the most complicated country in the world, with scores of nationalities and languages. The Russian Communists had developed a system for ruling this complicated society, and he may have meant to suggest that somewhat different methods would have to be used in other countries. The fact that the first Bolshevik revolution took place in Russia gave the Communist system a peculiarly Russian form. Had it taken place in China or Yugoslavia, the form would have been rather different, I believe.

"There were other inconsistencies. He obviously believed in the inevitability of world revolution. Yet at the same time he was a Great Russian imperialist first, and he was not prepared to jeopardize the Soviet state in order to push the revolution much farther west. But Poland, to him, was the traditional invasion route into Russia. Napoleon had come that way, also Hitler, and in Poland he was absolutely determined to keep control."

It was Roosevelt who opened the discussion of Poland at Yalta on February 6. Stalin, with every reason to believe that things were going his way inside Poland, had not raised the question during the first two plenary sessions. The United States, Roosevelt said, was farther away from Poland than either Russia or Britain, and distance sometimes provided a useful perspective. The American people on the whole were ready to accept the Curzon Line as Poland's eastern frontier, but there were six or seven million Poles in the United States who would like to see Lwow and the oil fields in Lwow province assigned to Poland. Although he was not insisting on this concession, it would make life easier for him at home, Roosevelt said, if the Soviet Union could "give something to Poland." He also proposed the creation of a presidential council of Polish leaders which could build a government based on five political parties, including the Communists. A government of that kind would be truly representative, he said, and deserve the support of all the great powers.[18]

Churchill, having long since conceded the Curzon Line frontier (even if Lwow were left to Russia), wanted Poland to be "mistress in her own house and captain of her soul." The main issue for him was no longer frontiers but Poland's independence. This was a question of honor, he insisted. It was for Poland's sake that Britain had gone to war in 1939 and she would not be content with any solution which did not leave the Poles free and independent. Why not form an interim government for the Poles in Yalta which could include such "good and honest" London Poles as Mikolajczyk, Grabski and Romer? Such a regime, if recognized by all three great powers, could then govern Poland until a free election became possible.

Stalin replied that if Poland was a question of honor for the British, for the Russians it was a question of life and death. Throughout history, Poland had been the corridor of attack against Russia from the west. To close this corridor to any future aggressor, the Soviet Union would have to insist upon a strong, independent, friendly Poland. As for the Curzon Line, it had been drawn by Lord Curzon and Clemenceau, not by the Russians. Lenin himself had opposed it. How could he and Molotov return to Moscow and "face the people" if they accepted less than those foreign statesmen had offered Russia back in Lenin's time? "Should we then be less Russian than Curzon and Clemenceau?"

Finally, he twitted Churchill for suggesting that a Polish government be created at Yalta, with no Poles present. "I am called a dictator and not a democrat," he said, "but I have enough democratic feeling to refuse to create a Polish government without the Poles being consulted." It would be difficult now to bring the Lublin and London Poles together. Moreover, the Lublin regime had a democratic base at least as broad as De Gaulle's in France, Stalin argued, and he had no reason to be dissatisfied with the present arrangement. While agents of the London Poles were killing Russians, attacking Red Army supply bases to seize arms and operating illegal radio transmitters, the government in Warsaw (i.e., the Lublin group) was doing its best to keep order. "As a military man," Stalin said, "I demand from a country liberated by the Red Army that there be no civil war in the rear. The men in the Red Army are indifferent to the type of government as long as it will maintain order and they will not be shot in the back. The Warsaw, or Lublin, government has not badly fulfilled this task."[19]

The crucial issue, Harriman had long felt, was not Poland's frontiers but the composition of its postwar government. Neither Britain nor the United States, in spite of their deep reservations about the attitudes of the London Poles, could accept the Provisional Government in Warsaw as at all representative of Polish opinion. It was beyond question a creature of Moscow. Roosevelt accordingly wrote a letter to Stalin on the evening of February 6 proposing a compromise: Let Bierut and Osubka-Morawski be invited to Yalta, together with such prominent Poles outside the government as Wincenty Witos, the prewar leader of the Peasant party, and Archbishop Sapieha of Cracow, both of whom had remained in Poland throughout the German and now the Russian occupations. Meeting together in Yalta, these respected national figures could help to shape a new Polish government, which would no doubt include certain Polish leaders from London such as Mikolajczyk, Grabski and Romer. The United States and Britain would then, Roosevelt said, be prepared "to examine with you conditions in which they would disassociate themselves from the London Government and transfer their recognition to the new provisional government." The proposal was shrewdly couched in terms of an appeal for the preservation of Allied unity:

> It seems to me that it puts all of us in a bad light throughout the world to have you recognizing one government while we and the British are recognizing another in London. I am sure this state of affairs should not continue and that if it does it can only lead our people to think there is a breach between us, which is not the case. I am determined that there shall be no breach between ourselves and the Soviet Union. Surely there is a way to reconcile our differences . . .
>
> You must believe me when I tell you that our people at home look with a critical eye on what they consider a disagreement between us at this vital stage of the war. They, in effect, say that if we cannot get a meeting of minds now when our armies are converging on the common enemy, how can we get an understanding on even more vital things in the future?[20]

This was not an appeal that Stalin could dismiss out of hand. The following day he said that he had tried to get the Lublin Poles on the telephone but unfortunately they were away in Cracow and Lodz. As for Witos, Sapieha and the others, he did not know their addresses and he was not sure they could be found in time to come to the Crimea. It was the flimsiest possible excuse. But before the President or the Prime Minister could put in a word, Stalin changed the subject abruptly. He said that although Molotov had prepared a draft proposal on Poland which to a certain extent met the President's ideas, it had not yet been translated. While waiting for the English text, Stalin added, "we might talk of Dumbarton Oaks."

With brilliant timing, Molotov then announced that the Soviet Union was prepared to accept the American formula for voting in the Security Council of the United Nations, a concession that Stalin had withheld for many months. (The American proposal provided for a great-power veto in voting on issues of substance, but expressly barred any party to a dispute before the Security Council from voting on it. Procedural matters were to be decided by the affirmative vote of any seven members.) This agreement on voting in the Security Council was the most concrete political achievement of the Yalta Conference. Molotov at the same time abandoned the original Soviet demand, made at Dumbarton Oaks the previous fall, that some or all of the sixteen Soviet Republics be admitted as original members. He reduced his demand at Yalta to "three or at least two" additional votes in the proposed United Nations Assembly for the Ukraine, White Russia and possibly also Lithuania. These Republics, he argued, had borne the greatest sacrifices in the war and it was "superfluous to explain" their importance in terms of size and population or in foreign affairs. Neither Roosevelt nor Churchill objected. "We all realized that Stalin would feel very much outnumbered," Harriman recalled, "and were greatly relieved that he had reduced his demand from sixteen to two additional votes." The three foreign ministers eventually worked out the details for the Ukraine and White Russia to be admitted, in effect giving the Soviet Union three votes.*

Molotov had presented his case as a contribution toward assuring "the maximum of unity among the three great powers in the question of peace and security after the war." It was an interesting echo—and an answer—to Roosevelt's appeal against breaching three-power unity over Poland. At the same time it effectively detoured the conference away from discussing the President's plan to summon the Polish leaders to Yalta. Roosevelt promptly hailed Stalin's concession, calling it "a great step forward which would be welcomed by all the peoples of the world," and Churchill expressed his "heartfelt thanks to Marshal Stalin and Mr. Molotov."

After a short intermission Molotov introduced the six-point Soviet proposal on Poland offering certain token concessions to the Western powers. The first of these was to allow minor digressions from the Curzon Line in favor of Poland, up to a distance of eight kilometers (five miles). The second consented to enlarging the Provisional Government in Warsaw by adding to it "some democratic leaders from Polish émigré circles." For the rest, the Soviet proposal fixed Poland's western frontier along a line from the city of Stettin in the north along

---

* Before leaving Yalta, Roosevelt had second thoughts about the effect upon American opinion when this decision was made known. He wrote to Stalin on February 10: "I am somewhat concerned lest it be pointed out that the United States will have only one vote in the Assembly. It may be necessary for me, therefore, if I am to ensure wholehearted acceptance by the Congress and the people . . . of our participation in the World Organization, to ask for additional votes in the Assembly in order to give parity to the United States." Stalin replied the following day: "I entirely agree with you that, since the number of votes for the Soviet Union is increased to three . . . the number of votes for the USA should also be increased." He added: "If it is necessary I am prepared officially to support this proposal."21 Roosevelt decided not to ask for more than one United States vote in the Assembly after the news of his arrangement with Stalin leaked to the New York *Herald Tribune* in late March. The newspapers, to his surprise, raised less objection to three votes for the Soviet Union than to the absurd notion that the United States also should claim three.

the Oder River and down to the western branch of the Neisse in the south. It provided for elections as soon as possible, to be organized by the enlarged Provisional Government; and it assigned the negotiations for enlarging the government to an Allied commission in Moscow made up of Molotov, Harriman and the British ambassador, Sir Archibald Clark Kerr.

Both Roosevelt and Churchill balked at the word "émigré." It was a word dating back to the French Revolution and in England at least, Churchill said, it meant a person who had been driven out by his own people. This was not true of the London Poles, who had been forced to leave their country by the brutal Nazi attack in 1939. They might be more accurately described as "Poles temporarily abroad."

On the frontier question, Churchill saw dangers in moving the Polish boundary too far to the west. "It would be a pity," he said, "to stuff the Polish goose so full of German food that it got indigestion." Some six million Germans would have to be removed from East Prussia and Silesia alone, Churchill estimated, and if the Poles also were to take over additional territory as far as the western Neisse, that would create even more of a problem. Stalin, in his most reassuring manner, said that most of the German population already had fled the region. There the day's discussion ended without a challenge by Roosevelt or Churchill to the main point of Molotov's proposal: that the existing, Soviet-fostered Warsaw regime was to remain in place. The Provisional Government could be enlarged by adding to it certain Poles who had been living in exile. Only the day before, Stalin had been saying how wrong it would be for the Great Powers to sit in Yalta and decide what kind of government Poland should have. Now he insisted that as far as the Soviets were concerned, the Lublin regime could not be replaced or substantially altered.

Again, on February 8, the Big Three wrestled with the problem of Poland to no effect. Roosevelt produced an American counterproposal, which Harriman had a hand in drafting. It authorized Molotov, Harriman and Clark Kerr to invite a representative group of Poles to Moscow for talks leading to the formation of a new Polish Government of National Unity. This was to be a government drawn from three groups—Warsaw, London and "other democratic elements inside Poland." To begin with, Bierut and Osubka-Morawski would represent the existing Provisional Government; Mikolajczyk and Grabski, the London Poles; and Witos and Archbishop Sapieha, the "other democratic elements." Meeting in Moscow under the guidance of Molotov and the two Western ambassadors, this assortment of Poles would be asked to form an interim government, pledged to the holding of free elections for a constitutional assembly. Once the constitution was ready, a permanent government could be elected and recognized by the three Allied governments.

Churchill quickly withdrew his own British counterproposal, explaining that with slight amendments he could support Roosevelt's. Molotov and Stalin lost no time, however, in attacking the American plan. It was one thing, the Russians argued, to enlarge the existing Polish government in Warsaw, but they would not accept a scheme to replace or even to change it greatly. In an eloquent appeal for unity, Churchill said the conference had reached its crucial stage. If the Allies went home still recognizing separate Polish governments, the world would see the conference as a failure and nothing else that was agreed to at Yalta would overcome this impression. The plain fact, he said, was that the British government could not accept the Lublin-Warsaw regime as broadly representative of the Polish people. Nor could it brush aside the London Poles, and the 150,000 Polish soldiers fighting with the Western Allies in France and Italy. That would be regarded as "an act of betrayal." The American record, while incomplete, catches part of the flavor:

> The Prime Minister made it clear that, speaking only for Great Britain, it would be said that the British Government had given way completely on frontiers, had accepted the Soviet view and championed it. To break altogether with the lawful government of Poland which had been recognized during all these five years of war would be an act subject to the most severe criticism in England. It would be said that we did not know what was going on in Poland—that we could not even get anyone in there to find out what was going on, and that we had accepted *in toto* the view of the Lublin government. Great Britain would be charged with forsaking the cause of Poland and he was bound to say that the debates in Parliament would be painful and, he might add, most dangerous to Allied unity.[22]

Stalin at this point smoothly turned aside Roosevelt's proposition while assuring Churchill that the situation was not so tragic as he had made it out. The Polish Provisional Government, he repeated, was popular and no less legitimate than De Gaulle's in Paris, although neither one had been elected. But the day was drawing near when elections could be held. Meanwhile the Allies ought to concentrate on essentials, and "deal with the reconstruction of the Provisional Government rather than attempt to set up a new one."

Roosevelt, who had said little during the heated debate, asked Stalin how soon elections might be held in Poland. In a month, the

Marshal replied, if there were no catastrophes on the fighting front. Taking encouragement from Stalin's promise of free elections, Roosevelt proposed that the Polish question be referred to the foreign ministers. The final agreement drafted by Stettinius, Molotov and Eden was approved on the evening of February 9:

> A new situation has been created in Poland as a result of her complete liberation by the Red Army. This calls for the establishment of a Polish Provisional Government which can be more broadly based than was possible before the liberation of Western Poland. The Provisional Government which is now functioning in Poland should be reorganized on a broader democratic basis with the inclusion of democratic leaders from Poland itself and from Poles abroad. This new government should then be called the Polish Provisional Government of National Unity.
>
> Mr. Molotov, Mr. Harriman and Sir Archibald Clark Kerr are authorized to consult in the first instance in Moscow with members of the present Provisional Government and with other Polish democratic leaders from within Poland and from abroad with a view to the reorganization of the present government along the above lines. The Polish Provisional Government of National Unity shall be pledged to the holding of free and unfettered elections as soon as possible on the basis of universal suffrage and secret ballot. In these elections all democratic and anti-Nazi parties shall have the right to take part and put forward candidates.

Roosevelt and Churchill have been bitterly criticized ever since Yalta for accepting those two paragraphs in their determination to avoid a split with Stalin. Harriman felt at the time that the language was far too vague and generalized. He and Bohlen agreed before leaving Yalta that there was bound to be trouble ahead.

"There was an expression we used at the embassy at the time—that trading with the Russians you had to buy the same horse twice," Harriman recalled. "I had that feeling about the Polish agreement and said as much to Bohlen. He agreed that the whole negotiation we had just completed at Yalta would have to be developed again from the ground up. We had established nothing more than the machinery for renegotiation.

"One of my great regrets was that we did not insist upon bringing the Polish leaders to Yalta. It had been proposed and I was strongly for it. When Stalin came up with the lame excuse that he didn't know where to find them, neither Roosevelt nor Churchill insisted. In better health, FDR might have decided to stay in Yalta until the thing was done. Some more acceptable compromise might have been worked out if Witos and Sapieha and the Lublin people had been brought down to Yalta.

"The President also gave in on another critical point, which I had particular reason to regret. That was in accepting Stalin's language that instead of creating a new Polish government, the existing Provisional Government should be reorganized to include 'democratic leaders from Poland itself and from Poles abroad.' I was gravely concerned because unless you knew whom you were talking about, that could be fudged. But Roosevelt was not ready to fight that one. No names were mentioned. There was no detailed discussion of the kind of government to be established. And Molotov was able to insist in the subsequent Moscow talks with Clark Kerr and myself that the reorganization called for nothing more than the addition of one or two non-Communist ministers, who had no real power, to the existing Lublin crowd."

Harriman also was to discover that Molotov would reinterpret the plain language concerning consultation "in the first instance in Moscow" with members of the existing Provisional Government and other Poles to mean that the men of Lublin would decide who should take part in the negotiations. It was clear to Harriman then, as it is now, that Roosevelt and Churchill, in accepting the language, had in mind nothing more than that the first meeting should be in Moscow rather than Warsaw.

The commitment to hold free elections was enshrined not only in the Polish agreement but also in the Declaration on Liberated Europe, signed at Yalta. The declaration reads in pertinent part:

> The establishment of order in Europe and the rebuilding of national economic life must be achieved by processes which will enable the liberated peoples to destroy the last vestiges of nazism and fascism and to create democratic institutions of their own choice. This is a principle of the Atlantic Charter— the right of all peoples to choose the form of government under which they will live—the restoration of sovereign rights and self-government to those peoples who have been forcibly deprived of them by aggressor nations.
>
> To foster the conditions in which the liberated peoples may exercise these rights, the three governments will jointly assist the peoples in any European liberated state or former Axis satellite state in Europe where in their judgment conditions require (a) to establish conditions of internal peace; (b) to carry out emergency measures for the relief of distressed peoples; (c) to form interim governmental authorities broadly

representative of all democratic elements in the population and
pledged to the earliest possible establishment through free
elections of governments responsive to the will of the people;
and (d) to facilitate where necessary the holding of such elections.

By present-day standards of rhetoric, the declaration sounds
grandiloquent. Roosevelt and Churchill had no choice but to take
Stalin at his word that free elections would be held, not only in
Poland but across Eastern Europe. Harriman has never believed, however, that more explicit language would have forced Stalin to honor
these commitments.

"I believed at the time that Stalin meant to keep his word, at
least within his own interpretation of 'free elections,' although I had
always expected that we would have trouble over those words. He
did not, in my judgment, sign the declaration with the intention of
breaking it. It seems to me a mistake to assume that Stalin had a fixed
plan to force Communist governments on all the countries of Eastern
Europe. He doubtless expected that the Red Army would be welcomed everywhere as a liberating force. I am inclined to believe that
the Communist leaders in these countries greatly overestimated their
popularity and reported in that vein to Moscow. In short, Stalin at first
mistakenly believed that there was little risk in promising free elections because the Communists were popular enough to win.

"It was after Yalta that he must have discovered he had been
misled about the depth of their popular support and then he changed
his mind. Hungary was a case in point. He did allow a free election
there in November, and the Communists polled barely seventeen percent of the vote against fifty-seven percent for the Smallholders party.
It seemed odd that a few months earlier the Smallholders, a peasant
party, also should have won the election for the city government of
Budapest over a combined slate of Communists and Social Democrats.
The reason, of course, was its anti-Communism. After that it didn't
take Stalin long to squeeze out the Smallholders, and he allowed no
more free elections in Hungary."

Harriman could not agree with George Kennan, his number two
in the Moscow embassy, that the Western Allies should have refused
to bargain with the Russians at Yalta. Kennan argued that instead of
trying to negotiate issues that were not negotiable, the rational course
was to divide Europe frankly into two spheres of influence and accept
no responsibility for whatever the Russians did in their sphere, because
the United States and Britain were too weak to affect it.[23]

"I could not—and cannot—agree with this position," Harriman
later observed. "I felt very strongly that it was absolutely necessary

for Roosevelt and Churchill to do everything they possibly could, to provide an opportunity for the peoples of Eastern Europe to develop governments that would be friendly to, but not the creatures of, Moscow. If they had failed to make the effort, they would have been condemned by history as having willfully sold out these countries. This was an honest attempt to build an orderly relationship with the Russians and there was a certain amount of give and take on our part in the hope of achieving orderly settlements. The fact that we tried and failed left the main responsibility for the Cold War with Stalin, where it belongs."

IN SPITE OF THE GRAVE TALK around the conference table, Yalta was not all solemnity. Stalin showed a surprisingly light touch in difficult moments as, for example, when Roosevelt said that he wanted the postwar election in Poland to be "the first one beyond question . . . like Caesar's wife." Stalin responded, "They said that about her but in fact she had her sins."

As the host at dinner in the Villa Koreis on February 8, Stalin outdid himself in paying tribute to Roosevelt and Churchill. Harriman had never seen Stalin in better form. He toasted the Prime Minister for his courage and staunchness, recalling the bitter months when Britain fought the Germans all alone, "irrespective of existing or potential allies." He knew of few examples in history, Stalin said, when the courage of one man had meant so much to the whole world.

Following Churchill's no less gracious response, Stalin raised his glass to the health of the President. For himself and for Churchill, he began, the war decisions had been relatively simple—their countries, after all, were fighting for their very existence. But, he said, there was a third man at the head of the table whose country had not been threatened with invasion but who, possessed of a broader conception of national interest, had been the chief forger of the weapons which had mobilized the world against Hitler. Stalin cited Lend-Lease as one of Roosevelt's most remarkable and vital achievements.

Kathleen Harriman, in behalf of Anna Boettiger and Sarah Churchill as well as herself, was tapped by her father to propose a toast in Russian after Stalin clinked glasses with all three and drank the health of "the ladies." Coached by Bohlen on one side and General Antonov on the other, she raised her glass "to those who had worked so hard in the Crimea for our comfort," adding that she had seen enough destruction wrought in the area by the Germans to realize what had been accomplished. "Jesus, I was scared," she wrote home afterward.

Miss Harriman also noted, in her letter, the unexpected presence at dinner of Lavrentia Beria, head of the NKVD and beyond question the most dreaded man in Russia. "He's little and fat with thick lenses, which give him a sinister look, but quite genial," she wrote. Clark Kerr offered a toast to Beria, describing him as the man "who looks after our bodies." Churchill was not amused. He walked over to the British ambassador and instead of clinking glasses shook his finger at him. "Be careful," Churchill said, "be careful."

Of all the Russians present, Beria was to be the one most directly concerned with the carrying out of an agreement, signed at Yalta on February 11 by General Deane for the United States and Lieutenant General A. A. Gryzlov for the Soviet Union, providing for the repatriation of liberated prisoners of war. The agreement was not, in fact, negotiated at Yalta and Roosevelt never saw the document. It was the product of a joint approach to the Soviet General Staff made exactly eight months earlier by General Deane and his British counterpart in Moscow, General Burrows. Their sole purpose was to make certain that American and British prisoners of war being held in camps soon to be overrun by the Red Army would be well cared for and swiftly returned home.[24] Not until January 19, 1945, however, and only after repeated interventions by George Kennan and Harriman with Molotov, had Deane succeeded in sitting down with Lieutenant General K. D. Golubev, deputy administrator of the Soviet Repatriation Commission, to discuss terms. The agreement, quickly negotiated in the days before the Yalta Conference and cleared with Eisenhower, also provided for the return to Russia of Soviet prisoners liberated by the Allies in Western Europe. It was inconceivable to Deane at the time that any appreciable number of the liberated Russians would refuse to return home. He had no reason to suspect that the Soviet state would treat as deserters all soldiers who had surrendered to the Germans.

"Our officers were thinking of the welfare of our own prisoners, some seventy-five thousand men, who without exception could not get home quickly enough," Harriman recalled. "We had no idea that hundreds of thousands of the Soviet citizens would refuse because they had reason to suspect they would be sent to their deaths or to Beria's prison camps. That knowledge came later."

Not a word in the agreement required the American and British commanders to forcibly repatriate Soviet citizens against their will. But the Russians insisted upon that cruel interpretation and the Western Allies went along until the spring of 1946, shipping trainload after trainload of former prisoners and slave laborers, including women and children, back to Russia. Eisenhower and his staff were fearful that if they did not send back the Soviet prisoners the Russians might seize upon one pretext or another to hold up the return of American prisoners from Eastern Europe.

THE YALTA CONFERENCE ENDED on February 11 with a flurry of amendments and minor excitements over drafting changes in the final communiqué. Churchill, Roosevelt and Stalin signed it at lunch, in that order. Roosevelt had suggested that Stalin sign first "because he has been such a wonderful host." Churchill, in a jocular mood, argued that he ought to sign first by reason of the alphabet and the fact that he was older than the rest. Stalin agreed, warning Churchill and Roosevelt that if his own name appeared first, people would say that he had led the conference.

Much against Harriman's advice, the President allowed his naval aide, Vice Admiral Wilson Brown, to persuade him to leave for Sebastopol after lunch. The crew of the U.S.S. *Catoctin*, moored in the harbor there, had been handling the coded communications between Livadia and Washington throughout the conference, and Admiral Brown urged the President to spend the night on board because, he said, it would boost morale.

"I was violently opposed to Brown's idea," Harriman recalled. "I wanted the President to spend the night at Yalta and leave refreshed the next morning. But Roosevelt, always a Navy man, agreed to go. It was a three-hour drive over twisting roads and when we reached the ship it was so hot on board that I almost collapsed myself. The President had a gastly night and I think it affected his health. At any rate, he looked tired and worn the next morning. I was indignant that Admiral Brown should have put him through this wholly unnecessary agony. He must have thought it was a plus for the Navy."

At five minutes to seven on Monday morning, February 12, the presidential party left the *Catoctin* for Saki Airfield, where *The Sacred Cow* was waiting to fly him to Egypt for meetings on board the *Quincy* with King Farouk of Egypt, Haile Selassie of Ethiopia and Ibn Saud of Saudi Arabia. Harriman waved goodbye, before flying north to Moscow with Stettinius to confront again the maddening intricacies of the Polish tragedy. It was the last time he saw Franklin Roosevelt.

CHAPTER XVIII

From Yalta
to Warm Springs

THE WAR IN THE WEST was moving toward its grand climax by the
time Roosevelt returned home. On March 1, as the President
rode up Pennsylvania Avenue to Capitol Hill to deliver his message to
the Congress, Eisenhower's armies in Europe were sweeping the Germans before them along an eighty-mile stretch of the Rhine frontier
from Düsseldorf down to Koblenz.

Buoyed by Stalin's agreement on conditions for establishing the
United Nations, Roosevelt spoke of the Yalta Conference as "a turning point—I hope in our history and therefore in the history of the
world." The Crimea decisions, he said, "ought to spell the end of the
system of unilateral action, the exclusive alliances, the spheres of influence, the balances of power, and all the other expedients that have
been tried for centuries—and have always failed." As for the stubborn
problem of Poland, Roosevelt said he was convinced that he had
worked out with Stalin and Churchill "the most hopeful agreement
possible for a free, independent and prosperous Polish state."

Churchill, addressing the House of Commons on February 27,
had dealt more specifically with the agreement on Poland and the great
unanswered questions still overhanging that country:

> The home of the Poles is settled. Are they to be masters in
> their own house? Are they to be free, as we in Britain and the
> United States or France are free? Are their sovereignty and
> their independence to be untrammelled, or are they to become
> a mere projection of the Soviet State, forced against their will

by an armed minority to adopt a Communist or totalitarian system? I am putting the case in all its bluntness. It is a touchstone far more sensitive and vital than the drawing of frontier lines. Where does Poland stand? Where do we all stand on this?

Most solemn declarations have been made by Marshal Stalin and the Soviet Union that the sovereign independence of Poland is to be maintained, and this decision is now joined in both by Great Britain and the United States. . . . The Poles will have their future in their own hands, with the single limitation that they must honestly follow, in harmony with their Allies, a policy friendly to Russia. That is surely reasonable. . . .

The impression I brought back from the Crimea, and from all my other contacts, is that Marshal Stalin and the Soviet leadership wish to live in honourable friendship and equality with the Western democracies. I feel also that their word is their bond.[1]

The war news from the western front was intoxicating enough to banish dark thoughts of trouble ahead. General Omar Bradley's 12th Army Group was rapidly pushing the battered Wehrmacht back across the Rhine while the Russians, holding their positions on the Oder, also struck northward to cut off the Baltic port of Danzig. On March 7 the U.S. First Army captured Cologne. Its 9th Armored Division, astonished to find the railroad bridge at Remagen weakened but intact, dashed across boldly the same day to open the first Allied bridgehead on the east bank of the Rhine.

Inside Poland and Rumania, however, where the fighting had ended weeks earlier, the march of events appeared to mock the high-flown promises written into the Yalta agreements. "The war is going wonderfully well again now," Kathleen Harriman wrote from Moscow to her sister in New York on March 8. "But the news is slightly dampened here by our gallant allies who at the moment are being most bastard-like. Averell is very busy—what with Poland, PWs and, I guess, the Balkans. The house is full of running feet, voices and phones ringing all night long—up until dawn."

Apart from Poland, Harriman's most pressing concern was the welfare of thousands of Americans liberated from German prisoner-of-war camps in East Prussia and western Poland by the advancing Red Army. Although the Russians had agreed at Yalta that American repatriation teams would have the right of "immediate access" to the camps and collection centers where the prisoners were waiting to be evacuated, repeated requests to the Soviet General Staff had been ignored or dismissed. Nor would the Russians allow American planes to fly into the liberated areas, although the Deane-Gryzlov agreement expressly provided that "each of the contracting parties shall be at liberty to use in agreement with the other party such of its own means of transport as may be available for the repatriation of its citizens."[2]

Harriman and Deane became so frustrated by Soviet refusals and evasions that they urged a direct presidential appeal to Stalin. On March 4, exactly three weeks after the signing of the prisoner agreement at Yalta, Roosevelt cabled Stalin asking permission for ten American planes, based in Poltava, to fly into Poland and pick up prisoners caught behind Red Army lines. Stalin refused. "There is no need at the moment for U.S. planes to fly from Poltava to Polish territory," he replied the following day. Stalin insisted that all the prisoners, except those too ill to travel, had been sent to Odessa on the Black Sea, the assembly point designated by the Russians, which was more than 600 miles from the interior of Poland where they had been liberated.

Harriman and Deane had good reason to question Stalin's assurances when three bedraggled American officers from a prisoner-of-war camp at Szubin, in northwestern Poland, made their way to Moscow after hitchhiking all the way across Poland and western Russia. The officers—Captain Ernest M. Gruenberg of New York, Second Lieutenant Frank H. Colley from Washington, Georgia, and Second Lieutenant John N. Dimmling, Jr., from Winston Salem, North Carolina—told a different story. They reported that some two hundred American prisoners had been left behind at Szubin when the Germans moved out. They told of thirty Americans in a Russian hospital at Wegheim. Hundreds more were wandering in the rear of the Red Army, searching for an American in authority and being ignored by the Russians. When Richard Rossbach, a nephew of Herbert H. Lehman, the former governor of New York, turned up among the prisoners at Odessa, Harriman ordered him to Moscow and put him up at Spaso House. Rossbach told of hiding out from the Russians for days, making his way to Warsaw and then being trundled all the way to Odessa in a boxcar. He spoke gratefully of the hospitality he and his companions had received from Polish peasants. But the Red Army men had been indifferent, taking little or no interest in the condition of the Allied prisoners.

Dismayed by all this testimony, Harriman on March 8 sent a message to Roosevelt disputing Soviet contentions that only 2,100 American prisoners had been liberated, of whom 1,350 had reached Odessa: "Our information received from our liberated prisoners indicates that there have been four or five thousand officers and enlisted men freed . . . there appear to be hundreds of our prisoners wandering about Poland trying to locate American contact officers for protection."

The Russians, under daily battering by Harriman and Deane, finally allowed one American officer and one Army doctor to enter Poland. But they were forbidden to move out of the city of Lublin. "I am outraged," Harriman cabled to Roosevelt after Molotov, on March 14, had slyly suggested that it was the Polish Provisional Government, not the Red Army, that was objecting to the entry of American officers. "The Soviet Government, I feel, is trying to use our liberated prisoners as a club to induce us to give increased prestige to the Polish Provisional Government by dealing with it," Harriman reported. The President, on March 17, tried once again to persuade Stalin:

> I cannot in all frankness understand your reluctance to permit American contact officers with the necessary means to assist their own people in this matter. This Government had done everything to meet each of your requests. I now request you to meet mine in this particular matter.

Again the answer was "No." The President was misinformed, Stalin replied on March 22. He contended that all the American prisoners were being well treated, better treated in fact than Soviet prisoners in American camps. If the matter had concerned him personally, he would, of course, "be ready to give way." But his Soviet commanders did not have the time to bother with "odd officers who, while having no relation to the military operations, need looking after, want all kinds of meetings and contacts, protection against possible acts of sabotage by German agents not yet ferreted out, and other things that divert the attention of the commanders and their subordinates from their direct duties."[3]

Infuriated by Stalin's reply, Harriman reported to Roosevelt on March 24:

> Stalin's statement that our liberated prisoners are in Soviet camps under good conditions is far from the truth. Soviet facilities in Odessa meet the barest minimum needs [although they] are improved as a result of the work of our contact officers and the American food, clothing and medical supplies that we have been able to furnish. Until arrival at Odessa the hardships undergone [by the prisoners] have been inexcusable. No effort whatsoever has been made by the Red Army until our men drifted into camps at Warsaw, Lodz, Lublin or Wrzenia, which the Red Army advertised as points of assembly. These are some hundreds of miles from the points of

liberation and our men would have starved if it had not been for the generosity and hospitality of the Polish people. Individual headquarters of the Red Army have sometimes given a meal to our men. On the other hand, reports indicate that in other places not only was nothing done but Red Army soldiers have taken wrist watches, clothing and other articles at the point of a gun . . .

It was preposterous, Harriman added, for Stalin to argue that the Red Army command in Poland could not be bothered with perhaps a dozen American officers, in light of all the help that the United States had sent to Russia over the war years. He urged the President to cable Stalin once again and to consider retaliatory steps, for example, by instructing Eisenhower to limit the movements of Russian contact officers in France. But Roosevelt had decided against further personal appeals. In a message to Harriman, dated March 26, he replied: "It does not appear appropriate for me to send another message now to Stalin . . . There may be some prospect of results from a further message . . . at a later date. Meanwhile you should make such approaches in Moscow as in your opinion will be of assistance to our intention to insure the best possible treatment of Americans who are liberated."

Roosevelt did pass on to the War Department Harriman's suggestion for reciprocal limitations on Soviet officers in France, although nothing more was done. The callousness of Stalin's attitude, however, profoundly affected Harriman's view of the prospects for postwar collaboration with Russia. He had long before cautioned the President and the State Department that American generosity was being misread in the Kremlin as weakness; he had advocated a "firm but friendly *quid pro quo* attitude" toward Russian demands and the White House had steadily declined his advice. Even the military professionals in Washington seemed fearful that a show of American toughness might prompt Stalin to conclude a separate peace with the Germans, or to break his promise of going to war against Japan. To Harriman, both these notions seemed ridiculous. Accordingly, on April 2, he cabled the President:

> Aside from the major questions which are causing concern in our relations with the Soviet Government there has been, starting some six weeks ago, an accumulation of minor incidents of which the following are only examples:
> On March 15 I personally requested a visa for General Eaker to come to Moscow to discuss the details of the establishment of air bases in the Budapest area in accordance with Marshal Stalin's agreement with you [at Yalta]. Although I

constantly pressed the Foreign Office, this request was not even answered and on March 23, when General Eaker was transferred from Italy [to Washington], it was withdrawn.

In getting approval for our air teams to visit Soviet-controlled territory for appraisal of bomb damage, and for our naval team to visit Gdynia, little or no progress has been made. Both proposals were agreed to in the Crimea.

General Deane and I on March 2 requested a visa for Colonel Ames [to be] sent here in connection with the bomb-damage appraisal project. He has been sitting in Teheran for a month and no reply has been given to a number of my requests.

General Deane has reported to the War Department that all our planes in Soviet and Soviet-controlled territory are grounded, affecting particularly the salvage of our combat planes coming down in these areas. 163 American combat flyers of stranded aircraft now in Poltava are thus held there.

Today Deane has sent to the War Department recommendations that drastic retaliatory measures be taken in the cases of Gdynia and our stranded aircraft. I earnestly recommend that these proposals be approved.

I feel certain that unless we do take action in cases of this kind, the Soviet Government will become convinced that they can force us to accept any of their decisions on all matters and it will be increasingly difficult to stop their aggressive policy. We may get some temporary repercussions, but if we stand firm I am satisfied it is the only way we can hope to come to a reasonable basis of give and take with these people.

Whatever we do, however, I am convinced it will not affect the Soviets' major determination to go all-out in the defeat of Germany nor what they may do in the Far East.

The Soviets decide to do things not to obtain our good-will but because they think their interests are being served. Conversely, the things we do to assist or please them do not obtain good-will from them. Failure to stand our ground is interpreted as a sign of weakness. We will get them to recognize our point of view only if we show them specifically that their interests are being adversely affected. It is my belief that if we adopt firm measures in several cases such as those Deane has proposed the Soviets will pay more attention to our requests in other matters of a more fundamental nature, such as those that may arise at the San Francisco conference. I am convinced that we will have greater difficulties as time goes on if we delay adoption of this policy.

In Rumania, King Michael had shown extraordinary courage in personally dismissing the pro-German government of Marshal Ion Antonescu the previous summer. He proclaimed the end of collaboration in a radio broadcast and offered to join forces with the Soviet Union. With the armistice, a new coalition regime had been established in Bucharest, committed to carry on the war alongside the Red Army. Here the Russians insisted upon a free hand, justifying their claim on the ground that Rumania was an immediate neighbor, that they had suffered more than the rest of the Allies from Antonescu's adherence to the Rome-Berlin Axis and that it was the Red Army which had driven the Germans out. An Allied Control Commission was set up to supervise the armistice but it was clearly subordinate to the Soviet high command. The American member, Brigadier General Cortland T. Van Rensselaer Schuyler, soon found that he could observe, he could complain, he could report to his government, but he had no power to act.

From the beginning Harriman had been under few illusions about the likely course of events in Rumania. On September 14, 1944, he had predicted that the Soviet high command would exercise unlimited control over the economic life of the country and unbridled police power as well. He foresaw the Russians dealing with the various political groups in the coalition—moderate conservatives, Socialists and Communists—to the degree that each accommodated Moscow's wishes. Two weeks after Yalta, Harriman's bleak forecast was being confirmed.

Ana Pauker and Gheorghe Gheorghiu-Dej, two tough Rumanian Communists who had sat out the war in Moscow, moved to create a political crisis that would bring down the coalition government, led by General Nicolae Radescu. General Schuyler warned Washington and the embassy in Moscow that the days of Radescu were numbered. In a long telegram, dated February 20, 1945, he defined the Soviet goal: to disintegrate the historic political parties of Rumania by creating a situation in which only a government of the left could maintain order. Four days later the Communist-led National Democratic Front staged a mass demonstration in Bucharest. When police fired a burst of gunfire over the heads of the crowd, the Communist press charged the government with a "massacre" and demanded Radescu's dismissal. The Premier defended himself in a radio broadcast, charging that a handful of Communists was attempting to subdue the nation by terror. For this he was sternly reprimanded by the Soviet member of the Allied Control Commission, who when pressed by the British and American members refused to call a meeting of the commission.

Both Clark Kerr and Harriman filed protests with Molotov. Harriman argued that political developments inside Rumania "should take an orderly course along the lines indicated in the Declaration on Liberated Europe, issued at the Crimea Conference." If they did not, then the United States would call for full consultation among the three governments, as provided in the declaration. In reply, Molotov and Vishinsky denounced the Radescu government, contending that it was incapable of maintaining order in the rear of the Red Army and supported by Fascist elements. Vishinsky arrived in Bucharest the following afternoon, insisting that he must see King Michael the same evening, and demanded that General Radescu's regime be replaced by a new government based on "the truly democratic forces of the country."

When the King temporized the next day, Vishinsky gave him "just two hours and five minutes to inform the public that General Radescu has been dismissed" and then stalked out, slamming the door as he went.

In Moscow, Harriman filed another protest with Molotov, reminding the Russians of their obligations (under the Atlantic Charter, the Yalta decisions and the Rumanian armistice agreement) to consult their allies and to maintain a broadly representative government instead of seeking to impose one drawn solely from the Communist-directed National Democratic Front. The protest proved fruitless. By nightfall of March 6 the King saw no alternative but to appoint Petru Groza, the Soviet choice, as Premier of a new coalition government. Thirteen of the seventeen ministers in the new Cabinet belonged to groups which Groza could command.

The United States and Britain refused to recognize the Groza regime because, in their view, it spoke for a minority of the Rumanian population. But the Soviet Union, eager to strengthen its chosen instrument, hastily announced that it would return to Rumania the province of northern Transylvania, which Hitler had awarded to Hungary. Molotov dismissed Harriman's sheaf of protests in a letter suggesting that the issue had "lost its keenness" now that a new government had been established in Bucharest. Washington could not agree that the issue was dead. It instructed Harriman to keep pressing for tripartite consultations on ways of fulfilling the Yalta commitments to free elections. He did so faithfully and Molotov kept brushing them aside.

In a message to Churchill, dated March 11, Roosevelt showed his full awareness of what was happening in Rumania:

I am fully determined, as I know you are, not to let the good decisions we reached at the Crimea slip through our hands and will certainly do everything I can to hold Stalin to their honest fulfillment. In regard to the Rumanian situation, Averell has taken up and is taking up again the whole question with Molotov, invoking the Declaration on Liberated Europe, and has proposed tripartite discussions to carry out these responsibilities. It is obvious that the Russians have installed a minority government of their own choosing, but . . . Rumania is not a good place for a test case. The Russians have been in undisputed control from the beginning and with Rumania lying athwart the Russian lines of communications it is more difficult to contest the plea of military necessity and security which they are using to justify their action. We shall certainly do everything we can, however, and of course will count on your support.[4]

Harriman's view from Moscow was anything but hopeful. On balance, however, he advised Washington on March 14 that Poland was the more promising test:

I recognize that the Rumanian situation is in many ways secondary in importance to Poland, and if we come to a point in our relations with the Soviet Government where we feel we must make a major issue, I believe that we would be on firmer grounds to do so in connection with Poland. Also, a serious and public issue over Rumania might prejudice our chances of a reasonable settlement regarding Poland.[5]

Even as he sent the March 14 message, Harriman had reason to wonder whether the prospect of a reasonable settlement in Poland was not fast becoming a pipe dream. The tripartite commission on Poland —Harriman, Clark Kerr and Molotov—had been meeting in Moscow since February 23. At the first session, Molotov took the position that the Poles designated by the Provisional Government in Warsaw must be invited to Moscow ahead of the others. He further demanded that the names of all others to be invited, whether from inside Poland or from London, must be approved in advance by the Warsaw group. In short, the men of Lublin, now installed in Warsaw by the Russians, must have veto power over invitations to any Poles outside their own circle. When Clark Kerr and Harriman objected that the commission must be free to invite whomever it chose, Molotov appeared to concede the point. It was just a matter of permitting Warsaw to "express an opinion" on the list of other Poles to be invited, the Foreign Minister said, in his most disarming manner. The commission's first message to Warsaw, accordingly, invited the Provisional Government to name its own representatives and listed eight other Poles whom the commission proposed to invite to Moscow: Mikolajczyk, Grabski and Romer from London; Archbishop Sapieha and old Witos from Poland; also Zygmunt Zulawski, a Socialist trade-union leader, Professor Franciszek Bujak, professor of chemistry at Lwow; and Professor

Stanislaw Kutrzeba, a Cracow historian who was president of the Polish Academy of Sciences. The last five names, incidentally, had been put forward at Yalta by Roosevelt, without objection from Stalin.

In reply, Warsaw accepted only Professor Kutrzeba. As for the London list, Warsaw blackballed Mikolajczyk, ostensibly because he had criticized the Yalta decisions, and Romer on the ground that he did not represent "any democratic tendency in Poland." Of the London group, only Grabski met with no Soviet objection. The wrangling over lists of names went back and forth for many weeks. The British and American governments had long since concluded that most members of the Polish government-in-exile had disqualified themselves by public expressions of distrust for the Soviet Union. But they held the participation of Mikolajczyk himself to be "a *sine qua non*," in the words of Clark Kerr. Since the death of Sikorski, Mikolajczyk had become the most respected of all the Poles in exile and was looked upon as a symbol of essential decency in the United States as well as Britain. On this point the Western ambassadors could not yield.

The resulting deadlock led the commission to invite a delegation from Warsaw on February 24 and then, at the insistence of Clark Kerr, to postpone the invitation just as Bierut, Osubka-Morawski and General Rola-Zymierski were preparing to leave for Moscow. Molotov made a similar reversal when, in response to complaints by the Western ambassadors that they had no reliable information out of Poland, he blandly suggested on February 27 that Britain and the United States might send observers to investigate—and then withdrew the offer two days later, contending that the self-respect of the Warsaw group must be taken into account. Molotov urged the British and Americans to approach the Warsaw government directly, because the Poles were bosses in their own country. This transparent attempt to force the Western powers to deal with the Warsaw regime, whose legitimacy they questioned, came to nothing. But Molotov's show of solicitude for Polish self-respect was to be repeated several times. When the question was discussed again on March 22, he solemnly declared that the very idea of admitting British and American observers by prearrangement with the Russians would "sting the national pride of the Poles to the quick."

Harriman came to believe that Molotov's stonewalling tactics had been carefully worked out in advance with the Warsaw regime during a visit to Moscow by Bierut immediately after Yalta. In an analytical message to Washington, dated March 7, he warned that time was on the side of Bierut's regime:

> The Lublin Government every day is becoming more and more the Warsaw Government and the ruler of Poland. I am

told, from eyewitness reports, that governmental machinery is being established under the direction of Warsaw throughout the recently liberated areas . . .

Molotov, if he is successful in inducing us to invite the Lublinites to Moscow before inviting any outside Poles, will be in the position of refereeing a discussion between Clark Kerr and myself on the one side and the Lublinites on the other, in which [they] will present sincere or trumped-up charges against each of our dangerous candidates . . .

I do not like even to suggest the thought of a breakdown of our conversations, but I recommend strongly that we now pursue no course on which we would not be willing, if Molotov continues to be unreasonable, to rest our case.

A month had passed since Yalta without the slightest move toward the creation of a Government of National Unity which could hold free elections. Although Churchill had carried the House of Commons in support of the Crimea decisions, eleven members of his government, alarmed over the news out of Poland, had abstained in a subsequent vote and two had resigned. His rising anxiety led the Prime Minister to draft a personal appeal to Stalin. He sent it to Roosevelt, who replied on March 10: "Our personal intervention, I feel, should be deferred until we exhaust every other possibility of bringing the Soviet Government into line." More messages followed. Churchill gave voice to his fears that the American and British governments might drift apart, that further delay served only Stalin's purpose. "It suits the Soviets very well to have a long period of delay," he wrote, "so that the process of liquidation of elements unfavourable to them or their puppets may run its full course."[6]

Roosevelt assured him that the Western Allies would stand together. Their disagreements were purely tactical, he wrote, not affecting the substance of the Polish question. But Churchill was not put off. The rising storm in Parliament and British public opinion would have to be faced. On March 13 he wrote again to Roosevelt:

I do not wish to reveal a divergence between the British and United States Governments, but it would certainly be necessary for me to make it clear [in Parliament] that we are in [the] presence of a great failure and an utter breakdown of what was settled at Yalta, but that we British have not the necessary strength to carry the matter further and that the limits of our capacity to act have been reached. The moment that Molotov sees that he has beaten us away from the whole process of consultations among Poles to form a new government, he will know that we will put up with anything.[7]

After detailed negotiation between the White House and 10 Downing Street, Harriman and Clark Kerr received instructions to present a joint memorandum to Molotov, reviewing the Yalta decisions on Poland. In this document, dated March 19, the British and American governments pointed out that there had been no agreement at Yalta sanctioning a veto for the Warsaw Provisional Government, or for the Soviet Union, in deciding which Polish leaders should be invited to Moscow. They also insisted that Mikolajczyk must be among the leaders called to consult with the three-power commission; proposed that the Polish leaders, once assembled in Moscow, should settle the composition of the new government among themselves, with the commission standing by to arbitrate, if necessary; revived the suggestion, already rejected by Molotov, that Allied observers be admitted into Poland; and called upon Warsaw to halt its purge of elements deemed unfriendly to the new regime.

The Soviet response showed a definite hardening of position. To consider the Provisional Government in Warsaw as merely one of three groups of Poles consulting together on the future of their country, Molotov argued, was "entirely incorrect" and a violation of the Yalta decisions. On the contrary, Warsaw must become "the nucleus" of the new Government of National Unity. Molotov found sanction for this interpretation in the fact that the Yalta communiqué contained no mention of "the Polish émigré government" in London. He insisted that only those Poles could be invited who were acceptable to all three members of the commission—thus reserving for himself the right to veto any name to which the Warsaw Poles might object. Harriman reminded Molotov on March 23 that at Yalta "there had been considerable discussion of the wording of the declaration and that the word 'enlarged,' as suggested by the Soviet delegation, had been rejected and the word 'reorganization' substituted."[8]

The deadlock was now confirmed. Under Churchill's prodding, Roosevelt conceded that the time had come for a personal approach to Stalin. In a message to the Prime Minister, dated March 29, the President acknowledged that in trying to compromise their differences with Stalin at Yalta they had placed

> somewhat more emphasis on the Lublin Poles than on the other two groups from which the new government is to be drawn . . . It by no means follows, however, and on this we must be adamant, that because of this advantage the Lublin group can in any way arrogate to itself the right to determine what Poles from the other two groups are to be brought in for consultation.[9]

Thus Roosevelt's message to Stalin, delivered by Harriman on April 1, carried a clear warning that the issue of Poland was the rock on which the wartime unity of the Allies could break apart:

> I cannot conceal from you the concern with which I view the development of events of mutual interest since our fruitful meeting at Yalta. The decisions we reached there were good ones and have for the most part been welcomed with enthusiasm by the peoples of the world, who saw in our ability to find a common basis of understanding the best pledge for a secure and peaceful world after this war. Precisely because of the hopes and expectations that these decisions raised, their fulfillment is being followed with the closest attention. We have no right to let them be disappointed. So far there has been a discouraging lack of progress made in the carrying out, which the world expects, of the political decisions which we reached at the conference, particularly those relating to the Polish question. I am frankly puzzled as to why this should be, and I must tell you that I do not fully understand in many respects the apparent indifferent attitude of your government . . .[10]

Roosevelt also mentioned the Allied disagreements over Rumania, saying that he failed to understand why that country was not being dealt with according to the principles of the Declaration on Liberated Europe. Attributing the lack of progress in the Polish commission to Soviet misinterpretations of the Yalta decisions, he then set down his own understanding of what had been agreed to seven weeks earlier:

• The Lublin regime was to have been reorganized "in such a fashion as to bring into being a new government." If the Russians continued to insist upon "a thinly disguised continuance" of the present Warsaw regime, then the American people would regard the Yalta agreement as having failed.

• It was the task of the Allied commission, not the Warsaw government, to decide which Poles were invited to Moscow for consultations. The United States would undertake not to veto any candidate Molotov might propose and he felt it was not too much to ask that Ambassador Harriman should be accorded the same right. If the list was agreed on beforehand, he would raise no objection to having the Lublin group arrive in Moscow ahead of the others.

To ensure political tranquillity inside Poland during the period of political consultation and government-building, Roosevelt urged, the Allies must use their influence with Warsaw and London respectively to end the wave of arrests by the Provisional Government and of counterattacks by its opponents. He also argued that in view of the responsibilities placed upon the Western ambassadors by the Yalta decisions, they had to be free to send representatives into Poland to see for themselves what was going on inside the country.

Roosevelt's personal intervention, reinforced by a message in similar vein from Churchill, had no effect. At the sixth meeting of the commission on April 2, Molotov refused even to discuss the messages from the President and the Prime Minister, since they had been addressed to Marshal Stalin. "Molotov was much more firm than ever tonight," Harriman reported, "in his opposition to Mikolajczyk and more open in his insistence that our guiding influence should be the opinion of the Warsaw Poles, as it was their government which was to be reorganized 'in accordance with the Crimea decision.'" No date was set for a further meeting. The break that Harriman had forecast appeared imminent:

> Judged on the conversation tonight we are at a breaking point [Harriman reported to Roosevelt]. However, it has been my experience in dealing with the Soviets in the past four years that sometimes they are toughest just before they are ready to make substantial concessions, providing they find they can't move us . . . I still believe that, confronted with a definite and firm decision on our part, there is a chance at least that the Soviet Government may yield and allow negotiations to continue.

On April 7 Stalin replied that the Polish discussions had reached a "dead end." For this he blamed Harriman and Clark Kerr. They had departed from the principles of the Yalta decisions, Stalin complained to Roosevelt, by refusing to recognize that the Lublin-Warsaw regime must be "the kernel" of the reorganized Government of National Unity. In his equally negative reply to Churchill, however, Stalin appeared to yield a point. He was prepared to use his influence with the Warsaw Poles, he said, to drop their objections to Mikolajczyk's participation if the former Polish Premier, in turn, agreed to make a public statement endorsing the Crimea decisions affecting Poland and declaring himself a supporter of friendly postwar relations with the Soviet Union.*

IT WAS A TIME OF FAINT HOPE for Allied officials, like Harriman, who were determined to preserve some semblance of common purpose into

---

* On April 15 Churchill was able to inform Stalin that Mikolajczyk had been to see him in London and had issued a declaration in which he accepted the Yalta decisions. "I consider that close and lasting friendship with Russia is the keystone of future Polish policy within the wider friendship of the United Nations," Mikolajczyk said in the declaration.

the postwar era. Ironically, the imminent collapse of Hitler's mighty war machine produced a new situation in which Stalin's deep-laid suspicions of Western purpose would surface more violently than ever before.

In late February, even as Harriman and Clark Kerr were beginning their arid discussions with Molotov in Moscow, word reached the Office of Strategic Services in neutral Switzerland that General Karl Wolff, the ranking SS officer in Italy, was trying to make contact with the Allies for the purpose of ending all German resistance in North Italy. After a preliminary investigation on the Allied side, Wolff was invited to turn up in Zurich for a meeting with Allen Dulles, then the OSS chief in Switzerland. Nothing was settled at the Zurich meeting. Dulles told Wolff that the Allies were not about to negotiate; their terms would have to be unconditional surrender. Wolff replied that he personally was ready to end the killing and would do his best to persuade Field Marshal Albrecht Kesselring, the German commander in chief in Italy, that surrender was the best course.

Dulles sent a detailed report to Allied headquarters in Caserta, where Field Marshal Sir Harold Alexander decided to follow up the first contact without waiting to hear what Kesselring had decided. He proposed to send his American deputy chief of staff, General Lyman Lemnitzer,* and his British chief intelligence officer, General Sir Terence Airey, to Switzerland for further discussions with Wolff.

On March 12, three days before Airey and Lemnitzer were to cross the Swiss border disguised as civilians, Harriman notified Molotov of the surrender discussions, handing him a copy of Alexander's detailed message to the Combined Chiefs of Staff in Washington and inviting the Soviet government's urgent comments. Molotov replied the same day: "Considering your communications very important, the Soviet Government does not object to the continuation of the negotiations of the Anglo-American officers with General Wolff. On its part, the Soviet Government would like officers representing the Soviet Military Command to participate in these negotiations." In view of the fact that the Russians had no diplomatic relations with Switzerland, Molotov added, they hoped the United States would help make it possible for three Soviet officers to enter the country and join the talks at Berne.

Harriman saw no justification for the Soviet request and so advised Washington. The Germans were merely proposing a military surrender, not a national capitulation, on what was, after all, an Anglo-American front. "The Soviets would never allow our officers, I am satisfied, to participate in a parallel situation on the eastern front," he

---

* General Lemnitzer advanced steadily after the war. He became Army Chief of Staff in 1959 and Chairman of the Joint Chiefs in 1960.

wrote. "Indeed I doubt whether they would even let us know of any negotiations for such a surrender." From the policy aspect, he saw no advantage for the Western Allies in acceding to the Soviet request. On the contrary, the Russians would read acquiescence as another sign of weakness and come back with even more untenable demands in the future. Finally, he warned that the Russians, if admitted to this highly preliminary meeting, might jeopardize the surrender by their "embarrassing demands." Deane supported Harriman's view in a separate message to General Marshall. The Russian demand made no more sense, Deane argued, than "if the United States were to insist on participating in possible future negotiations for the surrender of 28 to 30 German divisions now cut off in Latvia." He was certain, Deane added, that the United States would not ask to participate and even more certain that, if it did, the Russians would refuse.

The Combined Chiefs in Washington, having arrived at the same conclusion, replied to Molotov through Harriman and Clark Kerr that the only purpose of the meetings in Switzerland was to arrange for the bringing of German representatives to Caserta, where the surrender would be worked out. The Russians, they said, were welcome to send representatives to Caserta but Marshal Alexander alone "would be responsible for conducting the negotiations and for reaching decisions."

In his furious reply, Molotov called the British-American refusal "utterly unexpected and incomprehensible." He insisted that the contacts be broken off at once and that any idea of surrender negotiations without the participation of the Soviet Union must be ruled out. On March 17 Harriman offered Washington his own best guess as to the reasons behind the Soviet attitude:

> It is entirely possible that they do not believe us when we say the Berne negotiations are for the sole purpose of attempting to bring Kesselring's authorized representative to Caserta. They may think that the real negotiations will be at Berne, with the Caserta meeting as a rubber stamp. This is a procedure which . . . they themselves are capable of following. On the other hand, they may be fearful, or have information, that in addition to the armies in North Italy there may be other groups of Germans who are considering surrendering to us . . .
>
> The question of prestige may also be involved. They have contended to their people and the world that Germany has been defeated almost entirely through the efforts of the Red Army. It may be that with the thaws their advance in the east may be bogged down for a couple of months and if there is a

break in Italy, leading to one in the West, they wish to insure
being full participants in any major surrender.[11]

Once again at this point, Roosevelt addressed a message directly
to Stalin, explaining step by step how the German surrender overture
had been dealt with. He wanted Stalin to have all the facts, the President said, because it was possible that they had not been "correctly
presented" to him. He appealed to Stalin "as a military man" to understand that when there was a possibility of forcing the surrender of
enemy troops, it would be "completely unreasonable" to permit any
delay which could cause additional deaths among American soldiers.
He would not, in short, suspend the Berne contacts because of
Molotov's objection, which he found incomprehensible, and he asked
Stalin to explain the matter to his subordinates.

Stalin's answer, dated March 29, paid little heed to Roosevelt's
careful assurances. The reason the Russians were so suspicious, he said
bluntly, was that they feared the Germans were "opening the front to
the Anglo-American troops in Italy" for a sinister purpose—so they
could shift troops to the east and fight the Red Army all the harder.

> I must tell you for your information [Stalin added] that
> the Germans have already taken advantage of the talks with
> the Allied Command to move three divisions from Northern
> Italy to the Soviet front.
> The task of coordinated operations involving a blow at
> the Germans from the West, South and East, proclaimed at
> the Crimea Conference, is to hold the enemy on the spot and
> prevent him from manoeuvering, from moving his forces to
> the points where he needs them most. The Soviet Command
> is doing this. Field Marshal Alexander is not. This circum-
> stance irritates the Soviet Command and engenders distrust.[12]

Roosevelt's restrained reply reached the Moscow embassy on the
evening of March 31, while Harriman and Clark Kerr were at the
Kremlin discussing at long last the coordination of Allied thrusts from
east and west in the final battle for Germany.

Eisenhower had initiated the discussion by sending General Deane
an extraordinary message addressed to Stalin. Harriman and Clark
Kerr decided to deliver it personally, taking Deane and Admiral
Archer, his British counterpart, along to the Kremlin. They did not
know at the time that Eisenhower had failed to consult the Combined
Chiefs of Staff, or his British deputy, Air Chief Marshal Tedder, let
alone Roosevelt or Churchill. His plan of attack, as outlined in the
message to Stalin, was to by-pass Berlin. Instead, he proposed to en-
circle and isolate the Ruhr, and then to split the German armies by

driving in the direction of Erfurt-Leipzig-Dresden, there to join hands with the Red Army. Eisenhower's direct approach to Stalin infuriated Churchill and bitterly disappointed Montgomery, who until the change of plan had expected his 21st Army Group to lead the assault on Berlin. Now Hitler's capital was being left to the Red Army, a decision fraught with political consequences to which Eisenhower seemed totally oblivious. Stalin's reaction, after Harriman handed him the Eisenhower message in Russian translation, was affirmative but misleading. "Berlin," he said, "has lost its former strategic importance. The Soviet High Command therefore plans to allot secondary forces in the direction of Berlin."

Eisenhower's plan of attack was a good one, Stalin added. It would accomplish the main objective of cutting Germany in half. He would, of course, have to consult his Marshals and give a more definite reply the following day. Meanwhile he asked Deane and Archer whether they could verify Soviet intelligence estimates that the Germans had sixty divisions on the western front. They answered that Western intelligence had counted sixty-one. Did the Germans, Stalin asked, have any additional reserves in the west? Apparently not, the Allied officers responded. Stalin said he was greatly impressed by the number of German prisoners the Allies had taken in March, adding that he was certain this would help end the war very soon.

Harriman asked about Stalin's own forecast that the Red Army's operations might be bogged down at the end of March. Stalin replied that the spring floods had come early and now the roads were drying. He added that the Germans were still resisting strongly in the mountains of Czechoslovakia; they had concentrated ten armored divisions northeast of Lake Balaton in Hungary, and they still had sixteen divisions in Latvia. But all these enemy forces would soon be overcome. Stalin predicted that Hitler's forces would make their last stand in the mountains of western Czechoslovakia and Bavaria, repeating at this point his praise of Eisenhower's plan to split Germany in two. The direction of the Western attack, he said, was most favorable for a link-up with the Red Army.

Stalin's tone throughout this conversation was calm and friendly, in dramatic contrast to the sour suspicions he had poured out in his correspondence with Roosevelt over the Italian surrender contacts. When Harriman returned to Spaso House late that evening to find on his desk another message for Stalin, he wrote the President:

> I regret that I did not receive till after our talk your last message regarding the Berne meeting . . . In the mood he was in at the end of our conversation, I feel that if I had delivered your message to him personally I might have been able to

get to the bottom of the Soviets' strange behavior . . . It has
been my experience that Stalin always reacts immediately to
matters that are put up to him personally and we are thus able
to obtain more understanding of his attitude than is possible
from his written replies alone.

The Roosevelt message, delivered to Stalin the following day
through the Soviet Foreign Ministry, had been drafted with scrupulous
forbearance. The President said he was sorry that "an atmosphere of
regrettable apprehension and mistrust" had somehow been created
even though he and Stalin were in agreement on all the basic principles. He went over the facts once again: no surrender negotiations had
been entered into; the Berne meeting had the sole purpose of arranging
contact with the competent German officers and it had been fruitless;
if, and when, there were to be negotiations for the surrender in North
Italy, these would be conducted at Caserta in the presence of Soviet
military representatives. There could be no question of negotiating
with the Germans in any way that would permit them to transfer
troops to the eastern front. Unconditional surrender was the only basis.
    As for the accusation that three German divisions had been trans-
ferred to the east under cover of the surrender negotiations, Stalin had
been misinformed. Three divisions in fact had been pulled out of Italy
since the first of the year, Roosevelt said, but the last of these had
started moving about February 25—and that was "more than two weeks
before anybody heard of any possibility of a surrender." He reminded
Stalin that General Wolff was close to Heinrich Himmler, the chief,
and that his original purpose conceivably had been to sow suspicion
and distrust between the Allies. "There is no reason," Roosevelt
concluded, "why we should permit him to succeed in that aim."
    While the Roosevelt-Stalin correspondence was growing steadily
more bitter, almost everything that could have gone wrong with
General Wolff's secret arrangements did go wrong. Hitler had
abruptly recalled Field Marshal Kesselring from Italy to take command
of the western front. Wolff insisted on talking to Kesselring before
approaching General Heinrich von Vietinghoff, the new German
commander in chief in Italy. This meant a trip back to Germany, with
added delays and risks of exposure. Dulles heard not a word from
Wolff between March 19 and 30. Then the Americans learned that he
had managed to reach Kesselring and was now back in Italy. But
Wolff had received a personal warning from Himmler that he and his
family were under close watch. He did not dare appear in Switzerland
to make contact, as arranged earlier, with Generals Lemnitzer and
Airey at Locarno on April 2. Instead he sent his Italian intermediary,
Baron Luigi Parilli, who reported that Wolff had Von Vietinghoff's

support. Parilli hinted, however, that the German officers wanted permission to withdraw their troops across the Italian frontier after giving up their arms. The Allied officers replied that such an arrangement was out of the question.

Harriman believed that Stalin's intelligence agents in Germany must have got wind of Wolff's comings and goings and leaped to the false conclusion, based on incomplete information or rumors planted by German counterintelligence, that Wolff and Kesselring were plotting a surrender not only in Italy but along the whole of the western front. The fact that the Wehrmacht was clearly in a state of disintegration, offering steadily weaker resistance to the Allied armies in the west, was bound to make the plot theory seem even more plausible to Stalin.

Stalin, at any rate, deeply wounded Roosevelt by his reply on April 3, which bristled with ugly reproaches:

> You insist that there have been no negotiations yet.
> It may be assumed that you have not been fully informed. As regards my military colleagues, they, on the basis of data which they have on hand, do not have any doubts that the negotiations have taken place and that they have ended in an agreement with the Germans, on the basis of which the German commander on the western front, Marshal Kesselring, has agreed to open the front and permit the Anglo-American troops to advance to the east and the Anglo-Americans have promised in return to ease for the Germans the peace terms.
> I think that my colleagues are close to the truth. . . .
> I understand that there are certain advantages for the Anglo-American troops as a result of these separate negotiations in Berne or in some other place, since the Anglo-American troops get the possibility to advance into the heart of Germany, almost without any resistance on the part of the Germans, but why was it necessary to conceal this from the Russians . . .?[13]

Roosevelt found the accusation both painful and astonishing. Having trusted Stalin, he expected a degree of trust in return. Now accused of betraying his ally, of being a liar or a dupe of his most trusted aides, the President replied:

> . . . It would be one of the great tragedies of history if at the very moment of the victory, now within our grasp, such distrust, such lack of faith, should prejudice the entire undertaking after the colossal losses of life, materiel and treasure involved.

Frankly I cannot avoid a feeling of bitter resentment toward your informers, whoever they are, for such vile misrepresentations of my actions or those of my trusted subordinates.[14]

Stalin's great fear that the Western Allies might conclude a separate peace with Germany was matched, Harriman recalled, by the fear of some Pentagon officials that the Russians in turn would break the alliance and make their own deal with the enemy if the United States took a tougher line. The idea of a second Stalin-Hitler pact in 1945 seemed to Harriman out of the question.

"I never thought it was possible," he recalled. "Not that I doubted Stalin would do it if he could, but too many terrible things had happened between the Russians and the Germans. A deal at this stage was just impossible. Stalin must have believed, however, that a British-American deal was feasible. The Germans certainly wanted to surrender—and there were elements in Germany which would have preferred, beyond question, to surrender to us. That came out in the final armistice negotiations a month later when we had to insist that they surrender to the Russians as well as ourselves, in Berlin as well as in Rheims.

"The whole incident showed the depth of Stalin's suspicious nature. It had nothing to do with whether or not we had opened a Second Front when he called for it. It went deeper than that. He had been schooled to believe in the inevitability of a clash between the Soviet Union and what he used to call 'capitalist imperialism.' He did not trust us and he could not believe that we trusted or would deal fairly with him. That was why he swallowed all kinds of misinformation fed him by his intelligence people. It was as if he needed to believe that we were betraying him.

"The telegram he sent to Roosevelt was the most bitter, and the most insulting, I had seen. It went far beyond anything he had sent before. And it jarred Roosevelt into recognizing that the postwar period was going to be far less pleasant than he had imagined. The President was deeply hurt. It made him realize what we were up against.

"In fact, the violence of Stalin's reaction was less disturbing to those of us who had worked in Moscow than it was to Roosevelt. General Deane and I, particularly, had seen for ourselves how deeply suspicious Stalin could be. We had been through the long and painful negotiations over shuttle-bombing, the exchange of weather and intelligence information, the fruitless attempt to get bases in the Maritime Provinces for our bombers in the Far East. Stalin's suspicion of our motives always stood in the way of our getting things done."

The Berne incident led to no practical result, in any event. When General Wolff, through his Italian go-between, asked for various assurances going beyond unconditional surrender, Field Marshal Alexander flatly refused. Stalin's suspicions, in short, were wholly unjustified. But even as the peak of the inter-Allied crisis was passing, he could not stifle his dark imaginings. In reply to Roosevelt's angry message, Stalin found it "difficult to agree" that the lightning advance of the Allied armies in the west could be explained by the fact that the Germans were near defeat. "They continue to fight savagely with the Russians for some unknown [railway] junction, Zemljenica in Czechoslovakia, which they need as much as a dead man needs poultices," he complained, "but surrender without any resistance such important towns in Central Germany as Osnabrück, Mannheim, Kassel. Don't you agree that such behavior of the Germans is more than strange and incomprehensible?" He also defended his Soviet intelligence officers as modest, conscientious folk who had no intention of offending anyone. "Judge for yourself," he wrote to Roosevelt. The previous February General Marshall, in an effort to be helpful, had sent to the Soviet high command some detailed information about German plans on the eastern front. Stalin's Soviet agents had discovered, though not a moment too soon, he admitted, that Marshall's information was wrong and thereby avoided a catastrophe for the Red Army. As for Roosevelt and Churchill, he had never doubted their integrity and trustworthiness, Stalin said. He just happened to differ with them on the proper duty of one ally to another.[15]

It was hardly an apology, as Churchill pointed out, but Roosevelt decided not to prolong the controversy. In the last message he was to send Stalin, the President wrote:

> Thank you for your frank explanation of the Soviet point of view of the Berne incident which now appears to have faded into the past without having accomplished any useful purpose.
>
> There must not, in any event, be mutual mistrust, and minor misunderstandings of this character should not arise in the future. I feel sure that when our armies make contact in Germany and join in a fully coordinated offensive the Nazi armies will disintegrate.[16]

Before passing on this message to Stalin, Harriman suggested to the President that the word "minor" should be deleted. "The use of the word 'minor,' " the Ambassador suggested, "might well be misinterpreted here, since I must confess that the misunderstanding appeared to me to be of a major character."

Roosevelt would have none of it. Replying from Warm Springs,

Georgia, he instructed Harriman to make no change in the text of his
message to Stalin: "I do not wish to delete the word 'minor' as it is my
desire to consider the Berne misunderstanding a minor incident." The
date of the message was April 12, 1945.

To Churchill, the President had written the same day in much the
same vein:

> I would minimize the general Soviet problem as much as
> possible, because these problems, in one form or another, seem
> to arise every day, and most of them straighten out, as in the
> case of the Berne meeting.
> We must be firm, however, and our course thus far is
> correct.

The news of Roosevelt's death in Warm Springs reached Spaso
House during a farewell party the Harrimans were giving for John
Melby, who was being transferred to Washington. The embassy duty
officer called a few minutes past 1 A.M. to say that he had just heard
the news on a late broadcast. Kathleen Harriman took the call in an
adjoining room and then told her father. "Soon the Ambassador and
Kathleen came out looking very somber and buttonholed Melby,"
according to Meiklejohn's diary. The dancing ended abruptly, Meiklejohn remembered: "Everybody ganged up on me to turn off the
victrola and get everybody home." There was no announcement.
Harriman kept the tragic news to himself for a few moments. As soon
as the guests had left, the Spaso House regulars—Melby, Elbridge
Durbrow, Meiklejohn and Paddock—assembled in the Ambassador's
room with Harriman and Kathleen. They gravely considered the new
situation. Harriman then telephoned Molotov to tell him that Roosevelt was dead and request an appointment. The Foreign Minister,
evidently surprised by the call, insisted upon coming to Spaso House
himself in spite of the hour. Wringing Harriman's hand, the Foreign
Minister said he had come to express the deep sympathy of his government and of himself personally.

> He seemed deeply moved and disturbed [Harriman re-
> ported on April 13]. He stayed for some time talking about
> the part President Roosevelt had played in the war and in the
> plans for peace, of the respect Marshal Stalin and all the
> Russian people had had for him and how much Marshal Stalin
> had valued his visit to Yalta. I encouraged him to ask questions
> about President Truman and assured him that President
> Truman would carry on President Roosevelt's policies.
> Molotov in leaving said that the Soviet Government
> would have confidence in President Truman because he had

been selected by President Roosevelt. I have never heard Molotov talk so earnestly. I asked him to arrange for me to call on Marshal Stalin today. It is my purpose to reassure Stalin as to the continuation of our policies and make every effort to get us back as far as possible to the spirit and atmosphere of the Crimea Conference.

For a week before Roosevelt's death, Harriman had been planning to fly back to Washington so that he might explain to the President why, in his judgment, the Russians were being so difficult about carrying out the various Yalta decisions. Roosevelt himself had been worried —and had written Stalin personally—about the stubborn Polish deadlock, the unworthy suspicions brought to the surface by the Berne incident, high-handed Soviet actions in Rumania and what he saw as the mistreatment of American war prisoners by the Red Army in Poland. He also had been troubled by Stalin's refusal to send Molotov to San Francisco for the founding conference of the United Nations, scheduled to open on April 25. The President had written to Stalin a month earlier: "All sponsoring powers and the majority of the other countries will be represented by their Ministers of Foreign Affairs. I am afraid that Mr. Molotov's absence will be construed all over the world as a lack of comparable interest in the great objectives of this Conference on the part of the Soviet Government." Stalin had replied that while the Soviets attached great importance to the San Francisco Conference, Molotov would be forced to stay in Moscow because the Supreme Soviet was about to convene and his attendance there was "imperative."

Now that Harry Truman was President, it seemed to Harriman all the more important that he should return promptly to Washington. Stettinius disagreed. He sent word on April 13, after consulting Truman, that "now of all times it is essential that we have you in Moscow."

Harriman decided that he would ask Stalin to send Molotov to San Francisco, in spite of the prior refusal. That seemed to him the most effective signal of assurance Stalin could give that his policy of collaboration with Roosevelt would continue under the untried new President. "This was a very serious emotional moment," Harriman recalled. "Before I went over to see Stalin I had thought hard about what I might ask him to do. So it was no accident."

Stalin greeted Harriman in silence when they met at eight o'clock that evening, holding his hand for perhaps thirty seconds before asking him to sit down. He appeared deeply distressed and questioned the Ambassador closely about the circumstances of Roosevelt's death. He did not believe, Stalin said, that there would be any change in American policy under Truman. Harriman agreed that this would be true in those areas where the President had made his plans clear, such as the war and foreign policy. Truman had been a Roosevelt man in his Senate days, faithfully following the President's lead. He was a man whom Stalin would like, Harriman added, a man of action, not of words. According to his own account of the conversation, Harriman then started leading up to his main objective:

> On the other hand, I said that President Truman naturally could not have the great prestige that President Roosevelt enjoyed at the time of his death. Until he had become Vice President he was not especially well known in the United States because he had never sought publicity. The same was true abroad. This, in my opinion, could not help but cause a period of uncertainty, both internally and externally, not necessarily about the conduct of the war but on all foreign and domestic policy questions. The San Francisco Conference, for example, might well cause more difficulties. The American people did not know whether President Truman could carry through President Roosevelt's program . . .
>
> The American people knew that President Roosevelt and Marshal Stalin had close personal relations and that this relationship had a great effect on United States–Soviet relations. Marshal Stalin interjected: "President Roosevelt has died but his cause must live on. We shall support President Truman with all our forces and all our will." The Marshal then requested me to inform President Truman accordingly.
>
> . . . I said that I believed that the most effective way to assure the American public and the world at large of the desire of the Soviet Government to continue collaboration with us and the other United Nations would be for Mr. Molotov to go to the United States at this time. I suggested that he might stop in Washington to see the President and then proceed to San Francisco, even though he might remain there only for a few days . . . During these exchanges of remarks, Mr. Molotov kept muttering, "Time, time, time." . . .
>
> After a brief discussion between Mr. Molotov and Marshal Stalin as to the dates of the San Francisco Conference and the convening of the Supreme Soviet, Marshal Stalin inquired whether I was expressing my personal views. I made it clear that I was, but added that I felt completely confident that I was expressing the views of the President and the Secretary of State and that I felt sure that they would be ready to confirm what I had said. Marshal Stalin then stated categorically that

Mr. Molotov's trip to the United States, although difficult at this time, would be arranged . . .

The sending of Molotov was a public gesture on Stalin's part, a necessary gesture but no more than a gesture, Harriman felt. "It, of course, in no sense solves any of our basic difficulties," he wrote in a draft telegram to Stettinius which he decided not to send. The Secretary of State nevertheless agreed that thanks to Stalin's turnabout, Harriman ought to accompany Molotov to the United States. Before he could leave Moscow, however, the Ambassador had a great load of work and official duty to get through, including a memorial service for Roosevelt at the American embassy and one more meeting with Stalin.

The simple memorial service at the embassy on April 15 drew a silent, solemn crowd of four hundred in tribute to the memory of Franklin Roosevelt. Molotov was there, together with all his Assistant Commissars of Foreign Affairs except Litvinov, who was ill. Mikoyan came, bringing his principal assistants in the Commissariat of Foreign Trade; also General Antonov, representing the General Staff of the Red Army, Admiral Gavrilov of the Soviet navy, senior diplomats from each of the United Nations embassies and virtually every American in Moscow—embassy staff, soldiers and journalists. Moscow had never seen such an outpouring for a foreign statesman.

Sergeant G. E. Thomas of the American military mission, who had been a lay preacher, conducted the service. The mission choir led the singing of "Onward, Christian Soldiers," "O God Our Help in Ages Past" and "Nearer, My God, to Thee." In place of a eulogy, Harriman read Roosevelt's own prayer, offered at the time of the Allied landings in Normandy on June 6, 1944:

"God of the free, we pledge our hearts and lives today to the cause of all free mankind.

"Grant us victory over the tyrants who would enslave all free men and nations.

"Grant us faith and understanding to cherish all those who fight for freedom as if they were our brothers.

"Grant us brotherhood in hope and union, not only for the space of this bitter war, but for the days to come which shall and must unite all the children of the earth.

"We are all of us children of the earth—grant us that simple knowledge. If our brothers are oppressed, then we are oppressed. If they hunger, we hunger. If their freedom is taken away, our freedom is not secure.

"Grant us a common faith that man shall know bread and peace—that he shall know justice and righteousness, freedom and security, an equal opportunity and an equal chance to do his best, not only in our own lands but throughout the world.

"And in that faith let us march, toward the clean world our hands can make."

The same day, Harriman received a personal message from Hopkins, once again in failing health, who was in a Rochester, Minnesota, hospital:

> Dear Averell:
> I know what a great shock the President's death must have been. Over the years the President, as you well know, had become devoted to you and had the utmost confidence in your judgment. Many times after I left you at Yalta he spoke of what a great help you were to him. Surely the cause of a righteous peace has lost its greatest friend.
>
> HARRY HOPKINS

Hopkins had known the President's mind more intimately than any other associate. His frail health left the bereft Administration with no sure guide to Roosevelt's thoughts about the troubled peace ahead. The record of Roosevelt's correspondence with Stalin and Churchill in the last weeks of his life, however—above all the bitter exchanges over the Berne incident—suggest that he was losing confidence in Stalin's word and in the efficacy of appeals to morality or "world opinion." There is no persuasive evidence to suggest that he was disposed to abandon his efforts at winning Stalin's cooperation. But with the shriveling of his hope for understanding came the first outline of a more hard-boiled *quid pro quo* attitude, of the kind that Harriman had been advocating for months past.

It was more in sorrow than anger that Roosevelt had confided his change of heart to a handful of friends. To Anna Rosenberg, at luncheon on March 23, at the height of the Berne incident, Roosevelt said, "Averell is right. We can't do business with Stalin. He has broken every one of the promises he made at Yalta." Anne O'Hara McCormick, who had seen the President the day he left Washington for Warm Springs, later shared with Harriman her recollection of that final talk. The President told her that he had fully believed what he said in his report to the Congress on the Yalta Conference decisions. But he had found that Stalin was not a man of his word; either that or Stalin was not in control of the Soviet government.[17]

Harriman's own surmise was that Stalin, for all his vaunted personal power and unchallenged public authority, in fact listened to his colleagues in the Politburo and frequently changed his mind after policy discussions in that narrow circle. His refusal to permit free elections in Poland seemed to Harriman a case in point. "I believe Bierut told Stalin a few days after Yalta," Harriman later observed, "that if the election were held, any real democratic leader such as Mikolajczyk would have become the rallying point for an over-whelming majority of the Polish people. They must have decided that the risk was too great."

NOW NINE WEEKS HAD PASSED since Yalta. Although Truman had just taken office, he made clear to Churchill in a message dated April 13 that he looked upon Poland as a "pressing and dangerous problem" and that in spite of past disappointments he was ready for "another go" at Stalin.[18] The following day Stettinius instructed Harriman to see Stalin before leaving Moscow and to tell him that "the problem between our two countries which was causing President Roosevelt before his death the greatest concern was the failure thus far of the Polish negotiations."

At the height of the Polish crisis, an American air crew on a res-cue mission from the Poltava base had made matters worse by smug-gling out a young Pole disguised in a GI uniform. The immediate Soviet response was to order the grounding of the few planes that remained at Poltava and 163 airmen who had landed there in planes crippled by German gunners or had been evacuated to safety after crashing in Poland.

Stalin made a great deal of this escapade when Harriman went to see him on April 15, accompanied by Patrick J. Hurley, the American ambassador to China, who had stopped in Moscow on his way to Chungking in order to discuss the Yalta agreements with respect to the Far East. Hurley was aghast when Stalin accused the American Air Forces of having conspired with the anti-Communist Polish under-ground against the Red Army, and Harriman thundered back, "You're impugning the loyalty of the American high command and I won't allow it. You are actually impugning the loyalty of General Marshall."

For all his reputed toughness, Hurley was shocked by Harriman's blunt words, but Stalin replied in a mollifying tone. "I would trust General Marshall with my life," he said. "This wasn't he but a junior officer."

Harriman seized the opportunity to point out that Poland had be-come the principal issue clouding Soviet-American relations. Roose-velt had been trying to resolve it at the time of his death, he said, and Truman was just as determined to reach an understanding. He sug-gested that Stalin authorize Molotov to discuss Poland with Stettinius and Eden during his American visit and attempt to reach some agree-ment. Molotov grumbled that he had not known he was going to the

United States to talk about Poland. But Stalin assured Harriman that Molotov would go under instructions to find common ground with the Western Allies. "The sooner the better," he said, overruling his unhappy Foreign Minister.

On the way back to Spaso House, Hurley exclaimed that he had been afraid Harriman would come to blows with Stalin during their contretemps over the grounding of the Poltava airmen. Harriman had his mind on weightier matters as he prepared to fly back to Washington. He was filled with foreboding over the increasingly difficult task of reconciling American and Soviet objectives, whether in Europe or Asia.

After working out with the Russians a direct route that would take him over the Balkans to Italy and across the Atlantic by way of the Azores, Harriman left Moscow on April 17. He reached Washington in record time forty-eight hours later. The route he had chosen gave him a head start over Molotov, who preferred to fly the long way round—across Siberia and by way of Alaska—in an American plane which had been put at his disposal. The Ambassador thus had a chance to brief Truman, whom he was meeting for the first time, before Molotov's arrival in Washington.

CHAPTER XIX

Truman Takes Charge

A T NOON ON APRIL 20, five days after Roosevelt's burial at Hyde Park, Harriman met the new President for the first time. Stettinius introduced Harriman. He and Joseph C. Grew, Under Secretary of State, sat mostly silent as Truman asked Harriman to run down the list of urgent problems with the Soviet Union.

The Ambassador responded that the Soviet Union was pursuing two contradictory policies at the same time: a policy of cooperation with the United States and Great Britain and a policy of extending its control over the neighboring states of Eastern Europe. Some of Stalin's advisers, misreading American generosity as softness, had persuaded him that he could do pretty much as he pleased in Eastern Europe without challenge from the United States. His own judgment, Harriman said, was that the Russians needed American help in postwar reconstruction and would not, therefore, wish to break with the United States. For this reason, America could afford to stand firm on important issues without serious risk.

Truman interjected that he was not afraid of the Russians. He proposed to be firm but fair. "Anyway," he added, "the Russians need us more than we need them."

As the dialogue continued, Harriman was pleased to discover that Truman had read, and was thoroughly familiar with, the Yalta agreements and the Stalin-Roosevelt correspondence. "I gained great respect for Truman at once," he recalled, "because he had grasped so quickly many of the problems we were facing with the Soviet Union. Although I also was disturbed, during this first conversation and others that followed, because he kept saying—too often, I thought—that he was not equipped for the job, that he lacked experience and did not fully understand the issues.

SPECIAL ENVOY

"I was afraid that Truman was being overhumble. I was a little concerned that he would not grasp control of the presidency, that he might be indecisive. It wasn't very long before I got over that fear. He showed the right kind of humility, I thought. But he also showed that he had the capacity to make decisions."

Truman listened carefully that first day as Harriman explained that Stalin and his associates were laboring under the mistaken notion that it was a matter of "life and death" for the United States to increase its exports to Russia.[1] The Ambassador had in mind his talks with Molotov and Mikoyan on postwar assistance for the Soviet Union. They had taken for granted that the United States, fearing a postwar depression, would offer credits to the Soviet Union in order to create jobs at home.

A ridiculous idea, Truman said, interjecting again that he proposed to stand firm. There would be no departures from American principles or traditions to win favor with Stalin.

Harriman made plain to Truman his misgivings about what the Russians might be up to in Poland, Rumania and other neighboring countries. Stalin would not be content with control over the foreign policies of these countries, Harriman predicted. He also would impose secret police methods and extinguish freedom of speech. In short, Harriman said, a new "barbarian invasion of Europe" was under way, and the United States would have to determine its attitude toward these unpleasant developments without delay.

In spite of his blunt language, Harriman still believed the United States could arrive at a workable relationship with the Russians. But this would require the abandonment of American illusions that the Soviet government was likely soon to act in accordance with accepted principles of international behavior. Both sides would have to make concessions, he said, in the process of give-and-take.

Truman agreed that it would be unrealistic to expect 100 percent Soviet cooperation with American proposals. He hoped to get 85 percent.

After Harriman had exposed some of the intricacies of the Polish problem, he put a question to Truman: Would the President go ahead with plans for the United Nations, even if the Russians dropped out? The truth, Truman replied, was that without Russia there would be no world organization. It was not the answer Harriman had hoped to hear; he favored going ahead without the Russians if necessary. Before leaving, Harriman stopped for a private word with Truman.

"Frankly, one of the reasons that made me rush back to Washington," he said, "was the fear that you did not understand, as I had seen Roosevelt understand, that Stalin is breaking his agreements. My fear was inspired by the fact that you could not have had time to catch up with all the recent cables. But I must say that I am greatly relieved to discover that you have read them all and that we see eye to eye on the situation." Truman said he was glad that Harriman was going to be available to the American delegation at San Francisco. "And keep on sending me long messages," he added.[2]

Earlier that morning Harriman had expounded his views at greater length in the first of two staff conferences at the State Department. The time had come, he said, "to eliminate fear in our dealings with the Soviet Union and to show we are determined to maintain our position." He agreed with Under Secretary Grew's remark that the United States possessed great leverage in its relationship with the Russians. They wanted, for example, to be accepted in international society and feared more than anything else the prospect of confronting a united West. Hence one way to improve relations with the Soviet Union was to settle promptly America's differences with Britain and France.[3]

The next day Grew read Harriman a telegram from Ambassador Jefferson Caffery in Paris reporting that the French government was becoming increasingly worried about Russian expansion in Europe. Harriman remarked that the new French attitude had been developing gradually since De Gaulle's visit to Moscow in 1944. It pointed up the desirability of settling differences with the French as well as the British. Assistant Secretary James Clement Dunn reported that the State Department was making every effort to improve relations with France. The main point of difficulty, however, was De Gaulle's determination to send troops to Indochina in order to restore French control. (At Yalta, Roosevelt had opposed De Gaulle's plan. He had told Stalin that he favored a United Nations trusteeship for Indochina, leading to eventual independence.)

Harriman's opinion—which he expounded in talks at the Pentagon as well as at the State Department—was that Stalin's insistence upon a belt of weak, easily dominated neighboring states might not be limited to Eastern Europe. Once the Soviet Union had control of bordering areas, he said, it would probably attempt to penetrate the next layer of adjacent countries. He saw no virtue in waiting; the issue was best fought out as far to the east as possible.

When Grew asked what course of action he could recommend, Harriman argued for selective application of the *quid pro quo* treatment which he and Deane had been urging for months past. When the Russians, for example, had grounded all the American planes and pilots at Poltava, the United States should have responded by grounding Soviet planes at Fairbanks, Alaska. Unfortunately, the War Department had rejected this advice. As far as the new world organization was concerned, it was important to make the Russians understand that the United States was prepared to go ahead without them, even though we would be disappointed if they did not agree with the majority on charter arrangements. Another case where pressure could have been successfully applied, Harriman said, was Rumania. The Russians had first stripped the Rumanian oil fields of essential equipment, thereby reducing production, and then asked the United States to double the amount of petroleum they were receiving under the Lend-Lease program. Instead of agreeing, the United States should have pressed the Soviets to restore production in Rumania.

At the second State Department conference, on April 21, Grew asked Harriman how much real leverage the United States possessed in its dealings with the Soviet Union. The Ambassador replied that the Russians needed heavy machinery and machine tools from the United States, together with American know-how in fields such as the chemical industry, coal-mine mechanization, power development and railroad equipment. Besides, the Soviet Union was not as strong as many in the West imagined. The country was still "fantastically backward." It had no modern road system, railroad mileage was inadequate, and 90 percent of Moscow's population lived in wretched conditions. In short, he was not much worried about the Soviet Union's taking the offensive in the near future. "But they will take control of everything they can by bluffing," he added.

William L. Clayton, the Assistant Secretary of State for economic affairs, raised the question of Lend-Lease. All the newly liberated countries of Europe, he said, were asking for sugar, fats and oils. If these needs were to be met, there would not be enough left for the Russians. Harriman said there was no doubt in his mind that the liberated areas of Western Europe should have first priority. While he was satisfied that the Russians had actually needed the Lend-Lease supplies they received while the war was being fought, shipments could and should be reduced after the end of hostilities.

The postwar credit was another matter. Harriman said it was important that talks should begin promptly, even if they had to "drag along" until Congress adopted new legislation. The Johnson Act still barred loans or credits to Russia, and without new legislation it would be impossible to conclude an agreement.* The Ambassador cautioned against making long-term commitments to the Russians. The best method, Harriman said, "would be to make a one-year arrangement and see how that worked out before expanding it."

Questioned about the British attitude toward the Soviet Union, he said London felt even more strongly than Washington that Stalin must be held to the agreements he had signed at Yalta. But the British could

* The Johnson Act of 1934 prohibited the floating of public bond issues or government loans to foreign countries, including the Soviet Union, which had defaulted on earlier debts. Congress repealed this restriction in July 1945.

not go it alone. If the United States failed to support them, they would have no choice but to settle for a sphere-of-influence deal with Stalin.

Truman's first meeting with Molotov, the following day, April 22, was cordial. The President spoke of his admiration for Marshal Stalin and the Soviet people. He stood squarely behind all the agreements entered into by the late President Roosevelt, he said, and would do everything to follow along that path. Molotov expressed his pleasure at hearing Truman say that he was determined to continue Roosevelt's policy of friendship with Russia. The two talked briefly about Poland and the new world organization, agreeing that all outstanding differences ought to be settled on the basis of Yalta and Dumbarton Oaks, respectively. Truman then offered a toast to the good health of Marshal Stalin; Molotov amended it to include Churchill and the President as well. Truman said that he hoped to meet Stalin before long, and Molotov responded that Stalin, too, was eager to meet the President. When Molotov sat down to discuss Poland with Eden and Stettinius at the State Department, however, it became clear that the Moscow deadlock had simply been transferred to Washington.

Harriman and Clark Kerr, who took part in the three Washington sessions with the foreign ministers, had been over this ground before, time and again. Molotov clung doggedly to his fixed position: the Warsaw regime was the only one now functioning in Poland; it alone was mentioned in the Yalta declaration; hence, before inviting other Polish leaders, whether from London or from inside Poland, the Warsaw group would have to be consulted. Again he pressed for a settlement along the lines of the Tito-Subâsič agreement in Yugoslavia.* Stettinius rejected the precedent. The new Yugoslav government, he said, numbered twenty-one Tito supporters as against only six from abroad. Besides, Eden pointed out, there was not a word in the Yalta agreement about applying the Yugoslav formula to Poland. Molotov left no doubt that he would be perfectly willing to depart from the Yalta text on this point because, he said, with a 21–6 ratio in their favor "he felt that the Warsaw Poles would agree."

Stettinius had tried and failed to budge Molotov by warning him that the San Francisco Conference, and the future of the new world organization itself, would be in jeopardy if the Great Powers made no progress on Poland. On the afternoon of April 23 he glumly reported to the President, at a special White House meeting also attended by Stimson, Forrestal, Leahy, Marshall, King, Harriman and Deane, that "a complete deadlock had been reached on the subject of carrying out the Yalta agreement on Poland." Truman, who was about to see Molo-

---

* Dr. Ivan Subâsič, Premier of the Royal Government of Yugoslavia, had returned to Belgrade from London in February to join a united postwar government which received the blessing of Roosevelt, Churchill and Stalin at Yalta.

tov a second time, later in the day, tried out his arguments on the assemblage of presidential advisers. It was now or never, he said. The Yalta agreements so far had been a one-way street and that could not continue. He would go ahead with the plans for San Francisco and if the Russians did not care to join, they could "go to hell." He then asked each of the officials around the table to state his views.

Stimson, who spoke first by reason of seniority, favored caution. In the big military matters, he said, the Russians had kept their word; often they had done more than they promised. Their ideas of independence and democracy in areas they regarded as vital to Russian security were, of course, different from ours. The United States might be heading into very dangerous water if it did not first find out "how seriously the Russians took this Polish question." Marshall was equally cautious. He was not familiar with the politics of Poland, he said, but from the military point of view he thought it unwise to have a row with the Russians lest Stalin delay joining the war against Japan "until we had done all the dirty work."

The Secretary of War, alarmed over what he later described as the "rather brutal frankness" which Truman proposed to use with Molotov, evidently felt that Harriman and Deane had been too persuasive with the President in pressing for a tougher policy. That evening he wrote in his diary:

> They [Harriman and Deane] have been suffering personally from the Russians' behavior on minor matters for a long time, and they have been urging firmness in dealing on these smaller matters & we have been backing them up, but now they were evidently influenced by their past bad treatment & they moved for strong words by the President on a strong position.[4]

Forrestal, on the other hand, was hospitable to Harriman's views. Poland was not the only example, he said, of Russian determination to dominate adjacent countries in disregard of the Allies. He had felt for some time, Forrestal added, that the Soviets believed we would not object if they took over all of Eastern Europe. Better to have a showdown now than later. The Navy and the Air Forces, unlike the Army, had concluded that Russian help would not be needed in forcing the Japanese to surrender.

Leahy stood halfway between Stimson and Forrestal. He had left Yalta, he said, believing that the Russians would never allow a free government to operate in Poland. But the Yalta agreement on Poland could be read two ways and it would be a serious matter to break with the Russians. We should tell them, he said, that the United States stood for a free, independent Poland.

Harriman, in turn, pointed out that the real issue was whether the United States was to be a party to the Soviet program for dominating Poland. It seemed obvious to him that Stalin had changed his mind about free elections after hearing from Bierut that his regime had no hope of winning. The possibility of a break with the Russians could, if properly handled, be avoided. The President at this point said that he had no intention of delivering an ultimatum to Molotov.

Truman's clear intention was to be firm though not offensive. When Molotov walked into the Presidential office later that afternoon, however, Truman went straight to the point. He was sorry to learn that there had been no progress on the Polish question, he said. The United States had gone as far as it could to meet Stalin's demands, but it could not recognize a Polish government that failed to represent all democratic elements. He was determined to go ahead with plans for the new world organization, no matter what difficulties or differences might arise with regard to other matters. The President reminded Molotov that Roosevelt himself had warned Stalin on April 1 that no American policy, foreign or domestic, could succeed unless it enjoyed public confidence and support. Pointedly, he added that Congress would have to appropriate money for any postwar economic-assistance programs and he had no hope of getting such measures through Congress without public support. He hoped the Soviet government would bear this in mind.

Molotov replied that the only acceptable basis for Allied cooperation was that the three governments must deal with one another as equals, without one or two of the powers trying to impose their will on the third. All the United States was asking, Truman said, was that the Soviets should carry out the Yalta decision on Poland. Molotov countered that his government could not be considered to have violated the agreements because of abrogations by others.

Truman repeated, with rising sharpness of tone, that the United States was prepared to carry out loyally all the agreements signed at Yalta. He asked no more of the Soviet Union than that it, too, should observe them. He wanted friendship with Russia but he also wanted it clearly understood in Moscow that this called for mutual observance of the Yalta agreements, not a one-way street.

"I have never been talked to like that in my life," Molotov protested.

"Carry out your agreements," Truman shot back," and you won't get talked to like that."

Harriman, who was in the room, later recalled: "I was a little taken aback, frankly, when the President attacked Molotov so vigorously. I suppose it was true that Molotov had never been talked to so bluntly before by a foreigner. Although the idea that his sensibilities were offended seemed to me rather silly. Molotov had talked just as bluntly to other people. He could be rough and tough, as I had reason to know. I did regret that Truman went at it so hard because his behavior gave Molotov an excuse to tell Stalin that the Roosevelt policy was being abandoned. I regretted that Truman gave him the opportunity. I think it was a mistake, though not a decisive mistake."

Having failed to find agreement in Washington, the foreign ministers now transported their differences across the continent to San Francisco. Harriman went along, inheriting an elaborate penthouse suite at the Fairmont Hotel reserved for Cordell Hull, who at the last moment decided not to attend the United Nations conference. After all the long, wearying months in Moscow, Harriman felt that a little luxury was entirely justified. He briefly enjoyed the easy life of an adviser to Stettinius. He took part in the daily delegation meetings, talked with men he had known among the delegates from other countries and attended the United Nations conference sessions.

The schedule left plenty of time to see old friends and get back in the swing of American life. A steady stream of visitors came to call, among them a tall, skinny young naval officer named John F. Kennedy who dropped in for a drink one afternoon. Jan Masaryk, who had returned to Prague as Foreign Minister of the first postwar government of Czechoslovakia after spending the war years in London, came several times. Masaryk explained to Harriman why he voted with Molotov in the conference. Part of the deal President Beneš had made with the Russians, he said, was that while the Czechoslovaks were to be independent in their internal affairs, they were bound to conform to Moscow's directions in foreign policy. He urged Harriman to pay no attention to what he said or did, or how he voted, on matters in dispute between the Soviet government and the United States; the Czechoslovaks simply had to go along with Molotov. Harriman assured him that, of course, he understood the problem. Privately, he reflected that his old friend was having a most unhappy time.

On another occasion Masaryk described a more-or-less obligatory Sunday drive with Molotov through the countryside near San Francisco. Molotov seemed much impressed with the prosperity that surrounded him: tidy houses, carefully tended lawns and automobiles in every driveway, all of them owned by ordinary working-class Americans. He remarked to Masaryk, "Ah, what we could do if we organized this country!" The anecdote reminded Harriman of statements he had heard from Soviet leaders back in 1926, on his first visit to Moscow. It was most unfortunate, they had said, that the first Communist-ruled state should be a backward agrarian country like Russia. They could have done a much better job if the Bolsheviks had taken over industrialized Germany or even the United States.

Harriman, who had known Stettinius since the early New Deal days as a fellow member of the Business Advisory Council, felt that the Secretary of State's lack of diplomatic experience was offset by his ability to get along with people. The American delegation included Senator Arthur Vandenberg of Michigan, Senator Tom Connally of Texas, Representative Sol Bloom of New York and Harold Stassen of Minnesota—all men accustomed to making their voices heard. Harriman admired the way Stettinius as chairman conducted the daily meetings of the delegation. He gave everyone a chance to be heard and to express his views fully. Stettinius was not about to prejudice the prospects for bipartisan support of the United Nations by appearing to override the foreign-policy grandees of either party. He listened carefully and composed differences with great skill. The advisers to the delegation were high-powered too, such men as John Foster Dulles and Adlai Stevenson. Harriman watched Stassen with particular interest, having heard Roosevelt speak warmly of him as a potential Republican candidate for the presidency. "I considered him one of the most intelligent members of our delegation," Harriman recalled. "Stassen's questions were clear, to the point and refreshingly brief. His comments were incisive. I was very much impressed."

At one delegation meeting Harriman crossed swords with Nelson A. Rockefeller, then an Assistant Secretary of State concerned with inter-American matters, over the proposed admission of Argentina to UN membership. The Argentines had just issued a belated declaration of war against the Axis powers in order to qualify for admission, a formal act that came too late to conform to the Yalta agreement. The rest of the Latin American delegations, predictably, were pressing Argentina's cause, and through Rockefeller were seeking commitments of support from the United States. Molotov, just as predictably, was objecting to the admission of a state which had shown marked sympathies for Nazi Germany and thus failed to meet the test agreed to at Yalta.

Harriman took the position that the United States must keep its word, even if the Russians had broken theirs in Poland and elsewhere. Worried that the Soviets might use the seating of Argentina to demand admission for the Provisional Government of Poland, he argued in delegation meetings that the Argentine matter could wait until the Polish problem was sorted out. "I was very strongly for living up to our agreements with the Russians so that our behavior would be in stark contrast to theirs," he recalled. "We had agreed at Yalta that only countries which had declared war by March 1 should be admitted. But Rockefeller was totally committed to his Latin American clients. So I said to him, 'Nelson, are you the ambassador to the Argentine or the ambassador of the Argentine?' I was terribly worried that a deal would be made sealing the fate of Poland—and in those days I could be pretty blunt." Stettinius, in fact, voted to seat Argentina.

Rockefeller's total commitment to Argentina's cause exposed the American delegation, Stettinius in particular, to widespread criticism. The Washington *Post*, for example, in a May 1 editorial, ridiculed "the bush league diplomacy of the State Department headed by Secretary Stettinius." Molotov must know, the *Post* continued, "that at this crucial period of world history we consider that nothing is more precious after the maintenance of our principles than the preservation of the wartime community of interest between Moscow and Washington. All he can conclude is that incompetence has taken hold of our foreign relations. However, Molotov is not averse to playing poker with men who, compared with him, don't even know the rudiments of the game."

Harriman felt that Stettinius had gone too far in placating the Latin Americans. But he was sufficiently troubled by the euphoria regarding Soviet intentions that he encountered at San Francisco to offer the beleaguered Secretary of State his help. It seemed to him that many of the American journalists at the conference did not understand what a tough game Molotov was playing. With Stettinius' ready agreement, he arranged three off-the-record talks—one for working reporters in the Palace Hotel and two for groups of publishers, editors and commentators in his penthouse suite at the Fairmont.

Harriman's warnings that Stalin was not living up to his agreements alarmed certain of the journalists and touched off a memorable controversy. He explained that the Russians were seeking to control Eastern Europe, inflicting upon the recently liberated peoples of that region Communist dictatorships or coalition governments in which the Communists held the whip hand through terror and intimidation. He took much the same line as in the State Department meetings, warning that Stalin's idea of postwar security was in conflict with the Yalta agreements, while expressing the hope that a firm American stand could lead to better relations.

Many of the journalists published Harriman's warnings under their own signatures. Ernest K. Lindley, for example, wrote in *Newsweek*: "The Yalta agreements had hardly been proclaimed before the Russians began to back away from them. That the Russians were running out on their pledges was entirely plain to Roosevelt before he died." *Time*, in its issue for the same week of May 21, observed: "A commentary on the state of Big Power relations was Averell Harriman's state of mind when he headed back to Moscow. Harriman, usually a mild fellow, was ready to go to the mat."

Many of the news people, however, had come to San Francisco expecting a glimpse of that "clean world" promised by Roosevelt in his D-Day prayer, a world in which Russians and Americans, putting aside old rivalries and outworn ideologies, would construct an enduring peace together. They were not prepared for Harriman's outspoken message.

At one of his meetings with the press, the discussion became hotly argumentative. Harriman recalled saying, "We must recognize that our objectives and the Kremlin's objectives are irreconcilable. The Kremlin wants to promote Communist dictatorships controlled from Moscow, whereas we want, as far as possible, to see a world of governments responsive to the will of the people. We will have to find ways of composing our differences in the United Nations and elsewhere in order to live without war on this small planet."

Two of Harriman's listeners, Raymond Gram Swing and Walter Lippmann, were so shocked that they got up and left the room. (Swing called on Harriman the following year to apologize.) Harriman was amazed at the reaction. "I spoke calmly," he recalled. "I understated the case as I saw it. I said that in dealing with the Russians we had to have our guard up, but at the same time, to have a friendly hand outstretched. Some of the journalists appeared to accept my analysis, but others were not prepared to listen. Their faith in the future was great and they could not believe at the time that the Russians, who had suffered so deeply in the war, would not want to live amicably with their neighbors and with ourselves."

Some reporters with liberal leanings were sternly disapproving. Alexander Uhl, for example, in a dispatch to *PM*, the experimental tabloid then being published in New York, blamed Harriman by name for the rising disenchantment with Russia. Uhl wrote on May 28: ". . . a good deal of the wave of 'get tough with Russia' talk that went through the conference circles during the Polish dispute got a lot of its inspiration from Harriman, who was here at the time. Newspapermen who were present at one of his more select press meetings reported an extraordinary amount of venom in his attitude toward the Russians." This was one of the few times in Harriman's experience when the off-the-record rule was abused.

Charles van Devender, who in later years became Harriman's close friend and press secretary, ascribed the behavior of his colleagues to the pro-Russian climate of the times. The press found it extraordinary and somewhat inexplicable, he said, that this rich man could have spent so much time in the Soviet Union and yet somehow failed to see its essential virtues.

In Poland those Soviet virtues seemed less apparent than in San Francisco. Sixteen prominent Poles, all members of the anti-Hitler underground, had disappeared in late March after being lured from their homes by the promise of a meeting with Marshal Zhukov. Both

Eden and Stettinius had asked Molotov for information regarding their whereabouts. On the evening of May 3, as Stettinius walked into the Soviet consulate in San Francisco for a dinner meeting, Molotov told him almost casually that the missing Poles had been arrested and charged with "diversionist activities against the Red Army," which had led to the death of more than a hundred Russians.

President Truman was seriously disturbed, Stettinius told Molotov the following evening, at a meeting in his penthouse apartment at the Fairmont. Eden added that he was "astounded and shocked" by the arrest of the Polish leaders, whom the British government knew to be democrats and patriots with outstanding records of resistance to the Germans. Several of the missing men, in fact, had been so highly regarded that their names were included in the list for consultation with the tripartite commission in Moscow. Molotov said he could well understand that the President was upset but the Soviet authorities had no choice. The Poles would have to stand trial and while "it was possible that not all would be equally guilty," the principal figure among them, General Leopold Okulicki, was an avowed enemy of the Soviet Union. The truth would emerge at the proper time during their trial, he said.

On May 5 Stettinius held a press conference to register America's "great concern" over this development, pointing out that it was bound to have "a direct bearing on the working out of this Polish problem."

With Germany's resistance crumbling the three foreign ministers at this point broke off their talks on Poland in San Francisco. Eisenhower had reported to the War Department on May 4 that representatives of Admiral Karl Dönitz were on their way to his headquarters at Rheims, apparently to arrange for the final surrender. He informed the Soviet high command that he would accept only the surrender of the German forces on the western front, including Norway. Those facing the Russians would be required to surrender to the Russians. When the German emissaries asked to surrender to the Western Allies alone, Eisenhower refused, adhering honorably to the Allied agreement. Stalin's suspicions, in short, had been totally refuted. Yet he kept the great news from the Russian people for almost two full days after the signing of the surrender. Kennan, in charge of the Moscow embassy during Harriman's absence, offered Washington his theory: "For Russia peace, like everything else, can come only by ukase and the end of the war must be determined not by the true course of events but by decision of the Kremlin. Among the lesser injuries for which the Germans may have to answer to Russia when the smoke has cleared away, perhaps not the least may be their willfulness in capitulating at a time and place not selected by the Kremlin."

Until the last moment, Stalin apparently feared a betrayal. In his message to the Soviet people, published in the Moscow newspapers of May 10, Stalin indicated that "knowing the wolflike conduct of the German leaders" he had delayed the announcement until he was absolutely certain that enemy troops had actually laid down their arms. "Now we can state with full certainty that there has come the historic day of the final rout of Germany," he declared.

Harriman and Bohlen flew back to Washington together on May 9. On the way they discussed the alarming deterioration in Soviet-American relationships since the Yalta Conference and what could be done to arrest it. Bohlen suggested that perhaps Hopkins might be sent to Moscow to talk with Stalin. "I jumped at the idea," Harriman recalled. "Stalin had told me of his respect for Hopkins' courage and determination. He had been particularly impressed that Hopkins should have made the long trip to Russia in July 1941 in spite of his ill health. Stalin also knew that Hopkins was Roosevelt's most intimate and loyal associate. I was concerned, however, whether Hopkins would be well enough to stand the rough trip. So, before proposing the mission to Truman, I went to see Hopkins. I found him ill and feeble in the little Georgetown house he was renting."

Harriman outlined the need as he saw it to reassure Stalin that the United States had not departed from Roosevelt's fundamental policy. Hopkins' response was instantaneous and affirmative. "Although he appeared too ill even to get out of bed and walk across N Street, the mere intimation of a flight to Moscow converted him into the traditional old fire horse at the sound of the alarm," as Robert Sherwood has written.[5]

Now it was Harriman's task to persuade Truman. The President, who had never felt entirely comfortable with Hopkins, refused. Harriman could talk with Stalin himself, he said. But the Ambassador persisted, stressing Hopkins' special relationship with Stalin dating back to the desperate summer of 1941, and the need to do something quickly about arresting the drift in American-Soviet relations. Truman said he would need to think it over, and for several anxious days Hopkins lay in bed worrying that the plan would come to nothing. When the President at last sent for Hopkins to ask whether he felt strong enough to undertake the mission, his answer was an immediate "Yes."

As Harriman was making his final Washington rounds before returning to Moscow by way of London and Paris, the new President stumbled into a new and unnecessary uproar with the Russians. The war in Europe having ended, Truman issued an executive order which cut back drastically on Lend-Lease shipments not only to Russia but to Britain and France as well. The President later maintained that when Grew and Leo T. Crowley, the Foreign Economic Administrator, took the order to him on May 8, he had signed it without reading the text. The date, in fact, was May 11 and Crowley specifically cautioned the President to expect a sharp response from the Russians. They would, Crowley predicted, "be running all over town looking for help."[6]

Crowley's staff, moreover, had compounded the problem by interpreting the new directive more literally than Truman intended. Showing more zeal than judgment, Crowley's representative on the President's Soviet Protocol Committee insisted the following day that immediate orders be issued to stop loading supplies for the Soviet Union and that ships already on their way to Russian ports should be turned around on the high seas. The Roosevelt policy of "when in doubt, give" had been reversed to read "when in doubt, hold."

The Washington bureaucracy, in short, had blundered into the precise posture that Harriman had been trying to avoid: it led Stalin to believe that the new Administration was trying to extract political concessions through economic pressure. The true character of Harriman's policy recommendation had been recorded by Grew in a message to the Moscow embassy, dated May 10: "Our general attitude toward USSR on Lend-Lease should be firm while avoiding any indication of political bargaining or implications of threat."

Harriman and Clayton, shocked by the Lend-Lease termination, lost no time persuading Truman to countermand his order. Loading and sailing of ships bound for Russia was promptly resumed. But the propaganda damage had been done. As in the case of Truman's Dutch-uncle lecture to Molotov, the Lend-Lease interruption gave the Russians a further opportunity to charge the new Administration with a reversal of Roosevelt's policies.

Before leaving Washington, Harriman urged Truman to arrange a meeting with Stalin and Churchill as soon as possible. At a White House meeting on May 15, he argued against the President's preference for waiting until July:

> [Harriman] said he felt that the establishment of a basis for future relations with Russia and the settlement of these immediate issues [the treatment of Germany in defeat and the Polish question] could only be done at a tripartite meeting, that the longer the meeting was delayed the worse the situation would get, and that while he assumed of course that we were not prepared to use our troops in Europe for political bargaining, nevertheless, if the meeting could take place before we were in large measure out of Europe he felt the atmosphere . . . would be more favorable and the chances of success increased.

He said he felt that Stalin was not getting accurate reports from Molotov . . . and as a result had grown deeply and unjustifiably suspicious as to our motives, which he probably thought were designed to deprive him of the fruits of victory.[7]

Truman agreed. But he had a number of pressing domestic questions to deal with, including the preparation of a budget message before the end of the fiscal year, June 30, which would make it difficult for him to leave Washington before that date. The Ambassador pressed for a meeting within the next several weeks, cautioning Truman that he would be confronted with a far more difficult situation in Europe if he waited until July. After some discussion of possible meeting places (Alaska and Vienna were mentioned), Harriman again urged the President to fix the earliest possible date. Truman then agreed to consider early June, if that was acceptable to Stalin and Churchill.

During his last days in Washington, Harriman also prodded the State, Navy and War Departments to clarify their position on the Far East and Russia's imminent participation in the war against Japan. He put a series of specific questions to Grew, Forrestal and John McCloy, for example, at a meeting in the State Department on April 12:

- Should the Yalta agreements be re-examined in the light of Soviet violations and the fact that the war in Europe had now ended?
- How urgent or important was it that Russia should join the war against Japan?
- What if the Russians asked to participate in the military occupation of the Japanese home islands?
- At Yalta, Roosevelt had proposed a great-power trusteeship for Korea, and Stalin had replied that he saw no need for it if the Koreans could produce a satisfactory government of their own. What was the United States position now?
- Roosevelt also had talked of a UN trusteeship for French Indochina. Should that proposal now be dropped and the French be given a free hand?
- What was the American objective in Japan? Destruction or retention as a power in the Pacific?

Harriman felt the need for definite answers before returning to Moscow, in part because Stalin in their last conversation had asked him whether Truman was prepared to honor the Yalta agreement assigning to Russia the Manchurian ports and railroads, South Sakhalin and the Kuriles. "Since Stalin appeared to think that the question was open," Harriman recalled, "I thought we might as well look at it again. I found that nobody had any serious objection to going through with the agreement Roosevelt had made."

Stimson continued to believe, as he wrote in a letter from San Francisco to Grew on May 21, that "Russian entry will have a profound military effect in that almost certainly it will materially shorten the war and thus save American lives." He did not see that much good would come of trying to revise the Yalta accords. Stimson felt that Russia had the power to occupy Manchuria, Korea, Sakhalin and North China at will, whatever the United States might do. Only in the Kuriles could the United States hope to forestall Soviet designs and he advised against such a course. Even Forrestal, who had told Harriman that he believed Russian intervention would not be necessary because the war was pretty much won, saw no reason to set aside Roosevelt's secret agreement with Stalin.

As for the occupation of Japan, Stimson saw one advantage in assigning a zone to the Soviet Union: it would reduce the need for American manpower. He raised the possibility, however, that "our experiences with the Russians in the occupation of Germany may in the future lead to considerations which would point to the wisdom of exclusive occupation by our own forces."

With no more than half his questions answered, Harriman left for London on May 21 to talk with Churchill, and confer once again with Mikolajczyk, before going on to meet Hopkins in Paris. He found the Prime Minister doubly burdened. Quite apart from his alarm over Russian behavior and intentions in Poland, Yugoslavia and Germany, there was the matter of winning a general election in the first week of July. His coalition government, which had rallied the British peoples through the dismal years of disappointment and defeat, was about to resign. Churchill was plainly unhappy over Truman's reluctance to fix a date for the next Big Three conference. His great fear, as he had just cabled Truman, was that Stalin might "play for time in order to remain all-powerful in Europe when our forces have melted."

In a report to the President on May 23, Harriman wrote that Churchill was "gravely concerned over the developments with Russia" and did not believe that basic issues such as Poland could be settled "unless you and he meet with Stalin. He expressed the hope that this could be arranged as early as possible."

Mikolajczyk impressed Harriman as most pessimistic about developments inside Poland while at the same time totally out of sympathy with the "unrealistic attitude" of the London Poles. "His only hope is of course that you and the Prime Minister can ameliorate the present trend and prepare the way for free elections," Harriman added, in what amounted to one more argument for an early meeting with Stalin.

Four days after Harriman's conversation with Churchill, a second emissary from Washington arrived in London. This was Joseph E. Davies, a pre-war ambassador in Moscow whose personal record of sympathy for Stalin's Russia was written large in his book, *Mission to Moscow*, and the motion picture based upon it. Davies, a generous contributor to Democratic campaigns, hardly seemed the ideal man to persuade Churchill that he was being too hard on the Russians. That appears to have been Davies' conception of his mission to Chequers, where he spent the night of May 26 with the Prime Minister. According to his own written report, made after his return to Washington, Davies told Churchill that his recent warnings against the spread of Communism in Europe, and the threat of Soviet domination, put him in the same camp as Hitler and Goebbels. Churchill rejected indignantly the suggestion relayed by Davies that the President meet alone with Stalin somewhere in Europe before being joined by the Prime Minister. Unless the three met "simultaneously and on equal terms," Churchill said, he would not come. Stalin, meanwhile, had notified Churchill that he would be pleased to meet with him and Truman in the vicinity of Berlin "in the very near future." That left only the date to be settled.

"Sending Davies to London was one of the few gauche things Truman did during those first weeks in office," Harriman later observed, "although the original suggestion came from Steve Early, who saw it as a way of balancing Hopkins' mission to Stalin."

On May 24, Harriman joined Hopkins in Paris and the two lunched with General Eisenhower at his headquarters before flying on to Moscow. "The conversation at luncheon covered the wide range of problems we were having with the Russians," Harriman recalled. "Ike was concerned that although President Truman had named him as the American representative on the Allied Control Council for Germany, his Russian counterpart had not yet been appointed. The Soviets were still in sole control of Berlin. Hopkins agreed to raise the subject with Stalin. Ike told us that the Council ought to have wide authority in carrying out the policies agreed to by the Allied governments. He felt that if there was little interference from the bureaucrats, he could get along with the Russians, as soldier to soldier."

Returning to Moscow on the evening of May 25 after a long flight over the scarred landscape of Germany with Hopkins, his wife Louise and Bohlen, Harriman quickly arranged a meeting with Stalin for eight o'clock the following evening at the Kremlin. It was to be the first of six meetings, each remarkable for its extraordinary candor and rare good feeling. Hopkins hoped for solid results, above all an agreement on Poland. Harriman had been over that boggy ground too many times to look for miracles.

Stalin greeted Hopkins as an old friend, listening with obvious sympathy as Hopkins described the circumstances of Roosevelt's death. Lenin, too, had died of a cerebral hemorrhage, he recalled. Hopkins spoke of the President's confidence that the United States and Russia could work together in peace, as they had fought together in war. He mentioned Roosevelt's respect and admiration for Stalin, recalling his own mission to Moscow in July 1941, and the President's swift decision to help the Russians when so many people believed that Hitler inevitably would win the war in a matter of weeks. Now Americans and Russians together had broken Hitler's Reich. But in the past two months another great change had occurred, a worrying change for all those Americans who had believed in Roosevelt's policies, and that was the reason he had picked himself up from his sickbed to fly to Moscow at Truman's request.

The real reason Truman had sent him, Hopkins said, was that so many Americans were disturbed or alarmed over the trend of relations with Russia. He found it difficult to put his finger on the precise reason for this shift but the crucial point was that Truman would find it difficult to carry forward Roosevelt's policies of cooperation with Russia without the support of public opinion. And the deterioration in popular support, as he saw it, arose from "a sense of bewilderment at our inability to solve the Polish question." Unless the Polish matter was cleared up promptly, Hopkins said, the situation would get rapidly worse.

Stalin blamed the British Conservatives for that failure. All the Soviet Union asked for was a friendly Poland, but the British wanted to revive the prewar *cordon sanitaire*. Hopkins replied that neither the government nor the people of the United States had any such intention. Stalin replied that he was speaking only of England, whose Conservative leaders did not want to see a Poland friendly to the Soviet Union. Hopkins assured him that the United States, far from objecting, wanted to see friendly countries all along the borders of Russia. If that be so, Stalin responded, we can easily come to terms.

The task of trying to come to terms on Poland filled many hours of the Kremlin meetings that followed, beginning on May 26 and concluding on June 6. Although the favorable atmosphere of that first evening continued to the end of Hopkins' visit, and Stalin exposed his thoughts to Hopkins and Harriman as he had seldom exposed them to any foreign visitor, few solid agreements resulted.

At the second meeting, on May 27, Stalin put all his grievances on the table. They were not limited to Poland. There was, to begin with, the case of Argentina at the San Francisco Conference. The Big Three had agreed at Yalta that only states which had declared war on Germany before March 1 would be invited to San Francisco. He found it difficult to understand why Argentina (which had not declared war until March 27) could not have been asked to wait three months. What value was there in agreements among the major powers, Stalin asked, "if their decisions could be overturned by the votes of such countries as Honduras and Puerto Rico?"*

Harriman, who had clashed with Nelson Rockefeller at San Francisco on precisely this point, undertook to explain what had happened: in keeping with the Yalta decisions and at Molotov's request, Stettinius at San Francisco had asked the Latin American delegations to support the admission of the Ukraine and White Russia. They had agreed, and as Molotov would remember, they had kept their word. But the Latin ambassadors had tried to condition their vote for the Soviet Republics on American support for the admission of Argentina. Stettinius was still trying to persuade them that the Argentine matter ought to be postponed when Molotov had complicated matters by pressing for the admission of the Polish Provisional Government as well. In these complicated circumstances, the Secretary of State felt he had no alternative but to go along with Latin America and vote for Argentina.

Stalin let the matter drop at that point. What had been done could not be put right, he said, and in any event, the Argentine question belonged to the past.

Stalin's second grievance had to do with the Reparations Commission, which had been conceived at Yalta as a three-power body. Now the United States was insisting that France should become the fourth member. This seemed to him an insulting suggestion in view of the French military collapse. If France was to be a member, why not Poland and Yugoslavia, which had fought harder and suffered more at the hands of the Germans? Hopkins replied that the admission of France had seemed a logical step, since she was to be one of the four powers in occupation of Germany, but if the Russians objected, he felt certain the United States would not insist on French participation.

It was the Lend-Lease curtailment, above all, that rankled with Stalin. The manner in which it had been done, he said, was "unfortunate and even brutal." If the decision had been made in order to put pressure on the Russians, it was a fundamental mistake. While Truman's order had now been revoked, Stalin added, it had caused the Soviet government great concern. According to the American record of the conversation, "He said he must tell Mr. Hopkins frankly that if the Russians were approached frankly on a friendly basis much could be done, but that reprisals in any form would bring about the exact opposite effect."

Hopkins explained what had gone wrong: there had been a "tech-

* Stalin evidently meant Costa Rica.

nical misunderstanding" by one government agency that did not in any sense represent a policy decision by the United States government. The unfortunate decision to order the unloading of ships bound for Russia had in any case been countermanded within twenty-four hours. He had seen no tendency on the part of Washington officials at the policy level to deal with Lend-Lease for Russia in "arbitrary fashion."

Stalin acknowledged that the end of the war in Europe doubtless required the United States to reconsider the old Lend-Lease program. He readily agreed with Hopkins that throughout the history of Lend-Lease the United States had faithfully met its commitments. It also was true, he conceded, that while the Lend-Lease Act stipulated that the supplies provided were only for use in the war, the United States had interpreted this limitation in its broadest sense, making foodstuffs and other materials available to the Soviet Union, in addition to munitions. Hopkins concluded by saying that there was honest confusion in Washington about the legal aspects of Lend-Lease now that the war in Europe had ended. But he assured Stalin that the curtailment had no fundamental policy significance. The American record shows that Stalin accepted Hopkins' skillful explanation:

MARSHAL STALIN said he wished to make it clear that he fully understood the right of the United States to curtail Lend-Lease shipments to the Soviet Union under present conditions since our commitments in this respect had been freely entered into. Even two months ago it would have been quite correct for the United States to have begun to curtail shipments, but what he had in mind was the manner and form in which it was done. He felt that what was after all an agreement between the two governments had been ended in a scornful and abrupt manner. He said that if proper warning had been given to the Soviet Government there would have been no feeling of the kind he had spoken of; that this warning was important to them since their economy was based on plans . . .

MR. HOPKINS replied that what disturbed him most about the Marshal's statement was the revelation that he believed that the United States would use Lend-Lease as a means of showing our displeasure with the Soviet Union. He wished to assure the Marshal that however unfortunate an impression this question had caused in the mind of the Soviet Government, he must believe that there was no attempt or desire on the part of the United States to use it as a pressure weapon. He said the United States is a strong power and does not go in for those methods. Furthermore, we have no conflict of immediate interests with the Soviet Union and would have no reason to adopt such practices.

MARSHAL STALIN said he believed Mr. Hopkins and was fully satisfied with his statement in regard to Lend-Lease but said he hoped Mr. Hopkins would consider how it looked from their side.

Another Soviet complaint, swiftly disposed of, was Stalin's request that one third of the German fleet and merchant vessels captured by the Western Allies should be turned over to the Russians. It would be very unpleasant if, as he had heard, the United States and Britain now proposed to reject this Soviet claim, Stalin warned. Hopkins assured him that the United States had no objection to handing over the captured German vessels, adding that he believed the matter could be definitely settled at the forthcoming conference of Truman, Stalin and Churchill.

The sticking point, as Harriman had fully expected, was still Poland. Stalin raised the matter himself, saying he could not understand the American attitude. At Yalta, Roosevelt and Churchill had agreed with him that the Warsaw government should be reconstructed; and as anyone endowed with common sense could see, this meant the new government was to be formed "on the basis of" the existing regime. "Despite the fact that they were simple people [he said], the Russians should not be regarded as fools, which was a mistake the West frequently made."

Stalin had listened quizzically to Roosevelt's lectures at Yalta and Teheran on the vital importance of public opinion in America. When Hopkins, too, suggested that the Soviet Union must accommodate its behavior—doubtless also its security interests in Poland—to the fickle demands of American opinion, Stalin responded in a new, sharp tone. He for one, he said, would not attempt to use public opinion as a screen. He would speak only of the feeling in the Soviet government, a feeling that once the war had been won the Americans were acting as if they no longer needed the Russians. Hopkins, in self-defense, assured Stalin that he was not "intending to hide behind American public opinion" in presenting the American position on the Polish question. At this Stalin withdrew his remark, saying that he was afraid he had "cut Mr. Hopkins to the quick" and praising him as "an honest and frank man."

Not until the final meeting, on June 6, was the Polish discussion concluded. Hopkins repeatedly stressed that Poland was important chiefly "as a symbol of our ability to work out problems with the Soviet Union." Disavowing any special American interest in that country, he argued that the Polish people must have the right to choose their own government through free elections, not through unilateral Soviet actions. Stalin's arguments were thoroughly familiar: a weak, hostile Poland had served twice in a generation as the main corridor for German attacks on Russia; it was therefore in Russia's interest that Poland should be both strong and friendly. If the Poles wanted a parliamentary system, they could have it, and any talk of Sovietizing Poland was stupid; even the Warsaw leaders, some of whom were Communists, did not want the Soviet system. They wanted no collective farms and in this they were right because the Soviet system (as Harriman had heard Stalin say more than once) was "not exportable." It was a system developed from within, based on a set of conditions that did not exist in Poland. Yes, it was true, Stalin conceded, that Russia had taken unilateral actions in Poland, but only because she had been compelled to protect the rear of the Red Army as it advanced on Berlin. It would have been impossible, he said, to wait until the Allies had come to an agreement on Poland.

When the talk turned to the composition of the proposed Polish Government of National Unity, Stalin at first offered "four or five" places to representatives of groups other than Lublin who could be picked from the list submitted by the Western powers. Molotov at this point whispered to Stalin that the Warsaw Poles would accept only four, not five, new ministers. Mikolajczyk, however, could be one of them, Stalin said.

Encouraged by this token concession, Hopkins and Harriman reopened the question at their fourth meeting with Stalin, on May 30. Stalin had said he had no objection to a parliamentary system for the Poles, and Hopkins felt the need to explain what that term meant to Americans: freedom of speech and the right of assembly, together with the right of free movement and of free worship; all political parties except the Fascists must, without distinction, have the right to hold meetings and to spread their views through the press and radio; all citizens, moreover, must have the right to public trial, defense by counsel of their own choosing, and the right to habeas corpus. If Stalin could accept these principles, which had been agreed to at Yalta, he felt confident the Allies would soon find ways of solving the Polish problem.

Stalin replied that such freedoms could only be applied in time of peace, and even then with certain limitations. Why, even the British government in wartime had arrested and tried certain individuals in secret. As for freedom of worship, that was a right also proclaimed by the Russian Communist party at the time of the Revolution. But when the church had called on the faithful to refuse military service and the payment of taxes, there was nothing to be done but declare war on the church. Happily, Stalin added, the German invasion had wiped out this antagonism on the part of the church and it was now possible to restore freedom of worship in Russia.

At the fifth meeting, on May 31, Hopkins had pleaded for the sixteen Polish leaders arrested in March. In the eyes of the American people, he said, it looked as if some of these men had been arrested for political reasons and this had added fuel to the flames in the United States. Stalin replied that the arrested men had shot the Red Army in the back while it was liberating Poland. He could not guarantee that there would not be more arrests if the guerrilla attacks continued. Were all sixteen charged with the same crimes? Hopkins asked. No, Stalin replied, the majority were charged only with operating illegal radio transmitters. Hopkins said he was afraid the fate of the arrested Poles would interfere with the negotiations on the substance of the Polish problem. He suggested that those not charged with murder might be dealt with another way. Stalin conceded that leniency was possible, now that the war was over, but all of these men would have to stand trial. For that matter, Stalin added, he happened to know that General Eisenhower had arrested saboteurs operating in the rear of the Allied forces, and the British had certainly done so in Greece.

On the night of June 1 Stalin gave a dinner for Hopkins at the Kremlin. There were forty guests, seated at one long table in the ballroom named for Catherine the Great. Perhaps in deference to Kathleen Harriman and Mrs. Hopkins, who had received somewhat ambiguous invitations to come "if they wanted to"—and, of course, eagerly accepted—the vodka bottles disappeared early from the table. Stalin left the toasts to Molotov, contenting himself with occasional asides.

Hopkins took the occasion to talk privately with Stalin, pressing for the release of the arrested Poles, or at least of those not charged with killing Russians. "I told him that I believed we would have no insurmountable difficulties with getting the list of names approved for the group to consult with the Moscow Commission if these men could be released," Hopkins reported to Truman on June 3. "I made it perfectly clear to him that, while we knew nothing of the merits of the case based on our own investigation, the offenses apparently seemed far more serious to the Soviet than they did to us . . . I finally told him that he must believe me when I stated that our whole relationship was threatened by the impasse over Poland . . . I suggested that he release these particular prisoners outright and that he find a way to do it that would clearly indicate his desire to meet us part way."

But Stalin refused to budge. He would not release the Poles, he said, because their offenses were far more serious than the exiled Polish government in London had led the British and Americans to believe. He was prepared to credit Hopkins' warning that the arrest of the sixteen Poles was having an unfavorable effect on public opinion in

America and in Britain, and he would do whatever he could "to make it easy for Mr. Churchill to get out of a bad situation." But outright release was out of the question. The Poles would have to stand trial and he would try to deal leniently with them.*

Hopkins continued to press for the release of the Poles until his last day in Moscow. But he and Harriman came to believe that "it would be a mistake to make this a condition to agreement on the list of names and the starting of the consultation in Moscow promptly," as he reported to Truman on June 3. Stalin had finally agreed that Mikolajczyk, Stanczyk and an architect named Julian Zakowski should be invited from London, together with Archbishop Sapieha or Witos, Zulawski and Kutrzeba and two nonparty men from inside Poland. Truman approved the list and Churchill, after consulting Mikolajczyk, agreed that Hopkins had "obtained the best solution we could hope for in the circumstances."[8] Although the deadlock over which Poles should be invited to Moscow had finally been broken, Churchill labored under no illusions. He wrote to Truman on June 4:

> While it is prudent and right to act in this way at this moment I am sure you will agree with me that these proposals are no advance on Yalta. They are an advance upon the deadlock but we ought by now, according to Yalta and its spirit, to have had a representative Polish Government formed. All we have got is a certain number of concessions on outside Poles to take part in preliminary discussions out of which some improvements in the Lublin Government may be made.
>
> I cannot feel therefore that we can regard this as more than a milestone in a long hill we ought never to have been asked to climb. I think we ought to guard against any newspaper assumptions that the Polish problem has been solved or that the difficulties between the Western Democracies and the Soviet Government on this matter have been more than relieved. Renewed hope and not rejoicing is all we can indulge in at the moment.[9]

Harriman fully shared Churchill's long-term pessimism over Poland. He felt, however, that the Hopkins visit had helped to clarify other important questions left open or ambiguous at Yalta. Stalin made clear, for example, that he no longer favored the dismemberment of Germany. Here again, he said, the British were at fault. They had

---

* The trial took place in June 1945, according to Soviet plan. While the prosecution was able to assemble all the witnesses it needed, no witnesses were called for the defense, ostensibly because of "transport difficulties." Fourteen of the Poles were found guilty as charged and promptly sentenced to Soviet prison terms ranging from ten years to four months.

made clear in the London meetings of the European Advisory Commission that Churchill had never seriously intended to break up Germany into a number of smaller states. The British, he complained, had chosen to interpret the Yalta decision as nothing more than a threat "to hold over the Germans' heads in the event of bad behavior." Moreover, Ambassador Winant had raised no objection. So dismemberment was dead. Hopkins said that was not his understanding. He knew that Truman still favored placing the Ruhr and the Saar under international control. When pressed by Harriman, Stalin agreed to keep an open mind and to discuss the matter further when he met with Truman and Churchill in July. But he did not believe the British would accept even the detachment of the Ruhr and Saar regions.

A more pressing question was the establishment of the Allied Control Council in Berlin. Three weeks had passed since the surrender and the Red Army was still in sole occupation of Hitler's shattered capital. Hopkins reminded Stalin that General Eisenhower had already been appointed the American representative on the Council, which ought to meet and get to work. He hoped that Eisenhower's Soviet counterpart would be named soon. Stalin replied that he proposed to appoint Marshal Zhukov. He readily agreed with Harriman, at a subsequent meeting, that the military men would need to operate under a single policy directive. Otherwise, he said, the Germans would certainly try to play off one against the other. Harriman argued for a minimum of political interference with the work of the Allied generals who, in effect, would govern Germany in defeat. Stalin, who never had shown great confidence in his marshals, disagreed. Military men were so intensely practical, he said, that left to their own devices, they were easily fooled.

Hopkins also raised the unsettled question of Korea's future once the Japanese had been driven out. After careful study, he said, the United States government had concluded that the best answer was a period of trusteeship (not less than five or ten years and not more than twenty-five) to prepare the Koreans for independence. The trustees would be the United States, Great Britain, China and the Soviet Union. Stalin wholeheartedly accepted the suggestion.

If the future of Korea received short shrift from Stalin, he showed intense interest in the future of China. The discussion opened with a reminder from Hopkins that General Marshall and Admiral King were anxious to learn when exactly the Soviet Union would make war on Japan. At Yalta, Stalin had committed himself to join the war within two or three months after the German surrender. Now, in response to Hopkins' question, he said that his forces in the Far East would be in position by August 8. But the actual date of the operation, he added, would depend on the execution of his secret agreement with Roosevelt

—and this would require Chiang Kai-shek's consent. If Chiang accepted his political demands, then the Red Army would move against Japan in August. Hopkins said it was his recollection that first Roosevelt and now Truman had been waiting for word from Stalin before approaching Chiang. That was correct, Stalin said. They had agreed to postpone telling the Generalissimo until the principal Soviet troop movements were under way. Now he thought he would raise the question directly with T. V. Soong, the Chinese Foreign Minister, who was expected to visit Moscow after the San Francisco Conference.

Hopkins observed that Ambassador Hurley had been working to reconcile Chiang's Kuomintang government with the Chinese Communists and that he would welcome Stalin's views on how unity could be accomplished. Stalin replied that he had no specific plan. All could agree that China ought to become a stable, integrated country, not an aggregation of separate little states like nineteenth-century Germany. She would need economic help and that could come only from the United States, he said. Stalin expanded on this idea later in the evening, in response to a question from Harriman:

> He said the United States must play the largest part in helping China to get on [its] feet; the Soviet Union would be occupied with its own internal reconstruction and Great Britain would be occupied elsewhere.
>
> MR. HOPKINS said he hoped the Marshal understood that we had no exclusive interest in China or the Far East and that we did not wish to see any other nation kept out.
>
> MARSHAL STALIN replied that he fully understood that but that what he had meant was that the United States was the only country that had sufficient capital and personnel to be really of assistance to China in the immediate postwar period.

Harriman followed this remarkable statement by probing for Soviet political designs on Manchuria or other parts of China. What if Hurley's unification efforts had failed, for example, by the time that Soviet troops entered Manchuria? In response, Stalin disclaimed any effort to tamper with the sovereignty of the Chinese over Manchuria or any other part of the country. The Soviet Union, he said, had no territorial claims with regard to China, not even in Sinkiang. He was prepared, furthermore, to deal with Chiang rather than the Chinese Communists, as the American record shows: "In regard to the Generalissimo, the Marshal said he knew little of any Chinese leader but that he felt that Chiang Kai-shek was the best of the lot and would be the one to undertake the unification of China. He said he saw no other possible leader and that, for example, he did not believe that the Chinese Communist leaders were as good or would be able to bring about the unification of China."

Harriman then put the question: Would Chiang's government be allowed to organize the civil administration in Manchuria once the Red Army had marched in? Again Stalin's answer was unequivocal: "Marshal Stalin replied that . . . in Manchuria as in any part of China where Soviet troops went the Chinese administration would be set up by Chiang."

Perhaps the most solid achievement of the Hopkins-Harriman talks with Stalin came on the final day, June 6. The question of voting procedures in the proposed Security Council of the new world organization had been wrestled with at Dumbarton Oaks, again at Yalta and finally at San Francisco, without final resolution. Ambassador Gromyko, who had taken Molotov's place at the head of the Soviet delegation at San Francisco, had just restated the obdurate position of his government on the night of June 1. The Soviet government, he said, would not permit any dispute or threatening situation to come before the Security Council unless all five of the great powers agreed that it should be heard. He was demanding, in short, the right to veto not only enforcement action by the Security Council but also its agenda. Stettinius had sent an anguished cable to Harriman the next day, suggesting a direct appeal to Stalin on the theory that he may not have fully understood what Gromyko was up to in San Francisco. The United States could not possibly yield on this point, Stettinius added. "In our opinion the whole proposed world organization would then become a farce."

Hopkins, who was not familiar with the details, left the argument to Harriman, although Bohlen's minutes of the June 6 meeting do not make this clear. The Ambassador recalled that the United States had long since agreed that the veto power should apply to enforcement actions voted by the Security Council. At Yalta, moreover, the heads of government had agreed that parties to any dispute must abstain from voting when the Council was considering methods for the peaceful settlement of disputes. The Americans had believed that this Yalta formula effectively safeguarded the right of any member to bring any dispute before the Council for its consideration. Now this right was being challenged by Gromyko, who demanded the right to veto even the agenda of the Council. He earnestly hoped, Harriman said, that Russia would go along with the United States, Britain, France and China, all of whom stood together on this question.

Molotov countered Harriman's appeal with the customary reply that the Soviet position was based squarely on the Crimea decisions. The veto must apply, he argued, even to deciding whether or not the Security Council should take up any given question. At this point

SPECIAL ENVOY

Stalin interrupted. Bohlen, who was interpreting, heard Stalin remark to Molotov in Russian that he thought it was an insignificant matter and that the Russians ought to accept the American position. Eavesdropping on that conversation, Bohlen got the impression that "the Marshal had not understood the issues involved and had not had them explained to him."

Stalin promptly overruled Molotov, telling Hopkins and Harriman that he was prepared to accept the American position on the technical point at issue. He treated the concession as a trifling matter, the kind of issue raised deliberately by small nations in order to make trouble between the great powers. Just because a nation was small did not necessarily mean that it was innocent, he said. After all, two great wars had begun over small nations.

On June 8, after Hopkins had left Moscow, Harriman summed up the results of their talks with Stalin in a message to the President:

> In presenting your views and in explaining the most important matters, particularly Poland, which were causing us concern, Harry did a first-rate job. I am afraid Stalin does not, and never will, fully understand our interest in a free Poland as a matter of principle. He is a realist . . . and it is hard for him to appreciate our faith in abstract principles. It is difficult for him to understand why we should want to interfere with Soviet policy in a country like Poland, which he considers so important to Russia's security, unless we have some ulterior motive . . .
>
> I told you, I believe, that I was certain that Molotov did not report to Stalin accurately and in fact truthfully in all cases. This was brought out again in our talks. It is clear also that Molotov is far more suspicious of us, and less willing to view matters in our mutual relations from a broad standpoint, than is Stalin. The fact that we were able to see Stalin six times and deal directly with him was a great help. Many of our difficulties could be overcome if it were possible to see him more frequently . . .
>
> Our last talk, on voting procedure, was most interesting. It was clear that the Marshal had not understood at all the issue between us. In spite of Molotov's explanation and defense of the Soviet position, Stalin waved him aside and accepted our position . . .
>
> In conclusion, I feel that Harry's visit has been ever more successful than I had hoped. Although there are and will continue to be many unsolved problems with the Soviet Govern-

ment, I believe that his visit has produced a much better atmosphere for your meeting with Stalin.

For Harriman, the Hopkins visit also paid a breathing dividend or two. During the showing of a newsreel at the end of the June 1 dinner for Hopkins, Harriman had admired the spirited horse ridden in the May Day parade by General Antonov before he took the salute. As soon as Stalin discovered that Harriman was an experienced horseman, he announced that he would present the Ambassador with two Russian horses. Three days later Kathleen Harriman wrote to her sister Mary:

> Today a general called officially (when he made the appointment through Russ Deane he refused to say what was the reason). Anyway, Russ and Ave both figured something terrible had come up as it's unprecedented for the Russians to call on us.
>
> A half hour later Ave came upstairs with a document beautifully covered in red leather—the pictures and pedigrees of two horses, the one which Ave had admired in the movie (English-bred) and the other a Don Basin horse, for me apparently. The first is named Fact, the second Boston. Now we've really got to scurry around and find a dacha with a stable to put them in.*

* Stabling the gift horses turned out to be no problem for the Harrimans. They were kept at the cavalry riding school in Moscow, where the Harrimans rode them frequently. When Harriman and Kathleen left Moscow at the conclusion of his embassy, the horses were shipped to the United States and lived out their days at the Arden estate in Harriman, New York.

CHAPTER XX

Japan Surrenders

O N July 2, 1945, as President Truman was preparing to leave
Washington for his first meeting with Stalin and Churchill,
Harry Hopkins resigned. He wrote to Harriman in Moscow:

> I am terribly sorry I won't see you in Berlin but I am sure
> my decision is the right one because I have every chance of
> really getting well now. I hope to be able to clear my affairs
> up in two or three weeks and get off on a long holiday some-
> where.
> I have taken a job in New York as Impartial Chairman
> of the Ladies Cloak and Suit Industry . . . they are paying
> me a reasonably good salary and the work is not going to be
> too hard. Then I am going to get busy writing a book so, all
> in all, I will have plenty to do.

Hopkins had been at Roosevelt's right hand throughout the
turbulent New Deal years and the long war just ending. Now the
new President was picking his own team. By the end of June he had
replaced four members of the Roosevelt Cabinet. Tom Clark succeeded Francis Biddle as Attorney General; Robert Hannegan took
Frank Walker's place as Postmaster General; Clinton Anderson became Secretary of Agriculture, replacing Claude Wickard; and Lewis
Schwellenbach succeeded Frances Perkins at the Labor Department.
Stettinius, too, was on the way out. At the President's request, his
resignation had been deferred until the conclusion of the San Francisco Conference. Truman then appointed James F. Byrnes of South
Carolina as Secretary of State. Although Byrnes had been to Yalta
with Roosevelt, his foreign-policy experience was meager. Harriman

felt that Byrnes had been chosen with other considerations—chiefly the presidential succession—in mind. Lacking a Vice President, Truman had to reckon with the constitutional proviso that the Secretary of State would be next in line to succeed him.* Byrnes had served in the House of Representatives and the Senate as well as on the Supreme Court before he resigned to become Roosevelt's chief lieutenant for the home front. He possessed all the political experience that Stettinius so clearly lacked.

Through May and June, Churchill had pressed Truman to advance the date of the Big Three conference. Time was working in Stalin's favor, the Prime Minister warned, as the American Army thinned its ranks in Europe to reinforce the Pacific theater for the climactic attack on the Japanese home islands. He also tried to persuade the President not to surrender the territory captured by the Americans when they had overrun the boundaries of the Soviet occupation zone to a depth of 120 miles. "I fear terrible things have happened during the Russian advance through Germany to the Elbe," Churchill had written to Eden at San Francisco, in a message he also sent to Truman on May 11. "The proposed withdrawal of the United States Army . . . would mean the tide of Russian domination sweeping forward 120 miles on a front of 300 or 400 miles. This would be an event which, if it occurred, would be one of the most melancholy in history." Churchill argued that the Allied troops should not move back "until we are satisfied about Poland and also about the temporary character of the Russian occupation of Germany . . ."[1]

The Prime Minister also had invited Truman to visit England before he went to Germany, promising him "a great reception from the British nation." He was deeply hurt when Truman replied that he wanted to avoid any suspicion on Stalin's part that the British and Americans were "ganging up" against him. He would be pleased to visit England after the conference, Truman wrote, but not before. His reply suggested to Churchill that powerful influences in Washington had somehow persuaded Truman that he must "stand between Britain and Russia as a friendly mediator," as if the United States were

---

* The first act of presidential succession, passed in 1792, provided for the succession (after the Vice President) of the President *pro tempore* of the Senate and the Speaker of the House, in that order. A second act, passd in 1886, was in force at the time that Truman succeeded Roosevelt. In the absence of a Vice President, it provided that the succession should devolve on the heads of the Executive Departments, in order of their establishment. The Department of State being the first of the Executive Departments, Byrnes would have been in line to succeed Truman in the event of his resignation, removal, death or inability to serve. The 1886 statute was revised in 1947 to provide for the succession of the Speaker of the House, the President *pro tempore* of the Senate and the heads of the Executive Departments, in that order.

not itself a party to their disagreements.² Confessing his disappointment, Churchill agreed that "no question of ceremonial should intervene" with plans for the Potsdam meeting. But he continued to sound the alarm over troop withdrawals from Europe. On May 12 he sent Truman another message, speaking for the first time of an "iron curtain" in the center of Europe:

> What will be the position in a year or two, when the British and American armies have melted and the French has not yet been formed on any major scale, when we may have a handful of divisions, mostly French, and when Russia may choose to keep two or three hundred on active service?
>
> An iron curtain is drawn down upon their front. We do not know what is going on behind. There seems little doubt that the whole of the regions east of the line Lübeck-Trieste-Corfu will soon be completely in their hands. To this must be added the further enormous area conquered by the American armies between Eisenach and the Elbe, which will, I suppose, in a few weeks be occupied, when the Americans retreat, by the Russian power. . . .
>
> . . . it would be open to the Russians in a very short time to advance if they chose to the waters of the North Sea and the Atlantic.³

Truman was not swayed, however, by Churchill's dark vision of a Russian-dominated Europe. Both the State and War Departments opposed using the presence of American troops in territory destined for Russian occupation as a bargaining counter. Hopkins counseled the President that an American failure to pull back from advanced positions would appear to violate a solemn agreement, made in good faith six months earlier, and was bound to be misunderstood not only in Russia but in the United States as well. Truman accordingly advised Churchill on June 11: "I am unable to delay the withdrawal of American troops from the Soviet zone in order to use pressure in the settlement of other problems." There was also the practical consideration that the Russians had made clear they would not allow the Allied Control Council to begin functioning in Berlin until American and British troops had withdrawn from the Soviet zone. "I am advised that it would be highly disadvantageous to our relations with the Soviet to postpone action in this matter until our meeting in July," Truman added. Churchill did not wholly conceal his bitter disappointment. "Obviously we are obliged to conform to your decision," he wrote back. "I sincerely hope that your action will in the long run make for a lasting peace in Europe."⁴

Harriman's view, even in the long retrospect of thirty years, was that Churchill's proposal that the Allies stand on the Elbe in order to force a political settlement in Eastern Europe would have altered none of the fundamental facts, except to make the United States and Britain wholly responsible for the Cold War. "The zonal boundaries had been drawn in advance," he recalled, "because we all felt it was important not to clash with the Russians over territorial questions. Our Chiefs of Staff thought the zonal arrangement agreed to in London was entirely satisfactory. Of course, they had misjudged the actual situation on the ground, overestimating the speed of the Soviet advance from the east and underestimating the depth of the Allied penetration from the west. But I cannot criticize them for that. No one could have foreseen with any degree of accuracy exactly how the final battle for Germany would come out. The important thing was that we had made an agreement with the Russians, specifying which army should occupy what territory; and that we honored it. If we had refused to withdraw from the Soviet zone in Germany, the Russians undoubtedly would have refused to pull out of the zone assigned to us in Austria—and Austria would probably be a Soviet satellite today.

"It is important to remember that we still had a war to win in the Pacific; our military plans called for a massive redeployment of American troops from Europe to the Far East. I am not persuaded that by refusing to withdraw from the Elbe we could in fact have forced the Russians to allow free elections, and the establishment of freely elected governments, in Eastern Europe. They did allow a free election in Hungary and the Communist party lost miserably. But the government established after this election in 1945 was soon squeezed out by the threat of Russian power.

"There was no way we could have prevented these events in Eastern Europe without going to war against the Russians. A few American officers—and some of the French—talked of doing just that. But I cannot believe that the American people would have stood for it, even if the President had been willing, which he was not."

On June 21 Vishinsky told Harriman that the conference would have to be held at Potsdam, southwest of the former capital, because Berlin was so totally destroyed. Truman, Churchill and Stalin would stay at Babelsberg, once the motion picture capital of Germany, a three-mile drive from the Cecilienhof Palace in Potsdam, where the formal conference sessions would take place.

The prospects for arriving at some kind of Polish settlement before Potsdam had quickened in mid-June. With deep misgiving, Mikolajczyk and Jan Stanczyk had flown to Moscow from London to open talks with the Lublin Poles and the oddly named third category of "Poles from within Poland," that is, non-Communists who had suffered through the German occupation and the Russian liberation at home. Until the last moment, Mikolajczyk had balked. When Radio Moscow announced on June 14 that the trial of the sixteen arrested Polish leaders was about to begin, Mikolajczyk was still in London. He notified the Foreign Office the following day that in view of the trial announcement, which he read as a signal that the Kremlin would not permit real negotiations among the Poles, he would refuse to go. It took the last-minute persuasions of Churchill ("You have put your foot in an open door and should not miss this occasion") to get Mikolajczyk on the plane.[5]

Once in Moscow, however, the talks went more swiftly than Harriman or Clark Kerr had expected. At Molotov's opening-day reception for the Polish visitors, Harriman observed that "the four Poles from within Poland, including the two named by Molotov, showed an almost emotional desire to see broader representation in the new government."

Bierut, who came to lunch at Spaso House with Osubka-Morawski on June 17, left Harriman with the impression that the Lublin Poles at long last were "ready to compromise in bringing into the government new personalities to satisfy American opinion." At a British embassy cocktail party, Osubka-Morawski made clear that Lublin had decided, presumably under pressure from Molotov, to make room for Mikolajczyk. "You, sir," he said to Clark Kerr, "can further ensure the success of the conference by not giving Mr. Mikolajczyk a visa so that it will be impossible for him to return to England."

"With all my heart," the British ambassador replied. "I promise you that I shall do that—keep him here until success is assured."

"We want him to return to Poland," Osubka-Morawski added, "where he can gather around him all the elements of the Peasant party and make it one great unified party which will work for Poland."

If Osubka-Morawski meant what he said, the British ambassador interjected, then he ought to say it directly to Mikolajczyk. Clark Kerr called Mikolajczyk over and Osubka-Morawski repeated how much the Lublin Poles wanted him back in Poland. As Harriman was leaving the reception, the Lublin leader added a cautionary note. He said to the Ambassador's Polish-language interpreter, "Please be sure to tell Mr. Harriman how important it is for Mr. Mikolajczyk not to fail this time. Ask him to tell Mr. Mikolajczyk that he must not fail, because this is his last chance—and he will be unable to try again if he fails now."

In this now-or-never atmosphere an agreement was finally worked out on June 21 by the Poles themselves to broaden the Warsaw Provisional Government. Mikolajczyk agreed to become Vice Premier and Minister of Agriculture, one of three new Peasant party ministers. Stanczyk became Minister of Labor and Social Welfare, the only Socialist minister admitted from London. Wladyslaw Kiernik, a prominent Peasant party leader who unlike Mikolajczyk had spent the war years in Poland, joined the government as Minister of Public Administration, and Czeslaw Wycech, another Peasant party man, became Minister of Education.

But the Lublin group kept the real levers of power in its own hands through its control of the police and the army. Bierut, whom the State Department belatedly identified as having been a Comintern agent for more than twenty years, was still President of the Polish National Council, and Osubka-Morawski stayed as Premier.[6]

Both Harriman and Clark Kerr admonished Molotov and the assembled Poles that formation of the new coalition government was only a first step toward fulfillment c he Yalta decision. They served notice that until a truly free election was held, the British and American governments could not consider that decision carried out. Harriman promptly asked for—and received—assurances that elections would be held. He also requested assurances of freedom of assembly for all legitimate parties during the electoral campaign and of amnesty for political prisoners. "These were answered in generalities," Harriman reported to Washington, "but Bierut assured me that the principle of amnesty was already accepted and that he expected 80% of those now under arrest would be set free." His report continued:

> I must in frankness report that this settlement had been reached because all the non-Lublin Poles are so concerned over the present situation in Poland that they are ready to accept any compromise which gives some hope for Polish independence and freedom for the individual . . .
>
> One could not help but gain the impression that Molotov and the Warsaw Poles were in high spirits and that the other Poles were seriously concerned but hoped that because of the trust they had shown in the good faith of Moscow the Poles would gain a freer hand to conduct their own affairs. I personally am much relieved that there is a settlement agreed to by the Poles and see no reason why we should not accept it.

President Truman accepted it, announcing on July 5 that he was establishing diplomatic relations with the newly formed Polish Provisional Government of National Unity and noting that the Warsaw regime had confirmed in writing "its intention to carry out the provisions of the Crimea decision with respect to the holding of elections." Churchill took the step the same day, a more painful step in his case because it meant severing relations with the government-in-exile to which the British had extended hospitality and protection throughout the war. The Prime Minister made clear, however, in a note to the Soviet government that he was "by no means satisfied" with the assurances that free elections would be held in Poland and that he reserved the right to raise the question at the Potsdam meeting.

Before he left Moscow, Mikolajczyk shared with Harriman his bleak misgivings about the future. "Mikolajczyk told me, 'I have grave doubts whether I will succeed,' " Harriman recalled, "his implication being that the Communists would not stick to the agreement just concluded in Moscow. 'However I will do everything I can to make it work.' I remember his closing words most clearly. 'I may never see you again,' he said. It was clear to me that he went to Warsaw with a heavy heart, fully aware that once the government was established—and to some extent strengthened by his participation—he might be arrested and executed."*

Another major issue of particular concern to Harriman which had not been settled at Yalta was the postwar relationship between Russia and China. Stalin's demands in Manchuria would have to be negotiated before he made a firm commitment to enter the war against Japan. In Washington on June 9, Truman had received the Chinese Foreign Minister, T. V. Soong, and had given him an account of the secret agreement entered into at Yalta. In Chungking on June 15, Ambassador Hurley had passed on the same information to Chiang Kai-shek. Chiang received the news calmly, although, as Harriman had predicted to Roosevelt at Yalta, he found it hard to swallow Moscow's insistence upon "pre-eminent interests" in the Manchurian ports and railroads and a "lease" on the Port Arthur naval base. Both smacked

---

* In spite of his dramatic farewell, Mikolajczyk was to see Harriman again at Babelsberg within the same month of July. He had been sent from Warsaw with President Bierut and Vice Premier Wladyslaw Gomulka to lobby for American and British recognition of the Oder-Neisse frontier. Mikolajczyk, in a separate meeting with Harriman, Dunn and Matthews, handed them two memoranda "with the special request that his name never be associated with them." His brief stay in Poland had persuaded Mikolajczyk that Poland could not be free and independent in present conditions. Only the Communist party enjoyed the full freedom promised to all, he reported, and "fair elections are impossible as long as the Soviet troops and the NKVD remain in Poland." The Russians, moreover, were dismantling factories and ripping up railroad tracks in East Prussia, Silesia and other former German territories which they had unilaterally assigned to Polish administration. He urged the United States to consider recognizing the proposed new frontier in the west on condition that the Russians honor their Yalta commitments. Byrnes took the position, however, that the frontier could be settled only at the peace conference. "I was quite unhappy that he left it open for the future," Harriman recalled. "It seemed to me that if you allowed the Poles to settle and administer the territory, even without title, you would never get it changed again. I also feared the effect inside Germany of leaving the frontier unsettled. It could have led to the worst kind of *revanchism*. Happily, however, Chancellor Adenauer kept the agitation under control after the war, and Willy Brandt, in my judgment, earned high marks by putting the issue to rest after almost thirty years of uncertainty."

of the discredited past when European powers controlled the Chinese treaty ports. In a message relayed to Harriman by way of Washington, Hurley nevertheless reported from Chungking:

I am convinced that Soviets and China will be able quickly to reach an agreement.

'Pre-eminent' and 'Lease' are the two words in the Yalta decision that are still causing most trouble. China will endeavor to make terms agreeable to Soviets but under specific definitions rather than under general terms. China wishes to avoid the use of words that are in conflict with territorial integrity and independent sovereignty but is agreeable to meeting the terms.[7]

On June 30 Soong arrived in Moscow to negotiate with Stalin the terms that Chiang was disputing. Day by day the Chinese Foreign Minister kept Harriman informed of his talks at the Kremlin. Outer Mongolia was the first sticking point. Stalin was insisting that China must recognize the independence of Outer Mongolia, although the Yalta agreement called for nothing more than recognition of the status quo, under which that former province of Imperial China for some thirty years past had been an autonomous state under Russian protection.

Soong protested to Stalin that no Chinese government could survive if it ceded Outer Mongolia, thus abandoning a claim which the Russians themselves had acknowledged in 1913 and again in 1924. "He explained to me," Harriman reported on July 3, "that it was a matter of principle deep in Chinese psychology and that although they recognized that they could not exercise suzerainty over Outer Mongolia at the present time, the Chinese would be unwilling to support a government which gave up Chinese claims to this territory for all time."[8]

Harriman in later years recalled, "I found that Soong was not at all concerned with some of the things that worried us. He felt it was a tremendous achievement to have Stalin recognize the sovereignty of Chiang Kai-shek's National Government over Manchuria. He was far less concerned than we had been about such details as whether Chinese or Russian troops would guard the railroad or who would be the Port Master of Dairen. I saw him almost every day and urged him to be more firm."

The Soong-Stalin talks had not been completed when Harriman left Moscow for Berlin on July 13 to attend the Potsdam Conference. Soong had identified the main obstacles to agreement and flown back to Chungking for consultations with Chiang. He would return to Moscow after Potsdam to conclude the negotiation.

On the five-hour flight to Berlin, Harriman and Edward Page of the embassy staff noted the changing landscape below: small herds of cattle grazing in the fields, deserted villages, little railroad traffic, deep trenches scarring the battlefields where Russians had fought German invaders for hundreds of miles westward from Moscow. Even from an airplane, flying at 200 miles an hour, the crossing of the old Polish border was easily marked: solid farmhouses and barns, hard-surfaced roads, much larger herds of cattle. "Poland, from the air, looks a hundred times more prosperous than Russia," Page wrote in his account of the journey. On the German side of the Oder, the landscape changed again: villages totally destroyed, tank tracks and shell craters defacing the green fields, most bridges destroyed. "Area from Oder to Berlin seemed to be completely deserted with no people in the villages or fields and no smoke coming out of those farms that were not destroyed," Page noted.

Berlin, their destination, was a wasteland of crumbled brick and stone, whole blocks of apartment houses and factories having been toppled into the streets as if a sulky child had smashed his sand castle in blind rage. Harriman recalled the shock he felt in driving through the ruins of Berlin. He had been mentally prepared for the destruction of war but not for the depredations that followed: "When I saw how completely the Russians had stripped every factory they could get their hands on, I realized that their conception of surplus tools and machinery which could be taken from Germany was far tougher than we could ever agree to. The Reparations Commission had been meeting in Moscow before Potsdam, talking endlessly about percentages, and all this time the Russians had been helping themselves to everything of any value in the Eastern zone and in Berlin. I decided after seeing the situation for myself that while there was nothing we could do to stop the Russians from taking whatever they wanted out of their own zone, we ought to give them nothing from the Western zones. Otherwise the American taxpayer would have to pay the bill for feeding the Germans, who could not possibly support themselves with all their industrial machinery transported to Russia."

Harriman found Babelsberg, on Lake Griebnitz, a little sanctuary intact amid the surrounding wreckage. The President had been assigned a three-story stucco villa at 2 Kaiserstrasse, once the home of a German film executive now serving with a labor battalion in the Soviet Union. Churchill lived two blocks away, at 23 Ringstrasse, and Stalin was billeted in a third requisitioned villa about a mile from the Little White House. All had been stripped of their original furnishings when the Russians moved into the area and then quickly refurnished for the conference.

Harriman shared a comfortable bungalow with Page and his personal assistant, Robert Meiklejohn. Edwin W. Pauley, the American representative to the Allied Reparations Commission in Moscow, and Robert D. Murphy, Eisenhower's political adviser, lived next door.

Truman arrived on the afternoon of July 15, having crossed the Atlantic on the heavy cruiser *Augusta* and flown the rest of the way in *The Sacred Cow*. The eight-day crossing gave him an unbroken opportunity for concentrated study of the issues to be dealt with at Potsdam. Each day on shipboard the President held staff meetings with Secretary Byrnes; Benjamin V. Cohen, the newly appointed counselor of the State Department; H. Freeman Matthews, chief of the European Affairs Division; Admiral Leahy; and Bohlen. James Clement Dunn, principal adviser to Byrnes, had flown to Europe ahead of the presidential party. By the time Truman reached Babelsberg, he had read and absorbed a vast amount of detail about such intricate problems as the administration of Germany in defeat. Once again, as in their first meeting some eight weeks earlier in Washington, Harriman found the President astonishingly well prepared.

Churchill brought with him the customarily large British delegation, this time including the Labor party leader, Clement Attlee. The Prime Minister was determined to ensure a certain continuity of British policy just in case the voters turned him out of office in mid-conference, as they turned out to have done when the official count was announced on July 26. "The defeat took him completely by surprise," Harriman recalled. "I remember Eden telling me in June that the soldier vote would be unpredictable. But Beaverbrook had advised the Prime Minister to call the election just as soon as the war in Europe was over and had assured him that he would win easily. It turned out to be bad advice. Beaverbrook was, of course, an extraordinarily successful newspaper publisher, but his business judgments seemed to me shrewder than his political judgments.

"He used to tell me about his papers and why the *Daily Express* was such an enormous success. 'I made it a lively paper for all the family,' he would say. 'It's a paper that can be on every breakfast table and any member of the family can read it.' It struck me as somewhat strange that a man who could produce such a popular newspaper should have failed to understand what ordinary Englishmen, including his own readers, were thinking."

Churchill and Eden did not, of course, return to Potsdam after flying to London to receive the election results. Attlee came back on July 28 as Prime Minister, bringing with him the new Foreign Secretary, Ernest Bevin. The change of administration had been carried out smoothly with only a two-day interruption in the schedule of plenary meetings. Some members of the American delegation, Admiral Leahy in particular, at first showed a degree of apprehension that the Labor government would turn away from Churchill's policies. But Harriman, who had learned to know Bevin and Attlee well during his London years, reassured the doubters. Forrestal, among the first Americans to look up Bevin for a private talk, recorded in his diary for July 29:

> [Bevin] said in answer to my questions that the only in-dustries [the Labor government] proposed to nationalize were power, railroads, mines and textiles up to spinning mills. He indicated he had no use for [Harold] Laski.* He spoke highly and appreciatively of Anthony Eden. He said he was quite familiar with tactics of the Communists because he had had to deal with them in his own labor unions in England.
>
> I asked him a question about the Emperor in Japan, whether he thought we ought to insist on destruction of the Emperor concept along with the surrender. He hesitated and said this question would require a bit of thinking, but he was inclined to feel that there was no sense in destroying the instrument through which one might have to deal in order to effectively control Japan. He then made a rather surprising statement—for a liberal and a labor leader: "It might have been better for all of us not to have destroyed the institution of the Kaiser after the last war . . . It might have been far better to have guided the Germans to a constitutional monarchy rather than leaving them without a symbol and therefore opening the psychological doors to a man like Hitler."[9]

Terminal was the code name Churchill had chosen for the Pots-dam Conference. The exhilaration that characterized Teheran and Yalta now had given way to a wary recognition that alliances, like the men who forge them, are not eternal. With Roosevelt dead and Churchill defeated at the polls, only Stalin remained. Germany lay in ruins and Japan staggered toward surrender. With the external peril at long last overcome by a mighty common effort, the Allied powers fell back into less fraternal attitudes.

The first agreement reached at Potsdam was to establish a Council of Foreign Ministers that would begin the task of peacemaking. France and China would be admitted; and the council would draft peace treaties for Italy, Rumania, Bulgaria, Hungary and Finland. Peace with Germany was to be deferred until a German government "adequate for the purpose" had been created. Meanwhile, the Germans were to be treated as a conquered people under rules decreed by the military

---

* Forrestal had developed a powerful, abiding antipathy for Harold J. Laski, the British political scientist who at the period was chairman of the Labor party's executive committee. His name recurs frequently in the diary, customarily wearing the Forrestal tag of "extreme Left-winger."

commanders of the four Allied powers, meeting periodically in Berlin as the Allied Control Council.

Both Harriman and Cohen were distinctly uneasy about setting up the Allied Control Council in Berlin, 110 miles deep inside the Soviet zone. They suggested a new seat of government at the junction of the British, American and Soviet zones which would be equally accessible to all three. Byrnes, who felt it was too late to be proposing new arrangements, left the question of access to be worked out by Eisenhower and Montgomery with Zhukov—a grave error, in Harriman's view, for which the Allies were to pay a heavy price. Eisenhower, who had his own ideas about how to get along with the Russians, discounted the dangers. After all, military men abhorred war more than any civilian.

What price the Germans should pay for the devastation they had visited on much of Europe preoccupied the foreign ministers and the heads of government through most of the Potsdam meeting. Harriman's initial shock at seeing how the Russians had stripped the Western sectors of Berlin had led him to argue against the taking of Soviet reparations from Germany as a whole. He and Pauley agreed that each of the occupying powers should be limited to reparations only from its own zone. Will Clayton opposed the Harriman-Pauley view, arguing that the Russians were entitled to 25 percent of the industrial equipment to be taken from the Western zones. Byrnes finally compromised between these conflicting American views. On July 23 he proposed to Molotov that while each of the occupying powers should be free to take whatever equipment it wanted from its own zone, the Russians could get additional reparations from the Western zones in exchange for food and coal from the east. Molotov eventually accepted the zonal principle, but he kept pressing for a fixed amount of additional reparations from the Ruhr, the heart of Germany's coal and steel industries, which was under British occupation.

When Byrnes offered the Soviet Union one quarter of the Ruhr's surplus capacity, or 12 percent from the combined Western zones, Molotov balked. He asked for a specified amount, mentioning the figure of $2 billion. Byrnes refused to put a dollar value on the amount of reparations from the west. On July 31 Stalin abandoned the fight for a fixed sum. He asked for 15 percent from the Western zones in exchange for food and materials from the east plus 10 percent in free reparations, apart from what the Russians were taking out of their own zone.* A bargain was struck on that basis, in effect denying the Russians "a hand in the Western zones," as Harriman expressed it.

---

* In fact, few deliveries from the Western zones were carried out, because the Russians failed to deliver corresponding quantities of coal and food from the east.

For Harriman, who had been so deeply involved in the discussions at Yalta and Teheran, Potsdam proved a personal disappointment. "Jimmy Byrnes played his cards very close to his vest," he recalled, "and he would seldom consult me. On certain issues—reparations, for example, which greatly concerned me—I managed to express my point of view and, of course, I sat in all the plenary sessions. But Byrnes had brought his own people from the State Department—Ben Cohen, Jimmy Dunn and 'Doc' Matthews—and I was not alone in being ignored. Stimson also had plenty of free time. So we sat in the sun together outside his villa talking about when and how the Japanese might be brought to surrender, and how to deal with the Russians after the war."

Stimson shared Harriman's feeling of being kept at arm's length by the new Secretary of State. "He [Byrnes] gives me the impression that he is hugging matters in this Conference pretty close to his bosom, and that my assistance, while generally welcome, was strictly limited in the matters in which it should be given," Stimson recorded in his diary on July 19.[10]

The following day Stimson showed Harriman a paper he had dictated on the importance of freedom of speech in liberalizing Russia. The Ambassador impressed the Secretary of War as gloomy about the prospect that the Soviet system after the war would evolve in a more liberal direction: "I talked with him for a long time regarding the matter and, in view of his intelligence and capacity, such a despairing view from him troubled me a great deal."[11]

Harriman's impression of Byrnes did not improve as the days passed. "He seemed to have gone to Potsdam with the idea that it was going to be a good deal like the Senate," he recalled. "When there was controversy, he would pour oil on the waters. I had the impression that he looked on the Potsdam discussions as an argument between Stalin and Churchill, and that he was going to mediate between the two.

"I didn't like the relationship with Byrnes. So I went to Truman and said, 'I'm ready to stay in Moscow, if you want me to, until the Japanese war is over. Then I want to get out and go home.' The President agreed."

The debate about when the war could be expected to end, and whether the Russians were still needed to help in the final defeat of Japan, had preoccupied the top layers of American officialdom for many weeks before Potsdam. The Combined Chiefs of Staff presented to Truman and Churchill on the morning of July 24 a written report listing the steps to be taken in bringing about Japan's defeat at the earliest possible date. "Russian entry into the war against Japan should be encouraged," the document read, in part. "Such aid to her [Rus-

sia's] war-making capacity as might be necessary should be provided."
The President had not the slightest doubt that the Chiefs' advice was
sound. "Of course my immediate purpose was to get the Russians into
the war against Japan as soon as possible . . ." he later wrote.[12]

Harriman had long since made up his mind that although the
defeat of Japan could be accomplished without Soviet assistance,
there was no way to keep Stalin from declaring war at the last
moment and sending his troops into Manchuria, by way of regaining
(at a minimum) the ports and railroads that Imperial Russia had lost
to the Japanese in the war of 1904–5. The Ambassador had raised the
question with the War, Navy and State Departments a month after
Roosevelt's death: Was it still advisable or necessary that Russia should
join the war against Japan? The answers varied. But neither Stimson
nor Forrestal had seen any reason at the time to upset or revise the
Roosevelt-Stalin agreement concluded at Yalta. Two new and startling
developments occurred just before the first Truman-Stalin-Churchill
meeting in the Cecilienhof at Potsdam on July 17. The first was an
exchange of telegrams on July 11 and 12 between the Japanese Foreign
Minister Shigenori Togo and his ambassador in Moscow, Naotake
Sato, which had been intercepted by U.S. naval intelligence. Togo suggested that Emperor Hirohito would be prepared to make peace with
the Allies if, through the good offices of the Soviet Union, the United
States and Britain could be persuaded not to insist upon unconditional
surrender.

The second was a coded message from Washington, dated July
16 and addressed to Stimson at Babelsberg. It read:

> Operated on this morning. Diagnosis not yet complete but
> results seem satisfactory and already exceed expectations.
> Local press release necessary as interest extends great distance.
> Dr. Groves pleased. He returns tomorrow. Will keep you
> posted.[13]

The message had been sent by George L. Harrison, president of
the New York Life Insurance Company. In Stimson's absence, Harrison was acting as chairman of the so-called Interim Committee set up
to advise the President on "questions of policy relating to the study of
nuclear fission." The successful operation Harrison had in mind was,
of course, the explosion early that morning of a ball of plutonium
about the size of a grapefruit on top of a 100-foot steel tower at the
Alamagordo Air Force Base in the New Mexico desert. And "Dr.
Groves" was the commanding general of the Manhattan District
project, Major General Leslie R. Groves.

Harrison's first message (a second followed the next day, providing more details) reached Stimson at seven-thirty in the evening.

He took it at once to the Little White House on Kaiserstrasse, where he showed it to Truman and Byrnes. Stimson noted in his diary that both men "of course were greatly interested, although the information was still in very general terms."[14] The following day Stimson saw Churchill to pass on the astonishing news that "the atomic bomb is a reality." He found the Prime Minister "intensely interested and greatly cheered up," according to Stimson's diary entry for July 17, but "strongly inclined" against sharing the news with Stalin.[15]

Harriman had learned about the bomb project from Churchill and his scientific adviser, Lord Cherwell, during their first trip to Washington together in 1941 for the Arcadia conference. It was then that Churchill had offered to pool British scientific knowledge and manpower with the early work on nuclear fission that was being done in the United States. Roosevelt's acceptance of the offer had given birth to the Manhattan Project. Harriman had not, however, followed its development closely over the intervening years.

"I knew they were pursuing it," he recalled. "Stimson had talked to me about the project in May. But I did not know until Potsdam that the first explosion was scheduled for the third week of July. It had never played a role in my thinking about our relations with the Russians. The importance of the bomb project, in my conception, was that we had to get it before Hitler did.

"In Potsdam I had a number of talks with Stimson. The bomb was very much on his mind. He worried about the dangers for mankind that were implicit in this new weapon. Stimson was one statesman who recognized even then, in July of 1945, before Hiroshima, that the leaders of the United States had a major obligation to keep this terrible weapon under control. It's utter nonsense to look back now and treat the whole thing as cut-and-dried, as if we all knew that on a particular morning in July the bomb would be tested and it would be certain to work; I keep remembering that Admiral Leahy bet an apple that it would not work. Just as it is nonsense to believe—as some historians apparently do—that Truman postponed the Potsdam Conference in order to have the bomb go off before the end of his meeting with Stalin. There were far too many uncertainties for that kind of planning. The idea of using the bomb as a form of pressure on the Russians never entered the discussions at Potsdam. That wasn't the President's mood at all. The mood was to treat Stalin as an ally—a difficult ally, admittedly—in the hope that he would behave like one."

On July 24 Truman walked over to Stalin during a break in the conference and told him about the bomb. "I casually mentioned to Stalin that we had a new weapon of unusual destructive force," the President wrote in his memoirs. "The Russian Premier showed no special interest. All he said was that he was glad to hear it and hoped we would make 'good use of it against the Japanese.' "[16]

Bohlen watched Stalin's face carefully as he heard the news. He later wrote: "So offhand was Stalin's response that there was some question in my mind whether the President's message had got through. I should have known better . . ."[17] In fact, the Russians were already at work on their own nuclear bomb, and as Marshal Zhukov has written in his memoirs, Stalin sent back immediate orders to accelerate the program.

Harriman's first clue that Truman's disclosure had come as no great surprise was supplied by Molotov soon after Potsdam. "We were talking about Japan and the bomb," Harriman recalled, "when Molotov looked at me with something like a smirk on his face and said, 'You Americans can keep a secret when you want to.' The way he put it convinced me that it was no secret at all. We now know that thanks to Klaus Fuchs and others, the Russians were in possession of the salient facts about our development of the bomb before Potsdam. The only element of surprise, I suppose, was the fact that the Alamagordo test had been successful. But Stalin, unfortunately, must have known that we were very close to the point of staging our first test explosion."

There had never been much question in the minds of Truman, Churchill and their advisers that the bomb, if it could be made to work, should be used to shorten the war. With Hitler dead and his Third Reich in ruins, Japan now presented the only possible target. As Churchill has written of his talks with Truman at Potsdam: "The historic fact remains, and must be judged in the after-time, that the decision whether or not to use the atomic bomb to compel the surrender of Japan was never even an issue. There was unanimous, automatic, unquestioned agreement around our table; nor did I ever hear the slightest suggestion that we should do otherwise."[18]

A month before Alamagordo, Truman had approved General Marshall's plan for a two-phase invasion of the Japanese home islands. The American Sixth Army, under command of General Walter Krueger, was to land on the island of Kyushu on or about November 1. Four months later there was to be a second invasion with the Eighth and Tenth armies going ashore on Honshu and striking across the Tokyo plain. Marshall had estimated that it would take until the late autumn of 1946 before the Japanese, who could be expected to resist desperately as they had in each of the Pacific island battles at a terrible cost in American lives, were brought to their knees. Suddenly the bomb had made Marshall's invasion plan obsolete. Conceivably Japan could be forced to surrender without expending, according to Marshall's estimate, a half-million additional American lives. Conceivably there was no further military reason for urging Stalin to join the war in the Far East; although, as Harriman had recognized long before Potsdam, there was no way to prevent his entry at the last moment for his own reasons.

As for the Japanese peace feeler received in Moscow, Stalin asked first Churchill and then Truman what he should do about it. On July 18 he handed the President a copy of the note received from Foreign Minister Togo, together with a message from Emperor Hirohito. It was his "heart's desire," the Emperor wrote, to see the war terminated, and for this purpose he proposed to send Prince Fumimaro Konoye to Moscow to negotiate terms for peace. As long as the United States and Britain insisted upon unconditional surrender, however, he saw no alternative but to continue the war "for the sake of survival and the honor of the homeland."

Stalin asked Truman whether he thought it worthwhile to answer the Emperor's message. The President replied that he had no respect for the good faith of the Japanese. After a brief discussion, Stalin proposed a stalling maneuver. He would send back a general message, pointing out that the character of the proposed Konoye mission had not been made clear and in this way "lull the Japanese to sleep." Truman agreed.[19]

Exactly a week had gone by since the receipt of Togo's first message in Moscow. For eight days afterward the President and his advisers tinkered with the draft of an ultimatum, prepared before they left Washington, calling upon Japan to surrender unconditionally. He wanted it issued from Potsdam as a demonstration to the Japanese "that the Allies were united in their purpose."

Stimson and Byrnes disagreed sharply, however, on a crucial point. The Secretary of War had insisted on writing into the proclamation an assurance that the Japanese in defeat could keep the institution of the monarchy. This would satisfy their need to avoid dishonor, he felt, and might well lead to an early surrender, ruling out any need to use the bomb on Japan. The Secretary of State and the Joint Chiefs of Staff, on the other hand, opposed any mention of the monarchy. Let the Japanese decide for themselves whether or not they wanted an emperor, the Secretary of State argued, and thereby avoid starting "a controversy among ourselves about the position of the Emperor." It was Byrnes who prevailed.

With the concurrence of Chiang Kai-shek and Churchill, the ultimatum was finally issued on July 26 from Potsdam. The Russians had not been consulted, even though they were pledged to make war on Japan in less than two weeks. Byrnes wanted it that way; he preferred to end the war without the Russians, if possible. Calling on the Japanese government to accept unconditional surrender, the proclamation warned that refusal would mean the country's "prompt and utter destruction." There was no mention of the monarchy's future, only a promise that the Allied occupation forces would be withdrawn as soon as a peacefully inclined and responsible Japanese government was established "in accordance with the freely expressed will" of the people. Nor was there any specific warning of new and more terrible weapons in store, only a hint that the Allies now possessed a power to destroy "immeasurably greater" than the power which had laid waste the German homeland.

Truman's purpose in broadcasting the Potsdam proclamation around the world, as he later wrote, was "to afford Japan a clear chance to end the fighting" before the first atomic bomb was dropped. But there was reason to doubt that the Japanese government understood the awful alternative. The hint of destructive powers "immeasurably greater" than those which had leveled Germany may have been overly subtle. It probably also lost something in translation. The Japanese Premier, Admiral Baron Kantaro Suzuki, at any rate, appeared to dismiss or reject the ultimatum at a press conference on July 28 in Tokyo. He found nothing new in the joint proclamation, Suzuki said, adding (in the translation of the Foreign Broadcast Intelligence Service in Washington) that "there is no other recourse but to ignore it entirely and resolutely fight for the successful conclusion of this war." Scholars, diplomats and journalists have debated ever since whether Suzuki in fact had intended to reject the ultimatum, or to stall for time while Togo kept trying to interest the reluctant Russians in mediating more favorable terms. The President, who read Suzuki's statement as a flat rejection, saw no alternative now. He ordered the Strategic Air Forces to drop the bomb as soon after August 3 as the weather in the far Pacific would permit. On August 6, the fourth day of his journey home after Potsdam, Truman received word from Stimson, as he was lunching with members of the *Augusta*'s crew, that the mission had been carried out:

> Big bomb dropped on Hiroshima August 5 at 7:15 P.M. Washington time. First reports indicate complete success which was even more conspicuous than earlier test.

"This is the greatest thing in history," Truman exclaimed to the Navy men surrounding him. "It's time for us to get home."[20]

CHINA WAS HARRIMAN'S CHIEF PREOCCUPATION during the last days at Potsdam. With Soong about to return to Moscow, and the Russians apparently determined to march into Manchuria on August 8, he felt the need for firm support from Washington. On July 28 Harriman had warned Byrnes in a memorandum:

> China is not in a position to resist unaided the present exaggerated Soviet demands. Since the United States is involved by the Yalta agreement in the contemplated settlement between China and the Soviet Union, I believe it is in our interest that the President give his interpretation of the Yalta agreements, specifically in connection with the differences over the arrangements for the port of Dairen and the operations of the railroads. I am fearful that unless this is done, Soong will be forced to make concessions which are at variance with our fundamental policies towards China and adverse to our national interests.

At the same time, Harriman stressed the importance of persuading Stalin to put in writing the oral assurances he had given at the time of the Hopkins visit in May that the Soviet Union would support the Open Door policy in China, with specific application to Manchuria. He pointed out that a declaration to this effect would give the United States an opportunity to deal directly with the Soviet Union in the event that Stalin abused his new privileges there.

Byrnes made no response. As time was running out, and the Secretary of State was about to leave for Washington, Harriman wrote out the instructions he wanted from the State Department in order to counter Stalin's stepped-up demands on China, and handed them to "Doc" Matthews on July 31. As the sole American witness, apart from Bohlen, to Roosevelt's tête-à-tête with Stalin on the Far East, Harriman could state with complete authority what the President had—and had not—agreed to at Yalta.

The instructions Harriman had requested came back to him on August 5, in a message from Byrnes, who was returning to the United States with Truman on board the *Augusta*, repeating his own language almost word for word. The Ambassador promptly told Stalin that Soong had already made all the concessions called for in the Yalta agreement and that the President hoped Stalin would not press him further; that Roosevelt had rejected the original Soviet proposal for a lease on Dairen, insisting instead that it be internationalized as a free port; and that Truman would be grateful for written assurances of Stalin's support for the American Open Door policy, to be published at the same time as the Soviet-Chinese agreement.

Soong saw Stalin on August 7 and reported to Harriman the following morning. Although Dairen was still a sticking point, they had agreed on arrangements for the use of Port Arthur as a Soviet naval base, Soong said, and for joint operation of the Manchurian railroads by a Chinese-Russian company. But Stalin had raised a wholly new and disturbing question: he now demanded the right to seize Japanese properties in Manchuria as trophies of war. Harriman's quick reading of Stalin's intentions was prophetic. He warned Washington:

> It would be possible for the Soviets, if they define war trophies as they did in connection with Germany . . . to strip Manchuria of certain of its industries and to obtain permanently complete industrial domination of Manchuria . . .
>
> This is another case where Stalin has increased his appetite and I recommend that we resist his demands . . .

The State Department sent back an indignant message pointing out that the United States had never recognized the puppet state of Manchukuo, set up by the Japanese after they had seized the territory in the thirties. It regarded Manchuria as an integral part of China, and if any country deserved special consideration in reparations to be taken from Japan, it was China. Although Stalin made no further mention of war trophies in his subsequent talks with Chiang Kai-shek's Foreign Minister, other pressures were building irresistibly.

When Harriman on August 8 appealed, in Truman's name, for an easing of Soviet demands on the Chinese, Stalin's testy reply was that the Manchurian ports and railroads had been built by Russians in czarist times. After all, he was giving the Chinese a half-interest in the railroads and restoring Chinese sovereignty in Manchuria, he said. Yet the ungrateful Chinese were treating the Russians as unwelcome guests. Harriman reported to the President:

> The Generalissimus concluded by asking me to tell you that he had no intention of encroaching on the sovereignty of China, saying that he would consider any other course dishonorable, that he would guarantee full freedom of trade in the port of Dairen and on the railroads and that, as far as Russia was concerned, he would respect the Open Door policy but that, of course, he could take no responsibility for the Chinese.
>
> It is difficult for me to believe, in spite of Stalin's assurances, that there can be a truly free port under Soviet management with security control by Soviet secret police and I see in the Yalta agreement nothing which would obligate us to support an arrangement of the kind described.

On the same day, Molotov sent for Harriman and Clark Kerr to tell them that the Soviet Union would consider itself at war with Japan on August 9. Stalin had decided not to wait until the Chinese met his terms, lest the Japanese surrender to the Americans before his troops had crossed the frontier into Manchuria. By the time that Harriman saw Stalin again on August 9, the day the second atomic bomb was dropped on Nagasaki, the Red Army had moved into Manchuria. "Stalin said that his advance troops had already crossed the frontiers of Manchuria both from the west and the east, not meeting heavy resistance on any front, and had advanced 10 or 12 kilometers in some sections," Harriman reported the same evening. It was clear that the bomb had forced Stalin's hand.

> In discussing the Japanese situation [Harriman added] he said that he thought the Japanese were looking for a pretext to set up a government that would surrender and he thought that the atomic bomb might give this pretext. He showed great interest in the atomic bomb and said that it could mean the end of war and aggression but that the secret would have to be well kept.
>
> He said that [the Russians] had found in Berlin laboratories in which the Germans were working on the breaking of the atom but that he did not find that they had come to any results. Soviet scientists had also been working on the problem but had not been able to solve it.

As the Red Army pushed toward Harbin and Changchun, Stalin stepped up the pressure on China. He warned Soong that if the Sino-Soviet agreement was not swiftly concluded, "the Communists will get into Manchuria." On August 13 he presented a new demand that China pay for the feeding of Soviet troops in Manchuria. According to Harriman's report of that conversation, Stalin explained to Soong that it was the practice of the Red Army to live off the land; as he did not wish to requisition food from the Chinese, they had the choice of providing currency for Russian purchases or letting the Russians issue their own currency, which China would then have to redeem. Soong replied that the Russians ought to pay for their food, as the American Army was doing, because China was a poor country. "Russia is a poor country too," Stalin rejoined.

In the end Soong submitted, accepting a Soviet harbor master for the ostensibly free port of Dairen, half of which would be leased to the Soviet Union for thirty years. He also agreed that China would recognize Outer Mongolia's independence, following a plebiscite to confirm the wishes of the populace. The final Sino-Soviet agreement was signed on August 14.

But the Open Door declaration, which Truman had asked Stalin to put in writing for publication at the same time, proved elusive. Harriman had raised the question with Stalin personally on August 8 and he had replied, "This will be done." That amiable Soviet attitude had vanished, however, when Harriman saw Molotov on August 14. The Foreign Minister remarked that Stalin now felt there was no need for a written declaration; his oral assurances ought to be sufficient; besides, no such declaration had been foreseen at Yalta. Harriman pressed harder, arguing that the way to allay public suspicions of Russian intent in Manchuria was to issue a public declaration. Molotov refused to budge. Under instructions from Truman, Harriman asked to see Stalin once more. On August 27 he told Stalin that while the President found his private assurances of respect for the Open Door in China satisfactory, it was important that the American people as well should know the Soviet attitude. Again Stalin sounded willing enough.

"We Soviets believe that the Open Door policy is better than the policy of colonial seizure," he said. "The English, however, might not like this policy. Their policy vis-à-vis China has been lagging behind. The Open Door policy is more progressive. We can make such a statement."

Harriman assured Stalin that the British government, too, would welcome a declaration from him in support of equal trading opportunities in China, including Manchuria, for all friendly nations. Stalin said again that he was willing as long as Chiang Kai-shek did not object, and the matter appeared to have been settled.

"By and large," Harriman recalled, "Dr. Soong got most of the things that he thought were important. The agreement was hailed the world over. Chiang welcomed it. So did Henry Luce.* It was chiefly the status of Outer Mongolia that bothered Chiang, although I could not see that it changed anything so far as the internal regime was concerned. The Mongolian regime had been pro-Russian and it remained pro-Russian. Soong made it clear to me that the Chinese never gave up their claim to a square foot of real estate that had belonged to them. He once said, 'I will not be able to go back home if I give up Chinese rights in Outer Mongolia.'

"I learned something quite important from that conversation. When Communist China many years later attacked India over the

---

* In an editorial published on September 10, 1945, *Life* magazine expressed deep satisfaction with the Soong-Stalin agreement:

Twelve days after Japan gave up there was announced in Moscow and Chungking an agreement which was as great a victory for common sense as the defeat of Japan was for armed might. The Soong-Stalin treaties contain less ammunition for pessimists than any diplomatic event of the last 20 years. The signatures of two men have done as much to ensure peace as all our flying fortresses . . .

Two strong and subtle men, both revolutionaries since youth, sat down in Moscow and discovered that each needed and wanted a long peace to complete his particular revolution. So they negotiated out every major issue between Russia and China . . .

Peace, lively but genuine peace, is therefore the outlook.

McMahon Line boundary in the Himalayas, Chiang supported the position of Mao Tse-tung and Chou En-lai. Political differences aside, Peking and Taipei were taking the same, traditionally Chinese, position.

"Our insistence on the Open Door policy was in keeping with American tradition, I suppose. But its meaning had changed since the nineteenth century. We were not seeking any special concessions in Manchuria or elsewhere, and it was not that we feared that the Chinese would slam the door shut. Our concern was that the Russians might set up a People's Republic in Manchuria and keep everybody else out. The plain fact was that Stalin did not need a treaty with Chiang to attain his objectives in the Far East. He could and would have occupied the Liaotung Peninsula without it. What the pact accomplished for him was to lend the appearance of legality to what he was determined to take in any event."

Spaso House was in constant turmoil through the month of August: Pauley and Isadore Lubin talking reparations with the Russians and the British; a dozen congressmen visiting Moscow for the first time; and General Eisenhower receiving a hero's welcome with Marshal Zhukov as his host and guide. For Kathleen Harriman, the embassy hostess, it was a trying and exhilarating period. She wrote to her sister in New York: "Ave's just returned with the news that Russia's at war with Japan. I wonder how many people will attribute it to the atomic bomb. I'm going off on the town to see the reaction. There will be no joy, unless I'm very mistaken."

The end of the war in Europe had been a tremendous emotional release for Muscovites, leading to a boisterous siege of the American embassy by thousands of cheering, waving Russians. The news that Russia was again at war, however briefly, could hardly have been expected to gladden hearts in Moscow. But the newspapers made much of the Red Army's unopposed advance into Manchuria. Although the Hiroshima bombing had been reported briefly on August 7, the Nagasaki bomb was ignored. Editorials commenting on the Japanese capitulation made no mention of the atomic bomb. It was as if the Red Army in Manchuria had delivered the *coup de grâce*.

At midnight on August 10 Molotov called in Harriman and Clark Kerr to discuss the Japanese surrender. The Potsdam declaration had been issued on July 26. After fifteen days of bitter wrangling between warhawks and peacemakers in Tokyo, and the obliteration of two industrial cities, the Emperor himself had tipped the scales toward peace in a message transmitted through the Swiss and Swedish governments. Now the Japanese government announced that it was prepared to accept the Potsdam terms with a single condition: that the act of surrender would not prejudice "the prerogatives of the Emperor as the sovereign ruler." The Soviet government was skeptical, Molotov said, because the Japanese were trying to impose conditions. "He gave every indication that the Soviet Government was willing to have the war continue," Harriman noted at the time. The Soviet army had advanced 170 kilometers into Manchuria, Molotov said, and the advance would continue. This was the Soviet government's "concrete reply" to the Japanese request for surrender terms.

Harriman had yet to respond when George Kennan burst into the room with a message just received from Washington asking the Soviet government to join the United States in dealing promptly with the Japanese surrender offer in order to end hostilities quickly. Washington took the position that the Emperor and the Japanese high command must sign the terms of surrender, issue orders to their armed forces to stop the fighting and give up their arms. Once this was done, subject to the authority of the Supreme Commander of the Allied powers, the Emperor could remain in keeping with the Potsdam formula—that the ultimate form of government was to be determined by "the freely expressed will of the Japanese people."

Harriman pressed Molotov for an immediate reply, stressing that the Emperor alone could issue orders to all Japanese troops to end the fighting. When Molotov promised an answer the following day, Harriman insisted upon getting it before the night was out.

At two o'clock in the morning Harriman and Clark Kerr were called back to Molotov's office and heard him read a brief statement:

> "The Soviet Government considers that the above-mentioned reply should be presented in the name of the principal powers waging war against Japan.
>
> "The Soviet Government also considers that, in case of an affirmative reply from the Japanese Government, the Allied Powers should reach an agreement on the candidacy or candidacies for representation of the Allied High Command to which the Japanese Emperor and the Japanese Government are to be subordinated."

Russia, in short, was associating itself with the American reply to the Japanese surrender offer but was now raising a new question about the Supreme Allied Commander. The text of the official memorandum, written by Page, catches part of the flavor of the pre-dawn duel that followed:

> THE AMERICAN AMBASSADOR inquired as to the exact meaning of the last sentence.
>
> MR. MOLOTOV pointed out that there was not a combined command in the Far East; therefore it would be necessary to reach agreement as to the Allied representative or representatives who would deal with the Japanese.

THE AMERICAN AMBASSADOR inquired whether this was a
concrete acceptance of the United States proposal.

MR. MOLOTOV replied that the American proposal did not
contain the name of any representative which had been agreed
upon by the principal Allies. The United States Government
should make some suggestion and the Allies could subsequently
agree as to who the Supreme Commander would be.

MR. HARRIMAN stated that this was utterly out of the
question. He knew that the Soviet reply would be unsatis-
factory to his government. It gave veto power to the Soviet
Government in the choice of the Supreme Commander—no
person could be appointed without Soviet agreement. He inquired whether the Soviet Government would be ready to
accept MacArthur.

MR. MOLOTOV replied [that] he did not know, he thought
so; however, he would have to consult his government.

THE AMERICAN AMBASSADOR stated that consultation was
one thing; however, as the Soviet reply now stood, it gave
veto power to the Soviet Government. It gave only qualified
approval. His Government surely would not accept it.

MR. MOLOTOV replied that it was conceivable that there
might be two Supreme Commanders, [Marshal] Vasilievsky
and MacArthur.

THE AMERICAN AMBASSADOR thereupon informed Mr. Molotov in no uncertain terms that this was absolutely inadmissible.

Harriman's own recollection was that his actual words were: "I
reject it in the name of my government." In fact, he was acting without instructions, a liberty he had taken in the conviction that Washington would back him up.

Molotov stiffly requested that Harriman should transmit the
Soviet reply to Washington, "whether he liked it or not." He would
do so, of course, Harriman replied, but he wanted to call Molotov's
attention to the fact that the United States had been fighting the
Japanese for four years and Russia had been in the war exactly two
days. It was unthinkable that the Supreme Commander should be
anyone but an American. Molotov, somewhat heatedly, said that he
would not reply because if he did he would have to make a comparison
with the European war.

"I went back to General Deane's office, which was our communications center," Harriman recalled, "and was just dictating to a
stenographer what I had done—and why I had done it—when the
telephone rang. It turned out to be Pavlov, the Soviet interpreter,
calling for Molotov. He said that Molotov had consulted Stalin and

that there had been a misunderstanding. Stalin had not meant that the Russians would have to agree on the choice of the Supreme Commander. He wanted only to be consulted. I insisted that the wording would have to be changed. They agreed to drop the language about the Allies having to 'reach an agreement' in favor of the single word 'consult.' I also wanted to get rid of the possibility that there would be more than one candidate for the Supreme Commander's job. I asked Pavlov to tell Molotov that the two words 'or candidacies' in his text would have to come out. He called back in a few minutes and said that Molotov had agreed to delete them. So the matter was settled that same night.

"My great fear, of course, was that if we had accepted Molotov's language we would be in for a long negotiation and they would finally insist that in exchange for agreeing to MacArthur they should have Hokkaido as a Soviet zone of occupation. Stalin had mentioned that ambition to Hopkins and myself, so I was alert to the possibility, and Stalin no doubt had it very much in mind.

"Jack McCloy told me some years later that it was a good thing I had been very firm that night and got the Russians to change their position without consulting Washington, because our government was so keen to get the fighting stopped that it would have accepted almost anything the Russians came back with. No one in Washington was thinking about the future of Japan, McCloy said. They were thinking only about the end of the war."

ON AUGUST 14 Japan accepted the terms of surrender. Truman appointed General MacArthur the Supreme Allied Commander, authorizing him to receive the surrender in behalf of Russia, China, Britain and the United States. The long war had ended at last. When the news reached Moscow at about one o'clock in the morning on August 15, Spaso House was filled with Russian guests, including Marshal Zhukov, attending a late reception for General Eisenhower. The party was just winding down when Harriman brought in the surrender announcement. "After that," Kathleen wrote home, "we had a very hard time getting rid of some of our drunker Soviet guests. I took a great shine to Marshal Zhukov. He's very genial & fun & apparently easy to work with. Once during the evening he called Eisenhower 'Ike'—a great departure for a Soviet."

The Eisenhower visit impressed Harriman as a genuine outpouring of long-suppressed feeling by the Russian people. "It was a real hero's welcome," the Ambassador recalled. "Zhukov was Ike's host and he came in and out of the embassy as no Russian had done before. I remember going to a soccer game with the two of them. Between periods, the announcer told the crowd of sixty thousand or more that they had two honored guests—General Eisenhower and Marshal Zhukov. Both men got to their feet and the cheers in the stadium surpassed anything I had ever heard. I had never seen such enormous enthusiasm anywhere. It was clear to me that next to Roosevelt himself, Eisenhower had become the human symbol of cooperation between our two countries. There was no question in my mind that the Russian people wanted that cooperation, that closeness, to continue after the war. Even the top people relaxed a little during the visit.

"Stalin invited Eisenhower, myself and General Deane to stand with him and the Soviet leadership on top of Lenin's tomb as they reviewed an enormous physical culture parade. I believe it was the first time that representatives of a foreign government had been honored this way. Oddly enough, Eisenhower stood beside Zhukov rather far down on the right. I was placed between President Kalinin and Stalin, presumably because I represented the President of the United States. It was an ordeal in a way. We were on our feet for five hours while tens of thousands of gymnasts from the various Soviet Republics moved through Red Square performing their routines. We had heard that Stalin was in poor health at the time. But he stood there like a rock—so I did too. From time to time I glanced longingly at some comfortable-looking chairs at the back of the platform but I didn't dare give in to my exhaustion. After a while, however, we began to move around from one group to another, chatting while the gymnasts went by. I walked over to talk to Molotov and remarked on the impressive spectacle. He asked me whether we had anything like it in the United States. I explained that our sport spectacles were rather different with only a handful of players and tens of thousands of spectators.

" 'This is very important,' Molotov remarked, 'because it develops the military spirit.' It was one of the few times I saw him let down his guard."

Eisenhower had come to Moscow with some definite ideas of his own about the postwar future. He told Harriman that he was convinced his friend Zhukov was going to succeed Stalin. After that, he predicted, the United States would have no major difficulties in dealing with the Soviet Union. He had linked arms with Zhukov repeatedly in soldierly toasts to peace, Eisenhower assured Harriman, and he was confident that a new era of friendly relations lay ahead. Both Harriman and Deane tried to persuade Eisenhower that he was being unrealistic. All good Communists, they pointed out, shared a horror of "Bonapartism"—their word for the taking over of a revolution by military men; it was an article of faith with them that the party must remain supreme.

"I told Ike that when the war was behind us, the Soviet military brass would seldom be seen in Moscow," Harriman recalled. "He was not persuaded and when, at a Kremlin banquet in his honor, Marshal Zhukov entered the reception room at Stalin's side, Ike pointed this out to me as evidence that he was right. I explained that Zhukov's appearance beside Stalin was a courtesy to him, that if the Secretary of State had been the guest of honor, it would have been Molotov who stood at Stalin's side."

The argument between Harriman and Eisenhower continued in a friendly way long after the war. Only after Zhukov had been downgraded to a lesser command at Odessa did Eisenhower acknowledge that he had been wrong. Like General Marshall, Eisenhower was slow to understand the crucial importance of the Communist party in setting Soviet policy. The fact that Stalin had honored his military commitments during the war was paramount in the thinking of both men. Marshall, in particular, refused to concede that the United States was facing a time of trouble with the Russians until he had to deal with Molotov, face to face, at the final Council of Foreign Ministers meeting in Moscow in the spring of 1947.*

Harriman, nevertheless, regretted that Eisenhower never revisited the Soviet Union as President of the United States. Nikita Khrushchev revoked his invitation to Eisenhower in 1960, during the uproar over the U-2 incident. "The great tragedy of the U-2," Harriman recalled, "was that Ike never went back to Moscow. The reaction of the people would have been overwhelming. Ordinary Russians still remembered Eisenhower with affection as the living symbol of our wartime cooperation. I have no doubt they would have responded to his warmth, his smile, his outgoing personality. I am convinced that a visit from Eisenhower at that time would have had a lasting effect on Soviet public opinion."

Stalin clearly had been favorably impressed by Eisenhower. "General Eisenhower is a very great man," he said to Harriman after the 1945 visit, "not only because of his military accomplishments but because of his human, friendly, kind and frank nature. He is not a *grubyi* like most military [men]." Passing along this rare compliment to Eisenhower, who had returned to Frankfurt, Harriman explained that "*grubyi*" was the Russian word for a man of coarse, brusque manners and added, "You evidently sold a bill of goods while you were here."

---

* General Walter Bedell Smith told Harriman that when he was appointed ambassador to Russia in 1946, Marshall said to him, "You must talk to Harriman, of course, in view of his long experience. But you ought to discount what he says. The Russians gave him a hard time and that made him too pessimistic."

BY LATE AUGUST, Harriman felt that his wartime mission to Moscow was substantially accomplished. He had helped to work out with Molotov the arrangements for the first Council of Foreign Ministers, which was about to begin the peacemaking in London. In a message to Byrnes on August 23, the Ambassador suggested that they meet in London before the sessions opened so that he might report personally on his conversations with Stalin and Molotov since Potsdam. Harriman warned of trouble ahead over the control machinery for Japan. "We will, I anticipate, have some difficulty in Korea," he added, "as it is my impression that the Soviets want to dominate this country in spite of Stalin's agreement that it should develop its independence through a four-power trusteeship. I believe the Soviets are feeling their way with us to see how far they can go with their unilateral objectives in the Far East." He also mentioned the need to discuss with Byrnes arrangements for his resignation as ambassador to the Soviet Union.

Byrnes's reply the following day impressed Harriman as brusque to the point of rudeness: "In the early days of the meeting, I am afraid I shall be so engaged . . . that I will not have the time to have any satisfactory talks with you. I suggest that you come to London about the 20th of September." There was not the faintest suggestion that Harriman's advice would be welcomed by the new Secretary of State in dealing with Molotov at the London meeting. "I was infuriated by Byrnes's reply," Harriman recalled. "Of course I wanted to talk to him about my resignation, but I was far more interested in telling him what had happened in Moscow. It was not, I think, a matter of personalities. Jimmy Byrnes just did not care to be confused by other people's judgments. To be treated in this cavalier manner by a man who refused to listen merely increased my determination to get out at the earliest possible moment." Harriman, accordingly, wrote to Truman on August 30:

> At Potsdam, as you may recall, I had the opportunity to explain to you that I had taken a commitment to President Roosevelt to remain in Moscow until Russia came into the war against Japan but that I hoped I could be relieved soon thereafter. Now that the war is ended, and certain basic agreements have been reached, we are entering a new phase in our relations with the Soviet Union. I feel that this is the appropriate moment for me to leave . . . I want to leave as soon as possible but naturally wish to do so in a manner to cause the least inconvenience to you and Secretary Byrnes.

In the personal letter to Hopkins, dictated on September 6 but apparently never sent, Harriman confirmed his decision to quit:

Truman has always been very cordial with me but I don't know just where I stand with Byrnes, although he supported me in working out the Chinese matter. I gather the agreements have been well received everywhere. I had a bit of a tussle with Molotov over accepting MacArthur as Supreme Commander. I feel these two things end my work for President Roosevelt.

CHAPTER XXI

Farewell to Moscow

THE COUNCIL of Foreign Ministers—established at Potsdam to draw up peace treaties with the former Axis satellite countries—met at Lancaster House in London on September 11. Rather than wait in Moscow until Byrnes agreed to see him, Harriman decided to spend a few days with General Eisenhower in Germany in order to get some feel for the developing situation there. Kathleen and General Deane flew to Frankfurt with him. Eisenhower received them warmly, suggesting that all four go down to Cap d'Antibes on the French Riviera, where he had a villa reserved. "Ike had been too busy for a vacation until then," Harriman recalled. "So we could hardly refuse, even though I regretted not getting to see something of Germany under Allied occupation. We had a very pleasant time, played a bit of bridge and sat in the sun, but after a couple of days Eisenhower was called away to Frankfurt. I began to get restless, so Kathleen and I went to London on September seventeenth. By that time Jimmy Byrnes was up to his ears in trouble."

Byrnes had insisted that the council meet formally twice a day in order to get its work done promptly. Far from saving time, however, the breakneck schedule left no opportunity for informal meetings with the Russians, the British or the Chinese at which ideas could be exchanged and quiet understandings worked out. "In other words," Harriman noted at the time, "no one really knew what was the point of view of any of the other delegates except through the endless open meetings. Instead of *saving* time, this procedure was an endless time-consumer. The morning meetings lasted two and a half to three hours, and the afternoon meetings three and a half to four hours. Everyone became exhausted, with nerves frayed."

Both Byrnes and Bevin, the new British Foreign Secretary, lacking experience as diplomatic negotiators, soon managed, in their separate ways, to offend Molotov. At one session Bevin became so incensed over Molotov's line of argument that he was reminded, he said, of the Hitler philosophy. Molotov jumped to his feet as soon as Bevin's words were translated and started marching out of the room.

"I had long since learned that you can be critical of the Russians but you can't compare them to Hitler," Harriman recalled. "Bevin could not have been expected to know that, I suppose. Molotov, at any rate, was in a state of controlled fury. I watched him closely as he moved toward the door and it seemed to me that he was torn between walking out—which might well have broken up the conference—and staying. The room was very crowded. I had the impression that Molotov was doing everything he could to put more people between himself and the door, so that he wouldn't get out too fast. Then Bevin began to talk and, of course, he said, 'I apologize if I have offended you.' Molotov stopped, turned around and took his place again at the table.

"I happened to see Bevin in the corridor after the meeting. I had known him intimately during the war and he was quite obviously crestfallen over the incident. He felt that he had committed a major gaffe in what was, after all, his first international conference as the principal representative of the United Kingdom. He had been to Potsdam, but Attlee had been in charge there. Bevin's point of view was not all that different from Eden's. But where Eden would have prefaced a tough statement with suave assurances about how greatly the British valued their relations with the Russians and how helpful they were trying to be, Bevin was a blunt instrument.

"He appeared ashamed to have shown his ignorance of diplomatic manners. I urged him to be himself, not to deviate from his blunt-spoken ways and assured him that in the long run he would get along better with the Russians that way. But he walked on to luncheon, depressed and humiliated."

Byrnes was having his own troubles with Molotov. Hopes for a peace treaty with Italy had been frustrated by the Soviet Foreign Minister's unyielding demands in behalf of Yugoslavia over the Venezia Giulia region surrounding Trieste. The treaties with Rumania, Bulgaria and Hungary, although far less complicated, also were derailed when Molotov suddenly announced on September 22 that France, a full member of the Council of Foreign Ministers, had no right to take part in the treaty talks on the technical ground that she had not been a signatory to the armistice agreements with the Balkan countries. China also was to be excluded, although the foreign ministers of both countries had participated in all the discussions since September 11 without opposition from Molotov.

The Secretary of State, increasingly alarmed by Molotov's aggressive and arbitrary attitude, in his turn had refused to discuss a Soviet proposal for the establishment of an Allied control commission in Tokyo to set policy for the occupation of Japan. Harriman, through his own efforts some six weeks earlier, had blocked Molotov's demands for veto power over the selection of General MacArthur as the sole Supreme Commander in Tokyo. But now that the war was over, he saw no reason for refusing to consult the Russians on occupation policy, as long as MacArthur had the last word. Byrnes, however, was not prepared to discuss the matter and kept brushing it aside—a tactic which, Harriman felt, fed Russian suspicions that the American policy was to shut them out of Japan entirely. In one private session Molotov became so exasperated by Byrnes's stalling tactic that he accused the United States of trying to set itself up as "dictator to the world."

"We can't get away with this brush-off," Harriman warned in a note he slipped to James Clement Dunn for Byrnes's attention. "The Sec. should say that the U.S. Gov. is prepared to supply full information to Soviet & is always ready to consider its views, but this meeting is not the place to consider policies." The same day, September 24, Harriman sent the Secretary of State a more formal memorandum, applauding his firmness while at the same time counseling him not to overdo it:

> . . . we must not minimize the importance of doing everything we can to disarm [the Russians'] unwarranted suspicions. For example, you know how suspicious the Soviets were up to the very end that we were prepared to make a separate peace with the Germans. They are undoubtedly fearful that we are now ready to use Japan against them.

On September 27, in a second memorandum to Byrnes, Harriman expanded his argument:

> There can be no doubt that the Soviet Government will continue to press us for a prompt agreement on Soviet participation in the control of Japan. I feel it is of importance that we should come to a decision as soon as possible on how far we are ready to allow them to participate and notify them promptly. I am afraid we are arousing unnecessarily their suspicions, which will react . . . in other Far Eastern matters, particularly the withdrawal of Soviet troops from Manchuria in favor of the Chinese. I believe that to satisfy them it will be necessary to agree to establish at once a control commission for Japan . . . Following the pattern of the Balkan control commissions, it should be clear, however, that General Mac-Arthur as Supreme Commander has the final voice . . .

"I feel strongly," Harriman concluded, "that it is very much in the interests of our long-term relations to act voluntarily rather than appear to be forced unwillingly into concessions."

Again, the following day, Harriman tried to move the reluctant Byrnes to action with a third memorandum, analyzing Molotov's tactics. "Molotov," he wrote, "has used the unsettled questions regarding the control of Japan to attempt to divert attention from his unilateral position in the Balkans to our unilateral action in the Pacific. May I suggest that we have a full discussion this morning of all your advisers before any further steps are taken?"

The highly tentative outcome was a letter from Byrnes to Molotov on September 29, based on a draft by Harriman and Bohlen, explaining that the Secretary of State had not meant to reject the Soviet proposal, only to postpone its consideration until he could consult the President and the War Department after his return to Washington. That cooled the issue temporarily, although Molotov grumbled at being put off.

During the final days of the stalemated London meeting, Byrnes at last overcame his disinclination to seek advice. He found time to listen to Harriman, Dunn, Bohlen, Cohen and John Foster Dulles. Each of the advisers, Cohen excepted, felt that further discussions would lead nowhere. Harriman noted at the time: "Byrnes had been reluctant to take this position up to the very end and, if Molotov had proposed some reasonable compromise, I believe he would have accepted it. On the other hand, Molotov gave him no opportunity to do so." Byrnes then contrived to have the new Chinese Foreign Minister, Wang Shi-chieh, who was presiding that day, declare the London meeting at an end on October 2.

While in London, Harriman discovered that he was not alone in regretting and resenting Byrnes's cavalier way with advisers, or allies. Both Bevin and A. V. Alexander, First Lord of the Admiralty in the new Labor government, complained to Harriman that they had been embarrassed repeatedly by unilateral American actions, taken without the careful consultation the British had come to expect in the days of Hopkins, Hull and Stettinius. "They were ready to support American policies provided they had a chance to thrash out questions before we took decisions," Harriman noted at the time, "but it was very embarrassing for . . . their new Labor Government when they had to defend matters with which they did not agree and on which they had not had a chance to express their views. Again this was a question of Byrnes going ahead without consultation."

Not until the end of the conference did Harriman have the opportunity to discuss his resignation with Byrnes at dinner. Faced with new difficulties, the Secretary of State asked the Ambassador to remain in Moscow. "Now that we are in this jam," he said, "you'll have to wait and get the train back on the rails." Harriman agreed to stay on a while longer. He recommended that Truman send him a telegram to be delivered to Stalin personally. This would create an opportunity to find out from Stalin himself "the basic questions which were disturbing the Russians," instead of renewing the battle of London with Molotov.

Harriman set out for Moscow on October 4, stopping in Berlin, Vienna and Budapest on the way. He found both the Deputy Military Governor, General Lucius D. Clay, and Ambassador Robert D. Murphy in Berlin disturbed over the sudden postponement of Marshal Zhukov's planned visit to the United States the same week. Murphy and Clay, according to Harriman's notes, put this piece of news together with the breakdown of the foreign ministers conference, Russian stalling on Allied decisions already agreed to at lower levels and a new pattern of guarded behavior on the part of Soviet officers in Berlin.

Did all these signs portend a more difficult period ahead? It was difficult to say. In Vienna, the evidence was contradictory. Generals Mark Clark and Alfred Gruenther told Harriman that they believed the sudden recall to Moscow of Colonel General Alexei Zheltov, the deputy commander of Soviet forces in Austria, and of his political adviser, might have been connected with the failure of the London conference. On the other hand, Marshal Ivan S. Koniev, Zheltov's superior, had put in a most cordial appearance at a reception in Vienna for Harriman and John McCloy, who was visiting from Washington. "I found a tendency both in Berlin and Vienna," Harriman noted at the time, "to think that the politicians were making their work more difficult, and to attach exaggerated importance to the cooperation they had been able to obtain from the Russians in what were, in fact, relatively small matters. In other words they have not really gotten down to the big issues in either place. There is no doubt, however, that the Russians are trying to play ball."

In Budapest, Harriman found the official Americans—Arthur Schoenfeld and Major General William S. Key—"much bucked up" by the fact that the Russians had allowed a free election in the city. The Smallholders, the anti-Communist Peasant party, had just won a clear, unexpected majority and Budapest was jubilant. "Jack McCloy and I wanted to go to the American mission," Harriman recalled, "but we couldn't get in the door. There was an enormous crowd celebrating the victory under the American flag. It made me feel very humble to recognize how much these people looked to the United States as the protector of their freedom. They expected so much of us—and there was so little that we could do. That scene in front of the American mission had its influence, I am sure, in persuading me that we ought to go on pressing the Russians to live up to their commitments. I simply could not accept the view that we ought to walk away and let the Russians have their sphere of influence in Eastern Europe, to do with as they chose."

Harriman found the shops in Budapest far better stocked than those in Vienna, but he wondered how long that could continue in view of the fact that the Russians had 800,000 troops in Hungary, living off the land. Already the Soviets were demanding a 50 percent share in all major Hungarian industries, including Danube River shipping. Harriman noted in his account of the journey: "It is interesting that the behavior of the Red Army soldiers has created basic enmity among the peoples in all countries occupied, which will cause difficulty for Soviet foreign policy."

Moscow was rife with rumor when Harriman returned. It started with an October 10 announcement by Tass, the Soviet news agency, that Stalin had left the capital "for a rest" at an undisclosed location. Kennan and the embassy staff knew of no precedent for such an announcement. It was the first time anyone could remember that Stalin's movements had been reported in the press before his return to Moscow; also the first public suggestion that Stalin, the man of steel, might need a rest. Rumors that he might be dead, or gravely ill, swept the city, including the diplomatic corps. At this moment Truman sent Harriman a message specifying (exactly as he had recommended) that it must be delivered to Stalin personally. The President's purpose was to get the interrupted dialogue with the Russians reopened.

On October 15 Harriman went to see Molotov, who told him that Stalin was not dealing with affairs of state during his rest period. Molotov offered to pass on the message from President Truman. But Harriman refused, explaining to the Foreign Minister that he was under instructions to deliver it personally, and adding, "I can wait till he gets back." Molotov explained that Stalin would be away for a month and a half. "Where is he?" Harriman asked. "I'll be glad to join him." Molotov, looking faintly incredulous, said he would see whether that was possible. Three days later he advised Harriman that Stalin would be pleased to receive him at Gagra, in the Crimea, on October 24.

"We flew south in overcast weather with little visibility," Harriman wrote in his notes of the journey, "but as we approached Rostov the weather cleared up and it became warm and brilliantly sunny over the Black Sea. The Caucasus Mountains on our left, snow-covered and majestic, with foothills extending down to the sea coast, were especially impressive after the dull, flat Moscow countryside. The rugged coast itself with its countless sanatoriums and rest homes, its vineyards, farms and tiny villages, nestled in the hills, was most beautiful from the air . . . At several thousand feet these buildings, painted white, pink, light blue or yellow, with their gardens, parks and recreational facilities, gave one the impression of the Riviera. This was quickly lost, however, when we got down to earth and were faced with the usual state of unrepair which is so common in the Soviet Union, the drab, sordid, and bedraggled people and the pathetic little villages with their dirty, empty shops."

After an hour's drive from Adler Airport over winding coastal roads, Harriman was delivered to a fine white stucco villa which (as Stalin later told him) had been the vacation retreat of Lavrenti Beria, chief of the NKVD, when he was Secretary General of the Communist party in Georgia. The guesthouse was surrounded by acres of vineyards and fruit trees—lemon, apple and pear. Like other grand pre-Revolutionary houses reserved for the Soviet leadership, it was screened from public view by a tall green fence and heavily guarded. After a bite of supper Harriman and Page, his interpreter, were taken to Stalin's villa in a government limousine, passing through the main gate on the coastal road and then climbing steadily up a steep, winding mountain road cut from sheer rock. Two massive wooden gates, studded with iron, swung open at the approach of Harriman's car and after a short walk between privet hedges on either side, he was escorted into a small building where Stalin greeted him warmly at the front door.

Stalin led the way into a mahogany-paneled room with a desk and several chairs in one corner. It was here that he worked while on vacation—his first in nine years, Stalin told Harriman. The Ambassador replied that he felt badly about interrupting Stalin's vacation to talk business, but he had been instructed to deliver a message from President Truman. Stalin read the message carefully in Russian translation. Then he looked up and said: "The Japanese question is not touched upon here."* His opening remark (and the discussion that followed) squarely confirmed Harriman's warnings to Byrnes at the London conference in September—which the Secretary of State had stubbornly disregarded—that the Russians were determined to reach an understanding on the control procedures for Japan.†

---

* The Truman message briefly reviewed certain of the procedural disagreements of the London Council of Foreign Ministers without mentioning the squabble over Allied control of Japan. Assuring Stalin that he remained faithful to the Yalta accords and the policies of Franklin Roosevelt, the President offered to accept a narrowing of the treaty-drafting procedure on condition that the Soviet Union agree to call a peace conference of all the "principally interested states," which would give final approval to the treaties.

† In his memoir *All in One Lifetime*, Byrnes later wrote: "When Harriman reported back to Washington, his [Stalin's] reply was surprising. Stalin apparently was not particularly interested in our recognizing these two Balkan states and turned the conversation away from Europe to the control of Japan."[1] The

The Ambassador, who had received no detailed instructions on the President's position, nevertheless gave Stalin a comprehensive account of the attitude in Washington as he understood it. Some of what he said was based on information he had received; some on surmise. In the first stage of accepting the surrender, the Japanese were being disarmed by the United States Army alone, he said. Following the surrender and disarmament, however, the United States could be expected to invite the participation of a limited number of Russian, Chinese and British forces, although there would be no separate zones of occupation. Harriman added that Washington also was considering the establishment of a military council in which the commanding generals of the Allied forces would meet and discuss all policy questions with MacArthur. If they failed to agree, then MacArthur would have the last word.

Stalin said he was very grateful for the information. He realized that by raising the question of the control machinery he was "placing the Ambassador in an embarrassing position." Harriman replied that he did not believe there was a topic that he and Stalin could not discuss together frankly.

The Soviet position, as explained by Stalin, was that the only proper term to use, in describing the Allied control machinery for Japan, was "control commission," not "control council." A control council was appropriate for Germany, which had no government of its own, but "there was a government in Japan and it was therefore more proper to speak of . . . a control commission."

To reassure Harriman that a control commission would in no way diminish MacArthur's authority, Stalin made the point that in Hungary and Rumania, where there were only Soviet troops, the last word had been reserved for the Soviet chairmen of the respective control commissions. In short, far from objecting to MacArthur's supremacy in Tokyo, Stalin appeared to find a happy precedent in Budapest and Bucharest.

It went without saying [he said to Harriman] that the United States representative, General MacArthur, should be the permanent chairman of the Control Commission and should have the final voice. However, if there were other troops on the Japanese islands, as there were in Germany, the effect would be to restrict the rights of General MacArthur. This was not desirable. In order to preserve the freedom of action of MacArthur it might perhaps not be advisable to

---

Harriman memoranda of September 24, 27 and 28 leave no room for doubt that Byrnes had received fair warning of Stalin's attitude a month earlier.

send . . . troops [of other countries] to Japan. This was more logical.

When Harriman returned at seven o'clock the following evening to resume the discussion, however, Stalin sounded far less agreeable. He complained that the Soviet government had never been consulted or even informed about policy decisions affecting Japan:

> The Soviet Union had its self-respect as a sovereign state. No decisions made by MacArthur were being transmitted to it. In point of fact the Soviet Union had become an American satellite in the Pacific. This was a role it could not accept. It was not being treated as an ally. The Soviet Union would not be a satellite of the United States in the Far East or elsewhere. These were the reasons [why] Mr. Molotov had raised the question of control machinery in London.

Harriman protested that it had never been Truman's intention to disregard the views of the Soviet Union. The President wanted to consult the Russians on all questions of mutual interest, and Japan certainly was one of them. If there had been a misunderstanding, Harriman said, this was the moment to straighten it out. But Stalin was not to be mollified. He listed a number of specific grievances: MacArthur, for example, had ordered certain changes in the Japanese government without informing the Russians of the reasons for his action; the Japanese press and radio were being allowed to denounce the Soviet Union; and certain senior Japanese commanders, who should have been locked up as war criminals, were still at liberty. "It would be more honest," he said, "if the Soviet Union were to quit Japan than to remain there as a piece of furniture."

In reply, Harriman argued that the United States had been trying for months past to establish an advisory commission in Washington for the express purpose of consulting its Pacific allies on occupation policy, but the Russians had failed to send a representative. The advisory commission was an "incorrect solution," Stalin rejoined. The only correct one was an Allied control commission in Tokyo. But it might be better for all concerned, Stalin said, if the Soviet Union were to step aside and let the Americans do as they wished in Japan. Then, for the first time, Stalin suggested that the Soviet Union might pursue a go-it-alone policy after the war:

> The Soviet Union would not interfere. For a long time the isolationists had been in power in the United States. He had never favored a policy of isolation, but perhaps now the Soviet Union should adopt such a policy. Perhaps, in fact, there was nothing wrong with it.

As Harriman understood him, Stalin was not proposing to embrace isolation in the classical American pattern, but he was weighing a policy of unilateral action. It was clear to the Ambassador that Stalin never would entrust the real security interests of the Soviet Union to collective arrangements which, in the final analysis, rested on the good will of other nations. "A policy of isolation," Harriman felt, meant a policy of maintaining Soviet domination throughout Eastern Europe and using the Communist parties in Western Europe and elsewhere as a means of expanding Russian influence. Stalin would not rely on the United States or other Western powers for economic assistance. Nor would he count upon their military cooperation in the future.

Bruised pride certainly played its part in Stalin's outburst. The Russians, he said, had maintained twenty to forty divisions on the Manchurian frontier for the past ten years and they had contributed seventy divisions to the final defeat of Japan. No one could say that the Soviet Union had done nothing, he added. In fact, he had been "ready to help the United States by landing troops on the Japanese islands," but his offer had been rejected.*

But something more than wounded feelings seemed to lie at the bottom of Stalin's sudden contemplation of isolationism. The statement that he personally had never favored such a policy but now saw "nothing wrong with it" could be read as one piece of evidence that the Soviet leadership had discussed and settled upon a new policy for the postwar period, a policy of increased militancy and self-reliance.

Harriman came away from his talks with Stalin persuaded that Molotov had been acting under instructions even when he was being most obstreperous over seemingly minor points of procedure. At Gagra, Stalin at first had taken the position that separate peace conferences should be called to deal with each of the former Axis satellites, including Italy. Only those Allied countries should be invited which had actually waged war against the satellite in question. Harriman argued for a single peace conference on the ground that "the European war was one war," that each of the satellites had assisted Hitler in its way and that all the Allied countries had a right to be consulted on the terms of the peace. Brazil, for example, having sent two divisions to fight in Italy, should be invited to the peace conference, but Costa Rica and Haiti, which had declared war without fighting, should not.

Reassured that the Europeans would not be overwhelmed by a

---

* At this point in the memorandum of Harriman's second conversation with Stalin at Gagra, the interpreter (Edward Page) added a note of his own: "When Stalin made this remark it was quite obvious from the tone of his voice and from the expression on his face that he was still very irked at our refusal to permit Soviet troops to land at Hokkaido."

swarm of Latin Americans representing countries obedient to Washington, Stalin finally gave ground. He agreed to reconvene the Council of Foreign Ministers in order to draft treaties with Bulgaria, Finland, Hungary, Italy and Rumania, with a single peace conference to follow. But he strenuously opposed the participation of China, Norway, the Netherlands, Belgium, Luxembourg, Poland and India in the peace conference. Harriman argued that each of the countries Stalin proposed to blackball had fought one Axis power or the other in what was, after all, a single war. Norway, Holland and Belgium, for example, had been overrun by the Nazis. They were vitally interested in the peace. Norway and Holland, moreover, even after they were occupied by the Germans, had thrown their navies and their merchant shipping into the battle. But Stalin was adamant. If the Americans insisted on their inclusion, he said, the Soviet Union would demand separate seats at the peace conference for each of its sixteen Socialist Republics. They, too, had fought and suffered. When Harriman shifted his ground, emphasizing that China was a permanent member of the United Nations Security Council, Stalin brushed off the argument. The United Nations, he said, was a question for the future; the peace treaties had to be settled now.

Harriman decided that nothing would be gained by prolonging the argument. Thanking Stalin for the extraordinary opportunity to talk at length with him while he was on vacation, Harriman got up to leave. It was important, he felt, that he should return to Moscow in order to communicate more swiftly with Washington. Stalin had the last word. "I have received you not only as the Ambassador of the United States but as a friend," he said. "It will always be so."

On his return to Moscow, Harriman set about his assigned task of getting the Council of Foreign Ministers back on the rails. He opened a series of talks with Molotov on the still-aggrieved question of Russia's role in the occupation of Japan. They spent many hours together disputing over words. The State Department, for example, now offered through Harriman to set up an Allied military council, consisting of Russian, Chinese and British generals, to consult with MacArthur in Tokyo. Molotov insisted that it had to be called an Allied control commission, not a military council. In their Gagra talks, Stalin had assured Harriman that MacArthur would have the "final word" in any Allied council or commission that might be set up. But Molotov now objected to what he described as an ornamental role for the Russian representative. "They are fearful that the Soviet Government will constantly be faced with a *fait accompli*," Harriman reported to Washington on November 13. "Japan has for two generations been a constant menace to Russian security in the Far East and the Soviets wish now to be secure from this threat." Molotov in fact was demanding veto power, while Harriman kept rejecting any arrangement that would bar the United States from issuing policy directives to MacArthur until it had the unanimous consent of the Big Four powers, Russia included.

"In all the discussions," Harriman recalled, "I was very thorough, also very liberal when it came to consultation with the Russians on policy questions, but very firm on the matter of keeping the power in American hands. So long as MacArthur had the last word, I could not see that it made a great deal of difference whether we called it a commission or a council. We should, I felt, have set this up rapidly, making concessions on matters of form. Instead, Washington fussed and fumed over little details. The instructions I was getting from the State Department showed a great lack of understanding. If they had acted on the suggestions I made after seeing Stalin at Gagra, we might have settled the whole business in October, but they dragged it out until December. In one message Byrnes actually said that he preferred to wait and hear further from the Soviet government before entering into discussions with other departments of our own government.

"In other words, he was more worried about dealing with the War Department, and with MacArthur, than he was about dealing with Stalin. It was a stupid performance because Stalin had made it abundantly clear to me that for him the question of Japan was linked with the peace treaties for Rumania and Bulgaria. He would not move on the Balkan countries until he had received satisfaction on Japan. And in Eastern Europe, time was on Stalin's side. The longer we delayed, the more entrenched the Communist bureaucracies became. I had seen it happen in Poland. The longer these new Communist-dominated governments were allowed to operate unhampered by free elections, the more surely did they consolidate their power and arrest or exile any independent national leaders; to the point where even if the Russians had been tempted to make concessions they would have met with resistance from the men they had installed in power.

"It seemed to me absurd to suggest that Stalin sat in the Kremlin and issued orders, as if he were Hitler. It was a different form of control that he exercised. The facts of life, as I saw them, were that these local Communist leaders were gaining a position in their own countries which it was important for the Kremlin to maintain. They were sitting on populations that, except in Bulgaria, were at least seventy to eighty percent anti-Russian and anti-Communist. And I have no doubt that they said to Stalin, 'If you dare to hold free elections, you will lose the country.' The Hungarian national election in which the Communist party got only seventeen percent of the vote must have been a shock."

During the short, dark days of autumn 1945, the political climate in Moscow became notably bleak and chilly. At the theater one evening Harriman had "a most disquieting conversation of a few sentences" with Litvinov, which he reported to Washington on November 22:

> He [Litvinov] told me that he was disturbed by the international situation, that neither side knew how to behave toward the other, and that this was the underlying reason for the breakdown of the London conference and the subsequent difficulties. I suggested that time might cool the strong feelings that had been aroused. He replied that in the meantime, however, other issues were developing. I suggested that it might clear the atmosphere if we came to an understanding about Japan. He replied that other issues would then confront us.
>
> When I asked him what we, for our part, could do about it, he replied, "Nothing."

"What can you do about it?" Harriman asked.

"Nothing," Litvinov replied. "I believe I know what should be done but I am powerless."

"You are extremely pessimistic," Harriman remarked.

"Frankly, between us, yes," Litvinov softly replied.

Litvinov had been extremely disgruntled since his recall from Washington two years earlier. He detested Molotov, who had supplanted him as Foreign Minister, and his advice (as Harriman surmised) had evidently been disregarded by the government. Yet Litvinov's fairly direct suggestion that matters were bound to get worse, regardless of what the United States did in its relations with the Soviet Union, struck Harriman as significant.

There were other signs of a new hard line, disseminated through the press and at party meetings. With remarkable unanimity, the handful of Soviet writers and artists who were encouraged to mix with foreigners now talked in wounded tones about an aggressive new American policy toward the Soviet Union. "Why has America become so aggressive?" they asked. "Why is she interfering with Soviet attempts to bring democracy to the Balkans? Why is she threatening the Soviet Union with the atomic bomb?"

Harriman saw no reason for despair but the "tentative interpretation" he sent back to Washington was somber:

> To sum up the above, together with Stalin's comment that the Soviet Union may have to pursue an isolationist policy, it appears that since Molotov could not get what he wanted at

the London conference, the Soviet Government . . . has been pursuing to the fullest extent possible a policy of unilateral action to achieve their concept of security in depth.

Vishinsky and other Soviets have attempted to stiffen the lines in Bulgaria and Rumania. Tito has broken with Subasic.* The Chinese National Government has been double-crossed and Manchuria has been turned over to the Chinese Communists. Revolt has been fostered under Red Army protection in Iranian Azerbaijan. Renewed pressure for bases has been brought on Norway and Turkey . . .

Thus it would appear that Molotov's policy following the London breakdown has been to seize the immediate situation to strengthen the Soviet position as much as possible through unilateral action and then probably to agree to another meeting of the Foreign Ministers. We would at that time be faced with a number of entrenched Soviet positions and *faits accomplis.*

The increasingly unilateral nature of Soviet policy became more marked after the London conference. George Andreychin, the remarkable Bulgarian-American revolutionary whom Harriman had first met as Trotsky's English-language interpreter, back in 1926, attributed the change primarily to the atomic bomb. The ruling group in the Kremlin, filled with pride over the Red Army's strength at the end of the war in Europe, Andreychin said, had been shocked to learn that America's possession of the bomb once again exposed Russia's comparative weakness. It was to conceal their weakness, he told Harriman during a surreptitious visit to Spaso House on October 30, that the Russians now were being so aggressive.

Andreychin had emigrated to the United States as a young man and joined the Industrial Workers of the World. Arrested for draft evasion during World War I, he had jumped bail in Seattle and escaped to Russia, where he became associated with Trotsky. This association, and to a lesser extent his friendship with William C. Bullitt, the first American ambassador to the Soviet Union, had landed Andreychin in Soviet jails more than once. A chronic victim of the revolution he had once espoused, Andreychin had been expelled from the Communist party.

Now he had come to say goodbye to Harriman, having finally received permission to go home to Bulgaria with his wife and two

---

* Subâsič resigned in October, complaining that the terms of his agreement with Josip Broz Tito, the Communist leader, had not been carried out.

daughters, and to offer his advice to the American mission in Sofia. Andreychin was distinctly apprehensive about talking frankly with Harriman except in the bathroom, over the rush of water in the basin to blanket their conversation. He knew, Andreychin said, that dictaphones had been installed in Spaso House before Bullitt's arrival in 1934; in fact, part of the evidence used against him by the Russians had been based on recordings of his conversations with Bullitt.

With the noisy tap turned up high, in spite of Harriman's assurances that the building had been checked and rechecked for listening devices, Andreychin talked freely. Molotov and Vishinsky, he said, had become the makers of Soviet foreign policy because Stalin had no independent sources of information about the outside world. The war-weary Russian people remained friendly, however, more friendly to the United States than to Britain. To offset their daily diet of propaganda, he said, the United States ought to start a shortwave radio service in the Russian language, broadcasting as much information as possible about American life and thought. Even the modest mimeographed bulletin which Harriman had inaugurated on his arrival as ambassador in 1943 had its value, Andreychin said, because it gave a limited number of Soviet officials untainted access to the speeches and press conferences of President Truman and other American leaders. He remarked, for example, that members of the ruling group had underlined and carefully discussed a provocative sentence in a statement by John Foster Dulles to the effect that "There will be no bloc of Western powers if the United States can avoid it."

Public opinion had its effect even in the Soviet Union, Andreychin maintained. For this reason, any abrupt reversal of policy required a tremendous purge. He cited the bloody purges of the thirties in connection with the Moscow trials, making the point that Stalin's shift to a policy of collaboration with Nazi Germany required the ruthless elimination of all Soviet officials who might have balked at accepting the change. In the same way, Andreychin said, any attempt to break with the United States would call for a new purge, eliminating thousands of Russians from their present positions of influence.*

Andreychin's observations tended to confirm Harriman's own impressions on a number of points, including the crucial effect of the atomic bomb in creating a new siege mentality among the Soviet leaders (and the importance of inaugurating Russian-language broad-

---

* Harriman was to see Andreychin once again—at the Paris Peace Conference in the summer of 1946, where he reappeared as a member of the Bulgarian delegation staff. "I never did find out what contact, if any, he had made with our people in Sofia," Harriman recalled. "But we talked freely in Paris and he gave me some very good steers. My great regret was that he never wrote the story of his extraordinary life. It would have been a document of major importance."

casts to the Soviet Union).* On November 27 Harriman sent Byrnes his personal assessment:

One must bear in mind the fact that high Soviet governmental and party leaders have lived throughout their lives in [an] almost constant state of fear or tension, beginning with the days when they were conspirators in a revolutionary movement . . . They feared capitalistic encirclement and dissension within the ranks of the party, leading to two ruthless purges . . . The German invasion all but destroyed them. There must have been a feeling of tremendous relief when the tide of war turned. With victory came confidence in the power of the Red Army and in their control at home, giving them for the first time a sense of security, for themselves personally and for the revolution, such as they had never before had.

In September, 1941, it will be recalled, Stalin told me that he was under no illusions, the Russian people were fighting, as they always had, "for their homeland, not for us," meaning the Communist Party. He would never make such a statement today. The war has assisted in the consolidation of the revolution in Russia. They determined that the Red Army should be kept strong, and industry developed to support it, so that no power on earth could threaten the Soviet Union again. Political steps were taken to obtain defense in depth, disregarding the desires and interests of other peoples . . .

Then, suddenly, the atomic bomb appeared and they recognized it as an offset to the power of the Red Army. This must have revived their old feeling of insecurity. They could no longer be absolutely sure that they could obtain their objectives without interference . . . This attitude partially explains Molotov's aggressiveness in London . . . The Russian people have been aroused to feel that they must again face an antagonistic world. American imperialism is included as a threat to Russia.

It is in no sense intended that this message should suggest any course [of policy or action]; it is sent only as a partial explanation of the strange psychological effect of the atomic bomb on the Soviet leaders' behavior.

* On November 21 Harriman strongly urged William Benton, Assistant Secretary of State for Public Affairs, to establish a powerful American transmitter somewhere in Europe "which would cover Eastern Europe as well as Russia in native languages." Benton, in reply, welcomed the idea, praising Harriman's "constructive suggestions" about the programs and policies of what was to become the Voice of America.

In Moscow that first winter at peace, the Kremlin-watchers fell back increasingly on surmise and supposition to explain the apparent change in Kremlin attitudes toward the Western powers. George Kennan's sensitive antennae had registered a tremor in the power structure as far back as October, when the press had announced Stalin's departure from Moscow "for a rest." In a memorandum to Harriman, dated December 11, Kennan wrote: "I now feel fairly confident that my original impression was correct: that there has been some change in Stalin's status and that he is no longer the decisive factor in the evolving and promulgating of Soviet policy and action in foreign affairs." Harriman disagreed sharply. "I see no evidence to draw this conclusion," he wrote at the top of Kennan's memorandum. "He may let Molotov become Premier again or Zhukov, chief Marshal of the Red Army. But there is no evidence so far that Stalin will not still be the boss in all matters that interest him."*

In Washington at the same period, even the possessors of the bomb were gripped by spasms of insecurity. Ambassador Hurley, having tried and failed to reconcile the Chinese Nationalists with the Communists, resigned on November 26 with a trumpet blast against seven Foreign Service officers whom he accused of favoring "the Chinese Communist armed party and the imperialist bloc of nations whose policy it was to keep China divided against herself." He later named the offending officers, in hearings before the Senate Foreign Relations Committee, as George Atcheson, John Stewart Service, John Carter Vincent, John Paton Davies, Fulton Freeman, Arthur Ringwalt and John K. Emmerson. Hurley's salvo opened the melancholy chapter of the "Who lost China?" witch hunt in Washington. Harriman, who made no particular effort to conceal his low opinion of Hurley, responded with an unsolicited testimonial to the career service in general and to John Paton Davies in particular. He wrote to Byrnes in praise of Davies and a second officer who had served under Hurley in China before being transferred to his own staff. "I have found both men loyal to the policies of the Government and competent in carrying out the work that has been assigned to them," Harriman added. "Though I am not anxious to become involved in a public controversy, I am making this statement for the record and if you feel it would serve a useful purpose I am willing to have it used publicly either now or in the future."

* Stalin remained the dominant figure in the Soviet leadership until his death in 1953. In the latter years of his life, as Khrushchev told Harriman in 1959, he became more and more suspicious of his associates. "He trusted no one," Khrushchev said. "When we were called to his office, we never knew whether we were going to see our families again."

Byrnes, meanwhile, had been having second thoughts about the failure of the London Council of Foreign Ministers. On November 23 he instructed Harriman to propose a mid-December meeting with Molotov and Bevin in Moscow. This time France and China were to be excluded by harking back to the Yalta decision that the foreign ministers of Russia, Great Britain and the United States should hold regular consultations every three or four months. Molotov was delighted to accept. "It is a good thing," he said to Harriman on November 24, "that Mr. Byrnes recalled that the three of us could meet independently." Characteristically, however, Byrnes had failed to consult Bevin before approaching Molotov. He also had stipulated, in a message to Harriman, that the conference must end by December 24 so that he could be home in Washington for Christmas. Harriman cautioned against a fixed deadline, pointing out that winter weather conditions in Russia had a way of disrupting flight plans and that "much might be accomplished in an extra day or two" if the conference developed favorably. "Although I recognize there is some value to you in having a deadline," he wrote to Byrnes on November 27, "on balance I am fearful that Molotov may attempt to take advantage of it."

Byrnes was obstinate. When Bevin objected on several grounds— there simply was not time enough to prepare a successful meeting, for example, and the exclusion of France and China was bound to raise suspicion—Byrnes threatened to go to Moscow without him. Lord Halifax, the British ambassador in Washington, complained, "You've got us in a bit of a hole." But the Secretary of State prevailed. He and his party reached Moscow in a blizzard on December 14, making clear to Harriman at the outset that he was no more ready to consult or take advice than he had been in London. Having carried the main burden of the inconclusive talks with Stalin and Molotov regarding Soviet participation in the control of Japan, Harriman suggested that question should have first place on the foreign ministers' agenda, in view of the high priority Stalin had assigned to it during their talks. He also counseled Byrnes to discuss the matter privately with Molotov before raising it formally.

"My idea," Harriman recalled, "was to get full information on the exact position of the Soviets before we went any further and see whether there was any possibility of working out a compromise. Byrnes seemed to agree but when he met Molotov at noon on December 15, he did not mention the matter, Then, at five P.M., when the conference opened at the Spiridonovka Palace, Molotov seemed willing to discuss the order in which agenda items should be listed. But Byrnes again made no suggestion. Instead he presented papers on the Japanese question and the drafting of the Balkan peace treaties which took no account of my discussions with Stalin at Gagra and without showing them to me in advance. It was typical of the way Byrnes did his business.

"After that first meeting I asked him whether I should draft a telegram for the President, reporting on the discussions, or whether he preferred to draft it himself. He said that he was not going to send any telegrams. I argued that this was customary, but he remained adamant. 'The President has given me complete authority,' Byrnes said. 'I can't trust the White House to prevent leaks.' I thought it was preposterous for any Secretary of State to show such disregard for the President's position. Byrnes no doubt was always jealous of Truman. He had gone to the Chicago convention in 1944 expecting Truman to nominate him for the vice presidency, and although the nomination was thrust upon Truman, Byrnes still appeared to feel that he had been double-crossed."

The Moscow conference made slow progress in the beginning. But after a few days, both sides made face-saving concessions. Byrnes, at long last, agreed to establish an Allied council in Tokyo—including American, Soviet, Chinese and British Commonwealth representatives —to consult with MacArthur on occupation policy, although the Supreme Commander was not obliged to take the Council's advice. Molotov was content with the final text, which read: "He [MacArthur] will consult and advise with the Council *in advance of the issuance of orders* on matters of substance, *the exigencies of the situation permitting. His decisions upon these matters shall be controlling*" (authors' italics).

In the case of the Balkan states, the shoe was on the Russian foot. With the Red Army in total control, Molotov resisted all efforts by Bevin and Byrnes to broaden the existing governments or to allow truly free elections as the price of Western recognition. On the snowy night of December 23, Byrnes called on Stalin (with Harriman and Bohlen) to appeal against Molotov's stonewalling attitude. The Secretary of State told Stalin that he had held up publication of a critical report on conditions in Rumania and Bulgaria by Mark Ethridge, editor of the Louisville *Courier-Journal*, but that he would have to publish it unless a solution was found in Moscow.* If Byrnes published the Ethridge report, Stalin said, then he would ask the Soviet writer Ilya Ehrenburg, who was just as impartial, to publish his views.

---

* Ethridge had traveled to both countries at Byrnes's request. Although Communists were a minority in both countries, he found, they dominated the governments to a large extent through "front" organizations. Russian protestations of noninterference, Ethridge wrote, "are almost certainly insincere, for their constant and vigorous intrusion into the internal affairs of those countries is so obvious to an impartial observer that Soviet denial of its existence can only be regarded as the reflection of a party line dictated from above."

That would be most unfortunate, Byrnes responded, as the two reports would tend to separate rather than unite Americans and Russians. He urged Stalin to suggest some plan that would allow representatives of the leading political parties in Rumania and Bulgaria to take their places in government, as provided in the Yalta agreement, and thus qualify for American recognition. "Surely it would be possible to find persons who were both representative of these parties and at the same time friendly to the Soviet Union," Byrnes said.

Contending that the Soviet Union asked nothing more of its neighbors than that they should not be hostile, Stalin acknowledged that some non-Communists could meet this test. Although he hesitated to interfere in the affairs of other countries, Stalin said, "perhaps the Bulgarian Parliament could be advised to include some members of the loyal opposition in the new government . . ." In the case of Rumania, he added, "it might be possible to make some changes in the government there which would satisfy Mr. Byrnes and Mr. Bevin." For example, the Rumanians might perhaps be persuaded to make room in their government for one representative each from the National Peasant party and the Liberal party, so long as people like Iuliu Maniu, president of the National Peasant party, Dinu Bratianu, president of the National Liberal party, and Niculae Lupu, another Peasant leader, were excluded.

Neither Bohlen nor Harriman thought much of Stalin's concession, but Byrnes leaped at it. In a matter of minutes he and Stalin had agreed that a tripartite commission including Vishinsky, Harriman and a British representative should go to Bucharest and work out arrangements with the Rumanian government. As for Bulgaria, the Russians would take care of that situation on their own. The United States and Britain, in turn, would recognize the governments of Bulgaria and Rumania as soon as they were restructured. Stalin's token concessions, of course, did not alter the brute facts or in any way loosen his grip on Eastern Europe.

The Moscow meeting also dealt for the first time with plans for the control of atomic energy. Byrnes had brought with him as an adviser Dr. James B. Conant, the president of Harvard University, in the hope of starting an exchange of views with Soviet scientists on the nuclear future. "Conant was ready to talk, but nothing happened," Harriman recalled. "Fairly obviously, Stalin was not going to allow it. Any discussions would have to be conducted on a government-to-government basis." Although that hope was dashed, Molotov readily accepted Byrnes's hastily drafted proposal to establish an Atomic Energy Commission at the United Nations which would, by stages, prepare proposals to limit the use of atomic weapons, set up a system of safeguards and provide for the exchange of fundamental scientific information. The Byrnes proposal, based on a prior declaration by Truman, Attlee and Prime Minister Mackenzie King of Canada, left the American nuclear monopoly intact. For that reason, Harriman believed, Molotov showed no special interest in the subject, except to insist that the UN Commission should report to the Security Council instead of the General Assembly. The Russians apparently felt constrained to discount the importance of nuclear matters as long as the United States alone possessed the detailed knowledge and engineering experience to build atomic bombs.

Stalin himself had laid down the official line that only the weak could be frightened by the bomb. At a Kremlin banquet, however, when Molotov made a clumsy joke to the effect that Dr. Conant might have smuggled a piece of the bomb into the Soviet Union in his vest pocket, Stalin got to his feet. "This is too serious a matter to joke about," he said, in a show of anger. "I raise my glass to the American scientists and what they have accomplished. We must now work together to see that this great invention is used for peaceful ends."[2] Conant responded in the same hopeful vein. But as far as the Soviet public was concerned, the exchange never took place. Not a word was published in the Moscow newspapers.

Conant, still hopeful that Americans and Russians could share scientific information, had sent Byrnes a memorandum, dated Moscow, December 17, outlining the steps that might be taken. Upon the signing of a treaty that would embody a workable system of inspection and control, he wrote, the United States should let other nations have "full details of the electromagnetic method of separating Uranium 235." Six months later, "full details of the gaseous diffusion process" should be made known (if the control system was functioning satisfactorily) and, a year after that, the method for producing plutonium. In the final stage, the United States would "dismantle all its bombs and place the material in storage or in industrial power plants, if it has been agreed that no other nation will construct atomic bombs."

It was not until December 24 that Byrnes sent a telegram to the President reporting "complete agreement as to the peace conference and resumption of the work on peace treaties with Italy and enemy Balkan states." He added: "As a result of a long conference with Stalin yesterday afternoon, I now hope that we can make forward step towards settling the Rumania-Bulgaria problems. We also discussed the Chinese situation, Iran and atomic energy . . . The situation is encouraging and I hope that today we can reach final agreement on the questions outstanding and wind up our work tomorrow."

Harriman found the discussion of China particularly illuminating, although Byrnes made no further mention of it in his sketchy report, the only one he bothered to send back during eleven days in Moscow.

Both Stalin and Molotov had been constantly pressing Byrnes for the removal of 50,000 United States Marines from North China. Byrnes explained that they would be withdrawn as soon as General Marshall, who had just been sent to China as the President's special representative, could arrange a truce between the Nationalists and the Communists in order to permit the disarming and deportation of some 325,000 Japanese troops stranded in the north by the armistice. Stalin predicted that Chiang Kai-shek would lose his influence with the Chinese people if he depended on foreign troops to get rid of the Japanese. "All Chinese are boastful," he said, "and tend to exaggerate both the size of their own forces and those of their opponents." Where was Chiang's army of 1,500,000 men, anyway?

Byrnes responded that he wished he knew where Chiang's troops were, but according to his information, there were no more than 50,000 of them in the North China region. Scornfully Stalin remarked that 50,000 ought to be enough to disarm the defeated Japanese. He boasted that in Mukden twenty-five Soviet aviators had taken the surrender of two Japanese army corps. Stalin then inquired about the number of Communist troops in the Tientsin area. According to Mao Tse-tung, Byrnes replied, there were 600,000. Stalin scoffed at Mao's claim. "All Chinese," he said again, "are boasters."

Harriman left the Kremlin that evening less impressed by Stalin's continuing scorn for the Chinese Communists than by the manifest weakness of Chiang. It seemed to him at the time that the Generalissimo, by keeping the bulk of his troops in the south, was leaving a vacuum in Manchuria and the north to be filled at will by Mao's Communists with the cooperation of the Russians.

With the conclusion of the foreign ministers meeting on December 26, two days behind Byrnes's schedule, Harriman at last was free to wind up his affairs in Moscow, except for a trip to Bucharest with Vishinsky and Clark Kerr which would place the seal of Allied approval on the broadening of the Rumanian government.

Byrnes himself flew back to Washington without consulting or informing Truman of the outcome in Moscow. When the President received word that Byrnes had asked for air time on all radio networks so that he might report to the people on the results of the conference, the President was furious. He ordered the Secretary of State to join him immediately on board the presidential yacht *Williamsburg*, and there, according to Truman's memoirs, administered a memorable tongue-lashing.

HARRIMAN, MEANWHILE, HAD GONE TO BUCHAREST with Vishinsky and Clark Kerr on December 28, for consultations with King Michael and an assortment of Rumanian politicians. After only a few hours in

SPECIAL ENVOY

Bucharest, Harriman and Clark Kerr recognized that their leverage was severely limited. They found the Bucharest government at Vishinsky's beck and call. Petru Groza, whom Vishinsky had forced on the King as Premier in March 1945, impressed Harriman as "very genial on the surface but unscrupulous," a faithful follower of the Russian line, although not himself a Communist. The government in fact appeared to be directed by such hard-line Communists as Ana Pauker and Gheorghiu-Dej. Both Vishinsky and Groza pledged themselves to hold free elections as soon as possible, assuring the American and British ambassadors that freedom of speech, press, assembly and religion would be respected. In line with the Moscow agreements, they also agreed to take into the government Emil Hatieganu, to represent the National Peasant party, and Mihai Romniceanu of the National Liberals. Both came in, however, as ministers without portfolio who could safely be ignored.

Harriman found it difficult to believe that free elections would be allowed in Rumania, in spite of the formal commitments made by Vishinsky and Groza. A truly free vote, he felt, was bound to return an anti-Russian government; hence no election answering that description would be held. Vishinsky told Harriman, with every appearance of confidence, that Groza's National Democratic Front would win 70 percent of the vote; the Peasant party, 20 percent; and the National Liberals, 10 percent.*

"No doubt there will be fixed voting and all kinds of pressure brought to bear on the people," Harriman predicted in a talk with the officers and attachés of the American embassy after his return to Moscow. "Russia will exploit Rumania for the benefit of Russia," he added. "Whether the Rumanians have enough national feeling to stand up to the Russians . . . remains to be seen."[3] †

Harriman came away from Bucharest with real admiration for King Michael, who at grave personal risk had turned his countrymen against the Germans. Even the Russians showed a certain grudging respect for the young King's courage and his tremendous popular appeal, although his reign under a Communist regime was bound to be short and stormy. It was a mark of special favor that when Michael abdicated under duress in late 1947, he was allowed to take into exile at

---

* When the postwar election was held on November 19, 1946, Groza's coalition managed by fraud and intimidation to improve on Vishinsky's confident prediction. Groza claimed no less than 89 percent of the vote.

† In later years Harriman was pleased to acknowledge that the Rumanians had rediscovered their national feeling, visible chiefly in their independent foreign policy. "They have shown more vigor than I thought they possessed," he remarked, "although the present government of Nicolae Ceausescu is at least as dictatorial in its internal policies as any in Eastern Europe except Bulgaria."

least a few of the royal family's possessions, including a number of valuable paintings.

The Queen Mother also impressed Harriman as a woman of uncommon grace and courage. He recalled traveling to Sinaia with Vishinsky and Clark Kerr after the signing of the agreement for a luncheon with Michael and the Queen Mother at their castle in the Carpathian Mountains. "I borrowed a Ford car from General Schuyler for the drive to Sinaia," Harriman recalled. "He assigned an American sergeant to drive me up there, with little American flags fluttering from the front fender. Kathleen and I sat in the back seat. Eddie Page sat up front with the driver. We were cheered by the villagers wherever we passed. No thought of danger entered my head, or I would not have brought Kathleen along. It never occurred to me that we needed protection.

"As we entered the mountains, however, we passed Vishinsky's convoy. One of the Soviet cars had broken down. He had six cars altogether, two in front and three behind, all filled with Soviet security guards. The Russians at the time had nine hundred thousand troops in Rumania; we had only Schuyler's staff of perhaps a hundred. Yet we felt entirely comfortable with our uniformed sergeant at the wheel. Vishinsky evidently did not regard the natives as friendly."

While in Rumania, Harriman encountered Marshal F. I. Tolbukhin at an official reception and fell into a long conversation with him about the junction of the American and Russian armies at Linz, Austria, at the end of the war. Tolbukhin had met General George S. Patton on that memorable occasion, and as he relived the moment, spoke proudly of their respective military achievements. The Soviet marshal had carefully worked out in kilometers the distances that he and Patton had traversed. He had fought the Germans all the way from Stalingrad to Linz, commanding Soviet army groups in their westward sweep across Bulgaria, Yugoslavia, Hungary and Austria, while Patton, after the campaigns in North Africa and Sicily, had fought his way across Europe from the Normandy beaches through France and Germany into Austria.

"Tolbukhin said he had a photograph of himself with Patton, who had just been killed in an automobile accident," Harriman recalled. "He asked if I would deliver it to Mrs. Patton. I said that I would be glad to do so, that I was sure it would be a great comfort to her, and suggested that he ought to inscribe it. He promised to do this and send the photograph to me. Unfortunately, that was the last I heard of the matter, although Tolbukhin had spoken of Patton with such intensity of emotion that I felt he fully intended to send it. Perhaps the NKVD intervened. It was profoundly depressing to me that a man of Tolbukhin's importance should have been debarred, presumably for political reasons, from doing this simple, human thing."

At the end of his mission to Rumania, Harriman flew to London for a few days to report on the reorganization of the Bucharest regime. Byrnes was there with a large American delegation to attend the first session of the newborn United Nations General Assembly. Although the Secretary of State, after the chilly Moscow experience, showed Harriman more personal cordiality, other members of the delegation were plainly disgruntled. Both Senator Connally and Senator Vandenberg complained to Harriman that Byrnes was ignoring them. "We didn't know how lucky we were to have Stettinius until we got Byrnes," Vandenberg remarked.

Harriman recorded his London impressions in a memorandum:

> Had a long talk with Frank Walker [the former Postmaster General] in which he told me of President Truman's dissatisfaction at Byrnes' plowing ahead without consultation and his own wonder whether Byrnes would last. He said the Senators were dissatisfied with the inadequate information and treatment they had received from Byrnes. Incidentally, I got this same idea but in less detail from almost everyone I talked to. It seems that Byrnes is pursuing his policy of not consulting anybody and making up his own mind. The Delegation is in the same mood (this came from Foster Dulles) . . . They do give Byrnes credit for capacity, but do not like the atmosphere of lack of frankness and opportunism which he is creating. All unanimously feel that the distinction of American foreign policy . . . created by Roosevelt and Hull, and carried on by Stettinius, is now being lowered by Byrnes . . .
>
> Byrnes is letting the British slip away from us, not because of any disagreement on policy but purely by offending them through his unwillingness to consult and what Bevin considers his somewhat overbearing attitude. It must be remembered that Bevin as a labor leader has a certain sensitivity which comes from his background.
>
> I sent a box of *pâté de foie gras*, brought from Bucharest, to Bevin and received a message of thanks. He said that he and Mrs. Bevin wanted to know what it was. This incident shows . . . his complete lack of any false pride.
>
> I feel that Bevin is forthright, frank and courageous but not yet sufficiently sure of himself to carry through to a conclusion the things that he starts.[4]

The Labor government, Harriman recognized, could ill afford an independent foreign policy, in spite of Bevin's distaste for Byrnes and his high-handed methods. Having mortgaged her future to pay for the war, Britain was on the edge of bankruptcy. "England is so weak she must follow our leadership," Harriman said to his staff at the embassy after returning from London. "She will do anything that we insist [upon] and she won't go out on a limb alone."

As for the Russians, Harriman believed they did not feel strong enough to push their differences with the United States to the point of an open break. "I am not discouraged," he said at his valedictory staff meeting in Moscow. "But I think we have a long, slow scrape ahead. So much depends on how much effort the American people are willing to put forward." From what he had heard in London, a great many Americans had grown weary of world responsibility, wanting nothing more (as he put it) than to "go to the movies and drink Coke." But support for a more forceful foreign policy was growing at the same time. "The boys coming home [from the war] don't want it to happen again," he said. He found it "interesting and encouraging" that Byrnes was now being criticized across the United States for being too conciliatory.

On January 20 Harriman called on Molotov at the Commissariat of Foreign Affairs to say goodbye. He was going home by way of the Far East, the Ambassador said, and he would resign upon his return to the United States. Molotov appeared somewhat chagrined, saying that he deeply regretted the Ambassador's departure. Harriman explained that he had been away from home for five years. His wartime service was now at an end. Although he could not say what he would do in the future, he felt that he could not entirely divorce himself from Soviet-American relations. Molotov urged him not to "stand aloof from politics." The Ambassador, he said, "had done a great deal in the cause of Soviet-American relations." It would be a pity if he had nothing more to do with them as a private citizen.

Harriman told Molotov that Harry Hopkins was seriously ill and that it was unlikely he would ever again play a part in American politics. Molotov expressed regret over the news, remarking that Hopkins was a tenacious man of great internal strength and that the Soviet government always thought well of him.

On January 23 Harriman called on Stalin for the last time. He found "the Generalissimus" perfectly content with the role assigned to the Russians in the occupation of Japan. "Matters are proceeding well in Japan," Stalin said, "because the United States and the Soviet Union have found common ground." He volunteered the information that Chiang Ching-kuo, the son of Chiang Kai-shek, had been to Moscow in

Harriman's absence to press for Soviet mediation in the civil strife between the Nationalists and the Chinese Communists.

Stalin said he had assured the younger Chiang, whom he described as "capable and clever," that Moscow recognized the Nationalist government in Chungking as the legitimate government of China. But he had refused Chiang's request that he play the mediator, because he was "not sure" that the Communists would accept his views. The Soviet government, Stalin said, "had poor contacts with the Communists," having recalled its three representatives from Yenan. His own impression was "that the Communists would not agree with the position of the Soviet Government on China." If he were to attempt mediation and fail, Stalin added, then the Soviet government would be placed in "an embarrassing situation."

Harriman interjected that the United States also might find itself in a difficult situation if General Marshal, who was in China "trying to knock the Communist and Nationalist heads together," failed in his mission.

Stalin responded that he had told the younger Chiang, when he continued to press for Soviet mediation, that Moscow would "not take the initiative" with the Chinese Communists. If the Communists asked for his advice, he would give it willingly, Stalin added. In fact, he had said to Chiang Ching-kuo, he was prepared to advise the Communists to end the civil war and try to reach an agreement with Chiang's government. But they had not asked for his advice. Harriman inquired about the possibility as Stalin saw it of reconciling the warring factions in China. Stalin discounted the political differences between the Communists and the Nationalists. The main obstacle was personal mistrust. "Chiang Kai-shek does not trust Mao, and Mao does not trust Chiang," he said. The Chinese Communists, he insisted, had no wish to "Sovietize" the country. "There was no Soviet system in Yenan," he said, according to Page's memorandum of the conversation. "It would be stupid for the Communists to strive for Sovietization. The main difference lay in the fact that the Communists wished to introduce full democracy in China as soon as possible. Chiang Kai-shek desired to introduce a less complete form of democracy and was in no hurry to do so."

When Harriman turned the discussion toward Korea, Stalin grumbled that he was receiving "little good news" from that corner of the world. Although the Moscow conference had approved plans for a four-power trusteeship in December, he had been informed that American representatives in Korea now were backing away from that decision. They were saying that only the Russians favored a trusteeship for Korea, when, in fact, it was Roosevelt who had first proposed it.

"The Soviet Government does not need a trusteeship any more than the United States," Stalin said. "If both countries consider it desirable, the trusteeship can be abolished."

Harriman, who would be in Korea within a few days, said he hoped to see for himself what was going on there. The United States government, he added, would certainly fulfill the Moscow decision, pointing out that there had been less disagreement on Korea than on any other question discussed by the foreign ministers in December. He knew, the Ambassador said, that Byrnes looked on the Korean experiment as "a splendid chance to demonstrate how the United States and Soviet Governments could work together."

In response to a question from Harriman, Stalin said that he still opposed the retention of the Emperor, whether as an individual or an institution, in Japan. "The Japanese Emperor," he said, "is not needed by us or by the Japanese people." He was a pole of attraction for the militarists and it would be better for all concerned to get rid of him, Stalin added. All the democratic and liberal elements had been destroyed, he said, but if they should come to the surface again these men would want a President, not an Emperor, for their leader.

Before inviting Stalin to speak his mind on the future of Soviet-American relations, Harriman suggested that he might be taking too much of the Generalissimus' time. Not at all, Stalin replied. Harriman then asked whether Stalin shared the view expressed by some persons that the political and social concepts of America and Russia were in such sharp conflict that they could not be composed. Of course, the two countries had different social and political concepts, Stalin replied, "but these related only to the internal policies of the two countries." With respect to foreign affairs it seemed to him that Russians and Americans "could find common ground," as the war period and the months since the war had demonstrated. Stalin then posed a question in return. The American press had been writing, he said, that the Soviet government had failed to raise the question of postwar credits or a loan from the United States. He had the impression that if the Russians were to raise the question, the Americans "would meet them halfway." Was his impression correct?

Stalin's question confirmed Harriman's belief that as late as January 23, 1946, the Soviet government had not yet decided whether to press for a large American loan. It also helped to explain why Molotov had failed to raise the matter with Byrnes in Moscow a few weeks earlier. The Soviet leadership evidently had not made up its mind.

Responding to Stalin's question, Harriman said that he felt certain the United States would be prepared to discuss "past and future economic collaboration," including the question of a loan. Harriman explained that the British had been the first of the Allies to open negotiations for a postwar loan, and most of the Washington officials concerned had been concentrating on the British settlement.

There had been "quite a bit of criticism" of the British settlement in Congress, Harriman added, and Byrnes was anxious to see it approved before taking up a Soviet loan request. That was why Byrnes had waited for Molotov to raise the matter when he was in Moscow but the Soviet Foreign Minister had not mentioned it. As in the case of the British, Harriman said, a settlement of the Lend-Lease account would have to be part of the negotiation. Would that procedure be acceptable to the Soviet government? Stalin replied that it would. The Ambassador then inquired whether, in fact, the Soviet government wished to negotiate an American loan.

Stalin replied that he was prepared to enter into negotiations but not if the United States attached the kind of "offensive" conditions talked about by a group of congressmen which had visited Moscow in September. (The congressional group, headed by Representative William M. Colmer of Mississippi, had published a report calling on the Soviet government to withdraw its occupation forces from Eastern Europe, make "full and frank disclosure" of its economic statistics, end press censorship and stop siphoning relief supplies from neighboring countries in order to qualify for American loans.)*

Harriman said that he had not read the congressmen's report and could not, therefore, discuss it. He felt satisfied, however, that he would find in Washington a desire to seek common ground with the Soviet Union, in spite of the fact that "American public opinion was puzzled by the difficulties the United States Government had faced in its relations with the Soviet Union and although there was some increase in fear that these difficulties might be irreconcilable." This state of mind, he added, necessarily would have "a definite bearing on what the present Administration could do with regard to a loan and its amount and conditions."

Stalin agreed that a settlement of economic questions would "serve to dispel many of the doubts" which existed between Russians and Americans. He said again that he was ready to enter into negotiations. Harriman promised to take up the matter with Truman on his return to Washington.

Addressing a personal word to the Ambassador as they shook hands on parting, Stalin said he hoped that Harriman would continue to take an interest in Soviet-American affairs. He had been a friend of

---

* Kennan, who escorted the congressmen to the Kremlin on September 14, had a private word with Stalin at the close of the interview. "Our troops are going to get out of those Eastern European countries and things will be alright," Stalin said. "Tell your fellows not to worry about those countries."

many years and had shown in the early days, when help was needed, that he could be counted upon. Stalin had not forgotten the manganese concession or Harriman's personal role in the inauguration of Lend-Lease assistance to Russia. He asked the Ambassador to extend his best wishes to President Truman and to the ailing Hopkins, once again speaking of him with great warmth.

Harriman left the Kremlin that January evening with his mind still in conflict about the enigmatic character of Josef Stalin. They had talked together dozens of times since the desperate autumn of 1941, when the Germans were beating at the gates of Moscow. Stalin had been bitterly abusive time and again, as when he accused the Western allies of bad faith over the lack of a Second Front or the cancellation of the Arctic convoys. Toward the Poles he had been downright brutal. Yet in his personal relations with Harriman, Stalin was never less than courteous and at times totally disarming.

There was his startling admission, after more than seven weeks of denouncing the Warsaw uprising and refusing any help, that the Poles, after all, had risen up against the Germans with good reason. He also could hail the Normandy landing as perhaps the greatest feat of arms ever accomplished, this after denouncing the British and the Americans throughout 1942 and 1943 for not invading Western Europe.

Other accounts suggest that Stalin lost his nerve at the time of Hitler's attack in June 1941. Yet he pulled himself and the country together to become, in Harriman's judgment, an extraordinarily effective war leader, knowledgeable and decisive, who directed the battle for Russia with remarkable attention to detail in nightly conferences by telephone with his field commanders. More than once in his conversations with Harriman, Stalin had compared the fighting effectiveness of his Red Army with the disintegration of the Russian front in World War I under the unfortunate Czar Nicholas. The people of Russia had always fought bravely for "the Motherland," Stalin said, "but we gave them guns while the Czar gave them only axe staves." Following the disaster of the German attack, he also had directed the relocation and reconstruction of Russia's essential industries behind the Urals and had demonstrated, in his talks with Harriman, an unexpected sensitivity to civilian morale among the many nationalities that made up the Soviet Union.

But there was always the darkly suspicious side of Stalin's character, which appeared to turn him into another man, as at the time of the Berne incident. Driven by fear that the Western Allies might make a separate peace with Hitler, leaving Russia to face the onslaught alone, he could hurl the grossest of false accusations at Roosevelt.

Harriman, who had seen both sides of Stalin, reflected: "It is hard for me to reconcile the courtesy and consideration that he showed me personally with the ghastly cruelty of his wholesale liquidations. Others, who did not know him personally, see only the tyrant in Stalin. I saw the other side as well—his high intelligence, that fantastic grasp of detail, his shrewdness and the surprising human sensitivity that he was capable of showing, at least in the war years. I found him better informed than Roosevelt, more realistic than Churchill, in some ways the most effective of the war leaders. At the same time he was, of course, a murderous tyrant. I must confess that for me Stalin remains the most inscrutable and contradictory character I have known—and leave the final judgment to history."

CHAPTER XXII

"The Center of Power
Is in Washington"

H IS MISSION TO MOSCOW COMPLETED, Harriman started for home
in the third week of January by way of the Far East. Kathleen,
Bob Meiklejohn, Eddie Page and Brigadier General William L. Ritchie
flew with him to New Delhi, Chungking, Shanghai, Tokyo and Seoul,
in an Air Force plane provided by Byrnes, before setting out across the
Pacific. "Among the matters unsettled at the end of the Moscow conference," Harriman recalled, "was the question of whether we ought
to let the Soviet Union send occupation troops to Japan. Some in the
War Department still thought it might be a good idea—because it
would allow us to bring home more GIs. This sort of thinking terrified
me. I wanted to make certain that General MacArthur understood
how the Russians were treating us in Europe, to be sure that he was
not taken in. I also was very keen to see General Marshall in Chungking and to have a look at Korea, where we were still committed to
set up a four-power trusteeship with the Russians, the Chinese and
the British."

Field Marshal Wavell, now the Viceroy of India, welcomed
Harriman to New Delhi as an old friend, recalling their first meeting in
Cairo almost five years earlier, when Rommel had routed the British
forces in the Western Desert and Hitler was about to launch his invasion of Russia. Harriman then flew on to China over "the hump"
route, which he had recommended to Roosevelt in 1942. It was a
dramatic flight even in peacetime. Climbing steadily, the plane traced
the silvery ribbon of the Ganges River, then through Assam up the
valley of the Brahmaputra, across upper Burma and over the spec-

tacular gorges of Yunnan. The weather turned foul toward the end of the long flight, but the pilot set his plane down safely in the rocky riverbed that served as the airport of China's wartime capital.

Harriman found both General Marshall and Generalissimo Chiang Kai-shek eager to hear his views on postwar Soviet policy. They listened closely in a late-afternoon meeting, followed by dinner, at Chiang's country residence outside Chungking on January 28, as Harriman described his recent talks with Stalin: how the Soviet dictator had discounted the ideological differences between Chiang's Nationalists and Mao's Communists and predicted success for Marshall's efforts to unify the two Chinas. Yet the mediation effort was not going well. And there was deep trouble in Manchuria, where in spite of Stalin's assurance to T. V. Soong that "we will not be greedy," the Red Army was claiming the right to seize much of the industrial equipment installed by the Japanese as war booty. At Chiang's request, Harriman explained that in his judgment Soviet policy had become increasingly unilateral in the past six months. After the Allied disagreements over the occupation arrangements for Japan, the Russians had shown increasing reluctance to relax their hold on Manchuria and nothing had come of Stalin's promise to proclaim the Open Door policy there.

Chiang observed that his son, Chiang Ching-kuo, had raised the matter during his visit to Moscow in 1945 and that Stalin "after waiting for two minutes, answered that he thought the Open Door policy was as dangerous to a nation as foreign military invasion." Chiang's son, stressing the Chinese government's belief in the Open Door, had finally wrung from Stalin a reluctant promise to support it. But Marshal Rodion K. Malinovsky, commander in chief of Soviet forces in the Far East, now was threatening to carry off whole industrial plants from Manchuria. After a second long talk with Chiang, Harriman reported to Washington on January 30:

> Malinovsky has indicated that the Russians were willing to leave this equipment in Manchuria providing they receive shares of stock in the enterprises. He demands a 51% interest in heavy industries and a 49% interest in light industries. The Generalissimo estimates that the specific industries involved represent about 70% of Manchurian industry previously under control of the Japanese.

Chiang told Harriman that under no circumstances would he let the Russians have 51 percent of the stock in any enterprise; that would violate the Chinese law forbidding foreign control of any industry. But he appeared willing to offer the Soviet Union "a substantial interest" in many of the Manchurian industries rather than risk their outright removal to Russia, which would destroy the economic life of the region. In a cable to Truman and Byrnes, Harriman warned:

It seems to me that this is a case of vandalism and theft. The industrial equipment is of great value in place [but] has relatively small value if removed. Also, Stalin made it clear to President Roosevelt at Yalta that his demands for entry into the war were fully met by the agreement then reached. This is another case of the Russians attempting to obtain more at a later date.

If we now acquiesce in the Russian demands for the ceding by China of an interest in these important industrial enterprises in return for their abandonment of their demands for war booty, Russia will dominate Manchurian industry and economy, which will seriously affect American commercial interests and the whole policy of the Open Door. You will recall that in my conversation with Stalin in August, he accepted the Open Door Policy and agreed to make a public announcement to that effect. However, this has never been done.

General Marshall has advised the Generalissimo to delay his negotiations on the above matters until the agreement with the [Chinese] Communists is concluded. The Generalissimo has accepted the advice.

After dinner on January 29, when the other guests had left, Chiang confided his long-term doubts to Harriman and Marshall. He asked the Ambassador to tell President Truman how he felt:

That he was prepared to work hard for unification, but he wanted the President to know that he did not believe that even if an agreement were concluded the Communists would live up to it. It was the Soviet Government's intention to keep China split. He had had many years of experience. The Russian policy had consistently been to keep the conflict going, in the hope of expanding Communist and Soviet influence. He also wanted the President to realize that General Marshall must stay after the agreement had been concluded or else there was utterly no hope of the agreement working out. He thought there was a chance of success if General Marshall remained.

Marshall remarked that Chiang was being oversuspicious. Harriman said that he believed Stalin wanted an agreement and "would tell the Communists to make it work," but that if Chiang did not live up to the agreement and failed to make progress in liberalizing China, the

Communists were bound to gain strength and seize their opportunity.

Harriman asked Chiang that evening why he did not get rid of the corrupt warlords and bureaucrats in his entourage. These men were doing great harm to China's reputation, he said, frankly urging the Generalissimo to liberalize his regime by bringing in representatives of the Democratic League and prominent intellectuals. Chiang replied that he would be glad to break with the warlords if the United States stopped pressing him to make peace with the Communists. But if he was required to bring the Communists into the government, Chiang added, he would need strong political support; and his main support came from precisely the two groups Harriman wanted him to drop, the warlords and the bureaucrats.

"I began to realize how very weak Chiang was in political terms," Harriman recalled. "Having also discussed the outlook with John Davies in Moscow, I could not see Chiang destroying the Communist forces in battle or regaining control of Manchuria. The best we could hope for, I thought, was a divided China with the Communists holding the northern part of the country and Chiang controlling the south. I assumed that Chiang would survive and I suppose I underestimated the Communists. Ironically, it was Stalin himself who helped persuade me that they were too weak to take over the whole of China."

T. V. Soong met Harriman in Shanghai on January 31, his last day in China. On condition that Harriman keep the information secret, Soong disclosed how astonishingly frank Stalin had been with Chiang Ching-kuo about his ambitions in Eastern Europe and the Far East:

> Stalin told the Generalissimo's son that it was his intention to strengthen himself everywhere that he could in the domination of his adjacent areas and to attain as many strategic positions as was possible at this time. In this he referred to Eastern Europe and other areas.
>
> Discussing the strategic situation in the Far East, Stalin said that it was the Soviet Government's intention to industrialize Siberia during the next fifty years. During that period he considered there was no chance that the United States would want war and this would give him time to strengthen his weak position in the East. He said that China and the Soviet Union must work together and that the production of Manchurian industry was essential to the carrying out of the industrialization of Siberia, which could not be accomplished otherwise.

Soong then mentioned one of his own conversations with Stalin in Moscow which had greatly disturbed him. Stalin had said he wanted to be China's friend. When Soong replied that it was China's policy to be friendly with both the Soviet Union and the United States, Stalin replied, "You are either with us, or against us." China, in short, would have to choose between Moscow and Washington. Stalin's statement confirmed Soong in his belief that the Russians were determined to dominate postwar China.

In spite of his personal misgivings about the Marshall mission, Harriman told Soong it was absolutely essential that the National Government "make a deal for the unification of China" with the Communists. "Whether it is right or wrong," Harriman added, "the American people would not support a civil war and the Communist movement . . . could be combatted only by strengthening the main body of China economically through a liberal and aggressive economic policy to improve the living conditions of the Chinese people."

Soong argued the point, but finally acknowledged that Chiang "did not appreciate the importance of developing an aggressive, liberal economic policy." He also agreed with Harriman that Chiang seemed blind to any alternative but the military defeat of the Communists. Fearful that Chiang was being less than sincere with General Marshall, Harriman remarked that all too often "the Generalissimo appeared to agree" with Marshall "and then did not fully support the agreement." Soong did not quarrel with Harriman's estimate. Chiang, he said, had "an Oriental mind" and did not fully understand how definitely such agreements were interpreted in the West.

Nothing that Harriman had seen or heard in China altered the conviction he had brought with him from Moscow: that it was a mistake for the United States to assume the mediator's role in China. "I still think it would have been wiser to take Stalin at his word," Harriman recalled. "He had agreed to support Chiang. Indeed, he talked of the Generalissimo time and again as the only possible leader of China. We should have taken the same position, left the political negotiations to the Chinese, and invested our energies in a major effort to make of Chiang a more appealing, more effective leader. When Harry Hopkins and I saw Stalin in June 1945, he told us—and the record bears out my recollection—that Chiang was the only Chinese leader capable of unifying the country. He also told us that China would need a lot of economic help and that it could only come from the United States. So he was perfectly prepared to see us play a more assertive role than we did. I doubt that Stalin was aware—any more than I—of the degree to which Chiang's influence in the country had deteriorated during the war and the influence of the Communists had grown."

FLYING ON to Tokyo, Harriman had a series of talks with General MacArthur, interrupted by a brief visit to Korea, where he conferred twice with the American commander, Lieutenant General John R. Hodge. MacArthur's appraisal of the postwar outlook for relations with the Soviet Union impressed Harriman as well informed. "I did not find myself in disagreement with anything he said," Harriman noted in a February 1 memorandum of their first conversation. "Among the things on which he commented was the Russian maintenance of a large military establishment, their aggressive policies in connection with their neighboring countries and the extremely skillful, dangerous penetration of the Communist [parties] in all countries, through their propaganda and political programs."

For MacArthur's benefit, Harriman then outlined the development of Soviet policy in the Far East. Although Stalin had committed himself to support a four-power trusteeship for Korea in order to prepare the country for self-government, Harriman said, it was his opinion that the Russians now were determined to establish "political domination," as they had in Eastern Europe, in order "to expand their narrow strategic position in the Far East."

Citing the Soviet demands for war booty in Manchuria, Harriman added that he feared the Russians would make similar demands on Korea. "Since Japanese industrial properties comprise most of the industry of Korea," he said, "the Russians would, if we stood by, be able to obtain industrial domination of Korea. It was obvious they wished Korean industry to support the development of Siberia, as well as thus attain for the Soviet Government a strong strategic position in the Far East from which they could penetrate into China proper. I explained that all this was at complete variance with the Yalta agreement, which included the recognition of Chinese sovereignty in Manchuria . . . the Russians had been paid in full for their agreement to enter the war against Japan" but they were now trying to raise the price.

When Harriman read to MacArthur the telegrams he had sent to Byrnes from Chungking, recommending a firm stand against the Soviet booty demands in Manchuria, MacArthur observed, "I would not change a word."

During the visit to Seoul, Harriman cautioned General Hodge against trying to form a Korean government in the south that would claim authority over the country as a whole. It was important to leave the door open for eventual unification. Hodge replied that his plan was to set up a Korean Governing Council limited to representatives of "democratic groups" in South Korea. The main obstacle to an independent South Korea, the general added, was its dependence on the Communist-ruled north for fertilizers, coke, bituminous coal and electricity. The south was poor in resources and had little to offer in exchange for the materials it needed. The north was short of food, however, because the Russian troops in occupation were living off the land.

General Hodge at this point asked Harriman how he would advise dealing with the Russians in Korea. He and his staff, the general said, "were somewhat inhibited by a fear of breaking things up completely if they got too tough with the Russians." According to the memorandum of that February 3 conversation, Harriman replied:

> Little ground would be gained by being considerate or attempting to establish good will by generous gestures. At the same time, the Soviets are aware of the fact that they are backward and they are very sensitive. We must, therefore, always indicate a willingness to be friendly and fair, but lay it on the line when we have to . . .
>
> When it comes to setting up a Provisional Government, [Harriman] thought there would have to be some joint agreement between Russia and the United States as to what our attitude toward Korea was going to be, and a general agreement that we want her independence. There must be a settlement of occupation costs and at that time the question of who is to get Japanese properties will come up. His contention was that all Japanese property, except arms equipment, was available for reparations, to be disposed of by the allies as a whole to the countries which suffered from Japanese aggression. He would think the Koreans would be entitled to those industrial properties . . . Soviet unilateral action in taking reparations should not be condoned. If they cannot be prevented from taking properties by force, he thought the United States should let them know that it was opposed . . . and publicly state its views.

Even though he was about to leave government service, Harriman's sense of responsibility for the future of Korea led him to recommend that officers experienced in dealing with the Russians should be assigned to Seoul. The first of these, Charles Thayer, was transferred from Bucharest to Seoul, as a political adviser to General Hodge, at Harriman's suggestion. He also strongly urged Byrnes to insist that General Deane be assigned to Korea as the commanding general. Byrnes in fact later recommended Deane's appointment. But the War Department, which was reserving the important postwar commands for officers who had made their reputations in combat, turned him down because he had been a staff officer. "I thought it was a tragic mistake," Harriman recalled. "Hodge was a very decent man but Deane had more direct experience of dealing with the Russians and more political understanding, I felt, than any other senior officer. I believe we would have done much better in Korea if an officer of Deane's experience and quality had been sent to Seoul. But the Army decided otherwise. Offered the choice of retiring as a major general or being demoted to a brigadier general, he retired and went to California, where he started a new career in the wine business. The country lost the services of a wise and uniquely qualified officer."

On his return to Tokyo, Harriman found MacArthur deeply troubled over the conviction and pending execution of Lieutenant General Tomoyuki Yamashita for war crimes against the Allies. The Supreme Court had just upheld the death sentence, on appeal from a court martial, and MacArthur showed "considerable emotion" as he read to Harriman his reluctant order to carry out the execution. According to Harriman's notes:

> General MacArthur explained that this had been a difficult decision for him to make as he . . . had accepted the unconditional surrender of General Yamashita . . . He then went on to discuss the current war crimes trial of [Lieutenant General Masaharu] Homma. Here the situation was different in that Homma had defeated his [MacArthur's] forces [in the Philippines].

MacArthur explained that after President Roosevelt had ordered him to Australia in 1942, leaving Major General Jonathan M. Wainwright in command at Corregidor, Homma had violated the rules of war by refusing to accept the surrender of the fortress unless Wainwright at the same time surrendered all the American forces in the Philippines, including the troops on Mindanao who were not under his command. MacArthur found this action by Homma indefensible. Struggling to contain his emotions, he got up "on the pretense of getting a glass of water," Harriman noted, but in fact to conceal the tears that were running down his face.

Although Harriman was "tremendously interested" in MacArthur's talk about the doomed campaign in the Philippines, he turned the conversation at the first opportunity to more immediate matters, chiefly the role of the Russians in the occupation of Japan. He mentioned Stalin's complaints that Lieutenant General K. Derevenko, who had signed the Japanese surrender instrument for the Soviet Union, was being ignored and treated "as a piece of furniture" in Tokyo. MacArthur "took violent exception to Stalin's accusations." He had talked repeatedly with Derevenko, MacArthur insisted, but the Russian "had shown no understanding of the problems and had been unwilling to express his views on any subject." Harriman explained to MacArthur that Soviet generals were not permitted to express personal opinions. They had to wait for specific instructions from Moscow.

> I suggested to General MacArthur [Harriman noted] that
> he keep General Derevenko informed, as he had in the past,
> but that he should not expect Derevenko to take any responsi-
> bility. I therefore thought General MacArthur would be wise
> if he did not hold up any action beyond a reasonable length of
> time for Derevenko to receive word from Moscow. I pointed
> out that if I had been personally better informed of the treat-
> ment he had accorded General Derevenko, when Stalin made
> his accusations I would have had a splendid opportunity to
> contradict him at the time. Undoubtedly General Derevenko
> . . . had to clear his own record and had perhaps blamed
> MacArthur for many things that were not in accordance with
> the facts . . .

As they were saying goodbye, MacArthur asked Harriman what
he was going to do when he returned home. Harriman replied that
he would return to private life. MacArthur suggested that Harriman ought to take a job under his command, mentioning the post of
High Commissioner for Korea. Harriman thanked the Supreme Commander, saying he would be glad to work for him in any capacity but
that he wanted to stay in the United States. "If I get too discouraged
and hungry," he added, "I may take you up on the proposition."

With that the two parted, not to meet again until 1950, after the
Korean War broke out. Although Harriman played a part in President
Truman's subsequent decision to relieve MacArthur of his command,
the general apparently bore him no grudge. When they met for the
last time in New York on May 6, 1963, at a dinner given by Henry
Luce for the men and women who had been portrayed on the cover
of *Time* over its first forty years of publication, MacArthur greeted
Harriman warmly. "You were the first one to warn me to be careful
of the Russians," he said. "It helped me a lot. I have always been grateful to you."

ON THE WAY HOME from Japan (by way of Okinawa, Guam and
Hawaii), Harriman was dismayed to find that the elaborate supply and
repair system the United States had strung across the Pacific had been
largely destroyed by the so-called point system, under which servicemen were demobilized in accordance with their length of service.
"This was no orderly demobilization and reduction of our military
forces," he recalled. "It was a case of destroying in just a few months

what it had taken years to build. Our plane had flown many thousands of miles and would ordinarily have been grounded for repairs. But we found there was no place in the whole Pacific area, short of Hawaii, with a full complement of mechanics to do the job. It was an easy way to satisfy the people at home, who wanted their boys back. We got through to Hawaii all right. But I felt our military effectiveness in the Pacific had been destroyed prematurely by the blind workings of the point system."

As soon as he reached Washington in the second week of February, Harriman reported to Truman, Byrnes and the State-War-Navy Coordinating Committee (SWNCC) on his farewell talks with Stalin and Molotov. He was prepared to urge a prompt resumption of serious negotiations with the Russians for a postwar credit but discovered that Byrnes had anticipated him by a day or two. The talks were to drag on for many months without a conclusion.

A few days after Harriman's return to Washington, President Truman accepted his resignation "with great reluctance." In a personal letter dated February 14, the President wrote:

> During the war you were called upon to perform many missions of great importance and on every occasion you discharged your duty in a manner that contributed to our victory and reflected credit upon your Government.
>
> In accepting your resignation I want you to know that I am satisfied all thoughtful Americans will share my feeling of gratitude to you for the services you have rendered your country.

The following day, at a State Department news conference, Byrnes pinned the Medal of Merit on Harriman's lapel, praising his "magnificent service" to the country. Speaking to the reporters afterward, Harriman reflected on his long absence. "I primarily want to come back to my own country," he said. "This is where I belong and where I want to live my life. Five years is a long time and I want to get to know this country again."

A reporter asked Harriman for his assessment of Stalin's February 9 speech in Moscow, in which he had appeared to stress the incompatibility of Communism and capitalism. His plain implication that future wars were inevitable until the world economic system was reformed had alarmed several high officials. Others, less hostile to the Soviet Union, saw in the Stalin speech an appeal to the war-weary population of Russia to rally behind the new five-year plan.

Harriman had not had time to study the speech carefully, he said, but it was important to remember that public statements by high Soviet officials "are directed primarily to their own people." In response to a follow-up question, Harriman expanded his view. "The Russian people are tired," he said. "They have made great sacrifices during this war. They are now asked to enthusiastically support another five-year plan and that plan will mean hard work. It will mean building up the equipment of the country, which means a relative minimum of consumer goods; therefore I would assume it was necessary to explain to them what the objectives were, and ask them to support [the] program enthusiastically for the future benefit of the country."

Why, then, another reporter asked, had Stalin failed to acknowledge the wartime help that Russia had received from the United States and Britain? Harriman replied the Russians had been suspicious of foreigners for generations past and were all too aware of their country's backwardness. They suffered from a national "inferiority complex." Americans generally were under no such handicap; thus General Marshall could feel free to praise the Red Army for its great contribution to the Allied victory. If the Russian people, on the other hand, were told that "they could not have won without American help, it would give them a sinking feeling."

Washington was not of one mind on the meaning and portent of recent Soviet moves. The Red Army had marched into Manchuria and showed no sign of leaving. The Russians also remained in occupation of Iran's Azerbaijan province, disregarding their wartime undertaking to withdraw their forces six months after the termination of hostilities. They had used their veto in the United Nations Security Council for the first time on a trifling matter involving the presence of British and French forces in Lebanon, not a question that was vital to Soviet national security. On the day following Harriman's Washington press conference—February 16, 1946—the Canadian government announced the arrest of twenty-two individuals, charged with trying to steal information on the atomic bomb for the Soviet Union. The Canadian spy case, which had been broken by the defection of a Russian embassy clerk, alarmed a good many Americans in high places. The Azerbaijan dispute, meanwhile, had blown up into the first full-scale crisis of the newborn United Nations. George Kennan, who had stayed on in Moscow after Harriman's departure, received a cable from the State Department asking for an explanation of recent Soviet behavior. He responded with an 8,000-word dispatch, dated February 22, which came to be known thereafter as the Long Telegram.

For the Russians, he wrote, the world was divided into two irreconcilable blocs, between which there was no possibility of peaceful coexistence. Their postwar policy would be directed toward dividing and weakening the capitalist nations, while at the same time strengthening their own Socialist camp. Kennan stressed that the motivation for this policy lay in the need of the Kremlin to justify its harsh rule. "[Marxism] is the fig leaf of their moral and intellectual respectability," he wrote. "Without it they would stand before history, at best, as only the last of that long succession of cruel and wasteful Russian rulers who have relentlessly forced their country on to ever new heights of military power in order to guarantee internal security for their initially weak regime."[1]

Harriman found himself in substantial agreement with Kennan's analysis. On February 26 he sent a copy of the Long Telegram to his old friend James Forrestal, remarking that in view of Forrestal's "interest in the philosophy of the present Soviet leaders," Kennan's dispatch was "well worth reading." To Kennan in Moscow, Harriman sent a brief personal message: "Congratulations on your long analytical message of February 22d."

Forrestal considered the Kennan telegram so important that he had it mimeographed and distributed to all members of the Truman Cabinet in any way concerned with foreign and military affairs. In a matter of days, accordingly, the official Washington attitude hardened perceptibly. Harriman felt that Forrestal's intervention was decisive. Kennan believed that had the Long Telegram been sent several months earlier, it would have gone into the State Department files, largely unnoticed.[2] The puzzling behavior of the Russians in Iran, Manchuria and the United Nations—reinforced by Forrestal's enthusiastic backing—made the difference.

Byrnes signaled the new policy in a speech on February 28 before the Overseas Press Club in New York. The United States, he said, "will not and we cannot stand aloof if force or the threat of force is used contrary to the purposes and principles of the [United Nations] charter." No nation, he said, had the right to station troops on the territory of another state without its consent. No nation had the right to seize enemy property before reparations agreements had been concluded. "If we are to be a great power," Byrnes concluded, "we must act as a great power, not only to ensure our own security but in order to preserve the peace of the world."

At this crucial moment Winston Churchill (who had been vacationing in Florida since January) traveled to Fulton, Missouri, for a speech on March 5 in which he spoke of an "iron curtain" descending across Europe from Stettin in the Baltic to Trieste in the Adriatic. Harriman, who saw the former Prime Minister in Washington a few days afterward, found him "very pleased with the reaction to his Fulton speech and anxious to get my view as to whether it had been beneficial or otherwise." Churchill was even more outspoken in this private talk of an hour and a quarter than he had been in Missouri. According to Harriman's notes:

He was very gloomy about coming to any accommodation with Russia unless and until it became clear to the Russians that they would be met with force if they continued their expansion. He agreed with my analysis that we are dealing not only with Russia as a national entity but with . . . the additional missionary force of a religion. He mentioned the fact that in his own immediate entourage he had had two men—I inferred they were scientists—to whom they had given terms of life imprisonment because they had taken blueprints and other secret documents and delivered them in person to the Russians in London. He said these men had no feeling that they were bound by patriotism or duty to their country but felt that they were acting according to the dictates of a much higher moral code . . .

Referring to the Russians, he said they had no understanding of such words as "honesty," "honor," "trust" and "truth" —in fact that they regarded these as negative virtues. They will, he said, try every door in the house, enter all the rooms which are not locked, and when they come to one that is barred, if they are unsuccessful in breaking through it they will withdraw and invite you to dine genially that same evening.

Toward the end of their long talk, Harriman asked Churchill about certain of his spur-of-the-moment speeches during the war. He used to wonder and worry, Harriman confessed, whether the Prime Minister would find a way to complete his sentence when he launched into a long, involved statement without a text. Churchill's response was that he had learned early in his career "not to worry about where the verb came." He had once put much the same question to Arthur Balfour, Foreign Secretary in the Lloyd George coalition cabinet of 1919, Churchill recalled. "Balfour's reply was, 'After covering what I want to say, when I come to the first sentence that has a grammatical ending I sit down.' "

Harriman had just been called back to Washington to see Byrnes, who offered him the embassy in London. It would be a fine way to end his career in government, Byrnes said. Harriman refused. He did not much care for Byrnes. He had been separated from his family for five years during the war and his real career was in business, not diplomacy.

Byrnes told Harriman he must see the President because it was Truman who wanted him back in London. In a taxi on the way over to the White House, Harriman marshaled his thoughts. He knew exactly what he wanted to say in declining the appointment. But Truman gave him no opportunity. "I want you to go to England," the President said. "There is a very dangerous situation developing in Iran. The Russians are refusing to take their troops out—as they agreed to do in their treaty with the British—and this may lead to war. I must have a man in London who knows the British, a man I can trust."

Harriman's firm resolve evaporated. "When do you want me to go?" he asked. "Just as soon as you can get there," the President replied.

"So I got up and started out of the room," Harriman recalled. "Then I suddenly remembered what I had planned to say. 'Mr. President,' I said. 'I hope you realize that I'm not looking on this as a regular appointment. I don't want to go to London for a full term. This, you say, is an emergency. As soon as the emergency is over, I'd like to come home.' He said, 'All right, I'll remember that.' And that was the end of it."

As Ambassador to the Court of St. James's, Harriman spent less than six months in London. By the time of his arrival in April the Russians had agreed to withdraw their troops from Azerbaijan, and the Iranian crisis disappeared from the front pages of the newspapers. Harriman's relations with the Labor government were warm and friendly. The Ambassador had learned to know Attlee, Bevin and other leaders of the Labor party when they served in Churchill's coalition cabinet during the war. Like a good many others, he underestimated Attlee in the beginning. "I thought of him as a compromise between the trade-union wing of the party and the intellectuals," Harriman recalled. "He gave the impression of being anything but forceful, a retiring man who did not throw his weight around. But as I learned to know him better I realized that he was much more than that. He was a real leader in his own right, a man consistently underrated. In his own quiet way, Attlee had the ability to bring the quarrelsome elements in his party together."

Harriman's good relations with British Labor soon brought him the bitterest kind of reproaches from Lord Beaverbrook, who tended to confuse his American friend's personal loyalty to Churchill with loyalty to the Conservative party, now in opposition. Harriman had been invited to address the annual miners' gala in Durham; so also had Prime Minister Attlee. They spoke from separate platforms at separate times. Attlee used the occasion to answer, with uncharacteristic sharpness, some of the attacks upon him by Churchill and other Conservatives. Although Harriman did not see or hear Attlee at Durham, certain of the morning newspapers the next day lumped their remarks together, giving the false impression that the Ambassador had been present when the Prime Minister delivered his political counterattack.

The next day Beaverbrook told Harriman that Churchill was greatly upset, so upset that he was going to lodge a formal complaint in the House of Commons. The American Ambassador, Beaverbrook snorted, had no business taking part in Labor party politics. Harriman told Beaverbrook that a complaint of the kind Churchill had in mind would be a godsend. There had never, he said, been the slightest objection or criticism when American ambassadors talked to British chambers of commerce or other business organizations. He had attended a nonpolitical labor rally and he would make no excuses for it. "I told Beaverbrook," Harriman recalled, "that it would do me untold good with the government and public if Churchill complained that I was in such close touch with British Labor. Nothing more came of it. Max was always trying to create trouble and this time he failed. As for Churchill, I think he was justified in raising an eyebrow because the British press had reported, erroneously as it happened, that Attlee and I had spoken at the same meeting and presumably from the same platform. Attlee, in any event, had been the target of one of Churchill's nastier pieces of sarcasm and I gather he replied in kind with a personal attack. Churchill never mentioned the matter to me when he discovered that I had been nowhere near Attlee that afternoon."

In one of his first talks with Attlee, Harriman found the Prime Minister gravely disturbed by the passage of the McMahon Act. This piece of legislation had the effect of revoking the wartime partnership between the United States and Britain, which had led to the successful development of the atomic bomb. Harriman, who believed that the British in the beginning had made a larger scientific contribution than the Americans, regretted the restrictive nature of the new legislation. "They had given us everything they had during the war," he recalled. "Now the Congress of the United States made it illegal even to exchange information with the British. I thought it was shameful. The British were determined to develop their own nuclear capability and we were suddenly debarred from helping them."

It took some wangling on Harriman's part but he succeeded in arranging an invitation for Lord Portal, who was in charge of the British nuclear program, to visit the United States with several of his scientists. Portal and his associates were shown as much of the atomic energy facilities in the United States as the law allowed. When Harriman asked Portal on his return whether the visit had been satisfactory, he agreed, adding, "We learned a lot of things that we should not do."

During the summer of 1946, Harriman was summoned to Paris by Byrnes to handle the Rumanian peace-treaty negotiations. He made short work of the treaty after a private talk with his Soviet counterpart, Dimitri Manuilsky. "I remember saying to him that we could spend many weeks arguing about the treaty terms in big public meetings," he recalled. "My suggestion was that we should sit down together quietly, identify the serious difficulties and try to compose them quickly. The net result was that we got our treaty settled long before the treaties with Hungary or Italy."

Harriman had just returned to London when Byrnes went from Paris to Stuttgart and on September 6 delivered a speech which in effect reversed the American policy toward defeated Germany. The principle that Germany must be treated as an economic unit, held dear by State Department planners, gave way to the acceptance of a divided country. "If complete unification cannot be secured," Byrnes said, "we shall do everything in our power to secure maximum possible unification." In practical terms this meant the eventual merger of the British and American zones of occupation, since the Russians and the French for different reasons could be expected to refuse. Byrnes also endorsed the idea of a German provisional government in the merged zones, which was to become the germ of the West German Federal Republic.

With his Stuttgart speech, Byrnes called the turn toward a tougher line with the Russians. Ironically, in view of his posthumous reputation as the toughest of the "Get tough with Russia" school, Forrestal had written to Harriman on September 4, 1946:

> There is nothing much new here except the same impression which I am sure you get out of American newspapers, namely the growing disillusionment about Russia. Just as you and I felt there was too great a swing pro-Russia three years ago, I am a little fearful that it may swing too strongly the other way now. We are in danger, I think, of succumbing to the great American temptation to see things precisely in black and white terms . . .
> China troubles me a lot. Again Americans are overprone to look for black-and-white solutions and certainly, as I am sure you will agree, there is no such thing possible. I fear we will reach the point where finally our people will get bored and say to hell with it and pull out.

The open challenge to Byrnes came from the former Vice President, Henry A. Wallace, in a speech at Madison Square Garden in New York on September 12. Its unintended effect was to cut short Harriman's stay in London. Wallace, now Secretary of Commerce, had already criticized Churchill's Fulton speech. Now he took aim at Byrnes and the Truman Administration's toughened foreign policy. Wallace insisted that the postwar world was divided into separate spheres of influence. "We should recognize," he said, "that we have no more business in the political affairs of Eastern Europe than Russia has in the political affairs of Latin America, Western Europe and the United States." In an unmistakable challenge to the Byrnes policy, he warned: "We are reckoning with a force which cannot be handled successfully by a 'Get tough with Russia' policy. 'Getting tough' never brought anything real and lasting—whether for schoolyard bullies or business or world powers. The tougher we get, the tougher the Russians will get." Wallace added, "Just two days ago, when President Truman read these words, he said that they represented the policy of his administration." Truman later admitted that Wallace had shown him a copy of the speech and that he had raised no objection after scanning it quickly. Two days after the speech was delivered, however, the President explained to reporters that he had not approved the content of the Wallace speech, only his right to deliver it. When Wallace on September 16 announced his intention of making more foreign-policy speeches, Byrnes threatened to resign unless the Secretary of Commerce was silenced. Four days later Truman announced that Wallace had been fired.

Far from the scene of battle, Harriman read all this in the London newspapers and wondered whether Truman would ask him to take Wallace's place in the Cabinet. When Truman called him on the transatlantic telephone two days later, he happened to be lunching with Churchill at Chartwell. Churchill's butler announced the call, saying that it would be a moment or two before the connection was made. As they waited, Churchill wondered, "What do you suppose the President wants to talk about?" Harriman predicted rather firmly that Truman would offer him Wallace's job as Secretary of Commerce. He asked Churchill whether he ought to accept. "Absolutely," Churchill replied. "The center of power is in Washington."

When Truman's voice came on the line, Harriman's guess was confirmed. "I want you to come home and be Secretary of Commerce," the President said. Showing no surprise, Harriman asked, "When do you want me there?"

"You don't seem to understand," Truman said. "I want you to be Secretary of Commerce."

"Yes, sir, I understand and I'll be only too glad to do it," Harriman replied. "When do you want me there?"

Truman wasted no words: "Just as soon as you can conveniently do it."

Next day, Harriman started his round of official goodbyes.

SOURCE NOTES

Unless otherwise indicated, all notes, memoranda and other documents are from Harriman's files. Certain of the messages published here can also be found in the State Department volumes titled *Foreign Relations of the United States, Diplomatic Papers* (FRUS). Any minor differences in wording can be attributed to the paraphrasing of diplomatic dispatches, designed to protect government codes.

In addition, we have consulted the following manuscript collections for related material:

At the Franklin Delano Roosevelt Presidential Library in Hyde Park—the Harry Hopkins Papers, the Map Room File, the President's Secretary's File, the President's Personal File and the Official File;

at the Princeton University Library—nonrestricted portions of the George F. Kennan Papers and the James V. Forrestal Papers;

from the Yale University Library—the Henry L. Stimson Diaries;

at the Department of State and the Federal Records Center at Suitland, Maryland—the Moscow Embassy Post Files;

at the Houghton Library, Harvard University—the Joseph C. Grew Papers.

I All Aid to Britain, Short of War

1. Harriman memorandum, dictated March 11, 1941, at Bermuda, en route to London.

2. Winston S. Churchill, *The Second World War*, 6 vols. (Boston,

Houghton Mifflin, 1948–1953). Vol. I, *The Gathering Storm*, pp. 440–41.

3. *Ibid.*, Vol. II, *Their Finest Hour*, pp. 24–25.

4. *Ibid.*, pp. 574–75.

5. Robert E. Sherwood, *Roosevelt and Hopkins* (New York, Harper, 1948), p. 243.

6. Admiralty memorandum, Harriman file.

7. Churchill, Vol. III, *The Grand Alliance*, p. 154.

8. Sherwood, *Roosevelt and Hopkins*, p. 284.

9. Letter from R. P. Meiklejohn to Knight Woolley, March 21, 1941.

II How to Be "Something and Somebody"

1. Churchill, *The Grand Alliance*, p. 307.

2. *Ibid.*, p. 312.

3. The details of Edward Henry Harriman's career are drawn from *E. H. Harriman*, a biography, in two volumes, by George Kennan (Boston and New York, Houghton Mifflin, 1922). The author was, in fact, the great-uncle of George F. Kennan, the career diplomat who served in the Moscow embassy with Averell Harriman during World War II.

4. John Muir, *Edward Henry Harriman* (New York, Doubleday, Page & Co., 1911). Privately printed.

5. Trotsky's interpreter was George Andreychin, a Bulgarian revolutionary who had fled to the United States before World War I and joined the International Workers of the World. Arrested for refusing military service in the United States, he went to Russia. In the great purge of 1935, Andreychin was sent to a prison camp, presumably to erase the taint of his association with Trotsky. Harriman was to meet him again in Moscow during World War II and at the Paris Peace Conference in 1946.

III "The British Can Hold Out but They Cannot Win Alone"

1. Churchill, *Their Finest Hour*, pp. 557–58.

2. Churchill, *The Grand Alliance*, pp. 421–22.

3. *Ibid.*, p. 423.

4. Harriman memorandum of conversation, dated Cairo, July 5, 1941.

5. Churchill, *The Grand Alliance*, p. 477.

6. Averell Harriman to Kathleen Harriman and Pamela Churchill, undated. Mrs. Churchill, then the wife of Captain Randolph Churchill, befriended the Harrimans, father and daughter in London. She married Leland Hayward, the American theatrical producer, after her divorce from Churchill. She is now Mrs. Averell Harriman. The Harrimans were married in 1971 following the death of Hayward and of Mrs. Marie Harriman.

7. Churchill, *The Grand Alliance*, p. 444.

8. Sherwood, *Roosevelt and Hopkins*, p. 417.

9. FRUS (*Foreign Relations of the United States*), *1941*, Vol. I, *General, the Soviet Union* (Washington, D.C., Department of State, 1958), p. 826.

IV Red Wolves in the Kremlin

1. Some eighty-four separate warnings and clues, including a number of red herrings, are catalogued in *Codeword Barbarossa*, by Barton Whaley (Cambridge, Mass., The MIT Press, 1973).

2. The Malinovsky quotation (from the *Soviet Journal of Military History*, No. 6 [1961], p. 7) is printed in *Stalin and His Generals*, edited by Seweryn Bialer (New York, Pegasus, 1969).

3. Churchill, *The Grand Alliance*, pp. 456–57.

4. *Ibid.*, pp. 457–58.

5. *Ibid.*, p. 458.

6. *Ibid.*, p. 453.

7. *Loc. cit.*

8. Harriman memorandum, dictated en route to Archangel, September 25, 1941.

9. Harriman unpublished recollections, October 21, 1953.

10. Thayer memorandum, September 29, 1953.

11. Harriman notes on the third meeting with Stalin, September 30, 1941.

12. Memorandum of the same conversation by Lord Beaverbrook, September 30, 1941.

13. *Ibid.*

14. Thayer memorandum, *op. cit.*

15. Harriman memorandum on return to London from Moscow, October 4–10, 1941.

V   Pearl Harbor: "At Least There Is a Future Now"

1. Thayer memorandum, *op. cit.*

2. FRUS, *1941*, Vol. I, p. 909.

3. Personal note on conversation with Churchill, October 15, 1941.

4. FRUS, *1941*, Vol. I, pp. 194–95.

5. Churchill, *The Grand Alliance*, p. 605.

6. *Ibid.*, p. 609.

7. The quotations from shipboard conversations with Churchill are drawn from Harriman's notes, recorded on board the *Duke of York*.

8. Minutes of the meeting on December 25 between the British and American Chiefs of Staff, quoted by Sherwood in *Roosevelt and Hopkins*, p. 455.

9. Churchill, *The Grand Alliance*, p. 630.

VI   No End of Defeats

1. Harold Nicolson, *Diaries and Letters, 1939–45* (New York, Atheneum, 1967), p. 205.

2. Herbert Feis, *Churchill, Roosevelt, Stalin,* 2d ed. (Princeton University Press, 1967), p. 40.

3. Cited in Churchill, Vol. IV, *The Hinge of Fate*, p. 214.

4. Quoted in Maurice Matloff and Edwin Snell, *Strategic Planning for Coalition Warfare, 1941–42* (Washington, D.C., Office of the Chief of Military History, Department of the Army, 1953), p. 156.

5. *Ibid.*, p. 175.

6. FRUS, *1942*, Vol. III, *Europe* (1961), pp. 542–43.

7. *Ibid.*, pp. 536–38.

8. *The Memoirs of Cordell Hull,* 2 vols. (New York, Macmillan, 1948).

9. Sherwood, *Roosevelt and Hopkins*, p. 526.

10. FRUS, *1942*, Vol. III. For the memoranda of Roosevelt's conversations with Molotov, see pp. 566–83.

11. Sherwood, *Roosevelt and Hopkins*, p. 563.

12. *Ibid.*, pp. 574–75.

13. *Ibid.*, p. 577.

14. Churchill, *The Hinge of Fate*, p. 342.

15. FRUS, *1942*, Vol. III, p. 598.

16. Details on the Arctic convoys are drawn from Report on the Harriman Mission, by R. P. Meiklejohn, an unpublished manuscript; and from Churchill, *The Hinge of Fate*, pp. 255–76.

17. Churchill, *The Hinge of Fate*, pp. 381–82.

18. Henry L. Stimson and McGeorge Bundy, *On Active Service in Peace and War* (New York, Harper, 1947), p. 425.

19. Sherwood, *Roosevelt and Hopkins*, p. 602.

VII To Moscow Again, with Churchill

1. *War Memoirs of Charles de Gaulle*, Vol. II, *Unity, 1942–1944* (New York, Simon and Schuster, 1959), pp. 14–15.

2. Churchill, in *The Second World War*, Vol. IV, *The Hinge of Fate*, p. 474, has written: "In the afternoon [of August 11], in the garden of the British Legation, there was a long conference with Averell Harriman and various high British and American railway authorities, and it was decided that the United States should take over the whole Trans-Persian railway from the Gulf to the Caspian." Harriman's clear recollection, confirmed by his notes, is that the decision was not made until after the return from Moscow at a meeting in Cairo on August 21.

3. *Ibid.*, p. 475.

4. *Ibid.*, p. 486.

5. The final arrangement worked out by General Bradley was that Soviet pilots would pick up the planes in Alaska and fly them across to Siberia. Except for a few special flights, the Soviet authorities refused to authorize deliveries by American air crews. Harriman at first attributed this attitude to Soviet fears of antagonizing the Japanese. He later came to believe that the Soviet authorities, for more traditional reasons of internal security, wanted to keep foreigners from mixing with the population.

6. Handwritten note by Harriman on the dinner talk with Stalin, August 14, 1942.

7. *Ibid.*

8. The account of Churchill's late-evening visit to Stalin's living quarters

is drawn from *The Hinge of Fate*, pp. 495–99; the notes of Major Birse; and Harriman's notes, written after he had listened to the Prime Minister's exuberant account the following morning.

VIII *"I Prefer a Comfortable Oasis to the Raft at Tilsit"*

1. The Sherwood quotation is from a profile of Harriman by E. J. Kahn, published in *The New Yorker* (May 10, 1952).

2. Churchill, *The Hinge of Fate*, p. 530.

3. *Ibid.*, p. 532.

4. FRUS, *1942*, Vol. III, p. 676.

5. Mark W. Clark, *Calculated Risk* (New York, Harper, 1950), p. 130.

6. FRUS: *The Conferences at Washington and Casablanca, 1943* (1968), p. 509.

7. Churchill, *The Hinge of Fate*, p. 649.

8. FRUS: *Washington and Casablanca*, p. 494.

9. *Ibid.*, p. 666.

10. *Ibid.*, pp. 675–76.

11. *Ibid.*, p. 594.

12. *Ibid.*, p. 603.

13. *Ibid.*, p. 656.

14. *Ibid.*, pp. 610–11.

15. *Ibid.*, p. 642.

16. Sherwood, *Roosevelt and Hopkins*, p. 683.

17. Churchill, *The Hinge of Fate*, p. 681.

18. FRUS: *Washington and Casablanca*. For transcript of Roosevelt–Churchill press conference, see pp. 726–31.

19. Churchill, *The Hinge of Fate*, p. 686.

20. Sherwood, *Roosevelt and Hopkins*, p. 696.

21. FRUS: *Washington and Casablanca*. See Roosevelt's press conference notes, pp. 836–39.

22. *Ibid.* See footnote, p. 506.

23. *Ibid.*, p. 635.

24. Churchill, *The Hinge of Fate*, p. 686.

25. FRUS: *Washington and Casablanca*, p. 506.

26. Churchill, *The Hinge of Fate*, p. 695.

IX Interlude at Sea

1. Edward J. Rozek, *Allied Wartime Diplomacy: A Pattern in Poland* (New York, John Wiley, 1958), p. 126.

2. *Stalin's Correspondence with Churchill, Attlee, Roosevelt and Truman, 1941–45*, 2 vols. (Moscow, Foreign Languages Publishing House, 1957; London, Lawrence & Wishart, 1958). Vol. I, p. 129.

3. *Ibid.*, p. 127.

4. *Ibid.* For text of Stalin's message, see p. 132.

5. *Ibid.*, p. 133.

6. *Ibid.*, p. 138.

X Farewell to London

1. Sherwood, *Roosevelt and Hopkins*, p. 737.

2. The British historian A. J. P. Taylor, denying that Churchill ever advocated an invasion of the Balkans, has written: "He merely retained his illusion, now thirty years old, that there was somewhere an easy backdoor into Germany and hoped to win the war by some unexpected miracle instead of by heavy fighting. Gallipoli was never far from his mind—as an example, not as a warning. Even now, he was unrepentant." See Taylor, *English History, 1914–1945* (New York, Oxford University Press, 1965), p. 573.

3. Hull memoirs, Vol. II, p. 1248.

4. FRUS: *The Conferences at Cairo and Teheran, 1943* (1961), pp. 10–11.

5. *Ibid.*, p. 13.

6. *Ibid.*, pp. 17–18.

7. FRUS: *The Conferences at Washington and Quebec, 1943* (1970), p. 448.

8. Stimson and Bundy, *On Active Service in Peace and War*, pp. 436–38.

9. FRUS: *Washington and Quebec*, p. 901.

10. *Ibid.*, pp. 1086–87.

11. Forrest C. Pogue, *George C. Marshall, Organizer of Victory, 1943–1945* (New York, Viking, 1973), p. 70.

12. Hull memoirs, Vol. II, p. 1255.

XI   "I Have Come as a Friend"

1. Churchill, *The Hinge of Fate*, p. 562.
2. FRUS, *1943*, Vol. I, *General* (1963), p. 602.
3. *Ibid.*, pp. 589–90.
4. John R. Deane, *The Strange Alliance* (New York, Viking, 1947), pp. 19–21.
5. FRUS: *Cairo and Teheran*, pp. 45–46.
6. *Ibid.*, p. 70.
7. *Ibid.*, pp. 71–72.
8. *Ibid.*, p. 147.
9. Hull memoirs, Vol. II, p. 1315.
10. FRUS, *1943*, Vol. I, pp. 638–39.
11. *Ibid.*, pp. 624–27.
12. The penciled notes passed between the British and American delegations are included in the Harriman Papers.
13. FRUS, *1943*, Vol. I, pp. 686–87.

XII   Teheran—"Friends in Fact, in Spirit and in Purpose"

1. Deane, *The Strange Alliance*, p. 38.
2. FRUS: *Cairo and Teheran*, p. 82.
3. *Ibid.*, pp. 327–29.
4. *Ibid.*, p. 361.
5. *Ibid.*, p. 514.
6. *Ibid.*, p. 513.
7. *Ibid.*, p. 512.
8. *Ibid.*, p. 531.
9. *Ibid.*, p. 539.
10. Churchill, Vol. V, *Closing the Ring*, pp. 373–74.
11. FRUS: *Cairo and Teheran*, p. 554.

12. *Ibid.*, p. 583.

13. *Ibid.*, p. 594 ff.

14. *Ibid.*, p. 599.

15. Churchill, *Closing the Ring*, p. 401.

16. *Ibid.*, p. 405.

XIII "The History of War Has Never Witnessed Such a Grandiose Operation"

1. *Memoirs of Dr. Eduard Benes: From Munich to New War and New Victory* (Boston, Houghton Mifflin, 1954), pp. 265–66.

2. Deane, *The Strange Alliance*, p. 53.

XIV Poland, the Touchstone

1. FRUS, *1944*, Vol. III, *The British Commonwealth and Europe* (1965), pp. 1240–43.

2. *Stalin's Correspondence*, Vol. I, p. 196.

3. FRUS, *1944*, Vol. III, pp. 1249–57.

4. *Ibid.*, pp. 1268–70.

5. Rozek, *Allied Wartime Diplomacy*, p. 22.

6. *Ibid.*, pp. 237–42.

7. Milovan Djilas, *Conversations with Stalin* (New York, Harcourt, 1962), p. 114.

XV Warsaw—The Doomed Uprising

1. Stanislaw Mikolajczyk, *The Rape of Poland: Pattern of Soviet Aggression* (New York, McGraw–Hill, 1948), p. 69.

2. *Stalin's Correspondence*, Vol. I, p. 249.

3. *Ibid.*, p. 254.

4. *Ibid.*, p. 255.

5. Poland, Official Government Documents, Vol. CLVI, Document 243. Quoted in Rozek, *Allied Wartime Diplomacy*, p. 255.

6. Churchill, Vol. VI, *Triumph and Tragedy*, p. 216.

7. *Ibid.*, pp. 227–28.

8. FRUS, *1944*, Vol. IV, *Europe*, p. 1011.

9. From Poland, Official Government Documents, Vol. VII, Document 3. Quoted in Rozek, *Allied Wartime Diplomacy*, p. 272.

10. Mikolajczyk, *The Rape of Poland*, pp. 98–99.

11. Deane, *The Strange Alliance*, p. 246.

XVI   Molotov's "Unconventional Request" for Postwar Credits

1. FRUS: *The Conferences at Malta and Yalta, 1945* (1955), p. 296.

2. Deane, *The Strange Alliance*, p. 256.

3. FRUS: *Malta and Yalta*, pp. 319–21.

XVII   Yalta

1. Churchill, *Triumph and Tragedy*, p. 344.

2. Sherwood, *Roosevelt and Hopkins*, p. 845.

3. FRUS: *Malta and Yalta*, p. 39.

4. Anthony Eden, *The Reckoning* (Boston, Houghton Mifflin, 1965), p. 375.

5. Churchill, *Triumph and Tragedy*, p. 348.

6. V. I. Chuikov, *The Capitulation of Hitler's Germany;* quoted in Diane Shaver Clemens, *Yalta* (New York, Oxford University Press, 1970), p. 86.

7. G. K. Zhukov, *On the Berlin Axis;* reprinted in Bialer, *Stalin and His Generals*, p. 510.

8. FRUS: *Malta and Yalta*, pp. 395–96.

9. *Ibid.*, p. 396.

10. *Ibid.*, p. 769.

11. William D. Leahy, *I Was There* (New York, McGraw–Hill, 1950), p. 318.

12. Edward R. Stettinius, *Roosevelt and the Russians* (New York, Doubleday, 1949), pp. 92–96.

13. Churchill, *Triumph and Tragedy*, p. 390.

14.   FRUS: *Malta and Yalta*, p. 617.

15.   *Ibid.*, pp. 899–900.

16.   Sherwood, *Roosevelt and Hopkins*, p. 861.

17.   *Ibid.*, p. 860.

18.   FRUS: *Malta and Yalta*, pp. 677–78.

19.   *Ibid.*, pp. 669–70.

20.   *Ibid.*, pp. 727–28.

21.   *Ibid.*, pp. 966–68.

22.   *Ibid.*, p. 721.

23.   Quoted in Charles E. Bohlen, *Witness to History* (New York, Norton, 1973), pp. 175–76.

24.   For the text of the prisoner agreement, see FRUS: *Malta and Yalta*, p. 985.

XVIII *From Yalta to Warm Springs*

1.   Churchill, *Triumph and Tragedy*, pp. 400–1.

2.   See FRUS: *Malta and Yalta*, pp. 985–87; for bilateral Agreement Concerning Liberated Prisoners of War.

3.   *Stalin's Correspondence*, Vol. II, pp. 196–97.

4.   FRUS, *1945*, Vol. V, *Europe*, pp. 509–10.

5.   *Ibid.*, pp. 511–12.

6.   Churchill, *Triumph and Tragedy*, p. 424.

7.   FRUS, *1945*, Vol. V, pp. 159–60.

8.   *Ibid.*, p. 180.

9.   *Ibid.*, p. 189.

10.   *Ibid.*, p. 194.

11.   FRUS, *1945*, Vol. III, *European Advisory Commission, Austria and Germany* (1968), pp. 733–34.

12.   *Stalin's Correspondence*, Vol. II, pp. 200–1.

13.   FRUS, *1945*, Vol. III, p. 742.

14.   *Ibid.*, p. 746.

15.   *Ibid.*, pp. 749–51.

16. *Ibid.*, p. 756.

17. The conversation with the *New York Times* columnist Anne O'Hare McCormick is recorded in a Harriman memorandum dated January 25, 1954.

18. FRUS, *1945*, Vol. V, p. 211.

XIX   *Truman Takes Charge*

1. Bohlen memorandum on first Truman-Harriman meeting: FRUS, *1945*, Vol. V, *Europe*, pp. 231–34. The notion that the United States needed Russia as an export market to avoid a postwar depression had been mentioned to Stalin by both Donald Nelson and Eric A. Johnston on their visits to Moscow.

2. Harry S. Truman, *Memoirs*, 2 vols., Vol I, *Year of Decisions* (New York, Doubleday, 1955), p. 72.

3. Official minutes of Secretary of State's staff committee, April 20 and 21, 1945. FRUS, *1945*, Vol. V, pp. 839–46.

4. Henry Lewis Stimson Diaries, Yale University Library, New Haven, Vol. LI, p. 63.

5. Sherwood, *Roosevelt and Hopkins*, p. 887.

6. Grew memorandum of conversation with Crowley, May 11, 1945. Joseph C. Grew Papers, Houghton Library, Harvard University.

7. Bohlen memorandum of May 15 conversation between Truman, Grew and Harriman.

8. FRUS, *1945*, Vol. V, p. 334.

9. *Ibid.*, p. 321.

XX   *Japan Surrenders*

1. FRUS: *The Conference of Berlin (Potsdam), 1945.* 2 vols. (1960). Vol. I, pp. 6–7.

2. Churchill, *Triumph and Tragedy*, p. 572.

3. *Ibid.*, p. 573.

4. FRUS, *1945*, Vol. III. See pp. 133–35 for Truman's message and Churchill's reply.

5. Rozek, *Allied Wartime Diplomacy*. See pp. 387–90 for a detailed account.

6. FRUS: *Berlin*, Vol. I, p. 718.

7. FRUS, *1945*, Vol. VII, *The Far East and China*, p. 908.

8. *Ibid.*, pp. 911–12.

9. The Forrestal diary entry is published in FRUS: *Berlin*, Vol. II, p. 477.

10. Stimson Diaries, Yale University Library, Vol. LII, p. 27.

11. *Ibid.*, p. 30.

12. Truman memoirs, Vol. I, p. 323.

13. FRUS: *Berlin*, Vol. II, p. 1360.

14. *Ibid.* See footnote 2 for Stimson's diary entry of July 16.

15. *Ibid.*, p. 47, for diary entry of July 17.

16. Truman memoirs, Vol. I, p. 416.

17. Bohlen, *Witness to History*, p. 237.

18. Churchill, *Triumph and Tragedy*, p. 639.

19. FRUS: *Berlin*, Vol. II, pp. 1587–88.

20. Truman memoirs, Vol. I, p. 421.

XXI   Farewell to Moscow

1. James F. Byrnes, *All in One Lifetime* (New York, Harper, 1958), p. 319.

2. James B. Conant, *My Several Lives* (New York, Harper, 1970), p. 482.

3. Transcript of Harriman's talk to officers and attachés of the embassy in Moscow on January 22, 1946.

4. Harriman memorandum, dictated in London, January 13, 1946.

XXII   "The Center of Power Is in Washington"

1. George F. Kennan, *Memoirs, 1925–1950* (Boston, Atlantic Monthly-Little, Brown, 1967), p. 550.

2. *Ibid.*, p. 295.

INDEX

About the Authors

W. Averell Harriman has had a distinguished career in both public life and private industry. He served as chairman of the board of the Union Pacific Railroad and chairman of the Executive Committee of the Illinois Central, and was an active partner in the banking firm of Brown Brothers Harriman Company. He worked for Roosevelt's New Deal as administrator for the NRA and also for three years as chairman of the Business Advisory Council of the Department of Commerce. During the war he served as Special Representative of President Roosevelt in England and as Ambassador to Russia. Under President Truman he was Ambassador to Britain, Secretary of Commerce, and European administrator of the Marshall Plan. He was Governor of New York State and later served in the Kennedy and Johnson administrations as Under Secretary of State for Political Affairs and Ambassador-at-Large. His two previous books are *Peace With Russia?* (1959) and *America and Russia in a Changing World* (1971).

Elie Abel, Godfrey Lowell Cabot Professor and Dean of the Graduate School of Journalism, Columbia University, has been a reporter and broadcaster for many years. He served as foreign correspondent for the North American Newspaper Alliance and the *New York Times*, as Washington Bureau Chief of the Detroit *News* and, for NBC, as Chief of the London Bureau and Diplomatic Correspondent. He has won the George Foster Peabody Award and two Overseas Press Club Awards. He wrote *The Missile Crisis* (1966) and was co-author of *Roots of Involvement: The U.S. in Asia 1784–1871* (1971).